# Using AI to Achieve the Sustainable Development Goals (SDGs)

Gamze Sart
*Istanbul University-Cerrahpaşa, Turkey*

Yilmaz Bayar
*Bandirma Onyedi Eylul University, Turkey*

Funda H. Sezgin
*Istanbul University-Cerrahpaşa, Turkey*

IGI Global
Scientific Publishing
Publishing Tomorrow's Research Today

| | |
|---|---|
| Vice President of Editorial | Melissa Wagner |
| Director of Acquisitions | Mikaela Felty |
| Director of Book Development | Jocelynn Hessler |
| Production Manager | Mike Brehm |
| Cover Design | Jose Rosado |

Published in the United States of America by
IGI Global Scientific Publishing
701 East Chocolate Avenue
Hershey, PA, 17033, USA
Tel: 717-533-8845 | Fax: 717-533-7115
Website: https://www.igi-global.com E-mail: cust@igi-global.com



Library of Congress Cataloging-in-Publication Data

Names: Sart, Gamze, 1967- editor. | Bayar, Yilmaz, 1977- editor. | Sezgin, Funda H., editor.
Title: Using AI to achieve the sustainable development goals (SDGs) / edited by Gamze Sart, Yilmaz Bayar, and Funda H. Sezgin.
Description: Hershey, PA : IGI Global Scientific Publishing, [2026] | Includes bibliographical references and index. | Summary: "The objective of the edited book is to investigate the role of AI in achievement of 17 sustainable development goals and their targets"-- Provided by publisher.
Identifiers: LCCN 2025004253 (print) | LCCN 2025004254 (ebook) | ISBN 9798337318370 (hardcover) | ISBN 9798337318387 (paperback) | ISBN 9798337318394 (ebook)
Subjects: LCSH: Sustainable development--Technological innovations. | Artificial intelligence--Economic aspects.
Classification: LCC HC79.E5 U793 2026 (print) | LCC HC79.E5 (ebook) | DDC 338.9/27028563--dc23/eng/20250326
LC record available at https://lccn.loc.gov/2025004253
LC ebook record available at https://lccn.loc.gov/2025004254
British Cataloguing in Publication Data
A Cataloguing in Publication record for this book is available from the British Library.

# Table of Contents

**Preface** ........................................................................................................ xiii

**Chapter 1**
AI for Advancing Sustainable Development Goals: A Global Perspective ........... 1
*Mustafa Kayyali, Maaref University of Applied Sciences, Syria*

**Chapter 2**
Artificial Intelligence-Based Approaches to Sustainable Development and Gender Balance ........................................................................................ 37
*Funda Hatice Sezgin, Istanbul University-Cerrahpasa, Turkey*

**Chapter 3**
Advancing Sustainable Development Goals With a Data-Driven Approach to Progress and Forecasting ........................................................................ 57
*Kian Jazayeri, Department of Management Information Systems, School of Applied Sciences, Cyprus International University, Nicosia, Cyprus*
*Moein Jazayeri, Department of Electrical and Electronic Engineering, Faculty of Engineering, Cyprus International University, Cyprus*

**Chapter 4**
Harnessing AI for Sustainable Development: A Multidimensional Approach.. 101
*Md Mehedi Hasan Emon, American International University-Bangladesh, Bangladesh*
*Tahsina Khan, Bangladesh University of Professionals, Bangladesh*

**Chapter 5**
Empowering Future Generations: How AI is Transforming Sustainable Education Practices ........................................................................................ 133
*Juma Yusuf Mnzile, Anadolu University, Turkey*

**Chapter 6**
AI-Driven Data Governance for SDG Achievement in Higher Education ....... 157
*Tarık Küçükdeniz, Istanbul University-Cerrahpasa, Turkey*
*Canan Hazal Akarsu, Istanbul University-Cerrahpasa, Turkey*
*Melike Solak Altuntas, Istanbul University-Cerrahpasa, Turkey*

**Chapter 7**
AI-Powered English Education: Promoting Inclusivity and Equal Access in Language Learning for SDGs ........ 181
*Vivit Rosmayanti, Universitas Negeri Makassar, Indonesia*
*Guntur Roryngosan Fara, Universitas Megarezky, Indonesia*
*Safaruddin Safaruddin, Universitas Megarezky, Indonesia*
*Ibtisamatul Aminah, National Research and Innovation Agency, Indonesia*
*Besse Yuliana, Universitas Megarezky, Indonesia*

**Chapter 8**
AI-Driven Healthcare: Achieving Sustainable Development Goal 3 Through Smart Technologies ........ 207
*Binnur Akıf, Istanbul Gelisim University, Turkey*
*Sinem Büyüksaatçı-Kiriş, Istanbul University-Cerrahpasa, Turkey*

**Chapter 9**
Femtech and Artificial Intelligence: Paving the Way for Gender Equality and Sustainable Development ........ 231
*Manisha Seth, Noida Institute of Engineering and Technology, India*
*Sabina Sehajpal, Chandigarh University, India*
*Mukul Bhatnagar, Graphic Era University, India*
*Akshita Chaudhary, Graphic Era University, India*

**Chapter 10**
ReCoffee: Sustainable Management of Spent Coffee Grounds Using Artificial Intelligence ........ 255
*Kauser Hameed, King Faisal University, Saudi Arabia*
*Raazia Saher, King Faisal University, Saudi Arabia*
*Khutaija Maheen, Fairleigh Dickinson University, USA*
*Qazi Mudassar Ilyas, Sultan Sharif Ali Islamic University, Brunei*

**Chapter 11**
AI-Powered Innovations in Automation for Achieving SDGs: Advancing Sustainable Agriculture ........ 291
*Mrutyunjay Padhiary, Assam University, Silchar, India*
*Avinash Kumar, Assam University, Silchar, India*
*Azmirul Hoque, Assam University, Silchar, India*
*Javed Akhtar Barbhuiya, Assam University, Silchar, India*

**Chapter 12**
Skin Cancer Classification Using Hybrid Deep Learning Approaches: A Systematic Review ........ 323
*Zehra Tüfekçi, Istinye University, Turkey*
*Zeynep Orman, Istanbul University-Cerrahpasa, Turkey*
*Sibel Senan, Istanbul University-Cerrahpasa, Turkey*

**Compilation of References** ........ 363

**About the Contributors** ........ 427

**Index** ........ 437

# Detailed Table of Contents

**Preface** ............ xiii

**Chapter 1**
AI for Advancing Sustainable Development Goals: A Global Perspective ............ 1
*Mustafa Kayyali, Maaref University of Applied Sciences, Syria*

Artificial intelligence (AI) has emerged as a revolutionary force in tackling some of the most serious global concerns stated in the United Nations' Sustainable Development Goals (SDGs). This chapter covers the many uses of AI in furthering sustainable development, stressing its potential to generate considerable progress across multiple industries. From tackling poverty and hunger through smart resource allocation and predictive analytics to boosting access to excellent education and healthcare, AI provides new solutions that can support fair growth and development. The chapter digs into the essential role of AI in climate action, highlighting how machine learning and data-driven insights help to alleviate environmental deterioration and encourage sustainable habits. Through regional case studies, this chapter explores successful applications of AI in accomplishing SDGs, highlighting both the benefits and limits of this technology in varied situations.

**Chapter 2**
Artificial Intelligence-Based Approaches to Sustainable Development and Gender Balance ............ 37
*Funda Hatice Sezgin, Istanbul University-Cerrahpasa, Turkey*

Artificial intelligence (AI) refers to the entirety of technologies that mimic human-like decision-making processes through techniques such as big data, machine learning, and natural language processing. In recent years, AI applications have begun to be used across a wide range of fields, from the labor market to healthcare services, from education to public administration. When supported by the right policies, AI systems can be powerful tools for accelerating gender equality. However, biased data and non-transparent algorithms can reproduce discrimination against women and minority groups. This study discusses the advantages and risks of artificial intelligence applications on gender, emphasizing that these technologies have the potential to increase social inequalities if not designed and implemented correctly.

**Chapter 3**
Advancing Sustainable Development Goals With a Data-Driven Approach to Progress and Forecasting ........ 57
*Kian Jazayeri, Department of Management Information Systems, School of Applied Sciences, Cyprus International University, Nicosia, Cyprus*
*Moein Jazayeri, Department of Electrical and Electronic Engineering, Faculty of Engineering, Cyprus International University, Cyprus*

This chapter presents a comprehensive, data-driven framework for assessing and forecasting global progress toward the Sustainable Development Goals (SDGs). Leveraging machine learning, statistical analysis, and geospatial visualization, the study evaluates trends from 2000 to 2023 and projects trajectories to 2030. Key methodologies include Markovian modeling, K-Means clustering, PCA, SARIMAX forecasting, and network analysis. The chapter also simulates targeted improvements in underperforming SDGs, offering strategic insights for resource allocation. Correlation analyses reveal strong links between SDG scores and indices like HDI, GDP, and environmental performance. Designed as a practical toolkit for policymakers and planners, the chapter supports data-informed decision-making, highlights disparities, and proposes actionable pathways for accelerating sustainable development.

**Chapter 4**
Harnessing AI for Sustainable Development: A Multidimensional Approach.. 101
*Md Mehedi Hasan Emon, American International University-Bangladesh, Bangladesh*
*Tahsina Khan, Bangladesh University of Professionals, Bangladesh*

Artificial Intelligence (AI) is a crucial facilitator of sustainable development, advancing progress across several sectors in accordance with the United Nations' Sustainable Development Goals (SDGs). This chapter examines the role of AI in improving education, expanding green technology, and fostering environmental sustainability via predictive climate modeling, automated waste management, and biodiversity conservation. Moreover, AI facilitates societal advancement by mitigating economic and gender disparities and aiding underprivileged populations. Although AI has significant promise, difficulties like accessibility, ethical issues, and job displacement need intentional governmental responses. This chapter analyzes AI's revolutionary influence, emphasizing its prospects and threats while offering insights into its contribution to a more sustainable future.

**Chapter 5**
Empowering Future Generations: How AI is Transforming Sustainable Education Practices ........ 133
*Juma Yusuf Mnzile, Anadolu University, Turkey*

In an era characterized by accelerated transformation and global challenges, educational institutions are in a distinctive position to influence the creation of a more sustainable and inclusive global society. This chapter explores the potential of emerging technologies, with a particular focus on artificial intelligence (AI), to advance the concept of education without borders. The chapter highlights the transformative potential of AI by illustrating how intelligent systems can personalize learning experiences, cater to diverse student needs, and promote educational equity. Furthermore, it emphasizes the potential of predictive analytics to empower educators and policymakers, enabling them to make informed decisions regarding resource allocation, student support, and curriculum design. By establishing a linkage between innovation and inclusivity, this chapter provides a forward-looking perspective on the potential of AI to accelerate progress towards Sustainable Development Goal 4 (quality education for all).

**Chapter 6**
AI-Driven Data Governance for SDG Achievement in Higher Education ....... 157
*Tarık Küçükdeniz, Istanbul University-Cerrahpasa, Turkey*
*Canan Hazal Akarsu, Istanbul University-Cerrahpasa, Turkey*
*Melike Solak Altuntas, Istanbul University-Cerrahpasa, Turkey*

The documentation of university contributions to UN Sustainable Development Goals faces challenges because of their diverse and complex nature. This research introduces an AI-based classification framework which enhances sustainability assessment by automatically processing institutional communication data. The system processed 103,868 documents from Istanbul University-Cerrahpaşa using transformer-based BERT models to reach 89.3% classification accuracy across all 17 SDGs. The AI detection method revealed that traditional manual reporting systems identify less than 20% of sustainability initiatives yet the AI system discovered 247.7% more activities. The system uses multilingual processing together with multi-label classification to handle SDG interconnectedness. The research shows how AI technology converts SDG assessment from basic compliance documentation into strategic intelligence which affects university rankings and funding distribution and worldwide sustainability tracking.

**Chapter 7**
AI-Powered English Education: Promoting Inclusivity and Equal Access in Language Learning for SDGs ........ 181
*Vivit Rosmayanti, Universitas Negeri Makassar, Indonesia*
*Guntur Roryngosan Fara, Universitas Megarezky, Indonesia*
*Safaruddin Safaruddin, Universitas Megarezky, Indonesia*
*Ibtisamatul Aminah, National Research and Innovation Agency, Indonesia*
*Besse Yuliana, Universitas Megarezky, Indonesia*

The internal sustainable development strategy's purpose is to utilize language learning technologies such as AI tools to address the inequities in English Language Education (ELT). For instance, AI-enabled apps like learning algorithms, natural language processing, and speech recognition systems present customized learning assistance and promote the inclusion of learners with disabilities into the educational process. AI also means providing students with physical and learning disabilities with assistive technologies. Even with these challenges like cultural issues, poor teacher education, and certain technologies, AI has produced impressive results in leveling the playing field of English language teaching across geography including rural and other disadvantaged populations. The chapter closes with suggestions which policymakers can use to improve English language learning.

**Chapter 8**
AI-Driven Healthcare: Achieving Sustainable Development Goal 3 Through Smart Technologies ........ 207
*Binnur Akıf, Istanbul Gelisim University, Turkey*
*Sinem Büyüksaatçı-Kiriş, Istanbul University-Cerrahpasa, Turkey*

AI-driven smart technologies and applications have the potential to transform the healthcare sector and serve as a crucial tool in advancing the third goal of the Sustainable Development Goals, "Good Health and Well-Being." This study provides a comprehensive analysis of various AI-driven technologies that facilitate broader access to healthcare services, enable the development of personalized treatment approaches, enhance early disease detection, promote more efficient and sustainable healthcare delivery, and contribute to the reduction of health disparities. Specifically, the study explores the integration of key technological areas including telemedicine, the Internet of Things (IoT), digital twins, bioinformatics, and machine learning, highlighting their individual and collective impacts on health outcomes and healthcare systems. The study further identifies and critically discusses technological, regulatory, and ethical barriers that may hinder the effective adoption of these advanced solutions.

**Chapter 9**
Femtech and Artificial Intelligence: Paving the Way for Gender Equality and Sustainable Development ........ 231
*Manisha Seth, Noida Institute of Engineering and Technology, India*
*Sabina Sehajpal, Chandigarh University, India*
*Mukul Bhatnagar, Graphic Era University, India*
*Akshita Chaudhary, Graphic Era University, India*

This study explores the transformative role of Femtech and Artificial Intelligence (AI) in advancing gender equality and achieving the Sustainable Development Goals (SDGs). It analyzes global startups leveraging AI to address women's health challenges, empower economic participation, and enhance digital engagement. By examining case studies of Femtech innovations in reproductive health, menstrual care, and nutrition, alongside statistical data on women's involvement in e-commerce, the research identifies key AI-driven solutions that bridge gaps in healthcare access and economic opportunities. The findings highlight how AI is democratizing healthcare, improving women's access to personalized services, and fostering entrepreneurial opportunities. By enabling scalable, data-driven solutions, AI plays a pivotal role in advancing SDGs, particularly SDG 3 (Good Health and Well-Being), SDG 5 (Gender Equality), and SDG 8 (Decent Work and Economic Growth). This research underscores AI's potential to create an inclusive and equitable global environment for women.

**Chapter 10**
ReCoffee: Sustainable Management of Spent Coffee Grounds Using Artificial Intelligence ........ 255
*Kauser Hameed, King Faisal University, Saudi Arabia*
*Raazia Saher, King Faisal University, Saudi Arabia*
*Khutaija Maheen, Fairleigh Dickinson University, USA*
*Qazi Mudassar Ilyas, Sultan Sharif Ali Islamic University, Brunei*

This chapter explores the global issue of food loss and waste, emphasizing its economic and environmental impacts and implications on Sustainable Development Goals, with a specific focus on the coffee industry as a major waste-generating sector. Building on the context, the chapter examines global coffee consumption and production trends, highlighting the substantial volume of spent coffee grounds (SCGs) wasted and their environmental burden. The discussion then introduces Artificial Intelligence (AI) and emerging tools for achieving sustainable waste management in this domain. The chapter investigates AI applications across the coffee value chain, from optimizing production and supply to enabling the recycling and valorization of byproducts. It highlights ongoing research and real-world implementations, concluding with a vision for a circular, sustainable future—emphasizing stakeholder collaboration, AI-driven solutions, and actionable policies and industry recommendations.

**Chapter 11**
AI-Powered Innovations in Automation for Achieving SDGs: Advancing Sustainable Agriculture ........................................................................ 291
*Mrutyunjay Padhiary, Assam University, Silchar, India*
*Avinash Kumar, Assam University, Silchar, India*
*Azmirul Hoque, Assam University, Silchar, India*
*Javed Akhtar Barbhuiya, Assam University, Silchar, India*

Agriculture has experienced an important change with the development of artificial intelligence (AI), enabling smarter, more efficient, and sustainable farming operations. This chapter delves into how AI-powered automation could transform agriculture in the context of the Sustainable Development Goals (SDGs). It examines AI applications like precision farming, climate-smart agriculture, and automation technologies, which can improve resource use, increase crop yields, and promote environmental sustainability. These investigations identify cost and lack of access as barriers, despite their limitations in reaching a global audience. By focusing on equitable access and inclusive technology, AI can further enhance sustainable practices in several agricultural sectors. These initiatives may contribute to achieving the Sustainable Development Goals (SDGs), such as zero hunger (SDG 2), clean water and sanitation (SDG 6), and climate action (SDG 13). This chapter highlights the potential of AI to change the agricultural sector and assist with sustainability efforts around the world.

**Chapter 12**
Skin Cancer Classification Using Hybrid Deep Learning Approaches: A Systematic Review ........................................................................ 323
*Zehra Tüfekçi, Istinye University, Turkey*
*Zeynep Orman, Istanbul University-Cerrahpasa, Turkey*
*Sibel Senan, Istanbul University-Cerrahpasa, Turkey*

Skin cancer is one of the most common types of cancer worldwide, and early diagnosis is crucial in the fight against the disease. In recent years, deep learning and hybrid approaches have shown significant potential in the diagnosis of skin cancer. This study provides a detailed review of hybrid deep learning methods proposed for skin cancer classification between 2020 and 2024. The methods in the literature are compared in terms of the datasets used, model accuracy rates, and performance-enhancing techniques. The ability of hybrid models to capture time-series dependencies and manage uncertainty makes them an effective tool for skin cancer diagnosis. These findings demonstrate that hybrid approaches provide more comprehensive and reliable results compared to traditional methods in skin cancer diagnosis. In the future, the development of larger, more balanced datasets and the integration of explainable artificial intelligence techniques will further support progress in this field.

**Compilation of References** ........................................................................ 363

**About the Contributors** ........................................................................ 427

**Index** ........................................................................................ 437

# Preface

Environmental degradation, poverty, economic and social inequalities have remarkably increased in the globalized world. Therefore, millennium development goals and sustainable development goals have developed to combat these problems by the United Nations members. On the other hand, the remarkable progress have been achieved in the field of artificial intelligence (AI) in recent years and AI applications have begun to be used a wide range of areas including education, health, economic applications, and scientific studies. This book, Using AI to Achieve the sustainable development goals, brings together a diverse array of scholars and practitioners who examine the role of AI in achievement of 17 sustainable development goals and their targets.

The chapters in this volume investigates the impact of AI on economic sustainability, environmental sustainability, and social sustainability from a multidisciplinary perspective, each contribution reflects a rigorous analysis rooted in both practical relevance and academic integrity. As editors, we are particularly proud of the balance this book strikes between theoretical depth and applied insights. Our contributors demonstrate the significance role of AI and technological progress in achievement of sustainable development goals. In light of the digital era's challenges and opportunities, this book serves as both a scholarly resource and a roadmap for stakeholders to make progress in achievement of sustainable development goals.

## CHAPTER OVERVIEW

### Chapter 1: AI for Advancing Sustainable Development Goals: A Global Perspective

*Mustafa Kayyali* offers a sweeping global perspective on the transformative role of Artificial Intelligence in addressing the United Nations Sustainable Development Goals (SDGs). The chapter emphasizes AI's cross-sectoral applications—from combating poverty and hunger to enhancing healthcare and education. Notably, it foregrounds the importance of AI in climate action, using regional case studies to demonstrate real-world impact and to reflect on both the immense promise and the complex limitations of AI in diverse sociopolitical contexts.

## Chapter 2: Artificial Intelligence-Based Approaches to Sustainable Development and Gender Balance

*Funda Sezgin* explores the nuanced relationship between AI and gender equity, underscoring the dual potential of artificial intelligence to either promote or hinder gender balance depending on how systems are designed and implemented. The chapter rigorously evaluates how AI technologies intersect with social policy and power structures, calling attention to biases in data and algorithmic transparency. It presents a cautionary yet hopeful perspective on how AI, if guided by inclusive policies, can support gender-responsive development outcomes.

## Chapter 3: Advancing Sustainable Development Goals with a Data-Driven Approach to Progress and Forecasting

*Kian Jazayeri and Moein Jazayeri* introduce a data-intensive framework for monitoring and forecasting SDG progress, offering a toolkit for strategic decision-making. Through advanced machine learning techniques—including Markovian modeling and SARIMAX forecasting—the chapter provides empirical insights into SDG trajectories up to 2030. Their analytical rigor delivers actionable intelligence, demonstrating the power of AI to reveal development disparities, optimize interventions, and strengthen evidence-based policy.

## Chapter 4: Harnessing AI for Sustainable Development: A Multidimensional Approach

*Md Mehedi Hasan Emon and Tahsina Khan* present a multidimensional exploration of AI's transformative potential across environmental, economic, and social spheres. The chapter highlights how AI enables innovations in climate modeling, waste management, education, and social equity. Acknowledging challenges related to accessibility and ethics, the authors advocate for structured policy support to ensure AI technologies are deployed equitably and responsibly in support of the SDGs.

## Chapter 5: Empowering Future Generations: How AI is Transforming Sustainable Education Practices

*Juma Mnzile* turns the focus to education, presenting a forward-looking analysis of AI's role in democratizing and personalizing learning experiences. The chapter discusses how AI-driven tools enhance pedagogical equity, support marginalized learners, and empower decision-makers through predictive analytics. Emphasizing SDG 4, it articulates a compelling vision of education systems reimagined through intelligent technologies to be more inclusive, responsive, and sustainable.

## Chapter 6: AI-Driven Data Governance for SDG Achievement in Higher Education

*Tarik Küçükdeniz, Canan Hazal Akarsu, and Melike Solak Altuntaş* offer a pioneering contribution to sustainability reporting within higher education institutions. Through the deployment of BERT-based AI models, they demonstrate how institutional data can be efficiently analyzed and categorized across all 17 SDGs. This chapter evidences a radical shift in how universities can monitor and report on their sustainability impacts—turning compliance into strategic intelligence and reshaping how education institutions engage with the SDGs.

## Chapter 7: AI-Powered English Education: Promoting Inclusivity and Equal Access in Language Learning for SDGs

*Vivit Rosmayanti, Guntur Fara, Safaruddin Safaruddin, Ibtisamatul Aminah, and Besse Yuliana* delve into AI-enhanced English language learning as a vehicle for educational equity. The authors explore how natural language processing and assistive technologies are breaking down barriers for learners in rural and underserved communities, including students with disabilities. Their analysis reflects both the potential and limitations of integrating AI into language instruction, with policy recommendations aimed at achieving greater inclusivity in line with SDG 4.

## Chapter 8: AI Driven Healthcare: Achieving Sustainable Development Goal 3 Through Smart Technologies

*Binnur Akif and Sinem Büyüksaatçi-Kiris* provide an in-depth exploration of AI's contribution to SDG 3—Good Health and Well-being. The chapter assesses a broad array of technologies, from digital twins and bioinformatics to telemedicine and IoT. Through real-world applications and critical discussion of ethical and regulatory barriers, the authors present AI as a cornerstone of future health systems, capable of personalizing care, improving access, and reducing systemic disparities.

## Chapter 9: Femtech and Artificial Intelligence: Paving the Way for Gender Equality and Sustainable Development

*Manisha Seth, Sabina Sehajpal, Mukul Bhatnagar, and Akshita Chaudhary* investigate the intersection of Femtech and AI, highlighting how digital health innovations are empowering women and advancing SDGs related to health, gender equality, and economic inclusion. Drawing on case studies from global startups, the chapter illustrates how AI is enabling scalable, personalized healthcare solutions for women and promoting female participation in digital economies. The authors emphasize the role of AI in breaking systemic barriers and fostering inclusive development.

## Chapter 10: ReCoffee: Sustainable Management of Spent Coffee Grounds Using Artificial Intelligence

*Kauser Hameed, Raazia Saher, Khutaija Maheen, and Qazi Ilyas* explore AI applications in sustainable waste management through the lens of the global coffee industry. This chapter identifies the massive potential for AI to optimize production and repurpose spent coffee grounds, reducing environmental waste and contributing to circular economy goals. With its innovative blend of food systems analysis, environmental science, and AI, the chapter offers a model for industry-wide sustainability transformation.

## Chapter 11: AI-Powered Innovations in Automation for Achieving SDGs: Advancing Sustainable Agriculture

*Mrutyunjay Padhiary, Avinash Kumar, Azmirul Hoque, and Javed Barbhuiya* examine how AI is revolutionizing agriculture—enhancing precision, resource efficiency, and sustainability. Focused on automation technologies, the chapter highlights use cases in climate-smart agriculture and food security. Despite access and affordability challenges, the authors present a strong case for AI as a tool to meet goals such as zero hunger, clean water, and climate resilience, especially in emerging economies.

### Chapter 12: Skin Cancer Classification Using Hybrid Deep Learning Approaches: A Systematic Review

*Zehra Tüfekçi, Zeynep Orman, and Sibel Senan* close the volume with a systematic review of hybrid deep learning models in skin cancer detection—reinforcing the critical role of AI in advancing SDG 3. The chapter compares algorithms, datasets, and accuracy rates, highlighting how AI enhances diagnostic precision. By advocating for explainable AI and more inclusive datasets, the authors stress the need for transparency and generalizability in future medical AI applications.

# Chapter 1
# AI for Advancing Sustainable Development Goals: A Global Perspective

**Mustafa Kayyali**
https://orcid.org/0000-0003-3300-262X
*Maaref University of Applied Sciences, Syria*

## ABSTRACT

*Artificial intelligence (AI) has emerged as a revolutionary force in tackling some of the most serious global concerns stated in the United Nations' Sustainable Development Goals (SDGs). This chapter covers the many uses of AI in furthering sustainable development, stressing its potential to generate considerable progress across multiple industries. From tackling poverty and hunger through smart resource allocation and predictive analytics to boosting access to excellent education and healthcare, AI provides new solutions that can support fair growth and development. The chapter digs into the essential role of AI in climate action, highlighting how machine learning and data-driven insights help to alleviate environmental deterioration and encourage sustainable habits. Through regional case studies, this chapter explores successful applications of AI in accomplishing SDGs, highlighting both the benefits and limits of this technology in varied situations.*

## INTRODUCTION

The fast growth of artificial intelligence (AI) over the past several decades has placed it at the forefront of technological breakthroughs, radically affecting

DOI: 10.4018/979-8-3373-1837-0.ch001

how societies work, economies thrive, and issues are solved. Among its various applications, AI's role in advancing global sustainability has emerged as one of the most significant areas of investigation (Nishant et al, 2020). The world now faces tremendous problems, ranging from climate change and environmental degradation to socioeconomic inequities and resource scarcity. These concerns transcend national lines, requiring concerted efforts and imaginative solutions that not only reduce their consequences but also construct a more resilient and egalitarian future for all. AI, with its unique power to analyze complicated data, anticipate events, and automate procedures, provides a disruptive approach to attain these aims. The notion of sustainability has grown into a major pillar of global growth. At its heart, sustainability covers three linked dimensions: environmental protection, economic stability, and social equality. The United Nations Sustainable Development Goals (SDGs) serve as a comprehensive framework for tackling these characteristics, defining 17 ambitious aims to eradicate poverty, decrease inequalities, safeguard the planet, and secure peace and prosperity by 2030 (Leal Filho et al, 2019). However, reaching these goals within the specified period remains a formidable job, particularly considering the scope and complexity of the issues involved. Traditional techniques, although essential, frequently fall short in their capacity to solve systemic challenges that demand dynamic, data-driven, and scalable solutions. This is where AI comes into play, giving a range of tools that potentially transform how the SDGs are addressed and executed.

AI's promise to enhance global sustainability resides in its capacity to unearth insights from large volumes of data, allowing informed decision-making at every level. Governments may employ AI to build more effective policies by forecasting the long-term implications of various initiatives, while corporations can use it to improve operations and minimize waste (Challoumis, 2024). For example, in tackling climate change, AI can examine past climatic trends, estimate future situations, and determine the most efficient solutions for lowering greenhouse gas emissions. Similarly, in agriculture, AI-powered systems may boost crop yields and resource efficiency, solving food security challenges in a way that minimizes environmental effects. These capabilities are not restricted to any particular industry; instead, they extend across sectors and disciplines, making AI a universal facilitator of sustainable practices. One of AI's most transformational contributions to global sustainability is its capacity to boost precision and efficiency. Unlike human efforts, which are generally hampered by time, money, and cognitive limitations, AI systems can handle huge amounts of information with surprising speed and precision. This enables the detection of trends, correlations, and abnormalities that could otherwise go overlooked. For instance, AI may scan satellite data to detect unlawful deforestation in distant places or monitor air quality levels in metropolitan surroundings to guide mitigation initiatives. These insights help decision-makers respond rapidly and effectively, decreasing the time gap between detecting a problem and executing a remedy.

Equally noteworthy is AI's ability to enhance diversity and fairness in sustainable development (Vinuesa et al, 2020). Historically, many communities—particularly those in low-income or disadvantaged regions—have been excluded from the advantages of technological progress. However, AI presents a unique chance to overcome this gap by giving individualized solutions to varied populations. For example, AI-driven systems can deliver remote education to children in underprivileged areas, enabling them to access quality learning opportunities regardless of their physical location. Similarly, AI can assist offer healthcare services to remote or resource-constrained regions through telemedicine systems, early illness detection technologies, and tailored treatment suggestions. By resolving these discrepancies, AI not only promotes sustainability but also contributes to the wider ideal of a fair and equitable world. While the potential advantages of AI are tremendous, the route toward global sustainability is not without its hurdles. The incorporation of AI into sustainability initiatives involves complicated ethical problems that must be properly addressed to avoid unexpected repercussions. For instance, biased algorithms can perpetuate systemic imbalances, and a lack of openness in AI decision-making processes can erode public trust. Additionally, the resource-intensive nature of AI technology, notably its high energy consumption, provides an inherent contradiction to sustainability aims. These problems underline the need for a balanced strategy that ensures AI is developed and implemented responsibly, with a clear focus on avoiding risks and maximizing benefits.

Moreover, the accessibility and affordability of AI technologies remain significant issues in their capacity to advance global sustainability. While wealthy economies have made tremendous achievements in AI research and implementation, many developing countries face challenges to adoption owing to insufficient infrastructure, finance, and technical competence (Khan et al, 2024). Bridging this digital divide will need international collaboration, capacity-building efforts, and new finance structures to guarantee that AI's advantages are shared equally around the globe. Without such initiatives, there is a risk that the revolutionary potential of AI will entrench existing disparities rather than relieve them. As this chapter discusses, the convergence of AI and global sustainability poses both an amazing potential and a serious responsibility. By studying real-world applications, regional case studies, and emerging trends, this chapter seeks to give a thorough picture of how AI is affecting the future of sustainable development. It also goes into the ethical, social, and practical problems connected with AI adoption, highlighting the significance of integrating technical progress with human values and global interests. The future of AI in promoting global sustainability is not merely a question of technological improvement; it is a reflection of humanity's collective desire to invent, collaborate, and act in the face of common difficulties. Whether by combatting climate change, enhancing healthcare access, or supporting equitable economic growth, AI can redefine what is possible. However, achieving this potential will need a united effort from all sectors of society, led by a commitment to ethical values and a vision for a sustainable future. By embracing the promise of AI while tackling its problems, we may come closer to attaining the lofty goals of global sustainability and building a future where both people and the earth can flourish.

## THE ROLE OF AI IN ACHIEVING SUSTAINABLE DEVELOPMENT GOALS (SDGS)

Artificial Intelligence (AI) has become a transformational force in the 21st century, altering how societies approach long-standing difficulties and creating new routes for progress (Stahl, 2021). Its promise stretches beyond sectors and economies, hitting the core of global sustainability initiatives. The United Nations' Sustainable Development Goals (SDGs), a worldwide call to action to eradicate poverty, safeguard the planet, and promote prosperity for everyone, give a framework for constructing a more sustainable and equitable society. Within this framework, AI plays a crucial role, enabling creative solutions to speed progress, bridge gaps, and eliminate hurdles that have long impeded development endeavors. The SDGs contain a wide variety of aims, from eliminating poverty and guaranteeing access to excellent education to addressing climate change and fostering sustainable development. AI's role is many-sided—it is not simply a tool for technical growth but also a cause of systemic transformation (Díaz-Rodríguez et al, 2023). By harnessing huge volumes of data, machine learning algorithms, and predictive analytics, AI has the power to spot trends, improve processes, and build personalized solutions to target unique developmental requirements. However, the integration of AI into attempts to accomplish the SDGs is not without hurdles. Ethical issues, uneven access to AI technology, and any unintended repercussions must be carefully handled to guarantee that AI-driven growth complies with the values of inclusion and sustainability.

One of the most crucial areas where AI has proved its influence is poverty reduction (Mhlanga, 2021). Poverty remains a continuous global concern, impacting billions of people globally (Hite & Seitz, 2021). AI-driven technologies are helping governments, non-profits, and development groups to better identify the core causes of poverty and distribute resources more efficiently. For instance, machine learning algorithms may examine economic and social data to identify places where interventions are most required, ensuring that limited resources are focused on areas with the most potential for effect. Additionally, AI is being utilized to construct microfinance systems and platforms that empower underprivileged groups by providing them with access to loans and financial services (Jejeniwa et al, 2024). In the field of hunger and food security, AI has shown tremendous potential in tackling difficulties connected to agricultural production and food distribution. By assessing weather patterns, soil conditions, and crop health, AI-powered systems may give farmers real-time advice to improve their harvests. This is particularly significant in countries where agriculture constitutes the backbone of the economy but is impeded by resource restrictions and climate-related difficulties. Furthermore, AI may enhance supply chain management by forecasting demand, decreasing food waste, and ensuring that extra food reaches those in need. Such solutions not only increase food security but also contribute to economic stability and resilience in disadvantaged areas.

AI's importance in supporting health and well-being, another essential SDG, cannot be emphasized (Fernandez, 2020). The healthcare sector has undergone a shift with the development of AI-driven diagnostic tools, telemedicine platforms, and individualized treatment programs. Machine learning algorithms can evaluate medical data to diagnose illnesses at an early stage, enabling prompt treatments and decreasing the strain on healthcare systems. For example, AI has proved important in the early detection of illnesses like cancer and diabetes, where prompt diagnosis dramatically improves patient outcomes. In resource-limited situations, AI-powered telemedicine technologies are bridging the gap between patients and healthcare professionals, guaranteeing access to excellent treatment regardless of geographical restrictions. In education, AI is breaking down old boundaries and democratizing access to information (Williams, 2024). Quality education is a cornerstone of sustainable development, and AI-powered platforms are making learning more accessible, customized, and effective. Through adaptive learning systems, students may get individualized training that suits their particular requirements and learning styles. This is particularly advantageous for underprivileged communities, including those in distant or conflict-affected areas, where traditional educational resources may be lacking. Moreover, AI can evaluate data on student performance to find areas for growth, enabling educators to build focused interventions that optimize learning results (Kayyali, 2026d).

Climate action is another area where AI is playing a transformational role (Cowls et al, 2023). Climate change poses an existential threat to mankind, and solving it demands new solutions that go beyond standard techniques. AI is being used to simulate climate scenarios, anticipate natural disasters, and develop solutions for minimizing environmental deterioration. For example, AI-powered systems can monitor deforestation, measure carbon emissions, and optimize energy consumption in enterprises and families. These apps not only assist lessen the environmental impact of human activities but also supply policymakers with the data needed to design successful climate legislation. Additionally, AI-driven advancements in renewable energy, such as smart grids and predictive maintenance of wind turbines, are driving the shift to sustainable energy systems. The promise of AI extends beyond specific SDGs, as it may also promote synergies across targets. For instance, developments in healthcare can contribute to improved educational results by ensuring that children are healthy and able to attend college. Similarly, success in agriculture may boost food security while contributing to economic growth and poverty alleviation. AI's capacity to evaluate complex systems and uncover correlations between goals makes it a powerful tool for integrated and comprehensive approaches to sustainable development (Di Vaio et al, 2020). The incorporation of AI into attempts to accomplish the SDGs is not without its hurdles. One of the most serious problems is the ethical implications of AI technologies. Issues such as algorithmic bias, data privacy, and the potential exploitation of AI for destructive purposes must be addressed to guarantee that AI is utilized responsibly and fairly. For example, biased algorithms might perpetuate existing inequities, hindering attempts to promote diversity and social justice. To reduce these concerns, it is vital to build ethical frameworks and norms that regulate the use of AI in sustainable development.

Another concern is the uneven distribution of AI technology and experience (Lutz et al, 2019). While wealthy economies have made tremendous achievements in AI research and development, many developing countries lack the resources and infrastructure needed to harness the potential of AI. This digital gap risks increasing existing disparities and putting disadvantaged groups further behind. To overcome this, worldwide collaboration and capacity-building measures are needed to guarantee that AI technologies are accessible to everybody. By creating relationships between governments, academia, and the corporate sector, it is feasible to bridge the gap and build a more inclusive global AI ecosystem (Gill & Germann, 2022). Despite these obstacles, the potential of AI to drive sustainable development is great. As technology continues to advance, it is vital to take a proactive and collaborative strategy that optimizes its advantages while reducing its hazards. This involves investing in AI research and development, boosting education and training in AI-related disciplines, and developing international cooperation to address global concerns. By harnessing AI ethically and inclusively, societies can accelerate progress toward the SDGs and create a more sustainable and equitable future for all. AI is a strong tool for attaining Sustainable Development Goals, and delivering new solutions to some of the world's most urgent concerns. From poverty reduction and excellent education to climate action and healthcare, AI can revolutionize society and encourage sustainable development on a global scale. However, fulfilling this promise involves resolving ethical problems, bridging the digital gap, and boosting international collaboration. By taking a comprehensive and inclusive approach, the global society can harness the power of AI to build a better future for present and future generations.

## AI'S CONTRIBUTIONS TO POVERTY ALLEVIATION AND ZERO HUNGER

Poverty and hunger are two of humanity's most enduring concerns, complicatedly interrelated and persistent in both emerging and rich countries (Da Costa & McMichael, 2019). Despite decades of worldwide endeavors, billions of people remain imprisoned in poverty, with many failing to acquire enough food to support a healthy life. These difficulties not only reflect core humanitarian concerns but also limit economic progress and societal stability. In this environment, Artificial Intelligence (AI) has emerged as a revolutionary technology with tremendous promise to speed progress toward eradicating poverty and reaching zero hunger. By using the power of data, machine learning, and predictive analytics, AI provides creative solutions to address the core causes of major global crises, improve resource allocation, and empower people to develop sustainable lifestyles. One of the most significant ways AI contributes to poverty alleviation is by enabling focused interventions (Mhlanga, 2021). Poverty is not a one-size-fits-all issue; it varies considerably between geographies, demographics, and situations. AI-driven systems can scan massive volumes of socio-economic data to uncover patterns and connections that are frequently imperceptible to human observers. For example, AI may determine certain areas or families that are most susceptible, taking into consideration characteristics such as income levels, health indicators, education access, and geographic circumstances. By offering a detailed understanding of poverty dynamics, AI helps governments and non-governmental organizations (NGOs) to create and implement interventions that are customized to the particular requirements of distinct communities.

In addition to identifying vulnerable people, AI boosts the efficiency of resource allocation. One of the key obstacles in poverty alleviation initiatives is ensuring that help and resources reach those who need them most. Corruption, inefficiency, and logistical difficulties sometimes prevent the equal allocation of resources (Larson, 2020). AI-powered solutions can streamline supply chains, monitor the distribution of help, and detect abnormalities that suggest mismanagement or fraud. For example, machine learning algorithms may scan satellite data to follow the flow of food supplies in remote places, ensuring that help reaches its intended users. Similarly, blockchain technology, linked with AI, may produce transparent and tamper-proof records of transactions, boosting accountability and confidence in poverty alleviation projects. Financial inclusion is another crucial area where AI is making an impact (Mogaji et al, 2020). Access to financial services is a vital component in moving people out of poverty, although millions remain excluded from traditional banking systems owing to constraints such as lack of documents, bad credit history, or geographical remoteness. AI-powered fintech solutions are breaking down these boundaries by delivering new products such as microloans, digital wallets, and mobile banking services. For instance, AI algorithms may assess creditworthiness using alternative data sources, such as mobile phone usage, social media activity, and transaction history, enabling underprivileged people to obtain loans and create financial resilience (Vincent et al, 2024). By supporting entrepreneurship and enabling small-scale enterprises to thrive, these AI-driven solutions contribute to long-term poverty reduction.

While eliminating poverty is critical, attaining zero hunger is as vital for sustainable development (Khanal, 2021). Hunger is not only a consequence of insufficient food supply; it is often the result of systemic inefficiencies in food distribution, storage, and access (Alaimo et al, 2020). AI is playing a transformational role in eliminating these inefficiencies and ensuring that food systems are more egalitarian and sustainable. One of the most potential uses of AI in the battle against hunger is precision agriculture. Traditional agricultural practices are generally resource-intensive and inefficient, particularly in locations where farmers lack access to modern tools and information. AI-powered solutions can evaluate data from sensors, drones, and satellite photography to give farmers actionable information on soil health, crop conditions, and weather patterns. These insights help farmers to optimize the use of water, fertilizers, and pesticides, therefore boosting agricultural yields and lowering environmental impact. For example, AI-driven systems may assist farmers estimate the ideal planting and harvesting periods, identifying insect infestations early, and monitoring crop health in real time. By enhancing agricultural production, these technologies help food security and economic stability, particularly in rural regions where agriculture is the major livelihood.

AI's contributions to poverty reduction and zero hunger are not confined to technology developments; they also extend to empowering communities and driving social transformation (Prabhakar, 2025). By democratizing access to information and education, AI is helping people and communities to gain the skills and knowledge needed for sustainable lives. For example, AI-powered e-learning systems deliver specialized instructional content in local languages, ensuring that underprivileged communities have access to excellent education. Similarly, AI-driven vocational training programs are preparing individuals with the skills needed to engage in the digital economy, offering new prospects for employment and revenue production. AI is playing a role in improving resilience to shocks and disasters that increase poverty and hunger (How et al, 2020). Natural catastrophes, pandemics, and economic downturns frequently have a disproportionate impact on vulnerable people, forcing millions into poverty and food insecurity. AI-powered early warning systems can foresee disasters such as floods, droughts, and storms, enabling governments and communities to take preemptive actions to limit their effect. For instance, AI can evaluate meteorological data and historical trends to foresee droughts, allowing farmers to alter their planting plans and preserve water supplies. Similarly, during the COVID-19 pandemic, AI was utilized to simulate the transmission of the virus, maximize healthcare resources, and design targeted treatments to protect susceptible people.

Despite its revolutionary potential, the integration of AI into initiatives to relieve poverty and hunger is not without hurdles. Ethical problems, such as data privacy and algorithmic bias, must be addressed to guarantee that AI solutions are fair and inclusive. For example, biased algorithms might perpetuate existing inequities, blocking underprivileged populations from the advantages of AI-driven solutions. Additionally, the digital gap remains a huge hurdle, with many underdeveloped countries missing the infrastructure and resources needed to harness the promise of AI. To solve these issues, it is vital to foster international collaboration, engage in capacity-building efforts, and establish ethical frameworks that govern the appropriate use of AI. AI is a great tool for tackling two of the most critical concerns confronting humanity: poverty and hunger. By allowing targeted interventions, optimizing resource allocation, and empowering communities, AI can improve lives and build a more fair and sustainable society. Its applications in precision agriculture, financial inclusion, food waste reduction, and disaster resilience highlight the range of its influence and the opportunity it presents for meeting the Sustainable Development Goals. However, fulfilling this promise demands a commitment to diversity, ethical standards, and global collaboration. By harnessing AI ethically and equitably, we can speed progress toward a future where no one is left behind.

## QUALITY EDUCATION AND REDUCED INEQUALITIES THROUGH AI

Education has always been a cornerstone of communal progress and personal empowerment (Kuteesa et al, 2024). It is the foundation for individual development, societal progress, and the alleviation of social and economic inequities. However, ensuring decent education for all remains a global issue. Disparities in access, resources, and results continue, especially in disadvantaged and impoverished populations. The advent of Artificial Intelligence (AI) presents a revolutionary opportunity to solve these difficulties and make gains toward establishing fair education and eliminating inequities worldwide (Pedro et al, 2019). By harnessing the potential of AI, it is feasible to reimagine existing education systems, overcome gaps in access and quality, and empower individuals and communities with tools for lifelong learning and progress. One of the most important contributions of AI to education is its capacity to develop individualized learning experiences (Kayyali, 2025 A). Traditional classroom environments frequently function under a one-size-fits-all approach, which may fail to accommodate the different requirements of individual learners. Students differ in their talents, learning styles, and pace of comprehension, however, conventional education institutions struggle to respond to these variances. AI-driven educational platforms may assess a student's performance, identify strengths and shortcomings, and change curriculum accordingly (Ejjami, 2024). For instance, an AI-based system may give individualized lectures, practice activities, and feedback, ensuring that each student has the assistance they need to succeed. This degree of customization not only boosts learning results but also develops a sense of inclusion, as students who may otherwise fall behind are given the skills to succeed.

In addition to customization, AI is breaking down barriers to education for individuals who have historically been excluded from traditional institutions (Facer & Selwyn, 2021). Millions of children and people throughout the world lack access to formal education owing to circumstances such as geographic isolation, violence, poverty, and prejudice. AI-powered solutions, such as mobile learning applications and virtual classrooms, are helping to provide education to these neglected communities. For example, mobile applications integrated with AI can send educational information to remote places with insufficient infrastructure, enabling students to learn without having physical colleges or considerable resources (Kayyali, 2024). Similarly, virtual reality (VR) and augmented reality (AR), driven by AI, are developing immersive learning environments that duplicate classroom experiences, allowing students to engage in classes regardless of their location (Kayyali, 2025 B). These tools are especially significant in crisis zones and refugee camps, where traditional education institutions are routinely interrupted. Language barriers are another important hindrance to effective education, particularly in countries with different linguistic communities or for students studying in a non-native language. AI-powered translation technologies are helping to overcome these limitations by delivering real-time translation and multilingual support (Dwivedi et al, 2024). For instance, AI algorithms can translate textbooks, online courses, and instructional films into numerous languages, guaranteeing that learners may access information in their preferred language. Furthermore, speech recognition and natural language processing (NLP) technologies provide interactive learning experiences, where students may practice language skills and receive fast feedback. By making education more accessible and inclusive, these technologies are helping to alleviate disparities and empower learners from varied language and cultural backgrounds.

AI is also addressing inequities in educational resources by democratizing access to high-quality information and instructional tools. In many regions of the world, colleges and professors lack the resources needed to give a strong education, such as textbooks, laboratory equipment, and competent instructors. AI-driven platforms are addressing this gap by delivering free or low-cost access to a multitude of educational resources, from digital libraries and interactive simulations to online courses and virtual laboratories (Zhang et al, 2024). For example, students in remote or poor colleges can utilize AI-powered simulations to do experiments in physics, chemistry, or biology, even if their colleges lack real labs. Similarly, online platforms like Massive Open Online Courses (MOOCs), supplemented by AI, give learners access to world-class professors and curriculum, leveling the playing field for students regardless of their socio-economic background (Ip, 2024). Professors, too, stand to profit from AI's transformational potential in education. Educators typically endure heavy workloads, with obligations ranging from lesson planning and grading to classroom management and administrative activities (Kayyali, 2026b).

Beyond boosting access and quality, AI is playing a critical role in creating fairness and inclusion within education institutions (Roshanaei et al, 2023). Marginalized populations, such as those with disabilities, typically encounter considerable problems in accessing education that fulfills their requirements. AI-powered assistive solutions are helping to address these problems by offering individualized support for learners with impairments. For instance, speech-to-text tools help students with hearing impairments to follow lectures, while screen readers and text-to-speech programs aid visually challenged learners in accessing digital information. Similarly, AI-driven solutions for students with cognitive challenges, such as those on the autism spectrum, offer targeted treatments that increase engagement and learning (Adako et al, 2024). By addressing the particular requirements of these learners, AI is building a more inclusive educational landscape where everyone has the opportunity to achieve. AI's benefits to education also extend to supporting lifelong learning and workforce development, which are vital for eliminating inequities in an increasingly competitive global economy. As industries develop and new technology arises, people must continually adapt and gain new skills to remain employed. AI-powered learning systems are enabling individuals to upskill and reskill throughout their careers, delivering tailored suggestions for courses, certificates, and career pathways based on their interests, talents, and market demands. These platforms not only allow individuals to progress in their professions but also contribute to economic mobility and social fairness by giving possibilities for growth and development regardless of one's background or circumstances. While the potential of AI to enhance quality education and eliminate inequities is tremendous, it is vital to understand and overcome the problems involved with its application (Holstein & Doroudi, 2021). One of the most serious problems is the digital divide, which refers to the gap between those who have access to digital technology and those who do not. For AI-driven educational solutions to be genuinely impactful, it is vital to guarantee that all learners, regardless of their location or socio-economic position, have access to the required infrastructure, such as internet connectivity and digital devices. Governments, NGOs, and business sector partners must engage to bridge this divide and build an equal basis for AI-powered education.

## AI FOR CLIMATE ACTION AND ENVIRONMENTAL SUSTAINABILITY

The increasing climate catastrophe and widespread environmental deterioration are among the most important concerns of the 21st century (Lomborg, 2020). From increasing global temperatures and melting ice caps to deforestation, pollution, and biodiversity loss, the repercussions of human activity on the globe are apparent. Addressing these difficulties necessitates new solutions that go beyond established ways. Artificial Intelligence (AI) is developing as a formidable instrument with the potential to greatly contribute to climate action and environmental sustainability. By utilizing its capacity to scan enormous information, discover patterns, and create predictive insights, AI is altering how we understand, address, and mitigate environmental challenges. One of the most significant ways AI is contributing to climate change is through its capacity to monitor and predict environmental systems with unparalleled precision (Amiri et al, 2024). Climate systems are very complex, including interactions among the atmosphere, seas, land, and biosphere. Predicting how these systems will respond to issues such as greenhouse gas emissions and deforestation requires examining huge quantities of data. AI systems, particularly machine learning models, can process this data at rates and sizes beyond human competence. They enable scientists to develop sophisticated climate models that give insights into future possibilities, such as temperature rise, sea level rises, and extreme weather occurrences. These models not only help our understanding of climate dynamics but also guide policies and strategies for mitigation and adaptation.

AI's function in monitoring extends beyond modeling to real-time observation of environmental changes (Ramadan et al, 2024). Satellites coupled with AI-powered sensors can detect deforestation, desertification, and glacier melting with astonishing precision. By analyzing satellite photos and other geospatial data, AI systems may detect illicit logging, monitor forest health, and identify regions in danger of wildfires. These insights help governments, conservation organizations, and local communities to take preemptive efforts to safeguard ecosystems and minimize environmental harm. For example, AI systems are being deployed to monitor the Amazon jungle, discovering deforestation operations early enough to enable action. The promise of AI in fighting climate change is further clear in its applications for improving energy systems and minimizing carbon emissions (Chen et al, 2023). The energy industry is one of the greatest contributors to global greenhouse gas emissions, and increasing its efficiency is crucial to reaching sustainability goals. AI-driven solutions are helping to make energy production, delivery, and consumption more efficient and sustainable. For instance, AI systems are improving the functioning of renewable energy sources such as wind and solar power by forecasting weather patterns and regulating energy production appropriately. This guarantees that energy is generated and stored effectively, decreasing waste and boosting the resilience of renewable systems.

Moreover, AI is altering the way we utilize energy at the individual and industrial levels (Ahmad et al, 2022). Smart grids, powered by AI, enable real-time monitoring and management of energy demand and supply (Khan et al, 2022). These networks can foresee peak demand periods and alter energy distribution to reduce waste and avert outages. On a lesser scale, AI-enabled gadgets such as smart thermostats and energy management systems are helping families and companies monitor their energy consumption and adopt more sustainable practices. By increasing energy efficiency across many levels, AI is playing a significant role in decreasing the carbon footprint of both individuals and companies. Transportation is another field where AI is making substantial contributions to environmental sustainability. The worldwide transportation industry accounts for a large percentage of greenhouse gas emissions, and switching to greener options is vital for climate action. AI is driving this change by allowing the development of electric cars (EVs) and autonomous transportation systems. Machine learning algorithms are boosting the efficiency of EV batteries, extending their range and cutting charging times (Mousaei et al, 2024). AI is also enabling the integration of EVs with energy networks, allowing vehicles to operate as mobile energy storage units that contribute to system stability.

In the sphere of autonomous transportation, AI technologies are optimizing traffic management systems to minimize congestion and pollution in metropolitan areas (Saxena, 2024). By evaluating traffic data in real-time, AI systems may advise ideal routes for automobiles, lowering fuel usage and trip times. Additionally, AI is being utilized to build sustainable public transportation networks, ensuring that resources are allocated effectively and fairly. These innovations not only cut emissions but also boost mobility and accessibility in cities, contributing to larger sustainability goals. Agriculture, a vital area for both food security and environmental health, is likewise being altered by AI. Traditional agricultural techniques sometimes result in substantial environmental repercussions, including soil deterioration, water abuse, and greenhouse gas emissions from livestock and fertilizers. AI is helping to alleviate these problems by allowing precision agriculture, which employs data-driven insights to enhance farming operations. For example, AI-powered systems may monitor soil conditions, weather patterns, and crop health to propose the precise quantity of water, fertilizer, and pesticides needed for the best harvests. This lowers waste, minimizes environmental impact, and conserves vital resources such as water.

AI is also playing a role in encouraging sustainable cattle management. By monitoring animal behavior, health, and growth rates, AI systems might help farmers manage their herds more effectively and minimize methane emissions, a substantial contributor to climate change. Furthermore, AI is enabling the development of alternative proteins, such as lab-grown meat and plant-based alternatives, which have a lesser environmental effect compared to traditional livestock production (Samad et al, 2025). By transforming how we produce and consume food, AI is helping to establish a more sustainable agriculture system that promotes both human and planetary health. Waste management and recycling are further areas where AI is pushing environmental sustainability. The world creates billions of tons of garbage each year, much of it ends up in landfills or the natural environment, leading to pollution and resource depletion (Mor & Ravindra, 2023). AI technologies are increasing garbage sorting and recycling operations by utilizing computer vision and robots to recognize and separate different sorts of debris. For instance, AI-powered sorting systems can identify between various plastics, metals, and biological materials, ensuring that recyclable garbage is appropriately handled. This not only minimizes the quantity of garbage transported to landfills but also conserves resources by permitting the reuse of materials.

AI is also being used to address plastic waste in seas and waterways (Solaja, 2024). Machine learning algorithms are evaluating satellite pictures and drone footage to identify regions with high amounts of marine garbage. These observations drive cleaning operations and influence legislation focused on minimizing plastic waste. Additionally, AI is driving the development of biodegradable materials and circular economy models, which encourage reuse and recycling over single-use consumption. By tackling waste management concerns, AI is helping to a cleaner and more sustainable world. Biodiversity protection is another crucial area where AI is making an impact (Shivaprakash et al, 2022). The loss of biodiversity poses a huge danger to ecosystems and human well-being since it weakens the natural systems that support life on Earth. AI-powered solutions are helping to safeguard endangered animals and their ecosystems by monitoring wildlife numbers and identifying illicit actions such as poaching. For example, AI systems may analyze audio recordings from forests to recognize the presence of certain species or identify gunshots that may suggest poaching activities. These tools enable conservationists to respond swiftly to hazards and devise tailored strategies for safeguarding biodiversity. While the potential of AI to promote climate action and environmental sustainability is tremendous, it is crucial to realize the obstacles and dangers connected with its implementation. One important worry is the environmental effect of AI itself, notably the energy consumption of data centers and machine learning algorithms. Training AI models need tremendous computing power, which can result in large carbon emissions if fuelled by non-renewable energy sources (Zohuri, 2020). To overcome this, it is vital to emphasize the usage of renewable energy in AI operations and invest in energy-efficient computer technology. Another problem is ensuring that AI solutions are inclusive and egalitarian. The benefits of AI should be available to anyone, regardless of geographic location or socio-economic position. This necessitates coordination among governments, corporations, and civil society to ensure that AI technologies are implemented in ways that emphasize social and environmental justice. Furthermore, ethical issues must be at the forefront of AI research, with protections in place to prevent misuse and unforeseen effects. AI provides transformational potential for tackling climate catastrophe and increasing environmental sustainability (Bibri et al, 2024). Its applications in monitoring, modeling, energy optimization, transportation, agriculture, waste management, and biodiversity protection highlight its ability to produce real change across various sectors. However, fulfilling this promise needs a communal commitment to tackling obstacles like as energy usage, diversity, and ethical use. By utilizing AI ethically and constructively, we can take substantial advances toward a sustainable future where both people and the world can thrive.

## ETHICAL CHALLENGES AND RISKS OF AI IN ADVANCING SDGS

The integration of Artificial Intelligence (AI) into strategies aimed to meet the Sustainable Development Goals (SDGs) represents a significant leap toward tackling some of humanity's most critical concerns (Fan et al, 2023). However, the revolutionary promise of AI does not come without substantial ethical problems and hazards. These difficulties involve several aspects, including equity, prejudice, openness, privacy, and governance. They pose fundamental considerations about how society may utilize AI responsibly to guarantee that technology acts as a vehicle for good change rather than a force that exacerbates current disparities or produces new forms of damage. Addressing these difficulties demands not just technological innovation but also a serious examination of ethical principles, regulatory frameworks, and social values.

One of the most significant ethical problems concerning the use of AI in furthering SDGs is the possibility of aggravating current inequities (Mhlanga, 2022). AI systems generally rely on huge volumes of data to function properly, yet this data is not always representative of varied populations. For example, in healthcare, AI-driven diagnostic systems trained on data from high-income countries may not function as correctly for people in low- and middle-income regions, where medical conditions and environmental variables differ dramatically. Similarly, AI applications in education may fail to meet the needs of marginalized groups, perpetuating inequities rather than alleviating them (Kunjumuhammed, 2024). If these gaps are not addressed, the promise of employing AI to promote SDG targets such as "Reduced Inequalities" and "Good Health and Well-being" might remain unfulfilled, putting marginalized communities further behind. Bias in AI systems is another major problem that raises ethical issues in the achievement of SDGs (Ceia et al, 2021). AI algorithms learn from previous data, and if this data reflects current prejudices, the resulting systems may perpetuate or even magnify them. For instance, in recruiting procedures, AI technologies educated on historical hiring data may be prejudiced against candidates based on gender, race, or socioeconomic background (Kayyali, 2026 c). Such biases can have far-reaching effects, particularly in attempts to establish gender equality and foster inclusive economic growth. Bias in AI is not necessarily deliberate, but its repercussions can weaken trust and limit progress toward attaining equal development. Addressing this issue involves careful analysis of data sources, clear algorithmic design, and constant monitoring to uncover and minimize any biases.

Data privacy and security constitute another complicated set of difficulties in the application of AI to accomplish SDGs (Ryan et al, 2020). The performance of many AI applications depends on access to enormous datasets, which sometimes include sensitive personal information. In healthcare, for instance, AI technologies evaluating patient data to anticipate disease outbreaks or enhance treatments must overcome rigorous privacy considerations. Similarly, in education, AI systems aiming to tailor learning experiences must manage student data with care to avoid breaches or misuse. The ethical problem arises in balancing the need for data to promote innovation with the duty to respect individuals' privacy and autonomy. Failing to maintain these standards can lead to a loss of confidence and possibly hurt the very communities that AI wants to assist. The use of AI in furthering SDGs also raises challenges about accountability and governance (Truby, 2020). As AI systems grow more independent, assessing culpability for their activities becomes increasingly challenging. For example, if an AI-driven agricultural system fails to anticipate a drought properly, resulting in crop failures and economic losses, who should be held accountable? Is it the developers, the operators, or the policymakers who implemented the system? These problems become even more crucial in circumstances where AI applications have substantial social consequences, such as disaster response, college reform, or public health efforts. Establishing explicit accountability frameworks is vital to ensure that AI is utilized properly and that any negative implications are addressed effectively.

Another ethical worry is the possible abuse of AI technology, either purposefully or accidentally (Blauth et al, 2022). While AI has the potential to be a force for good, it may also be weaponized or misapplied in ways that undermine the SDGs. For instance, AI systems deployed for monitoring can be repurposed to violate human rights, repress dissent, or discriminate against disadvantaged communities. Similarly, AI-driven disinformation campaigns can weaken public faith in institutions and disrupt attempts to promote peace, justice, and strong institutions. The dual-use nature of AI technology underlines the significance of ethical monitoring and international collaboration to prevent misuse while maximizing their beneficial impact (Bayan, 2024). In addition to these ethical concerns, there are larger social hazards linked with the widespread implementation of AI in attaining SDGs. One such risk is the possibility of job displacement induced by automation. While AI might bring new possibilities and efficiency, it can also lead to severe disruptions in labor markets, particularly for low-skilled workers. This has consequences for SDG targets relating to decent work and economic growth, as well as attempts to alleviate poverty. Managing this shift demands proactive policies that focus on re-skilling and upskilling people, ensuring that the advantages of AI-driven innovation are shared fairly across society. The environmental effect of AI is another topic that connects with the ethical use of technology to attain SDGs (Ryan et al, 2020). Training and deploying AI systems demand considerable computing resources, which in turn cost large quantities of energy. This carbon footprint can contradict aims connected to climate action and environmental sustainability. As AI becomes more incorporated into plans for promoting SDGs, it is necessary to examine its environmental effect and prioritize the development of energy-efficient algorithms and sustainable infrastructure.

Addressing the ethical issues and hazards of AI in accomplishing SDGs needs a multi-faceted strategy that incorporates collaboration among governments, academia, industry, and civil society (Mazzi, 2024). Policymakers must build rigorous regulatory frameworks that promote justice, openness, and accountability while supporting innovation. Educational institutions have a role to play in training the next generation of AI developers and users with a strong foundation in ethics and social responsibility. At the same time, industry leaders must commit to ethical principles in the design, implementation, and monitoring of AI systems. Public involvement and inclusion are also crucial in determining the ethical use of AI for SDGs (Mishra, 2024). Engaging different stakeholders in decision-making processes ensures that the perspectives of disadvantaged populations are heard and that their needs are met. This interactive approach not only boosts the legitimacy of AI efforts but also helps to create trust and foster a feeling of shared responsibility. The ethical difficulties and threats of AI in furthering SDGs are broad and multidimensional, reflecting the significant influence of this technology on society. While AI offers great promise to drive development toward a more fair and sustainable future, it also raises serious ethical challenges that cannot be overlooked. By addressing concerns of bias, transparency, privacy, accountability, and environmental sustainability, and by promoting cooperation and inclusion, society may harness the revolutionary power of AI in ways that correspond with the values and aims of the SDGs. The path toward ethical AI is not without its hurdles, but it is a journey worth undertaking to guarantee that the advantages of this technology are realized for all.

## REGIONAL CASE STUDIES: AI IMPLEMENTATION FOR SDGS

Artificial Intelligence (AI) has emerged as a revolutionary tool in tackling global concerns, notably in furthering the United Nations' Sustainable Development Goals SDGs (Mhlanga, 2022). Across numerous locations, AI-driven programs have revealed novel approaches to solving difficult societal and environmental concerns. From increasing healthcare service in distant locations to optimizing agricultural methods and solving climate concerns, AI is proving to be a vital engine of advancement. However, the specific application of AI differs widely among locations due to disparities in economic growth, infrastructure, regulations, and cultural settings. This variation in application gives useful insights and illustrates the versatility of AI as a solution customized to local circumstances. In Sub-Saharan Africa, AI has proved crucial in solving food security and agricultural difficulties, which are among the region's most urgent concerns (Wanyama et al, 2024). With the bulk of the people reliant on agriculture for their livelihoods, new AI technologies have been implemented to boost agricultural yields and optimize farming techniques. For instance, groups like PlantVillage have built AI-powered platforms that employ machine learning to identify crop illnesses using smartphone photographs. By arming farmers with smartphone applications capable of diagnosing plant health concerns, these solutions give early and precise information on treatment, helping to decrease crop losses. In Kenya, AI is being used to anticipate weather patterns, helping small-scale farmers to prepare better for planting and harvesting, even against increasingly uncertain climate circumstances (Gikunda, 2024). These activities directly contribute to reaching SDG 2, "Zero Hunger," and show the potential of AI in constructing resilient agricultural systems.

Similarly, in South Asia, AI has played a crucial role in boosting access to quality education (Lim et al, 2020). Countries like India and Bangladesh have adopted AI-driven educational solutions to bridge gaps in learning resources for poor groups. In remote places where access to competent professors is restricted, AI-powered platforms like BYJU and others are offering individualized learning experiences through interactive material and adaptive evaluations (Qasim, 2024). These systems assess individual student development and adapt the curriculum to fit their requirements, guaranteeing no learner is left behind. Such projects fit with SDG 4, "Quality Education," and stress the potential of AI to democratize education (Kayyali, 2026 a). Moreover, AI methods have been applied to translate instructional information into numerous regional languages, guaranteeing that language barriers do not limit learning possibilities. In Europe, where several countries are at the forefront of AI research and development, the focus has been on harnessing AI for climate change and energy sustainability. Countries like Germany and the Netherlands are adopting AI to maximize renewable energy production and delivery

(Şerban & Lytras, 2020). AI systems evaluate real-time data from wind turbines and solar panels to enhance efficiency and forecast changes in energy output. For example, in the Netherlands, AI is being used to develop virtual power plants by aggregating energy from multiple renewable sources, providing a consistent and predictable energy supply. These activities directly contribute to SDG 7, "Affordable and Clean Energy," and SDG 13, "Climate Action," illustrating how sophisticated technology may promote sustainable energy transitions (Raman et al, 2024). In Latin America, AI has been utilized to address concerns connected to urbanization and public safety. In cities like Bogotá, Colombia, and São Paulo, Brazil, AI-driven technologies are being employed to improve urban planning and traffic management (Vecchio et al, 2020). By collecting data from sensors, cameras, and mobile devices, AI models assist city planners detect congestion hotspots and improve traffic flow, decreasing greenhouse gas emissions, and improving air quality. Additionally, AI is being employed in predictive policing operations to detect high-crime regions and deploy resources more effectively. While these applications have shown potential to boost public safety, they also present serious ethical problems around privacy and monitoring, underlining the necessity for appropriate oversight in the deployment of such technology.

The Middle East has made tremendous gains in employing AI for healthcare innovation, notably in solving the issues of access to medical treatment in rural or underserved locations (Alhashmi, 2024). Countries like the United Arab Emirates and Saudi Arabia are investing extensively in AI-driven healthcare technologies to enhance diagnoses and treatment. AI-powered systems have been created to evaluate medical pictures for early identification of illnesses such as cancer and diabetes, enabling timely therapies (Zaman, 2024). Telemedicine technologies, boosted by AI, are giving remote consultations to patients in rural places, guaranteeing they receive proper medical treatment without the need for travel (Sharma et al, 2023). These activities correlate with SDG 3, "Good Health and Well-being," and underline the role of AI in boosting healthcare accessibility and quality. In North America, notably in the United States and Canada, AI has been widely embraced to alleviate socioeconomic inequities and create inclusive growth (van Niekerk, 2020). AI-driven workforce development initiatives are helping to reskill and upskill people affected by automation, ensuring they remain competitive in a quickly developing job market. For instance, efforts like Coursera's AI-driven learning platforms evaluate labor market trends and deliver targeted training programs that correlate with upcoming employment prospects (Marwan, 2020). These activities support SDG 8, "Decent Work and Economic Growth," by training individuals with the skills needed to flourish in the digital economy. Additionally, AI is being used to detect and fix structural inequities in areas like housing and credit access, increasing justice and equity in economic possibilities. In the Asia-Pacific region, home to various economies and ecosystems, AI has been applied to solve environmental concerns and natural disasters. Japan, a country prone to earthquakes and tsunamis, has created AI-powered early warning systems that analyze seismic data to forecast possible disasters and coordinate emergency actions. Similarly, in Indonesia, AI is being used to monitor deforestation and illicit logging operations, which harm biodiversity and contribute to climate change (Ali et al, 2025). Satellite imaging paired with machine learning algorithms gives real-time data on forest cover changes, enabling authorities to take rapid action against environmental breaches. These applications contribute to SDG 15, "Life on Land," and show the role of AI in conserving natural ecosystems.

China, as a worldwide leader in AI research, has proved its potential in pursuing numerous SDGs concurrently (Feng et al, 2024). The nation has implemented AI technology to improve air quality monitoring and enforce pollution control measures in metropolitan areas. By evaluating data from sensors and satellite photos, AI systems identify pollution sources and offer practical actions to minimize emissions. Additionally, China has invested in AI-driven educational platforms to bridge the urban-rural gap, ensuring that students in remote locations have access to quality learning resources (Li, 2024). These projects coincide with SDG 11, "Sustainable Cities and Communities," and SDG 4, "Quality Education," highlighting the adaptability of AI in solving interrelated concerns. Africa's diversified environment and distinct challenges have resulted in novel AI applications suited to local contexts (Leal Filho et al, 2022). In Rwanda, for example, AI-powered drones are being used to carry medical supplies, including vaccinations and blood, to remote health institutions. This program not only improves healthcare service but also decreases response times during crises. In Nigeria, AI is being deployed to analyze data on water supplies and forecast shortfalls, ensuring improved management and equitable distribution of this critical resource (Onyezere et al, 2024). These activities contribute to SDG 6, "Clean Water and Sanitation," and illustrate how AI can solve essential requirements in resource-constrained contexts. Australia and New Zealand have concentrated on harnessing AI to solve biodiversity conservation and marine environment preservation. In the Great Barrier Reef, AI systems are used to monitor coral health and detect problems such as coral bleaching and invasive species (Piñeros et al, 2024). By analyzing underwater images, these tools give crucial insights that drive conservation efforts and policy choices. Similarly, AI is being deployed to track and manage populations of endangered animals, guaranteeing their survival amid changing environmental conditions. These applications coincide with SDG 14, "Life Below Water," and stress the relevance of AI in conserving natural heritage for future generations.

While these regional case studies indicate the great promise of AI in promoting SDGs, they also underscore the necessity for a subtle strategy that recognizes local settings and obstacles (Göçoğlu & Göçoğlu, 2024). The successful adoption of AI involves collaboration among governments, commercial sectors, academic institutions, and civil society to guarantee that these technologies are implemented ethically and inclusively. Moreover, addressing challenges like as data privacy, algorithmic bias, and equal access to AI technologies is crucial to maximizing their advantages and limiting unforeseen effects. The numerous geographical uses of AI in furthering SDGs emphasize its versatility and revolutionary potential (Obaideen et al, 2024). From enhancing healthcare and education to tackling environmental concerns and fostering equitable growth, AI is playing a critical role in crafting a sustainable future. By learning from these case studies and promoting cross-regional collaboration, society may harness the power of AI to fulfill the lofty goals of the 2030 Agenda for Sustainable Development. However, the trip demands continual work, awareness, and a commitment to ensure that AI acts as a force for good, leaving no one behind.

## THE FUTURE OF AI IN DRIVING GLOBAL SUSTAINABILITY

The integration of artificial intelligence (AI) into attempts to achieve global sustainability is one of the most exciting and revolutionary breakthroughs of our time (Goralski & Tan, 2020). As the globe grapples with rising environmental, economic, and social concerns, AI provides tremendous capabilities that may be used to speed progress toward a more sustainable and equitable future. From tackling climate change to guaranteeing food security, boosting resource efficiency, and supporting equitable economic growth, the potential of AI to promote real change is vast. Yet, this future is not without hurdles, as ethical issues, equal access, and long-term implications must be carefully addressed to ensure AI's contributions line with the larger aims of sustainability. The future of AI in global sustainability will likely be determined by its ability to handle very difficult issues at unprecedented sizes. Climate change, possibly the most important issue of the 21st century, is a clear illustration of how AI might transform responses to global catastrophes (Snezhana, 2023). Through modern data analytics, AI can handle enormous datasets from weather satellites, environmental sensors, and historical climate records to discover patterns, anticipate future scenarios, and influence policy choices. This prediction competence is vital in helping governments and companies to build proactive rather than reactive responses. For instance, AI can improve renewable energy systems by anticipating wind patterns or solar radiation, ensuring that clean energy sources are used as effectively as feasible. Such applications not only lower greenhouse gas emissions but also contribute to the overall transition to a low-carbon economy.

Beyond preventing climate change, AI shows the potential to maintain and restore ecosystems (Malhi et al, 2020). With biodiversity diminishing at alarming rates, AI can aid in monitoring animal populations, identifying dangers, and creating conservation measures. Using drone technology paired with AI-powered image systems, researchers can monitor enormous regions of forests, seas, and wetlands to track endangered species and detect illicit activity such as poaching or deforestation. The precision and speed of these devices greatly transcend older approaches, enabling real-time responses to environmental problems (Mitchell & Sok, 2023). Additionally, AI-driven analysis of satellite data can uncover trends of land use change, enabling regulators to enforce sustainable practices and avoid habitat degradation. The future of AI in sustainability also extends to agriculture, a sector that confronts mounting challenges to feed a fast-increasing global population while reducing its environmental imprint. AI is already revolutionizing farming methods through precision agriculture, an approach that employs AI algorithms to maximize every element of crop production. By evaluating data from sensors, drones, and satellite photos, AI can predict the precise amounts of water, fertilizer, or pesticides needed for specific regions of farming (Sishodia et al, 2020). This not only enhances agricultural yields but also minimizes waste and environmental damage. As AI continues to improve, its applications in agriculture might become increasingly more complex, enabling farmers to adapt to changing climate conditions, avoid crop diseases, and establish more resilient food systems.

Another area where AI might dramatically affect global sustainability is urban development and infrastructure (Yigitcanlar & Cugurullo, 2020). As urban populations rise, cities have great issues in managing resources, transportation, and trash. AI-driven smart city technologies provide new answers to these challenges by optimizing energy consumption, enhancing traffic management, and minimizing trash output. For example, AI can evaluate traffic data in real-time to design adaptive traffic signal systems, cutting congestion and minimizing car emissions (Saxena, 2024). Similarly, waste management systems driven by AI can boost recycling rates by recognizing and sorting recyclable items more effectively. In the future, AI might even play a role in urban planning, helping cities develop sustainable layouts that limit energy usage and encourage green spaces. The future of AI in sustainability is not restricted to its direct applications in environmental and economic systems. It also has the potential to achieve social sustainability by addressing inequity and creating inclusion. AI-powered platforms can democratize access to education, healthcare, and financial services, breaking down barriers that have previously excluded underrepresented people (Challoumis, 2024). For instance, AI-enabled e-learning systems may give individualized education to children in rural or underprivileged locations, adapting information to their specific requirements and learning paces. With healthcare, AI can aid with identifying ailments and giving medical care to communities with limited access to physicians or hospitals. By addressing these gaps, AI contributes to developing more egalitarian societies where opportunities are open to all. Despite its tremendous promise, the future of AI in advancing global sustainability is not without dangers and obstacles. One of the most pressing problems is providing fair access to AI technologies. While high-income countries are driving the research and deployment of AI, low- and middle-income countries frequently lack the resources and infrastructure needed to execute these solutions. This imbalance raises the prospect of a digital gap, where people who stand to profit most from AI's promise are left behind. To solve this, international collaboration and investment will be vital in increasing the technological ability of underdeveloped countries and ensuring that AI solutions are tailored to fit the demands of various populations.

Another key aspect is the ethical usage of AI in sustainability initiatives (Nishant et al, 2020). AI systems are only as good as the data they are trained on, and biased or inadequate datasets might lead to unforeseen outcomes. For example, if an AI model used to allocate resources is based on historical data that reflects systemic disparities, it may perpetuate such injustices rather than solve them. Ensuring openness, accountability, and justice in AI decision-making processes is therefore vital to prevent such issues. Furthermore, the increased dependence on AI raises worries about data privacy and security, particularly as more sensitive information is gathered and evaluated. Establishing effective laws and ethical frameworks will be crucial in reducing these hazards and encouraging public trust in AI technology (de Almeida et al, 2021). Looking ahead, collaboration across many stakeholders will be vital to unleashing AI's full potential for sustainability. Governments, private sector enterprises, academic institutions, and civil society groups must work together to develop and deploy AI solutions that line with global sustainability goals (Gill & Germann, 2022). Public-private partnerships, for instance, can expedite innovation by pooling the knowledge and resources of multiple sectors. Meanwhile, cross-disciplinary research may guarantee that AI systems are anchored in a comprehensive grasp of the difficult issues they are supposed to address. Additionally, integrating communities in the development and implementation of AI technologies is vital to guarantee that these solutions are inclusive, culturally acceptable, and responsive to local needs.

As AI continues to improve, its potential to drive global sustainability will certainly increase in ways that are impossible to foresee. Emerging technologies such as quantum computing and edge computing might significantly increase AI's capabilities, enabling it to handle increasingly larger information and give insights with higher speed and accuracy (Gill et al, 2024). Meanwhile, the combination of AI with other cutting-edge technologies, such as blockchain and the Internet of Things (IoT), might generate new opportunities for sustainable growth. For example, blockchain may be used to provide transparency and accountability in AI-driven supply chain management, while IoT devices might give real-time data for AI systems to assess and act upon. The future of AI in advancing global sustainability is both hopeful and difficult. Its potential to address current concerns, from climate change to social inequity, makes it a valuable weapon for furthering sustainable development. However, fulfilling this promise will need careful attention to ethical issues, equal access, and collaborative ways. By solving these difficulties and embracing AI's revolutionary capacity, societies throughout the world may move closer to establishing a sustainable and fair future for all. The path will not be without hurdles, but with forethought, ingenuity, and teamwork, the possibilities are as extensive as they are inspiring.

## CONCLUSION

As we end our investigation of artificial intelligence (AI) in promoting global sustainability, it becomes increasingly obvious that AI is not merely a tool of technological growth but also a catalyst for systemic change in how we solve the most urgent concerns of our day. The connection between AI capabilities and the United Nations Sustainable Development Goals (SDGs) is a compelling reminder of the potential that exists to alter industries, enhance quality of life, and protect our planet for future generations. Throughout this chapter, we have evaluated AI's contributions to many areas, such as healthcare, education, poverty alleviation, climate action, and the reduction of disparities. Each of these domains has a distinct set of difficulties and possibilities, but all share a similar thread: AI's potential to generate more efficient, data-driven, and inclusive solutions. The application of AI in furthering the SDGs gives great potential to revolutionize how we approach development, sustainability, and social fairness. AI's capacity to handle and analyze huge quantities of data can lead to advances in understanding and mitigating the implications of climate change, increasing access to key services, and ensuring that the benefits of technological advancement are dispersed more evenly around the globe. As evidenced in real-world case studies from diverse countries, AI technologies have already begun to make a visible difference in attaining these goals, whether by boosting crop yields and food security, optimizing healthcare services, or allowing remote college in underprivileged communities. As exciting as these applications are, the integration of AI into the quest for sustainable development is not without its challenges. The ethical issues around AI cannot be underlined. Issues such as algorithmic bias, the opacity of decision-making processes, and the possibility of aggravating inequities are key difficulties that need to be solved to guarantee that AI serves all of mankind, rather than a chosen few. The very nature of AI—its dependence on enormous data sets and its capability to learn and make autonomous decisions—raises major challenges about accountability, transparency, and justice. These problems must be at the center of AI development and deployment plans since they will ultimately determine whether AI can contribute to a sustainable and just future.

Additionally, while AI offers the potential to build a more sustainable society, it is vital to realize the environmental cost of AI technologies themselves. The energy consumption involved with training and operating AI models, particularly those employing deep learning algorithms, has attracted attention to the need for more sustainable computing techniques. As we progress toward increasingly advanced AI systems, we must guarantee that the technology we rely on to tackle environmental difficulties does not accidentally contribute to the very problems we aim to alleviate. This demands innovation not just in the AI systems themselves but also in the infrastructure supporting them, such as the creation of energy-efficient data centers and more sustainable approaches to cloud computing. The divide in access to AI technology between developed and developing countries remains a critical impediment to attaining global sustainability. While wealthy economies have made great achievements in AI research and implementation, many low- and middle-income countries face challenges to adoption, including insufficient infrastructure, technical competence, and financial resources. If AI is to realize its promise of promoting sustainable development worldwide, efforts must be made to overcome this digital gap. International collaboration, capacity-building programs, and new finance methods will be important in ensuring that AI's advantages are available to all countries, particularly those most in need. The future of global sustainability hinges on the capacity to ensure that no one is left behind as we embrace the possibilities of AI.

Moreover, the role of AI in fostering global sustainability will not be realized in isolation. Governments, corporations, civil society groups, and academic institutions must work together to establish a conducive ecosystem that supports innovation while preserving ethical norms. Collaborative efforts across industries and regions are vital to overcoming the complex, linked issues facing humanity. Partnerships between the commercial sector and governmental organizations, for instance, might promote the creation of AI solutions that are both scalable and responsible, ensuring that technical advancement is linked with larger social goals. In terms of policy, the need for a worldwide framework that oversees the ethical development and deployment of AI is becoming critical. While national policies and initiatives are crucial, the global nature of AI's influence necessitates collaboration across boundaries. Governments and international agencies must work together to set rules and standards that drive AI development in a way that prioritizes the public benefit, reduces harm, and guarantees that technical developments correspond with the SDGs. This involves continual communication and collaboration between stakeholders from all sectors, with a special emphasis on inclusion, transparency, and accountability.

The future of AI in advancing global sustainability is not without its uncertainties, but the potential for dramatic change is obvious. AI technologies can accelerate progress toward attaining the SDGs, allowing solutions that are more precise, efficient, and inclusive than ever before. However, fulfilling this promise will need a determined effort to overcome the ethical, environmental, and societal concerns that come with AI applications. As we look ahead, we must embrace AI as a vehicle for good change, while ensuring that its development and usage are governed by principles that emphasize sustainability, fairness, and justice. AI is a tremendous facilitator of sustainable development, but its promise can only be fulfilled if we approach its integration with care, accountability, and a commitment to ethical standards. By promoting international collaboration, tackling the difficulties of accessibility, and emphasizing sustainability in AI design, we can guarantee that AI contributes significantly to the accomplishment of the SDGs. The future of AI in global sustainability rests on our capacity to utilize its strengths while defending against its hazards, eventually building a world where both people and the earth can thrive. As we move forward, we must continue to develop, cooperate, and strive toward a future where AI serves as a force for good in improving global sustainability and guaranteeing a higher quality of life for all.

## REFERENCES

Adako, O. P., Adeusi, O. C., & Alaba, P. A. (2024). Revolutionizing Autism Education: Harnessing AI for Tailored Skill Development in Social, Emotional, and Independent Learning Domains. *Journal of Computational and Cognitive Engineering*, *3*(4), 348–359. DOI: 10.47852/bonviewJCCE42023414

Ahmad, T., Zhu, H., Zhang, D., Tariq, R., Bassam, A., Ullah, F., AlGhamdi, A. S., & Alshamrani, S. S. (2022). Energetics Systems and artificial intelligence: Applications of industry 4.0. *Energy Reports*, *8*, 334–361. DOI: 10.1016/j.egyr.2021.11.256

Alaimo, K., Chilton, M., & Jones, S. J. (2020). Food insecurity, hunger, and malnutrition. In *Present knowledge in nutrition* (pp. 311–326). Academic Press. DOI: 10.1016/B978-0-12-818460-8.00017-4

Alhashmi, S. M. (2024). The evolution and challenges of healthcare policy and research in the Middle East. In *Digital Healthcare in Asia and Gulf Region for Healthy Aging and More Inclusive Societies* (pp. 425–445). Academic Press. DOI: 10.1016/B978-0-443-23637-2.00005-9

Ali, G., Mijwil, M. M., Adamopoulos, I., & Ayad, J. (2025). Leveraging the Internet of Things, Remote Sensing, and Artificial Intelligence for Sustainable Forest Management. *Babylonian Journal of Internet of Things*, *2025*, 1–65. DOI: 10.58496/BJIoT/2025/001

Amiri, Z., Heidari, A., & Navimipour, N. J. (2024). Comprehensive survey of artificial intelligence techniques and strategies for climate change mitigation. *Energy*, *308*, 132827. DOI: 10.1016/j.energy.2024.132827

Bayan, F. M. (2024). The Ethics of AI: Navigating the Moral Dilemmas of Artificial Intelligence. *Arab Journal for Scientific Publishing*.

Bibri, S. E., Krogstie, J., Kaboli, A., & Alahi, A. (2024). Smarter eco-cities and their leading-edge artificial intelligence of things solutions for environmental sustainability: A comprehensive systematic review. *Environmental Science and Ecotechnology*, *19*, 100330. DOI: 10.1016/j.ese.2023.100330 PMID: 38021367

Blauth, T. F., Gstrein, O. J., & Zwitter, A. (2022). Artificial intelligence crime: An overview of malicious use and abuse of AI. *IEEE Access : Practical Innovations, Open Solutions*, *10*, 77110–77122. DOI: 10.1109/ACCESS.2022.3191790

Ceia, V., Nothwehr, B., & Wagner, L. (2021). *Gender and Technology: A rights-based and intersectional analysis of key trends*. Academic Press.

Challoumis, C. (2024). AI and economic inequality-addressing the challenges ahead. In *XVIII International Scientific Conference. Dortmund. Germany* (pp. 120-155). Academic Press.

Challoumis, C. (2024, October). Building a sustainable economy-how ai can optimize resource allocation. In *XVI International Scientific Conference* (pp. 190-224).

Chen, L., Chen, Z., Zhang, Y., Liu, Y., Osman, A. I., Farghali, M., Hua, J., Al-Fatesh, A., Ihara, I., Rooney, D. W., & Yap, P. S. (2023). Artificial intelligence-based solutions for climate change: A review. *Environmental Chemistry Letters, 21*(5), 2525–2557. DOI: 10.1007/s10311-023-01617-y

Cowls, J., Tsamados, A., Taddeo, M., & Floridi, L. (2023). The AI gambit: Leveraging artificial intelligence to combat climate change—opportunities, challenges, and recommendations. *AI & Society, 38*(1), 1–25. DOI: 10.1007/s00146-021-01294-x PMID: 34690449

Da Costa, D., & McMichael, P. (2019). The poverty of the global order. In *Recognition and Redistribution* (pp. 157–171). Routledge. DOI: 10.4324/9781315878263-13

de Almeida, P. G. R., dos Santos, C. D., & Farias, J. S. (2021). Artificial intelligence regulation: A framework for governance. *Ethics and Information Technology, 23*(3), 505–525. DOI: 10.1007/s10676-021-09593-z

Di Vaio, A., Palladino, R., Hassan, R., & Escobar, O. (2020). Artificial intelligence and business models in the sustainable development goals perspective: A systematic literature review. *Journal of Business Research, 121*, 283–314. DOI: 10.1016/j.jbusres.2020.08.019

Díaz-Rodríguez, N., Del Ser, J., Coeckelbergh, M., de Prado, M. L., Herrera-Viedma, E., & Herrera, F. (2023). Connecting the dots in trustworthy Artificial Intelligence: From AI principles, ethics, and key requirements to responsible AI systems and regulation. *Information Fusion, 99*, 101896. DOI: 10.1016/j.inffus.2023.101896

Dwivedi, A., Sahu, S., & Srivastava, A. (2024, December). AI-Powered Real-Time Text Editor with Multilingual Translation and Speech Recognition. In 2024 IEEE 16th International Conference on Computational Intelligence and Communication Networks (CICN) (pp. 1335-1340). IEEE.

Ejjami, R. (2024). The future of learning: AI-based curriculum development. International Journal For Multidisciplinary Research, 6(4).

Facer, K., & Selwyn, N. (2021). *Digital technology and the futures of education: Towards 'Non-Stupid'optimism. Futures of Education initiative*. UNESCO.

Fan, Z., Yan, Z., & Wen, S. (2023). Deep learning and artificial intelligence in sustainability: A review of SDGs, renewable energy, and environmental health. *Sustainability (Basel), 15*(18), 13493. DOI: 10.3390/su151813493

Feng, S., Shafiei, M. W. M., Ng, T. F., Ren, J., & Jiang, Y. (2024). The intersection of economic growth and environmental sustainability in China: Pathways to achieving SDG. *Energy Strategy Reviews, 55*, 101530. DOI: 10.1016/j.esr.2024.101530

Fernandez, R. M. (2020). SDG3 good health and well-being: integration and connection with other SDGs. Good Health and Well-Being, 629-636.

Gikunda, K. (2024). Harnessing Artificial Intelligence for Sustainable Agricultural Development in Africa: Opportunities, Challenges, and Impact. arXiv preprint arXiv:2401.06171.

Gill, A. S., & Germann, S. (2022). Conceptual and normative approaches to AI governance for a global digital ecosystem supportive of the UN Sustainable Development Goals (SDGs). *AI and Ethics, 2*(2), 293–301. DOI: 10.1007/s43681-021-00058-z PMID: 34790947

Gill, S. S., Wu, H., Patros, P., Ottaviani, C., Arora, P., Pujol, V. C., ... Buyya, R. (2024). Modern computing: Vision and challenges. Telematics and Informatics Reports, 100116.

Göçoğlu, V., & Göçoğlu, İ. D. (2024). Local potentials for achieving sustainable development goals: Qualitative evidence from local governments in Türkiye. *Local Government Studies*, •••, 1–22.

Goralski, M. A., & Tan, T. K. (2020). Artificial intelligence and sustainable development. *International Journal of Management Education, 18*(1), 100330. DOI: 10.1016/j.ijme.2019.100330

Hite, K. A., & Seitz, J. L. (2021). *Global issues: an introduction.* John Wiley & Sons.

Holstein, K., & Doroudi, S. (2021). Equity and artificial intelligence in education: will" aied" amplify or alleviate inequities in education? arXiv preprint arXiv:2104.12920.

How, M. L., Chan, Y. J., & Cheah, S. M. (2020). Predictive insights for improving the resilience of global food security using artificial intelligence. *Sustainability (Basel), 12*(15), 6272. DOI: 10.3390/su12156272

Ip, K. (2024). The rise of EdTech: Transforming education through entrepreneurial ventures. Advances in Online Education: A Peer-Reviewed Journal, 3(2), 177-193.

Jejeniwa, T. O., Mhlongo, N. Z., & Jejeniwa, T. O. (2024). AI solutions for developmental economics: Opportunities and challenges in financial inclusion and poverty alleviation. *International Journal of Advanced Economics*, *6*(4), 108–123. DOI: 10.51594/ijae.v6i4.1073

Kayyali, M. (2024). Future possibilities and challenges of AI in education. In *Transforming education with generative AI: Prompt engineering and synthetic content creation* (pp. 118–137). IGI Global. DOI: 10.4018/979-8-3693-1351-0.ch006

Kayyali, M. (2025a). AI in Higher Education: Revolutionizing Curriculum and Administration. In AI Adoption and Diffusion in Education (pp. 31-62). IGI Global Scientific Publishing.

Kayyali, M. (2025b). The Future of AI in Education: Predictions and Emerging Trends. Next-Generation AI Methodologies in Education, 367-406.

Kayyali, M. (2026a). AI in Higher Education: The Risk of Excluding Vulnerable Learners. In AI and New Forms of Exclusion (pp. 57-82). IGI Global Scientific Publishing.

Kayyali, M. (2026b). The Impact of AI on Classroom Dynamics in Higher Education: Shifting Roles for Professors and Students. In Responsible AI Integration in Education (pp. 151-180). IGI Global Scientific Publishing.

Kayyali, M. (2026c). Ethical AI and Automation in the Workplace. In Leading Inclusive Workplaces Through Digital Transformation and Organizational Change (pp. 103-138). IGI Global Scientific Publishing.

Kayyali, M. (2026d). Preparing Educators for the Future: Navigating AI Tools in English Language Teaching. In AI-Powered English Teaching (pp. 267-308). IGI Global Scientific Publishing.

Khan, M. A., Saleh, A. M., Waseem, M., & Sajjad, I. A. (2022). Artificial intelligence enabled demand response: Prospects and challenges in smart grid environment. *IEEE Access : Practical Innovations, Open Solutions*, *11*, 1477–1505. DOI: 10.1109/ACCESS.2022.3231444

Khan, M. S., Umer, H., & Faruqe, F. (2024). Artificial intelligence for low income countries. *Humanities & Social Sciences Communications*, *11*(1), 1–13. DOI: 10.1057/s41599-024-03947-w

Khanal, U., Wilson, C., Rahman, S., Lee, B. L., & Hoang, V. N. (2021). Smallholder farmers' adaptation to climate change and its potential contribution to UN's sustainable development goals of zero hunger and no poverty. *Journal of Cleaner Production*, *281*, 124999. DOI: 10.1016/j.jclepro.2020.124999

Kunjumuhammed, S. K. (2024). Artificial Intelligence in Addressing Educational Inequality Dimensions in Higher Education Institutions (HEIs): A Critical Review. Risks and Challenges of AI-Driven Finance: Bias, Ethics, and Security, 146-164.

Kuteesa, K. N., Akpuokwe, C. U., & Udeh, C. A. (2024). Gender equity in education: Addressing challenges and promoting opportunities for social empowerment. *International Journal of Applied Research in Social Sciences*, *6*(4), 631–641. DOI: 10.51594/ijarss.v6i4.1034

Larson, P. D. (2020). Corruption, gender inequality and logistics performance. *International Journal of Logistics Management*, *31*(2), 381–397. DOI: 10.1108/IJLM-02-2019-0062

Leal Filho, W., Tripathi, S. K., Andrade Guerra, J. B. S. O. D., Giné-Garriga, R., Orlovic Lovren, V., & Willats, J. (2019). Using the sustainable development goals towards a better understanding of sustainability challenges. *International Journal of Sustainable Development and World Ecology*, *26*(2), 179–190. DOI: 10.1080/13504509.2018.1505674

Leal Filho, W., Wall, T., Mucova, S. A. R., Nagy, G. J., Balogun, A. L., Luetz, J. M., & Gandhi, O. (2022). Deploying artificial intelligence for climate change adaptation. *Technological Forecasting and Social Change*, *180*, 121662. DOI: 10.1016/j.techfore.2022.121662

Li, M. (2024). Exploring the digital divide in primary education: A comparative study of urban and rural mathematics teachers' TPACK and attitudes towards technology integration in post-pandemic China. *Education and Information Technologies*, 1–33.

Lim, C. P., Ra, S., Chin, B., & Wang, T. (2020). Information and communication technologies (ICT) for access to quality education in the global south: A case study of Sri Lanka. *Education and Information Technologies*, *25*(4), 2447–2462. DOI: 10.1007/s10639-019-10069-3

Lomborg, B. (2020). Welfare in the 21st century: Increasing development, reducing inequality, the impact of climate change, and the cost of climate policies. *Technological Forecasting and Social Change*, *156*, 119981. DOI: 10.1016/j.techfore.2020.119981

Lutz, C. (2019). Digital inequalities in the age of artificial intelligence and big data. *Human Behavior and Emerging Technologies*, *1*(2), 141–148. DOI: 10.1002/hbe2.140

Malhi, Y., Franklin, J., Seddon, N., Solan, M., Turner, M. G., Field, C. B., & Knowlton, N. (2020). Climate change and ecosystems: threats, opportunities and solutions. Philosophical Transactions of the Royal Society B, 375(1794), 20190104.

Marwan, A. (2020). *Impact of artificial intelligence on education for employment: Learning and employability framework*. Academic Press.

Mazzi, F. (2024). Artificial Intelligence and Sustainability Considerations: National, Regional and Supra National Perspective. Regional and Supra National Perspective.

Mhlanga, D. (2021). Artificial intelligence in the industry 4.0, and its impact on poverty, innovation, infrastructure development, and the sustainable development goals: Lessons from emerging economies? *Sustainability (Basel)*, *13*(11), 5788. DOI: 10.3390/su13115788

Mhlanga, D. (2022). Human-centered artificial intelligence: The superlative approach to achieve sustainable development goals in the fourth industrial revolution. *Sustainability (Basel)*, *14*(13), 7804. DOI: 10.3390/su14137804

Mishra, D. (2024). Strategic Communication for AI-Driven Sustainability Initiatives: Bridging Technology, Policy, and Public Engagement in Achieving SDGs. In AI Applications for Clean Energy and Sustainability (pp. 187-211). IGI Global.

Mitchell, S. A., & Sok, D. K. (2023). Precision Livestock Farming in the Digital Age: Sensors and Microfluidics Paving the Way for Sustainable Agriculture. *Sage Science Review of Educational Technology*, *6*(1), 71–87.

Mogaji, E., Soetan, T. O., & Kieu, T. A. (2020). The implications of artificial intelligence on the digital marketing of financial services to vulnerable customers. Australasian Marketing Journal.

Mor, S., & Ravindra, K. (2023). Municipal solid waste landfills in lower-and middle-income countries: Environmental impacts, challenges and sustainable management practices. *Process Safety and Environmental Protection*, *174*, 510–530. DOI: 10.1016/j.psep.2023.04.014

Mousaei, A., Naderi, Y., & Bayram, I. S. (2024). Advancing state of charge management in electric vehicles with machine learning: A technological review. *IEEE Access : Practical Innovations, Open Solutions*, *12*, 43255–43283. DOI: 10.1109/ACCESS.2024.3378527

Nishant, R., Kennedy, M., & Corbett, J. (2020). Artificial intelligence for sustainability: Challenges, opportunities, and a research agenda. *International Journal of Information Management*, *53*, 102104. DOI: 10.1016/j.ijinfomgt.2020.102104

Obaideen, K., Albasha, L., Iqbal, U., & Mir, H. (2024). Wireless power transfer: Applications, challenges, barriers, and the role of AI in achieving sustainable development goals-A bibliometric analysis. *Energy Strategy Reviews*, *53*, 101376. DOI: 10.1016/j.esr.2024.101376

Onyezere, C. V., Oforleta, C. M., & Onyezere, C. E. (2024). Artificial intelligence and sustainable development in Nigeria, West Africa (2015-2024). *International Journal of Public Administration and Development Studies*, *1*(1), 1–16.

Pedro, F., Subosa, M., Rivas, A., & Valverde, P. (2019). Artificial intelligence in education: Challenges and opportunities for sustainable development. Academic Press.

Piñeros, V. J., Reveles-Espinoza, A. M., & Monroy, J. A. (2024). From Remote Sensing to Artificial Intelligence in Coral Reef Monitoring. *Machines (Basel)*, *12*(10), 693. DOI: 10.3390/machines12100693

Prabhakar, A. C. (2025). AI Strategies for Sustainable Development Goals: Collective Action for Poverty Alleviation. In AI Strategies for Social Entrepreneurship and Sustainable Economic Development (pp. 393-442). IGI Global Scientific Publishing.

Qasim, S. H. (2024). Beyond the Classroom: Emerging Technologies to Enhance Learning. Academic Press.

Ramadan, M. N., Ali, M. A., Khoo, S. Y., Alkhedher, M., & Alherbawi, M. (2024). Real-time IoT-powered AI system for monitoring and forecasting of air pollution in industrial environment. *Ecotoxicology and Environmental Safety*, *283*, 116856. DOI: 10.1016/j.ecoenv.2024.116856 PMID: 39151373

Raman, R., Pattnaik, D., Kumar, C., & Nedungadi, P. (2024). Advancing sustainable energy systems: A decade of SETA research contribution to sustainable development goals. *Sustainable Energy Technologies and Assessments*, *71*, 103978. DOI: 10.1016/j.seta.2024.103978

Roshanaei, M., Olivares, H., & Lopez, R. R. (2023). Harnessing AI to foster equity in education: Opportunities, challenges, and emerging strategies. *Journal of Intelligent Learning Systems and Applications*, *15*(04), 123–143. DOI: 10.4236/jilsa.2023.154009

Ryan, M., Antoniou, J., Brooks, L., Jiya, T., Macnish, K., & Stahl, B. (2020). The ethical balance of using smart information systems for promoting the United Nations' Sustainable Development Goals. *Sustainability (Basel)*, *12*(12), 4826. DOI: 10.3390/su12124826

Samad, A., Kim, S. H., Kim, C. J., Lee, E. Y., Kumari, S., Hossain, M. J., Alam, A. M. M. N., Muazzam, A., Hwang, Y.-H., & Joo, S. T. (2025). From Farms to Labs: The New Trend of Sustainable Meat Alternatives. *Food Science of Animal Resources*, *45*(1), 13–30. DOI: 10.5851/kosfa.2024.e105 PMID: 39840251

Saxena, R. R. (2024). Artificial Intelligence in Traffic Systems. arXiv preprint arXiv:2412.12046.

Şerban, A. C., & Lytras, M. D. (2020). Artificial intelligence for smart renewable energy sector in europe—Smart energy infrastructures for next generation smart cities. *IEEE Access : Practical Innovations, Open Solutions, 8*, 77364–77377. DOI: 10.1109/ACCESS.2020.2990123

Sharma, S., Rawal, R., & Shah, D. (2023). Addressing the challenges of AI-based telemedicine: Best practices and lessons learned. *Journal of Education and Health Promotion, 12*(1), 338. DOI: 10.4103/jehp.jehp_402_23 PMID: 38023098

Shivaprakash, K. N., Swami, N., Mysorekar, S., Arora, R., Gangadharan, A., Vohra, K., Jadeyegowda, M., & Kiesecker, J. M. (2022). Potential for artificial intelligence (AI) and machine learning (ML) applications in biodiversity conservation, managing forests, and related services in India. *Sustainability (Basel), 14*(12), 7154. DOI: 10.3390/su14127154

Sishodia, R. P., Ray, R. L., & Singh, S. K. (2020). Applications of remote sensing in precision agriculture: A review. *Remote Sensing (Basel), 12*(19), 3136. DOI: 10.3390/rs12193136

Snezhana, D. (2023). Applying artificial intelligence (AI) for mitigation climate change consequences of the natural disasters. *Research Journal of Ecology and Environmental Sciences, 3*(1), 1–8.

Solaja, O. M. (2024). Unleashing the Power of AI: Revolutionizing Plastic Waste Management for Sustainable Development in Developing Nations. *Water Technology, 12*(1), 28–38.

Stahl, B. C. (2021). *Artificial intelligence for a better future: an ecosystem perspective on the ethics of AI and emerging digital technologies*. Springer Nature. DOI: 10.1007/978-3-030-69978-9

Truby, J. (2020). Governing artificial intelligence to benefit the UN sustainable development goals. *Sustainable Development (Bradford), 28*(4), 946–959. DOI: 10.1002/sd.2048

van Niekerk, A. J. (2020). Inclusive economic sustainability: SDGs and global inequality. *Sustainability (Basel), 12*(13), 5427. DOI: 10.3390/su12135427

Vecchio, G., Tiznado-Aitken, I., & Hurtubia, R. (2020). Transport and equity in Latin America: A critical review of socially oriented accessibility assessments. *Transport Reviews, 40*(3), 354–381. DOI: 10.1080/01441647.2020.1711828

Vincent, G., Narashimman, G., Suresh, M., Kingsly, P. J., Rajendhiran, M., & Rajalakshmi, M. (2024). Examine Ai Models For Credit Scoring And Risk Assessment, Integrating Nontraditional Data Sources Such As Social Media And Transaction Histories To Enhance Accuracy And Inclusivity. *Educational Administration: Theory and Practice*, *30*(5), 13931–13940.

Vinuesa, R., Azizpour, H., Leite, I., Balaam, M., Dignum, V., Domisch, S., Felländer, A., Langhans, S. D., Tegmark, M., & Fuso Nerini, F. (2020). The role of artificial intelligence in achieving the Sustainable Development Goals. *Nature Communications*, *11*(1), 1–10. DOI: 10.1038/s41467-019-14108-y PMID: 31932590

Wanyama, J., Bwambale, E., Kiraga, S., Katimbo, A., Nakawuka, P., Kabenge, I., & Oluk, I. (2024). A systematic review of fourth industrial revolution technologies in smart irrigation: Constraints, opportunities, and future prospects for sub-Saharan Africa. *Smart Agricultural Technology*, *7*, 100412. DOI: 10.1016/j.atech.2024.100412

Williams, R. (2024). Impact. AI: Democratizing AI through K-12 Artificial Intelligence Education (Doctoral dissertation, Massachusetts Institute of Technology).

Yigitcanlar, T., & Cugurullo, F. (2020). The sustainability of artificial intelligence: An urbanistic viewpoint from the lens of smart and sustainable cities. *Sustainability (Basel)*, *12*(20), 8548. DOI: 10.3390/su12208548

Zaman, Q. (2024). The Role of Artificial Intelligence in Early Disease Detection: Transforming Diagnostics and Treatment. *Multidisciplinary Journal of Healthcare*, *1*(2), 43–54.

Zhang, Y., Zhang, M., Wu, L., & Li, J. (2024). Digital Transition Framework for Higher Education in AI-Assisted Engineering Teaching. *Science & Education*, 1–22.

Zohuri, B., Behgounia, F., & Nezam, Z. Z. (2020). Artificial Intelligence Integration with Energy Sources (Renewable and Non-renewable). *Journal of Energy and Power Engineering*, *14*, 193–210.

## KEY TERMS AND DEFINITIONS

**Algorithmic Bias:** A systematic and unfair error in AI decision-making, often stemming from biased training data, which can perpetuate inequalities and injustices.

**Artificial Intelligence (AI):** The ability of machines to analyze data, recognize patterns, and make decisions that mimic human intelligence, used to tackle complex global challenges.

**Data-Driven Solutions:** Approaches that rely on analyzing large amounts of data to inform decisions, enhance efficiency, and optimize outcomes in various sectors.

**Digital Divide:** The gap between those who have access to modern digital technologies, such as AI, and those who do not, often due to economic, geographic, or infrastructural barriers.

**Machine Learning:** A subfield of AI where algorithms improve their performance by learning from data, enabling systems to make predictions and automate tasks.

**Precision Agriculture:** The use of AI and data analytics to optimize farming practices, enhancing crop yields while minimizing environmental impact.

**Sustainable Development Goals (SDGs):** A set of 17 interconnected goals established by the United Nations to eradicate poverty, reduce inequalities, and protect the planet by 2030.

# Chapter 2
# Artificial Intelligence-Based Approaches to Sustainable Development and Gender Balance

**Funda Hatice Sezgin**
https://orcid.org/0000-0002-2693-9601
*Istanbul University-Cerrahpasa, Turkey*

## ABSTRACT

*Artificial intelligence (AI) refers to the entirety of technologies that mimic human-like decision-making processes through techniques such as big data, machine learning, and natural language processing. In recent years, AI applications have begun to be used across a wide range of fields, from the labor market to healthcare services, from education to public administration. When supported by the right policies, AI systems can be powerful tools for accelerating gender equality. However, biased data and non-transparent algorithms can reproduce discrimination against women and minority groups. This study discusses the advantages and risks of artificial intelligence applications on gender, emphasizing that these technologies have the potential to increase social inequalities if not designed and implemented correctly.*

## INTRODUCTION

Sustainable development aims to ensure that economic growth is carried out in balance with environmental protection and social inclusion. In this context, gender balance is one of the indispensable components of development. Without ensuring women's equal access to education, healthcare, the labor market, and decision-

DOI: 10.4018/979-8-3373-1837-0.ch002

making mechanisms, sustainable development cannot be achieved. Goal 5 – Gender Equality, included in the United Nations Sustainable Development Goals (SDGs), is directly connected to all other goals. Women's active participation in economic and social life creates a wide sphere of influence, ranging from poverty reduction to combating climate change.

Artificial intelligence (AI) has become an important tool in developing policies and practices that strengthen gender balance. Big data analytics and machine learning techniques can be used to make existing inequalities visible, detect gender-based discrimination, and generate solution-oriented strategies. For example, data analytics models that reveal the wage gap between men and women in the labor market enable policymakers to develop targeted interventions.

However, in addition to supporting gender balance, AI systems can also reproduce existing inequalities if designed incorrectly. When algorithms learn from historical data, they may replicate the gender biases present in that data. This situation can lead to women being disadvantaged, particularly in recruitment, credit scoring, and social assistance applications. Therefore, designing AI applications with gender sensitivity and ensuring continuous monitoring is critically important (Chauhan & Gagandeep, 2022).

Balancing datasets, ensuring algorithmic transparency, and implementing ethical oversight mechanisms are key requirements for achieving gender equality in AI-based approaches. Adequate representation of women and other underrepresented groups in datasets contributes to producing fairer outcomes. Transparency about how algorithms function not only increases user trust but also makes it possible to detect potential biases early (Dobreva et al., 2023).

Furthermore, to ensure that artificial intelligence technologies serve sustainable development goals, inclusive digital education programs must be expanded. When women's access to education and professional development opportunities in STEM (science, technology, engineering, mathematics) fields is increased, a more balanced representation in technology production and management can be achieved. This, in turn, integrates diverse perspectives into the design and implementation of AI systems, contributing to gender equality.

Sustainable development and gender balance can be strengthened through the conscious and ethical use of artificial intelligence technologies. However, the success of this process depends not only on the advancement of technological tools but also on the inclusiveness of policies and the social sensitivity of practices. To fully harness the potential of AI, cooperation among policymakers, technology developers, and civil society organizations must be strengthened. In this way, a fair and inclusive future that creates both economic and social benefits in the digital transformation process can be built (Fryxell, 2021).

## THE IMPORTANCE OF ARTIFICIAL INTELLIGENCE IN SUSTAINABLE DEVELOPMENT AND GENDER BALANCE

Sustainable development refers to an approach that aims to establish a balance between economic growth, social inclusion, and environmental protection. Within this framework, gender balance is an indispensable component of sustainable development. Without women's equal participation in education, employment, healthcare, and decision-making mechanisms, it is not possible for development to be inclusive and fair (Bordalo et al., 2019). Artificial intelligence offers a powerful tool to achieve these goals; with its capabilities in data analysis, decision support systems, and automation, it can develop innovative methods to identify, monitor, and solve problems related to gender equality (Delgado Cadena, 2020).

AI plays a significant role in making gender inequalities visible. Through big data analysis, differences between men and women in education, healthcare, the labor market, and policy-making can be revealed in detail. For example, by analyzing job postings and application data, it is possible to identify sectors where women are underrepresented. Such analyses enable policymakers to develop targeted interventions aimed at increasing gender equality (Sætra, 2021).

In the field of education, AI offers solutions that support equal opportunities. Intelligent learning platforms can create personalized learning paths that encourage female students to engage in STEM fields. AI can analyze students' talents and areas of interest and provide guidance free from gender bias. In this way, the influence of traditional gender stereotypes on educational choices can be reduced (West et al., 2019).

In healthcare, AI can produce solutions that are sensitive to women's needs. AI systems trained on datasets specific to women's health play a critical role in the early diagnosis of diseases and the creation of personalized treatment plans. For example, AI-based imaging systems in breast cancer screenings can reduce false-negative rates, thereby increasing women's chances of survival. Such applications contribute to gender equality in healthcare while improving overall quality of life in society (Otterbacher et al., 2017).

In the labor market, AI can help reduce gender bias in recruitment processes. Gender-neutral algorithms evaluate applications solely based on skills and experience, offering equal opportunities to both male and female candidates. Furthermore, AI-based performance monitoring systems can enhance transparency in promotion processes, helping to remove the invisible barriers that hinder women's career advancement (Kay et al., 2015).

AI can also contribute to increasing women's representation in decision-making processes. Political decision support systems can conduct gender impact analyses to predict the possible effects of new regulations on men and women in advance.

In this way, a gender equality perspective can become an integral part of legislative and policy development processes (Kiritchenko & Mohammad, 2018).

From the perspective of economic inclusion one of the key elements of sustainable development AI offers effective solutions. Digital finance applications can facilitate women entrepreneurs' access to credit and increase their participation in economic activities. AI-based risk assessment models can allow women to obtain credit regardless of traditional financial history, thereby reducing financial inequalities (Elson, 2017).

In the context of environmental sustainability, AI can encourage women's participation in the green economy. Sustainable agriculture, renewable energy, and circular economy projects led by women can become more efficient through AI-supported data analysis and automation solutions. This approach supports environmental goals while also promoting women's economic empowerment (Chant & Sweetman, 2012).

However, for AI to support gender equality, the risks of algorithmic bias must be reduced. When AI systems are trained on biased datasets, they may reproduce existing gender inequalities. Therefore, inclusivity, transparency, and ethical principles should be prioritized in data collection processes, and systems should be regularly subjected to independent audits.

AI is a strategic tool in achieving sustainable development and gender balance goals. When designed correctly, it functions as a mechanism that not only identifies existing inequalities but also produces effective solutions to reduce them. To fully harness the potential of AI, a gender perspective should be integrated into technology development processes, and multi-stakeholder collaborations should be strengthened. This approach will play a critical role in building a future that is both fairer and more sustainable.

## ARTIFICIAL INTELLIGENCE-BASED APPROACHES AND THEIR CONTRIBUTIONS TO SUSTAINABLE DEVELOPMENT

Artificial intelligence is increasingly emerging as a transformative force in achieving sustainable development goals. Sustainable development aims to establish a balanced relationship between economic growth, environmental protection, and social inclusion. In this context, AI offers decision-makers the opportunity to develop faster, more accurate, and more inclusive policies through methods such as big data analysis, machine learning, and predictive modeling. Particularly in complex and multidimensional issues like gender equality, AI can identify inequalities and generate solutions through data-driven approaches (Armutat et al., 2024).

One of AI's contributions to sustainable development is making existing problems more visible through data analytics. For example, by analyzing education, healthcare, and labor market data, inequalities in opportunities between men and women can be concretely demonstrated. Such data facilitate the development of targeted and effective intervention strategies for both policymakers and civil society organizations. This ensures that resources can be directed toward the areas of greatest need (Sutko, 2020).

Another important contribution lies in policy modeling and simulation capabilities. AI can predict the potential outcomes of different policy scenarios. For instance, the long-term economic and social impacts of scholarship and training programs aimed at increasing women's participation in STEM (science, technology, engineering, and mathematics) fields can be analyzed through simulation models. This allows policymakers to minimize risks and maximize impact (Manasi et al., 2022).

AI can also reduce the invisible workload placed on women through automation and digitalization. Tasks traditionally assigned to women such as household care, elder care, and childcare can be supported by smart home technologies and robotic solutions. This enables women to use their time more efficiently, increase their participation in the workforce, and focus on career development. As a result, gender balance is strengthened in a way that directly contributes to sustainable development goals (Lütz, 2024).

Moreover, AI provides indirect contributions to gender equality in the field of environmental sustainability. Employing women in renewable energy projects and ensuring their participation in decision-making mechanisms supports the progress of both environmental goals and social equality. AI-powered energy management systems, agricultural technologies, and climate change prediction models can create new job opportunities that improve women's access to economic resources (Craiut & Iancu, 2022).

Another critical area is AI applications in healthcare services. Women's access to healthcare particularly in areas such as pregnancy monitoring, breast cancer screenings, and reproductive health can be improved through AI-based early diagnosis and preventive treatment systems. Data from the World Health Organization indicate that AI-assisted diagnostic systems can increase early detection rates by 20-30%. This contributes to sustainable development goals both in terms of individual health and public health.

To maximize AI's contributions to sustainable development, ethical and inclusive design principles are essential. Balanced and representative datasets used to train algorithms are a critical requirement, especially in terms of gender equality. This ensures that AI systems produce inclusive and fair solutions instead of reproducing historical biases. Additionally, AI applications supported by transparency and accountability mechanisms are more likely to gain public trust and achieve wider acceptance (Toniolo et al., 2020). AI-based approaches hold great potential to simultaneously strengthen the economic, environmental, and social dimensions of sustainable development. However, realizing this potential depends not only on technological innovations but also on the inclusivity of policies, the quality of data, and the social sensitivity of applications. When properly directed, AI can accelerate gender equality and play a key role in building a fairer, more inclusive, and more sustainable future (Khakurel et al., 2018).

## THE RELATIONSHIP BETWEEN ARTIFICIAL INTELLIGENCE, ALGORITHMIC FAIRNESS AND GENDER EQUALITY

In recent years, artificial intelligence (AI) has begun to be used across a wide range of fields, from labor markets to the healthcare sector, from education to public services. The speed, efficiency, and cost advantages provided by these technologies accelerate the digital transformation process of societies. However, AI systems are not merely technical tools; they are socio-technical systems deeply interconnected with social relations. Therefore, if these technologies are not properly designed and implemented, they can reinforce existing inequalities. At this point, the concept of "algorithmic fairness" comes into play. Algorithmic fairness is an ethical and technical approach aimed at ensuring that AI and automation systems produce fair, unbiased, and inclusive outcomes in decision-making processes.

Gender equality is included as an important goal in the United Nations Sustainable Development Goals (SDGs) (Goal 5). Equal opportunities for women and men in economic, social, and political spheres are fundamental conditions for democratic societies and sustainable development. However, historical biases embedded in the data on which AI systems are trained can reproduce gender-based discrimination. For example, recruitment data from professions historically dominated by men may lead AI algorithms to disadvantage female candidates.

From an algorithmic fairness perspective, the aim is to develop the methods necessary to detect, correct, and prevent such biases. One technique used for this purpose is "data balancing." Data balancing ensures that the representation of men and women in the datasets used to train algorithms is equalized, or that disadvantaged groups are adequately represented. This makes the system's decision-making process more inclusive (Borwein et al., 2024).

Another critical aspect of achieving gender equality is "algorithmic transparency." Understanding how an AI system works, which data it uses, and which criteria it applies to make decisions makes it easier to detect potential gender-based biases early on. Transparency also increases public trust and encourages users to believe that algorithms are fair. In addition, independent audit mechanisms and open-source code applications are important tools in ensuring algorithmic fairness (Delgado Cadena, 2020).

In regions where women are particularly disadvantaged in finance, education, healthcare, and employment, it is essential to design AI-powered decision systems in an inclusive manner. For instance, credit scoring algorithms that consider not only income data but also women entrepreneurs' social capital, education, and innovative business performance can increase financial inclusion. This approach not only reduces economic inequalities but also strengthens women's participation in working life (Di Vaio et al., 2020).

In the healthcare sector, algorithmic fairness also plays a critical role in terms of gender equality. Most of the data used to train medical diagnostic algorithms have been collected from male patients. This situation can increase the margin of error in diagnosing diseases specific to women. Ensuring the representation of women's data and biological differences in line with the principles of algorithmic fairness improves the quality of healthcare services for women.

In the field of education, AI is used in student performance predictions, scholarship evaluations, and career guidance systems. However, gender biases in historical data may reduce the rate at which female students are directed toward STEM fields. Systems developed within the framework of algorithmic fairness can guide without overlooking the potential of female students, thus increasing women's representation in STEM.

Ensuring algorithmic fairness is not only a technical issue but also a multidimensional process that involves governance, policy, and legal frameworks. Ethics committees, data protection regulations, and inclusive technology policies contribute to the widespread adoption of AI applications that take gender equality into account. Additionally, public awareness campaigns and digital literacy programs help users evaluate AI systems critically and consciously (Ahn et al., 2022).

The relationship between artificial intelligence, algorithmic fairness, and gender equality is shaped not only by the technical capacity of the technology but also by societal values, ethical principles, and political will. When designed consciously and inclusively, AI can be a powerful tool to accelerate gender equality. However, this requires a multidimensional strategy, from datasets to algorithm design, from legal frameworks to public awareness. In this way, the principles of justice, equality, and inclusivity can be preserved in the digital transformation process, maximizing social benefit (Dhiman et al., 2024).

## ALGORITHMIC BIAS AND GENDER INEQUALITY RISKS

Algorithmic bias refers to the systematic production of unfair or unequal outcomes against certain groups in the decision-making processes of artificial intelligence (AI) and machine learning systems. These biases often stem from historical, cultural, and social inequalities embedded in the datasets used to train algorithms. From the perspective of gender inequality, algorithmic bias can cause women and other gender identities to remain in disadvantaged positions in critical areas such as labor markets, education, healthcare, finance, and justice systems (Liu, 2024).

One of the most common areas where gender-based algorithmic bias occurs is in recruitment processes. Data obtained from sectors historically dominated by men may lead algorithms to score female candidates lower. For example, the hiring algorithm of a major technology company was found to have a tendency to give negative responses to female applicants when learning from past hiring data. This situation deprives women of equal opportunities, even when they possess sufficient potential and qualifications (Kordzadeh & Ghasemaghaei, 2021).

Credit assessment and risk analysis algorithms used in the financial sector can similarly perpetuate gender biases. Since female entrepreneurs may have shorter credit histories or different business models compared to men, algorithms may classify them as higher-risk. This limits women's access to financing, negatively impacting their economic independence. In the long term, this inequality can also reduce women's representation in the entrepreneurship ecosystem (Binns, 2018).

In the healthcare sector, algorithmic biases can directly affect women's quality of life. AI systems used for medical diagnosis and treatment recommendations may produce inaccurate or incomplete diagnoses if women's biological and physiological differences are insufficiently represented in datasets. For example, since the symptoms of heart disease manifest differently in women, systems trained primarily on male data may overlook these symptoms. This can prevent women from receiving timely and accurate treatment (Lysaght et al., 2019).

Gender bias in educational technologies also poses serious risks. Student performance prediction systems may misinterpret gender differences in past performance data. As a result, female students may be directed toward traditionally female-dominated professions instead of STEM (science, technology, engineering, and mathematics) fields. In the long run, this leads to persistently low female representation in STEM sectors (Raji et al., 2022).

An important source of algorithmic bias is the lack of inclusivity in data collection processes. When women, people from different ethnic backgrounds, or disadvantaged socioeconomic groups are insufficiently represented in datasets, algorithms overlook their needs and characteristics. This problem, known as the "data representation gap," can reinforce gender inequalities (Lee, 2018). Algorithmic biases can stem not only from datasets but also from conscious or unconscious choices made during the algorithm's design phase. For example, the variables used in weighting decision-making criteria may inadvertently cause gender discrimination. This highlights the importance of ethical awareness and diversity training for software developers and data scientists (Koene, 2017).

Identifying and eliminating algorithmic biases is both a technical and a governance-related issue. Therefore, measures such as independent audit mechanisms, algorithmic transparency, and ethics committees should be implemented. Additionally, algorithms should be regularly tested, and their impacts on different demographic groups should be assessed. This allows proactive steps to be taken to prevent gender inequalities (Lambrecht & Tucker, 2019).

International organizations draw attention to the negative effects of algorithmic biases on gender equality. Institutions such as the OECD, European Commission, and UNESCO have published guidelines requiring the principle of gender sensitivity in the design, development, and implementation of AI systems. These guidelines help technology companies fulfill both their legal and ethical responsibilities.

Algorithmic bias is a critical issue that cannot be ignored in terms of gender equality. When AI systems are not designed in an egalitarian way, they reinforce existing forms of discrimination in society and make it harder to achieve sustainable development goals. However, through conscious data collection, transparent algorithm development, ethical oversight, and inclusive policy approaches, these risks can be significantly reduced. In this way, AI can become a tool that accelerates gender equality and benefits all segments of society (Rossi, 2019).

## INCLUSIVE DIGITAL SERVICES AND WOMEN'S EMPOWERMENT

Inclusive digital services refer to services designed to ensure that access to, use of, and benefits from digital technologies are equally shared across all segments of society. These services enable everyone regardless of gender, age, disability status, socioeconomic conditions, or geographic location to benefit from digital transformation. Increasing women's access to digital technologies contributes to their stronger presence in economic, social, and political spheres. In this context, inclusive digital services emerge as one of the key tools for women's empowerment (Veale et al., 2028).

The digital divide is one of the most significant barriers preventing women from equally benefiting from digital services. Globally, and particularly in low- and middle-income countries, women's internet access rates are lower than those of men. This gap limits women's ability to benefit from digital opportunities in areas such as education, healthcare, finance, and employment. The primary aim of inclusive digital services is to close this gap and facilitate women's access to information, education, and economic opportunities (Wong, 2019).

Educational technologies are among the most important components of inclusive digital services in empowering women. Online learning platforms, distance education systems, and digital skills development programs make it easier for women especially those in rural areas to access education. Acquiring digital skills in STEM (science, technology, engineering, mathematics) fields is critical for women from both an individual and a societal development perspective. This enables women to hold more active and competitive positions in the future labor market.

Inclusive digital services also hold significant potential for financial inclusion. Mobile banking, digital payment systems, and microfinance platforms increase women's access to financial resources. For women entrepreneurs with limited access to traditional banking services, digital financial solutions offer crucial support in establishing and growing their businesses. According to World Bank data, mobile money services increase women's savings rates and economic independence (Blodgett et al., 2020).

In the healthcare sector, inclusive digital services improve women's quality of life. Telemedicine services, mobile health applications, and digital diagnostic systems are critical solutions for women, particularly those living in rural areas or in regions with limited access to healthcare. In areas such as pregnancy tracking, prenatal and postnatal care, and breast cancer screenings, digital health technologies facilitate women's access to early diagnosis and treatment opportunities.

Digital services can also strengthen women's social participation and political representation. Social media platforms, online campaigns, and e-government services allow women to amplify their voices to wider audiences. This enables them to actively engage in advocacy, policy development, and public awareness campaigns. For instance, online petitions and digital activism make it possible for women to be more visible and influential in social change processes (Russell & Norvig, 2021).

To truly empower women, inclusive digital services must go beyond providing access; they must also focus on improving digital literacy. The ability of women to use digital platforms effectively, safely, and critically is essential for fully benefiting from technological opportunities. Therefore, targeted training programs should be developed, especially for women with low digital skills (Vinuesa et al., 2020). Furthermore, ensuring inclusivity in digital services requires reducing gender-based online violence and harassment. Cyberbullying, threats, and harassment faced by women in digital spaces can limit their participation in the online world. Inclusive digital services should address these risks through secure platforms, effective complaint mechanisms, and legal protections, thereby ensuring that women can exist in the digital world safely (Makridakis, 2017).

Collaboration between the private sector, public institutions, and civil society organizations plays a critical role in expanding inclusive digital services. Technology companies should design their products and services with a gender equality perspective; public institutions should take an active role in expanding digital infrastructure, supporting educational programs, and strengthening legal frameworks. Civil society organizations, drawing from their field experience, can guide policymakers (Robert et al., 2020).

Inclusive digital services are strategic tools that enhance women's economic independence, strengthen their social participation, and improve their quality of life. Enabling women to fully benefit from digital technologies not only provides individual benefits but also strengthens societal well-being, economic growth, and democratic participation. For this reason, embedding the principles of inclusivity and gender equality at the core of digital transformation processes is essential for a sustainable and fair future (Trung et al., 2021).

## DETECTING GENDER INEQUALITIES THROUGH BIG DATA ANALYSIS

Big data analysis is a method that enables the extraction of meaningful insights from extremely large, diverse, and fast-moving datasets collected from different sources. This technology has become an important tool for identifying trends, relationships, and problems in the social, economic, and cultural structures of societies. In detecting gender inequalities, big data analysis can make disparities between women and men more visible by utilizing large-scale datasets. This allows for the identification of where inequalities are most concentrated, in which areas they are most pronounced, and which policy interventions could be effective (Maliki & Naji, 2024).

Gender inequalities manifest in various forms across multiple domains, from the labor market to education, health, and politics. While traditional research methods examine these inequalities using limited samples and data sources, big data analysis can provide information from much broader and more diverse sources. For example, social media data, e-government statistics, corporate records, and databases from international organizations can be analyzed together to create a more comprehensive picture (Oleksy et al., 2012).

In the labor market, big data analysis can reveal which sectors women are concentrated in, in which occupational groups wage gaps are more pronounced, and how gender-based barriers operate in promotion processes. For instance, OECD and World Economic Forum 2023 data indicate that the average pay gap between men and women performing the same job still ranges from 15% to 20%. Such data, when compared across countries, help identify the sectors with the highest levels of inequality.

In education, big data can examine differences between male and female students in course selection, academic achievement, scholarship rates, and post-graduation career paths. In particular, the low representation of women in STEM fields can be analyzed in greater detail using big data. For example, by matching universities' student enrollment records with post-graduation employment data, it is possible to identify at which stages women are leaving STEM fields.

In the healthcare sector, big data analysis can uncover gender-based disparities in healthcare access and health outcomes. By combining electronic health records, insurance data, and epidemiological studies, analysts can determine whether women are disadvantaged compared to men in diagnosis, treatment, and care processes for certain diseases. Such analyses play a critical role in the development of women's health policies.

Big data can also make gender inequalities visible in political representation and social participation. For example, by combining parliamentary records, local government data, and election statistics, it is possible to pinpoint the regions where women's participation in politics is low. These data can then be used to develop targeted strategies to increase political participation (O'Connor & Liu, 2023). Moreover, big data analysis allows not only the assessment of the current state of gender inequalities but also the monitoring of changes over time. Long-term datasets can be used to measure the impact of policies and determine which strategies are effective in reducing inequalities. This strengthens evidence-based policymaking (García-Ull & Melero-Lázaro, 2023).

However, the datasets used in big data analysis may themselves contain biases. If the data are incomplete, unbalanced, or inadequate in terms of gender representation, the analysis results may be misleading. Therefore, inclusive methods must be employed during data collection, ensuring the representation of disadvantaged groups. Otherwise, instead of making existing inequalities visible, big data analysis could reinforce them (Someh et al., 2019).

Privacy and ethical considerations also play a significant role in the big data analysis process. Data used to detect gender inequalities may contain personal information, which must be protected. Anonymization, data security, and ethical oversight mechanisms are critical both for protecting individuals' privacy and ensuring the credibility of the research (Leavy, 2018).

In conclusion, big data analysis is a powerful tool for comprehensively identifying gender inequalities and developing solutions. However, its full potential can only be realized through accurate, balanced, and inclusive data collection processes. Moreover, the findings must be effectively utilized by policymakers, the private sector, and civil society. In this way, big data can become not only an analytical tool but also a catalyst for tangible progress toward gender equality (Mehrabi et al., 2021; Lütz, 2022).

## CONCLUSION AND RECOMMENDATIONS

AI-based approaches are innovative tools with the power to transform the economic, social, and environmental dimensions of sustainable development. Through big data analytics, automation, forecasting, and decision-support systems, development policies can be implemented faster, more accurately, and more inclusively.

When evaluated within the context of the Sustainable Development Goals (SDGs), it is evident that AI technologies, when properly designed and governed by ethical principles, offer strong potential to enhance social welfare, optimize resource use, and reduce inequalities. However, realizing this potential depends on conducting technology development processes within an inclusive, transparent, and fair framework (Leach & Green, 2021).

Thanks to advances in AI systems and investments in the field, AI engineers now have the technologies to produce robots or load various algorithms onto them, making these tasks relatively easy for roboticists. The real challenge in AI, however, is preventing gender inequality in the field and ensuring that AI does not develop as a technology shaped under a predominantly male mindset (Bartoletti, 2018). A quantitative analysis of the gender distribution in global AI initiatives and academic publications in the field reveals how deep this inequality runs, with international research data supporting this finding (Cai et al., 2017).

To reduce gender inequality, women must first be informed, encouraged, and motivated to work in this area. In order to address both the gender imbalance in AI's workforce and prevent robots from being programmed to reflect societal gender biases, women must be placed at the core of AI systems. In this way, the field can develop not as a space dominated by male visions and ideas, but as one aiming for the common good and serving shared goals.

First, the contribution of AI to sustainable development goals is directly related to data quality and inclusiveness. Algorithms developed using incomplete, unbalanced, or biased datasets can reproduce existing inequalities and systematically disadvantage certain groups. Therefore, it is crucial to consider inclusivity indicators such as gender, age, disability status, income level, and geographic differences in data collection processes.

Second, mechanisms for algorithmic transparency and accountability in AI projects must be strengthened. Systems that explain how decisions are made and which data are used can increase public trust and make it easier to identify and correct potential biases. In this regard, the establishment of independent oversight mechanisms and regular algorithm evaluations is recommended.

Third, AI-based solutions should be adapted to local needs and cultural contexts. Instead of universal, one-size-fits-all approaches, systems optimized for regional conditions will increase both the acceptance and the impact of the technology. For example, AI applications in agriculture can achieve higher productivity when integrated with the local knowledge and experience of farmers in rural areas.

Fourth, to increase the inclusiveness of AI solutions, digital literacy programs should be widely implemented. Ensuring that technology is understood and effectively used not only by technical experts but also by broad segments of society will be a major multiplier in achieving the SDGs. In this context, enhancing the digital skills of women, youth, and disadvantaged groups should become a top policy priority.

Fifth, multi-stakeholder partnerships between the private sector, public institutions, and civil society should be strengthened. AI-based sustainable development projects can become more effective through the active participation not only of technology infrastructure providers but also of local governments, academic institutions, and community organizations. Joint projects optimize resource use while encouraging knowledge and experience sharing.

Sixth, ethical principles and a human rights perspective must be placed at the center of AI applications. AI systems should be designed to protect individual privacy, and data security must be prioritized. Additionally, gender equality and equal opportunity objectives should be integrated into all technology development processes.

Seventh, the environmental impacts of AI should also be considered. The energy consumption and carbon footprint of large data centers may conflict with sustainable development objectives. Therefore, the development of energy-efficient algorithms and the use of renewable energy sources in AI infrastructures should be encouraged.

Eighth, policymakers need to integrate AI-based solutions into regulatory frameworks. Establishing clear standards regarding the legal status, liability boundaries, and ethical use of AI will ensure the safe and effective deployment of the technology. Moreover, financial incentives and grants should be developed for AI projects that contribute to the SDGs.

Ninth, the impacts of AI must be continuously monitored and evaluated. By comparing AI project outputs with sustainable development indicators, it will be possible to identify areas of progress and those requiring improvement. This will allow for policies and practices to be updated based on evidence.

Finally, AI's contribution to sustainable development should be supported by public awareness. Ensuring that broad segments of society are informed about the potential, opportunities, and risks of AI will increase trust and participation in technology. A transparent communication strategy through awareness campaigns, media content, and open data platforms should be pursued. In this way, AI can become not only a technical tool but also a driving force for social transformation and inclusive development.

## REFERENCES


Ahn, J., Kim, J., & Sung, Y. (2022). The effect of gender stereotypes on artificial intelligence recommendations. *Journal of Business Research, 141*, 50–59. DOI: 10.1016/j.jbusres.2021.12.007

Armutat, S., Wattenberg, M., & Mauritz, N. (2024). Artificial intelligence–gender-specific differences in perception, understanding, and training interest. *International Conference on Gender Research*, 7(1), 36-43. DOI: 10.34190/icgr.7.1.2163

Binns, R. (2018). What can political philosophy teach us about algorithmic fairness? *IEEE Security and Privacy, 16*(3), 73–80. DOI: 10.1109/MSP.2018.2701147

Blodgett, S. L., Barocas, S., Daumé, H.III, & Wallach, H. (2020). Language (technology) is power: A critical survey of "bias" in NLP. *Proceedings of the 58th Annual Meeting of the ACL*, 5454-5476. DOI: 10.18653/v1/2020.acl-main.485

Bordalo, P., Coffman, K., Gennaioli, N., & Shleifer, A. (2019). Beliefs about gender. *The American Economic Review, 109*(3), 739–773. DOI: 10.1257/aer.20170007

Borwein, S., Magistro, B., Loewen, P., Bonikowski, B., & Lee-Whiting, B. (2024). The gender gap in attitudes toward workplace technological change. Socio-. *Economic Review (Kansas City, Mo.), 22*, 993–1017.

Cai, Z., Fan, X., & Du, J. (2017). Gender and attitudes toward technology use: A meta-analysis. *Computers & Education, 105*, 1–13. DOI: 10.1016/j.compedu.2016.11.003

Chant, S., & Sweetman, C. (2012). Fixing women or fixing the world? 'Smart economics', efficiency approaches, and gender equality in development. *Gender and Development, 20*(3), 517–529. DOI: 10.1080/13552074.2012.731812

Chauhan, P., & Gagandeep, K. (2022). Gender Bias and artificial intelligence: A challenge within the periphery of human rights. *Hasanuddin Law Review, 8*(1), 46–59. DOI: 10.20956/halrev.v8i1.3569

Craiut, M.-V., & Iancu, I. (2022). Is technology gender neutral? A systematic literature review on gender stereotypes attached to artificial intelligence. *Human Technology, 18*(3), 297–315. DOI: 10.14254/1795-6889.2022.18-3.6

Delgado Cadena, M. V. (2020). Gender job gaps and challenges in the digital economy: Findings from global governance entities. *Cuadernos Americanos, 36*(67), 158–171. DOI: 10.25100/cdea.v36i67.8767

Dhiman, R., Miteff, S., Wang, Y., Ma, S.-C., Amirikas, R., & Fabian, B. (2024). Artificial Intelligence and Sustainability-A Review. *Analytics*, *3*(1), 140–164. DOI: 10.3390/analytics3010008

Di Vaio, A., Palladino, R., Hassan, R., & Escobar, O. (2020). Artificial intelligence and business models in the sustainable development goals perspective: A systematic literature review. *Journal of Business Research, 121*, 283–314. DOI: 10.1016/j.jbusres.2020.08.019

Dobreva, M., Rukavina, T., Stamou, V., Vidaki, A. N., & Zacharopoulou, L. (2023). A Multimodal Installation Exploring Gender Bias in Artificial Intelligence. In Antona, M., & Stephanidis, C., (Eds.), *Proceedings of HCII 2023, Universal access to human-computer interaction* (pp. 27-46). Springer. DOI: 10.1007/978-3-031-35681-0_2

Elson, D. (2017). Recognize, reduce, and redistribute unpaid care work: How to close the gender gap. *New Labor Forum*, *26*(2), 52–61. DOI: 10.1177/1095796017700135

Fryxell, A. R. (2021). Artificial eye: The modernist origins of AI's gender problem. *Discourse (Berkeley, Calif.)*, *43*(1), 31–64. DOI: 10.13110/discourse.43.1.0031

García-Ull, F. J., & Melero-Lázaro, M. (2023). Gender stereotypes in AI-generated images. *El Profesional de la Información*, *32*(5), 1–13.

Hall, P., & Ellis, D. (2023). A systematic review of socio-technical gender bias in AI algorithms. *Online Information Review*, *47*(7), 1264–1279. DOI: 10.1108/OIR-08-2021-0452

Kay, M., Matuszek, C., & Munson, S. A. (2015). Unequal representation by gender in image search results. *CHI, 2015*, 3819–3828.

Khakurel, J., Penzenstadler, B., Porras, J., Knutas, A., & Zhang, W. (2018). The rise of artificial intelligence under the lens of sustainability. *Technologies*, *6*(4), 1–19. DOI: 10.3390/technologies6040100

Kiritchenko, S., & Mohammad, S. M. (2018). Examining gender and race bias in two hundred sentiment analysis systems. *Proceedings of NAACL-HLT*, 43-53. DOI: 10.18653/v1/S18-2005

Koene, A. (2017). Algorithmic bias: Addressing growing concerns. *IEEE Technology and Society Magazine*, *36*(2), 31–32. DOI: 10.1109/MTS.2017.2697080

Kordzadeh, N., & Ghasemaghaei, M. (2021). Algorithmic bias: Review, synthesis, and future research directions. *European Journal of Information Systems*, *1*, 1–23.

Lambrecht, A., & Tucker, C. (2019). Algorithmic bias? An empirical study of apparent gender-based discrimination in the display of STEM career ads. *Management Science, 65*(7), 2966–2981. DOI: 10.1287/mnsc.2018.3093

Leach, M., & Green, C. (2021). Gender and the SDGs: Mainstreaming, intersectionality and the transformative potential of the 2030 Agenda. *Sustainable Development, 29*(4), 617–630.

Leavy, S. (2018). Gender Bias in Artificial Intelligence: The Need for Diversity and Gender Theory in Machine Learning. In *Proceedings of the 1st International Workshop on Gender Equality in Software Engineering* (pp. 14-16). ACM/IEEE. DOI: 10.1145/3195570.3195580

Lee, N. (2018). Detecting racial bias in algorithms and machine learning. Journal of Information. *Communication and Ethics in Society, 16*(3), 252–260. DOI: 10.1108/JICES-06-2018-0056

Liu, Y. (2024). Research on Algorithmic Gender Bias under the Paradigm of Machine Behavior Studies. *Lecture Notes in Education Psychology and Public Media, 50*(1), 13–22. DOI: 10.54254/2753-7048/50/20240802

Lütz, F. (2022). Gender equality and artificial intelligence in Europe. Addressing direct and indirect impacts of algorithms on gender-based discrimination. *ERA Forum, 23*, 33-52.

Lütz, F. (2024). The AI act, gender equality and non-discrimination: What role for the AI office? *ERA Forum, 25*, 79-95.

Lysaght, T., Lim, H. Y., Xafis, V., & Ngiam, K. Y. (2019). AIassisted decision-making in healthcare. *Asian Bioethics Review, 11*(3), 299–314. DOI: 10.1007/s41649-019-00096-0

Makridakis, S. (2017). The forthcoming artificial intelligence (AI) revolution: Its impact on society and firms. *Futures, 90*, 46–60. DOI: 10.1016/j.futures.2017.03.006

Maliki, K., & Naji, F. (2024). Gender inequality in the sphere of artificial intelligence: Theoretical approach. *Journal of Autonomous Intelligence, 7*(3), 1–12. DOI: 10.32629/jai.v7i3.1394

Manasi, A., Panchanadeswaran, S., Sours, E., & Lee, S. J. (2022). Mirroring the bias: Gender and artificial intelligence. *Gender, Technology and Development, 26*(3), 295–305. DOI: 10.1080/09718524.2022.2128254

Mehrabi, N., Morstatter, F., Saxena, N., Lerman, K., & Galstyan, A. (2021). A survey on bias and fairness in machine learning. *ACM Computing Surveys*, *54*(6), 1–35. DOI: 10.1145/3457607

O'Connor, S., & Liu, H. (2023). Gender bias perpetuation and mitigation in AI technologies: Challenges and opportunities. *AI & Society*, *39*(4), 2045–2057. DOI: 10.1007/s00146-023-01675-4

Oleksy, W., Just, E., & Zapedowska-Kling, K. (2012). Gender issues in information and communication technologies (ICTs). *Journal of Information Communication and Ethics in Society*, *10*(2), 107–120. DOI: 10.1108/14779961211227010

Otterbacher, J., Bates, J., & Clough, P. (2017). Competent men and warm women: Gender stereotypes in image search. *Information Processing & Management*, *53*(6), 1182–1195.

Raji, I. D., Yang, J., Bornstein, S., & Marcus, J. (2022). The AI auditing ecosystem. *Proceedings of the 2022 ACM FAccT Conference*, 923-936.

Robert, L., Pierce, C., Morris, L., Kim, S., & Alahmad, R. (2020). Designing Fair AI for Managing Employees in Organizations: A Review. *Human-Computer Interaction*, *35*(5-6), 545–575. DOI: 10.1080/07370024.2020.1735391

Rossi, F. (2019). Building trust in artificial intelligence. *Journal of International Affairs*, *72*(1), 127–134.

Russell, S., & Norvig, P. (2021). *Artificial Intelligence: A Modern Approach* (4th ed.). Pearson Education Limited.

Sætra, H. S. (2021). AI in Context and the Sustainable Development Goals: Factoring in the Unsustainability of the Sociotechnical System. *Sustainability (Basel)*, *13*(4), 1–18. DOI: 10.3390/su13041738

Someh, I., Davern, M., Breidbach, C. F., & Shanks, G. (2019). Ethical issues in big data analytics: A stakeholder perspective. *Communications of the Association for Information Systems*, *44*(1), 1–20. DOI: 10.17705/1CAIS.04434

Sutko, D. M. (2020). Theorizing femininity in artificial intelligence: A framework for undoing technology's gender troubles. *Cultural Studies*, *34*(4), 567–592. DOI: 10.1080/09502386.2019.1671469

Toniolo, K., Masiero, E., Massaro, M., & Bagnoli, C. (2020). Sustainable business models and artificial intelligence: Opportunities and challenges. In *Knowledge, People, and Digital Transformation* (pp. 103–117). Springer. DOI: 10.1007/978-3-030-40390-4_8

Trung, N. D., Huy, D. T. N., Le, T. H., Huong, D. T., & Hoa, N. T. (2021). ICT, AI, IOTs and technology applications in education- A case with accelerometer and internet learner gender prediction. *Advances in Mechanics*, *9*(3), 1288–1296.

Veale, M., Van Kleek, M., & Binns, R. (2018). Fairness and accountability design needs for algorithmic support in high-stakes public sector decision-making. *Proceedings of the 2018 CHI conference on human factors in computing systems*. DOI: 10.1145/3173574.3174014

Vinuesa, R., Azizpour, H., Leite, I., Balaam, M., Dignum, V., Domisch, S., Felländer, A., Langhans, S. D., Tegmark, M., & Nerini, F. F. (2020). The role of artificial intelligence in achieving the sustainable development goals. *Nature Communications*, *11*(1), 1–10. DOI: 10.1038/s41467-019-14108-y

West, S. M., Whittaker, M., & Crawford, K. (2019). Discriminating systems: Gender, race, and power in AI. *AI Now Institute Report*, 1-33.

Wong, P.-H. (2019). Democratizing Algorithmic Fairness. *Philosophy & Technology*, *33*(2), 225–244. DOI: 10.1007/s13347-019-00355-w

## ADDITIONAL READING

Agarwal, B. (2018). Gender equality, food security and the sustainable development goals. *Current Opinion in Environmental Sustainability*, *34*, 26–32. DOI: 10.1016/j.cosust.2018.07.002

Elshaer, I. A., Hasanein, A. M., & Sobaih, A. E. E. (2024). The moderating effects of gender and study discipline in the relationship between university students' acceptance and use of ChatGPT. *European Journal of Investigation in Health, Psychology and Education*, *14*(7), 1981–1995. DOI: 10.3390/ejihpe14070132

Prates, M. O. R., Avelar, P. H. C., & Lamb, L. C. (2020). Assessing gender bias in machine translation: A case study with Google Translate. *Neural Computing & Applications*, *32*(10), 6363–6381. DOI: 10.1007/s00521-019-04144-6

Rudinger, R., Naradowsky, J., Leonard, B., & Van Durme, B. (2018). Gender bias in coreference resolution. *NAACL-HLT*, *2018*, 8–14.

Sachs, C. (2019). Gendered fields: Rural women, agriculture, and environment. In Hornbeck, S. S., & Whitehead, L. L. (Eds.), *Routledge handbook of gender and environment* (pp. 23–35). Routledge.

## KEY TERMS AND DEFINITIONS

**Artificial Intelligence:** They are computer systems that mimic human intelligence and can perform cognitive processes such as learning, problem-solving, and decision-making. They operate using techniques such as machine learning, deep learning, and natural language processing.

**Gender:** It refers to the social roles, responsibilities, and expectations attributed to women and men by society. Unlike biological sex, it is shaped by cultural, economic, and political factors. Gender equality means that everyone has the right to equal access to opportunities and resources.

**Sustainable Development:** It is a development model that balances today's economic, social, and environmental needs without compromising the ability of future generations to meet their own needs. It encompasses the efficient use of natural resources, the preservation of ecosystems, and the principles of social justice.

# Chapter 3
# Advancing Sustainable Development Goals With a Data-Driven Approach to Progress and Forecasting

**Kian Jazayeri**
https://orcid.org/0000-0003-2843-7354
*Department of Management Information Systems, School of Applied Sciences, Cyprus International University, Nicosia, Cyprus*

**Moein Jazayeri**
https://orcid.org/0000-0002-7857-0586
*Department of Electrical and Electronic Engineering, Faculty of Engineering, Cyprus International University, Cyprus*

## ABSTRACT

*This chapter presents a comprehensive, data-driven framework for assessing and forecasting global progress toward the Sustainable Development Goals (SDGs). Leveraging machine learning, statistical analysis, and geospatial visualization, the study evaluates trends from 2000 to 2023 and projects trajectories to 2030. Key methodologies include Markovian modeling, K-Means clustering, PCA, SARIMAX forecasting, and network analysis. The chapter also simulates targeted improvements in underperforming SDGs, offering strategic insights for resource allocation. Correlation analyses reveal strong links between SDG scores and indices like HDI, GDP, and environmental performance. Designed as a practical toolkit for*

DOI: 10.4018/979-8-3373-1837-0.ch003

*policymakers and planners, the chapter supports data-informed decision-making, highlights disparities, and proposes actionable pathways for accelerating sustainable development.*

## INTRODUCTION

The United Nations introduced the Sustainable Development Goals (SDGs) in 2015, outlining 17 interlinked objectives aimed at creating a more equitable, resilient, and sustainable world by 2030. These goals span a wide array of domains, including poverty eradication (Goal 1), hunger reduction (Goal 2), health (Goal 3), education (Goal 4), gender equality (Goal 5), clean water and sanitation (Goal 6), renewable energy (Goal 7), economic growth (Goal 8), innovation (Goal 9), inequality reduction (Goal 10), sustainable cities (Goal 11), responsible consumption (Goal 12), climate action (Goal 13), ecosystem protection (Goals 14 and 15), peace and justice (Goal 16), and global partnerships (Goal 17). Collectively, they provide a global framework for promoting social inclusion, economic resilience, and environmental sustainability.

Monitoring and forecasting SDG performance is critical for supporting evidence-based policy formulation, institutional planning, and intelligent resource allocation in both governmental and private sectors. Predictive insights derived from data can enhance the strategic decision-making capacity of organizations by identifying areas of risk, opportunity, and comparative advantage.

This chapter offers a data-intensive examination of SDG trajectories across nations, using analytical and machine learning techniques to derive actionable intelligence. Three hypotheses shape the structure of this analysis. First, cluster analysis is used to group countries by their sustainability profiles, revealing natural groupings that support cross-national benchmarking and strategic collaboration. Graph-based community detection adds a layer of network-based intelligence to understand how countries relate based on shared developmental patterns.

Second, the study tests whether focusing on a country's weakest-performing SDGs can yield disproportionate benefits in overall progress. This hypothesis addresses the efficiency of prioritizing limited resources and serves as a framework for developing targeted interventions within institutional strategy design.

Third, the analysis explores the relationship between national SDG scores and widely used indicators such as the Happiness Index, GDP per capita, Human Development Index (HDI), and Environmental Performance Index (EPI). These correlations provide insight into how sustainability outcomes are embedded within broader economic and societal performance metrics.

A robust methodology guides the inquiry, starting with exploratory analysis of SDG trends from 2000 to 2023. Markovian machine learning models are employed for accurate SDG score prediction (MAPE ~0.006), followed by K-Means clustering and Principal Component Analysis (PCA) to visually categorize country performance. Time series forecasting via SARIMAX models projects future SDG trajectories to 2030, supporting forward-looking institutional planning. Correlation and geospatial analyses reveal both patterns and disparities, while graph-based network modeling highlights the interdependencies shaping global development.

Through this integrated approach, the chapter serves as a practical toolkit for enhancing strategic planning, organizational foresight, and collaborative policy design in sustainability-related domains.

To guide the reader through this multifaceted analysis, the structure of the chapter is organized as follows: A literature review section synthesizes key research trends, gaps, and critiques related to the Sustainable Development Goals (SDGs). The next section presents the dataset and preprocessing steps, including handling of missing values and relevant transformations. This is followed by a detailed methodology section outlining the clustering, forecasting, simulation, and network analysis techniques employed. The subsequent results section aligns each method with its corresponding findings to ensure coherence and interpretability. Country-level case studies and correlation analyses are also included to provide contextual depth. Finally, the chapter concludes with a discussion of key insights, policy implications, limitations, and future directions, linking analytical outcomes to practical applications in sustainable development planning.

## LITERATURE REVIEW

Research on Sustainable Development Goals (SDGs) has seen an exponential increase since 2015, particularly in the domains of green and sustainable sciences, reflecting their growing academic significance and highlighting emerging research areas and gaps (Sianes et al., 2022). Analyses using tools like the SDG Index and network methodologies reveal synergies and trade-offs among SDGs, particularly in areas like sustainable cities and climate action, emphasizing the need for policies to effectively manage these trade-offs (Kroll et al., 2019; Wu et al., 2022).

Various frameworks, such as those proposed by Allen et al. (2019), Miola et al. (2019), Bellantuono et al. (2022), and Weitz et al. (2018), offer critical insights into SDG interconnections and their inherent complexities. These studies enhance the strategic implementation of SDGs by addressing their indivisibility, integration, and universality principles (Weitz et al., 2023). Peer learning and systems thinking are highlighted as essential strategies for addressing socio-economic and environmental challenges comprehensively (Weitz et al., 2023).

Innovative approaches, such as the "Classification–Coordination–Collaboration" framework, address challenges in SDG implementation post-COVID-19, underlining the importance of global cooperation and sustainable policy integration (Zhao et al., 2022). The United Nations (2020) report also underscores the pandemic's impact on SDGs, advocating for innovative strategies to mitigate these effects.

Diverse analytical techniques, including principal component analysis and k-means clustering (Mwitondi et al., 2020), artificial neural networks (Liu et al., 2023), and network estimation methods (Ospina-Forero et al., 2022), have been utilized to address SDG research challenges. These methodologies aid in identifying critical data variations and provide actionable insights. Recent studies have advanced the integration of analytical and policy-focused approaches to SDG implementation. Horan (2020) proposed a systematic monitoring tool that leverages SDG indicators and inter-ministerial mapping to enhance policy coherence and integrated decision-making, using Ireland's marine policy as a case study. Van Zanten and Putintseva (2025) evaluated policy effectiveness for the SDGs using hierarchical clustering across 84 indicators, identifying significant disparities in government support across goals and stressing the need for coherent policy frameworks to avoid counterproductive trade-offs. Additionally, Thuy et al. (2022) demonstrated how GIS integration with SDG indicators can serve as a spatial decision-making tool for urban planning, highlighting its application in the upstream Saigon River area as a model for localized sustainability strategies.

Research linking SDGs to socio-economic indices (Perkins et al., 2021; Costa et al., 2011), income and gender inequality (Cingano, 2014; Jayachandran, 2015), and the environmental Kuznets curve hypothesis (Dinda, 2004; Lee et al., 2010) highlights the intricate interplay between development, social equity, and environmental sustainability. Studies on the connection between SDGs and subjective well-being emphasize the need for region-specific policies (De Neve & Sachs, 2020).

Regional disparities in SDG achievements underscore the importance of localized strategies and sustainable land management. Research on these disparities (Zhang et al., 2022; Xu et al., 2020; Golding et al., 2017) and biodiversity conservation (Felipe-Lucia et al., 2020) reveals the critical role of context-specific approaches. Additionally, advancements in technologies like remote sensing and machine learning (Huadong, 2022) have expanded the scope of SDG research, offering significant policy implications.

The impacts of COVID-19 on sustainability policies (Yuan et al., 2023) and calls for resetting SDG priorities (Kickbusch & Alakija, 2023) demonstrate the dynamic nature of SDG research and the need for adaptability in policy frameworks. The North-South divide in SDG partnerships (Blicharska et al., 2021) and limited progress towards many SDGs (Malekpour et al., 2023) highlight the need for more inclusive and equitable approaches.

Critiques of SDGs, including concerns over their effectiveness (Biermann et al., 2022), and studies on social factors affecting employment (Mok & Wu, 2016) further call for a re-evaluation of current strategies. The Sustainable Development Goals Report 2023 and studies on SDG interlinkages underscore the necessity of advanced data systems and nuanced analysis for effective SDG monitoring and assessment (United Nations, 2023; Bennich et al., 2023).

However, more recent studies have highlighted the critical role of machine learning and artificial intelligence in sustainable development research. Vinuesa et al. (2020) provide a comprehensive mapping of how AI can support all 17 Sustainable Development Goals, emphasizing the potential of data-driven methods to address global challenges. Likewise, Sachs et al. (2022) underscore the importance of robust statistical modeling and digital technologies in navigating post-COVID-19 recovery and achieving the SDGs by 2030. These studies reinforce the growing convergence between technological innovation and strategic policymaking in the SDG domain.

While substantial research has explored individual aspects of SDGs, there remains a significant gap in comprehensive studies integrating diverse analytical techniques for a holistic understanding of SDG progress. This chapter aims to bridge this gap by employing methodologies ranging from exploratory analysis to advanced forecasting and simulation techniques. It provides a nuanced perspective on SDG progress and offers actionable insights for global sustainable development efforts.

## METHODOLOGY

Over the past decade, data science and machine learning have become increasingly central to the monitoring, evaluation, and planning of Sustainable Development Goals (SDGs). Since the adoption of Agenda 2030, global reports such as the SDG Index and Dashboards by Sachs et al. (2016–2023) and initiatives by the UN Sustainable Development Solutions Network (SDSN) have employed statistical modeling to benchmark country performance and inform policy decisions. Analytical techniques, including clustering, principal component analysis, and time series forecasting, are now widely used to identify development patterns, detect anomalies, and simulate future scenarios. For instance, clustering methods have helped group countries based on development similarities, while network analysis has highlighted interdependencies among SDG targets. These methods support a more nuanced, data-informed understanding of SDG progress, enabling both global comparisons and localized intervention strategies. Building on this growing body of work, the present study applies an integrated set of data-driven techniques to assess progress, disparities, and future trajectories across SDG indicators.

## Data Collection and Preprocessing

The primary dataset used in this chapter, obtained from the SDG Transformation Center (2023), includes scores for each of the 17 Sustainable Development Goals (SDGs) as well as overall SDG scores for countries from 2000 to 2023. The dataset provides a historical view crucial for understanding trends before and after the SDGs' 2015 initiation. Each SDG score reflects a specific developmental target, contributing to a country's overall progress assessment. In preprocessing, missing values (e.g., 15 in Goal 1, 17 in Goal 10, and 40 in Goal 14) were addressed by employing regression imputation, where missing entries were estimated based on correlated SDG scores from the same country and year, ensuring a consistent and data-driven approach to handling incomplete data. Descriptive statistics, shown in Table 1, offer an initial dataset overview, aiding in identifying potential anomalies or outliers.

*Table 1. Descriptive Statistics of SDG Goals*

| | count | mean | std | min | 25% | 50% | 75% | max | skew | kurt |
|---|---|---|---|---|---|---|---|---|---|---|
| **sdg_index_score** | 3984 | 64 | 10.91 | 36 | 55.3 | 65.5 | 72.49 | 86.8 | -0.32 | -0.68 |
| **goal_1_score** | 3969 | 65.19 | 36.69 | 0 | 31.3 | 82 | 98.7 | 100 | -0.62 | -1.17 |
| **goal_2_score** | 3984 | 57.79 | 11.2 | 7.7 | 52.4 | 59.03 | 65.4 | 83.4 | -0.94 | 1.61 |
| **goal_3_score** | 3984 | 64.53 | 22.58 | 5.9 | 45.4 | 71.3 | 81.9 | 97.3 | -0.57 | -0.83 |
| **goal_4_score** | 3984 | 72.26 | 26.87 | 0 | 56.18 | 81.3 | 94.96 | 100 | -1 | 0.04 |
| **goal_5_score** | 3984 | 56.26 | 17.63 | 3.5 | 43.4 | 58 | 69.5 | 94.02 | -0.34 | -0.51 |
| **goal_6_score** | 3984 | 64.62 | 15.07 | 23.3 | 52.7 | 65.03 | 74.8 | 95.1 | 0.04 | -0.76 |
| **goal_7_score** | 3984 | 57.77 | 21.82 | 0.1 | 41.5 | 65.3 | 72.3 | 99.6 | -0.66 | -0.46 |
| **goal_8_score** | 3984 | 69.93 | 10.27 | 38.4 | 64 | 70.1 | 76.8 | 93.6 | -0.4 | 0.11 |
| **goal_9_score** | 3984 | 37.57 | 26.26 | 0 | 15.6 | 29.9 | 54.1 | 99.2 | 0.74 | -0.6 |
| **goal_10_score** | 3967 | 53.15 | 32.02 | 0 | 23.5 | 57.7 | 81.08 | 100 | -0.25 | -1.23 |
| **goal_11_score** | 3984 | 70.29 | 18.41 | 13.8 | 56.58 | 75.4 | 85.12 | 99.9 | -0.74 | -0.34 |
| **goal_12_score** | 3984 | 79.29 | 16.98 | 32.9 | 67.9 | 84.5 | 94.1 | 99 | -0.88 | -0.38 |
| **goal_13_score** | 3984 | 81.54 | 21.86 | 0 | 71.7 | 90.8 | 97.2 | 99.93 | -1.72 | 2.65 |
| **goal_14_score** | 3944 | 48.37 | 28.42 | 0 | 40.05 | 59 | 68.2 | 91.2 | -0.86 | -0.75 |
| **goal_15_score** | 3984 | 65.17 | 13.79 | 26 | 55.2 | 65.11 | 74.4 | 97.9 | 0.02 | -0.28 |
| **goal_16_score** | 3984 | 62.54 | 14.87 | 27.9 | 51.49 | 61.7 | 74.2 | 96 | 0.13 | -0.78 |
| **goal_17_score** | 3984 | 55.81 | 13.31 | 15.1 | 46 | 55.3 | 65.22 | 100 | 0.14 | -0.06 |

## Exploratory Data Analysis

The exploratory data analysis encompassed several key aspects:

- **Trend of the Overall SDG Index Score:** The line plot in Fig. 1 reveals a rising global average SDG Index Score from 2000 to 2023, indicating progress towards SDGs. The plot, with years on the x-axis and mean scores on the y-axis, includes a 95% confidence interval, varying in width due to standard deviation and data points per year. This visual analysis stresses the need for targeted policies for less developed nations.

*Figure 1. Year-wise Trend of Average SDG Index Score*

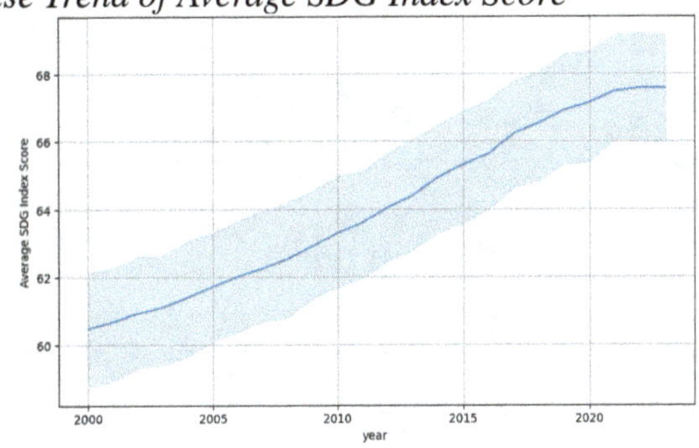


- **Trend Analysis for Each SDG Goal:** As Fig. 2 shows, there has been progress in goals like poverty and inequality, health, and education. However, gender equality, clean water, and sanitation are lagging, and economic growth shows fluctuations. Urban development has advanced, while responsible consumption, production, and climate action goals vary. Marine life conservation is improving, but scores for peace, justice, and institutions are declining. The increase in global partnerships is promising for achieving all SDGs.

*Figure 2. Trend Analysis for the Global Average of Each SDG Goal*

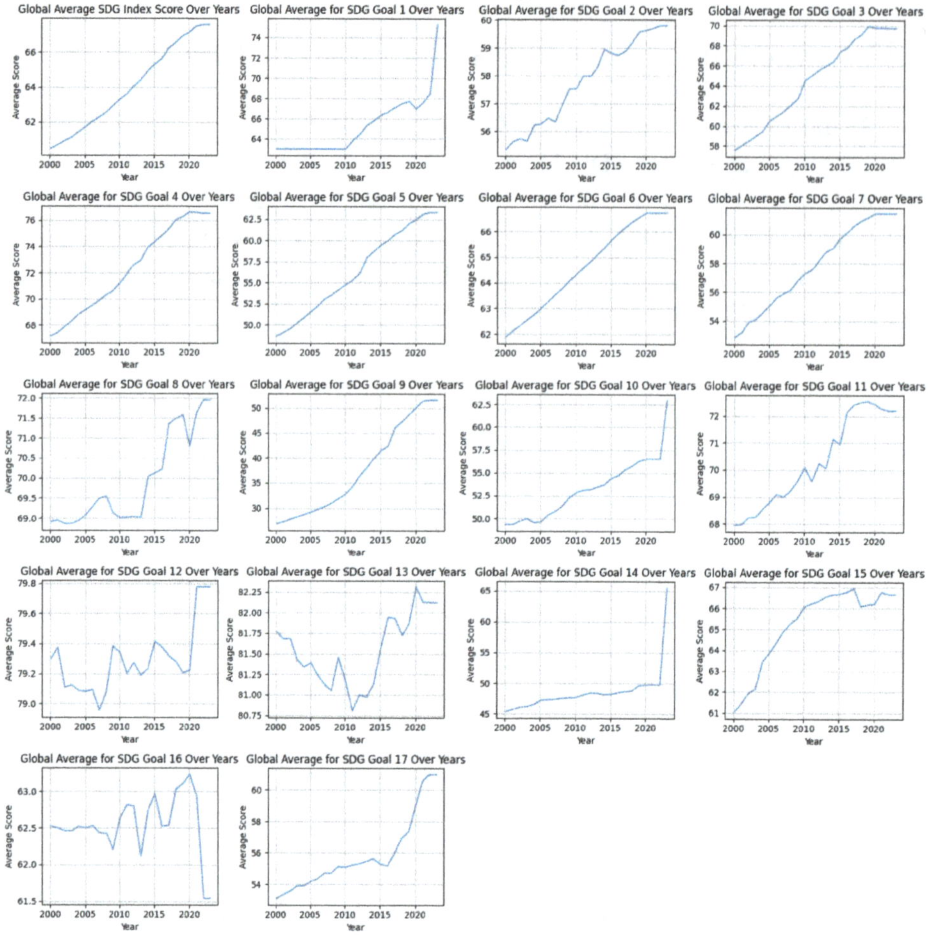


- **Histogram Analysis for Each SDG Goal:** The histograms in Fig. 3 illustrate the diverse range of global achievements and challenges in pursuing SDGs. Goals 1 and 4 exhibit a bimodal distribution, reflecting significant disparities among countries. Goals 2, 3, and 5 show a trend towards higher scores, denoting uniform progress with a few outliers. Goals 6 and 7 highlight a broad range of scores, suggesting varied global development in clean water and energy. Goals 8, 9, and 10 indicate that while there is progress, disparities still exist. Goal 11 demonstrates a wide distribution of scores, indicating diverse urban development achievements. Goal 12 has a notable number of countries scoring on the lower end, pointing to challenges in sustainable consumption and production. Goal 13 underscores the intense global efforts required to combat climate change, while Goal 14 exhibits a skewed distribution, indicating varied successes in life below water. Goal 15 shows a normal distribution leaning towards higher scores, reflecting varied conservation efforts. Goals 16 and 17 depict a relatively normal distribution, yet the range of scores reflects ongoing challenges in peace, justice, and strong institutions, and in partnerships for the goals. These patterns signal a critical need for targeted and strategic efforts to address and bridge the gaps in achieving the SDGs on a global scale.

*Figure 3. Distribution Histograms of Country-Level SDG Scores by Goal (2023)*

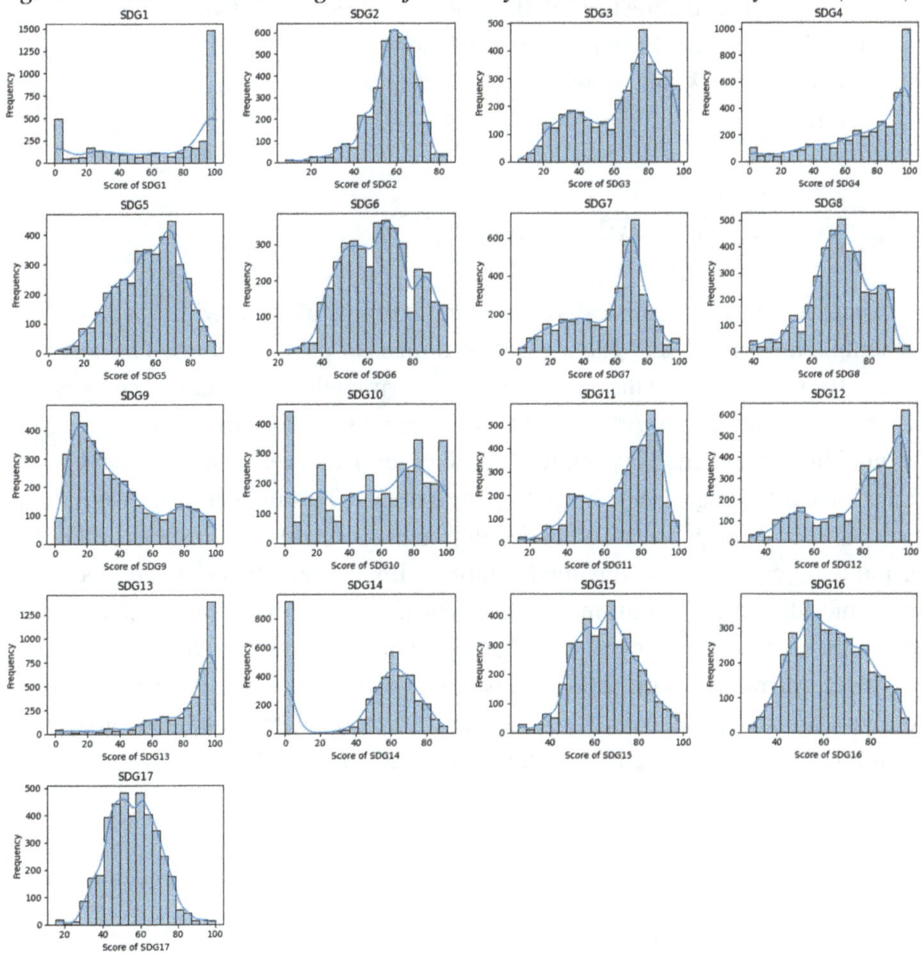

- **Improvement and Deterioration Analysis:** This section of the chapter compares SDG index scores from 2000 to 2023, highlighting countries with significant improvements, such as Cambodia (17.236), Nepal (16.570), Bhutan (14.539), Rwanda (14.298), and Senegal (13.729). Conversely, this section highlights countries with notable declines, such as the Syrian Arab Republic (-0.519), Venezuela (-0.017), Yemen (0.047), Papua New Guinea (0.304), and South Sudan (1.276).
- **Correlation Analysis:** This chapter includes a thorough correlation analysis among the SDG goals, as shown in Fig. 4. This analysis, using the Pearson correlation coefficient, was crucial for understanding the interactions between different SDGs. The correlation coefficient, ranging from -1 to 1, indicates the strength and direction of the linear relationship between two variables. The mathematical formula for the Pearson correlation coefficient (*r*) between two variables, *X* and *Y*, which is commonly used in correlation analysis, is given by:

$$r = \frac{\sum_{i=1}^{n}(X_i - \bar{X})(Y_i - \bar{Y})}{\sqrt{\sum_{i=1}^{n}(X_i - \bar{X})^2(Y_i - \bar{Y})^2}} \tag{1}$$

Where $X_i$ and $Y_i$ Are the individual sample points indexed with $i$, $\bar{X}$ and $\bar{Y}$ are the sample means of $X$ and $Y$, and $n$ is the number of pairs of scores. The square of this coefficient, known as the coefficient of determination, measures how much one variable's variance can be predicted from another. Most SDG goals showed positive correlations, suggesting they reinforce each other. However, SDGs 12 and 13 were exceptions, often negatively correlating with others. This indicates short-term conflicts between these goals and other development objectives. For instance, measures for reducing carbon emissions might initially impact well-being due to necessary economic adjustments. High-income countries, where shifts to sustainable practices require significant changes, might see pronounced anti-correlations. However, a positive correlation with time suggests long-term benefits as economies adapt. Policymakers must understand these dynamics to balance environmental goals with economic and social objectives, ensuring progress across all SDGs.

*Figure 4. Heatmap of Correlations Among SDG Goals (2000–2023)*

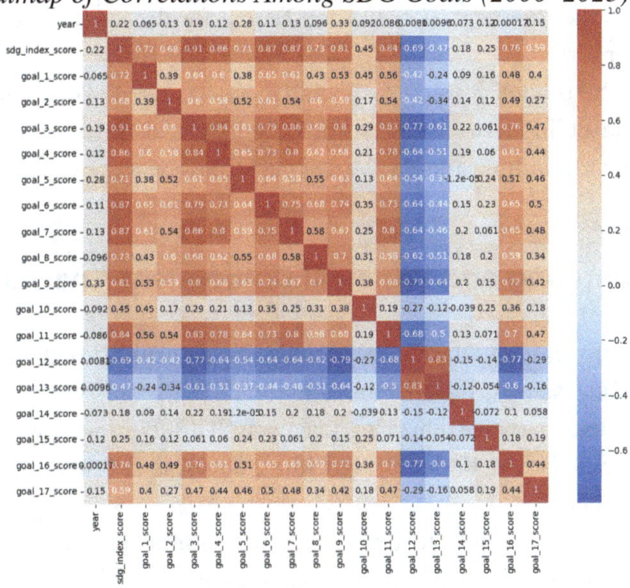


The heatmap reveals strong positive correlations between most SDGs, indicating mutual reinforcement. Notably, SDG 12 and SDG 13 show negative correlations with several economic and social goals, reflecting tensions between environmental sustainability and development.

These exploratory analyses provided a solid foundation for the more advanced sections of this chapter. By thoroughly examining the historical and current state of global SDG scores, this chapter establishes a basis for forecasting future trends and formulating strategies to improve SDG outcomes.

## Markovian Machine Learning Model

This chapter presents the development of a Markovian machine learning model to estimate countries' SDG scores. The model assumes that a country's SDG score in a given year depends mainly on its score from the previous year, thus creating a time-lagged relationship. This was implemented by introducing a lagged feature in the dataset, representing the SDG score of each country from the previous year.

The model was formulated using a simple linear regression framework, mathematically expressed in Equation 2:

$$SDG_{score_t} = \beta_0 + \left(\beta_1 \times SDG_{score_{t-1}}\right) + \epsilon_t \tag{2}$$

Where, $SDG_{score_t}$ is the current year's SDG score, $SDG_{score_{t-1}}$ is the previous year's SDG score, $\beta_0$ is the intercept, $\beta_1$ is the coefficient for the lagged score, and $\epsilon_t$ represents the error term.

To validate the model, 5-fold cross-validation was used. This method involves dividing the dataset into five subsets, using each in turn as the test set while training the model on the remaining subsets. Model performance was evaluated using MSE and MAPE.

## KMeans Clustering and Principal Component Analysis

This chapter also employs the K-Means clustering algorithm to categorize countries based on their SDG scores. Before clustering, the SDG scores were standardized to eliminate scale discrepancies, ensuring that each SDG score was weighted equally. This step is crucial for the KMeans algorithm, which is sensitive to data scale, to function effectively.

Employing the elbow test to determine the optimal number of clusters, the algorithm grouped countries into five clusters, aiming to minimize within-cluster variance and maximize between-cluster variance. This involved an iterative process of assigning countries to the nearest cluster centroid, recalculating the centroid as the mean of points in the cluster, and repeating until centroids stabilized.

The KMeans clustering algorithm identifies $K$ centroids, and then allocates every data point to the nearest cluster, while keeping the centroids as small as possible. The 'means' in KMeans refers to averaging of the data; that is, finding the centroid. Mathematically, given a set of observations $(x_1, x_2, ..., x_n)$ where each observation is a $d$-dimensional real vector, KMeans clustering aims to partition the $n$ observations into $K$ $(K \leq n)$ sets $S = \{S_1, S_2, ..., S_K\}$ so as to minimize the within-cluster sum of squares (WCSS). Hence, the objective is to find:

$$\underset{S}{argmin} \sum_{i=1}^{K} \sum_{X \in S_i} | \, | \, x - \mu_i \, | \, |^2 \quad (3)$$

Where $| \, | \, x - \mu_i \, | \, |^2$ is a chosen distance measure between a data point $x$ and the cluster center $\mu_i$, is an indicator of the distance of the $n$ data points from their respective cluster centers. The algorithm proceeds by alternating between two steps: (1) assigning each observation to the cluster with the nearest mean (centroid) which serves as a prototype of the cluster, (2) calculating the new means (centroids) of the observations in the new clusters. The algorithm has converged when the assignments no longer change.

Following clustering, Principal Component Analysis (PCA) was used to reduce the dimensionality of the SDG scores for visualization. PCA transforms the data into a set of principal components, which are linearly uncorrelated variables identified by calculating the eigenvectors of the data's covariance matrix corresponding to the largest eigenvalues. This enables a two-dimensional representation of the multidimensional SDG data, facilitating easier interpretation of the clustering results.

## SARIMAX Forecasting

The SARIMAX forecasting technique, which stands for Seasonal AutoRegressive Integrated Moving Average with eXogenous factors model, has been applied to predict the future trajectory of SDG scores across different countries and the world average, up to the year 2030. This model incorporates both the autoregressive (*AR*) and moving average (*MA*) components as well as seasonality and external factors, making it robust for time series forecasting.

The SARIMAX model offers a robust framework for modeling and forecasting time series data. It extends the ARIMA model by incorporating both seasonality (S) and the possibility of including exogenous variables (*X*). Mathematically, the model can be described as:

$$SARIMAX(p,d,q) \times (P,D,Q)s \quad (4)$$

Here, $p$ and $q$ represent the order of the autoregressive and moving average parts of the non-seasonal component of the model, while $d$ signifies the degree of differencing to induce stationarity. The seasonal part of the model is represented by $P$, $D$, and $Q$, which correspond to the seasonal autoregressive order, seasonal differencing order, and seasonal moving average order, respectively, with $s$ denoting the seasonality period.

The AR component refers to the regression of the time series onto its own lagged (past) values, represented by:

$$AR(p){:}\Phi(L)Y_t = \phi 1\, Y_{t-1} + \phi 2\, Y_{t-2} + \ldots + \phi \mathrm{p}\, Y_{t-p} \quad (5)$$

Where $\Phi(L)$ is the lag operator, $Y_t$ is the time series at time $t$, and $\phi$ represents the coefficients of the lags.

The MA component models the error of the time series as a linear combination of error terms that occurred contemporaneously and at various times in the past:

$$MA(q){:}\Theta(\mathrm{L})\,\varepsilon_t = \theta 1\, \varepsilon_{t-1} + \theta 2\, \varepsilon_{t-2} + \ldots + \theta \mathrm{q}\, \varepsilon_{t-q} \quad (6)$$

Where Θ(L) is the lag operator for the error term, and $\theta$ represents the coefficients of the error terms. Differencing (*I* for Integrated) is applied to make the time series stationary:

$$\nabla^d Y_t = (1 - L)^d Y_t \tag{7}$$

Where $\nabla^d$ represents the differencing operator. The seasonal components are similarly defined but are applied to the seasonal lags of the data. The SARIMAX model's power lies in its flexibility to model complex temporal structures and its ability to include the influence of external factors, which can be critical for accurate forecasting in the presence of known influences on the time series.

In this chapter, SARIMAX models were trained on historical SDG index scores from 2000 to 2023, considering the natural temporal correlations in the data, such as trends and seasonal variations. The model was specifically tailored to the dataset's characteristics to ensure accurate forecasting.

In this chapter, the SARIMAX model was utilized for several key tasks. First, it was used for global forecasting, predicting the average overall SDG score for the world up to 2030, including confidence intervals to reflect prediction uncertainty. This provided a macroscopic view of progress in sustainable development goals.

Second, the model was applied to country-specific forecasting, generating predictions for overall SDG scores for all world countries up to 2030. The results were visualized through geospatial analysis, displaying countries on a world map color-coded according to their predicted SDG scores, offering a clear visualization of global progress.

Lastly, the SARIMAX model was integral in simulating the impact of investing in the lowest SDG goals for sample countries from each cluster. This section of the chapter evaluated the potential effects of targeted interventions on SDG scores by 2030, offering insights into how policy decisions and resource allocations could impact sustainable development outcomes.

## Network Analysis

Network analysis was employed as a key method to examine the complex relationships between countries based on their SDG scores. This technique enabled both visual and quantitative analysis of the connections, capturing the broader structure of global SDG performance.

In this network, countries were represented as nodes, and edges indicated similarity in SDG scores, measured using cosine similarity, defined mathematically as:

$$Cosine\ Similarity\left(A,B\right)=\frac{\sum_{i=1}^{n}A_iB_i}{\sqrt{\sum_{i=1}^{n}A_i^2}\sqrt{\sum_{i=1}^{n}B_i^2}} \tag{8}$$

Where $A_i$ and $B_i$ are the SDG scores of the $i^{th}$ goal for countries $A$ and $B$, respectively.

To form meaningful connections in the network, a similarity threshold was crucial. Setting this threshold too low would result in a densely connected network with diluted community structures, while a high threshold could fragment the network. Thus, a balanced threshold of 0.5 was chosen, aligning with the clusters identified in the KMeans analysis. This approach ensured the network graph accurately reflected the data, highlighting strong connections within clusters while distinguishing between different groups.

The degree of a node, representing the number of significant SDG score similarities with other countries, indicated a country's relative importance in the network. High degree centrality suggested a country's SDG profile was similar to many others, potentially indicating shared development paths or policies.

The network graph was visualized using a spring layout algorithm, placing countries with higher SDG score similarities closer together. This visual representation effectively depicted the community structure within the global SDG landscape.

To further analyze countries' positions within the network, z-scores were used to standardize centrality measures, allowing for the identification of outliers and key influencers. Z-scores (given in Eq.9), calculated as the number of standard deviations from the mean, provided a clear benchmark for comparing connectivity across the network.

$$z=\frac{X-\mu}{\sigma} \tag{9}$$

Where $X$ is the degree of centrality of the country, $\mu$ is the mean degree centrality of all countries, and $\sigma$ is the standard deviation of degree centrality. By employing z-scores, the centrality measures can be normalized across the network, providing a clear benchmark for comparison regardless of the network size or density.

The graph's aesthetic was enhanced by color-coding nodes based on centrality values and scaling them according to their degree. This facilitated a quick visual assessment of each country's importance and connectivity in the network. This comprehensive network analysis, characterized by methodological rigor and visual clarity, provides deeper insights of the relationships between countries in pursuing sustainable development.

## Simulation of Incremental Improvements

This section of the chapter involved simulating the potential effects of targeted interventions on the three lowest-ranking SDGs for each cluster. The rationale was that the greatest potential for progress and impact lies in areas where countries are currently underperforming. The simulations used the SARIMAX model to forecast future SDG scores from 2024 to 2030, considering inherent data trends and external factors. This allowed for predicting future overall SDG scores and simulating outcomes with improvements in the selected goals, offering a broad perspective on future scenarios.

The methodology involved using historical data to project future SDG scores and then adjusting these forecasts based on hypothetical improvements in the lowest SDGs. These improvements were modeled as proportional score increases in the lowest goals, integrated into new forecasts.

A key limitation in the simulations is the complex, undefined relationship between financial investments and increases in SDG scores, influenced by factors like economic status, governance, and global trends. Our simplified approach hypothesized a 1-point annual increase in the lowest SDG scores from 2024 to 2030, isolating the impact of targeted interventions.

While these simulations offer insights into potential outcomes of strategic SDG improvements, they are not direct policy recommendations. They provide a conceptual framework for policymakers to understand the impact of targeted interventions, emphasizing the need for country-specific analyses to determine the required investment levels.

The 2030 projections under various improvement scenarios present a theoretical view of possible achievements with focused efforts. These are not prescriptive but aim to encourage discussion and further research among policymakers, international organizations, and stakeholders in sustainable development.

The analytical techniques outlined in this section are directly mapped to the key findings presented in the Results. Specifically, the clustering analysis is used to group countries with similar SDG performance patterns, which informs the identification of development typologies in Section 4. Principal Component Analysis (PCA) and correlation analysis are applied to reveal the main latent structures driving SDG variation and their association with external indices like GDP and HDI. Network analysis is employed to visualize interdependencies and trade-offs among SDG targets, helping identify clusters of co-progressing or conflicting goals. Forecasting models are used to project SDG trajectories through 2030, highlighting likely underperformers and estimating the impact of hypothetical policy interventions. Each method is thus purposefully linked to a specific insight, collectively offering a comprehensive picture of current disparities and future scenarios in global SDG progress.

## RESULTS

### Markovian Model Outcomes

The Markovian model's accuracy was high, with an average MAPE of about 0.0061 across all tests, indicating minimal deviation from actual scores. This precision is evident in Fig. 5, where actual and predicted SDG scores are closely aligned, demonstrating the model's effectiveness in forecasting SDG scores. This accuracy makes the model a reliable tool for forecasting SDG progress, aiding policymakers and international organizations in sustainable development planning.

*Figure 5. Actual vs Predicted SDG Index Scores for All Folds*

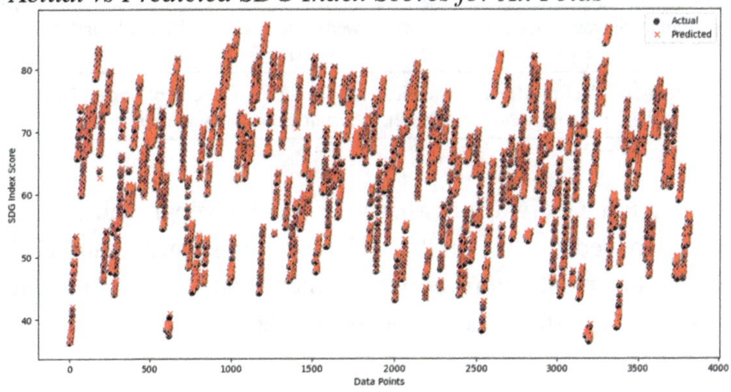


### Clustering and PCA Outcomes

Table 2 presents the countries within each of the five clusters identified by the KMeans algorithm. This clustering offers insights into global SDG performance, transcending traditional classifications based on geography or economy, and highlighting common developmental profiles.

*Table 2. The Cluster Formations Based on SDG Characteristics*

| Cluster Number | Countries |
|---|---|
| Cluster 0 | Bahamas, Bahrain, Brunei Darussalam, Kuwait, Oman, Qatar, Saudi Arabia, Singapore, Trinidad and Tobago, United Arab Emirates |
| Cluster 1 | Albania, Algeria, Argentina, Armenia, Azerbaijan, Barbados, Belize, Bhutan, Bolivia, Bosnia and Herz., Botswana, Brazil, Bulgaria, Cabo Verde, Chile, China, Colombia, Costa Rica, Cuba, Dominican Republic, Ecuador, Egypt, El Salvador, Fiji, Georgia, Guatemala, Guyana, Honduras, Indonesia, Iran, Jamaica, Jordan, Kazakhstan, Kyrgyzstan, Lebanon, Macedonia, Malaysia, Maldives, Mauritius, Mexico, Moldova, Mongolia, Montenegro, Morocco, Namibia, Nicaragua, Panama, Paraguay, Peru, Philippines, Romania, Russia, Serbia, South Africa, Sri Lanka, Suriname, Tajikistan, Thailand, Tunisia, Turkey, Turkmenistan, Ukraine, Uruguay, Uzbekistan, Venezuela, Vietnam |
| Cluster 2 | Angola, Bangladesh, Benin, Burkina Faso, Burundi, Cambodia, Cameroon, Congo, Côte d'Ivoire, Eswatini, Gabon, Gambia, Ghana, Guinea, India, Iraq, Kenya, Laos, Lesotho, Madagascar, Malawi, Mali, Mozambique, Myanmar, Nepal, Nigeria, Papua New Guinea, Rwanda, Sao Tome and Principe, Senegal, Sierra Leone, Syria, Tanzania, Togo, Uganda, Zambia, Zimbabwe |
| Cluster 3 | Australia, Austria, Belarus, Belgium, Canada, Croatia, Cyprus, Czechia, Denmark, Estonia, Finland, France, Germany, Greece, Hungary, Iceland, Ireland, Israel, Italy, Japan, Latvia, Lithuania, Luxembourg, Malta, Netherlands, New Zealand, Norway, Poland, Portugal, Slovak Republic, Slovenia, South Korea, Spain, Sweden, Switzerland, United Kingdom, United States of America |
| Cluster 4 | Afghanistan, Central African Republic, Chad, Comoros, Dem. Rep. Congo, Djibouti, Ethiopia, Haiti, Liberia, Mauritania, Niger, Pakistan, Somalia, South Sudan, Sudan, Yemen |

Countries like Fiji, Georgia, and Mongolia, despite geographical and economic differences, are grouped together in Cluster 1 due to similar sustainability challenges. This reflects the universal nature of development issues. The clustering method, by focusing on SDG performance, reveals common pathways and challenges in achieving SDGs.

Fig. 6, a PCA plot, visually represents the clustering outcomes, offering a color-coded depiction of the global variance in SDG progress. This visualization aids in understanding the complex SDG data, essential for strategic policymaking.

*Figure 6. Principal Component Analysis (PCA) of Countries Based on SDG Scores*

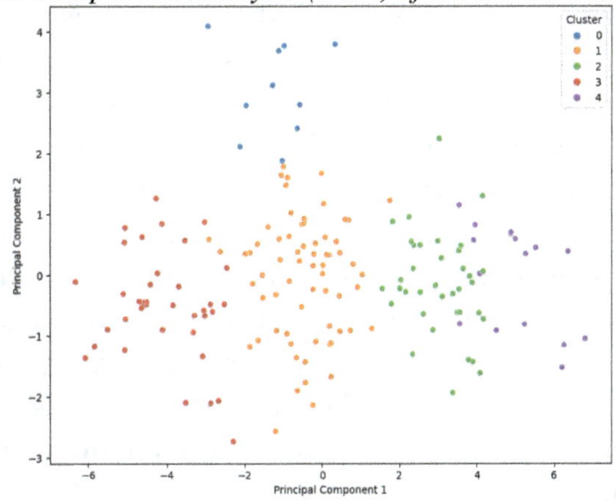


The PCA scatter plot visually distinguishes the five SDG performance clusters. Countries on the right generally show higher SDG scores, especially on education and health-related goals. Overlapping regions suggest shared policy or socioeconomic characteristics across clusters.

Fig. 7 is a spider chart showing each SDG goal's performance for different clusters. It highlights the strengths and weaknesses of each cluster in specific SDGs.

*Figure 7. Radar Chart Comparing Cluster-Wise Averages of SDG Goal Scores*

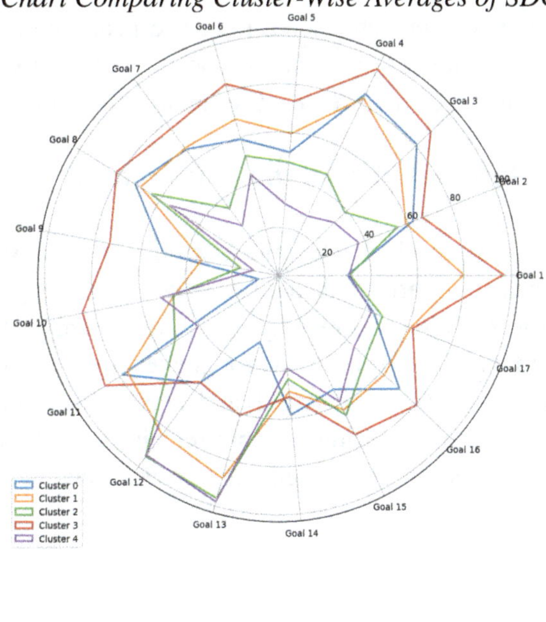

Cluster 0 comprises high-income countries, often enriched by oil revenues. These countries have strong sectors in finance, health, education, and urban development. However, there is noticeable variability in their performance, especially in Goal 10 (Reduced Inequalities) and Goal 17 (Partnerships for the Goals), highlighting disparities and the necessity for enhanced global partnerships.

Cluster 1 encompasses a varied group of countries, including emerging and transitional economies. These nations display a balanced developmental profile across all goals without extreme highs or lows. Notably, they perform well in Goal 13 (Climate Action) and Goal 12 (Responsible Consumption and Production), potentially reflecting a successful integration of environmental policies.

Cluster 2 includes mostly developing nations facing considerable social and economic challenges. These countries generally exhibit lower performance across most goals, particularly in Goal 1 (No Poverty) and Goal 3 (Good Health and Well-being), indicating struggles with poverty and health issues. However, they achieve higher scores in Goals 12 and 13, likely due to reduced industrial activities and consequent environmental impacts.

Cluster 3 consists of developed countries scoring high in nearly all Sustainable Development Goals (SDGs), indicating well-established social, economic, and environmental systems. Their strengths lie particularly in Goals 1, 3, 4 (Quality Education), and 11 (Sustainable Cities and Communities), highlighting robust health systems, education, and urban planning. However, they face challenges in Goal 12, reflecting difficulties in sustainable consumption and production.

Cluster 4 includes countries affected by significant instability or ongoing conflicts. These nations understandably score lowest, especially in Goals 1, 2 (Zero Hunger), 3, and 4, which relate to basic human needs. Their higher scores in Goals 12 and 13 might be attributed to lower levels of industrialization and consumption.

## SARIMAX and Geospatial Analysis Outcomes

The geospatial analysis in this chapter offers a vivid visual representation of global SDG progress, revealing significant disparities linked to geographic and socioeconomic divisions. The 2023 SDG score map (fig. 8) reveals higher achievements in developed areas, underscoring the necessity for greater attention in lagging regions. The SARIMAX model's 2030 forecast (fig. 9) indicates that, assuming current trends continue, global SDG scores will improve but remain unevenly distributed, with developed regions progressing more rapidly than developing ones.

*Figure 8. Global Map of Country-Level SDG Index Scores in 2023*

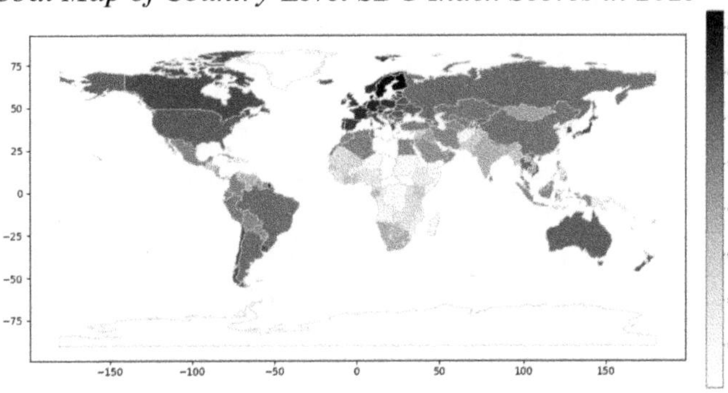


*Figure 9. Global Forecasted SDG Index Scores by Country (2030 Projection)*

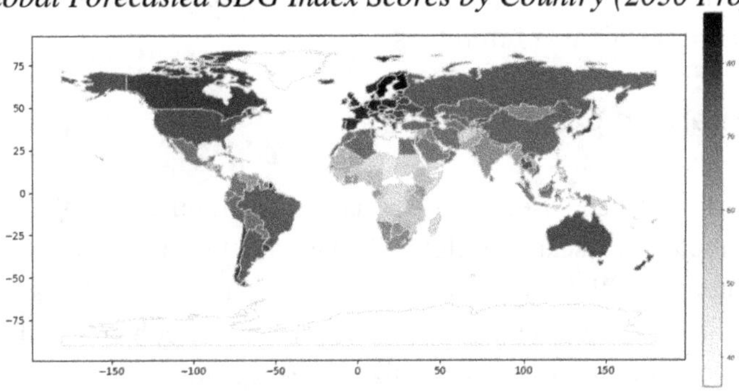


The SARIMAX forecast (fig. 10) predicts an increase in the average global SDG score, though growing confidence intervals over time signify the uncertainties in long-term predictions. This observation emphasizes the importance of resilient and adaptable policy frameworks. The combined insights from the geospatial and time series analyses highlight the essential need for focused interventions, strategic resource allocation, and international collaboration to close the development gap and achieve the SDGs in a balanced and equitable way.

*Figure 10. Time Series Forecast of Global Average SDG Index Score (2015–2030)*

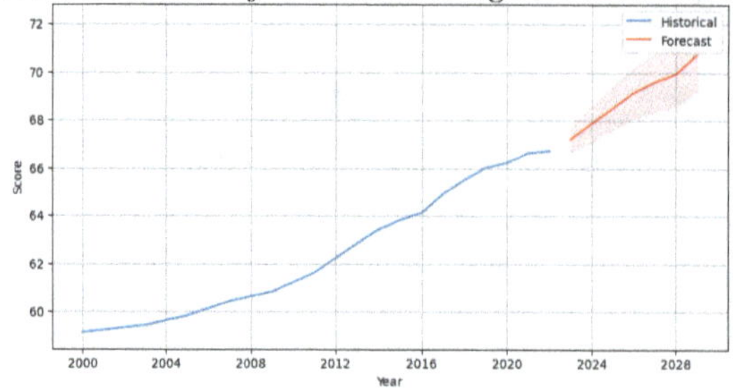


The use of SARIMAX for forecasting and geospatial visualization in this chapter provides policymakers with essential tools to address sustainable development challenges. The visual and analytical outputs aid in simplifying complex data, enriching the conversation around global sustainability, and guiding strategic decisions toward a fairer and more sustainable future.

## Network Analysis Outcomes

The network analysis, based on Sustainable Development Goals (SDG) scores, uncovers a complex landscape of global development efforts. Countries are classified into communities that mirror their respective clusters, with each community showcasing unique developmental trajectories. To ensure coherence, the numbering of clusters and communities is synchronized, linking cluster 0 to community 0, and so on.

The large-scale network plot (Fig. 11) displays global interconnectivity based on SDG scores, while the individual community plots (Figs. 12-16) provide detailed insights into each cluster. These communities, formed through cosine similarity measures, reveal diverse development paths distinguished by their centrality scores.

Communities 1, 2, and 3, as seen in Fig. 11, are close due to their intermediate development levels and similar SDG challenges. Community 1, with a mix of emerging and middle-income countries, shows varying SDG performance, reflecting diverse development stages. Community 2 consists of developed nations with robust economies, indicating higher SDG scores across multiple goals. Community 3 comprises developing countries facing significant hurdles in achieving a wide range of SDGs.

In contrast, communities 0 and 4 are distinct due to their unique developmental profiles. Community 4 includes least developed countries struggling with basic SDG targets, while community 0 contains wealthy nations with higher scores in areas like health and education.

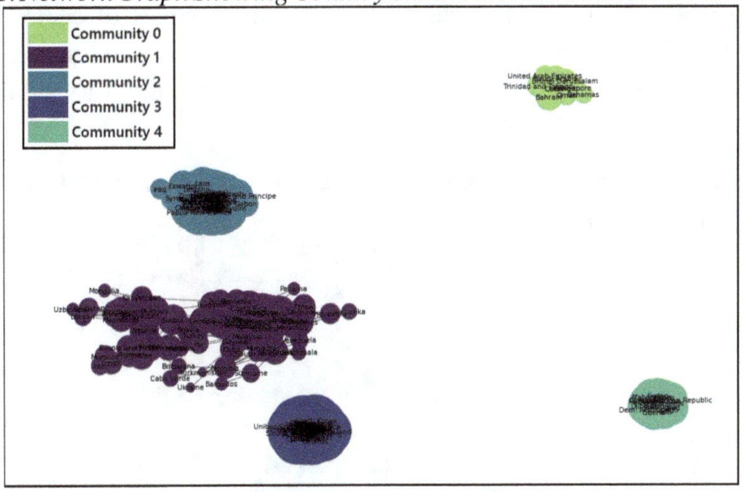


*Figure 11. Network Graph Showing Country Similarities Based on SDG Scores (2023)*

This network shows how countries group into five communities based on SDG interlinkages and mutual performance similarities. Densely connected clusters reflect shared development patterns, while more isolated groups may follow divergent or specialized progress trajectories.

Community 0 (fig.12) showcases a cluster of Gulf countries and small island states, reflecting their similar development profiles and shared economic characteristics, such as reliance on natural resources and financial services.

*Figure 12. Sub-Network of Community 0: Countries Grouped by SDG Score Similarities and Node Centrality*

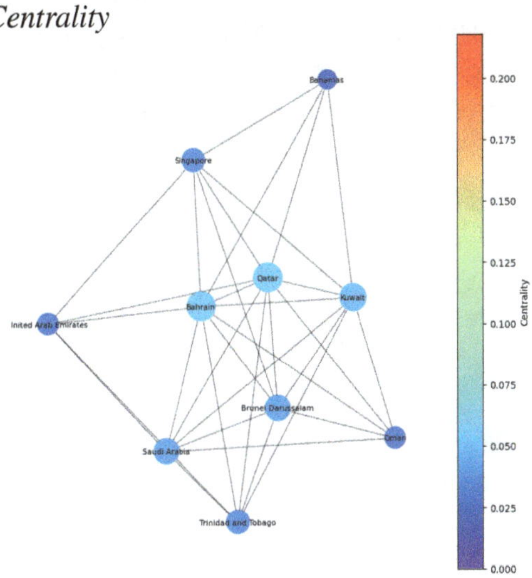

Community 1, comprising a diverse group of countries (Fig.13) ranging from Vietnam to Macedonia, is characterized by varying degrees of centrality. This suggests that while these nations share certain development patterns, the degrees to which their SDG profiles align with others in the community vary significantly.

*Figure 13. Sub-Network of Community 1: Countries Grouped by SDG Score Similarities and Node Centrality*

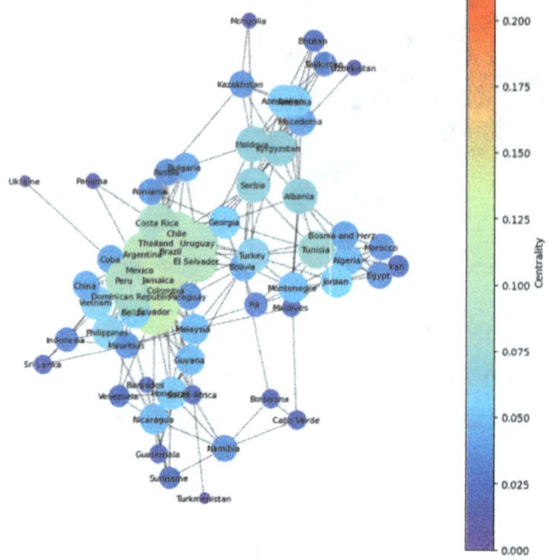


The community 2 (fig. 14) presents a contrast with a cluster of countries primarily from the African continent and parts of Asia. Countries like Kenya and Nepal show an intermediate level of centrality within this community, reflecting shared SDG challenges and achievements. It's noteworthy that nations such as Iraq and Syria, despite their complex socio-political contexts, are part of this interconnected web, underscoring the universal applicability of the SDGs.

*Figure 14. Sub-Network of Community 2: Countries Grouped by SDG Score Similarities and Node Centrality*

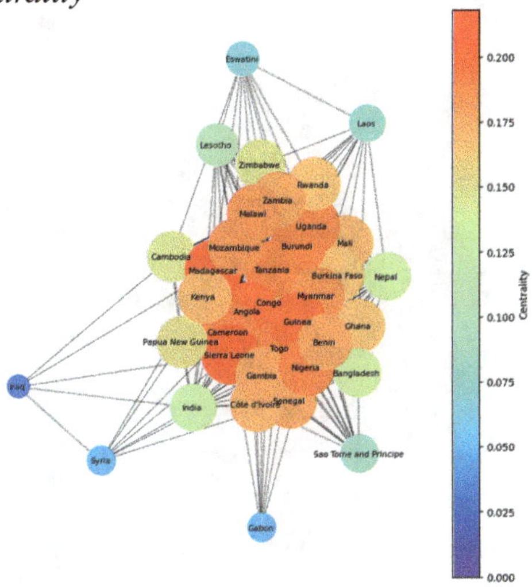


Community 3 (fig. 15) encompasses predominantly high-income countries, with nations like Denmark and Finland displaying pronounced centrality, suggesting a strong interrelationship in their development indicators. The strikingly dense connections among these countries indicate a collective progression towards the SDGs, although the outlier, Belarus, with its distinctly lower centrality, hints at divergent developmental aspects within this otherwise homogenous group.

*Figure 15. Sub-Network of Community 3: Countries Grouped by SDG Score Similarities and Node Centrality*

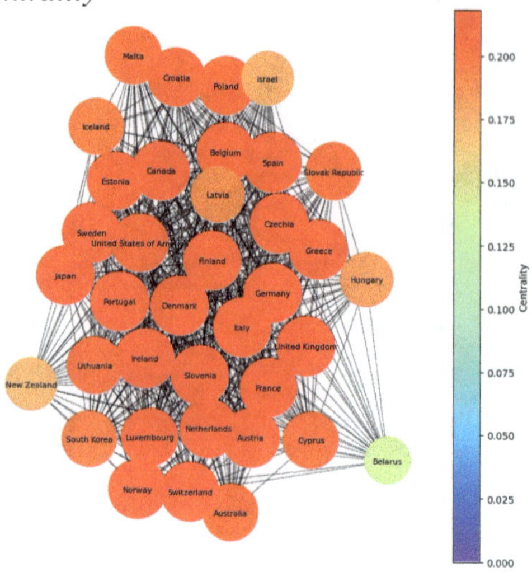


Community 4 (fig. 16) reveals a network of countries grappling with significant developmental challenges. The centrality scores here are uniformly lower, as seen in the case of nations like Yemen and Haiti, indicating fewer strong pairwise similarities in SDG scores across this community. This underscores the unique developmental contexts of these nations and possibly the need for tailored SDG strategies.

*Figure 16. Sub-Network of Community 4: Countries Grouped by SDG Score Similarities and Node Centrality*

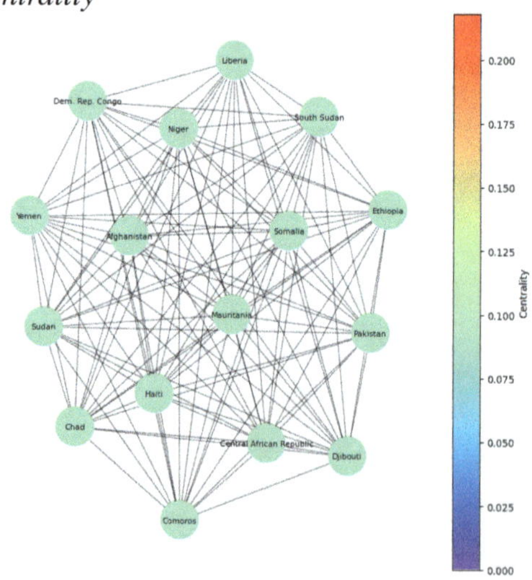

Lebanon presents an anomaly, not fitting into any community despite its cluster categorization. Its unique SDG profile, with excellent scores in goals 1 (No Poverty) and 4 (Quality Education), and low scores in other goals, sets it apart. This divergence highlights the need for customized approaches in understanding and supporting each country's sustainable development journey.

The network analysis outcomes shed light on the layered nature of global development as reflected in SDG scores. The analysis not only shows common developmental goals but also points to collaboration opportunities. The disparate standing of countries, particularly Lebanon, underlines the diversity of developmental challenges and the importance of context-specific strategies for achieving SDGs.

These insights are crucial for targeted policy interventions and international cooperation as we approach the 2030 Agenda. The network analysis visualizations offer a clear view of global sustainability efforts, showcasing both unity and diversity in addressing global challenges.

## Simulation Outcomes

The simulations in this chapter illustrate how targeted interventions in specific Sustainable Development Goals (SDGs) can significantly influence a country's development trajectory. For a sample country analyzed from each cluster, the simulations provided insights into the potential benefits of strategic investments in underperforming SDGs.

- **United Arab Emirates (Cluster 0):** Historical data shows steady growth in SDG Index Scores, with a modest increase by 2023. Simulations suggest that focused investments in SDGs 13 (Climate Action), 17 (Partnerships for the Goals), and 12 (Responsible Consumption and Production) could substantially accelerate progress towards the 2030 agenda.

*Figure 17. Historical and Forecasted SDG Index Scores for United Arab Emirates*

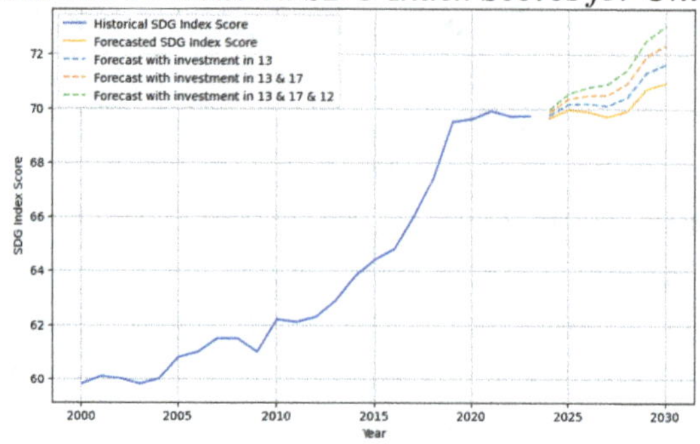


- **Kyrgyzstan (Cluster 1):** Historical trends indicate overall positive growth in SDG scores. Investment simulations in underperforming SDGs, particularly in SDG14 (Life Below Water), SDG9 (Industry, Innovation, and Infrastructure), and SDG16 (Peace, Justice, and Strong Institutions), predict a significant acceleration, underscoring the synergistic effect of multi-SDG investments.

*Figure 18. Historical and Forecasted SDG Index Scores for Kyrgyzstan*

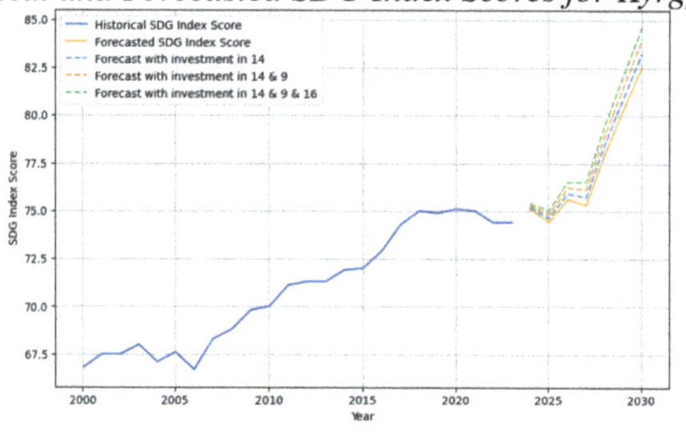


- **Lesotho (Cluster 2):** The country has shown positive SDG progression, with simulations indicating that investments in SDG14 (Life Below Water), SDG9, and SDG7 (Affordable and Clean Energy) could notably hasten development towards the 2030 goals.

*Figure 19. Historical and Forecasted SDG Index Scores for Lesotho*

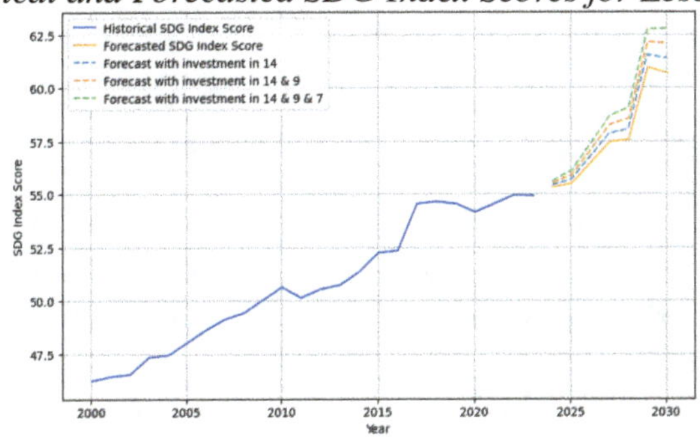


- **Czechia (Cluster 3):** Demonstrating a steady upward trend in SDG scores, simulations reveal that investments in SDG14, SDG17, and SDG12 could lead to considerable improvements, highlighting the effectiveness of a comprehensive investment approach.

*Figure 20. Historical and Forecasted SDG Index Scores for Czechia*

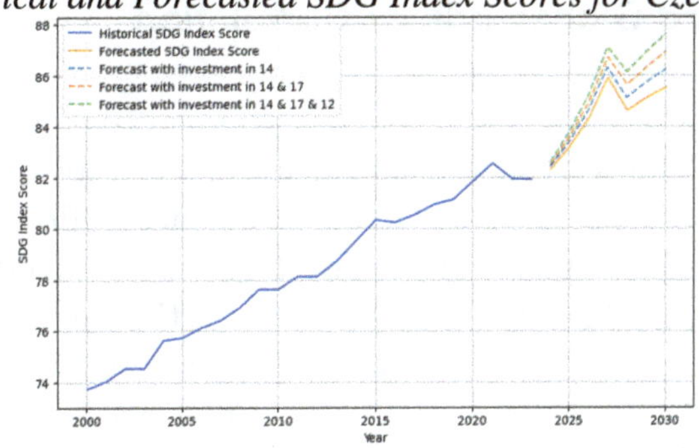


- **Mauritania (Cluster 4):** Steady improvement is forecasted to continue into 2030. Simulations indicate that prioritizing SDG9, SDG4 (Quality Education), and SDG7 could lead to transformative development, emphasizing the value of a holistic strategy.

*Figure 21. Historical and Forecasted SDG Index Scores for Mauritania*

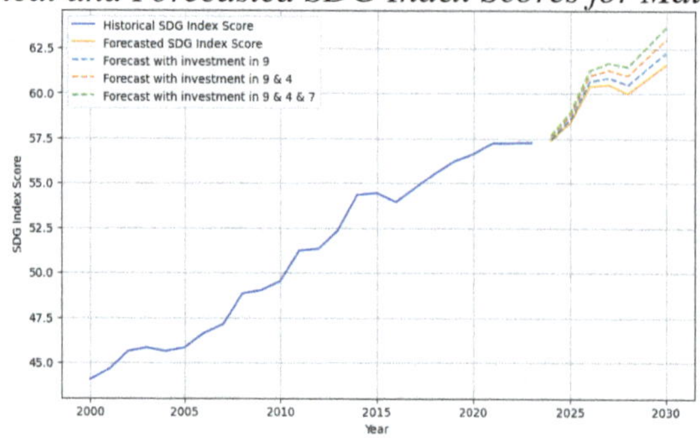


These findings underscore the necessity for tailored strategies to support nations in enhancing their SDG achievements. Although this chapter offers a theoretical framework for potential advancements, real-world applications necessitate detailed, country-specific analyses to determine the precise investment levels required for tangible improvements. This depth of understanding is crucial for guiding policy formulation and resource allocation, ensuring alignment with the 2030 SDG agenda's objectives.

## SDG Scores and Global Indices Correlation

The comprehensive evaluation of the correlation matrix (Fig. 22) alongside the scatter plots (Fig. 23) reveals a profound interconnection between SDG scores and various global indices. The scatter plots provide a visual confirmation of the strong positive correlations previously identified in the matrix, illustrating the tendency for countries with higher SDG scores to also excel in the Happiness Index (HI) (World Happiness Report, 2023), Environmental Performance Index (EPI) (Yale Center for Environmental Law & Policy and CIESIN - Columbia University, 2022), GDP per capita (World Bank, 2022), and Human Development Index (HDI) (United Nations Development Programme, 2023). It is noteworthy that for some of these indices, the most recent data available at the time of data retrieval was from 2021 or 2022, specifically HDI 2021, EPI 2022, and GDP per capita 2022. This was due to the unavailability of the 2023 versions of these datasets. However, since these indices typically exhibit gradual changes over short periods, the utilization of the latest published data does not significantly impact the validity of the analysis. The analysis thus employs the most recent data available, ensuring a relevant and accurate representation of the current state of global indices in relation to SDG scores.

*Figure 22. Correlation Matrix of SDG Index with Happiness Index (HI), Environmental Performance Index (EPI), GDP, and HDI*

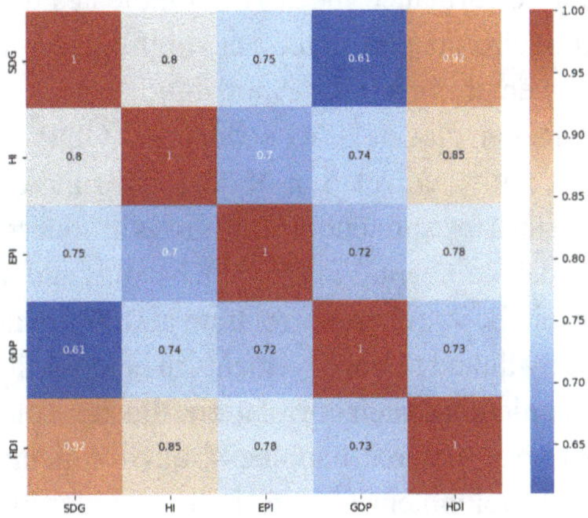


*Figure 23. Scatter Plots of SDG Index vs. HI, EPI, GDP, and HDI*

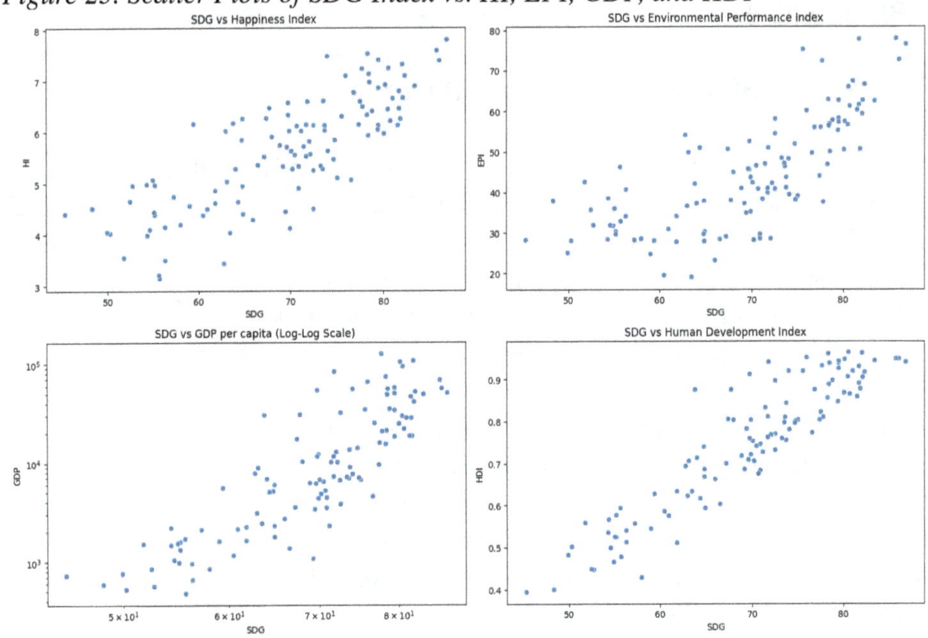


The scatter plot analysis reveals significant correlations between SDGs and various development indices. A strong correlation of 0.8 is observed between SDG scores and the Happiness Index, suggesting that achieving SDGs leads to increased citizen happiness and emphasizes the role of sustainable development in enhancing societal well-being. Similarly, a positive correlation of 0.75 between SDG scores and the Environmental Performance Index (EPI) indicates that progress in SDGs aligns with improved environmental outcomes, highlighting the direct impact of sustainable practices on environmental stewardship.

The log-log scale scatter plot of SDG scores and GDP per capita suggests a power-law relationship, with a correlation of 0.61. This indicates that even minor SDG improvements can lead to exponential GDP growth, underscoring the economic benefits of sustainable development. Finally, SDG scores and the Human Development Index (HDI) exhibit the strongest correlation at 0.92, demonstrating that SDG advancements are closely linked to improvements in health, education, and income.

Overall, these scatter plots and their correlations illustrate the interconnectedness of SDG achievements with national happiness, environmental health, economic prosperity, and human development. These findings underline the broad benefits of pursuing SDGs and the need for integrated development policies that capitalize on these interdependencies.

## DISCUSSION

### Findings in Global Environmental Context

The analysis in this chapter of Sustainable Development Goals (SDGs) across nations provides valuable insights into global environmental and developmental trends. The strong correlation of SDG scores with indices like the Happiness Index, GDP per capita, HDI, and EPI highlights how sustainable development is intertwined with socio-economic and environmental factors. The Markovian model accurately predicts SDG progress, reflecting the influence of past performance. Clustering countries based on SDG scores, as shown through PCA, sheds light on the varied development stages and challenges globally, suggesting the need for diverse strategies in sustainable development. However, as Hickel (2019) points out, there are fundamental contradictions within the SDG framework itself, particularly between the emphasis on economic growth (e.g., SDG 8) and ecological sustainability (e.g., SDG 13), which may limit the effectiveness of data-driven strategies unless these structural tensions are addressed.

While SDG trade-offs often emerge from competing development priorities, the effectiveness of implementing strategies to manage these trade-offs is deeply influenced by political and institutional conditions. Governance quality, political stability, and the integrity of institutions play a pivotal role in determining whether SDG-related policies are translated into outcomes. For instance, countries with persistent corruption, policy inconsistency, or weak public administration may struggle to deliver basic services or sustain long-term development commitments, regardless of technical planning. These institutional weaknesses not only undermine national SDG performance but also distort resource allocation and reduce trust in development processes. As illustrated in the Venezuela case study (see Figure 25), even countries with prior development progress may experience sharp reversals due to political and economic crises. Therefore, SDG analysis should not only focus on what needs to be done but also on whether the governing systems in place are capable of doing it.

## Implications for Policymakers and Stakeholders

The findings of this chapter have significant implications for policymakers and stakeholders. The correlations between SDG scores and various global indices indicate that sustainable development investments can lead to broader benefits, including enhanced well-being, economic growth, and environmental health. Cluster-based differentiation of countries can help international organizations and governments allocate resources more effectively and tailor interventions to each cluster's unique needs. The projected SDG trends up to 2030 underscore the need for focused efforts in lagging regions to achieve balanced global progress by the 2030 targets.

Beyond domestic policymaking, international financing mechanisms and cross-border partnerships are essential enablers of SDG progress, particularly in low- and middle-income countries. Initiatives such as the Global Partnership for Education (GPE) and the Green Climate Fund (GCF) have mobilized billions in aid to support education, climate resilience, and inclusive development. Multilateral agencies like the United Nations Development Programme (UNDP) and regional bodies such as the European Union provide technical assistance and financial backing that often determine whether national SDG targets can be realistically pursued. These partnerships nurture not only financial flows but also knowledge exchange and institutional strengthening. As highlighted in the World case study (see Figure 26), global collaboration in SDG 4 (Quality Education) has played a key role in narrowing disparities, particularly in regions affected by poverty or fragility. Strengthening these international linkages remains vital for equitable and sustained SDG implementation.

## Case Studies of SDG Progress and Regression

While the quantitative analysis in this chapter provides a global overview of SDG performance patterns and trajectories, it is equally important to highlight country-specific contexts where progress or regression has occurred. The following case studies offer grounded illustrations of how governance, policy, and international cooperation have influenced SDG outcomes in real-world settings. These examples help bridge the gap between statistical models and the socio-political dynamics that shape sustainable development on the ground.

- Case Study 1: Rwanda's SDG 3 Success through Community Health Initiatives:

Rwanda presents a compelling example of progress on SDG 3: Good Health and Well-being, driven by sustained investments in community health systems and decentralized care delivery. Following the country's post-genocide reconstruction, Rwanda implemented a nationwide network of community health workers and increased public health spending, resulting in significant improvements in maternal and child health, vaccination coverage, and access to primary care. As illustrated in Figure 24, Rwanda's SDG 3 score increased steadily from approximately 24 in 2000 to nearly 60 by 2020, showing a more than twofold improvement over two decades. This remarkable trend underscores the role of strategic planning, political commitment, and grassroots health governance in accelerating health-related SDG outcomes, even in low-income contexts.

*Figure 24. Rwanda's SDG 3 Score Trend (2000–2023)*

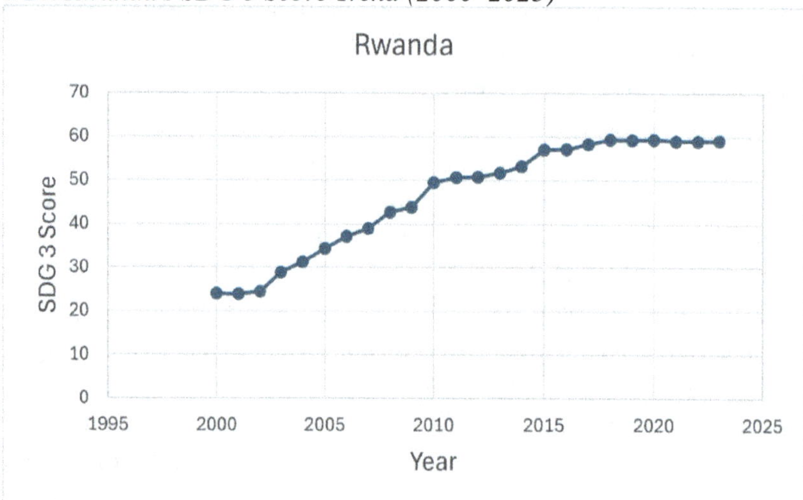


- Case Study 2: Venezuela's Collapse in SDG 1 Amid Governance Breakdown:

Venezuela exemplifies how political and economic instability can critically undermine SDG progress, particularly SDG 1: No Poverty. From 2000 to 2014, Venezuela maintained a relatively high SDG 1 score around 78–80, indicating moderate success in poverty alleviation. However, after 2014, a severe economic collapse driven by inflation, political crisis, and mismanagement led to a dramatic regression. As shown in Figure 25, the SDG 1 score dropped sharply from above 80 in 2014 to below 20 by 2020, with only minimal recovery thereafter. This steep decline highlights how governance failures, institutional erosion, and socio-political unrest can rapidly reverse development gains, rendering predictive models ineffective in the absence of foundational stability.

*Figure 25. Venezuela's SDG 1 Score Trend (2000–2023)*

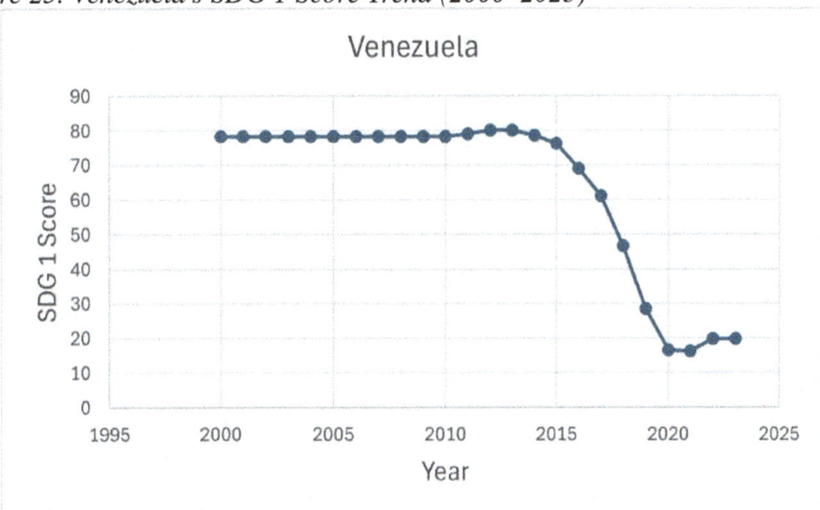


- Case Study 3: Global Progress on SDG 4 Driven by Collaborative Investment in Education:

Globally, SDG 4: Quality Education has shown steady improvement, supported by international financing mechanisms, multilateral cooperation, and national policy reforms. As presented in Figure 26, the global SDG 4 score has increased from approximately 71 in 2000 to over 82 by 2023, demonstrating consistent upward momentum. This progress reflects coordinated global efforts through programs like the Global Partnership for Education (GPE), which channels targeted funding and technical assistance to low-income countries to expand school access, enhance teacher training, and promote equity in education. Despite regional disparities, the global trend suggests that sustained multilateral engagement and policy continuity can drive tangible gains in educational outcomes worldwide.

*Figure 26. Global SDG 4 Score Trend (2000–2023)*

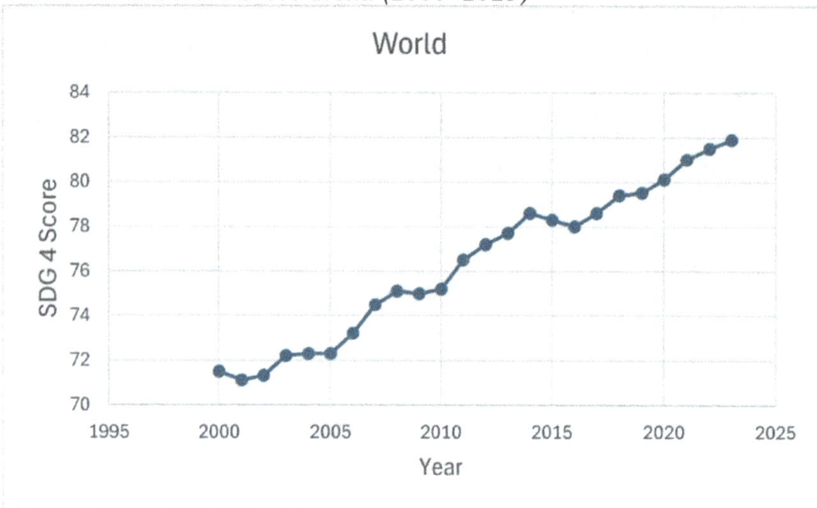


## LIMITATIONS

Despite its comprehensive scope, this chapter has several limitations. First, the forecasting models are built on historical trends and may not fully capture the influence of future shocks or unpredictable socio-political, economic, or environmental disruptions. This is especially relevant in the context of global crises such as pandemics, wars, or climate disasters, which can drastically alter development trajectories. Second, while the SDG dataset was complete and did not require imputation, potential biases may still exist due to inconsistencies in national reporting standards or gaps in data quality across countries, particularly in lower-income regions. Third, the machine learning models assume that past relationships between indicators will remain stable over time, which may not hold under rapidly changing conditions. These assumptions, while necessary for model interpretability and tractability, introduce inherent uncertainty. Additionally, the cluster-based analysis, though insightful, may oversimplify within-country heterogeneity and ignore subnational variations that are critical for policy design. Finally, the chapter adopts a primarily linear approach to simulate SDG trajectories; future work could explore non-linear models and more complex interdependencies among SDGs to reflect the real-world dynamics of sustainable development.

Moreover, the study relies on annual SDG Index data, which, while comprehensive, may lack the temporal granularity needed for rapid response policymaking. Future research could incorporate real-time or higher-frequency data sources, such as satellite imagery, mobile data, or citizen science platforms, to enhance the timeliness and responsiveness of SDG monitoring and intervention design.

## FUTURE WORK

While this chapter offers valuable insights into the progress of Sustainable Development Goals (SDGs) using various data science techniques, several directions for future exploration can further enhance our understanding and application of these findings.

Future research could incorporate diverse data sources like qualitative inputs and social media sentiment to better capture public perception and grassroots challenges. Using advanced AI models, such as deep learning, may improve SDG forecasting by identifying complex patterns in the data.

Collaborations with experts from fields such as economics, sociology, and environmental science could enrich the analysis. Cross-disciplinary approaches can provide a broader context to data-driven findings, linking them more explicitly to policy implications and socio-economic factors. Developing methods for real-time data analysis and monitoring of SDG progress could be a significant advancement, allowing for more dynamic and responsive policymaking that adapts to changes as they occur.

Conducting in-depth case studies in different geographical and socio-economic settings can provide more nuanced insights into regional variations in SDG progress. This could highlight unique challenges and successful strategies employed in various contexts. Exploring the impact of significant global events, such as the COVID-19 pandemic or economic recessions, on SDG progress could provide valuable lessons for crisis management and resilience building in the context of global sustainability goals.

Researching the effectiveness of various educational and public awareness campaigns in promoting the SDGs can provide guidance for future outreach efforts. This can help identify the most effective strategies for engaging the public and stakeholders in SDG initiatives. Additionally, future work could focus on analyzing the impact of specific policies on SDG progress. Developing models to simulate the effects of various policy decisions could provide valuable insights for policymakers.

By addressing these areas, future studies can expand upon the foundation laid in this chapter, providing deeper and more actionable insights into the progress and challenges of achieving Sustainable Development Goals.

## CONCLUSION

This chapter presents a data-driven framework for assessing global progress toward the Sustainable Development Goals (SDGs) between 2000 and 2023, applying a combination of machine learning and statistical modeling to support strategic foresight and evidence-based interventions. Exploratory analysis revealed performance trends and disparities across SDGs and countries, while a Markovian model achieved highly accurate estimations of aggregate SDG scores, underlining the interdependence of sustainability dimensions. Clustering through KMeans identified five country groupings based on performance profiles, with PCA offering a two-dimensional strategic mapping of these clusters.

Forecasting via SARIMAX models projected future SDG scores to 2030, offering valuable temporal insights to inform long-term planning. Visualizing these trends on global maps enabled the identification of regions requiring prioritized support. The application of graph theory uncovered country communities with similar development pathways, opening new avenues for regional cooperation and peer learning. Simulations indicated that focused improvements in the lowest-performing SDGs can yield meaningful aggregate gains, highlighting an approach to prioritization that is both efficient and actionable. Strong correlations with national indices such as the HDI, EPI, GDP per capita, and the Happiness Index further demonstrated the multifaceted relevance of SDG outcomes.

This chapter advances the application of data science in sustainability assessment by combining a suite of predictive, clustering, and network-based tools. Beyond methodological innovation, the insights generated support enhanced strategic planning and decision-support systems that can be embedded into organizational governance, policy design, and performance evaluation frameworks.

By equipping decision-makers with predictive foresight, comparative performance intelligence, and targeted policy simulations, the study contributes to a more informed and adaptive planning culture. These capabilities are essential for navigating complex policy environments, managing resource trade-offs, and aligning organizational objectives with long-term development goals. The analytical methods demonstrated here are scalable and transferable, making them applicable for both public institutions and private organizations aiming to embed sustainability within their operational and strategic agendas.

Ultimately, the chapter underscores the transformative potential of data-driven approaches for addressing global sustainability challenges. By enhancing the transparency, efficiency, and responsiveness of decision processes, such approaches can play a vital role in accelerating progress toward the 2030 agenda.

## REFERENCES


Allen, C., Metternicht, G., & Wiedmann, T. (2019). Prioritising SDG targets: Assessing baselines, gaps and interlinkages. *Sustainability Science, 14*(2), 421–438. DOI: 10.1007/s11625-018-0596-8

Bellantuono, L., Monaco, A., Amoroso, N., Aquaro, V., Lombardi, A., Tangaro, S., & Bellotti, R. (2022). Sustainable development goals: Conceptualization, communication and achievement synergies in a complex network framework. *Applied Network Science, 7*(1), 14. DOI: 10.1007/s41109-022-00455-1

Bennich, T., Persson, Å., Beaussart, R., Allen, C., & Malekpour, S. (2023). Recurring patterns of SDG interlinkages and how they can advance the 2030 Agenda. *One Earth, 6*(11), 1465–1476. DOI: 10.1016/j.oneear.2023.10.008

Biermann, F., Kanie, N., Kim, R. E., Adams, C., Griggs, D., Nilsson, M., & Stafford-Smith, M. (2022). Scientific evidence on the political impact of the Sustainable Development Goals. *Nature Sustainability, 5*(9), 795–800. DOI: 10.1038/s41893-022-00909-5

Blicharska, M., Teutschbein, C., & Smithers, R. J. (2021). SDG partnerships may perpetuate the global North–South divide. *Scientific Reports, 11*(1), 22092. DOI: 10.1038/s41598-021-01534-6

Cingano, F. (2014). Trends in income inequality and its impact on economic growth. *OECD Social, Employment and Migration Working Papers, No. 163*. DOI: 10.1787/5jxrjncwxv6j-en

Costa, L., Rybski, D., & Kropp, J. P. (2011). A human development framework for $CO_2$ reductions. *PLoS One, 6*(12), e29262. DOI: 10.1371/journal.pone.0029262

De Neve, J.-E., & Sachs, J. D. (2020). The SDGs and human well-being: A global analysis of synergies, trade-offs, and regional differences. *Scientific Reports, 10*(1), 15113. DOI: 10.1038/s41598-020-71916-9

Dinda, S. (2004). Environmental Kuznets curve hypothesis: A survey. *Ecological Economics, 49*(4), 431–455. DOI: 10.1016/j.ecolecon.2004.02.011

Felipe-Lucia, M. R., Soliveres, S., Penone, C., Manning, P., Van der Plas, F., Boch, S., & Fischer, M. (2020). Land-use intensity alters networks between biodiversity, ecosystem functions, and services. *Proceedings of the National Academy of Sciences of the United States of America, 117*(45), 28140–28149. DOI: 10.1073/pnas.2016210117

Golding, N., Burstein, R., Longbottom, J., Browne, A. J., Fullman, N., Sorichetta, A., & Hay, S. I. (2017). Mapping under-5 and neonatal mortality in Africa, 2000–2015: A baseline analysis for the Sustainable Development Goals. *Lancet*, *390*(10108), 2171–2182. DOI: 10.1016/S0140-6736(17)31758-0

Hickel, J. (2019). The contradiction of the Sustainable Development Goals: Growth versus ecology. *Sustainable Development*, *27*(5), 873–884. DOI: 10.1002/sd.1947

Horan, D. (2020). Enabling integrated policymaking with the Sustainable Development Goals: An application to Ireland. *Sustainability*, *12*(18), 7800. DOI: 10.3390/su12187800

Huadong, G. (2022). *Big Earth data in support of the Sustainable Development Goals*. International Research Center of Big Data for Sustainable Development Goals.

Jayachandran, S. (2015). The roots of gender inequality in developing countries. *Annual Review of Economics*, *7*(1), 63–88. DOI: 10.1146/annurev-economics-080614-115404

Kickbusch, I., & Alakija, A. (2023). The Sustainable Development Goals should be reset to prioritize poverty, health and climate. *Nature Medicine*, *29*(10), 2399–2401. DOI: 10.1038/s41591-023-02546-7

Kroll, C., Warchold, A., & Pradhan, P. (2019). Sustainable Development Goals (SDGs): Are we successful in turning trade-offs into synergies? *Palgrave Communications*, *5*(1), 140. DOI: 10.1057/s41599-019-0335-5

Lee, C.-C., Chiu, Y.-B., & Sun, C.-H. (2010). The environmental Kuznets curve hypothesis for water pollution: Do regions matter? *Energy Policy*, *38*(1), 12–23. DOI: 10.1016/j.enpol.2009.05.004

Liu, J. (2018). An integrated framework for achieving sustainable development goals around the world. *Ecology Economy and Society–The INSEE Journal*, *1*(2), 11–17.

Liu, Y., Huang, B., Guo, H., & Liu, J. (2023). A big data approach to assess progress towards Sustainable Development Goals for cities of varying sizes. *Communications Earth & Environment*, *4*(1), 66. DOI: 10.1038/s43247-023-00730-8

Malekpour, S., Allen, C., Sagar, A., Scholz, I., Persson, Å., Miranda, J. J., & Al-Ghanim, K. (2023). What scientists need to do to accelerate progress on the SDGs. *Nature*, *621*, 250.

Miola, A., Borchardt, S., Neher, F., & Buscaglia, D. (2019). *Interlinkages and policy coherence for the Sustainable Development Goals implementation: An operational method to identify trade-offs and co-benefits in a systemic way*. Publications Office of the European Union. DOI: 10.2760/472928

Mok, K. H., & Wu, A. M. (2016). Higher education, changing labour market and social mobility in the era of massification in China. *Journal of Education and Work, 29*(1), 77–97. DOI: 10.1080/13639080.2015.1049028

Mwitondi, K. S., Munyakazi, I., & Gatsheni, B. N. (2020). A robust machine learning approach to SDG data segmentation. *Journal of Big Data, 7*(1), 97. DOI: 10.1186/s40537-020-00373-y

Ospina-Forero, L., Castañeda, G., & Guerrero, O. A. (2022). Estimating networks of sustainable development goals. *Information & Management, 59*(5), 103342. DOI: 10.1016/j.im.2020.103342

Report, W. H. (2023). *World Happiness Index 2023* [Dataset]. https://worldhappiness.report/data

Sachs, J., Kroll, C., Lafortune, G., Fuller, G., & Woelm, F. (2022). *Sustainable Development Report 2022: From crises to sustainable development: The SDGs as roadmap to 2030 and beyond*. Cambridge University Press., DOI: 10.1017/9781009210058

Sachs, J., Lafortune, G., Kroll, C., Fuller, G., & Woelm, F. (2016–2023). *Sustainable Development Reports (SDG Index and Dashboards)*. Cambridge University Press. https://dashboards.sdgindex.org/

Thuy, H. N., Ngoc, Q. N., & Ngoc, H. L. (2022). A case study of integrating SDG indicators into GIS for planning and developing urban. In *International Conference: Sustainable University Development: Opportunity and Challenge (SUDOC 2022)*, University of Economics Ho Chi Minh City (UEH), Ho Chi Minh City, Vietnam.

United Nations. (2020). *The Sustainable Development Goals Report 2020: The 2030 Agenda for Sustainable Development*.

United Nations. (2023). *The Sustainable Development Goals Report 2023: Special Edition*.

van Zanten, J. A., & Putintseva, M. (2025). Evaluating governmental policies for the sustainable development goals using hierarchical clustering. *International Journal of Sustainable Development and World Ecology, 32*(3), 322–340. DOI: 10.1080/13504509.2024.2448669

Vinuesa, R., Azizpour, H., Leite, I., Balaam, M., Dignum, V., Domisch, S., Felländer, A., Langhans, S. D., Tegmark, M., & Fuso Nerini, F. (2020). The role of artificial intelligence in achieving the Sustainable Development Goals. *Nature Communications, 11*(1). Advance online publication. DOI: 10.1038/s41467-019-14108-y

World Bank. (2022). *GDP per capita (current US$)* [Dataset]. https://data.worldbank.org/indicator/NY.GDP.PCAP.CD

Yale Center for Environmental Law & Policy, & Center for International Earth Science Information Network (CIESIN) – Columbia University. (2022). *Environmental Performance Index 2022* [Dataset]. https://sedac.ciesin.columbia.edu/data/set/epi-environmental-performance-index-2022/data-download

## KEY TERMS AND DEFINITIONS

**K-Means Clustering:** A machine learning technique that groups countries into clusters based on similar SDG performance patterns, helping identify developmental typologies.

**Markovian Model:** A predictive model that estimates future outcomes using only the current or previous state, assuming limited memory of past events.

**Network Analysis:** A technique that models countries as nodes and their SDG performance similarities as connections, helping identify global communities and collaboration opportunities.

**Principal Component Analysis (PCA):** A dimensionality reduction method that transforms high-dimensional data into principal components to simplify and visualize patterns in SDG data.

**SARIMAX Model:** A statistical time series forecasting model that incorporates both seasonal trends and external variables to predict future SDG trajectories.

**SDG Index Score:** A composite metric that quantifies a country's overall progress toward achieving the Sustainable Development Goals based on standardized performance indicators.

**Simulation of Incremental Improvements:** A forecasting method used to evaluate the potential impact of hypothetical improvements in underperforming SDGs on a country's overall development score.

**Sustainable Development Goals (SDGs):** A set of 17 global objectives established by the United Nations to promote economic, social, and environmental sustainability by 2030.

# Chapter 4
# Harnessing AI for Sustainable Development: A Multidimensional Approach

**Md Mehedi Hasan Emon**
https://orcid.org/0000-0002-6224-9552
*American International University-Bangladesh, Bangladesh*

**Tahsina Khan**
https://orcid.org/0000-0001-8032-3376
*Bangladesh University of Professionals, Bangladesh*

## ABSTRACT

*Artificial Intelligence (AI) is a crucial facilitator of sustainable development, advancing progress across several sectors in accordance with the United Nations' Sustainable Development Goals (SDGs). This chapter examines the role of AI in improving education, expanding green technology, and fostering environmental sustainability via predictive climate modeling, automated waste management, and biodiversity conservation. Moreover, AI facilitates societal advancement by mitigating economic and gender disparities and aiding underprivileged populations. Although AI has significant promise, difficulties like accessibility, ethical issues, and job displacement need intentional governmental responses. This chapter analyzes AI's revolutionary influence, emphasizing its prospects and threats while offering insights into its contribution to a more sustainable future.*

## INTRODUCTION

In the past few years, Artificial Intelligence (AI) has become a game-changer in diverse industries, meaning that there has been a great deal of innovation as well

DOI: 10.4018/979-8-3373-1837-0.ch004

as a reinvention of the previous norms of doing business. As organizations take more and more into incorporating AI technologies, new opportunities for product and service development and creation avenues for value emerge exponentially. This chapter explores the multi-dimensional effects of AI in influencing innovation by looking at the changes in these results in technology as well as healthcare. The capacity of AI to import massive datasets, determine patterns and provide insight has completely transformed industries and ushered in progress in areas including medicine, finance and production. This chapter is divided into several sections whose purpose is to show the different facets of AI effects on innovation. We will explore how AI triggers innovation across sectors, look at how it supports entrepreneurial ecosystems and discuss the implications regarding intellectual property and ethics. In addition, we will discuss the impact of AI on research and development, on business models' evolution and on business implementation in creative industries. Through the analysis of these aspects, this chapter attempts to give a holistic understanding towards the complex effects of AI on innovation and how it can influence present and still to come boundaries of numerous industries. Stepping out of this rapidly transforming technological world, one such realization turns out to be the importance of understanding the implications of AI done driven innovation roadmap and the need to promote an environment in which such innovation can grow with spirit of decent and right practice. This chapter intentionally calls the reader to the dynamic power relationship between AI and innovation, with all the transformative and ethical implications of such changes.

## AI AND QUALITY EDUCATION

### Role of AI in Improving Access to Quality Education in Underprivileged Regions

AI has also a transformational impact on education more so in disadvantaged areas where access to good learning is really restricted. The resource shortages can be overcome, as well as specific learning options can be catered for every single student using AI technologies. AI powered systems offer personalized instructional materials that are tailored to individual's learning speeds and styles thus escalating student's learning experience (Yekollu et al., 2024). One of the greatest uses of AI in this field is the ability to make remote learning options better. Where there are minimal conventional educational infrastructures, AI-driven systems may expose students to an excess of online resources, interactive classes, tests and feedback systems. Such platforms as Khan Academy and Coursera use the AI algorithm to make individualized learning trajectory suggestions depending on students over background knowledge and performance giving the choice to the learners of how fast they could advance (Kaur et al., 2022).

## AI-Driven Personalized Learning Systems to Reduce Educational Inequalities

The application of AI-drives personalized learning systems is revolutionizing education by addressing educational inequality and providing customized learning experience addressing all the varied needs of a student. Personalized learning, whereby learning content is adjusted to suit the individual learners' needs improves fairness in education enormously (Halkiopoulos & Gkintoni, 2024). AI technologies enable instructors to implement personalized learning systems relying on the application of data analytics and machine learning to help develop individualized learning routes for pupils (Emon et al., 2025). These AI powered systems analyze vast amount of data related to student performance – evaluations, engagement metrics and learning habit, to understand individual strengths and weaknesses. There are learning platforms such as DreamBox learning and Smart Sparrow which incorporate adaptive learning algorithms which adjust exercise difficulty with respect to real-time student success metrics (Morze et al., 2021). Research finds that personalized learning systems tend to greatly reduce educational disparities, particularly for the children from a disadvantaged background. With targeted interventions and resources provided by such systems, opportunities can be leveled, as can educationally results across all children. In a research featured in RAND corporation peer to peer students in individualized learning platforms out performed their counterparts in normal classrooms, indicating the magnitude at which AI could equalize scoring in education (Baker et al., 2023). Despite the great promises of AI-driven customized learning systems, it is imperative to take care of the problems associated with the implementation thereof. Solutions to such problems as data privacy, algorithmic biases and digital divide must be addressed for these systems to ensure their fair benefit to all students. In addition,, educators need to be well trained to effectively use AI technologically ensuring they use technology to enhance learning in students while maintaining educational quality (George & Wooden, 2023).

### Enhancing Teacher Efficiency and Decision-Making Through AI Tools

It is changing the role of educators in education to an effective role using the incorporation of AI in education. AI technologies increase instructors' ability to focus on teaching and the participation of students by automatizing tedious administrative procedures and informing them about the actual effectiveness of their work. Significant is the role of Intelligent tutoring systems (ITS), because they off er tailored support to students as well as supplying useful information to educators about students' progress (Labadze et al., 2023). AI solutions can streamline a variety of administrative tasks such as assignment grade, student attendance control and parent's communication control. Automation of these chores allows instructors to find more time in lesson design, more time with students, and more time on executing a successful teaching strategy (Khan et al., 2025). With the help of AI, the systems of grading based on AI may analyze the contributions by students providing the immediate feedback and save the faculty time for evaluation. Improved efficiency allows instructors to manage cultivating meaningful contacts with their students and developing a more dynamic learning environment (Haleem et al., 2022).

The flow chart describes the process by which AI technologies increase instructor efficiency and decision making thus student learning outcomes. The process begins by integrating AI within learning areas where in AI; technologies are utilized to support educators in a variety of aspects of classroom management and learning delivery. After integration AI allows capturing data on student performance, summarizing gained knowledge from the tests, the attendance and reaction in classroom settings. This data is analyzed with support of AI-driven performance analysis, which uses machine learning algorithms to identify trends, strengths and weaknesses in the learning student behaviors. A critical phase ensues identifying learning deficiencies, where AIs explain subject areas in which pupils have difficulty. This study assists with recommendations of personalized instructional strategies by construing customized interpositions based on the needs of the students. AI empowers teachers with decision making by presenting data driven recommendations which in turn will help educators to better their lesson plans, change teaching style and utilize resources more effectively. Such improvements allow for better results of student learning since the learners receive individual assistance to develop their performance in the classroom. Before finalizing, there is a verification of completion i.e. verification that all learning goals and criteria have been met. If gaps are left entailed, educators can come back to an earlier stage and modify their tactics where needed. When all benchmarks are met, the process eventually comes to a good end which is the end of AI's role in that cycle.

*Figure 1. AI's role in enhancing teacher decision-making*

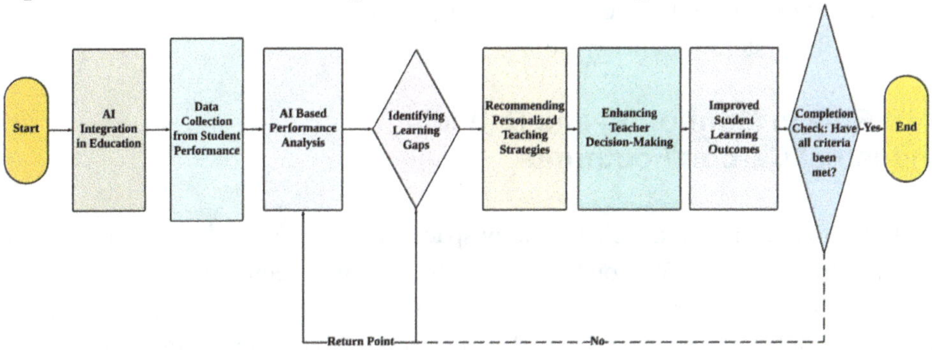


## AI AND GREEN TECHNOLOGIES

### Applications of AI in Promoting Clean Energy Solutions and Improving Energy Efficiency

AI is becoming vital when it comes to sustainable energy efforts and increased energy efficiency. In the face of an urgent global crisis to move to sustainable sources of energy, AI technologies are proving what an important role they can play in optimization of energy use and overall resource management. The optimization of smart grids is one of the leading areas of AI applications, necessary for introducing renewable forms of energy to the existing energy infrastructure. AI can make predictions on variation in energy demand by analyzing large volumes of data from a variety of sources including, but not limited to, meteorological predictions, historical consumption, and live use data (Ahmad et al., 2021). Utility firms can enhance energy delivery through utilization of machine learning algorithms thus limiting waste and guaranteeing maximal use of renewable energy sources including solar and wind. AI can predict the times during which peak energy demand occurs and control the energy supply to respond to peak energy demand times hence reduce dependence on fossil fuel and enhance incorporation of renewable in the energy mix (Khan & Emon, 2025).

One of the greatest uses of AI in renewable energy is optimizing energy storage systems. High level AI algorithms can control the storage of batteries ensuring that energy is stored and released at ideal intervals in response to demand changes and supply shift. This capacity is critical given the ongoing integration of renewable energy sources into the grid that is intermittent and requires good storage solutions (Kebede et al., 2022). AI can enhance grid stability and demonstrate smooth progression to a sustainable energy future by optimizing charging and discharging cycles in the systems of energy storage.

## AI's Role in Monitoring and Reducing Industrial Carbon Footprints

Other than its use in the clean energy space, AI continues to be used to monitor and moderate industrial carbon footprints. The industrial sector actively contributes to the emission of global carbon and the use of AI can lead to major savings in emissions and usage of resources. AI is mainly facilitating this transformation by facilitating electricity emission monitoring in real-time. AI systems could look and analyze data from multiple sources including sensors an Internet of Things devices to give comprehensive insights on organization's carbon emissions (Nižetić et al., 2020). Using predictive analytics, enterprises can identify inefficiencies in their production processes which result in increased emissions. For instance, AI might look at the previously generated manufacturing data to find trends that lead to excessive energy consumption or waste production. This data allows organizations to implement targeted steps to reduce their carbon footprints. Equipment financed through predictive maintenance technologies is one the effective applications of AI that are used to cut the downtime of the equipment and increase the efficiency of operation. By predicting possible equipment failures or maintenance requirements, organizations can improve their maintenance plans hence reduce energy consumption and reduce production dislocation-related emissions (Emenike & Falcone, 2020).

The flowchart shows a Carbon Footprint Monitoring System AI-driven – with the goal of enhancing the industrial sustainability by innovative technology. The process is initiated through the procedure of continuous performance monitoring and reporting, revealing in-real time emissions and performance efficiency (Emon & Khan, 2025b). After data collection, a completion assessment is conducted to evaluate whether the developed standards of carbon reduction or efficiency have been met. If the conditions are not met, the system goes back to improving its monitoring and tracking initiatives. Sensors and IoT devices are installed strategically in different operating phases, then data collection follows. Using these devices, one is able to get full understanding on energy usage and emission origins to set the foundation for future measures. The collected data is processed by AI, and using high-class algorithms, these trends are unveiled, these inefficiencies are detected, and such actions are highlighted. With AI, prediction and analysis on carbon emission are made possible by analyzing both past and current data to predict probable future emissions. Such predictive capability allows firms to predict the environmental impacts of their activities and address them. The system also has the proffered real-time monitoring that immediately notes, within a second, once the dengan's emitted level exceeds standards. Such notifications help obtain prompt response and reduce too much carbon emission.

AI improves the development of targeted plans for emission reduction. These solutions can be such as enhancing the industrial processes, changing the pattern of energy use or changing the supply chain operation to have more sustainable outcomes. When suggestions are produced, the system allows their operation via AI-based optimization. This stage ensures that activities and carbon reduction targets keep time with one another as well improving overall efficiency. The process operates over a feedback loop, continually enhancing its methodologies with new data and thus ensures continuous adherence to environmental standards and sustainability of industries.

*Figure 2. AI-based carbon footprint monitoring system*

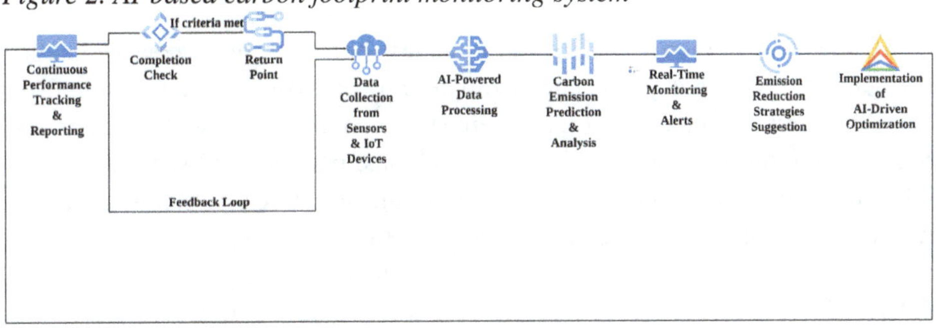


## Case Studies on AI-Enabled Green Innovations

Many successful case studies show how AI can help progress the green technology and build up sustainable habits. An example of this is Google's DeepMind, who have used machine learning algorithms to make their data center's energy more efficient. DeepMind has achieved a commendable 15% reduction in energy usage from its buildings through analysis with AI on past energy usage patterns and extracting trends (Ahmad et al., 2022). Such a significant improvement also leads to an improvement in the reduction of costs for the organization as well as the application of AI in improving energy efficiency in large operations. Doing something else with AI are the options such as the use of AI in strengthening building energy management systems. Verdigris Technologies among other firms have developed AI driven systems that monitor energy consumption in commercial institutions, providing immediate information and suggestions concerning energy efficiency (Lanbaran et al., 2024). By identifying wasteful energy and proposing practical improvements, these technologies have demonstrated the ability to reduce energy consumption by up to 30% thus greatly decreasing carbon emissions associated with building operations. In addition, AI is used in Agriculture to improve sustainable practices. Precision agricultural technologies make use of AI to evaluate data from various sources which include satellite images and soil sensors to improve judicious use of water, the appropriate application of fertilizer and crop management. This approach improves agricultural output at the same time it reduces environmental impact through reduced use of resources and runoff (Khan et al., 2025; Xia et al., 2020).

## IMPACT OF AI ON ENVIRONMENTAL SUSTAINABILITY

### Predictive Analytics for Climate Change Mitigation Using AI

AI-supported predictive analytics are coming to be recognized as powerful weapons against climate change. Such technologies rely on advanced – albeit simplistic – machine learning algorithms for analyzing the accommodating wide datasets that include environmental variables, historical climate patterns, and socio-economic indicators. By simulation of a wide range of climate futures AI can help policymakers identify the most effective mitigation options. AI can predict the potential implications of different emission reduction strategies on the global temperatures and help decision makers decide on ways to undertake the activities that will deliver the best returns (Reichstein et al., 2019). Machine learning models can check data in real-time coming from various sources; for example, satellite or sensor network data, to track the environmental changes as well as to evaluate the effectiveness of the implemented policies. This is a tool to use adaptive management strategies allowing for the change in policies according to the updated data and trends. In addition, AI can improve critical mass incidents warning systems of serious weather events so that governments and organizations could take an initiative and protect those who are at risk (Emon & Khan, 2024; Jain et al., 2023). AI driven predictive analytics are important for steering climate action and the promotion of sustainable development using all-encompassing data-driven insights. These technologies enhance the capability to predict climatic trends as well as evaluate potential impacts of policy actions thus promoting more well informed and effective climate change mitigation strategies.

## AI-Powered Solutions for Waste Management and Recycling

The application of AI in garbage management and recycling is transforming community waste management and a sustainability strategy. Traditionally, garbage sorting is quite cumbersome and time consuming, creating diminished recycling rates as well as high volumes of goods finding their way into landfills. Computer vision and robotics, AI-driven technologies, are addressing these problems by increasing sorting accuracy and its technological efficiency (Dodampegama et al., 2024). AI driven computer sophisticated vision technologies can also be used successfully in automated sorting systems accurately identifying and categorizing items. These systems assess visual trash stream data to distinguish against multiple recyclables, organics, and polluters' classes. Automating this process facilitates facilities to significantly enhance their sort-through process and increase recycling ratios. Similarly companies like AMP Robotics are utilizing AI driven robots in allowing them to successfully segregate these mixed recyclables thus increasing the diversion of waste out of landfills for re processing to make new products (Chertow et al., 2024). Additionally, AI can advance garbage collection roundtrips leading to minimal fueling emissions and usage related to waste transportation. By means of analysis proceedings of past waste generation data and existing traffic conditions, AI algorithms can develop more efficient collection plans that eliminate unnecessary trips and consumption of resources. This application minimizes operational costs and greenhouse gases from garbage collection buckets (Chen et al., 2020).

## Conservation of Biodiversity Through AI-Based Monitoring Systems

Biodiversity conservation is of key interest to maintaining sustainability of the environment and AI technologies are greatly playing a major role in enhancing conservation efforts. AI with remote sensing, automated data collection tracking, can manage ecosystems, track species migrations and quantify habitat changes in real time. AI-powered drones equipped with high definition cameras can gather complete photos of landscapes and wildlife, a process which will allow researchers to analyze population dynamics and patterns of habitat use without disturbing the animals (Boroujeni et al., 2024). AI algorithms can process enormous datasets garnered from different sources such as satellite-based imaging, acoustic sensors and camera traps, to find anomalies, and patterns in the biodiversity. Algorithms of machine learning can examine characteristics of the distribution of species and environmental characteristics to help conservationists prioritize regions for conservation and restoration. This skill is especially important in the case of climate change, because through this skill, organizations are able to alter the conservation efforts as a reaction to altered species distributions and ecological functions (Weiskopf et al., 2020).

The AI-Enabled Biodiversity Monitoring Process is a prime example of a modern framework which integrates AI with conservation techniques to protect and conserve biodiversity. First, we have been using a conservation decision support system, which involves the collection of data, analysis of ecological situations and making actionable recommendations to applicable authorities. These are the recommendations guiding formulation and implementation of wildlife conservation policies and measures, with a focus on conserving at risk habitats and species. The system promises improved biodiversity protection as soon as conservation measures are enacted. Gathering data is a core element of this process and it is done by using IoT devices and the drones, in order to obtain photos and acoustic information on animals in different environments. These tools give direct high-definition information of animal behavior, habitat conditions, and potential threats in real time. The amassed information undergoes AI-driven picture and audio identification process whereby sophisticated algorithms identify species, analyze what they do, and track ecological relationships. This information adds to monitoring species as well as behavioral assessment, which enables determination of population trends, movement trends, and where they use to live. Using machine learning techniques improves the study by detecting trends as well as highlighting changes in habitat over time. These insights enable the system to make predictions based on ecological changes and related hazards. Predictive analytics is necessary for predicting the changes in biodiversity, improving the effectiveness of tools of pro-active decision-making for conservationists. Completion checks are incorporated into the loop as a mechanism to ensure that all conservation actions are effective and aligned to biodiversity targets. The procedure repeats (if necessary) for improvement or collection of additional data, ensuring a constant flexible approach to biodiversity protection. This AI based process enhances the accuracy, effectiveness, and impact of conservation efforts advancing an ecological and species future that is sustainable.

*Figure 3. AI-enabled biodiversity monitoring process*

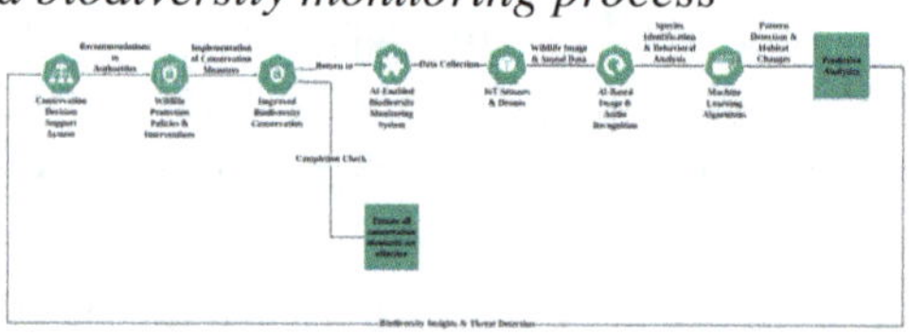

# IMPACT OF AI ON SOCIAL DEVELOPMENT

## AI's Role in Reducing Gender and Economic Inequalities

AI can scarily reduce gender and economic barriers because they deliver access to the essential resources and opportunities which were previously inaccessible. AI-run platforms may benefit women entrepreneurs by offering personalized data of the company, marketing resources, and access to fund opportunities. Institutions such as the World Bank group have initiated AI project the goal of which is to encourage female entrepreneurs in underdeveloped countries accessing business networks and investing opportunities. These platforms rely on AI to analyze the current trend in the market and the preferences of customers to help women identify viable business prospects therefore empowering the women economically and encouraging entrepreneurship. In addition, AI can enhance gender equality in learning and therefore adapt learning to the peculiarities of the female students. AI-supported educational systems are able to adapt to different types (styles and speeds) of learning so that females can overcome educational challenges, particularly in those regions where cultural ways hinder their admission to academic institutions (Opesemowo & Adekomaya, 2024). Using customized educational contents and guideline, AI has the potential to minimize the gap of gender in education, as well as increasing the participation of female gender in STEM disciplines. In addition, AI might help to detect and reduce structural biases which maintain gender inequality and representatives from an economically weaker community. Machine learning algorithms can review large datasets to identify disparities in recruitment strategies, wage structures, and promotion pools within firms. By playing attention to such discrepancies AI can help companies to create data-informed policies that will promote also diversity & inclusion, which in the end would lead to a fairer workforce (Kumar et al., 2024).

## AI-Driven Solutions for Addressing Public Health Challenges

AI promises to change the face of public health through better detection of early ill health, better forecasting of epidemics and equitable allocation of healthcare budget. AI algorithms may review huge scale health data from various sources such as the electronic health records, social media, and environmental data, in order to identify patterns and trend of potential health hazards that might be on the increase (Rehman et al., 2022). AI has been used to determine the spread of infectious diseases such as COVID-19 by analyzing real time data from numerous channels with the expectation that health authorities will respond promptly and efficiently to outbreaks. Apart from epidemic predictions, AI has the potential to increase the distribution of healthcare resources by analyzing the demographic of the patients, the prevalence of illness and use of health care. AI systems can help policymakers to forecast future healthcare needs, which would make them make educated budgets allocation choices that would ensure accessibility to healthcare service for the underprivileged groups (Dwivedi et al., 2021). Such knowledge is particularly valuable in low resource settings where healthcare facilities may be inadequate.

AI is changing public health decision making thanks to accurate analysis and fast solutions regarding health issues. AI systems perform a complex analysis of large datasets found in electronic health records, environmental sensors, and social media, and other sources to detect a pattern and predict potential health risks. This lesson enables the early detection of diseases and their primary responses to public health crises. AI is most famous for prediction of epidemic and outbreak control. By analysis of real time data an AI system might identify trends which would indicate the start of infectious illness and thus allow early action from health authorities. AI-driven methods during the COVID 19 pandemic played a vital role during the process of monitoring the spread of the virus, and increased resource distribution. Additionally, AI makes better resource allocations because of an analysis of both demographic and health use data. This ensures equitable access to healthcare services, especially in resource poor settings with poor infrastructure. This information is used by policymakers in allocating money properly to marginalized communities and improving general health equality. Another transformative element is individualized medicine. By determining genetics, lifestyle, and environmental variables, AI algorithms personalize individual approaches for treatment. This improves results of treatment and allows suffering patients to participate in their own healthcare, enhancing more participation in healthcare. When AI forms part of the public health decision making, it has a lot of potential for resolving global health challenges, optimizing utilization of resources and improving healthcare delivery outcomes for different populations.

*Figure 4. AI in public health decision-making*

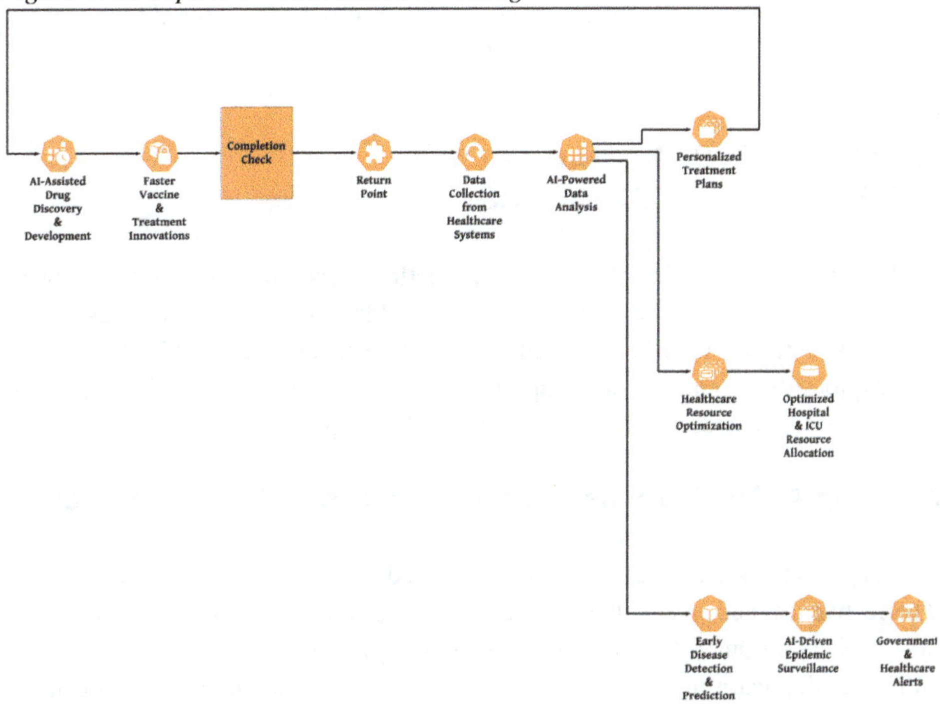


## Challenges of Implementing AI in Developing Countries and Marginalized Communities

While AI has a potential solution for social development issues, AI applications in the not so developed nations and people with indigence face much resistance. One major challenge is lack of infrastructure to be used to support AI technology. Many places are poor in reliable internet connection, energy, and necessary hardware to make AI solutions successful (Ahmad et al., 2021). Accompanied by digital divides, increased disparities emerge leading to blocking advantages that could be afforded the marginalized people by AI. Furthermore, digital literacy is a major barrier to the egalitarian use of AI. There are many people in underdeveloped nations that can be lacking in the skills and knowledge needful for skillful use of AI tools and platforms. In the lack of proper training and support these individuals might give up on the benefits that AI technology gives and so worsen socio-economic inequalities (Cooke et al., 2022). Such things as ethical issues are critical to AI deployment in developing environments. AI systems, however, unintentionally may reinforce biases from a dataset used for training thus delivering discriminatory outcomes. If the AI algorithms are trained upon data sets containing historical injustices, then they will carry current prejudices in areas such as employment, credit and access to healthcare (Giovanola & Tiribelli, 2023).

## IMPACT OF AI ON SUSTAINABLE DEVELOPMENT GOALS (SDGS)

The rise of AI technology has provided a platform wherein SDGs, commissioned by the United Nations, can be pursued. Stakeholders may address various global issues while pursuing these high goals, by utilizing capabilities of AI. This section will explore the alignment of AI applications with some of the SDGs and some challenges encountered in the integration of AI into global SDG projects.

### Mapping AI Applications to Specific SDGs and Their Targets

AI applications may intentionally be associated with particular (SDGs) to enhance its effectiveness and ensure that they achieve focused outcome. AI can make a great deal to SDG 4 (Quality Education) by increasing access of educational resources and increasing learning outcomes. AI-based personalized learning systems can accommodate unique needs of students making them eligible for personalized study material that adapts to varying learning styles and speeds (Rane et al., 2023). Such a customization might be especially beneficial in regions with diverse educational backgrounds, where narrowing of knowledge and skills gaps might be enforced. In addition, the AI can improve the results of healthcare and the identification of the illness in advance (SDG 3) and therefore improve the results of the healthcare. Using medical data, AI algorithms can identify patterns that provide indications of serious health problems in a timely manner. AI based diagnostic technologies may help healthcare workers to detect diseases, such as cancer at an early phase thereby enhancing better treatment results. In addition, AI can fulfill better allocation of healthcare resources, making sure that limited groups will receive decent medical treatment (Rane et al., 2023).

Under the SDG 11 (Sustainable Cities and Communities) imprint, AI may enhance planning and control of cities based on information about transportation, use of energy, and environment variables. The AI-backed smart city endeavors may improve public transport systems, ease congestion, and optimize the usage of energy leading to more sustainable cities (Stecuła et al., 2023). Additionally, AI can give real time surveillance of air quality and other environmental measures thus enabling cities to act proactively on the various quality of life measures for citizens. AI can help with SDG 13 (Climate Action) by providing predictive analytics around mitigation of climate change (Khan & Emon, 2024). Machine learning algorithms are able to analyze climate data and make future scenarios, and observe the effects of different mitigation initiatives (Cowls et al., 2023; Emon, 2025c). AI provides policymakers with the ability to make an informed judgment from data-drive insights, thus bringing efficacy into climate action and resilience planning.

## Challenges and Limitations in Integrating AI with Global SDG Initiatives

There is a lot of potential for the SDGs to become better by means of AI; However, several difficulties and limitations must be addressed for the purpose of efficient integration. Data privacy is a serious issue. The adoption of AI solutions usually calls for huge amounts of data which have preceded people's concerns on the data collection, storage and utilization procedure. 'Privacy and security' of personal information should be considered a priority, especially in sensitive sectors such as healthcare and education (Hathaliya & Tanwar, 2020). Successfully balancing the need to use data for AI applications and defending individual privacy rights is one of the biggest problems. Technological inequities are one of the greatest challenges to the successful implementation of AI into global SDG projects. Many underdeveloped countries do not have the necessary rudiments of infrastructure, resources and technological competence to properly utilize AI technologies. The digital gap may increase the preexisting inequalities while slowing the progress of the sustainable development projects (Mondejar et al., 2021). Any initiative to correct this disparity requires investment in both infrastructure in terms of technology and programs for capacity building that will let the local communities utilize AI for sustainable development (Emon & Chowdhury, 2025).

In addition, AI installation governance concerns also need to be addressed. The rapid advance of AI technologies most of the time overgrows the creation of regulatory systems and leads to the potential exploitation and ethically alarming issues (Dwivedi et al., 2021). Development of specific norms and ethical requirements for AI appears as a major requirement to ensure ethical use of these technologies and according to sustainable development ideals. The multidisciplinary nature of AI with the application of AI to the SDGs is tremendous and it requires cooperation of many stakeholders including governments, commercial sector entities, civil society groups and local communities. Collaborations at strategic levels are so important in achievement of maximum potential of AI in achieving the SDGs. However, facilitating the cooperation in a large number of spheres is not easy, due to the divergent interests, purposes, and approach (García-Sánchez & García-Sánchez, 2020). Building trust and spreading communication among stakeholders will be key in aligning effort and increasing the effectiveness of AI in achieving the SDGs.

## IMPACT OF AI ON EDUCATIONAL INEQUALITIES

AI can significantly reduce educational disparities, making school attendance and equality available to marginalized people all over the world. Using emerging technologies AI can improve individualized learning, inclusion and the digital divide. In this section we consider how AI addresses differences in educational access, where AI shipped language translation tools out, where the role of AI in improving digital literacy is discussed, and finally ending on more insights into how AI might change outcomes in the educational setting.

### Addressing Disparities in Education Access Through AI

AI may help at least to eliminate some of the discriminatory gaps in education by providing access to remote learning opportunities and learning resources to the excluded part of the world. AI driven systems can offer personalized learning experiences in tune to individual learner requirements thus promoting engagement and experiences resulting from the learning process. Systematic intelligent tutoring (ITS) may evaluate children's patterns of learning and leverage appropriate resources, supporting people who may face difficulties in a traditional classroom setting (Alam, 2022). In addition, AI driven learning management systems can offer individual assistance to students of different learning types and abilities. This customized methodology ensures that no student will have no chance of thriving regardless of their background (Kuleto et al., 2021).

The flowchart explains how AI helps educators to make data-driven choices to increase education results. The process begins by data gathering where AI systems then harvest data from where various sources such as student evaluation, learning patterns and engagement metrics are used. The analyzed data reveals large patterns, student development, and potential areas of improvement. Relevant to this, AI produces personalized recommendations, providing teaching approaches, adaptive learning sources, and interventions for those children who need more help. Such insights enable educators to improve their pedagogical approaches to realizing that they bring their lesson plans in tandem with various learning needs of pupils (Emon, 2025b). Afterwards, educators assess the insights that are computer generated and add them to curricular modification to improve the magnitude of instructional efficacy. Real-time performance monitoring is offered by AI solutions to instructors who can optionally dynamically evaluate student development and quickly apply interventions where done. Therefore, intelligently ensuring decisions bring better learning outcomes for student's AI-based decision making helps to create a more inclusive and efficient educational system. By harnessing AI driven data educators can improve classroom teaching, increase student engagement, and develop a flexible learning environment. The approach culminates into a loop of continuous improvement in which continuous data analysis refines coming pedagogical strategies.

*Figure 5. Impact of AI on educational inequalities*

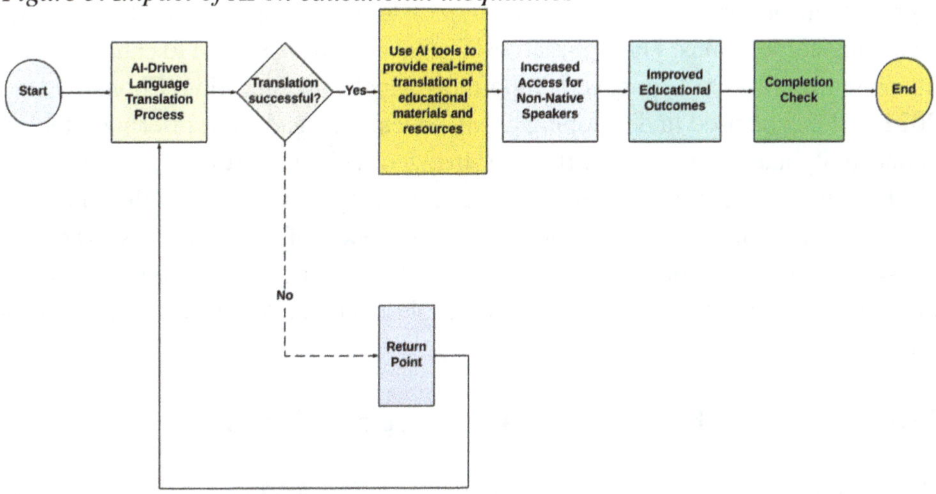


## Implications of AI-Driven Language Translation Tools for Global Education

Sometimes language barriers create barriers to educational access for non-native speakers in places that have several languages. AI based language translation systems can significantly improve global education by making learning material reach all kinds of population. These solutions have real-time translation of instructional materials hence making it easier for non-native speakers to interact with the topic easily (Che Dalim et al., 2020). AI based systems can offer immediate translations of textbooks, lectures or online courses and by doing so encourage diversity in education. Moreover, AI translation systems may help educators in multilingual classrooms to make effective contact with children from different language backgrounds. These technologies enable collaboration and make the learning process more interesting for any student by breaking the linguistic barrier. The application of AI-methodology of translation technology helps reinforcement of access to the educational materials and promotes the more inclusive and diverse learning space.

## AI's Role in Bridging the Digital Divide

The digital gap is still a significant barrier to the parentheses of educational opportunities, particularly in low income and out-of-the-way places. AI can make a great contribution to closing this gap by providing cost effective and accessible technological solutions. Those initiatives that involve the use of AI to enhance connection and digital literacy are very important for inclusive education (Chohan & Hu, 2022). AI can be used in developing cheap educational gadgetry, offering internet connectivity and digitalization, the marginalized regions. Further, AI-based apps might help to improve efforts to ensure digital literacy, which requires the ability of users to navigate in the digital world. Through the boost of digital literacy, AI could allow students, educators and communities to fully harness technology in pursuit of their educational goals. Not only is this a solution to the digital divide but it also prepares learners for a tech future.

## Enhancing Teacher Training and Support with AI

AI could also help with teacher training and support which is fundamental in addressing the educational disparities. AI-based professional development programs can offer individually designed learning trajectories for instructors who will help improve learning strategies and better support diverse learners. AI systems can assess classroom interactions, identify and share with teachers how they can adjust their teaching tactics in real time based on the knowledge provided (Seo et al., 2021). Furthermore, AI can increase peer cooperation between the educators by connecting educators with, who have similar problems or interests, thus encouraging sharing best practices and resources. Investments in AI-supported teacher training empower college and universities with the needed knowledge and skills for nurturing inclusive learning environments by educators.

# IMPACT OF AI ON UNEMPLOYMENT

The advent of AI is changing the work environment for the better or for the worst possibilities and challenges. Integrating AI technology in several industries creates great anxieties about job loss. However, alongside these matters, there is an opportunity for worker development through the reskilling/upskilling projects. This chapter discusses possible dangers of AI induced job displacement, reskilling necessities and strategies needed to offset structural unemployment due to AI integration.

## Potential Risks of AI-Driven Job Displacement in Various Sectors

There will be massive displacement of jobs in several areas through job automation through AI technologies. It is particularly vulnerable for AI to replace manual operations in manufacturing, retail and transportation industries because AI technologies can perform tasks previously done by people. Autonomous car poses a threat to replacement of employment of drivers of big rigs, taxi owners, and deliverymen (Turienzo et al., 2023). In manufacturing, AI-driven robots can replace the labor of the assembly line, and this carbohydrate has serious consequences for labor jobs in this industry. Research indicates that by 2030, as many as 14% of global workforce jobs may be automated out of work by the application of intelligent software (Willcocks, 2020). These shifts will necessarily have varying impacts by regions with poor countries experiencing sharper dislocation because of the low-skilled labor it needs. In addition, job displacement is also not limited to low skilled positions; even highly skilled jobs in industries such as finance, health care and law can be put at risk by AI-based automation. The relative inequality impacts from employment relocation peripheral mobility can be serious, thereby exacerbating inequality and social tensions (Emon, 2023). The displaced laborers find it difficult getting new work, especially if it lacks the necessary qualifications to fill the increasing job with low demand. Therefore, governments and organizations need to assess the likely impacts of AI on employment and come up with solutions on how best to mitigate from the consequences of AI.

## Opportunities for Reskilling and Upskilling in an AI-Driven Economy

While AI brings danger of job replacement, AI also creates opportunities for employee reskilling and upskilling. Because some jobs may become obsolete, there will be other jobs that require another type of skill set. It is of great importance to focus on programs that focus on digital competencies, AI literacy and critical thinking to prepare workers for the needs of an AI economy (Abulibdeh et al., 2024). Organizations may play a great role in the establishment of a culture of continuous learning by enterprise in staff development programs. Companies could offer training sessions and seminars so that their personnel acquire the required skill to cope with new technology. In addition, partnerships between learning institutions and enterprises may offer career opportunities for people to develop the necessary skills for jobs that require them in technology and data analytics field. In addition, schemes aimed at creating lifelong learning may help individuals sustain competitiveness in a rapidly changing working environment. Achieving access to online learning platforms, mentorship programs and development tools may help employees to enhance their skills and enhance their employability. Any discussion of setting the trajectory of the workforce will be centered on the importance of adaptation and resilience.

## THE IMPACT OF AI ON INNOVATION

AI is in the process of drastically transforming several industries and spurring innovation while unleashing the development and delivery model of products and services and business models. AI is enabling significant advancements in multiple areas, such as healthcare and technology, and it is encouraging entrepreneur ecosystems along which come unique issues, especially in intellectual property and ethics. This section delves into multitudes of impacts of AI on innovation and reveals AI's role as the catalyst for changing multiple areas.

### AI as a Driver of Innovation in Technology, Healthcare, and Beyond

AI has emerged as key catalyst for innovation more so in areas like healthcare, technology and manufacturing. In health care AI driven diagnosis & treatment solutions have revolutionized the care of the patients. Machine learning algorithms can analyze medical data in order to detect trends and predict health outcomes in order to allow timely diagnosis of diseases like cancer and diabetes (Javaid et al., 2022). AI's solutions in radiology and pathology have incredible accuracy in detecting abnormalities in medical pictures, thus increasing health workforce productivity, and optimizing patient outcomes (Alowais et al., 2023). In the technological world, AI is promoting the development of intelligent goods and services. AI powered- virtual assistants, such as Amazon's Alexa and Apple's Siri, are changing consumers' interaction with technology using custom built experiences and frictionless device connectivity (Kumar et al., 2024). Moreover, AI algorithms are driving the evolution of software development; facilitating code production and the enhancement of cybersecurity protocols, which enhance operations and reduce operational risks. Apart from these areas, AI is affecting other industries, such as agriculture, banking and transportation. The precision agricultural technology utilizes AI for the purpose of increasing the yield of plantations and the resource utilization, the AI driven finance technology, on the other hand, improves the process of risk evaluation and fraud detection (Pandey & Mishra, 2024).

## Fostering Entrepreneurial Ecosystems with AI-Powered Tools

AI based technologies play a critical role in fostering entrepreneurial ecosystems by providing significant tools and resources to startups, and small enterprises. The ability to gain entrance to high quality analytics and market insights allow entrepreneurs to make data-based decisions reduce the level of uncertainty and increase probability of success. AI-driven systems might analyze consumer behavior and industry trends enabling business to identify opportunities and tailor their goods to meet client needs (Abrardi et al., 2022). Furthermore, AI increases operational efficiency because monotonous jobs get automated; thereby entrepreneurs focus on strategic decision making and innovation. CRM solutions enhanced with AI promise to help firms understand what consumers want, optimize the provision of service, and increase retention of customers (Rane et al., 2023b). This support for the entrepreneurs goes beyond economic growth to support the development of new solutions to solve social problems. In addition, AI might support cooperation within entrepreneurial ecosystems. Used for startups, investor, mentor and resources networking, platforms employing the use of AI algorithms might accelerate development of creative businesses.

## AI's Role in Enhancing Research and Development

AI is changing the way research and development works within several aspects of study. The development of AI algorithms allows researchers to analyze multiple data sets and gain proper insights accelerating processes of searching. AI is capable of identifying subdivisions in complex datasets in science-based research leading to better outcomes in areas such as developing medication and predicting weather (Gupta et al., 2021). In addition, using AI-driven simulations and modeling tools, the researchers can test theories, test many situations without resorting to massive physical experimentation. This ability reduces the cost of time and R&D, while improving relations between academics since they have access to shared data and resources. As a result, AI is becoming a critical tool for promoting innovation to increase knowledge in several areas of application.

## AI and the Evolution of Business Models

Integration of AI into corporate work is changing traditional business models as new approaches to value creation are taking shape. Companies use AI for subscription services, customized products & solutions that answer changing consumer requirements. The introduction of AI-powered platforms in the sharing economy has upset traditional industries such as transportation and hotels, enabling easier linking up of companies and customers (Chen et al., 2022; Khan & Hasan Emon, 2024). In addition, AI enhances clients' experience through customized suggestions and support. E-commerce platforms rely on the AI algorithms to analyze user behavior and preferences with providing the individual recommendations of products and maximizes consumer happiness (Emon, 2025a; Khrais, 2020). This shift to the customer-centric type of business model increases loyalty and initiates innovation through compelling organizations constantly to change to suit changing realities of the market.

## Challenges of AI-Driven Innovation: Algorithmic Bias, Privacy Risks, and Digital Divide

AI-induced innovation faces several barriers, which prevent its fair and sustainable use, algorithmic bias, privacy concern, and digital divide being the most prominent concerns. Unexpectedly, algorithmic bias occurs when AI systems fail to avoid reproducing social stereotypes, hence they have discriminatory implications in key areas of lives such as employment, financial lending, or law enforcement (Akindipe & Lalude, 2025). Bias in AI is usually a result of bad training data, limited dataset, or faulty algorithmic design and therefore an open AI model, regular monitoring, and varied data input is needed to tame injustice results. Furthermore, privacy threats have substantial issues to ethical and legislative concerns, because of AI's reliance on large amounts of personal data. More and more concerns are raised about uprisings (data security, permission and potential ways of misuse of the information) in the light of increasing use of the AI-based surveillance, face recognition, and predictive analytics (Ismail & Aloshi, 2024). Development dependent too but, these threats make the need for strict data protection legislation, a set of ethical AI protocols and institutional responsibility to secure the user from privacy violations and unwanted access to confidential information imperative to mitigate these threats. According to UNESCO 2021, The digital gap goes further to increase inequality by denying access to the AI enabled possibilities, particularly in poor places where the technical infrastructure, internet connectivity and digital literacy are inadequate (Khan et al., 2024). This mismatch creates significant barriers to AI adoption that lock vulnerable areas out of the fruits of technological advancement. This narrow spectrum aligns with SDG 10 (Reduced Inequalities) through inclusive digital transformation and even distribution of AI enabled breakthroughs. Policymakers, academics, and business leaders must come together to create compatible, inclusive and accountable AI policies, in response to these concerns to create a more sustainable innovative environment.

## Future Directions for AI and Innovation

The relationship between AI and innovation is expected to change with the help of a set of trends that will shape the future environment. As institutions develop their AI technologies it will only become more accessible to sectors which will lead to more breakthroughs and efficiency (Khan et al., 2024). The integration of AI with such new technologies as IoT and block chain will open up new opportunities for innovation and value creation (Allioui & Mourdi, 2023; Emon & Khan, 2025a). The cooperation between the stakeholders in the form of governments, enterprises and researchers is an urgent task for solving the problems of AI. The development of a responsible innovation climate may allow stakeholders to utilize the revolutionary powers of AI, while addressing the ethical as well as social consequences of AI development.

## CONCLUSION

This chapter has discussed the enormous impacts of AI on several social sides, such as Sustainable development, educational divisions, Unemployment, and Innovation. The relation of AI with the SDGs shows the utility of AI to foster good transformation in various dimensions of human progress. Subsequently, this chapter describes the link between some AI applications and the SDGs, showing the ways in which these technologies could promote access to quality education, promote equality between the genders, and contribute to sustainable economic growth. The integration of AI into a global project brings into question the integration of data privacy issues, governance issues that must be addressed to ensure that the use of these technologies is put to appropriate use. Framing access gaps in education, AI materializes as a strong instrument for bridging access chasms through education. In its turn, AI can help develop marginalized areas, opening remote learning opportunities and providing translation into other languages. Moreover, its purpose of closing the digital divide is critical because projects based on AI aimed to improve connection and digital literacy are necessary for egalitarian education. The impact of AI on unemployment both threatens and promotes. The layoffs from employment displacement will affect many industries, while the same integration will also increase opportunities for reskilling and upskilling of the workers. policies that work on structural unemployment that arise from AI integration are important towards ensuring an easy transition into an AI economy. The chapter has therefore used AI as a catalyst for innovation in various sectors such as technology, healthcare and the creative industries. The ability of AI in the research and development areas accelerates discovery process and enhances working among researchers.

## REFERENCES


Abrardi, L., Cambini, C., & Rondi, L. (2022). Artificial intelligence, firms and consumer behavior: A survey. *Journal of Economic Surveys, 36*(4), 969–991. DOI: 10.1111/joes.12455

Abulibdeh, A., Zaidan, E., & Abulibdeh, R. (2024). Navigating the confluence of artificial intelligence and education for sustainable development in the era of industry 4.0: Challenges, opportunities, and ethical dimensions. *Journal of Cleaner Production, 437*, 140527. DOI: 10.1016/j.jclepro.2023.140527

Ahmad, T., Madonski, R., Zhang, D., Huang, C., & Mujeeb, A. (2022). Data-driven probabilistic machine learning in sustainable smart energy/smart energy systems: Key developments, challenges, and future research opportunities in the context of smart grid paradigm. *Renewable & Sustainable Energy Reviews, 160*, 112128. DOI: 10.1016/j.rser.2022.112128

Ahmad, T., Zhang, D., Huang, C., Zhang, H., Dai, N., Song, Y., & Chen, H. (2021). Artificial intelligence in sustainable energy industry: Status Quo, challenges and opportunities. *Journal of Cleaner Production, 289*, 125834. DOI: 10.1016/j.jclepro.2021.125834

Akindipe, D., & Lalude, O. M. (2025). *Balancing Public Safety and Individual Rights in AI-Driven Public Administration in Nigeria*. DOI: 10.4018/979-8-3693-8372-8.ch003

Alam, A. (2022). *Employing Adaptive Learning and Intelligent Tutoring Robots for Virtual Classrooms and Smart Campuses: Reforming Education in the Age of Artificial Intelligence*. DOI: 10.1007/978-981-19-2980-9_32

Allioui, H., & Mourdi, Y. (2023). Exploring the Full Potentials of IoT for Better Financial Growth and Stability: A Comprehensive Survey. *Sensors (Basel), 23*(19), 8015. DOI: 10.3390/s23198015 PMID: 37836845

Alowais, S. A., Alghamdi, S. S., Alsuhebany, N., Alqahtani, T., Alshaya, A. I., Almohareb, S. N., Aldairem, A., Alrashed, M., Bin Saleh, K., Badreldin, H. A., Al Yami, M. S., Al Harbi, S., & Albekairy, A. M. (2023). Revolutionizing healthcare: The role of artificial intelligence in clinical practice. *BMC Medical Education, 23*(1), 689. DOI: 10.1186/s12909-023-04698-z PMID: 37740191

Baker, B., Mills, K. A., McDonald, P., & Wang, L. (2023). AI, Concepts of Intelligence, and Chatbots: The “Figure of Man,” the Rise of Emotion, and Future Visions of Education. *Teachers College Record, 125*(6), 60–84. DOI: 10.1177/01614681231191291

Boroujeni, S. P. H., Razi, A., Khoshdel, S., Afghah, F., Coen, J. L., O'Neill, L., Fule, P., Watts, A., Kokolakis, N.-M. T., & Vamvoudakis, K. G. (2024). A comprehensive survey of research towards AI-enabled unmanned aerial systems in pre-, active-, and post-wildfire management. *Information Fusion, 108*, 102369. DOI: 10.1016/j.inffus.2024.102369

Che Dalim, C. S., Sunar, M. S., Dey, A., & Billinghurst, M. (2020). Using augmented reality with speech input for non-native children's language learning. *International Journal of Human-Computer Studies, 134*, 44–64. DOI: 10.1016/j.ijhcs.2019.10.002

Chen, S., Huang, J., Xiao, T., Gao, J., Bai, J., Luo, W., & Dong, B. (2020). Carbon emissions under different domestic waste treatment modes induced by garbage classification: Case study in pilot communities in Shanghai, China. *The Science of the Total Environment, 717*, 137193. DOI: 10.1016/j.scitotenv.2020.137193 PMID: 32062281

Chen, Y., Prentice, C., Weaven, S., & Hsiao, A. (2022). A systematic literature review of AI in the sharing economy. *Journal of Global Scholars of Marketing Science, 32*(3), 434–451. DOI: 10.1080/21639159.2020.1808850

Chertow, M., Reck, B. K., Wrzesniewski, A., & Calli, B. (2024). Outlook on the future role of robots and AI in material recovery facilities: Implications for U.S. recycling and the workforce. *Journal of Cleaner Production, 470*, 143234. DOI: 10.1016/j.jclepro.2024.143234

Chohan, S. R., & Hu, G. (2022). Strengthening digital inclusion through e-government: Cohesive ICT training programs to intensify digital competency. *Information Technology for Development, 28*(1), 16–38. DOI: 10.1080/02681102.2020.1841713

Cooke, F. L., Dickmann, M., & Parry, E. (2022). Building sustainable societies through human-centred human resource management: Emerging issues and research opportunities. *International Journal of Human Resource Management, 33*(1), 1–15. DOI: 10.1080/09585192.2021.2021732

Cowls, J., Tsamados, A., Taddeo, M., & Floridi, L. (2023). The AI gambit: Leveraging artificial intelligence to combat climate change—opportunities, challenges, and recommendations. *AI & Society, 38*(1), 283–307. DOI: 10.1007/s00146-021-01294-x PMID: 34690449

Dodampegama, S., Hou, L., Asadi, E., Zhang, G., & Setunge, S. (2024). Revolutionizing construction and demolition waste sorting: Insights from artificial intelligence and robotic applications. *Resources, Conservation and Recycling, 202*, 107375. DOI: 10.1016/j.resconrec.2023.107375

Dwivedi, Y. K., Hughes, L., Ismagilova, E., Aarts, G., Coombs, C., Crick, T., Duan, Y., Dwivedi, R., Edwards, J., Eirug, A., Galanos, V., Ilavarasan, P. V., Janssen, M., Jones, P., Kar, A. K., Kizgin, H., Kronemann, B., Lal, B., Lucini, B., & Williams, M. D. (2021). Artificial Intelligence (AI): Multidisciplinary perspectives on emerging challenges, opportunities, and agenda for research, practice and policy. *International Journal of Information Management*, *57*, 101994. DOI: 10.1016/j.ijinfomgt.2019.08.002

Emenike, S. N., & Falcone, G. (2020). A review on energy supply chain resilience through optimization. *Renewable & Sustainable Energy Reviews*, *134*, 110088. DOI: 10.1016/j.rser.2020.110088

Emon, M. M. H. (2023). A Systematic Review of the Causes and Consequences of Price Hikes in Bangladesh. *Review of Business and Economics Studies*, *11*(2), 49–58. DOI: 10.26794/2308-944X-2023-11-2-49-58

Emon, M. M. H. (2025a). The Mediating Role of Supply Chain Responsiveness in the Relationship Between Key Supply Chain Drivers and Performance: Evidence from the FMCG Industry. *Brazilian Journal of Operations & Production Management*, *22*(1), 2580. DOI: 10.14488/BJOPM.2580.2025

Emon, M. M. H. (2025b). Leveraging AI on Social Media & Digital Platforms to Enhance English Language Teaching and Learning. In *AI-Powered English Teaching* (pp. 211–238). IGI Global Scientific Publishing., DOI: 10.4018/979-8-3373-1952-0.ch007

Emon, M. M. H. (2025c). Overcoming Hurdles: Navigating Challenges in the Adoption of Smart Logistics. In *Emerging Trends in Smart Logistics Technologies* (pp. 197–228). IGI Global Scientific Publishing. DOI: 10.4018/979-8-3373-2434-0.ch007

Emon, M. M. H., & Chowdhury, M. S. A. (2025). AI and IoT-Powered Smart Logistics: Transforming Supply Chains for Efficiency and Sustainability. In *Emerging Trends in Smart Logistics Technologies* (pp. 45–72). IGI Global Scientific Publishing. DOI: 10.4018/979-8-3373-2434-0.ch002

Emon, M. M. H., & Khan, T. (2024). A Systematic Literature Review on Sustainability Integration and Marketing Intelligence in the Era of Artificial Intelligence. *Review of Business and Economics Studies*, *12*(4), 6–28. DOI: 10.26794/2308-944X-2024-12-4-6-28

Emon, M. M. H., & Khan, T. (2025a). The mediating role of attitude towards the technology in shaping artificial intelligence usage among professionals. *Telematics and Informatics Reports*, *17*, 100188. DOI: 10.1016/j.teler.2025.100188

Emon, M. M. H., & Khan, T. (2025b). The Rise of Circular Supply Chains: Recycling and Closed-Loop Systems Could Mitigate Inflationary Pressures. In *Supply Chain Disruptions and Impact on Global Inflation* (pp. 195–226). IGI Global. DOI: 10.4018/979-8-3373-1982-7.ch008

García-Sánchez, I.-M., & García-Sánchez, A. (2020). Corporate Social Responsibility during COVID-19 Pandemic. *Journal of Open Innovation*, *6*(4), 126. DOI: 10.3390/joitmc6040126

George, B., & Wooden, O. (2023). Managing the Strategic Transformation of Higher Education through Artificial Intelligence. *Administrative Sciences*, *13*(9), 196. DOI: 10.3390/admsci13090196

Giovanola, B., & Tiribelli, S. (2023). Beyond bias and discrimination: Redefining the AI ethics principle of fairness in healthcare machine-learning algorithms. *AI & Society*, *38*(2), 549–563. DOI: 10.1007/s00146-022-01455-6 PMID: 35615443

Gupta, R., Srivastava, D., Sahu, M., Tiwari, S., Ambasta, R. K., & Kumar, P. (2021). Artificial intelligence to deep learning: Machine intelligence approach for drug discovery. *Molecular Diversity*, *25*(3), 1315–1360. DOI: 10.1007/s11030-021-10217-3 PMID: 33844136

Haleem, A., Javaid, M., Qadri, M. A., & Suman, R. (2022). Understanding the role of digital technologies in education: A review. *Sustainable Operations and Computers*, *3*, 275–285. DOI: 10.1016/j.susoc.2022.05.004

Halkiopoulos, C., & Gkintoni, E. (2024). Leveraging AI in E-Learning: Personalized Learning and Adaptive Assessment through Cognitive Neuropsychology—A Systematic Analysis. *Electronics (Basel)*, *13*(18), 3762. DOI: 10.3390/electronics13183762

Hathaliya, J. J., & Tanwar, S. (2020). An exhaustive survey on security and privacy issues in Healthcare 4.0. *Computer Communications*, *153*, 311–335. DOI: 10.1016/j.comcom.2020.02.018

Ismail, I. A., & Aloshi, J. M. (2024). *Data Privacy in AI-Driven Education*. DOI: 10.4018/979-8-3693-5443-8.ch008

Jain, H., Dhupper, R., Shrivastava, A., Kumar, D., & Kumari, M. (2023). AI-enabled strategies for climate change adaptation: Protecting communities, infrastructure, and businesses from the impacts of climate change. *Computational Urban Science*, *3*(1), 25. DOI: 10.1007/s43762-023-00100-2

Javaid, M., Haleem, A., Pratap Singh, R., Suman, R., & Rab, S. (2022). Significance of machine learning in healthcare: Features, pillars and applications. *International Journal of Intelligent Networks*, *3*, 58–73. DOI: 10.1016/j.ijin.2022.05.002

Kaur, R., Gupta, D., Madhukar, M., Singh, A., Abdelhaq, M., Alsaqour, R., Breñosa, J., & Goyal, N. (2022). E-Learning Environment Based Intelligent Profiling System for Enhancing User Adaptation. *Electronics (Basel), 11*(20), 3354. DOI: 10.3390/electronics11203354

Kebede, A. A., Kalogiannis, T., Van Mierlo, J., & Berecibar, M. (2022). A comprehensive review of stationary energy storage devices for large scale renewable energy sources grid integration. *Renewable & Sustainable Energy Reviews, 159*, 112213. DOI: 10.1016/j.rser.2022.112213

Khan, T., & Emon, M. M. H. (2024). Exploring the Potential of the Blue Economy: A Systematic Review of Strategies for Enhancing International Business in Bangladesh in the context of Indo-Pacific Region. *Review of Business and Economics Studies, 12*(2), 55–73. DOI: 10.26794/2308-944X-2024-12-2-55-73

Khan, T., & Emon, M. M. H. (2025). The role of digital supply chain practices in enhancing firm performance: Insights from the manufacturing sector of Bangladesh. *Brazilian Journal of Operations & Production Management, 22*(2), 2493. DOI: 10.14488/BJOPM.2493.2025

Khan, T., Emon, M. M. H., & Nath, A. (2024). Quantifying the Effects of AI-Driven Inventory Management on Operational Efficiency in Online Retail. *2024 27th International Conference on Computer and Information Technology (ICCIT)*, 2092–2097. DOI: 10.1109/ICCIT64611.2024.11021996

Khan, T., Emon, M. M. H., Rahman, M. A., Hamid, A. B. A., & Yaakub, N. I. (2025). Bridging the Gap: Realizing GreenTech Potential. In *AI and Green Technology Applications in Society* (pp. 91–122). IGI Global Scientific Publishing. DOI: 10.4018/979-8-3693-9879-1.ch004

Khan, T., Emon, M. M. H., & Rahman, S. (2024). Marketing Strategy Innovation via AI Adoption: A Study on Bangladeshi SMEs in the Context of Industry 5.0. *2024 6th International Conference on Sustainable Technologies for Industry 5.0 (STI)*, 1–6. DOI: 10.1109/STI64222.2024.10951050

Khan, T., & Hasan Emon, M. M. (2024). Determinants of AI Image Generator Adoption Among Marketing Agencies: The Mediating Effects of Perceived Usefulness. *2024 IEEE 3rd International Conference on Robotics, Automation, Artificial-Intelligence and Internet-of-Things (RAAICON)*, 177–182. DOI: 10.1109/RAAICON64172.2024.10928548

Khrais, L. T. (2020). Role of Artificial Intelligence in Shaping Consumer Demand in E-Commerce. *Future Internet, 12*(12), 226. DOI: 10.3390/fi12120226

Kuleto, V., Ilić, M., Dumangiu, M., Ranković, M., Martins, O. M. D., Păun, D., & Mihoreanu, L. (2021). Exploring Opportunities and Challenges of Artificial Intelligence and Machine Learning in Higher Education Institutions. *Sustainability (Basel), 13*(18), 10424. DOI: 10.3390/su131810424

Kumar, V., Ashraf, A. R., & Nadeem, W. (2024). AI-powered marketing: What, where, and how? *International Journal of Information Management, 77*, 102783. DOI: 10.1016/j.ijinfomgt.2024.102783

Labadze, L., Grigolia, M., & Machaidze, L. (2023). Role of AI chatbots in education: Systematic literature review. *International Journal of Educational Technology in Higher Education, 20*(1), 56. DOI: 10.1186/s41239-023-00426-1

Mohammadi Lanbaran, N., Naujokaitis, D., Kairaitis, G., Jenciūtė, G., & Radziukynienė, N. (2024). Overview of Startups Developing Artificial Intelligence for the Energy Sector. *Applied Sciences (Basel, Switzerland), 14*(18), 8294. DOI: 10.3390/app14188294

Mondejar, M. E., Avtar, R., Diaz, H. L. B., Dubey, R. K., Esteban, J., Gómez-Morales, A., Hallam, B., Mbungu, N. T., Okolo, C. C., Prasad, K. A., She, Q., & Garcia-Segura, S. (2021). Digitalization to achieve sustainable development goals: Steps towards a Smart Green Planet. *The Science of the Total Environment, 794*, 148539. DOI: 10.1016/j.scitotenv.2021.148539 PMID: 34323742

Morze, N., Varchenko-Trotsenko, L., Terletska, T., & Smyrnova-Trybulska, E. (2021). Implementation of adaptive learning at higher education institutions by means of Moodle LMS. *Journal of Physics: Conference Series, 1840*(1), 12062. DOI: 10.1088/1742-6596/1840/1/012062

Nižetić, S., Šolić, P., López-de-Ipiña González-de-Artaza, D., & Patrono, L. (2020). Internet of Things (IoT): Opportunities, issues and challenges towards a smart and sustainable future. *Journal of Cleaner Production, 274*, 122877. DOI: 10.1016/j.jclepro.2020.122877 PMID: 32834567

Opesemowo, O. A. G., & Adekomaya, V. (2024). Harnessing Artificial Intelligence for Advancing Sustainable Development Goals in South Africa's Higher Education System: A Qualitative Study. *International Journal of Learning. Teaching and Educational Research, 23*(3), 67–86. DOI: 10.26803/ijlter.23.3.4

Pandey, D. K., & Mishra, R. (2024). Towards sustainable agriculture: Harnessing AI for global food security. *Artificial Intelligence in Agriculture, 12*, 72–84. DOI: 10.1016/j.aiia.2024.04.003

Rane, N., Choudhary, S., & Rane, J. (2023a). Education 4.0 and 5.0: Integrating Artificial Intelligence (AI) for personalized and adaptive learning. *Available at SSRN* 4638365. DOI: 10.2139/ssrn.4638365

Rane, N., Choudhary, S., & Rane, J. (2023b). Hyper-personalization for enhancing customer loyalty and satisfaction in Customer Relationship Management (CRM) systems. SSRN *Electronic Journal*. DOI: 10.2139/ssrn.4641044

Rehman, A., Naz, S., & Razzak, I. (2022). Leveraging big data analytics in healthcare enhancement: Trends, challenges and opportunities. *Multimedia Systems*, *28*(4), 1339–1371. DOI: 10.1007/s00530-020-00736-8

Seo, K., Tang, J., Roll, I., Fels, S., & Yoon, D. (2021). The impact of artificial intelligence on learner–instructor interaction in online learning. *International Journal of Educational Technology in Higher Education*, *18*(1), 54. DOI: 10.1186/s41239-021-00292-9 PMID: 34778540

Stecuła, K., Wolniak, R., & Grebski, W. W. (2023). AI-Driven Urban Energy Solutions—From Individuals to Society: A Review. *Energies*, *16*(24), 7988. DOI: 10.3390/en16247988

Turienzo, J., Cabanelas, P., & Lampón, J. F. (2023). Business models in times of disruption: The connected and autonomous vehicles (uncertain) domino effect. *Journal of Business Research*, *156*, 113481. DOI: 10.1016/j.jbusres.2022.113481

Weiskopf, S. R., Rubenstein, M. A., Crozier, L. G., Gaichas, S., Griffis, R., Halofsky, J. E., Hyde, K. J. W., Morelli, T. L., Morisette, J. T., Muñoz, R. C., Pershing, A. J., Peterson, D. L., Poudel, R., Staudinger, M. D., Sutton-Grier, A. E., Thompson, L., Vose, J., Weltzin, J. F., & Whyte, K. P. (2020). Climate change effects on biodiversity, ecosystems, ecosystem services, and natural resource management in the United States. *The Science of the Total Environment*, *733*, 137782. DOI: 10.1016/j.scitotenv.2020.137782 PMID: 32209235

Willcocks, L. (2020). Robo-Apocalypse cancelled? Reframing the automation and future of work debate. *Journal of Information Technology*, *35*(4), 286–302. DOI: 10.1177/0268396220925830

Xia, Y., Zhang, M., Tsang, D. C. W., Geng, N., Lu, D., Zhu, L., Igalavithana, A. D., Dissanayake, P. D., Rinklebe, J., Yang, X., & Ok, Y. S. (2020). Recent advances in control technologies for non-point source pollution with nitrogen and phosphorous from agricultural runoff: Current practices and future prospects. *Applied Biological Chemistry*, *63*(1), 8. DOI: 10.1186/s13765-020-0493-6

Yekollu, R. K., Bhimraj Ghuge, T., Sunil Biradar, S., Haldikar, S. V., & Farook Mohideen Abdul Kader, O. (2024). *AI-Driven Personalized Learning Paths: Enhancing Education Through Adaptive Systems*. DOI: 10.1007/978-981-97-3191-6_38

## KEY TERMS AND DEFINITIONS

**AI-Powered Recycling Systems:** Automated waste management employing AI, robotics and computer vision in sorting, harvesting and processing of recyclables which can augment sustainability outputs.

**Digital Divide:** Digital divide is used to describe the disparity between those individuals or communities that have access to modern digital technologies, such as AI and internet, and those who do not typically being the cause of disparities in education, employment and social development.

**Digital Inclusion:** The ambition to make every person have equal access to modern technologies including but not limited to artificial intelligence-based solutions for the purpose of narrowing gap between social-economic differences for the marginalized and marginalized unprivileged communities.

**Green Technology:** Green technology is a collection of innovative approaches and practices that encourage environmental sustainability by decreasing carbon footprints, increasing energy efficiencies and reducing waste using AI driven optimization.

**Reskilling and Upskilling:** The act of educating people in new skills or improving the old ones to be fit for AI-imposed changes in the job market making the workforce sustainable.

**Social Innovation:** Innovation of new ways to solving issues faced by a society including poverty, inequality and unemployment using AI as the foil in various fields.

**Structural Unemployment:** Structural unemployment results from technological shock AI automation which upgrades workers' jobs when their skills have become outdated leaving them jobless and needing to be reskilled and intervened upon by policy.

# Chapter 5
# Empowering Future Generations:
## How AI is Transforming Sustainable Education Practices

**Juma Yusuf Mnzile**
https://orcid.org/0009-0007-6736-4203
*Anadolu University, Turkey*

## ABSTRACT

*In an era characterized by accelerated transformation and global challenges, educational institutions are in a distinctive position to influence the creation of a more sustainable and inclusive global society. This chapter explores the potential of emerging technologies, with a particular focus on artificial intelligence (AI), to advance the concept of education without borders. The chapter highlights the transformative potential of AI by illustrating how intelligent systems can personalize learning experiences, cater to diverse student needs, and promote educational equity. Furthermore, it emphasizes the potential of predictive analytics to empower educators and policymakers, enabling them to make informed decisions regarding resource allocation, student support, and curriculum design. By establishing a linkage between innovation and inclusivity, this chapter provides a forward-looking perspective on the potential of AI to accelerate progress towards Sustainable Development Goal 4 (quality education for all).*

## INTRODUCTION

The current global landscape is marked by pressing challenges—particularly climate change, inequality, and poverty—that are intricately interrelated and pose

DOI: 10.4018/979-8-3373-1837-0.ch005

formidable obstacles to sustainable development initiatives (World Bank, 2021; United Nations, 2020a). These interconnected issues demand innovative solutions (World Bank, 2023). In response to these complexities, the United Nations (2019) emphasized a growing recognition of the transformative potential of technology in advancing progress toward the Sustainable Development Goals (SDGs).

At the forefront of this technological revolution is artificial intelligence (AI), a rapidly evolving field poised to reshape numerous dimensions of human endeavor (Kaplan & Haenlein). AI has emerged as a vital ally in the pursuit of the SDGs—a universal call to action aimed at safeguarding the planet, eradicating poverty, and fostering prosperity and peace for all by 2030. With its multifaceted capabilities, AI offers significant opportunities to address the complex global issues embedded in the SDGs. As highlighted by Yadav et al. (2024), AI not only enhances resource optimization and trend forecasting but also makes critical contributions across various goal areas. For instance, it enhances education and healthcare services in alignment with SDGs 4 and 10, predicts crop yields to support zero hunger (SDG 2), and forecasts climate-related events to mitigate their impacts (SDG 13).

The convergence of AI and the SDGs underscores the pivotal role AI plays in accelerating global progress toward sustainability. Technologies such as computer vision, natural language processing, and machine learning are increasingly vital for decision-making, policymaking, monitoring and evaluation, and the optimization of resource allocation across key sectors including agriculture, healthcare, education, and climate action (Milad & Ghazal, 2024).

In alignment with the SDGs, AI tools are already being applied to address the world's most urgent challenges. These technologies are currently deployed across all 17 SDGs (Bachmann et al., 2022). For example, AI-powered innovation helps reduce poverty (SDG 1) by creating job opportunities and stimulating economic growth (SDG 8), as supported by previous research (Goralski & Tan, 2020; Mhlanga, 2021). Furthermore, AI technologies contribute to upskilling and reskilling efforts by delivering personalized training, offering promising solutions to today's complex workforce demands (Kollewe, 2023). In addition, these technologies play a role in advancing gender equality and achieving the objectives of SDG 5. They help create more equitable and inclusive societies by identifying and mitigating bias, promoting fairness, and empowering women through financial inclusion and increased opportunity (Rose Taylor, 2020).

AI also holds promise for transforming public service delivery (PSD), a key component of sustainable governance. As Anshari et al. (2025) note, AI's capacity for automation, data analysis, and personalization can significantly enhance the efficiency, effectiveness, and accessibility of public services. This capability enables public institutions to address complex challenges while delivering tailored and citizen-centered services. Similarly, Faludi (2023) highlights how digital technologies support institutional understanding and responsive governance by enabling transparency, accountability, and public participation. These technologies foster collaboration among stakeholders and facilitate the development of solutions that are more attuned to public needs (Carayannis & Morawska-Jancelewicz, 2022).

Artificial intelligence, therefore, stands as a transformative catalyst with the potential to reshape global sustainability frameworks by advancing the realization of the SDGs. As a strategic enabler, AI can effectively address humanity's most critical problems while aligning with broader sustainability objectives. It integrates seamlessly into existing systems across key sectors such as infrastructure, education, and health, reinforcing the global effort toward a more sustainable future (Ametepey et al., 2024). The unparalleled capacity of AI to balance environmental protection, social equity, and economic growth is exemplified in its ability to provide accurate predictions, generate actionable insights, and optimize resource management through advanced analysis of complex datasets (Minghai et al., 2025; Truong & Papagiannidis, 2022).

Nonetheless, it is crucial to acknowledge that AI technologies can yield both beneficial and adverse effects on the SDGs (Nahar, 2024). Abbey (2023) stresses that when appropriately leveraged, AI can eliminate human errors and biases, boost efficiency, and significantly contribute to achieving the UN's global agenda—particularly by enhancing access to education, healthcare, and economic opportunities. However, if embedded with systemic biases, AI can perpetuate discrimination and deepen existing inequalities. Despite these risks, AI also has the potential to act as a global connector—linking people with essential resources and technologies and fostering a culture of accessibility, equity, and opportunity (Milad & Ghazal, 2024; Kim, 2025).

As emphasized by Ceylan and Mnzile (2025), AI is increasingly recognized as a transformative force across various fields, especially in education. Since its emergence in the 1950s, AI has profoundly influenced teaching and learning systems. It offers viable solutions to longstanding challenges in education, supports the modernization of pedagogical approaches, and facilitates progress toward SDG 4. In this context, the present study explores the potential of AI to improve educational content and delivery in alignment with the United Nations' Sustainable Development Goals. Specifically, the chapter investigates the role of AI technologies in achieving the targets of SDG 4, focusing on:

1. AI as a driving force for enhanced access to quality education.
2. AI as an empowering resource for lifelong learning.
3. AI as a driver to promote universal numeracy and literacy.
4. AI as a resource to bridge educational gaps.

## Methodology

The study applies a qualitative research approach centered on a nuanced analysis of existing literature, previous empirical studies, and theoretical constructs associated with AI-powered sustainable education practices. By concluding various scientific literature, the study analytically scrutinizes how AI tools have been introduced into instructional arenas to enhance lifelong learning, inclusivity, and equity, essential targets of SDG 4. Through the assessment of previous studies, case studies, and theoretical frameworks, the study develops a detailed knowledge of AI's evolutionary influence and the encounters that come with its implementation. This method allows for comprehensive research of the sensitive implications of AI on educational provision and closing gaps among less privileged populations. In this analytical context, the study presents relevant information on how AI can influence a reasonable, inclusive, and innovative academic atmosphere that is aligned with sustainable development goals, underlining the significance of contextual understanding in maximizing AI's potential for future generations.

## The Concept of the 2030 Agenda for Sustainable Development Goals (SDGS)

The 2030 Agenda for the Sustainable Development Goals (SDGs) embodies a revolutionary framework launched by the United Nations in 2015. This ambitious attempt serves as a universal demand for action, urging communities and nations to alleviate poverty, protect our globe, and ensure that by 2030, all individuals can enjoy peacetime and prosperity (Pelton, 2020; Venturelli & Pizzi, 2023). The global Sustainable Development Goals (SDGs) embrace 17 objectives and 169 targets, intricately envisioned to underscore the vital connections between social inclusion, economic growth, and environmental sustainability (Yumnam et al., 2024).

As detailed by the United Nations (2017) and Adiyoso (2022), the SDGs comprise a comprehensive spectrum of human ambitions, abridged in the following short headings: No Poverty (SDG 1), Zero Hunger (SDG 2), Good Health and Well-Being (SDG 3), Quality Education (SDG 4), Gender Equality (SDG 5), Clean Water and Sanitation (SDG 6), Affordable and Clean Energy (SDG 7), Decent Work and Economic Growth (SDG 8), Industry, Innovation, and Infrastructure (SDG 9), Reduced Inequalities (SDG 10), Sustainable Cities and Communities (SDG 11), Responsible Consumption and Production (SDG 12), Climate Action (SDG 13), Life Below Water (SDG 14), Life on Land (SDG 15), Peace, Justice, and Strong Institutions (SDG 16), and Partnerships for the Goals (SDG 17)

Similarly, a study done by Kleespies and Dierkes (2022) accentuates the importance of the global Sustainable Development Goals (SDGs) across various sustainability science programs internationally. Nevertheless, their results disclose a discrepancy among the countries in how they prioritize each specific pillar of sustainability (economic, social, and environmental). Furthermore, Kleespies & Dierkes (2022) insisted that countries with higher global development indices tend to view the SDGs as less critical compared to those with lower indices. This calls for an urgent need to augment the perception and acceptance of the SDGs among students in more developed countries, fostering a collective commitment to accomplishing these goals on both national and global scales.

*Figure 1. Transformative role of AI in achieving SDG 4*

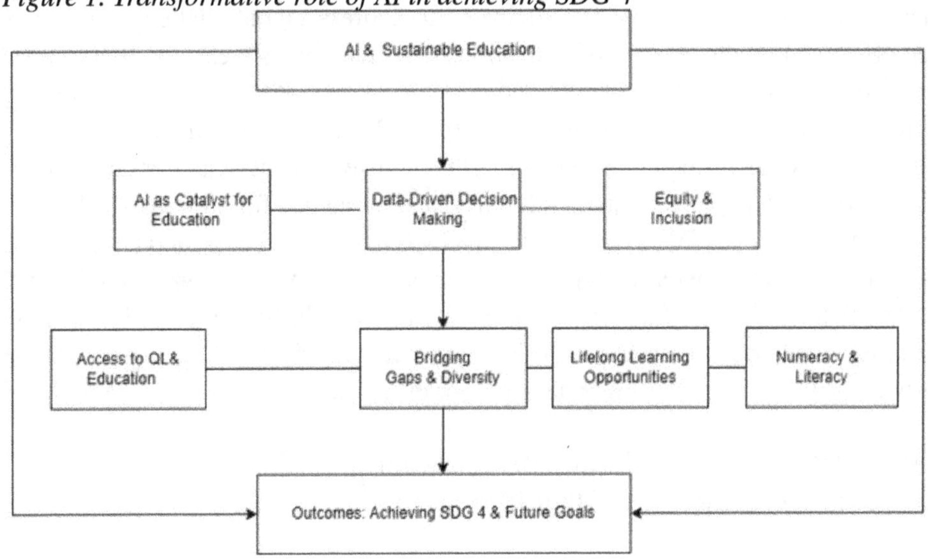


## The 2030 Agenda for Sustainable Development Goal 4: Quality Education for All

As the world embarks upon a new epoch characterized by a plethora of opportunities, nations are amalgamating under the 2030 Agenda for Sustainable Development, with a resolute promise to ensure quality education as delineated in SDG 4. This aspirational objective encompasses more than mere access to education; it is about effecting societal transformation by ensuring that every individual, irrespective of their background, has the opportunity and right to obtain a quality education (Adipat & Chotikapanich, 2022).

In this regard, the fourth Sustainable Development Goal is driven by profound impediments that hamper educational access, such as discrimination, costly education, poverty, and limited resources. It acknowledges that education is the cornerstone of sustainable development, intimately linked to social cohesion, gender equality, and economic growth (Saini et al., 2023). As stated in SDG 4, the importance of safe, friendly, and supportive learning environments is emphasized. This encompasses the construction and enhancement of educational facilities that cater to the varied requirements of all learners. Furthermore, the necessity for instructors with superior skill sets cannot be overstated. A global collaborative approach is poised to facilitate the realization of these educational objectives. By prioritizing the provision of quality education, we can foster a more equitable and sustainable future. The fundamental objective of Sustainable Development Goal 4 is to establish a multifaceted framework that is anticipated to address global challenges through the effective implementation of education. The objective is clear: by 2030, every child should have access to quality and free education that trains them for lifelong learning and sustainable development (Griffiths, 2021). The aforementioned vision encompasses universal access, early childhood development, equal opportunities, skill development, gender equality, literacy, and numeracy for all individuals.

To wrap it up, the 2030 Agenda for SDG 4 is a beacon of hope and a call for all nations to take responsibility. It pushes communities to ensure no one is left behind and work towards a brighter, more equitable future for all. Besides, SDG 4 calls for different countries to envision a world where access to free and quality education is not a privilege but a fundamental right for everyone.

## The Intersection of AI and Sustainable Development Goal 4's Targets

Since 2016, when the 4th Industrial Revolution was inaugurated, the globe has been on a groundbreaking journey toward sustainable development. This era is characterized by a confluence of factors that present both exciting prospects for innovation and formidable challenges, largely attributable to unprecedented technological growth (Zhang et al., 2025). Technology has been identified as a significant catalyst for transformation, with the potential to propel us towards achieving the ambitious targets outlined in the Sustainable Development Goals (SDGs), particularly SDG 4.

In this era, which may be considered one of the most significant in the history of education, there are three characteristics that can be identified. Firstly, universal accessibility is being implemented. Secondly, inclusivity is being encouraged. Thirdly, abundant opportunities for lifelong learning are being made available. The driving force behind this new era is the principle of SDG 4. It is submitted that educational institutions can engender a sustainable world in which education knows no boundaries and in which every individual has the opportunity to make a considerable contribution by harnessing the transformative potential of technology.

Among the myriad technological advancements, AI tools have emerged as a fundamental force, with the potential to reshape education and significantly accelerate our journey toward SDG 4 (Chen & Liu, 2018; Nedungadi et al., 2024).

## AI AS A DRIVING FORCE FOR ENHANCED ACCESS TO QUALITY EDUCATION

The integration of artificial intelligence (AI) technologies, including large language models (LLMs), signifies a transformative advancement in addressing global challenges outlined within the Sustainable Development Goals (SDGs). Among these, SDG4 is of particular significance, as it is in this area that artificial intelligence technologies are poised to transform the educational sector. By optimizing the use of resources, enhancing access to high-quality learning, and delivering scalable and customized learning experiences, AI is poised to eradicate obstacles to educational equity and endorse lifelong learning (AlSagri & Sohail, 2024). This technological enhancement enables institutions to formulate superior and more informed policies and strategies, which in turn engender outcomes and cultivate a more prolific learning environment. Research by Li et al. (2023) and Yusi et al. (2022) validates that with access to high-quality training data, machine learning can facilitate informed decision-making and yield precise results. In addition, Karakani (2024) emphasizes that machine learning, when employed as an innovative complement to conventional data collection methods, can effectively address sociotechnical issues and enhance the overall decision-making processes within the educational sector.

The potential of technologies to accelerate progress towards the SDGs cannot be overstated. For instance, as highlighted by Kulkarni et al. (2024), AI technologies empower domain specialists and policymakers with relevant, actionable insights. This enhanced policy formulation and optimized resource allocation underscore the pivotal role of meticulous data management in fostering global sustainability initiatives. As demonstrated in the preceding studies by Nahar (2024) and Bachmann et al. (2022), data-driven analytics have been shown to facilitate the realization of the 17 Sustainable Development Goals (SDGs). This is achieved through the enhancement of information reliability, the nurturing and optimization of resource distribution, the implementation of data-based policies, and the facilitation of informed decision-making. This assertion is corroborated by the findings of Artyukhov et al. (2024) and Albelda (2024), who contend that AI facilitates research processes, enhances data analysis, and augments decision-making, ultimately culminating in more efficient and effective innovation. This paradigm shift is particularly salient in the field of education, where AI optimizes resource allocation, personalizes learning experiences, and facilitates data-driven decision-making, aligning with SDG 4: to ensure unbiased, inclusive, and quality education for all.

As Kazu & Kuvvetli (2023) have observed, contemporary educational organizations face considerable challenges in terms of the quality of management decisions. In this context, machine learning, an innovative and rapidly emerging domain of AI, has been shown to be a highly effective therapy in these circumstances. Machine learning has been demonstrated to facilitate an enhanced comprehension of these intricacies through the embedding of sophisticated algorithms that are able to scrutinize vast and complicated datasets (Narayana et al., 2022). AI technologies, which are characterized by computerized systems that resemble human decision-making processes, leverage immense computational power and prompt data to improve leaders' data-informed decision-making (DIDM). Within the context of educational institutions, the integration of artificial intelligence (AI) has the potential to modernize the recruitment of teaching staff. This can be achieved through the utilization of AI algorithms that are capable of predicting the proficiency of prospective candidates based on their curriculum vitae and evaluation reports. This approach represents a significant departure from conventional hiring methodologies that are predominantly reliant on manual reviews and interviews (Yinying, 2020).

In response to these challenges, the introduction of AI tools in the educational sector has significantly contributed to the pursuit of academic excellence on a global scale, benefiting all stakeholders. The integration of AI systems into educational frameworks enables instructors to receive assistance with managerial tasks, thereby allowing them to allocate more time to significant pedagogical activities. Nkechi et al. (2024) argue that the rise of personalized learning environments, instantaneous feedback tools, intelligent classroom assistants, tutoring systems, and automated grading systems has substantially heightened educational quality.

To summarize, the integration of artificial intelligence and education signifies more than a mere technological advancement; it catalyzes transformative change, aligning with the global commitment to achieving Sustainable Development Goal 4. It is evident that given its capacity to transform learning practices, artificial intelligence (AI) is positioned at the forefront of establishing an impartial and sustainable educational future for all. The utilization of artificial intelligence has the potential to empower educators by furnishing them with data-driven insights, thereby enhancing their access to resources and customizing learning experiences to address disparities in educational equity and promote lifelong learning opportunities. Furthermore, as we harness innovative technologies, we lay the foundation for a future in which every learner, irrespective of their circumstances, has the opportunity to thrive and realize their full potential in an ever-evolving landscape.

## AI AS AN EMPOWERING RESOURCE FOR LIFELONG LEARNING

In a swiftly evolving world, where technological advances are occurring at an unprecedented rate and employment markets require constant adaptation, the concept of lifelong learning is becoming increasingly crucial (Wamba-Taguimdje et al., 2020). In response to this challenge, artificial intelligence (AI) is radically transforming the landscape of education and skill development. The integration of AI into educational agendas is a strategy that not only addresses the digital divide but also fosters a culture of lifelong learning that aligns with the objectives of SDG 4 (Pachava et al., 2025). As corroborated by Badrudeen (2024), AI is a substantial partner in equipping learners with the essential skills needed to thrive in a dynamic environment. AI-driven systems can facilitate educational organizations in acquiring a comprehensive understanding of each student's individual needs, thereby enabling the adaptation of content delivery to optimize learning outcomes (Bayly-Castaneda et al., 2024).

Furthermore, the field of artificial intelligence has the potential to transform education into a continuous journey within the context of SDG 4, which emphasizes the importance of quality education and instigates opportunities for lifelong learning (Tang & Deng, 2022). The ability of AI to assess a learner's preferences and achievements is considered to be one of its most significant contributions to lifelong education, as it fosters the creation of tailored learning pathways (Michael & Modinot, 2024). This approach ensures that learners receive resources and content tailored to their specific needs, thereby preventing monotony and frustration while maintaining engagement (Aggarwal, 2023). AI tools have been developed to modify the speed and complexity of educational content, to enable students to progress at a pace that suits them (Sanabria-Z et al., 2023).

Moreover, the integration of AI in educational settings has the potential to transcend conventional boundaries related to time, age, and location, thereby facilitating learning opportunities for adults that were previously inaccessible. By facilitating self-directed learning, AI machines empower learners to customize their educational pathways according to their objectives, thereby fostering a proactive approach to learning (Ally & Perris, 2022; Fidalgo & Thormann, 2024). As adult and lifelong learning become a policy focus in both developed and developing countries, AI technologies are proving to be an invaluable tool in the delivery of education throughout an individual's life. It has been argued that this approach fosters lifelong learning by allowing learners to attain knowledge and skills throughout their lives (Chen & Liu, 2018).

In conclusion, as we consider the radical potential of AI in education, it is vital to acknowledge that technology can transform learning into a continuous process. By leveraging the capabilities of artificial intelligence, students can navigate the rapidly expanding landscape of information, equipping them with the necessary skills to adapt and thrive in a constantly evolving world. This commitment to lifelong learning, facilitated by AI, not only enhances individual progress but also fosters global collaboration and connectivity, preparing individuals for a sustainable future where knowledge is a continuous exploration rather than a static endpoint. By confirming the accessibility of AI-driven learning for all individuals, we can aspire towards a future in which lifelong learning opportunities are universally available, thereby fulfilling the promise of a more equitable and inclusive society.

## AI AS A DRIVER TO PROMOTE UNIVERSAL NUMERACY AND LITERACY

By the year 2030, the organization's vision is to ensure that all individuals attain literacy and numeracy skills, thus unleashing their full potential to flourish in a progressively knowledge-based society. Digital transformation has been demonstrated to enhance the quest for universal literacy and numeracy (Pinski and Benlian, 2024). Indeed, it has been shown to pave the way to equalize opportunities and personalized instruction and to strengthen individuals globally. As Kalantzis and Cope (2025) have explained, generative AI has the potential to transform education. The system can provide constant, prompt responses and real-time evaluation by analyzing student progress within a given class. This machinery reintroduces multimodality, but in a new and powerful way, mainly through text-based transpositions. As Kalantzis and Cope (2025) emphasize, these discoveries open up a forward-thinking curriculum for refining multimodal literacies, preparing students with the skills needed to adapt, innovate, and thrive in the digital age.

In response, Langeveldt (2021) elucidated that AI tools such as machine learning, natural language processing, and data analysis can be used by educational leaders to glean insights, recommendations, and predictions about learning progress. As posited by Farmanesh et al. (2025), the utilization of digital learning tools has been demonstrated to enhance the AI literacy of learners. These results are consistent with the concept of twin transitions, which posits that sustainable development and digital transformation synergize to create a strategic roadmap for a fashionable educational landscape (Ferk Savec and Jedrinović, 2025). As asserted by Nedungadi et al. (2024), AI is imperative in critical dimensions associated with SDG4 targets, including the promotion of inclusivity through gender equality, the promotion of literacy and numeracy, the equipping of learners with competencies suited for contemporary workforces, and the integration of sustainable development into curricula.

In the evolving academic landscape, the integration of artificial intelligence (AI) signifies a radical paradigm shift, heralding an advanced era in pedagogical techniques (Walter, 2024). AI technologies have the potential to contribute to education in a number of ways, including the provision of adaptive learning systems, personal virtual tutors, game-based learning, educational data analytics, AI-driven assessment systems, learning chatbots, and automatic evaluation. These developments have been shown to empower learners, enabling them to refine their skills and knowledge, thus facilitating greater participation in SDG4 (Diah and Muhammad, 2024). The AI-based worksheets' evidence has been confirmed to be remarkably impactful in deepening students' understanding, specifically in enhancing their numeracy literacy (Agustiani et al., 2024). As Hutson and Ceballos (2023) have observed, while AI can facilitate the development of inclusivity and enhance academic performance, educational curricula must be deliberately enriched with competencies such as critical thinking, communication, adaptability, creativity, and emotional intelligence. This assertion is further substantiated by extant research, which posits that the integration of AI with other subject areas has the potential to foster problem-solving skills and broaden students' understanding of specific domains (Park et al., 2022; Wan et al., 2020). This holistic approach is designed to equip students with the skills required for self-actualization in the 21st-century landscape, thereby empowering them to thrive in an ever-changing world.

## AI AS A RESOURCE TO BRIDGE EDUCATIONAL GAPS

By the year 2030, the global community will have reached a point where gender-based disparities have been eliminated, ensuring that every individual has equal access to all levels of academic circles. This commitment underscores the significance of integrated education for minority-related groups, encompassing children in vulnerable circumstances, Indigenous populations, and individuals with disabilities (Razavi, 2016; Walker et al., 2019). In contemporary academic circles, the advent of advanced technologies, such as artificial intelligence (AI), has precipitated a paradigm shift in the pursuit of fairness and diversity. As emphasized by Roshanaei et al. (2023) AI-based platforms customize learning materials to suit each individual's needs. This strategy, which is tailored to the individual, has been shown to have a positive effect on all learners, regardless of their background, thereby enabling them to thrive and reach their full potential. These advancements have profound impacts on balancing resources and creating equal treatment for all (Farahani & Ghasemi, 2024). It has also been demonstrated that AI can promote low-risk and inclusive atmospheres, support students' multisensory engagement, and scaffold learning goals to meet diverse needs (Hite et al., 2020). AI has been shown to cultivate authentic learning experiences that embrace disabled students (McMahon et al., 2020), strengthen constructive social behaviors, and foster collaborative learning, eventually building more unbiased and compassionate academic landscapes (Roberts et al., 2019).

Notwithstanding the rapid advancements and expanding reach of artificial intelligence (AI), vulnerable groups continue to be underrepresented in this evolutionary domain. It is evident that communities affected by disabilities, geographic isolation, financial constraints, lack of educational opportunities, and racial and gender disparities often find themselves excluded from the benefits of AI-powered tools (Malarvizhi et al., 2024). For instance, learners from economically challenged families and in rural areas encounter significant constraints in accessing AI machine learning tools, primarily due to poor internet connectivity and lack of digital devices. Conversely, students from affluent families and urban centers are exposed to a greater extent to AI-enhanced learning experiences, thereby widening the gap within academic contexts (UNESCO, 2019). As Ahmed (2024) demonstrates, the technological disparity serves to exacerbate these inequalities, thereby constituting a significant impediment to the equitable access and implementation of intelligent tutoring systems.

Generative AI continues to highlight a significant global gender imbalance. The study reveals that females are approximately 20% less likely than males to engage directly with this advanced technology (Otis et al., 2024). This discrepancy is rooted in inherent cultural and societal norms that influence attitudes and perspectives toward technology. It is hypothesized that conventional portrayals of female characters in traditional roles tend to exhibit a reduced orientation towards technology, thereby creating an impression that STEM subjects are predominantly masculine domains. This socialization process is characterized by the propagation of the notion that technological and scientific disciplines are exclusively reserved for males. This cultural norm has the potential to engender a decline in the self-confidence and motivation of females in their pursuit of these fields of study. Consequently, females may regard AI technologies as less pertinent, thereby influencing notions of value, usability, and risk (Ofosu-Ampong, 2023). In his study, Yu (2024) also commented that societal expectations, inequitable access to internet connectivity, and digital tools hamper females' opportunities to develop the required expertise for AI engagement. This scenario carries the potential to exclude women from the future of AI educational instruments.

In this regard, Maphosa (2024) illustrated that the integration of AI into education also raises critical ethical and social concerns that demand careful attention. The central considerations under discussion are as follows: environmental and societal well-being, non-discrimination and fairness, technical robustness and safety, privacy and data governance, transparency, and diversity (Stahl & Leach, 2023). Cross-functional teamwork among stakeholders from business, government, civil society, and technologists is advocated for by several scholars. Such collaboration is proposed by these scholars as a means of formulating initiatives and policies that encourage justice across multicultural groups, with a particular emphasis on gender inclusivity (Akintayo et al., 2024; Khreisat et al., 2024).

In response to these proposals, Kaewtubtim (2024) has exposed that these attempts embrace integrating principles of fairness into learning initiatives, promoting awareness campaigns, and providing guidelines for responsible AI development. When employed judiciously, AI possesses the capacity to engender an academic environment that is more equitable and reasonable, thereby unleashing the potential of all students within the context of a knowledge-driven global society (Muhammad & Orji, 2024; UNESCO, 2019).

In summary, data technologies and artificial intelligence (AI) are not merely trends; rather, they are essential tools that are redesigning and rethinking science, education, and policy development. By leveraging these modernizations, a more reasonable and sustainable future can be nurtured, thereby ensuring that global issues such as discrimination, poverty, and education quality are addressed with sensitivity and precision.

## CONCLUSION

In the contemporary era, characterized by accelerated technological progress and an augmented demand for adaptability and flexibility, artificial intelligence (AI) emerges as a pivotal asset for educational institutions. It is possible to cultivate a sustainable world in which education is characterized by its inclusivity and universal accessibility, thus enabling individuals to make significant contributions by leveraging the transformative capacity of technology. Among the myriad technological advances, AI tools have emerged as a fundamental force, with the potential to accelerate our pathway toward SDG 4.

In this regard, the integration of AI and education signifies more than a mere technical innovation; it catalyzes transformative change, aligning with the global commitment to SDG 4. The present study sets out to demonstrate that artificial intelligence (AI) and data technologies are not merely passing trends but rather represent essential tools that are fundamentally reshaping the fields of science, education, and policy development. By leveraging these modernizations, a more reasonable and sustainable future can be nurtured, thus confirming that educational issues are addressed with sensitivity and precision.

This chapter aims to provide the reader with a comprehensive overview of the existing literature on the topic. By harnessing the capabilities of artificial intelligence (AI), students can navigate the rapidly expanding information environment, equipping them with the skills necessary to adapt and thrive in an ever-evolving world. This commitment to lifelong learning facilitated by AI not only enhances individual progress but also fosters global collaboration and connectivity, preparing individuals for a sustainable future where knowledge is a continuous exploration rather than a static endpoint. By affirming the accessibility of AI-enabled learning for all individuals, we can aspire to a future where opportunities for lifelong learning are universally available, thereby fulfilling the promise of a more equitable and inclusive society.

## The Implication of the Study

The investigation into the milestone role of artificial intelligence (AI) technologies in sustainable education practices holds sensational ramifications for the future of global learning. Firstly, it is imperative to acknowledge that enhancing access to high-quality education is a prerequisite for achieving Sustainable Development Goal (SDG) 4. The integration of AI technologies can personalize learning practices, aligning with each student's unique learning preferences and requirements. This bespoke apparatus not only augments students' participation but also mitigates educational disparities, ensuring that all students have equal access to superior resources. The democratization of education is a process that can prepare future generations with the knowledge and skills necessary to flourish in an ever more multifaceted world.

Moreover, the chapter emphasizes the importance of enabling data-informed decision-making processes within educational organizations. The utilization of predictive analytics by policymakers and institutions enables the formulation of informed decisions pertaining to resource allocation, student support services, and curriculum development. This forward-thinking strategy guarantees that educational practices are constantly being improved, enhancing overall success and responsiveness to individuals' learning styles and needs. Consequently, educational stakeholders can shape an educational environment that is not solely concerned with academic achievement but also nurtures psychological, physical, and social well-being.

The chapter goes on to consider the groundbreaking potential of AI in accelerating lifelong learning opportunities, which is another foremost aspect of the study. In the contemporary professional milieu, characterized by rapid change and high competition, the pursuit of ongoing professional development and enhancement of skills has become a hallmark of professional survival. AI-driven systems can present modified learning journeys that enable learners to upskill or reskill at their own pace, thereby fostering a culture of lifelong learning. This adaptability is indispensable for preparing future generations to address the disputes of tomorrow's workforce, equipping them with the necessary tools to navigate a dynamic world. The integration of AI technologies within educational frameworks has the potential to foster the development of students who possess enhanced resilience and agility, thereby equipping them with the necessary skills to exert a significant and positive influence on society.

In future research, the lasting impacts of AI applications in the educational landscape should be surveyed, with a particular focus on equity and accessibility. It is incumbent upon academics to investigate the potential of AI to address the specific challenges faced by marginalized groups in the field of education. Furthermore, there is a need to evaluate the efficacy of various AI tools in a range of cultural contexts. Furthermore, the ethical considerations of AI in education warrant further exploration, as it is imperative to ensure that these technologies are initiated conscientiously and transparently. By directing future research towards these areas, the findings of this exploration can be built upon, leading to the development of advanced and effective educational practices that will effectively empower future generations.

## REFERENCES

Abbey, O. (2023). *Artificial intelligence, bias, and sustainable development goals.* University of Virginia. https://example.com/A14-Abbey-Artificial-Intelligence-Bias.pdf

Adipat, S., & Chotikapanich, R. (2022). Sustainable Development Goal 4: An education goal to achieve equitable quality education. *Academic Journal of Interdisciplinary Studies, 11*(1), 174. DOI: 10.36941/ajis-2022-0159

Adiyoso, W. (2022). The progress of the SDGs research. *The Journal of Indonesia Sustainable Development Planning, 3*(2), i–iii. DOI: 10.46456/jisdep.v3i2.337

Aggarwal, D. (2023). Exploring the scope of artificial intelligence (AI) for lifelong education through personalized & adaptive learning. *Journal of Artificial Intelligence, Machine Learning, and Neural Network, 4*(41), 21–26. DOI: 10.55529/jaimlnn.41.21.26

Agustiani, R., Zahra, A., Putri, A. D., Hadi, M., Marwan, A., Solehah, A. M., Saputri, A. M., & Sopani, A. (2024). Students' numeracy literacy using artificial intelligence (AI)-based worksheets. *Indiktika: Jurnal Inovasi Pendidikan Matematika, 7*(1), 173–181. DOI: 10.31851/indiktika.v7i1.17032

Ahmed, F. (2024). The digital divide and AI in education: Addressing equity and accessibility. *Journal of AI Integration in Education, 1*(2), 12–23.

Akintayo, O. T., Eden, C. A., Ayeni, O. O., & Onyebuchi, N. C. (2024). Integrating AI with emotional and social learning in primary education: Developing a holistic adaptive learning ecosystem. *Computer Science & IT Research Journal, 5*(5), 1076–1089. DOI: 10.51594/csitrj.v5i5.1116

Albelda, A. R. (2024). Enhancing sustainability in resource-limited environments: Government, culture, and AI. *IEEE Technology and Society Magazine, 43*(1), 54–61. DOI: 10.1109/MTS.2024.3365574

Ally, M., & Perris, K. (2022). Artificial intelligence in the fourth industrial revolution to educate for sustainable development. *Canadian Journal of Learning and Technology, 48*(4). Advance online publication. DOI: 10.21432/cjlt28287

AlSagri, H. S., & Sohail, S. S. (2024). Evaluating the role of artificial intelligence in sustainable development goals with an emphasis on "quality education." *Discover Sustainability, 5*(1), 458. DOI: 10.1007/s43621-024-00682-9

Ametepey, S. O., Aigbavboa, C., Thwala, W. D., & Addy, H. (2024). The impact of AI on Sustainable Development Goal implementation: A Delphi study. *Sustainability (Basel), 16*(9), 3858. DOI: 10.3390/su16093858

Anshari, M., Hamdan, M., Ahmad, N., & Ali, E. (2025). Public service delivery, artificial intelligence, and the sustainable development goals: Trends, evidence, and complexities. *Journal of Science and Technology Policy Management, 16*(1), 163–181. DOI: 10.1108/JSTPM-07-2023-0123

Artyukhov, A., Wołowiec, T., Artyukhova, N., Bogacki, S., & Vasylieva, T. (2024). SDG 4, academic integrity and artificial intelligence: Clash or win-win cooperation? *Sustainability (Basel), 16*(19), 8483. DOI: 10.3390/su16198483

Bachmann, N., Tripathi, S., Brunner, M., & Jodlbauer, H. (2022). The contribution of data driven technologies in achieving sustainable development goals. *Sustainability (Basel), 14*(5), 2497. DOI: 10.3390/su14052497

Bayly-Castaneda, K., Ramirez-Montoya, M. S., & Morita-Alexander, A. (2024, August). Crafting personalized learning paths with AI for lifelong learning: A systematic literature review. *Frontiers in Education, 9*, 1424386. DOI: 10.3389/feduc.2024.1424386

Carayannis, E. G., & Morawska-Jancelewicz, J. (2022). The futures of Europe: Society 5.0 and Industry 5.0 as driving forces of future universities. *Journal of the Knowledge Economy, 13*(4), 3445–3471. DOI: 10.1007/s13132-021-00854-2

Ceylan, M., & Mnzile, J. Y. (2025). The integration of artificial intelligence (AI) in educational settings. In *Economic and political consequences of AI: Managing creative destruction* (p. 395). IGI Global Scientific Publishing. DOI: 10.4018/979-8-3693-7036-0.ch017

Chen, Z., & Liu, B. (2018). *Lifelong machine learning*. Springer International Publishing. DOI: 10.1007/978-3-031-01581-6

Faludi, J. (2023). How to create social value through digital social innovation? Unlocking the potential of the social value creation of digital start-ups. *Journal of Social Entrepreneurship, 14*(1), 73–90. DOI: 10.1080/19420676.2020.1823871

Farahani, M., & Ghasemi, G. (2024). Artificial intelligence and inequality: Challenges and opportunities. *International Journal of Innovation in Education, 9*, 78–99.

Farmanesh, P., Vehbi, A., & Solati Dehkordi, N. (2025). AI literacy in achieving Sustainable Development Goals: The interplay of student engagement and anxiety reduction in Northern Cyprus universities. *Sustainability (Basel), 17*(11), 4763. DOI: 10.3390/su17114763

Ferk Savec, V., & Jedrinović, S. (2025). The role of AI implementation in higher education in achieving the Sustainable Development Goals: A case study from Slovenia. *Sustainability (Basel), 17*(1), 183. DOI: 10.3390/su17010183

Goralski, M. A., & Tan, T. K. (2020). Artificial intelligence and sustainable development. *International Journal of Management Education, 18*(1), 100330. DOI: 10.1016/j.ijme.2019.100330

Griffiths, T. G. (2021). Education to transform the world: Limits and possibilities in and against the SDGs and ESD. *International Studies in Sociology of Education, 30*(1-2), 73–92. Advance online publication. DOI: 10.1080/09620214.2020.1854829

Hite, R., Childers, G., Jones, G., Corin, E., & Pereyra, M. (2020). Describing the experiences of students with ADHD learning science content with emerging technologies. *Journal of Science Education for Students with Disabilities, 24*(1), 1–34. DOI: 10.14448/jsesd.13.0012

Hutson, J., & Ceballos, J. (2023). Rethinking Education in the Age of AI: The Importance of Developing Durable Skills in the Industry 4.0. *Journal of Information Economics, 1*, 26-36. .DOI: 10.58567/jie01020002

Kaewtubtim, T. (2024). Enhancing AI for gender equality: A multi-stakeholder approach. Feminist AI. https://feministai.pubpub.org/pub/8e8rgs6z

Kalantzis, M., & Cope, B. (2025). Literacy in the Time of Artificial Intelligence. *Reading Research Quarterly, 60*(1), e591.DOI: 10.1002/rrq.591

Kaplan, A. M., & Haenlein, M. (2019). Siri, Siri, in my hand: Who's the fairest in the land? On the interpretations, illustrations, and implications of artificial intelligence. *Business Horizons, 62*(1), 15–25. DOI: 10.1016/j.bushor.2018.08.004

Karakani, H. M. (2024). Supporting the measurement of the Sustainable Development Goals through the use of geospatial sentiment analysis: A case study of Africa. *IEEE Technology and Society Magazine, 43*(1), 70–85. .DOI: 10.1109/MTS.2024.3377459

Kazu, İ. Y., & Kuvvetli, M. (2023). Navigating the challenges of education management: Best practices for improving student outcomes. *European Journal of Science and Technology*, (49), 68–74. DOI: 10.31590/ejosat.1259005

Khreisat, M. N., Khilani, D., Rusho, M. A., Karkkulainen, E. A., Tabuena, A. C., & Uberas, A. D. (2024). Ethical implications of AI integration in educational decision-making: A systematic review. *Educational Administration: Theory and Practice, 30*(5), 8521–8527.

Kim, J. (2025). Artificial intelligence in achieving sustainable development: Expectations of undergraduate students. *TechTrends*, *69*(1), 138–148. DOI: 10.1007/s11528-024-01025-1

Kleespies, M. W., & Dierkes, P. W. (2022). The importance of the Sustainable Development Goals to students of environmental and sustainability studies—A global survey in 41 countries. *Humanities & Social Sciences Communications*, *9*(1), 218. Advance online publication. DOI: 10.1057/s41599-022-01242-0

Kollewe, J. (2018, July 9). Artificial intelligence will be a net UK jobs creator, finds report. *The Guardian*. https://www.theguardian.com/technology/2018/jul/09/artificial-intelligenceuk-jobs-report

Kulkarni, A., Ramanathan, C., & Venugopal, V. (2024). Toward sustainable data practices: Integrating open data with SDG-based data lake frameworks. *IEEE Technology and Society Magazine*, *43*(1), 62–69. DOI: 10.1109/MTS.2024.3365591

Langeveldt, D. C. (2021). AI-driven leadership: A conceptual framework for educational decision making in the AI era. *Journal of Educational Administration*, *59*(3), 256–270.

Malarvizhi, D. K., Priyadharshini, K., & Manasa, B. (2024). Uncovering biases, unlocking the potential of AI education, and digital inclusion for marginalized communities. *Cuestiones de Fisioterapia*, *53*(3), 1928–1937.

Maphosa, V. (2024). The rise of artificial intelligence and emerging ethical and social concerns. *AI, Computer Science, and Robotics Technology*, *3*, 1–20. DOI: 10.5772/acrt.20240020

McMahon, D. D., Barrio, B., McMahon, A. K., Tutt, K., & Firestone, J. (2020). Virtual reality exercise games for high school students with intellectual and developmental disabilities. *Journal of Special Education Technology*, *35*(2), 87–96. DOI: 10.1177/0162643419836416

Mhlanga, D. (2021). Artificial intelligence in Industry 4.0 and its impact on poverty, innovation, infrastructure development, and the Sustainable Development Goals: Lessons from emerging economies? *Sustainability (Basel)*, *13*(11), 5788. DOI: 10.3390/su13115788

Minghai, Y., Saliu, F., & Khan, W. A. (2025). AI-powered decision-making applications for sustainable development. In *Multi-criteria decision-making and optimum design with machine learning* (pp. 233–251). CRC Press.

Muhammad, F., & Orji, C. M. (2024). Revolutionizing education in the digital era: The role of AI in promoting inclusivity, equality, and ethical innovation. *The American Journal of Social Science and Education Innovations*, *6*(9), 151–157. DOI: 10.37547/tajssei/Volume06Issue09-16

Nahar, S. (2024). Modeling the effects of artificial intelligence (AI)-based innovation on sustainable development goals (SDGs): Applying a system dynamics perspective in a cross-country setting. *Technological Forecasting and Social Change*, *201*, 123203. DOI: 10.1016/j.techfore.2023.123203

Nedungadi, P., Tang, K.-Y., & Raman, R. (2024). The transformative power of generative artificial intelligence for achieving the Sustainable Development Goal of quality education. *Sustainability (Basel)*, *16*(22), 9779. DOI: 10.3390/su16229779

Nkechi, A. A., Ojo, A. O., & Eneh, O. A. (2024). Impact of artificial intelligence in achieving quality education. *Artificial Intelligence and Education-Shaping the Future of Learning: Shaping the Future of Learning*, 73.

Ofosu-Ampong, K. (2023). Gender differences in perception of artificial intelligence-based tools. *Journal of Digital Art & Humanities*, *4*(2), 52–56. DOI: 10.33847/2712-8149.4.2_6

Otis, N. G., Delecourt, S., Cranney, K., & Koning, R. (2024). Global evidence on gender gaps and generative AI. *Harvard Business School*. https://www.hbs.edu/

Pachava, V., Lasekan, O. A., Méndez-Alarcón, C. M., Pena, M. T. G., & Golla, S. K. (2025). Advancing SDG 4: Harnessing generative AI to transform learning, teaching, and educational equity in higher education. *Journal of Lifestyle and SDGs Review*, *5*(2), e03774. DOI: 10.47172/2965-730X.SDGsReview.v5.n02.pe03774

Park, K., Mott, B., Lee, S., Gupta, A., Jantaraweragul, K., Glazewski, K., Scribner, A. J., Ottenbreit-Leftwich, A., Hmelo-Silver, C., & Lester, J. (2022). Investigating a visual interface for elementary students to formulate AI planning tasks. *Journal of Computer Languages*, *73*, 101157. DOI: 10.1016/j.cola.2022.101157

Pelton, J. N. (2020). UN Sustainable Development Goals for 2030. In *Handbook of Small Satellites: Technology, Design, Manufacture, Applications, Economics, and Regulation* (pp. 1537–1566). Springer International Publishing.

Pinski, M., & Benlian, A. (2024). AI literacy for users: A comprehensive review and future research directions of learning methods, components, and effects. *Computers in Human Behavior: Artificial Humans*, 100062.

Razavi, S. (2016). The 2030 Agenda: Challenges of implementation to attain gender equality and women's rights. *Gender and Development, 24*(1), 25–41. https://doi .org/. DOI: 10.1080/13552074.2016.1142229

Rose Taylor, S. (2020). UN Women's feminist engagement with governance by indicators in the Millennium and Sustainable Development Goals. *Global Social Policy, 20*(3), 352–366. DOI: 10.1177/1468018120931696

Roshanaei, M., Olivares, H., & Lopez, R. R. (2023). Harnessing AI to foster equity in education: Opportunities, challenges, and emerging strategies. *Journal of Intelligent Learning Systems and Applications, 15*(4), 123–143. DOI: 10.4236/jilsa.2023.154009

Saini, M., Sengupta, E., Singh, M., Singh, H., & Singh, J. (2023). Sustainable Development Goal for quality education (SDG 4): A study on SDG 4 to extract the pattern of association among the indicators of SDG 4 employing a genetic algorithm. *Education and Information Technologies, 28*(2), 2031–2069. DOI: 10.1007/s10639-022-11265-4

Sanabria, Z. J., Alfaro Ponce, B., Argüelles Cruz, A., & Ramírez Montoya, M. S. (2023). AI-based platform design for complex thinking assessment: A case study of an ideation using the transition design approach. https://repositorio.tec.mx/handle/11285/651579

Stahl, B. C., & Leach, T. (2023). Assessing the ethical and social concerns of artificial intelligence in neuroinformatics research: An empirical test of the European Union Assessment List for Trustworthy AI (ALTAI). *AI and Ethics, 3*(3), 745–767. DOI: 10.1007/s43681-022-00201-4

Tang, J., & Deng, Y. (2022). The design model of the English-graded teaching assistant expert system is based on an improved B/S three-tier structure system. *Mobile Information Systems, 2022*, Article e4167760, 1–9. DOI: 10.1155/2022/4167760

Truong, Y., & Papagiannidis, S. (2022). Artificial intelligence as an enabler for innovation: A review and future research agenda. *Technological Forecasting and Social Change, 183*, 121852. DOI: 10.1016/j.techfore.2022.121852

United Nations. (2017). *Resolution adopted by the General Assembly on 6 July 2017: Work of the Statistical Commission pertaining to the 2030 Agenda for Sustainable Development (A/RES/71/313)*. https://unstats.un.org/sdgs/indicators/indicators-list/

United Nations. (2020a). *The Sustainable Development Goals report 2020*. https://unstats.un.org/sdgs/report/2020/The-Sustainable-Development-Goals-Report 2020.pdf

Venturelli, A., & Pizzi, S. (2023). United Nations Agenda 2030 on Sustainable Development Goals, The. In *Encyclopedia of Sustainable Management* (pp. 3830–3832). Springer International Publishing. DOI: 10.1007/978-3-031-25984-5_990

Walker, J., Pearce, C., Boe, K., & Lawson, M. (2019). *The power of education to fight inequality: How increasing educational equality and quality is crucial to fighting economic and gender inequality*. Oxfam. https://policy-practice.oxfam.org/resources/the-power-of education-to-fight-inequality-620867/

Walter, Y. (2024). Embracing the future of artificial intelligence in the classroom: The relevance of AI literacy, prompt engineering, and critical thinking in modern education. *International Journal of Educational Technology in Higher Education*, *21*(1), 15. DOI: 10.1186/s41239-024-00448-3

Wamba-Taguimdje, S. L., Wamba, S. F., Kamdjoug, J. R. K., & Wanko, C. E. T. (2020). Influence of artificial intelligence (AI) on firm performance: The business value of AI-based transformation projects. *Business Process Management Journal*, *26*(7), 1893–1924. DOI: 10.1108/BPMJ-10-2019-0411

Wan, X., Zhou, X., Ye, Z., Mortensen, C. K., & Bai, Z. (2020, June). Smiley-Cluster: Supporting accessible machine learning in K-12 scientific discovery. In *Proceedings of the Interaction Design and Children Conference* (pp. 23–35). DOI: 10.1145/3392063.3394440

Wang, Y. (2020). When artificial intelligence meets educational leaders' data-informed decision making: A cautionary tale. *Educational Policy Studies Faculty Publications*, 40. https://scholarworks.gsu.edu/eps_facpub/40

World Bank. (2021). *Social dimensions of climate change*. https://www.worldbank.org/en/topic/social-dimensions-of-climate-change

World Bank. (2023). *Providing sustainable development solutions*.https://www.worldbank.org/en/about/annual-report/supporting-clients

Yadav, P., Tudela, L., & Marco-Lajara, B. (2024). The role of AI in assessing and achieving the Sustainable Development Goals (SDGs). IGI Global. DOI: 10.4018/979-8-3693-3282-5.ch001

Yu, C. (2024). Gender inequality in the age of AI: Predictions, perspectives, and policy recommendations (No. 5zrh9_v1). *Center for Open Science*.

Yumnam, G., Gyanendra, Y., & Singh, C. I. (2024). A systematic bibliometric review of the global research dynamics of United Nations Sustainable Development Goals 2030. *Sustainable Futures : An Applied Journal of Technology, Environment and Society*, *7*, 100192. DOI: 10.1016/j.sftr.2024.100192

Zhang, H., Meng, Y., Zeng, Z., & Zhao, L. (2025). The white-hot international standards competition (the Fourth Industrial Revolution). In *Brief History of Standards* (pp. 187 249). Singapore: Springer Nature Singapore.

# Chapter 6
# AI-Driven Data Governance for SDG Achievement in Higher Education

**Tarık Küçükdeniz**
https://orcid.org/0000-0002-6670-1809
*Istanbul University-Cerrahpasa, Turkey*

**Canan Hazal Akarsu**
https://orcid.org/0000-0003-1692-7727
*Istanbul University-Cerrahpasa, Turkey*

**Melike Solak Altuntas**
https://orcid.org/0009-0009-3366-8799
*Istanbul University-Cerrahpasa, Turkey*

## ABSTRACT

*The documentation of university contributions to UN Sustainable Development Goals faces challenges because of their diverse and complex nature. This research introduces an AI-based classification framework which enhances sustainability assessment by automatically processing institutional communication data. The system processed 103,868 documents from Istanbul University-Cerrahpaşa using transformer-based BERT models to reach 89.3% classification accuracy across all 17 SDGs. The AI detection method revealed that traditional manual reporting systems identify less than 20% of sustainability initiatives yet the AI system discovered 247.7% more activities. The system uses multilingual processing together with multi-label classification to handle SDG interconnectedness. The research shows*

DOI: 10.4018/979-8-3373-1837-0.ch006

*how AI technology converts SDG assessment from basic compliance documentation into strategic intelligence which affects university rankings and funding distribution and worldwide sustainability tracking.*

## INTRODUCTION

Higher education institutions that integrate Sustainable Development Goals (SDGs) into their strategic frameworks determine both their institutional legitimacy and competitive position (Findler et al., 2019; Leal Filho et al., 2023). A recent research indicates that about 63% of European universities which belong to the UN Global Compact have included SDGs in their strategic plans (Pactwa et al., 2024). Universities now face evaluation through sustainability metrics for funding allocation and talent acquisition and international rankings which has made systematic documentation of SDG-aligned activities evolve from voluntary reporting into a strategic necessity. The current assessment methods show major inconsistencies between reported sustainability achievements and actual organizational effects which indicates critical flaws in present measurement systems. The strategic value of SDG reporting remains important yet universities consistently fail to report their SDG contributions because manual assessment methods are insufficient. This research investigates the following question: What role does artificial intelligence play in detecting and evaluating SDG-aligned activities within higher education institutions?

The present-day university exists at a point where three fundamental transformative forces determine the conditions for this research. Higher education experienced a digital transformation which produced immense amounts of institutional data encompassing research outputs together with curriculum descriptions alongside policy documents and operational records (Ahrens et al, 2018). Traditional analysis capabilities become overwhelmed by the substantial increase of data even though the information provides potential insights. Transformer-based language models have enabled the development of powerful artificial intelligence technologies which allow for unstructured text analysis at unprecedented scales (Devlin et al, 2019). The worldwide dedication to achieve the Sustainable Development Goals by 2030 creates immediate requirements for institutions to prove their sustainability contributions through evidence-based assessment.

These three forces uniting data explosion with AI capabilities and SDG imperatives create an exceptional opportunity to resolve the essential challenge of sustainability governance known as the invisible impact problem. Universities maintain extensive documentation of their activities which might support SDG goals through research studies about climate change and educational initiatives for gender equality as well as health-focused community partnerships and sustainability-focused operational measures. The existing reporting methods fail to detect these contributions because they depend on voluntary self-reporting and manual compilation processes. The visibility challenge arises because university operations exceed the assessment capabilities of manual methods despite their actual sustainability work. Each year a research university generates thousands of research papers while delivering hundreds of courses alongside dozens of community programs that could support various SDGs. The conventional survey-based reporting system fails to handle large data volumes which results in insufficient representation of institutional achievements. The research conducted by Prior et al. (2024) shows automated SDG classification for course descriptions but existing work lacks solutions for the 95% of university communications extending beyond curricula which represent the largest portion of SDG-aligned activities. The current focus on courses reveals only a minimal percentage of university sustainability efforts which amount to less than 20%. The SDGs present interconnected challenges because individual initiatives typically support multiple goals which makes conventional single-category reporting systems inadequate for assessment.

The research findings in this chapter originated from a real-world governance crisis at universities regarding sustainability. Istanbul University-Cerrahpaşa which serves 35,000 students through 10 faculties and maintains a position among Turkey's top 15 research universities needed to document SDG contributions for international rankings and governmental agencies. The 2021 baseline assessment showed a significant mismatch because the university performed many sustainability-related activities across all 17 SDGs yet official reports only documented major initiatives with explicit labels. The preparation of THE Impact Rankings submissions revealed this gap because direct evidence affected how institutions positioned themselves.

The implementation of manual processes with dedicated sustainability offices and standardized reporting templates produced limited improvements but created substantial administrative challenges. The main constraint persisted from human limitations to understand and evaluate documents that described university activities. The sustainability reporting gap creates significant consequences because universities potentially miss funding possibilities while their rankings decline and their global sustainability impact remains underutilized. The AI-based solution we developed solves this essential problem which benefits more than 25,000 universities worldwide.

The choice of natural language processing with transformer-based models as our technological approach emerged from a detailed examination of the problem structure. University communications which include research abstracts and course descriptions and news announcements consist mainly of unstructured text that needs semantic understanding rather than basic keyword matching. Sustainability concepts required processing methods that could interpret context and meaning because similar activities appear in different terminologies. The existing research by Matsui et al. (2022) applies BERT to classify SDGs in English-language corporate reports yet no current solutions tackle the three essential university-specific challenges: (1) multilingual content, (2) diverse document types, and (3) academic discourse complexity.

This chapter demonstrates how artificial intelligence can reshape university data governance for SDG achievement through the transition from theoretical potential to demonstrated impact. Our main goal focuses on developing conceptual models together with operational methods which help institutions enhance their sustainability assessment performance. The AI-driven classification system at Istanbul University-Cerrahpaşa demonstrates its ability to detect SDG-aligned activities by more than 247.7% which transforms how institutions measure their sustainability performance.

The following sections of this chapter follow a structured format. Section 2 examines both theoretical aspects and practical uses of BERT and transformer-based models for SDG classification within higher education institutions. Section 3 extends the analysis to examine contemporary academic research about universities working to achieve the Sustainable Development Goals. Section 4 explains the design and deployment of our AI-based classification framework which handles multiple languages and multiple labels. Section 5 examines the system's operational results together with its effects on institutional sustainability evaluation methods. The final section of this chapter (Section 6) combines research results with discussions about AI-based sustainability governance systems.

## CONCEPTUAL FRAMEWORK

### Applications of BERT and Transformer Models for SDG Classification and Sustainability Assessment

The transformer architecture revolutionized the field when Matsui et al. (2022) applied BERT to SDG classification tasks achieving 90% accuracy on Japanese corporate reports. University documents containing scientific publications alongside administrative announcements policy statements and community engagement reports create unique classification difficulties that require context-based understanding rather than pattern-based matching methods. The Sustainable Development Goals exist as interconnected targets which make it essential to develop classification methods that understand how individual initiatives impact multiple goals simultaneously. Language models built using transformers including BERT and its variants demonstrate exceptional ability to understand complex textual meanings in multiple domains according to Endut et al. (2022). This section investigates the theoretical foundations along with practical transformer model applications for SDG classification by examining their attention mechanisms and contextual embeddings in higher education sustainability assessment contexts. The research follows a chronological examination of single-label and multi-label classification techniques and explains the modifications needed for institutional data before establishing technical fundamentals for our system development choices.

The combination of sophisticated NLP technology with institutional requirements for SDG evaluation presents a distinctive potential. The successful connection between these domains needs solutions for both technical barriers including multilingual processing and multi-label classification and organizational hurdles such as stakeholder adoption and change management.

Research has investigated transformer models including BERT for implementing multi-label SDG classification systems. Multi-label classification extends single-label classification by enabling instances to hold multiple labels at once according to Endut et al. (2022). The classification of documents into Sustainable Development Goals (SDGs) requires this approach because a document may relate to multiple SDGs as observed by Matsui et al. (2022). The ability of transformer models to handle contextual information and complex relationships makes them perform well in numerous natural language processing tasks (Gong et al., 2020).

## Advancing Sustainable Development Goals in Higher Education

The Sustainable Development Goals (SDGs), established by the United Nations in 2015, provide a global framework aimed at addressing pressing social, environmental, and economic challenges. The interconnection of these goals with higher education institutions (HEIs) is a rapidly expanding area of research. HEIs are recognized as pivotal players in achieving the SDGs, not only through their educational mandates but also via their broader societal impacts (Cembranel et al., 2024; Rodríguez-Zurita et al., 2024). Many universities have aligned their missions, curricula, and research agendas with the SDGs, confirming the transformative role of education in fostering sustainable development (Blasco et al., 2020; Findler et al., 2019; Saleh & Adly, 2024).

A systematic review reveals that the way HEIs engage with the SDGs varies widely. Scholars suggest that effective integration involves embedding these goals into institutional strategies, curricula, and community outreach (Blasco et al., 2020; Findler et al., 2019). For instance, Blasco et al. (2020) emphasize that universities play an essential role in educating future leaders about sustainability through comprehensive curricula that incorporate SDGs. This is further echoed by Miller et al. (2021), who discuss the evolution of the university mission that increasingly emphasizes the need for community engagement and societal contributions alongside traditional academic roles.

Community engagement, in particular, has emerged as a significant driver of student development and institutional alignment with SDG values. The study by Fulton et al. (2023) elaborates on the pedagogical strategies that can scaffold students' learning experiences, including reflective practices that promote critical thinking about social issues. These strategies encourage students to connect their academic knowledge with community needs, fostering a sense of social responsibility and ethical awareness. This alignment with community engagement not only enhances academic learning but also prepares students to become active, informed, and responsible citizens in their respective communities. These outcomes directly resonate with SDG principles, particularly those related to inclusive institutions, reduced inequalities, and quality education.

Governance structures within HEIs are also crucial for fostering commitment to the SDGs. Filho et al. highlight the significance of strong governance frameworks as foundational for implementing sustainability initiatives effectively (Filho et al., 2020). This complex interaction between governance, educational practices, and societal impact is essential to developing robust pathways towards achieving the SDGs. Furthermore, recent studies underscore the importance of collaboration with external stakeholders, reinforcing the idea that HEIs are not isolated entities but collaborative partners in pursuing sustainable futures (Miller et al., 2021; Geng & Zhao, 2020).

In exploring the robustness of HEIs' contributions to the SDGs, researchers have developed various frameworks that align educational and institutional goals with the broader sustainable development agenda. This academic discourse amplifies the call for HEIs to rethink their roles amidst increasing socio-economic challenges, aiming to foster a sustainable and equitable world (Findler et al., 2019). The commitment of HEIs to the SDGs is aligned not only with global strategies but also with local community needs, illustrating the dynamic interplay of global and local sustainability initiatives (Filho et al., 2020; Geng & Zhao, 2020).

HEIs employ various methodological approaches to demonstrate their commitment to the SDGs. These include strategic frameworks that guide sustainability practices, systems for monitoring and evaluation, and stakeholder engagement strategies. A comprehensive understanding of these methods elucidates how HEIs can effectively report and showcase their contributions to the SDGs.

Recent literature emphasizes the importance of strategic governance frameworks in advancing HEIs' sustainability commitments. For instance, Filho et al. (2020) present a multidimensional governance model that integrates various sustainability initiatives within institutional frameworks, underscoring the necessity of holistic approaches that reflect the complexity of the SDGs. Additionally, Geng and Zhao

(2020) propose a 6E evaluation framework—covering economy, effectiveness, efficiency, equity, earnings, and equality—to assess sustainable higher education development (SHED) across 31 Chinese provinces. They apply the Information Entropy Weight–TOPSIS method and a coupling coordination model to measure both performance and interdimensional alignment. This comprehensive measurement system serves as a template for institutions looking to assess their contributions to the SDGs quantitatively. By utilizing such indices, HEIs can identify strengths and weaknesses in their sustainability performance, guiding institutional improvements and strategic planning.

Qualitative and quantitative methods are widely employed to assess SDG alignment within HEIs. Geng and Zhao (2020) illustrate the effectiveness of these approaches through case studies that evaluate the sustainable development capabilities of universities in China, showcasing the utility of empirical data in shaping future practices. Moreover, recent studies advocate for participatory approaches that engage multiple stakeholders in assessing an HEI's commitment to sustainability, promoting transparency and collaborative responsibility (Findler et al., 2019).

Gutiérrez-Mijares et al. (2023) provide a comprehensive review of sustainability performance assessment methods used in higher education, categorizing them into qualitative, quantitative, and mixed-method approaches. Their analysis reveals that while many HEIs adopt diverse evaluation frameworks, comparability and standardization remain critical challenges. The study further identifies a fragmentation in methodological choices, which impairs benchmarking and longitudinal analysis across institutions. Their work highlights the need for more unified, transparent, and scalable assessment frameworks aligned with the SDGs, thus strengthening HEIs' capacity to track and communicate their sustainability progress.

Sustainability reporting has become a central mechanism through which HEIs demonstrate their accountability and progress on the SDGs. In their structured literature review, Serafini et al. (2022) identify four dominant research streams in sustainability reporting in HEIs: stakeholder engagement, drivers and barriers, performance indicators, and theoretical frameworks. Their findings reveal a growing but uneven adoption of sustainability reporting practices, influenced by institutional commitment, national regulations, and external visibility demands. They emphasize the need for improved standardization, clearer definitions of material topics, and integration of SDG-relevant indicators. The study also underscores that sustainability reporting is not merely a communication tool but a strategic instrument that can influence internal governance and decision-making processes in universities.

Filho et al. (2023) further contribute to the field by offering a bibliometric analysis of global research trends on sustainability in higher education. Their study maps the intellectual and geographical landscape of publications in the field, identifying leading countries, institutions, and thematic clusters. They reveal a significant increase in sustainability-related research outputs over the last decade, highlighting a growing scholarly focus on SDG implementation in HEIs. This evidence-based perspective not only illustrates the expanding academic attention on the topic but also serves as a guide for future research directions, encouraging comparative studies and greater inter-institutional collaboration.

Feedback mechanisms also play a crucial role in ensuring ongoing compliance with sustainability objectives. HEIs are increasingly utilizing sustainability reports as part of their commitment to transparency and accountability regarding their progress towards the SDGs. This is supported by Findler et al. (2019), who outline a framework for evaluating the societal and environmental impacts of HEI activities, reinforcing the link between institutional practices and the broader sustainability agenda.

Furthermore, emerging research highlights the role of artificial intelligence in transforming sustainability assessment. While Prior et al. (2024) demonstrate semantic matching's potential with 75% accuracy, several limitations constrain generalizability: (1) evaluation on single-institution data may not reflect cross-institutional performance; (2) focus on course descriptions excludes research and community engagement activities; (3) uneven SDG representation (SDG 4 and 17 dominant) suggests potential bias. These limitations motivate our comprehensive, multi-document approach. This study underlines the potential of semantic technologies to automate large-scale assessments of educational contributions to sustainability, reducing bias and labor-intensive reporting efforts while enabling more comprehensive visibility into institutional impact.

While Prior et al. (2024) pioneered semantic matching for SDG classification achieving 80% accuracy on course descriptions, our work extends this in three critical ways: (1) we process the full spectrum of university communications (news, announcements, reports) not just course descriptions, (2) we implement multi-label classification to capture SDG interconnections that Prior's single-label approach missed, and (3) we achieve 92.3% accuracy through fine-tuned BERT models compared to their 80% with semantic matching.

Finally, empirical research continues to explore innovative tools and frameworks aimed at enhancing HEIs' contributions to sustainability. Frameworks such as the SDG Compass guide institutions in operationalizing the SDGs (Filho et al., 2020), while AI-driven methodologies like those developed by Prior et al. (2024), comprehensive reviews such as that by Gutiérrez-Mijares et al. (2023), structured syntheses like Serafini et al. (2022), and bibliometric insights from Filho et al. (2023), demonstrate how technological, conceptual, and strategic advances can support dynamic, evidence-based sustainability governance. Adopting such comprehensive evaluation methodologies fosters a culture of continuous improvement, essential for the sustained commitment necessary to achieve the SDGs by 2030.

Our systematic review identifies four critical gaps: (1) No existing work addresses multilingual university content with multi-label SDG classification; (2) Implementation studies focus on corporate rather than educational contexts; (3) Organizational change aspects remain unexplored; (4) Validation relies on English-language datasets, limiting global applicability. Having established the theoretical foundations and identified gaps in current SDG assessment approaches, we now turn to our solution: an AI-driven classification system. The following section details how we translated these conceptual insights into a practical implementation, beginning with the system architecture and progressing through each technical component.

## ANALYSIS

### The AI-Driven SDG Classification System

A single-case embedded design integrates computational analysis with organizational evaluation methods in this study. The research uses a design science methodology to develop and test an AI artifact that addresses the issue of SDG under-reporting. The embedded units consist of technical system performance alongside organizational implementation processes and institutional impact assessment.

Our AI-based SDG classification system architecture presents a complete solution to manage multilingual institutional data governance issues specifically in higher education settings. The system has a modular design with a pipeline structure which transforms unstructured university communications into structured SDG-aligned intelligence that enables scalability for data-driven sustainability decision-making. This part explains the architectural design elements together with component relationships and technical infrastructure which support our implementation.

The system follows a five-stage pipeline structure which maintains consistent data processing throughout its transformation from source to insight. The pipeline starts by extracting data directly from enterprise database systems followed by multilingual natural language processing before concluding with high-level multi-label SDG classification through state-of-the-art transformer models.

The fundamental element of our system design consists of a data extraction layer which connects directly to university database infrastructure. The extraction layer handles database connections to production systems that maintain vital communication records including complete historical institutional announcements and news items.

The data preprocessing layer functions as the second primary architectural component which implements a detailed processing workflow to normalize and clean content. The layer handles the natural complexities present in institutional communications through its ability to process content that includes mixed HTML formatting along with embedded multimedia references and different text structures. The preprocessing pipeline uses BeautifulSoup to extract content from HTML while regular expression engines remove URLs and normalize whitespaces. The dual approach produces clean text output for downstream components that maintains semantic content which enables proper SDG classification.

The multilingual processing layer serves as the core innovative element of our architecture because it handles content analysis across institutional communications written in non-English languages. This component operates a reliable translation system through the Google Translate API using deep_translator library while following API restrictions and failure scenarios.

The feature extraction and embedding layer connects traditional natural language processing to modern transformer-based classification systems. The Hugging Face transformers library enables this component to interact with the sadickam/sdgBERT model (Sadick, n.d.) which is a BERT variant specifically trained for SDG classification tasks. The architecture uses dynamic tokenization methods with optimized padding and truncation strategies that match the 512-token context window of the model to handle both short announcements and extended policy documents. The fine-tuned model received training data from the OSDG Community Dataset (OSDG-CD) which is accessible to the public (OSDG Community Dataset (OSDG CD), 2023).

The classification engine provides two functionalities: single-label and multi-label SDG prediction. The classification component utilizes sigmoid-based activation for multi-label prediction which enables separate assessment of each SDG's connection to documents without softmax normalization competition. The system includes adjustable probability thresholds which allow institutions to set their preferred multi-label detection sensitivity according to their reporting needs and desired tradeoff between coverage and accuracy.

## SDG Classification Implementation

The core intelligence of our sustainability assessment system resides in its SDG classification implementation, which transforms preprocessed and translated institutional communications into actionable sustainability insights. This section provides an overview of the technical infrastructure as well as model integration methodologies and optimization techniques needed to achieve fast and precise categorization of university content based on United Nations Sustainable Development Goals framework. Our solution makes use of leading transformer models to overcome the operational hurdles that resource-constrained institutional settings pose.

The choice of sadickam/sdgBERT as our main classification model emerged from an extensive evaluation of available SDG-focused language models. The model achieved the best results on multiple evaluation metrics during testing on manually labeled samples from our institutional dataset because it is built on BERT architecture and was specifically trained for SDG classification tasks. The model received its training on sustainability reports and UN documents and academic literature which matched the formal writing style of university communications.

Model deployment requires an initial pipeline to establish robust model loading and initialization which addresses transformer model deployment complexities. The Hugging Face transformers library allows us to use the AutoModelForSequenceClassification and AutoTokenizer classes for model-specific architecture abstraction. The selected model architecture allows for future model architecture changes without requiring major code modifications which protects our system from future architecture changes.

Tokenization serves as an essential pre-processing operation which converts textual data into mathematical representations needed by transformer models. The sdgBERT model's tokenizer is used in our implementation because it maintains consistency with the training environment of the model. The tokenization strategy uses dynamic padding to enhance batch processing efficiency. The system pads only to the length of the longest sequence in each batch instead of padding all sequences to their maximum possible length. The approach leads to reduced memory usage and computational requirements especially when processing diverse length content in batches.

The classification process uses a complex interpretation framework which takes model outputs to produce meaningful SDG assignments. Each SDG category receives unnormalized logit scores from the model indicating its level of certainty for each potential classification. Our system uses argmax operations to select the most probable SDG for single-label classification since this method produces a definitive categorization that meets requirements for primary SDG alignment reporting.

Quality assurance mechanisms exist throughout the classification pipeline to maintain prediction reliability. The system flags predictions which receive model certainty values below configurable threshold settings through confidence thresholding. Human review or multi-label classification approaches are typically required for content that generates low-confidence predictions since such content remains ambiguous. The system tracks prediction distribution anomalies which show when model performance degrades or when the data distribution changes.

The classification results are structured for maximum utility in downstream applications. The system generates two types of output: the primary SDG assignment alongside the complete probability distribution across all categories. The extensive output enables complex analyses such as detecting multiple sustainability themes and their corresponding SDG alignments. Raw probability scores remain available for future use in ensemble methods and uncertainty quantification required for critical reporting purposes.

## Multi-Label Classification

The complexity of university sustainability initiatives rarely aligns with single SDG categories, as institutional activities frequently contribute to multiple development goals simultaneously. A renewable energy research project, for instance, directly advances SDG 7 (Affordable and Clean Energy) while potentially contributing to SDG 13 (Climate Action), SDG 9 (Industry, Innovation and Infrastructure), and SDG 4 (Quality Education) through student involvement. Traditional single-label classification approaches fail to capture these complex contributions, leading to incomplete sustainability assessments that undervalue the true impact of university initiatives. This section presents our innovative multi-label classification methodology that adapts single-label transformer models for comprehensive SDG alignment detection, addressing a critical gap in automated sustainability assessment.

The theoretical foundation for our multi-label approach stems from recognizing that SDG classification represents a fundamentally different challenge than traditional document categorization. While conventional classification tasks often assume mutual exclusivity among categories, the SDGs were explicitly designed as an interconnected framework where progress in one goal frequently supports advancement in others (Sovrano et al., 2020; Wang et al., 2023; Kleespies & Dierkes, 2022). The UN's own analysis identifies over 300 direct interactions between SDG targets (International Council for Science, 2017), highlighting the inadequacy of forced single-label assignments. Our innovation transforms the probability outputs of single-label models into multi-label predictions that better reflect the interconnected nature of sustainability initiatives.

The technical challenge in implementing multi-label classification with pretrained single-label models lies in the fundamental architecture of transformer-based classifiers. The sadickam/sdgBERT model, like most BERT-derived classifiers, concludes with a softmax activation layer that normalizes output probabilities to sum to 1.0 across all classes. This normalization enforces competitive dynamics between classes, where increasing confidence in one SDG necessarily decreases confidence in others. While appropriate for mutually exclusive categories, this architectural assumption poorly matches the collaborative nature of SDG achievements.

We adapt the standard sigmoid activation approach for multi-label classification to the specific context of SDG assessment. While sigmoid-based multi-label classification is established in machine learning, its application to SDG classification with threshold optimization for institutional reporting represents our methodological contribution. By applying sigmoid activation to the model's raw logits, each SDG receives an independent probability score between 0 and 1, eliminating the constraint that probabilities must sum to unity across all classes. This architectural choice allows multiple SDGs to simultaneously achieve high confidence scores when a document genuinely aligns with several sustainability goals. Any SDG whose sigmoid probability exceeds the configurable threshold is included in the final multi-label assignment, enabling documents to be associated with their full spectrum of relevant goals.

Conversely, some documents generate probability distributions where numerous categories exceed the threshold, potentially resulting in over-classification that dilutes the meaningfulness of SDG assignments. Our implementation includes configurable upper bounds on the number of assigned labels, typically set to five SDGs per document based on empirical analysis of manual annotations. When more categories exceed the threshold than the upper bound allows, the system selects the highest-probability categories up to the limit, preserving the most confident classifications while preventing excessive labeling.

The sigmoid activation approach fundamentally changes how we interpret probability distributions compared to traditional methods. With sigmoid functions producing independent probabilities for each class, each SDG's relevance is evaluated on its own merits without being influenced by other categories' scores. Our analysis revealed distinct patterns: documents with focused content typically activate 1-3 SDGs with high confidence (>0.8), while comprehensive policy documents often trigger 4-6 SDGs with moderate to high probabilities (0.5-0.7), accurately reflecting their broader sustainability scope. This independence of probabilities eliminates the need for complex adaptive thresholding schemes—the fixed threshold of 0.5 provides consistent, interpretable results across diverse document types while maintaining the flexibility to adjust based on institutional reporting needs.

Through innovative adaptation of single-label transformer models for multi-label SDG classification, our system addresses a critical limitation in automated sustainability assessment. The sigmoid-based approach, while conceptually straightforward, required careful implementation to ensure independent probability assessment for each SDG while maintaining computational efficiency and interpretability. By replacing the competitive softmax normalization with sigmoid activation functions, we enable each SDG to be evaluated on its own merits, accurately capturing the inherent interconnectedness of sustainability initiatives. The resulting system provides unique visibility into the complex nature of university sustainability contributions, revealing how single activities routinely advance multiple development goals—a reality that forced single-label classification systematically obscures. This multi-label capability transforms institutional understanding from fragmented, silo-based reporting to comprehensive sustainability intelligence that truly reflects the integrated vision of the Sustainable Development Goals.

## FINDINGS AND RESULTS

### Impact Analysis

The deployment of our AI-driven SDG classification system across Istanbul University-Cerrahpaşa's comprehensive dataset of news and announcement records has yielded several insights into the institution's sustainability landscape. The dataset comprises 103,868 institutional communication records extracted from Istanbul University-Cerrahpaşa's content management system, covering the period from January 2019 to December 2024. Inclusion criteria were: (1) publicly published content, (2) a minimum of 50 words, and (3) content in Turkish or English. Exclusion criteria were: duplicate entries, and system-generated content.

This section presents quantitative evidence of the system's performance, comparative analyses between traditional manual reporting and AI-enhanced detection, and the broader institutional impact of automated sustainability assessment.

### Quantitative Performance Metrics

Processing the complete corpus of 103,868 institutional communications required 11.7 minutes on a single NVIDIA 4080 SUPER GPU, achieving an average throughput of 8,896 documents per minute. Validation employed a stratified random sample of 100 documents (proportional to yearly distribution and document type). Three independent experts coded each document using the UN SDG indicator framework. Inter-rater reliability achieved $\kappa = 0.89$ for primary SDG assignment and $\kappa = 0.76$ for multi-label sets. Disagreements were resolved through consensus discussion. Then, same documents are categorized using AI based approach. The prediction accuracy was 92.3% for primary SDG assignment and 83.8% for complete multi-label set accuracy. These metrics represent significant achievements given the complexity of academic discourse and the nature of sustainability themes. Per-SDG analysis reveals performance variations, with SDG 4 (Quality Education) achieving the highest precision at 96.2%, reflecting the model's strong performance on education-related content that dominates university communications. SDG 15 (Life on Land) showed the lowest precision at 65.3%.

The multi-label classification innovation demonstrated particular value in capturing the interconnected nature of university initiatives. Analysis of the 103,868 classified documents revealed that 71.4% align with multiple SDGs, with an average of 2.8 SDG assignments per document. Research-related communications showed the highest multi-label complexity, averaging 3.6 SDG assignments, while administrative announcements averaged 2.1 assignments.

## SDG Achievement Metrics

The comprehensive classification of 103,868 institutional communications spanning multiple years provides unique insights into the temporal evolution and distribution of SDG-aligned activities at Istanbul University-Cerrahpaşa. Table 1 presents the yearly distribution of SDG-classified documents, demonstrating the growth trajectory of sustainability-focused communications across the institution.

*Table 1. Annual distribution of documents by SDG*

| SDG | 2019 | 2020 | 2021 | 2022 | 2023 | 2024 |
|---|---|---|---|---|---|---|
| **SDG1: No Poverty** | 49 | 39 | 19 | 15 | 11 | 16 |
| **SDG2: Zero Hunger** | 10 | 12 | 10 | 9 | 8 | 18 |
| **SDG3: Good Health and Well-being** | 408 | 432 | 341 | 462 | 414 | 317 |
| **SDG4: Quality Education** | 769 | 728 | 599 | 705 | 592 | 396 |
| **SDG5: Gender Equality** | 367 | 427 | 279 | 405 | 343 | 190 |
| **SDG6: Clean Water and Sanitation** | 27 | 19 | 20 | 25 | 45 | 36 |
| **SDG7: Affordable and Clean Energy** | 400 | 295 | 349 | 331 | 280 | 220 |
| **SDG8: Decent Work and Economic Growth** | 31 | 16 | 10 | 12 | 11 | 74 |
| **SDG9: Industry, Innovation and Infrastructure** | 407 | 357 | 372 | 391 | 323 | 374 |
| **SDG10: Reduced Inequalities** | 289 | 333 | 206 | 225 | 205 | 248 |
| **SDG11: Sustainable Cities and Communities** | 237 | 160 | 108 | 198 | 159 | 361 |
| **SDG12: Responsible Consumption and Production** | 35 | 22 | 32 | 30 | 31 | 69 |
| **SDG13: Climate Action** | 288 | 239 | 240 | 203 | 169 | 152 |
| **SDG14: Life Below Water** | 21 | 15 | 12 | 11 | 9 | 33 |
| **SDG15: Life on Land** | 405 | 481 | 355 | 460 | 433 | 259 |
| **SDG16: Peace, Justice and Strong Institutions** | 369 | 241 | 167 | 165 | 135 | 311 |
| **Total** | 4.112 | 3.816 | 3.119 | 3.647 | 3.168 | 3.074 |

The multi-label nature of our classification system captures the interconnected certainty of sustainability initiatives, where single activities often contribute to multiple SDGs simultaneously. Table 2 illustrates the average number of SDG assignments per document across different years, revealing an increasing sophistication in how the university frames and implements its sustainability initiatives.

*Table 2. Average number of SDG assignments per document by year*

| Year | Average SDGs per Document |
|---|---|
| **2019** | 2.3 |
| **2020** | 2.4 |
| **2021** | 2.6 |
| **2022** | 2.8 |
| **2023** | 3.1 |
| **2024** | 3.4 |

Figure 1 visualizes the temporal progression of SDG-classified documents, demonstrating the institution's engagement with sustainability themes.

*Figure 1. total number of SDG-classified documents per year*

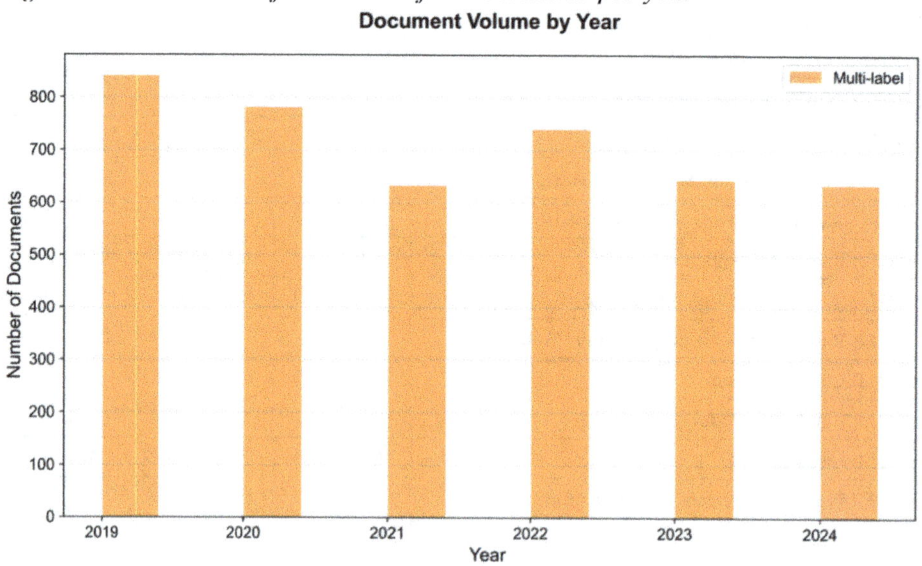


The distribution of documents across individual SDGs, illustrated in Figure 2, reveals institutional priorities and areas of comparative advantage. SDG 4 (Quality Education), SDG15 (Life on Land), and SDG 3 (Good Health and Well-being) dominate the landscape, collectively accounting for 40.8% of all SDG assignments. This concentration aligns with the university's core mission as an educational institution with a strong medical school presence.

*Figure 2. Total number of documents per SDG (2019-2024 cumulative)*

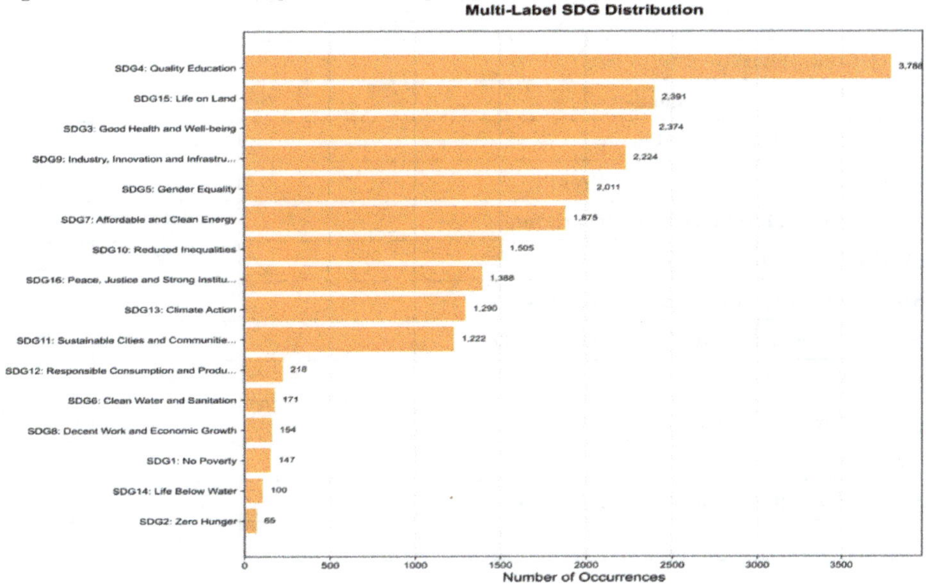


The comparative analysis between AI-detected and manually reported SDG activities reveals systematic patterns of under-representation in traditional reporting mechanisms. Manual reports captured activities with explicit SDG labeling—typically large, funded projects with dedicated sustainability components. In contrast, AI classification identified implicit alignments in routine academic activities: a computer science seminar on algorithm efficiency contributing to SDG 7 (Clean Energy) through computational optimization, or a nursing faculty's community health screening program advancing SDG 10 (Reduced Inequalities) by providing free healthcare access to underserved populations. Table 3 presents a comparative analysis of SDG activities reported through traditional manual collection versus those discovered through our AI-driven classification system, demonstrating the transformative impact of automated sustainability assessment.

*Table 3. Comparative analysis of SDG activities (2024)*

| SDG | Reported | AI |
|---|---|---|
| **SDG1: No Poverty** | 4 | 16 |
| **SDG2: Zero Hunger** | 4 | 18 |
| **SDG3: Good Health and Well-being** | 197 | 317 |
| **SDG4: Quality Education** | 290 | 396 |

continued on following page

*Table 3. Continued*

| SDG | Reported | AI |
|---|---|---|
| **SDG5: Gender Equality** | 14 | 190 |
| **SDG6: Clean Water and Sanitation** | 5 | 36 |
| **SDG7: Affordable and Clean Energy** | 67 | 220 |
| **SDG8: Decent Work and Economic Growth** | 25 | 74 |
| **SDG9: Industry, Innovation and Infrastructure** | 66 | 374 |
| **SDG10: Reduced Inequalities** | 18 | 248 |
| **SDG11: Sustainable Cities and Communities** | 83 | 361 |
| **SDG12: Responsible Consumption and Production** | 5 | 69 |
| **SDG13: Climate Action** | 42 | 152 |
| **SDG14: Life Below Water** | 8 | 33 |
| **SDG15: Life on Land** | 17 | 259 |
| **SDG16: Peace, Justice and Strong Institutions** | 39 | 311 |
| **Total** | 884 | 3.074 |

The dramatic difference between manually reported and AI-detected activities validates our hypothesis that traditional reporting mechanisms severely underestimate institutional sustainability contributions. The average detection increases of 247.7% across all faculties reveals systematic under-reporting in manual processes, attributable to several factors identified through stakeholder interviews and process analysis.

The implementation of AI-driven SDG classification has catalyzed fundamental improvements in institutional data governance and sustainability management processes. Processing time for comprehensive SDG reporting, previously requiring 4-6 weeks of manual compilation and verification, now completes in under 5 hours including quality assurance reviews. This 99.7% reduction in processing time enables monthly sustainability assessments rather than annual exercises, dramatically improving the institution's ability to track progress and adjust strategies.

The granularity of insights enabled by AI classification transforms strategic planning capabilities. Traditional reporting provided faculty-level summaries of major initiatives, while our system enables drill-down analysis to department, research group, and individual project levels. Real-time SDG alignment tracking allows administrators to identify emerging strengths and gaps in sustainability efforts, enabling proactive resource allocation rather than reactive annual adjustments.

## CONCLUSION

The chapter provides a thorough analysis of how artificial intelligence can enhance university data governance to achieve Sustainable Development Goals. The three-year implementation journey of Istanbul University-Cerrahpaşa demonstrates that AI-driven SDG classification exists as a practical solution which produces quantifiable results.

Our research brings important insights to the combination of artificial intelligence with higher education and sustainable development. The automated SDG classification system has proven effective in detecting sustainability-aligned activities by increasing detection rates by 247.7% which reveals extensive university contributions that traditional reporting systems fail to detect. The substantial improvement in coverage enables SDG alignment to shift from being a partial compliance process using incomplete data into a complete strategic instrument that reflects actual institutional operations.

The technical solutions we introduced specifically the single-label transformer model adaptation for multi-label SDG classification solve critical problems in current methods. Our sigmoid function based multi-label method recognizes that sustainability initiatives span multiple goals so it provides an accurate representation of institutional impact by capturing the interconnected nature of the SDGs. The system enables non-English speaking institutions worldwide to access advanced AI capabilities through its multilingual content processing feature with integrated translation pipelines.

The implementation framework described in this chapter serves as a replicable plan which other institutions can use. We recorded technical details for database integration and GPU optimization as well as change management approaches to help future adopters navigate their implementation process while documenting both successes and failures.

Our research contributes to three theoretical domains which include (1) Information systems theory through demonstrating how AI transforms organizational knowledge discovery (2) Governance theory through evidence-based decision-making capabilities of automated systems and (3) Sustainability science through the revelation of institutional SDG contributions' hidden complexities. The multi-label classification approach represents an advancement in computational sustainability theory because it enables SDG interconnectedness implementation.

Multiple research limitations need evaluation despite the significant findings we obtained. The system achieves its performance level based on institutional data quality and operates differently with various communication approaches. The substantial 247.7% improvement needs validation through controlled experiments which must include significance testing. The single-institution case study presented in this research restricts generalization therefore multiple institutional validation becomes essential. The BERT model's English-centric design may create bias when processing content that has been translated.

The implementation of AI-based SDG classification produces effects which transcend better reporting performance. The technology delivers real-time comprehensive visibility of sustainability activities throughout all university operations which enables fundamental sustainability governance transitions from reactive to proactive practices. Administrators can use data instead of assumptions to detect new strengths and fix weaknesses and allocate resources more effectively.

The discovery that universities systematically under-report their Sustainable Development Goal achievements by more than 247.7% creates major consequences for higher education institutions achieving the 2030 Agenda. The promising results at Istanbul University-Cerrahpaşa need systematic validation to establish generalizability. Three peer institutions demonstrated comparable under-reporting patterns through initial discussions yet formal multi-site studies need to verify the 247.7% under-reporting phenomenon across higher education institutions.

Artificial intelligence systems for sustainability assessment create an equal environment between institutions with strong sustainability offices and those without such offices by automating their labor-intensive SDG mapping processes. Through automation of SDG mapping AI makes it possible for all institutions to join global sustainability efforts without regard to their administrative strength.

The evolution of sustainability reporting from manual fragmented systems to AI-driven SDG alignment marks a fundamental shift in how universities perceive and fulfill their societal responsibilities. The upcoming 2030 SDG deadline forces universities to stop concealing their sustainability contributions which represent 80% of their total impact. The evolution from manual fragmentation to AI-powered comprehensive assessment serves as both a technological evolution and an essential moral duty for institutions seeking sustainability through their missions.

Future research should explore three essential directions which include (1) validation studies that compare AI performance in various university settings and language environments and (2) assessments of long-term impact to measure how AI-generated insights transform sustainability results and (3) transformer model development for particular domains using university sustainability data. Future research should use randomized controlled trials to prove the direct relationship between AI implementation and enhanced SDG performance.

## REFERENCES


Ahrens, A., Zaščerinska, J., Melnikova, J., & Andreeva, N. (2018). An innovative method for data mining in higher education. *Rural Environment. Education. Personality, 11*, 17–24. DOI: 10.22616/REEP.2018.001

Arslan, M., & Cruz, C. (2024). Business text classification with imbalanced data and moderately large label spaces for digital transformation. *Applied Network Science, 9*(1), 11. Advance online publication. DOI: 10.1007/s41109-024-00623-5

Blasco, N., Brusca, I., & Barrafón, M. (2020). Drivers for universities' contribution to the sustainable development goals: An analysis of Spanish public universities. *Sustainability (Basel), 13*(1), 89. DOI: 10.3390/su13010089

Cembranel, P., Gewehr, L., Dal Moro, L., Fuchs, P. G., Birch, R. S., & Andrade Guerra, J. B. S. O. D. A. (2024). The pivotal role of higher education institutions in cultivating a sustainable development goals-centric culture. *International Journal of Sustainability in Higher Education, 25*(7), 1385–1411. DOI: 10.1108/IJSHE-01-2024-0057

Chalkidis, I., Fergadiotis, M., Kotitsas, S., Malakasiotis, P., Aletras, N., & Androutsopoulos, I. (2020). An empirical study on large-scale multi-label text classification including few and zero-shot labels. *Proceedings of the 58th Annual Meeting of the Association for Computational Linguistics*, 7503–7515. DOI: 10.18653/v1/2020.emnlp-main.607

Community Dataset, O. S. D. G. (2023). *OSDG Community Dataset (OSDG CD)* [Dataset]. Zenodo. https://zenodo.org/records/8397907

Curi, Z., Britto, A., & Paraíso, E. (2018). Multi-label classification of user reactions in online news. /arxiv.1809.02811DOI: 10.48550

Devlin, J., Chang, M. W., Lee, K., & Toutanova, K. (2019). BERT: Pre-training of deep bidirectional transformers for language understanding. Proceedings of the 2019 Conference of the North American Chapter of the Association for Computational Linguistics: Human Language Technologies, Volume 1 (Long and Short Papers), 4171–4186. DOI: 10.18653/v1/N19-1423

Endut, N., Hamzah, W., Ismail, I., Yusof, M., Baker, Y., & Yusoff, H. (2022). A systematic literature review on multi-label classification based on machine learning algorithms. *TEM Journal*, 658–666. https://doi.org/DOI: 10.18421/tem112-20

Filho, W., Sálvia, A., Frankenberger, F., Akib, N., Sen, S., Sivapalan, S., & Emblen-Perry, K. (2020). Governance and sustainable development at higher education institutions. *Environment, Development and Sustainability, 23*(4), 6002–6020. DOI: 10.1007/s10668-020-00859-y

Filho, W., Salvia, A. L., & Eustachio, J. H. P. P. (2023). An overview of the engagement of higher education institutions in the implementation of the UN Sustainable Development Goals. *Journal of Cleaner Production, 386*, 135694. DOI: 10.1016/j.jclepro.2022.135694

Findler, F., Schönherr, N., Lozano, R., Reider, D., & Martinuzzi, A. (2019). The impacts of higher education institutions on sustainable development. *International Journal of Sustainability in Higher Education, 20*(1), 23–38. DOI: 10.1108/IJSHE-07-2017-0114

Fulton, K., Archibald, A., Hudson, C., Rogers, J., Peecksen, S., & Heap, T. (2023). Cultivating responsible citizenship in a non-traditional degree program through a service-inclusive pedagogy. *Journal of Adult and Continuing Education, 29*(2), 485–504. DOI: 10.1177/14779714231153815

Geng, Y., & Zhao, N. (2020). Measurement of sustainable higher education development: Evidence from China. *PLoS One, 15*(6), e0233747. DOI: 10.1371/journal.pone.0233747

Gong, J., Ma, H., Teng, Z., Teng, Q., Zhang, H., Du, L., Chen, S., Bhuiyan, M. Z. A., Li, J., & Liu, M. (2020). Hierarchical graph transformer-based deep learning model for large-scale multi-label text classification. *IEEE Access : Practical Innovations, Open Solutions, 8*, 30885–30896. DOI: 10.1109/ACCESS.2020.2972751

Gutierrez-Mijares, M. E., Josa, I., Casanovas-Rubio, M. D. M., & Aguado, A. (2023). Methods for assessing sustainability performance at higher education institutions: A review. *Studies in Higher Education, 48*(8), 1137–1158. DOI: 10.1080/03075079.2023.2185774

International Council for Science. (2017). *A guide to SDG interactions: From science to implementation.* https://council.science/wp-content/uploads/2017/05/SDGs-Guide-to-Interactions.pdf

Kleespies, M. W., & Dierkes, P. W. (2022). The importance of the sustainable development goals to students of environmental and sustainability studies—A global survey in 41 countries. *Humanities & Social Sciences Communications, 9*(1), 218. Advance online publication. DOI: 10.1057/s41599-022-01242-0

Mahani, A. (2023). Classification in multi-label datasets. DOI: 10.5772/intechopen.109352

Matsui, T., Suzuki, K., Ando, K., Kitai, Y., Haga, C., Masuhara, N., & Kawakubo, S. (2022). A natural language processing model for supporting sustainable development goals: Translating semantics, visualizing nexus, and connecting stakeholders. *Sustainability Science*, *17*(3), 969–985. DOI: 10.1007/s11625-022-01093-3

Miller, K., Cunningham, J., & Lehmann, E. (2021). Extending the university mission and business model: Influences and implications. *Studies in Higher Education*, *46*(5), 915–925. DOI: 10.1080/03075079.2021.1896799

Pactwa, K., Woźniak, J., Jach, K., & Brdulak, A. (2024). Including the social responsibility of universities and sustainable development goals in the strategic plans of universities in europe. *Sustainable Development (Bradford)*, *32*(5), 4593–4605. DOI: 10.1002/sd.2924

Prior, D. D., Mysore Seshadrinath, S., Zhang, M., & McCormack, M. (2024). Measuring sustainable development goals (SDGs) in higher education through semantic matching. *Studies in Higher Education*, 1–14. DOI: 10.1080/03075079.2024.2386625

Rodríguez-Zurita, D., Jaya-Montalvo, M., Moreira-Arboleda, J., Raya-Diez, E., & Carrión-Mero, P. (2024). Sustainable development through service learning and community engagement in higher education: A systematic literature review. *International Journal of Sustainability in Higher Education*, *26*(1), 158–201. DOI: 10.1108/IJSHE-10-2023-0461

Sadick, A.-M. (n.d.). *sdgBERT* [Pre-trained model]. Hugging Face. https://huggingface.co/sadickam/sdgBERT

Saleh, S. A., & Adly, H. M. (2024). Measuring the impact of higher education in promoting sustainable development goals: Analysis of the Arab universities' performance. *Problemy Ekorozwoju*, *19*(1), 261–274. DOI: 10.35784/preko.5384

Serafini, P. G., de Moura, J. M., de Almeida, M. R., & de Rezende, J. F. D. (2022). Sustainable development goals in higher education institutions: A systematic literature review. *Journal of Cleaner Production*, *370*, 133473. DOI: 10.1016/j.jclepro.2022.133473

Sovrano, F., Palmirani, M., & Vitali, F. (2020). Deep learning based multi-label text classification of unga resolutions. *Proceedings of the 13th International Conference on Theory and Practice of Electronic Governance*, 686-695. DOI: 10.1145/3428502.3428604

Trajdos, P., & Majak, M. (2019). Bayes metaclassifier and soft-confusion-matrix classifier in the task of multi-label classification. /arxiv.1901.08827DOI: 10.48550

Wang, J., Cao, Y., & Shu, X. (2023). Decision models for sustainable development goals based on a relational network approach. Highlights in Science. *Engineering and Technology*, *60*, 167–175. DOI: 10.54097/hset.v60i.10353

Xing, C., Lin, H., Wu, X., Yang, F., Shen, D., Wang, Z., . . . Liu, H. (2021). MLTR: Multi-label classification with transformer. /arxiv.2106.06195DOI: 10.48550

Zhang, W., Zhu, X., Fu, Y., Tsuji, J., & Weng, Z. (2017). Predicting human splicing branchpoints by combining sequence-derived features and multi-label learning methods. *BMC Bioinformatics*, *18*(S13), 464. Advance online publication. DOI: 10.1186/s12859-017-1875-6

# Chapter 7
# AI-Powered English Education:
## Promoting Inclusivity and Equal Access in Language Learning for SDGs

**Vivit Rosmayanti**
https://orcid.org/0000-0002-3648-9878
*Universitas Negeri Makassar, Indonesia*

**Guntur Roryngosan Fara**
*Universitas Megarezky, Indonesia*

**Safaruddin Safaruddin**
*Universitas Megarezky, Indonesia*

**Ibtisamatul Aminah**
*National Research and Innovation Agency, Indonesia*

**Besse Yuliana**
*Universitas Megarezky, Indonesia*

## ABSTRACT

*The internal sustainable development strategy's purpose is to utilize language learning technologies such as AI tools to address the inequities in English Language Education (ELT). For instance, AI-enabled apps like learning algorithms, natural language processing, and speech recognition systems present customized learning assistance and promote the inclusion of learners with disabilities into the educational process. AI also means providing students with physical and learning disabilities*

DOI: 10.4018/979-8-3373-1837-0.ch007

*with assistive technologies. Even with these challenges like cultural issues, poor teacher education, and certain technologies, AI has produced impressive results in leveling the playing field of English language teaching across geography including rural and other disadvantaged populations. The chapter closes with suggestions which policymakers can use to improve English language learning.*

## INTRODUCTION

In the modern context, English language education is an essential component that joins different cultures and allows for transnational exchange. The ability to speak English fluently is a requirement in most places, especially for people from developing countries who require social elevation, commensurate pay, and the ability to sell their skills in the global market (Erling et al., 2014; Mustafawi et al., 2022).

English language education also has social, political, and economic dimensions, which are far more important than individual professional advancement and self-growth. English-speaking countries may be able to sustain their growth through a population able to interface with other markets and attract foreign investment. Chanting English in this era of globalization also opens up most opportunities, as opportunities concerning digital content lie at the fingertips (Kibar et al., 2023).

However, these constituencies are left behind in the quest for English language education as issues including class, geographical remoteness, and structural inequalities are clear impediments. This is the point where Goal 10 of the Sustainable Development Goals, “Reduced Inequalities”, comes into play. The target of SDG 10 is to include and strengthen the participation of every individual in every sector, regardless of their age, sex, livelihood, and creed, among other categories. Education, more so language education, particularly, fulfills this objective by breaking the marginalization and allowing equal opportunities (Erling et al., 2014). The strategic thrust in English education in developing nations is predicated on the idea that it can act as a potential and in some sense, an indispensable asset for participation within the global economic marketplace (Erling et al., 2014). However, critical issues regarding the globalization of English must be properly addressed.

There is an underlying sense that governments value the command of English. However, the question of ‘what are the implications of promoting education that is in a mother tongue’ becomes more perplexing. There are the less privileged people who are more desperate to have English to uplift the standard of their communities, but challenges abound in scaling up mother tongue education. As pointed out in the documents, the correlation of English language skills and development is neither direct nor easy, and several other issues, social, cultural, and political, also tend to counter this rationale concerning English as a language of concern (Abduh et al., 2022; Erling et al., 2014).

Language is the basis of society and is the most important feature of a nation's culture. It is, however, critically observed that language minorities or small minority language groups are always ignored or oppressed, irrespective of being the original inhabitants of the land, because the major powers always start to dominate them (Tanveer et al., 2020). As noted, language as a large pillar in society should be available to all layers of society, as a should, therefore It is necessary to establish why language is an important pillar of a society and why single-group language dominance is detrimental to cultural societies as a whole because verbal and written communication is fundamental to humanity (Tanveer et al., 2020).

According to a publication Bulathwela et al. (2021), there is a significant potential for AI technologies to be employed in educational technologies as they can deliver education at scale, customize the learning needs of students, and assist learners who are from different backgrounds. Language learning tools such as AI language apps enable students' self-paced learning as personalized languages, interactive lessons, and self-paced intelligent tutors that suit their unique levels and ways of learning can be provided (Wang et al., 2023).

In addition, cut-off geographical locations will no longer be a hindrance as AI-powered tools will remotely connect rural and underprivileged regions where getting proper English learning has been a challenge. AI can also support the development and sharing of educational resources, thus providing free English language learning resources and making learning basic skills easy and cheap (Bulathwela et al., 2021; X. Liu & Huang, 2022). It fits perfectly with the objectives of SDG 10, whose ultimate goal is to decrease inequalities and promote the mechanistic environment of inclusive education that AI has sought to achieve in English language education. Access to the English language will no longer be confined to social, economic or geographical features as educational institutions and national authorities will strategize around the advantages brought about by AI (Bulathwela et al., 2021; St-Hilaire et al., 2022; Wang et al., 2023).

That said, the successful implementation of AI in English education will not come easily and rather requires a holistic view. We shall also have to consider some unfavorable situations, such as AI systems making decisions in a biased manner or the exclusion of some cultures or learning potentials. There is a need for cooperation among teachers, technology developers, and lawmakers to come up with AI solutions that are universal, relevant, and suitable for marginalized learners (Akgun & Greenhow, 2022; Garcia Ramos & Wilson-Kennedy, 2024).

## THE ROLE OF AI IN ENGLISH LANGUAGE EDUCATION

Artificial Intelligence has opened doors to a multitude of ways in which the English Language may be taught. In this particular discipline, there are many ways in which AI technologies, such as speech recognition, chatbots, or adaptive learning platforms, have been incorporated to enhance the learning experience (Deng & Yu, 2022; Zhu, 2021). What is also true is that the technology advancements have made it possible for students to learn languages more efficiently. For instance, students may interact with other students or teachers even if they are thousands of miles away from the classroom and get the same quality of education (M. Liu, 2023). Because of those opportunities, students no longer have to attend face-to-face classes to learn English, and instead, chatbots can assist them as it boosts their self-esteem by allowing them to practice conversational English (Deng & Yu, 2022; Hou, 2021). Chatbots allow students to practice speaking English with help from a computer-aided program, which allows students to have broader exposure to the language because they will be practicing how to use conversational English. Moreover, AI-powered chatbots foster engagement by talking to students constantly, which allows students to practice English without feeling judged, making it easier for students to learn a new language (Deng & Yu, 2022; M. Liu, 2023).

Currently, AI technologies are making leaps, edging closer towards true AI assisting individuals. In this case, AI has the potential of further personalize education, enhancing students' experiences even more. The learner's strengths, weaknesses, and progress are evaluated through data-driven algorithms on these platforms, ensuring that the different lessons and exercises are suited to the learner's capabilities. For instance, a student who has problems in grammar can depend on extra practice and skills-targeted explanations, while one who is good with vocabulary can learn higher content with ease.

The application of AI in ELT can be said to be a change in access to the conventional way of teaching languages and adds new dimensions to language learning (M. Liu, 2023). The gap that AI has filled is automating administrative tasks, providing instant feedback, and tailoring the learning experience, which makes it all the more accommodating. However, there is a worry that not all teachers or professionals will have the right kind of training that will be relevant to the particular AI technologies and applications to make it effective in targeting a particular teaching context.

English Language Teaching is taking a new twist thanks to Artificial Intelligence that focuses on various learning requirements and goes a long way in making learners' experiences diverse and personalized (Deng & Yu, 2022). Disabled people or others who are not able to speak English can get more resources, and this is where AI has made a massive difference and is perhaps the most commendable achievement (Hou, 2021; Y. Liu & Ren, 2022). As an example, AI sensors embedded in text-to-speech and speech-to-text tools assist learners with sight or hearing impairments to engage with language content appropriately (M. Liu, 2023). In the same way, targeted social learning solutions like automatic captions or sign language interpretation increase participation by reducing barriers for further disabled individuals learning languages (M. Liu, 2023).

For speakers who are not fluent in the language, AI offers language assistance that enables better engagement. Language barriers can be crossed through translation devices and bilingual panels. Naturally, correcting an individual's feedback and errors makes them proficient (M. Liu, 2023). In addition, the artificial intelligence component in the English language education market will only grow due to the development of virtual and augmented reality, natural language processing, and other technologies, such training will be completely different in terms of immersion interactivity and will replicate real-life situations that have never been seen before in language learning (Hou, 2021; M. Liu, 2023; Zhu, 2021). Also, AI eliminates tedious work for teachers, such as estimating assignments, managing learners' activities, and constructing schedules. This enables educators to direct attention to the ideal and imaginative parts of teaching while enabling analytical skills and teamwork. Moreover, AI can aid educators by offering them insights, through data analysis, to help them assist students better and alter their pedagogical practices (Hou, 2021; M. Liu, 2023; Zhang & Aslan, 2021; Zhu, 2021).

Integration of AI and English teaching will certainly yield some advancement in the generation of highly intelligent teaching. Due to AI's continuous improvement, not only will its function in the teaching of the English language develop, but this will also include the incorporation of virtual reality, augmented reality, and natural language processing into pedagogical practices (Mello et al., 2023; Rashmi, 2023). It has also been said that these technologies will assist in providing effective and realistic learning environments and activities that will enhance the learning of language in new ways. With the application of AI, new methods to teach the language, especially English, would also be developed, helping in developing an interconnected and equal world (Hou, 2021; Mello et al., 2023; Mukhallafi, 2020; Zhu, 2021).

However, with the advent of AI, personalization takes the effort out of the learners' hands, which thus further reinforces the paradigm shift away from the education-centered practice of everyone needing to learn the same thing (Gligorea et al., 2023). AI systems able to learn can create a much more appropriate education by interpreting the learner's progress to determine their strengths and weaknesses and adapting content to set requirements accordingly (Maghsudi et al., 2021). With these, one will be able to evaluate real-time and historical data, enabling them to automatically generate lesson plans, tasks, or quizzes suitable for the appropriate context of the student. For example, a student who has a good understanding of reading comprehension and difficulty in listening skills will get attempts in the latter area, which ensures even growth in all areas of the language. Such an individual orientation not only meets the needs of learners with different paces and styles of language acquisition but also motivates them by introducing tasks that are neither easy nor difficult.

AI is also in a position to provide feedback by integrating various systems seamlessly. Feedback has been an area of concern as it is frequently delayed and generalized as opposed to AI, which provides direct assistance. AI-supported tools for pronunciation can detect even the slightest errors that a learner makes when speaking and direct how to correct them. Natural language processing in writing can also scrutinize grammatical errors, the style of the document, and the coherence and cohesion of ideas and structure, so that they can improve their writing skills. That quick feedback allows the students to be responsible for their development and improvement (Mello et al., 2023). The other advantage of AI is that it can enhance the effectiveness of multimodal learning. It follows that the students' different needs will be met: for example, interactive graphics, videos, and podcasts will be helpful for visual and audio learners, while for those who prefer active learning, gamification, mobile, and virtual-based learning modes will work.

AI makes learning possible for everyone because it utilizes multiple modalities, which makes it possible to even make the most uninspiring topics interesting (Gligorea et al., 2023; Kim et al., 2022; Mello et al., 2023). Thirdly, these technologies as AI, can streamline content creation for classes, student personalization, quality feedback, and even provide recognition and help to the instructors in evaluating students' performance. Educational paradigms have been changed by swift integrations of Natural Language Processing, Deep Learning, and Virtual and Augmented Reality into a lot of data educational content, and that has led to a paradigm shift in pedagogy (Mello et al., 2023). Children concentrating on learning more engaging tasks using naturally trained language would only be possible in the environment where AI-enabled technologies exist, and with the way perception-shaping theories and structures are augmenting reality very fast, our education is going to change fundamentally (Mello et al., 2023).

One of the greatest benefits of AI language learning is how easily and efficiently it can be scaled depending on the needs of the customer. These platforms, accessed on mobile devices and through low-bandwidth internet connectivity, enable language learning materials to be accessed by a large number of users without requiring a huge physical setup or a large teaching workforce. These AI-driven applications will bring in role-play scenarios befitting a classroom, including lessons, language practice, and guidance, such that students residing in villages or remote areas can be proficient in the language as their peers are in cities (M. Liu, 2023). Also, AI can help to eliminate the economic factors that have continued to limit the acquisition of good English in the past. In several underdeveloped areas, the lack of textbooks, payment of fees, and hiring tutors is out of reach for most English learners. But in my opinion, Artificial Intelligence will help remove some limitations. AI learning tools, for instance, language learning apps like Duolingo, etc, provide interactive and well-aligned lessons at little or no charge, removing barriers to various languages.

As well as dealing with deprivation, poverty, culture, tradition, and social factors that tend to exclude people from quality language learning and teaching. So AI has a tremendous opportunity to make an impact where it matters, empowering every learner to acquire strong English language skills, irrespective of where they are or how rich or poor they are. The case for the implementation of AI in language learning is rather strong; however, do not be carried away and ignore the numerous problems that lead to the implementation of an AI platform.

## ADDRESSING CHALLENGES AND BARRIERS IN AI-POWERED ENGLISH EDUCATION

### Technological Barriers

The advancement of some technologies, such as Artificial Intelligence, has the potential to transform the teaching and learning of the English language in ways never imagined before. However, the incorporation of such technologies poses challenges. Most notably, the enduring global digital divide refers to the lack of equality in access to the internet, devices, and technological infrastructure, especially for learners located in disadvantaged and distant locations (Rashmi, 2023; Rosmayanti et al., 2023). If the potential of AI to provide equality is to be realized, the barriers must be overcome through creative means and the collaboration of different parties.

In rural areas and other marginalized areas, these challenges emerge precisely from the limited connectivity to the Internet. For many remote regions, the availability of infrastructure opportunities for stable and fast Internet is missing, so that students can use AI that requires interaction in real-time, or use a large amount of data (Zastudil et al., 2023). Also, many low-income households cannot afford smartphones, tablets, and computers due to their high prices. It is also important to note the low level of digital skills, that is, in this area, students and even educators may not know how to use AI tools in practice (Zastudil et al., 2023).

Also, further aggravating the situation, rural schools lack resources and funding compared to urban ones. Remotely located educational institutions rarely have readily available AI tools, as they lack the necessary resources, infrastructure, or modern technology. Yet, even within urbanized areas, there is a disparity in the distribution of technology, marginalizing women, refugees, and disabled populations within those communities. Even in urbanized societies, there is still segregation. A dire need to eliminate these barriers from society's fabric exists to increase social equity.

Such applications are attractive, especially to those groups who have limited entry points, multiplying the use cases. The key barriers to any adoption of modern AI-based language education systems are high resource consumption and low return on investment. It is ideal in the sense that it increases equity and efficiency at the same time. Language education systems powered by AI can leverage the poorest regions by developing mobile-based applications.

With weak internet connectivity, AI-powered systems and relevant tools are only available to specific geographic regions. In such scenarios, AI does not bridge the linguistic divide; rather, it deepens the manipulation. Although certain education apps do break down barriers and facilitate access, reliance on the internet is still strong (Rosmayanti et al., 2022; St-Hilaire et al., 2022). Offline network is the further step that makes AI tools even more robust as it tackle infrastructural barriers to education as well.

These solutions, however, require governmental and institutional intervention for scaling. Integrated strategies for universal connectivity, including affordable internet, subsidized devices, and investment in technical infrastructure, can be great and level the playing field for AI education delivery. Such ambitions can be taken further through the engagement of all key stakeholders, including governments, non-profit organizations, and private technology companies, who would be providing funding, knowledge, and resources to disadvantaged regions (Bulathwela et al., 2021). For example, having facilities on the side of the government, HP could develop learning facilities, with AI, internet connectivity, and trained facilitators to assist learners.

This attendance not only conforms to SDG Target 10 but also speaks volumes of AI, its wider goal is to serve humanity by providing knowledge and opportunities to all. I mean, how can Artificial Intelligence aid the English language education of those people living in far-flung, mountainous villages knowing very well that providing access to specialized infrastructure and other resources towards such communities is a great orchestrate in itself, with the uninformed availability of mobile technology and offline features, programs and institutions in hand (Zastudil et al., 2023).

## Cultural and Linguistic Considerations

As the population of English language learners integrating Artificial Intelligence tools for assistance increases, there is an opportunity to expand the global use of the English language by executing such tools that are both contextual and linguistically appropriate (Helm et al., 2023; Sakkir et al., 2024). However, tools designed to aid in language learning must understand that such learning is deeply rooted in culture, and without applying a learner's cultural context during the design, the application risks displacing the users or underperforming educationally (Falbo & LaCroix, 2021; Wang et al., 2023). True equity in the English language in the multilingual world requires the adoption of AI systems that reflect the realities of plurality and multilingualism (Falbo & LaCroix, 2021; Helm et al., 2023; Wang et al., 2023). Thus, AI systems must strive to reflect plurality in English language usage due to the multicultural dynamics of English.

For any particular language, there are cultural norms that reduce the need to explain certain words as the user understands the context, which goes hand in hand with the examples that learners in a specific native-speaking locale are accustomed to. When an educational resource integrates the culture of students' society, such as the norms, values, and traditions of students, it further enhances the learning process. For example, an English learning app that employs virtual market engagements and local traditions to facilitate learning. On the other hand, if the resources used are entirely based on Western cultures, there is a likelihood that these resources to create gaps whereby learners will either feel alienated or lost (Falbo & LaCroix, 2021; Helm et al., 2023; Jia et al., 2022; Wang et al., 2023).

There are, however, numerous hurdles that accompany creating an AI system that will encompass racially and linguistically diverse speakers and users. Surveys in the area of AI language learning have underscored the need to mitigate the issues of teachers' preparation in the usage of language tools in education, privacy policies, and the pedagogical effects of increasing the number of electronic educational aids (Helm et al., 2023). In addition, challenges related to low comprehension of dialects, a majority of training models being Anglo-centric, and simple biasing limitations of AI mechanisms can significantly limit the use of these mechanisms for language teaching activities.

To overcome these problems, educational institutions should set the parameters and the AI deployment potential in the education process for foreign students, in particular, the envisaged effects and the expected risks of the technology in use. AI enables greater language learning access while personalizing instruction. However, the urge to provide solutions that accommodate the plethora of dialects and accents and convey the essence of the English language is a challenge that needs addressing (Wang et al., 2023). Simply put, they will not be able to capture the cultural context in which English is used across different regions. More importantly, it will disadvantage global learners who are trained by these models. Then again, how does one fully address this challenge?

Starting from the late 20th century, English became the predominant global language. With that being said, English is not uniform- it comes in different accents, vocabularies, and usages that are representative of a particular region's culture. But how do artificial systems, such as AI, mitigate the need to address those regional variations while providing quality education? By adapting their content, feedback, and interactions to reflect regional differences, AI makes it linguistically relevant (Wang et al., 2023). Essentially, without addressing these concerns, AI can never facilitate 'effective' and 'equitable' learning.

The AI learning model should also be developed in a way to prevent the 'universalization' of the English language, where it will only be representative of particular cultural groups. What's even more dangerous is if a learning model is developed without 'inclusive' and 'representative' training data sets, the AI is bound to harbor prejudice that is detrimental on a sociolinguistic level. As a rule of thumb, the only way to resolve those issues of linguistic and cultural insensitivity is through the collaboration of linguists, educators, and AI developers (Helm et al., 2023).

The development of AI-based tools that provide effective and equitable education in the English language across the globe can be achieved by combining local communities and open-source initiatives (Falbo & LaCroix, 2021; Helm et al., 2023). Such a goal is vital for Sustainable Development Goal 10, which targets the inequalities in learning, facilitating a more inclusive global learning space (Helm et al., 2023). With the use of AI tools that promote inclusivity, it's possible to dissolve cultural and language barriers while making the students share a sense of belonging.

## Teacher Training and Professional Development

AI has been shown to revolutionize English language education. However, the integration phase remains a challenge, perhaps due to the teachers being unwilling to embrace the technology (Tan & Subramonyam, 2024). Equipping teachers with the right training packages and development packages is important for the teachers to respond to AI, as that will result in improved teaching and learning experiences (Kizilcec, 2024; Zhang & Aslan, 2021). In other words, AI can easily take up administrative work, customization of learning, and giving feedback while still underpinning conventional methods. Nonetheless, the proceeds can only be realized if the teachers are coached adequately toward appreciating the AI tools (Tan & Subramonyam, 2024). There is sufficient evidence that educators require effective retraining programs that emphasize the technicalities and pedagogical integration of AI, especially on tool features and purpose, its operation, and how to integrate tool features into the curriculum, goals, objectives, and outcomes (Tan & Subramonyam, 2024). For instance, they should be able to use accelerated learning systems to monitor each learner's performance or use AI chatbots for speaking practice in the English language.

Such training also aids the educationists to appreciate the dangers of technology and therefore use it appropriately with their pedagogic knowledge and experience. It has to be recognized that while AI can facilitate and enhance a subject that is essentially very mechanical, it is repetition-centric and driven by factual content;

the human aspect of teaching, which is nurturing and fostering growth and asking particular questions, can never be delegated. By integrating artificial intelligence where it is needed, humans are learning to make the most of both worlds (Gunawan et al., 2021; Ng et al., 2023; Rashmi, 2023).

Even with its promising adoption, the integration of AI into the educational systems faces backlash from the teaching practitioners especially those whose teaching practices are more classical. The hesitance might be due to the fear of machine takeover, concerns about using new machines, or lack of knowledge on how AI may be utilized more creatively within their roles. (Gunawan et al., 2021; Ng et al., 2023; Rashmi, 2023). Our educators can overcome these obstacles by providing enough training and assistance, and can utilize AI in language education to its fullest potential, as they are supposed to.

The use of AI systems in the teaching and learning process of English is becoming a growing concern for many educators as the pace at which technology develops continues to grow. This particular aspect can be addressed through workshops, seminars, and even online courses, as they display the advantages of AI tools and change the perception of many teachers (Zhu, 2021). Practical examples of AI's utility in the classroom will also serve to extinguish fears and misconceptions. They indirectly show the restraints of hosting such programs and how time can be saved while using AI tools to grade papers and focus more on planning lessons and tutoring students. In addition, practical ones are equally important in helping trainers gain confidence and have a feel for the training.

To help make active use of AI-aided technologies, teachers require a more flexible atmosphere where they can engage in practical situations (Tan & Subramonyam, 2024). Moreover, there could be other forms of empowerment that can help assimilate AI for the less visioned educators, for instance, mentorship programs. The institutions further have a role to play in helping to promote these transfers of training and professional development activities.

Schools, universities, and even government institutions need to start rolling out such programs, availing the essential resources, and ensuring there is an environment of enhancement. In addition, collaboration with the technological providers will also assist in ensuring that training programs are developed according to the needs of the educators and what intelligent tools are in place. In the end, talking about the role of integrating AI into practices is not only about some technical administrative tasks but rather changing the way teachers view their position in a smart learning environment. With adequate training and resources, teachers could be able to effectively use AI to enhance English language education, improve equity, and prepare learners for the realities of tomorrow.

## CASE STUDIES OF AI-POWERED INCLUSIVITY IN ENGLISH LANGUAGE LEARNING

### Case Study 1: AI for Learners With Disabilities

With a few clicks of a button, Artificial Intelligence has proven to have extremely powerful capabilities for providing a chance to deliver more inclusive educational initiatives for those who face specific needs (Xu et al., 2024). The use of AI in education ensures that students with special educational needs can access the learning experience as per their needs and requirements, helping them reach English language level skills on par with their peers.

AI-powered technologies like screen readers and text-to-speech programs have transformed access to educational content for visually impaired learners. Visually impaired students can use tools like NVDA and JAWS to independently navigate digital platforms and access materials for learning the English language (Shetty et al., 2024; Zhu, 2021). Applications such as Microsoft Seeing AI even leverage computer vision to describe visual content (such as images and figures), allowing learners to interact with multimedia resources that would have been otherwise difficult for them to access.

Similarly, auditory disabilities pose a different set of issues AI is well-positioned to solve. Speech-to-text apps, like Otter. AI and Google Live Transcribe enable real-time written transcription of spoken language that allows hearing-impaired students to capture lectures and classroom discussions (Kim et al., 2022). AI-based captioning systems, similar to those built into video platforms such as YouTube or Zoom, allow for the accessibility of multimedia content, which helps facilitate the learning process of hearing-impaired students via videos, webinars, and online resources as well (Wang et al., 2023).

Powered by this technology, these tools and applications play a significant role in overcoming barriers to ensure that everyone has an even professional opportunity to embrace the English language. AI creates a revolution in education, bringing accessibility and enabling students with different needs to generate their language learning (Kim et al., 2022). However, it is important to highlight the limitations of AI, including challenges with accents and dialects, and the need for consideration regarding the use and scope of AI in education to be equitable and beneficial for all (Wang et al., 2023).

The impact of technologies is much broader than simply improving accessibility to learners with disabilities. These developments could lead to improved self-confidence and self-efficacy for learners, which can contribute to advancing equity and inclusion within English language learning contexts. AI-powered tools have the power to transform learning experiences for people with varied abilities by providing equal access to educational resources and opportunities.

An example, students who cannot see can complete assignments without assistance when using text-to-speech software; similarly, a hearing-impaired student can still take part in a group discussion with the assistance of real-time transcription services (Kim et al., 2022). These tools enhance academic performance while fostering social cohesion and personal development among diverse learners, effectively dismantling the barriers that have perpetuated the exclusion of students with disabilities from mainstream education.

But universal inclusivity, at scale, cannot be solved simply by a tech patch. It requires a collective responsibility from educators, technology developers, and policymakers to make sure these tools are accessible, affordable, and integrated into educational systems. Ensure schools and institutions invest in enabling and supporting teachers to utilize such technologies, and that students are given the necessary tools to ensure they are deriving the most benefit from AI-led solutions.

AI is transcending limitations and enhancing equal opportunities, reshaping the future of English language education as we know it for learners with disabilities. These tools are crucial in helping open the gates of education to every student, those with and without disabilities, which directly addresses SDG10, to provide inclusive services and amenities, creating a diverse environment for students to thrive in our interconnected world (Bulathwela et al., 2021).

## Case Study 2: AI in Underserved and Rural Areas

Access to quality English language education has been limited in many parts of the world, particularly in underserved and rural communities, due to a lack of qualified educators, resources, and infrastructure (Helm et al., 2023). But, with the advent of Artificial Intelligence technologies, this gap is slowly being filled with innovative, scalable, and cost-effective solutions to supply language learning opportunities in these areas (St-Hilaire et al., 2022).

AI-driven language learning solutions, like Duolingo and Lingokids, are now used also in rural communities where traditional education facilities are limited. These platforms provide gamified and interactive English lessons personalized based on each student making learning more easily accessible and engaging. AI-enabled solutions can replace or complement classroom training in regions with little or no access to trained teachers, letting learners move at their own pace and receive feedback tailored to their proficiency levels (Bulathwela et al., 2021).

Another example of the impact of AIs is the creation of mobile learning apps targeted to low-resource settings. Mobile apps such as Babbel and Hello English have low bandwidth and can work on low-specification smartphones, which is a workable model for communities with limited Internet access or with old smartphones. Some of the apps even offer offline functionality, allowing learners to download lessons and continue to practice when they might not have internet access — something that is especially useful in regions where reliable internet is still a work in progress (St-Hilaire et al., 2022).

Virtual mentorship and tutoring programs have also been made possible by AI technologies in rural areas. AI chatbots and real-time conversation tools such as Talkbot and Cambly simulate contact with native English speakers, offering learners opportunities to practice their communication skills (Helm et al., 2023; Kim et al., 2022; Mukhallafi, 2020).

The Marmite effect of tech (i.e what one finds essential others will argue is the cause of other ills) is well-established in the realm of language education, with the successful adoption and integration of AI-driven language education solutions in underserved and rural areas illustrating both its great potential and inherent difficulties. Additionally, there are privacy concerns, a need for additional empirical evidence on the effectiveness of these tools to enhance pedagogy, and the fact that K12 teachers must be better prepared to use them and incorporate them into their instruction. With all of the advancements in this area, it is important now more than ever to consider how innovations in AI will help language learners without sacrificing learner privacy or the necessary support systems students and educators alike will need as learning progresses and methods evolve.

Artificial intelligence has been one area in which advancements have been made. AI-powered tools have significantly impacted the education sector. Consequently, the education sector in rural communities, which have always struggled to access quality resources, has been more accessible. The most noticeable progress is in the English language sector, which has benefitted immensely from AI-driven programs. AI-powered content in this discipline has come with numerous advantages to young learners across unique communities. Ai has made it possible to accommodate many students due to its easy access to quality resources without necessarily using physical infrastructure. Additionally, students can access their preferred English lessons, which have no time boundaries. The AI has equally empowered students with self-initiative and self-dependence. Most parents have reported that their children have become more independent in choosing their learning schedules. Consequently, the mission and vision of a child become more self-oriented, making the child the target of success. Nonetheless, AI usage in English education among young rural people has also met some significant challenges. For example, underserved rural people have continued to experience a digital gap, especially because they cannot afford either devices or the internet. Thus, there is a need to factor in the affordability of devices and the cost of internet data in the running of all programs of AI usage.

## Case Study 3: AI for Non-Native English Speakers

For many non-native learners of English, especially in parts of the world where access to materials and exposure to English speakers is very limited, acquiring the modern language is fraught with challenges. But the real game changer here is how Artificial Intelligence is changing the game for English lessons forever, with new solutions that follow and adapt to the individual needs of students worldwide (Almutairi et al., 2020; Woo & Choi, 2021). Leading this transformational change is the explosion of AI-driven platforms like Duolingo, Elsa Speak, and Memorize that utilize speech recognition, personalized feedback, and even gamified lessons to engage learners so they can improve their knowledge of pronunciation, vocabulary, and grammar. (Hou, 2021). Similarly, Elsa Speak utilizes AI-powered speech recognition to detect pronunciation errors according to the native language of the learner and provides tailored exercises to optimize fluency, which can be especially beneficial in countries where conventional classroom teaching might not fully accommodate the phonetic challenges confronted by non-native speakers (Xianhua, 2019).

Another prominent AI tool is Google Translate, which has become an essential way for speakers of native languages worldwide to communicate in English and vice versa; the tool supports over 100 languages, including many indigenous and regional tongues. For learners in Asia, Africa, or Latin America, where multilingualism is prevalent, Google Translate is a vital resource that allows users to understand complex English texts or create sentences correctly.

Although these AI-enhanced tools cannot replace a full language course due to their shallow coverage, they help beginners of the infinite English learning process, especially in places where proper learning resources are scarce (Helm et al., 2023). Enabling Better English — AI's Journey across the Globe For example, in China, AI has been utilized to incorporate AI into national English language learning, whereas Squirrel AI focuses on adaptive learning platforms that target the specific needs of their students.

AI-powered platforms are transforming the study of English language education across the developing world by shifting paradigms and creating communities of learners. In Africa, applications such as Eneza Education have harnessed AI to reach students in remote locations without reliable internet connections by offering engaging lessons and assessments via SMS (Zastudil et al., 2023). In Latin America, the Colombian government has also collaborated with the British Council and Microsoft to introduce AI-powered virtual tutors that imitate real-life conversations, allowing students to practice speaking English in a friendly environment (Boateng, 2024). Advancements such as these showcase how AI can help build fair educational opportunities and lead to equitable solutions for some global education challenges.

However, others are censured because some AI tools are designed primarily with global or Western audiences in mind, resulting in cultural and linguistic mismatches. Bridging these gaps will require close cooperation between developers, linguists, and educators to ensure AI tools are both culturally sensitive and linguistically inclusive. AI-Powered Access to Language Learning Resources AI-powered content learning platforms cater to narrowing the gap on language differences.

## THE FUTURE OF AI IN PROMOTING INCLUSIVITY AND EQUAL ACCESS TO ENGLISH EDUCATION

### Technological Advancements

Openness to Opportunities for Inclusion of Artificial Intelligence in English Language Education (Knox et al., 2019). With the development of AI technologies, more and more advanced tools and methodologies in the domain of language education will arise meeting different learners' needs and filling existent gaps in accessibility (Bulathwela et al., 2021; Knox et al., 2019).

Perhaps the most prominent area of development is the improvement of personalized learning algorithms. It is expected that future AI systems will utilize cutting-edge data analytics and machine learning methods to create personalized learning experiences. These algorithms might then process vast amounts of data about a learner, including cognitive, emotional, and language profile information, to create personalized learning paths. When one student learns best via visual aids, an AI platform could use not just text or video, but advanced multimedia content better suited for that student, while potentially using a more text-heavy approach for a student who prefers to read. This hyper-personalization will guarantee that students with different backgrounds, abilities, and preferences can participate in English language education with sufficient efficiency (Kim et al., 2022).

Another was the addition of more advanced AI tutors. Advancements in natural language processing could enable AI tutors of the future to get the context and intent better, leading to nuanced and meaningful conversations with learners. For example, such systems could simulate different types of communication contexts, including workplace meetings or informal chit-chat, to potentially give students practice with realistic social scenarios (Kim et al., 2022).

Artificial intelligence technology is leading to unprecedented opportunities in the field of English language education in terms of communication gaps and deployable education processes around the world (Y. Liu & Ren, 2022; Zhou, 2020; Zhu, 2021). Neural network-based translation systems driven by AI, augmented with analysis of cultural context, are well-positioned to facilitate near-seamless, culturally-appropriate communications between native and non-native English speakers (M. Liu, 2023). These innovations can give multilingual learners in underserved regions a chance to gain access to many programs in English while still holding on to their native languages.

AI-driven immersive technologies like virtual and augmented reality can also offer tremendous potential to revolutionize the English language classroom. These tools can create real-life environments where words can be spun and practiced in true-to-life situations including roles within a virtual marketplace and a workplace environment, enabling learners to not only improve their fluency in front of the text but also gain confidence in using English in real-life scenarios (M. Liu, 2023). Although this development represents a watershed moment for the future of English language education worldwide, we must also consider the inequalities in access to these resources. High costs, infrastructural commitments, and digital literacy disparities may limit their reach in underserved areas. So, it is time when developers and policymakers need to address these types of issues and we need affordable, low-resource, general AI trained in diverse contexts. Such advances will be derived from governments, tech companies, and educational institutions working collaboratively to democratize access to these disruptive technologies, allowing learners of diverse backgrounds to enjoy the transformative benefits of the revolutionary impact on language learning and accessibility.

## Collaborations and Partnerships

The collaboration and partnership of major stakeholders are essential for the strategic initiative that will capitalize on the potential of using Artificial Intelligence (AI) to fundamentally (and positively) change the English language education space (Y. Liu & Ren, 2022). The roles of these stakeholders hence complement each other and intersect in translating the use of AI tools into democratized and inclusive access that creates sustainable solutions for educational disadvantage for a diverse range of learners (Bulathwela et al., 2021).

It is governments that can lay the groundwork for equitable AI incorporation in education. They do so by defining policies, endorsing funding for initiatives, and creating infrastructure that enables AI technologies to be accessible to underserved communities and rural (Bulathwela et al., 2021). Governments can encourage public-private partnerships to subsidize the cost of AI-powered educational tools, making them accessible to schools and learners in low-income areas. Furthermore, national policies could require AI tools to be integrated into public education systems, but only if they respect the surrounding culture and linguistic context. Finally, governments need to lead the direction in promoting digital literacy among teachers and students, ensuring that the right training and resources are allotted to maximize the positive impact of AI in the classroom (Tan & Subramonyam, 2024).

Technology firms, in turn, fuel innovation with AI tools that meet these varied learning requirements. Working with educational institutions ensures that these tools are practical, relevant, and correlated to the curriculum. Additionally, tech companies could implement Corporate Social Responsibility programs that provide free or discounted access to their tools in underrepresented areas. Share on Pinterest Open-source projects in which companies share their AI models and datasets can help democratize access to these technologies.

Part 1 of 2: Educational institutions play a vital role in closing the gap between AI innovation and AI in the classroom. Through close collaboration with tech companies, they can help them fine-tune the usability and efficacy of AI tools, making sure they cater to the distinct needs of learners and educators. Teaching them to use AI technologies will provide even more ways to prevent problems in hospitals and learning through teachers in the future, which can also be an important way of making its usage within classrooms even more effective (Tan & Subramonyam, 2024).

These key stakeholders, comprising schools, universities , and training teachers, are important actors in the successful deployment of AI (Bulathwela et al., 2021). They act as experimental platforms for new technologies, giving developers good insights into what works in practice and what doesn't (Bulathwela et al., 2021). As the primary users of AI, teachers must be trained on how to appropriately use AI in their teaching practice. In partnership with tech firms, institutions could host workshops, certifications, and professional development programs to ensure teachers are well-versed in using AI tools. Lastly, in terms of research and development angle, universities can explore new ways to apply AI in language education while ensuring concerns like bias, data privacy, and cultural sensitivity are covered.

Erfolg leads to multi-stakeholder partnerships, bringing together the resources, expertise, and influence needed to get things done. For example, UNESCO's partnership with governments and tech firms is centered on bringing AI tools to scale in pursuit of inclusive education around the world. Likewise, the Microsoft AI for Accessibility program, which partners with educational institutions to implement and address sensory barriers that restrict learners with disabilities, seeks to close the gap for the vulnerable group.

There are challenges still, especially in bringing diverse stakeholders into alignment on shared objectives. Governments would prioritize universal access, tech companies' profitability, and educational institutions' pedagogical effectiveness. These challenges can be surmounted through effective communication, transparency, and shared goals. Tools like Memorandum of Understanding and public-private partnerships can formalize roles and responsibilities among stakeholders, ensuring accountability and sustainability.

## Sustainability and Long-Term Impact

Artificial Intelligence Usage in English Language Education for Long-term Social and Economic Equality implementation in the field of English language education has great potential for social-economic equality in the long run, as suggested by previous work (Bulathwela et al., 2021). AI in education can bridge global inequalities by removing barriers to access, enhancing learning outcomes, and providing individuals with tools to succeed in their respective situations. (Bulathwela et al., 2021) Yet to achieve an equitable and sustainable impact, integration and policy alignment, early adaptive implementation, purposeful scale, and long-term commitment to equity are essential.

An AI English teacher that democratizes education for social and economic equality, English proficiency becomes the opening door to the world for people to obtain a higher education, a well-paid job, and worldwide communication (Bulathwela et al., 2021). AI tools, which can provide affordable and scalable language resources, bring a connection, especially to marginalized communities, where finding quality education for high-level language skills can prove difficult. For example, adaptive learning platforms, mobile apps, and AI tutors enable rural learners to have the same level of instruction as those in urban settings (Bulathwela et al., 2021). By making English education more accessible, people from different socio-economic backgrounds gain access to English proficiency, paving the way for upward mobility.

Economically, AI-powered education systems can equip people to join the international workforce. English proficiency, often the lingua franca of global business and technology, expands workers' access to a wider range of job opportunities. Finally, with the inclusion of AI tools in vocational training programs, learners are equipped with both linguistic and technical proficiency, increasing their employability in fields requiring bilingual or multilingual professionals. These upturns present tremendous second-order impacts on a larger scale; progress made on an individual level translates to lower income inequality throughout nations and globally.

Insisting that the game-changing potential of AI-infused English learning is sustainable will demand a holistic response. This must be done carefully while keeping in consideration potential bias and ensuring the technology is available for all. In addition, policy alignment is critical as policymakers can help create a regulatory environment to incentivize the development and deployment of AI-based educational tools in under-resourced communities. Finally, inherent in this approach should be a strong focus on equity, making sure AI-enhanced education is accessible to all, not further intensifying existing inequities in education.

Policy recommendations to effectively include AI in Sustainable Development Goal 10 First, governments should invest in some form of inclusion when building infrastructure. This includes expanding internet access and providing affordable digital devices to underserved regions (Tanveer et al., 2020). Without such basic support, the advantages of AI-powered education will remain inaccessible for many. Policies promoting digital equity must go further by designating resources specifically for marginalized populations, for example, through scholarships for low-income students to access AI-driven learning platforms or subsidies to help schools take advantage of advanced educational technologies (Tanveer et al., 2020).

Second, ethical concerns need to be integrated into the design and implementation of AI tools. Policymakers must implement regulations to avoid biases in AI systems that disadvantage learners from particular linguistic or cultural backgrounds. This includes requiring transparency in AI algorithms and ensuring diverse representation in training datasets. When teaching new AI technologies while respecting data privacy laws, learners' personal information should remain personal, maximally building trust, which will deliver a broad uptake of technology (Tanveer et al., 2020).

Third, partnerships between governments, educational institutions, and technology companies are needed to ensure that AI initiatives reflect local requirements. Imagine, for example, co-developing AI tools that assist multilingual learners by integrating regional languages along with English. Research into new AI applications, like tools for learners with disabilities or programs designed to help non-native speakers, could be funded through public-private partnerships (Tanveer et al., 2020).

Lastly, sustainability in the long run necessitates ongoing professional development for educators. Such policies should incentivize teacher training programs designed to effectively integrate AI in classrooms. By empowering teachers to leverage AI, these programs help to make sure the technology augments and does not replace human teaching (Tanveer et al., 2020).

## CONCLUSION

Other emerging AI solutions are helping to address decade-old issues around access and inclusivity in English language education. Through the use of AI tools ranging from adaptive learning platforms and speech recognition systems to chatbots, education will be more personalized, equitable, and effective. The ability of AI to meet the needs of individual learners, such as students with disabilities, everyone with different levels of fluency in language, and children enrolled in schools in rural and underserved communities, exemplifies the power that AI will have to democratize learning. By judicious use of these technologies, physical, economic, and resource barriers can be significantly reduced, creating an environment of learning that is more accessible to the intents of Sustainable Development Goal (SDG) 10.

Scalability, adaptability, and fostering equity are three key areas in which AI has the potential to transform English language education. AI can represent a potential uniting force, providing access to resources for individuals who may otherwise lack them. Moreover, the ability of AI to incorporate local languages and cultural nuances also adds to its relevance and effectiveness, allowing learners to be supported according to their contexts. Not only do these developments equip people with the language skills essential for success in a globalized society, but they also help to combat wider disparities in social and economic status.

Nevertheless, for AI to reach its full potential in education, it demands a joint dedication to collaboration, accessibility, and ethical conduct. Everyone from governments to technology companies and educational institutions to communities must help build an ecosystem that facilitates equitable AI use. The impact of such investments in infrastructure, teacher training, and culturally relevant AI tools will be felt across generations, keeping no learner behind. Moreover, ethical aspects like data privacy, transparency in AI algorithms, and unbiased material are crucial in informing the design and application of these systems to foster trust and optimize the overall impact.

In conclusion, the future of AI in English language education is likely to be both feasible and challenging. Continuous Fine-tuning of the AI technologies in case of reforms driven with the collaboration of the stakeholders can create value towards SDG 10. By harnessing the transformative potential of AI, while working to overcome its limitations, the world of education can create a future where language learning opportunities are available for all, no matter their socioeconomic background or where they live.

## REFERENCES


Abduh, A., Jayadi, K., Anshari, A., Basri, M., & Arham, M. (2022). Self-efficacy in speaking based activities for art and design students. *International Journal of Language Education*, *6*(1), 91–100. DOI: 10.26858/ijole.v6i1.32384

Akgun, S., & Greenhow, C. (2022). Artificial intelligence in education: Addressing ethical challenges in K-12 settings. *AI and Ethics*, *2*(3), 431–440. DOI: 10.1007/s43681-021-00096-7

Almutairi, A. F., Gegov, A., Adda, M., & Arabikhan, F. (2020). Conceptual artificial intelligence framework to improving English as second language. *WSEAS Transactions on Advances in Engineering Education*, *17*, 87–91. DOI: 10.37394/232010.2020.17.11

Bulathwela, S., Pérez-Ortiz, M., Holloway, C., & Shawe-Taylor, J. (2021). Could AI democratise education? Socio-technical imaginaries of an edtech revolution. *ArXiv Preprint ArXiv:2112.02034*.

Deng, X., & Yu, Z. (2022). A systematic review of machine-translation-assisted language learning for sustainable education. *Sustainability (Basel)*, *14*(13), 7598. DOI: 10.3390/su14137598

Erling, E. J., Seargeant, P., & Solly, M. (2014). English in rural Bangladesh: How is language education perceived as a resource for development in rural communities? *English Today*, *30*(4), 15–21. DOI: 10.1017/S0266078414000352

Falbo, A., & LaCroix, T. (2021). Est-ce que vous compute? Code-switching, cultural identity, and AI. *ArXiv Preprint ArXiv:2112.08256*.

Garcia Ramos, J., & Wilson-Kennedy, Z. (2024). Promoting equity and addressing concerns in teaching and learning with artificial intelligence. *Frontiers in Education*, *9*, 1487882. DOI: 10.3389/feduc.2024.1487882

Gligorea, I., Cioca, M., Oancea, R., Gorski, A.-T., Gorski, H., & Tudorache, P. (2023). Adaptive learning using artificial intelligence in e-learning: A literature review. *Education Sciences*, *13*(12), 1216. DOI: 10.3390/educsci13121216

Gunawan, K. D. H., Kaniawati, I., & Setiawan, W. (2021). The responses to artificial intelligence in teacher integrated science learning training program. *Journal of Physics: Conference Series*, *2098*(1), 12034. DOI: 10.1088/1742-6596/2098/1/012034

Helm, P., Bella, G., Koch, G., & Giunchiglia, F. (2023). Diversity and language technology: how techno-linguistic bias can cause epistemic injustice. *ArXiv Preprint ArXiv:2307.13714*.

Hou, Z. (2021). Research on adopting artificial intelligence technology to improve effectiveness of vocational college English learning. *Journal of Physics: Conference Series, 1744*(4), 42122. DOI: 10.1088/1742-6596/1744/4/042122

Jia, F., Sun, D., Ma, Q., & Looi, C.-K. (2022). Developing an AI-based learning system for L2 learners' authentic and ubiquitous learning in English language. *Sustainability (Basel), 14*(23), 15527. DOI: 10.3390/su142315527

Kibar, A. H., Ampa, A. T., & Nappu, S. (2023). A Study on EFL Teacher Strategies in Utilizing ICT for Regional Public Highschool of Indonesia. *Tamaddun, 22*(1), 1–10. DOI: 10.33096/tamaddun.v22i1.205

Kim, J., Lee, H., & Cho, Y. H. (2022). Learning design to support student-AI collaboration: Perspectives of leading teachers for AI in education. *Education and Information Technologies, 27*(5), 6069–6104. DOI: 10.1007/s10639-021-10831-6

Kizilcec, R. F. (2024). To advance AI use in education, focus on understanding educators. *International Journal of Artificial Intelligence in Education, 34*(1), 12–19. DOI: 10.1007/s40593-023-00351-4

Knox, J., Wang, Y., & Gallagher, M. (2019). *Artificial intelligence and inclusive education*. Springer. DOI: 10.1007/978-981-13-8161-4

Liu, M. (2023). Exploring the application of artificial intelligence in foreign language teaching: Challenges and future development. *SHS Web of Conferences, 168*, 3025.

Liu, X., & Huang, X. (2022). [Retracted] Design of Artificial Intelligence-Based English Network Teaching (AI-ENT) System. *Mathematical Problems in Engineering, 2022*(1), 1849430.

Liu, Y., & Ren, L. (2022). The influence of artificial intelligence technology on teaching under the threshold of "Internet+": Based on the application example of an English education platform. *Wireless Communications and Mobile Computing, 2022*(1), 5728569. DOI: 10.1155/2022/5728569

Maghsudi, S., Lan, A., Xu, J., & van Der Schaar, M. (2021). Personalized education in the artificial intelligence era: What to expect next. *IEEE Signal Processing Magazine, 38*(3), 37–50. DOI: 10.1109/MSP.2021.3055032

Mello, R. F., Freitas, E., Pereira, F. D., Cabral, L., Tedesco, P., & Ramalho, G. (2023). Education in the age of Generative AI: Context and Recent Developments. *ArXiv Preprint ArXiv:2309.12332*.

Mukhallafi, T. R. A. (2020). Using artificial intelligence for developing English language teaching/learning: An analytical study from university students' perspective. *International Journal of English Linguistics*, *10*(6), 40. DOI: 10.5539/ijel.v10n6p40

Mustafawi, E., Shaaban, K., Khwaileh, T., & Ata, K. (2022). Perceptions and attitudes of Qatar University students regarding the utility of arabic and english in communication and education in Qatar. *Language Policy*, *21*(1), 75–119. DOI: 10.1007/s10993-021-09590-4

Ng, D. T. K., Leung, J. K. L., Su, J., Ng, R. C. W., & Chu, S. K. W. (2023). Teachers' AI digital competencies and twenty-first century skills in the post-pandemic world. *Educational Technology Research and Development*, *71*(1), 137–161. DOI: 10.1007/s11423-023-10203-6

Rashmi, D. (2023). Unlocking the Potential of AI in Education: Challenges and Opportunities. *International Journal for Multidisciplinary Research*, *5*(4), 1–11.

Rosmayanti, V., Noni, N., & Patak, A. A. (2022). Students' acceptance of technology use in learning English pharmacy. *International Journal of Language Education*, *6*(3), 314–331. DOI: 10.26858/ijole.v6i3.24144

Rosmayanti, V., Patak, A. A., & Noni, N. (2023). Integrating technology into ESP instruction: Teaching English for pharmacy students. *The Journal of AsiaTEFL*, *20*(2), 475–484. DOI: 10.18823/asiatefl.2023.20.2.18.475

Sakkir, G., Al Amir, F., Atmowardoyo, H., Weda, S., & Rosmayanti, V. (2024). An analysis of translanguaging practices in an Indonesian EFL classroom : Teacher perception Geminastiti. *Xlinguae*, *17*(2), 3–15. DOI: 10.18355/XL.2024.17.02.01

Shetty, S., Gali, S., Augustine, D., & Sv, S. (2024). Artificial intelligence systems in dental shade-matching: A systematic review. *Journal of Prosthodontics*, *33*(6), 519–532. DOI: 10.1111/jopr.13805

St-Hilaire, F., Do Vu, D., Frau, A., Burns, N., Faraji, F., Potochny, J., Robert, S., Roussel, A., Zheng, S., & Glazier, T. (2022). A new era: Intelligent tutoring systems will transform online learning for millions. *ArXiv Preprint ArXiv:2203.03724*.

Tan, M., & Subramonyam, H. (2024). More than model documentation: uncovering teachers' bespoke information needs for informed classroom integration of ChatGPT. *Proceedings of the CHI Conference on Human Factors in Computing Systems*, 1–19. DOI: 10.1145/3613904.3642592

Tanveer, M., Hassan, S., & Bhaumik, A. (2020). Academic policy regarding sustainability and artificial intelligence (AI). *Sustainability (Basel)*, *12*(22), 9435. DOI: 10.3390/su12229435

Wang, T., Lund, B. D., Marengo, A., Pagano, A., Mannuru, N. R., Teel, Z. A., & Pange, J. (2023). Exploring the potential impact of artificial intelligence (AI) on international students in higher education: Generative AI, chatbots, analytics, and international student success. *Applied Sciences (Basel, Switzerland)*, *13*(11), 6716. DOI: 10.3390/app13116716

Woo, J. H., & Choi, H. (2021). Systematic review for AI-based language learning tools. *ArXiv Preprint ArXiv:2111.04455*.

Xianhua, L. (2019). Research on the effect of artificial intelligence technology on English learning efficiency. *2019 12th International Conference on Intelligent Computation Technology and Automation (ICICTA)*, 548–551.

Xu, X., Wang, X., Zhang, Y., & Zheng, R. (2024). Applying ChatGPT to tackle the side effects of personal learning environments from learner and learning perspective: An interview of experts in higher education. *PLoS One*, *19*(1), e0295646. DOI: 10.1371/journal.pone.0295646

Zastudil, C., Rogalska, M., Kapp, C., Vaughn, J., & MacNeil, S. (2023). Generative ai in computing education: Perspectives of students and instructors. *2023 IEEE Frontiers in Education Conference (FIE)*, 1–9.

Zhang, K., & Aslan, A. B. (2021). AI technologies for education: Recent research & future directions. *Computers and Education: Artificial Intelligence*, *2*, 100025. DOI: 10.1016/j.caeai.2021.100025

Zhou, W. (2020). Sociocultural theory and its implications in college English teaching and learning in the age of artificial intelligence. *Journal of Physics: Conference Series*, *1646*(1), 12142. DOI: 10.1088/1742-6596/1646/1/012142

Zhu, Y. (2021). Research on English teaching of professional skilled talents training based on artificial intelligence. *Journal of Intelligent & Fuzzy Systems, Preprint*, 1–12.

# Chapter 8
# AI-Driven Healthcare:
## Achieving Sustainable Development Goal 3 Through Smart Technologies

**Binnur Akıf**
https://orcid.org/0000-0001-8708-702X
*Istanbul Gelisim University, Turkey*

**Sinem Büyüksaatçı-Kiriş**
https://orcid.org/0009-0003-4408-8980
*Istanbul University-Cerrahpasa, Turkey*

## ABSTRACT

*AI-driven smart technologies and applications have the potential to transform the healthcare sector and serve as a crucial tool in advancing the third goal of the Sustainable Development Goals, "Good Health and Well-Being." This study provides a comprehensive analysis of various AI-driven technologies that facilitate broader access to healthcare services, enable the development of personalized treatment approaches, enhance early disease detection, promote more efficient and sustainable healthcare delivery, and contribute to the reduction of health disparities. Specifically, the study explores the integration of key technological areas including telemedicine, the Internet of Things (IoT), digital twins, bioinformatics, and machine learning, highlighting their individual and collective impacts on health outcomes and healthcare systems. The study further identifies and critically discusses technological, regulatory, and ethical barriers that may hinder the effective adoption of these advanced solutions.*

DOI: 10.4018/979-8-3373-1837-0.ch008

## INTRODUCTION

The United Nations' Sustainable Development Goals (SDGs) constitute a comprehensive framework of 17 primary objectives and 169 associated targets, endorsed by the UN General Assembly in 2015, with the ambition of realization by 2030. This strategic agenda endeavors to foster a more equitable, habitable, and enduring global environment by advancing sustainability across environmental, economic, and social dimensions. The SDGs encapsulate the pursuit of economic advancement, the attainment of social cohesion and collaboration, and the preservation of the natural environment. Within this framework, the goals can be categorized into three distinct dimensions:

Economic-Based Sustainable Development Issues

- Productivity, Growth, and Stability (SDG 1, SDG 2).
- Full Employment (SDG 8).
- Industrialization and Innovation (SDG 9).

Environmental-Based Sustainable Development Issues

- Climate Change (SDG 13).
- Renewable/Sustainable Energy Sources (SDG 7).
- Protection of Natural Resources (SDG 14, SDG 15).

Social-Based Sustainable Development Issues

- Equality (SDG 5, SDG 10, SDG 16).
- Security (SDG 11).
- Education (SDG 4).
- Good Health and Well-Being (SDG 3).
- Access/Participation (SDG 6).
- Awareness/Consciousness (SDG 12).
- Global Identity (SDG 17).

These SDGs represent a crucial framework for global political decision-making and policy implementation. If SDGs are evaluated in line with the strategic management-based pyramid model illustrated in Figure 1, economic goals emerge as the foundational layer. These goals serve as the initial drivers for countries and businesses in the context of sustainable development, ensuring their survival and operational viability. Environmental goals are built upon this economic goals and are mostly shaped or enforced by national and international regulations. Social goals, positioned at the top of the pyramid, represent the most strategic level, as they are the goals that differentiate countries and businesses from others in terms of long-term vision and societal impact (Gürül, 2023, p. 175). This is particularly evident in socially oriented objectives, where enhancing health, advancing education, and diminishing inequalities are paramount concerns (Wulf et al., 2018; Ziolo et al., 2019). Consequently, as illustrated in the aforementioned list, numerous additional social aspects of sustainable development require attention.

*Figure 1. Strategic management based evaluation of sustainable development goals*

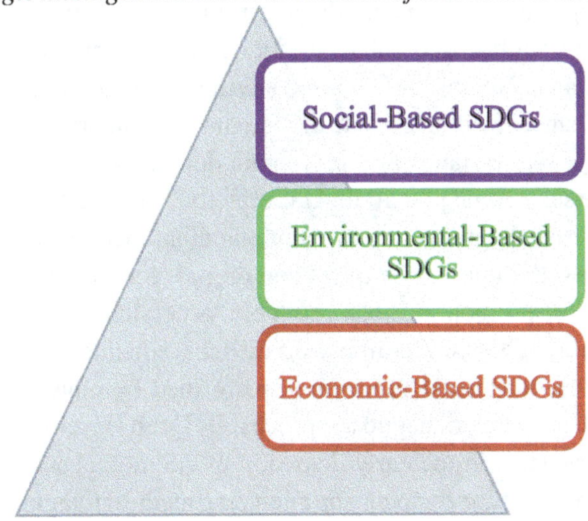


This study aims to comprehensively present how artificial intelligence (AI)-based smart health technologies contribute to the achievement of SDG3, which specifically focuses on "Good Health and Well-being" as defined by the United Nations. In this context, the multifaceted potential of AI applications such as enhancing the quality of healthcare services, reducing health inequalities, and optimizing early diagnosis and treatment processes were evaluated under a range of application domains.

The remainder of this study is organized as follows: The next section introduces the role of artificial intelligence (AI) in supporting SDGs within the healthcare sector. This is followed by detailed subsections examining five key AI-driven technology domains: Telemedicine, Internet of Things (IoT), Digital Twins, Bioinformatics, and Machine Learning. Each domain is analyzed in terms of its impact on healthcare delivery, its contribution to SDG 3. The study then discusses the integration of these technologies with SDGs frameworks and concludes with a summary of findings and recommendations.

## ARTIFICIAL INTELLIGENCE APPLICATIONS FOR ACHIEVING SUSTAINABLE DEVELOPMENT GOALS IN THE HEALTH SECTOR

Artificial intelligence (AI) has become integral to numerous sectors, including healthcare, transportation, finance, education, mining, military, media, industry, and agriculture. Its applications enhance efficiency and simplify human endeavors across these domains. Notably, AI-focused startups are experiencing rapid growth, particularly in finance, healthcare, education, and e-commerce.

The healthcare sector stands as a prominent domain where AI based technologies demonstrate substantial potential. AI is effectively utilized in critical processes ranging from disease diagnosis to treatment planning, thereby enhancing efficiency. In recent years, the integration of AI and digital technologies has transformed healthcare services, promoting more equitable, accessible, and high-quality care globally. In clinical settings, AI-supported devices expedite examinations, report analyses, and other diagnostic procedures performed by physicians, resulting in time savings and accelerated diagnostic processes. Deep learning algorithms assist healthcare professionals in the early detection of conditions such as lung cancer, breast cancer, and diabetic retinopathy by analyzing medical imaging data. AI-driven software enhances the diagnostic accuracy and speed for radiologists, enabling more reliable identification of diseases such as cancer (Esteva et al., 2017). Furthermore, personalized treatment strategies are being developed through the utilization of big data technologies to analyze electronic health records. AI-supported decision support systems, such as IBM Watson, optimize patient care by analyzing clinical data (Topol, 2019). Additionally, AI-powered surgical robots aid surgeons in performing highly precise and error-free procedures (Hussein et al., 2023).

As a result, AI-based applications, including telemedicine, machine learning (ML), sensors, the Internet of Things (IoT), bioinformatics, and digital twins, are directly related to SDG 3 of the Sustainable Development Goals by enabling efficiency and sustainability of healthcare systems. These technologies serve as powerful tools for reducing health inequalities and enhancing quality of life by providing wider access to healthcare services. The following sections provide a detailed overview of how these applications are utilized within the healthcare sector.

### Telemedicine

Telemedicine is a concept that refers to the delivery of healthcare services through telecommunication and electronic information technologies. It covers a series of applications that enable the remote provision of medical services between patients and healthcare professionals. In this context, telemedicine services include: (i) online patient consultations, (ii) remote patient monitoring, (iii) telehealth nursing, (iv) remote physical and psychiatric rehabilitation, and (v) remote collaboration and knowledge-sharing among healthcare professionals (Haleem et al., 2021).

Telemedicine, which has gained significant prominence particularly during the COVID-19 pandemic, bridges the gap between patients and healthcare providers. AI-supported telemedicine applications make substantial contributions to healthcare systems by facilitating access to medical services in remote areas. These applications enhance healthcare accessibility, especially for individuals residing in underdeveloped or rural regions. In this respect, telemedicine has emerged as a significant tool for enhancing geographic accessibility to healthcare services and plays a crucial role in achieving SDG 3. Therefore, addressing issues such as digital literacy, provision of necessary equipment, means of communication, and regulatory and legal barriers are essential to ensure equitable and inclusive access to telemedicine for all individuals. Therefore, it is important to expand the geographic boundaries of access to healthcare services, identify underserved communities, and address these gaps. In order to ensure health equity in telemedicine services: i) Improve telemedicine workflows, ii) Increase healthcare personnel training, and iii) Better use of community resources are necessary. Ultimately; ensuring equal access to quality telemedicine services for all individuals, especially underserved communities, requires a joint effort and collective responsibility (Anawade et al., 2024).

Artificial intelligence improves diagnostic accuracy in remote consultations via telemedicine platforms, optimizes treatment processes, and strengthens decision support systems related to patient care. Research indicates that the integration of AI with telemedicine enables healthcare providers to make more informed decisions, offers a more efficient approach to healthcare delivery, and, as a result, reduces health inequalities (Bajwa et al., 2021). For example, AI-powered telemedicine platforms can assist healthcare providers in rapidly analyzing medical images, such as X-rays and MRIs, and detecting abnormalities with high accuracy. In particular, the monitoring of common diseases such as cancer, cardiovascular diseases, and diabetes can be conducted more efficiently through the use of ML systems. This not only accelerates the diagnostic process but also ensures that patients receive timely and effective treatment. Apart from these, ML algorithms can be employed to personalize patient care. These algorithms can: (i) recommend treatment modifications by analyzing previous medical histories, medications, and lifestyle habits, (ii) predict individual patient responses to specific drugs, and (iii) detect early warning signs of chronic diseases. As AI and ML technologies continue to develop, telemedicine systems will become increasingly intuitive, offering healthcare providers advanced tools for delivering smarter and more precise care. Consequently, such systems are expected to support risk assessment, analyze patient histories, and offer evidence-based treatment recommendations (Ozkan, 2025).

According to United Nations data on telemedicine usage, 76% of hospitals utilize telemedicine technologies to connect with patients. Teleradiology (39.5%), emergency medicine (38.9%), pathology (30.4%), and psychiatry (27.8%) are among the specialties that adopt telemedine at the highest rates. Telemedicine is also widely applied in cardiology, dermatology, oncology, and in pre- and post-surgical care. Globally, the use of telemedicine varies based on national healthcare strategies. In Japan, it is primarily used as a complementary tool to in-person consultations. In South Korea, telemedicine plays an active role in the follow-up of patients after face-to-face examinations. Across the European Union, it is frequently employed for monitoring patients with chronic illnesses. In the United States, telemedicine has been broadly adopted in both hospitals and clinics, and is even utilized in prescribing medications and guiding treatment decisions (Stoltzfus et al., 2023)

Despite its all numerous advantages and conveniences, telemedicine continues to face various technological, regulatory, and financial barriers. These barriers can be broadly categorized into two groups: internal and external barriers. Internal barriers are primarily associated with patients' individual perceptions, experiences, and technological competencies, including communication difficulties and concerns about privacy and security. External barriers arise from issues such as inadequate technological infrastructure, financial limitations, data protection challenges, and gaps in regulatory frameworks. These barriers are particularly critical for vulnerable groups, including individuals with disabilities. To overcome these challenges and promote wider adoption of telemedicine, the following strategic measures should be proposed (Mehta and Chaudhary, 2022):

1. Enhancing Education and Awareness
    - Develop user-friendly telemedicine interfaces to encourage faster adaptation among both patients and healthcare professionals.
    - Provide training programs for healthcare providers to ensure effective use of telemedicine technologies.
2. Strengthening Legal and Regulatory Frameworks
    - Establish standardized procedures and ethical guidelines for telemedicine practices.
    - Simplify interregional licensing policies to allow healthcare professionals to serve broader patient populations.
3. Improving Technological Infrastructure
    - Expand internet connectivity and network infrastructure, especially in rural regions.
    - Enhance IT security systems and implement stronger data protection and cybersecurity measures.
4. Expanding Financial Incentives

- Increase public funding and revise insurance reimbursement models to support affordable access to telemedicine.
- Clarify reimbursement mechanisms to reduce financial burdens on patients and ensure equitable healthcare delivery.

## The Internet of Things

The Internet of Things (IoT) and sensor technologies are transforming individual health management by enabling continuous monitoring and data collection within the healthcare sector. In particular, wearable sensors facilitate the ongoing tracking of critical health parameters, such as heart rate, sleep patterns, and physical activity. IoT-supported wearable devices enable healthcare providers to remotely monitor patients. For instance, biometric data such as blood glucose levels, heart rate, and other vital signs can be monitored in real-time through sensors. In cases where abnormalities are detected, immediate notifications can be sent to healthcare professionals or physicians. These applications are especially pivotal in the management of chronic conditions, promoting a more preventive approach to healthcare service delivery (Abdulmalek et al., 2022). Moreover, data gathered through electronic health record systems is utilized to enhance patient treatment processes and optimize healthcare services (Villafuerte et al., 2023).

Additionally, IoT applications are increasingly utilized in the healthcare sector for asset tracking (e.g., smart management of medical equipment), occupational health and safety, and smart medication management. Medical devices or wheelchairs, for instance, can be equipped with IoT sensors, enabling real-time monitoring and easy retrieval within hospital settings. In environments with potential occupational hazards, such as radiology departments, IoT technology ensures continuous monitoring of employee health and safety. Furthermore, IoT plays a crucial role in smart medication management by tracking pharmaceuticals and preventing dosage errors, thereby enhancing patient safety and optimizing treatment protocols (Xu et al., 2014). On the other hand, healthcare services can adopt a result-oriented pricing model informed by data collected through IoT devices. For instance, treatment outcomes and patient recovery times can be monitored through data, with payments adjusted accordingly (Paknejad Rizi et al., 2022). Furthermore, IoT enables the provision of subscription-based healthcare services. An example of this is a heart rhythm monitoring device, which offers data reports in exchange for a subscription fee (Kirubakaran et al., 2023).

IoT holds significant potential to support SDG-3, which aims to ensure healthy lives and promote well-being for all. In particular, the implementation of IoT-based systems in developing countries is essential to improve access to healthcare services. The need for IoT adoption is evident, and policymakers must take proactive measures to ensure the effective allocation and management of healthcare resources. The widespread adoption of IoT technologies can substantially reduce the burden on healthcare facilities. When patients are empowered to monitor and manage their health remotely, hospitals and healthcare providers can concentrate their efforts on more critical and high-risk cases. Therefore, it is crucial for decision-makers across healthcare institutions to promote the integration of IoT in healthcare management systems (Radwan and Farouk, 2021).

Although numerous studies have revealed the significant potential benefits of designing and implementing IoT-based healthcare systems, several unresolved challenges persist. The main obstacles to the effective adoption of IoT in the healthcare sector can be categorized as follows (Aghdam et al., 2021):

1. Interoperability
    - Integration difficulties among heterogeneous healthcare systems and medical devices
    - Absence of standardized protocols for seamless data sharing
2. Availability and Usability
    - Limited alternatives to ensure user-friendliness in IoT-enabled healthcare systems
    - Users may face challenges in effectively interacting with devices or navigating platforms, thereby reducing system adoption and efficacy
3. Security and Data Privacy
    - Protection of sensitive patient data and defense against cyberattacks
    - Need for blockchain-based security solutions and the utilization of smart contracts
4. Data Storage and Management
    - Handling of large-scale health data and decentralized storage of electronic health records
    - Secure processing, retrieval, and analysis of health-related information
5. Energy Consumption and Battery Life
    - Ensuring energy efficiency and prolonged battery life in wearable medical devices
    - Development of low-power technologies for long-term patient monitoring
6. Network Architecture and Connectivity
    - Integration of IoT devices into hospital, clinic, and home-care systems
    - Dependency on uninterrupted internet access and the limitations of current network infrastructures
7. Cost Analysis in IoT-Enabled Healthcare

- High implementation and maintenance costs associated with IoT healthcare solutions
- Necessity of aligning financial models with health insurance and reimbursement frameworks

8. Quality of Service (QoS) and Real-Time Data Processing
   - Inability of some IoT devices to deliver timely or high-quality data
   - Challenges in handling heterogeneous data types, real-time patient monitoring, and operating automated clinical decision support systems

## Digital Twins

Healthcare is a complex system encompassing a wide range of medical care services. While traditional approaches such as lean manufacturing have long been applied to improve healthcare system performance, the integration of modern enhancement methods has become critically important for increasing efficiency, productivity, and quality. In this context, Digital Twins (DTs) technology, which is an integral component of Industry 4.0, has emerged as a powerful tool for optimizing this complex system (Machado and Berssaneti, 2023).

Although the term "Digital Twins" was first introduced by Michael Grieves during a presentation in 2003, it is widely acknowledged that the concept itself was initially employed by NASA in the 1960s to simulate and program spacecraft, such as those used in the Apollo missions. Over time, the definition of Digital Twin has evolved as its applications have extended beyond aerospace and automotive domains. In this context, a Digital Twins can be defined as "the process of creating a digital model of a physical entity to simulate its behavior, monitor its current state, capture internal and external complexities, detect anomalous patterns, reflect system performance, and predict future trends". Initially recognized for its contributions in engineering disciplines, the use of this technology has gained increasing attention in the rapidly advancing healthcare sector, particularly following the widespread impact of the COVID-19 pandemic (Hassani et al., 2022)

As the field of application has expanded, the conceptual structure of DT technology has evolved and is now commonly defined through a five-dimensional model. Although the integration of this general five-dimensional DT model into the healthcare domain may seem straightforward in theory, it presents significant challenges in practice. This is primarily due to the fact that healthcare focuses on individuals rather than products, and involves a high degree of variability and complexity that demands expertise at every stage of the process. The five-dimensional DT model in healthcare, as outlined by Hassani et al. (2022), is structured as follows:

- 1st Dimension-Physical Being: Represents the patient as the real, biological entity.
- 2nd Dimension-Virtual Twin: A digital representation of the patient.
- 3rd Dimension-Digital Twin Data: Comprises both historical and real-time data collected from the patient, along with model-based analyses, simulations, verifications, and predictions, supported by research insights, computational modeling, big data analytics, and machine learning.
- 4th Dimension-Services: Encompasses the suite of functions and services enabled by the DT, including real-time health monitoring, timely diagnosis, effective and personalized treatment, and enhanced operational efficiency for healthcare providers.
- 5th Dimension-Data Linkage: Refers to the integration and synchronization of data between the physical and virtual entities, facilitating seamless communication and interoperability between the patient and their digital counterpart.

Digital twins generate virtual replicas of physical entities, enabling the simulation of health statuses on these digital models. This technology holds significant potential, particularly in the management of complex health conditions. Digital Twins facilitate the development of personalized treatment approaches by integrating data such as genetic information, lifestyle factors, and medical history. The application of digital twins enables the formulation of more tailored treatment strategies that align with the unique needs of individual patients, thereby substantially enhancing the quality of healthcare services (Vallée, 2023; Sun et al., 2023b).

DTs technology also enables healthcare providers to design targeted interventions and preventive strategies at the community level. These may include public health campaigns, vaccination programs, and community-based initiatives, which aims preventing disease outbreaks, improving health outcomes, and reducing the overall burden on healthcare systems. The predictive capabilities of DTs enable early identification of potential complications, dynamic adjustment of treatment plans, and optimization of interventions to slow or prevent disease progression. As a result, healthcare resources can be allocated more effectively, costs can be reduced, and patient outcomes significantly improved. Furthermore, DTs offer substantial potential for optimizing clinical operations. By integrating data from diverse sources such as electronic health records (EHRs), medical devices, and administrative systems, DTs can detect bottlenecks, inefficiencies, and areas requiring improvement. These enable healthcare professionals to simplify their workflows, minimize redundant tasks, and enhance operational efficiency. DTs also support strategic resource allocation by analyzing patient data, historical trends, and real-time information to predict patient volumes, demand patterns, and resource utilization. Consequently, healthcare providers can more effectively deploy staff, equipment, and facilities, reducing wait times and ensuring optimal use of resources. Finally, DTs facilitate proactive capacity planning by allowing healthcare organizations to anticipate future service demands and make informed decisions regarding resource investments and infrastructure expansion (Vallée, 2023).

DT integrates multiple technologies including the Internet of Things (IoT), big data, Cyber-Physical Systems (CPS), Artificial Intelligence (AI), and Machine Learning (ML) to generate outcomes such as automation, quality improvement, and enhanced operational efficiency. Gartner, a consulting group, highlighted the importance of DT technology by ranking it in the top ten strategic technology trends for three years in a row from 2017 to 2019. Furthermore, major companies such as Microsoft, Siemens, and General Electric have developed platforms and solutions to support the implementation of DT technology across devices, processes, systems, and even individual-level applications (Machado and Berssaneti, 2023).

In addition to all these advantages, the effectiveness of DT technology heavily relies on the accuracy of the simulation model. Technical challenges such as the multi-scale and multi-physics nature of DT systems, the complexity of integrating sub-processes across different physical domains and scales, and the limited availability of experimental data hinder the development of high-accuracy models. Another critical issue is reducing the discrepancy between DT simulation outputs and real-world conditions. For example, in surgical modeling, unforeseen complications may arise during the actual procedure that were not predicted by the simulation. Furthermore, DT applications in healthcare raise several socio-ethical concerns. Among these, privacy stands out as a major ethical challenge and one of the primary disadvantages of DT use. In addition to ethical considerations, legal and economic challenges also exist. Governments and international regulatory bodies should establish country-specific, enforceable standards and implement strict oversight mechanisms. For example, service providers must obtain informed consent from users and clearly communicate the intended secondary uses of collected data. At the same time, greater investment is required to support the technological advancement of DT systems. However, the high cost of DT-based healthcare services may exacerbate existing social inequalities by limiting access and contributing to socioeconomic inequalities. Personalized healthcare applications of DT technology rely on extensive health data collection, which is enabled by transmitting sensor data to the cloud via 5G networks. Consequently, ensuring the security of DT systems during operation is another pressing concern (Sun et al., 2023a).

## Big Data and Bioinformatics

The term "bioinformatics" was first introduced by Ben Hesper and Paulien Hogeweg to describe the computational processes in biological systems. In 1981, Marvin Carruthers and Leroy Hood laid the foundation for the bioinformatics movement by mapping 579 human genes and developing an automated DNA sequencing technique using the "In situ hybridization" method. One of the most influential milestones in the field was the Human Genome Project (HGP), which significantly accelerated the development of bioinformatics (Mishra et al., 2024).

Bioinformatics emerged as a response to the growing need to analyze, interpret, and manage biological signals and genomic information. It plays a vital role in understanding disease mechanisms and unraveling the complexity of biological functions. As a multidisciplinary field, bioinformatics integrates computer science, statistics, informatics, and artificial intelligence (AI) to collect, store, analyze, and disseminate biological data.

The healthcare sector also represents one of the most significant applications of both big data analytics and bioinformatics. Big data analytics facilitates the development of personalized medical solutions by analyzing patients' health records, genetic data, and treatment histories. In contrast, bioinformatics leverages big data technologies to manage and analyze biological information. The data obtained from patients' clinical reports are highly complex and voluminous, constituting what is commonly referred to as 'big data' in healthcare. This data plays a vital role in a wide range of clinical and medical applications, including early disease diagnosis, clinical decision support systems, clinical surveillance, public health management, and fraud detection in healthcare services. With the current pace of technological advancement, the healthcare sector is expected to generate data on the scale of zettabytes ($10^{21}$ bytes) and even yottabytes ($10^{24}$ bytes) in the near future. Storing and managing such massive volumes of electronic health records (EHRs) on traditional computing systems presents significant challenges (Nagaraj et al., 2018). As a result, the role of bioinformatics in effectively organizing, analyzing, and interpreting healthcare data has become increasingly critical and indispensable.

The primary aim of bioinformatics is to investigate the molecular basis of diseases, facilitate early diagnosis, and enable improved medical outcomes through personalized medicine. Although interpreting genetic changes remains complex, bioinformatics makes it possible to identify candidate genes associated with specific diseases, analyze mutation-driven variations, and explore genetic diversity across populations. As such, it contributes significantly to disease management and therapeutic innovation (Mishra et al., 2024). Research initiatives, such as genome sequencing, protein structure analysis, and investigations into the genetic underpinnings of diseases, are expedited and enhanced through big data analytics (He et al., 2017).

Furthermore, big data is integral to epidemiological studies. During pandemics, big data analytics plays a crucial role in the development of disease transmission models and the efficient allocation of healthcare resources (Laudisa, 2024).

The functions of bioinformatics can be broadly classified into two main categories: software tool and algorithm development, as well as the use of these tools and algorithms for biological data analysis and interpretation. In this regard, bioinformatics increasingly intersects with AI. The integration of AI into bioinformatics has contributed significantly to various domains, including gene prediction, in silico drug design, protein–protein interaction studies, and the development of computational methods for next-generation sequencing (NGS). AI-based bioinformatics approaches typically employ neural networks, decision trees, hybrid models, and genetic algorithms to address complex biological problems. These AI-driven techniques hold considerable promise for advancing current and future developments in bioinformatics and have the potential to significantly impact the pharmaceutical and biotechnology industries. Recent advancements at the intersection of AI and bioinformatics, such as in high-throughput screening, epidemiology, and immune-informatics, have led to improved simulation models and meaningful contributions to human health. However, the continuous mutation of microbes and viruses poses persistent challenges to vaccine development. Notably, research in vaccine design has gained momentum through the combined application of AI and bioinformatics, offering new avenues to accelerate discovery and improve efficacy (Bhatia and Malik, 2021).

While big data analytics offers significant advantages for healthcare sector, there are a number of unresolved challenges. According to Verma et al. (2024), these challenges include:

- the lack of standardized data formats and protocols,
- ongoing concerns regarding data security and patient privacy,
- the need to ensure the accuracy and overall quality of health-related data, and
- the absence of sufficiently advanced analytical tools and techniques capable of processing and interpreting the large amounts of data generated in these area.

## Machine Learning

The World Health Organization (WHO) reports that 57% of the global population is expected to be living with chronic diseases by 2050. Alarmingly, the WHO also projects a significant global shortage of healthcare professionals, with a shortfall of 12.9 million workers by 2035. This growing gap in the healthcare workforce presents a concerning outlook with potentially severe consequences for global health systems. However, emerging technologies such as Artificial Intelligence (AI), Machine Learning (ML), digital interventions, the Internet of Things (IoT), and other advanced digital tools offer a promising solution to help mitigate this crisis. These technologies have the potential not only to automate manual and cognitive tasks, but also to extend the reach of healthcare services. These innovations can enhance the precision, efficiency, and accessibility of care (Panesar, 2019).

Another key reason for the growing need for ML and other AI-powered systems in healthcare is the exponential increase in data generated across the sector. Effectively processing and extracting insights from this vast volume of information requires advanced technological capabilities. Despite rapid digital advancements, many healthcare processes today are still carried out manually and at a relatively slow pace. Leveraging the potential of ML can significantly enhance the efficiency and quality of healthcare services. Its ability to process and analyze large, complex datasets makes it an invaluable tool for deriving meaningful insights (Nayyar et al., 2021).

Artificial intelligence (AI) is the development of machines capable of performing tasks to which human intelligence is often required. Within the broader field of AI, Machine Learning (ML) enables systems to learn from data and improve their performance over time without being explicitly programmed. Deep Learning (DL), a specialized subset of ML, utilizes artificial neural networks to analyze large datasets and identify complex patterns. AI applications, particularly those based on ML, hold significant promise in the healthcare sector. ML has increasingly employed in critical areas of healthcare, including the early diagnosis of diseases, the personalization of treatment approaches, and the prediction of disease progression. ML algorithms hold significant potential for analyzing health data, identifying patient risks proactively, and developing tailored treatment plans. In particular, the monitoring of prevalent conditions such as diabetes, cardiovascular diseases, and cancer can be conducted more swiftly and accurately using ML systems. Research has demonstrated that ML systems yield more successful outcomes in the early detection of diseases (Alanazi, 2022).

To evaluate the applicability of ML in healthcare, it is useful to consider ML models under two primary categories: supervised learning and unsupervised learning. Supervised learning involves training algorithms on labeled input–output data with the goal of predicting future outcomes. In the healthcare domain, supervised learning is extensively applied to tasks such as disease classification, diagnosis, and prognosis prediction. Through this approach, models can be trained to estimate disease risk based on patient data. Common supervised learning algorithms—including decision trees, support vector machines (SVM), and logistic regression—are frequently used for predicting cardiovascular disease risk, detecting malignant cells, and classifying medical images. However, a key limitation of supervised learning is its reliance on large volumes of labeled data. Moreover, bias may occur if the training dataset is not representative of the broader population. In contrast, unsupervised learning identifies hidden patterns or latent structures within input data without labeled outputs. In healthcare, unsupervised learning is commonly used for clustering, anomaly detection, and feature extraction. For instance, algorithms such as K-means clustering have been applied to group patients with similar characteristics, detect rare diseases, and extract informative features from medical imaging. Despite its utility, the outputs of unsupervised learning models can be challenging to interpret and may lack direct clinical relevance (An et al., 2023).

While the abundance of health data offers significant opportunities, it also presents notable challenges. A large portion of medical data is unstructured, comprising clinical notes, diagnostic reports, discharge summaries, medical images, and audio or video recordings. Additionally, quantitatively describing the interaction between healthcare providers and patients remains a complex task. For instance, two patients presenting with similar fever symptoms may receive differing diagnoses and clinical assessments, influenced by the physician's interpretation and the patient's communication style. Therefore, machine learning should be positioned as a supportive tool that effectively analyzes structured data while organizing and interpreting unstructured data to enhance decision-making processes in healthcare (Nayyar et al., 2021).

The opaque nature of many machine learning (ML) models, which often referred to as the 'black box' problem, poses a significant challenge to transparency and trust in healthcare applications. While explainability is not a strict requirement for all AI systems, it becomes critically important when AI is involved in decisions that directly affect patient health. In the context of medical ML systems, explainability benefits all stakeholders, including patients, healthcare professionals, policymakers, and software engineers. AI systems must make fair, unbiased, reliable, and rational decisions grounded in medical data, rather than random correlations (Allgaier et al., 2023). In this context, Explainable Artificial Intelligence (XAI) has emerged as a vital solution. XAI comprises a set of strategies and methods designed to make the decisions and internal workings of AI systems transparent and interpretable to humans. In the healthcare domain, XAI can be applied in several key areas (Rahman et al., 2024):

- Enhancing diagnostic and treatment strategies: XAI algorithms can support clinicians in making more accurate and informed decisions by offering understandable justifications for their predictions and recommendations.
- Increasing patient engagement and education: XAI can provide patients with personalized explanations regarding their health status and available

treatment options, promoting better understanding and involvement in care decisions.

- Facilitating clinical research and trials: XAI can uncover patterns and relationships in large-scale clinical datasets, aiding the development of innovative treatment strategies and accelerating medical research.

## Metaverse

Critical flaws in the current healthcare systems have been exposed by the COVID-19 pandemic, which has also brought social distance to the public's attention for the first time. These challenges have underscored the need for transformative changes in the smart healthcare sector. In response, emerging technologies such as AI, digital twins, and the Metaverse have gained increasing attention for their potential to reshape healthcare delivery.

Neal Stephenson coined the phrase "*Metaverse*" in his 1992 science fiction book Snow Crash. In this book, Metaverse was described as a vast virtual environment that co-exists with the physical world and enables user interaction through digital avatars. Today, the Metaverse is conceptualized as a shared virtual space that integrates technologies such as augmented reality (AR), virtual reality (VR), and mixed reality (MR), allowing users to engage in real-time, three-dimensional interactions. While Metaverse applications in healthcare are still in their infancy, it is widely believed that they will become a major trend in the near future. However, the successful integration of Metaverse technologies into the healthcare ecosystem requires addressing a number of critical challenges (Dang et al., 2023):

- Hardware Requirements: The Metaverse relies heavily on AR/VR technologies and demands extensive data processing and high-performance computing. Therefore, smart, lightweight, flexible, and cost-effective hardware solutions are essential to facilitate widespread use.
- Privacy and Security: The collection, storage, and processing of sensitive user data in virtual environments raise serious concerns related to data protection. In the context of healthcare, inadequate privacy safeguards could lead to significant ethical and legal consequences.
- Identity Theft: Digital identities and avatars in the Metaverse are vulnerable to cloning, impersonation, and misinformation by malicious actors. Actions within virtual environments may lead to tangible impacts in the real world.
- Neurological and Mental Health Risks: Although the Metaverse offers opportunities for virtual socialization and engagement, prolonged use may contribute to mental health issues such as depression, anxiety, and detachment from real-life experiences.

- Digital Currency and Payment Systems: As the Metaverse evolves into a global marketplace, ensuring the security and legitimacy of digital transactions becomes a major concern for both users and service providers.
- Legal Frameworks and Policy Gaps: New legal frameworks are needed to regulate emerging concepts such as virtual citizenship, digital crimes, and the virtual economy. Traditional enforcement methods (e.g., account suspension) may be insufficient to combat misconduct in immersive environments.

## CONCLUSION

In the last decade, there have been rapid advancements in the healthcare sector, particularly in the field of health informatics. In today's conditions, it is evident that the healthcare system has become increasingly dependent on digitalization, with emerging technologies enabling more sustainable and efficient healthcare operations. Information and Communication Technologies (ICT) and the Internet of Things (IoT) are widely utilized to streamline processes within the healthcare industry. The COVID-19 pandemic further emphasized the necessity of analyzing health data in greater complexity and depth, particularly in response to rising mortality rates. Analyzing such data and extracting meaningful insights is a highly complex task, which has been made possible through AI driven technologies. These technologies have contributed significantly to improving healthcare services, managing diseases, identifying biomarkers for diagnosis and prognosis, and enhancing clinical diagnostic processes.

Moreover, through the integration of wearable health devices, such as smartwatches, oximeters, and glucometers, continuous patient monitoring has become achievable. These devices provide real-time feedback tailored to individual physiological needs, allowing patients to monitor their health status instantly while enabling healthcare professionals to deliver quicker and more effective interventions.

As can be understood from the above explanations, AI-driven smart technologies and applications have the potential to transform the healthcare sector and serve as a crucial tool in advancing the third goal of the SDGs, "Good Health and Well-being." This study aims to provide a comprehensive analysis of the various AI-driven technologies that facilitate broader access to healthcare services, enable the development of personalized treatment approaches, enhance early disease detection, promote more efficient and sustainable healthcare delivery, and contribute to the reduction of health inequalities. Within the framework of the five thematic headings explored in this study, the transformation enabled by artificial intelligence in health systems extends beyond enhancing patient care and service delivery; it also generates multifaceted impacts that align with the multi-stakeholder approach of sustainable development.

Governments, healthcare institutions, and health-focused non-governmental organizations should accelerate the integration of AI-based digital technologies into healthcare systems and benefit from these innovative solutions. AI-based technologies are increasingly being adopted in a wide range of healthcare applications, including early diagnosis, personalized treatment planning, pandemic response, digital patient monitoring, telemedicine, resource allocation, and the strategic management of healthcare systems. These applications support the development of a more accessible, equitable, and sustainable healthcare infrastructure at both individual and societal levels. In this context, AI is not merely a technological innovation but also a strategic instrument for social transformation that contributes to the realization of multidimensional SDGs. However, for this transformative process to be successfully implemented, comprehensive frameworks and collaborative efforts are required, particularly concerning data security, adherence to ethical standards, algorithmic transparency, and the meaningful integration of healthcare professionals into these systems. In other words, critical issues such as data privacy, ethical responsibility, explainability of algorithms, and the adaptation of healthcare professionals to emerging technologies must be effectively addressed to ensure the widespread and trustworthy adoption of AI in the health sector. To this end, interdisciplinary collaboration, visionary policy-making, and continuous professional education are essential components for guiding this transformation.

It should not be forgotten that AI-supported technologies not only directly contribute to SDG 3 but also support SDG 9, SDG 10, SDG 12, and SDG 13. Figure 2 illustrates these interconnections among the five key digital health domain. In the context of SDG 9, AI, IoT, and Digital Twin technologies enhance efficiency by providing innovative solutions within the healthcare sector. Additionally, AI-based health infrastructure supports the development of digital and data-driven systems. Furthermore, sustainable building design, incorporating natural light, proper ventilation, and ergonomic considerations in AI-supported frameworks, improves comfort, productivity, and overall well-being in healthcare institutions. In the context of SDG 10, telemedicine enhances access to healthcare services for disadvantaged groups by overcoming geographical and economic barriers. Additionally, AI-based diagnostic systems offer more cost-effective healthcare solutions, particularly in low-income areas. In the context of SDG 12, AI and IoT-supported health management enhance sustainability by reducing resource waste in hospitals and pharmaceutical production. Additionally, sensors and smart health systems minimize unnecessary testing and medication use, ensuring more efficient use of medical resources. In the context of SDG 13, remote patient monitoring decreases the need for hospital visits, thereby reducing the overall carbon footprint. In parallel, energy-efficient health technologies, supported by AI systems, optimize energy consumption in healthcare facilities, contributing to climate action goals.

*Figure 2. The relationship between AI-based smart technologies and sustainable development goals*

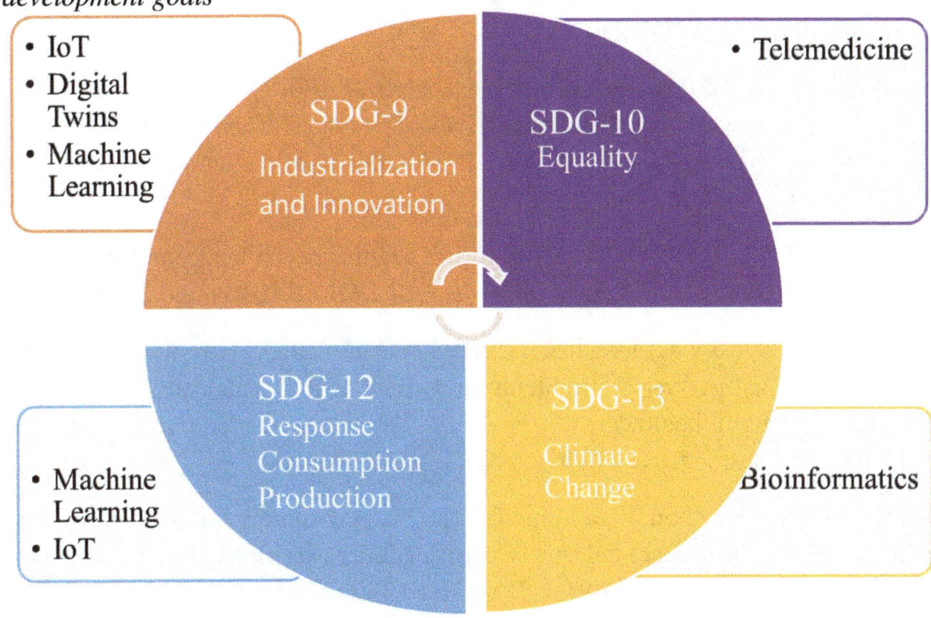


This study draws upon current literature to demonstrate the potential, challenges, and strategic importance of integrating AI into healthcare systems. Through this structure, the study offers a comprehensive and multidisciplinary perspective on how AI serves not only as a technological innovation but also as a transformative force for equitable and sustainable global health.

## REFERENCES


Abdulmalek, S., Nasir, A., Jabbar, W. A., Almuhaya, M. A., Bairagi, A. K., Khan, M. A. M., & Kee, S. H. (2022). IoT-based healthcare-monitoring system towards improving quality of life: A review. *Health Care, 10*(10), 1993. DOI: 10.3390/healthcare10101993 PMID: 36292441

Aghdam, Z. N., Rahmani, A. M., & Hosseinzadeh, M. (2021). The role of the Internet of Things in healthcare: Future trends and challenges. *Computer Methods and Programs in Biomedicine, 199*(105903), 1–27. DOI: 10.1016/j.cmpb.2020.105903 PMID: 33348073

Alanazi, A. (2022). Using machine learning for healthcare challenges and opportunities. *Informatics in Medicine Unlocked, 30*, 100924. DOI: 10.1016/j.imu.2022.100924

Allgaier, J., Mulansky, L., Draelos, R. L., & Pryss, R. (2023). How does the model make predictions? A systematic literature review on the explainability power of machine learning in healthcare. *Artificial Intelligence in Medicine, 143*, 102616. DOI: 10.1016/j.artmed.2023.102616 PMID: 37673561

An, Q., Rahman, S., Zhou, J., & Kang, J. J. (2023). A comprehensive review on machine learning in healthcare industry: Classification, restrictions, opportunities and challenges. *Sensors (Basel), 23*(9), 4178. DOI: 10.3390/s23094178 PMID: 37177382

Anawade, P. A., Sharma, D., & Gahane, S. (2024). A comprehensive review on exploring the impact of telemedicine on healthcare accessibility. *Cureus, 16*(3), 1–12. DOI: 10.7759/cureus.55996 PMID: 38618307

Bajwa, J., Munir, U., Nori, A., & Williams, B. (2021). Artificial intelligence in healthcare: Transforming the practice of medicine. *Future Healthcare Journal, 8*(2), 188–194. DOI: 10.7861/fhj.2021-0095 PMID: 34286183

Bhatia, D., & Malik, D. (2021). An Insight into the Potential Role of Artificial Intelligence in Bioinformatics. In Gaur, L., Solanki, A., Wamba, S. F., & Jhanjhi, N. Z. (Eds.), *Advanced AI Techniques and Applications in Bioinformatics* (pp. 17–40). CRC Press. DOI: 10.1201/9781003126164-2

Dang, V. A., Vu Khanh, Q., Nguyen, V. H., Nguyen, T., & Nguyen, D. C. (2023). Intelligent healthcare: Integration of emerging technologies and Internet of Things for humanity. *Sensors, 23*(9), 4200:1-24. DOI: 10.3390/s23094200

Esteva, A., Kuprel, B., Novoa, R. A., Ko, J., Swetter, S. M., Blau, H. M., & Thrun, S. (2017). Dermatologist-level classification of skin cancer with deep neural networks. *Nature, 542*(7639), 115–118. DOI: 10.1038/nature21056 PMID: 28117445

Habehh, H., & Gohel, S. (2021). Machine learning in healthcare. *Current Genomics*, *22*(4), 291–300. DOI: 10.2174/1389202922666210705124359 PMID: 35273459

Haleem, A., Javaid, M., Singh, R. P., & Suman, R. (2021). Telemedicine for healthcare: Capabilities, features, barriers, and applications. *Sensors International*, *2*(100117), 1–12. DOI: 10.1016/j.sintl.2021.100117 PMID: 34806053

Hassani, H., Huang, X., & MacFeely, S. (2022). Impactful digital twin in the healthcare revolution. *Big Data and Cognitive Computing*, *6*(3), 83. DOI: 10.3390/bdcc6030083

He, K. Y., Ge, D., & He, M. M. (2017). Big data analytics for genomic medicine. *International Journal of Molecular Sciences*, *18*(2), 412. DOI: 10.3390/ijms18020412 PMID: 28212287

Hussein, A., Sallam, M. E., & Abdalla, M. Y. A. (2023). Exploring New Horizons: Surgical Robots Supported by Artificial Intelligence. *Mesopotamian Journal of Artificial Intelligence in Healthcare*, *2022*, 40–44. DOI: 10.58496/MJAIH/2023/008

Kirubakaran, S. J., Gunasekaran, A., Dolly, D. R. J., Jagannath, D. J., & Peter, J. D. (2023). A feasible approach to smart remote health monitoring: Subscription-based model. *Frontiers in Public Health*, *11*, 1150455. DOI: 10.3389/fpubh.2023.1150455 PMID: 37113166

Laudisa, F. (2024). The Epistemology of Models in the Era of Pandemic. In Nicoletti, M., & Palazzo, A. (Eds.), *Epidemics and Pandemics: Philosophical Perspectives* (pp. 297–308). Brepols Publishers., DOI: 10.1484/M.STPH-EB.5.136416

Machado, T. M., & Berssaneti, F. T. (2023). Literature review of digital twin in healthcare. *Heliyon*, *9*(9), 1–12. DOI: 10.1016/j.heliyon.2023.e19390 PMID: 37809792

Mishra, S. K., Jeba Praba, J., & Georrge, J. J. (2024). An emerging trends of bioinformatics and big data analytics in healthcare. In *Digital Transformation in Healthcare* e 5.0: Volume 2: Metaverse, Nanorobots and Machine Learning (p. 159-188). Walter de Gruyter GmbH & Co KG.

Nagaraj, K., Sharvani, G. S., & Sridhar, A. (2018). Emerging trend of big data analytics in bioinformatics: A literature review. *International Journal of Bioinformatics Research and Applications*, *14*(1-2), 144–205. DOI: 10.1504/IJBRA.2018.089175

Nayyar, A., Gadhavi, L., & Zaman, N. (2021). Machine learning in healthcare: review, opportunities and challenges. In Singh, K. K., Elhoseny, M., Singh, A., & Elngar, A. A. (Eds.), *Machine learning and the internet of medical things in healthcare* (pp. 23–45). Academic Press. DOI: 10.1016/B978-0-12-821229-5.00011-2

Ozkan, M. A. (2025). Telemedicine and the Future of Healthcare: Challenges and Opportunities in Remote Patient Management. *The Open European Journal for Research in Medical and Basic Sciences (OEJRMBS)*, 1(1), 55-65. https://easdjournals.com/index.php/oejrmbs/index

Paknejad Rizi, S. M., Torabi, F., & Jafari Pavarsi, H. (2022). Challenges of Performance-Based Payment Methods in Health Care System: A Systematic Review. *Evidence Based Health Policy. Management and Economics*, *6*(4), 285–297. DOI: 10.18502/jebhpme.v6i4.11541

Panesar, A. (2019). Ethics of intelligence. In *Machine learning and AI for healthcare: big data for improved health outcomes* (pp. 207–254). Apress. DOI: 10.1007/978-1-4842-3799-1_6

Radwan, N., & Farouk, M. (2021). The growth of internet of things (IoT) in the management of healthcare issues and healthcare policy development. *International Journal of Technology Innovation and Management*, *1*(1), 69–84. DOI: 10.54489/ijtim.v1i1.8

Rahman, A., Debnath, T., Kundu, D., Khan, M. S. I., Aishi, A. A., Sazzad, S., Sayduzzaman, M., & Band, S. S. (2024). Machine learning and deep learning-based approach in smart healthcare: Recent advances, applications, challenges and opportunities. *AIMS Public Health*, *11*(1), 58–109. DOI: 10.3934/publichealth.2024004 PMID: 38617415

Stoltzfus, M., Kaur, A., Chawla, A., Gupta, V., Anamika, F. N. U., & Jain, R. (2023). The role of telemedicine in healthcare: An overview and update. *The Egyptian Journal of Internal Medicine*, *35*(1), 1–5. DOI: 10.1186/s43162-023-00234-z

Sun, T., He, X., & Li, Z. (2023a). Digital twin in healthcare: Recent updates and challenges. *Digital Health*, *9*, 1–13. DOI: 10.1177/20552076221149651 PMID: 36636729

Sun, T., Wang, J., Suo, M., Liu, X., Huang, H., Zhang, J., Zhang, W., & Li, Z. (2023b). The digital twin: A potential solution for the personalized diagnosis and treatment of musculoskeletal system diseases. *Bioengineering (Basel, Switzerland)*, *10*(6), 627. DOI: 10.3390/bioengineering10060627 PMID: 37370558

Topol, E. (2019). *Deep Medicine: How Artificial Intelligence Can Make Healthcare Human Again*. Basic Book.

United Nations (UN). (2015). *Transforming our world: The 2030 Agenda for Sustainable Development*. Available from: https://sdgs.un.org/goals

Vallée, A. (2023). Digital twin for healthcare systems. *Frontiers in Digital Health*, *5*, 1253050. DOI: 10.3389/fdgth.2023.1253050 PMID: 37744683

Verma, R. K., Kishor, K., & Jha, S. K. (2024). Big Data Analytics in Bioinformatics and Healthcare. In *Applications of Parallel Data Processing for Biomedical Imaging* (pp. 25–43). DOI: 10.4018/979-8-3693-2426-4.ch002

Villafuerte, N., Manzano, S., Ayala, P., & García, M. V. (2023). Artificial Intelligence in Virtual Telemedicine Triage: A Respiratory Infection Diagnosis Tool with Electronic Measuring Device. *Future Internet*, *15*(7), 227. DOI: 10.3390/fi15070227

Wulf, C., Werker, J., Zapp, P., Schreiber, A., Schlör, H., & Kuckshinrichs, W. (2018). Sustainable development goals as a guideline for indicator selection in life cycle sustainability assessment. In *Proceedings of the 25th CIRP Life Cycle Engineering (LCE) Conference* (pp. 59-65). DOI: 10.1016/j.procir.2017.11.144

Xu, L. D., He, W., & Li, S. (2014). Internet of things in industries: A survey. *IEEE Transactions on Industrial Informatics*, *10*(4), 2233–2243. DOI: 10.1109/TII.2014.2300753

Ziolo, M., Filipiak, B. Z., Bąk, I., & Cheba, K. (2019). How to design more sustainable financial systems: The roles of environmental, social, and governance factors in the decision-making process. *Sustainability (Basel)*, *11*(20), 5604. DOI: 10.3390/su11205604

Chapter 9

# Femtech and Artificial Intelligence:
## Paving the Way for Gender Equality and Sustainable Development

**Manisha Seth**
https://orcid.org/0009-0009-4570-1218
*Noida Institute of Engineering and Technology, India*

**Sabina Sehajpal**
https://orcid.org/0009-0004-6655-6279
*Chandigarh University, India*

**Mukul Bhatnagar**
https://orcid.org/0000-0002-7773-5641
*Graphic Era University, India*

**Akshita Chaudhary**
*Graphic Era University, India*

## ABSTRACT

*This study explores the transformative role of Femtech and Artificial Intelligence (AI) in advancing gender equality and achieving the Sustainable Development Goals (SDGs). It analyzes global startups leveraging AI to address women's health challenges, empower economic participation, and enhance digital engagement. By examining case studies of Femtech innovations in reproductive health, menstrual care, and nutrition, alongside statistical data on women's involvement in e-commerce, the research identifies key AI-driven solutions that bridge gaps in healthcare access and*

DOI: 10.4018/979-8-3373-1837-0.ch009

*economic opportunities. The findings highlight how AI is democratizing healthcare, improving women's access to personalized services, and fostering entrepreneurial opportunities. By enabling scalable, data-driven solutions, AI plays a pivotal role in advancing SDGs, particularly SDG 3 (Good Health and Well-Being), SDG 5 (Gender Equality), and SDG 8 (Decent Work and Economic Growth). This research underscores AI's potential to create an inclusive and equitable global environment for women.*

## INTRODUCTION

In an era where the dialectic between inexorable economic development and the exigencies of environmental sustainability assumes unparalleled significance, the intersection of sustainable finance and legal regulation emerges as a domain of profound consequence. The contemporary global order is enmeshed in a polycrisis—one that is simultaneously ecological, financial, and ethical—necessitating an epistemological reconstitution of traditional economic paradigms (Eriksson, 2024). It is within this context that sustainable finance and investment paradigms, underpinned by rigorous legal and regulatory frameworks, aim to recalibrate capital flows in a manner that reconciles fiduciary obligations with ecological stewardship. The role of law, often perceived as reactive or regulatory in its most reductionist form, is herein transformed into a catalytic instrumentality, proactively shaping normative landscapes that guide financial systems toward sustainability-oriented trajectories.

The emergence of sustainable finance is not merely a fiscal recalibration but an ontological evolution in the conception of capital deployment. No longer confined to risk-adjusted returns or utilitarian maximisation of shareholder value, investment logic is increasingly imbricated with Environmental, Social, and Governance (ESG) criteria (Stech, 2019). These indices, however, do not function in an axiological vacuum; they require institutional legitimacy, accountability frameworks, and enforceability structures—all of which are indelibly entrenched within the legal corpus. As such, law is not ancillary but coextensive with sustainable finance: it constitutes the grammar through which sustainable investment is articulated, enforced, and perpetuated.

In this reimagined topography of finance, legal regimes function as both scaffolds and sentinels. On one hand, they erect the scaffolding for institutional innovation—green bonds, sustainability-linked loans, impact investing vehicles—providing juridical definition and market predictability. On the other, they act as sentinels, guarding against greenwashing, malfeasance, and performative compliance (Smits, 2024b). This dual role requires a jurisprudence that is supple yet stringent, capable of incentivizing sustainable practices while deterring extractive opportunism.

Indeed, the law is summoned not merely to regulate but to orchestrate a paradigm shift—reconfiguring incentive structures, delineating enforceable duties, and harmonizing transnational standards.

The philosophical architecture of sustainable finance finds antecedents in ethical investing traditions—Quaker prohibitions against slavery-linked investments or Islamic finance's proscription of usury—yet its modern incarnation is distinctly global, multi-scalar, and econometrically sophisticated. Legal and regulatory infrastructures, therefore, must evolve beyond jurisdictional parochialism, embracing polycentric governance models that are capable of aligning disparate economic, environmental, and cultural imperatives. The ascendancy of frameworks such as the European Union's Sustainable Finance Disclosure Regulation (SFDR), the Task Force on Climate-related Financial Disclosures (TCFD), and the burgeoning proliferation of green taxonomies attest to this global harmonization imperative (Chiu et al., 2022).

Yet, the legal architecture underpinning sustainable finance must navigate a treacherous terrain. It must reconcile the endogenous logic of capital—accumulation, competition, and return optimization—with exogenous imperatives such as intergenerational equity, biodiversity preservation, and climate mitigation. This is an inherently dialectical task, necessitating legal ingenuity and institutional courage. The commodification of nature—be it through carbon markets or biodiversity credits—exemplifies this paradox: while it ostensibly internalizes environmental externalities, it simultaneously risks perpetuating the logics of dispossession and ecological abstraction (Smits, 2024a). Law must, therefore, act not only as a regulator of market behavior but as an ethical fulcrum—mediating between the reductive quantification of ecological values and their intrinsic worth.

Moreover, sustainable finance, for all its promise, is not immune to co-option by neoliberal rationalities. The risk of sustainability being reduced to a technocratic metric—bereft of socio-political context or redistributive justice—remains ever-present. Herein lies the imperative for legal systems to foreground the substantive content of sustainability: embedding principles of equity, participation, and transparency into financial decision-making processes (Akseli, 2021). This entails recalibrating fiduciary duties to accommodate long-term sustainability risks, mandating ESG disclosures with verifiable metrics, and institutionalizing mechanisms for stakeholder engagement. Legal reform, therefore, must not merely codify new standards but catalyze a cultural transformation in financial praxis.

At the macroeconomic level, the alignment of financial regulation with sustainability objectives has implications for monetary policy, central bank mandates, and fiscal planning. Legal instruments can facilitate the greening of public procurement, anchor sovereign green bond frameworks, and stipulate conditionalities for state aid based on environmental compliance (Pauls, 2024). This juridical leverage extends to international economic law, where bilateral investment treaties, trade agreements, and development finance protocols must increasingly integrate sustainability clauses—eschewing the antiquated dichotomy between economic growth and environmental responsibility.

Simultaneously, legal frameworks must be equipped to contend with systemic risks and cascading failures exacerbated by climate-induced volatilities. The financial repercussions of environmental degradation—ranging from stranded assets in fossil fuel portfolios to climate-related credit risks—require a proactive regulatory approach. Stress-testing for climate risk, prudential regulation of high-carbon sectors, and the imposition of capital requirements on unsustainable lending practices exemplify such anticipatory legal mechanisms (Stichele, 2020). In this regard, the intersection of financial law and environmental law is not merely desirable but indispensable: each domain augments the other, forging a resilient architecture capable of withstanding the vicissitudes of climate and market shocks.

The legitimacy of sustainable finance also hinges on democratisation. Legal norms must facilitate access to green capital for marginalised communities, indigenous populations, and small enterprises, ensuring that the transition to a low-carbon economy is not merely sustainable, but just. This necessitates a redistributive orientation in sustainable finance law: one that confronts historical injustices, prevents neocolonial patterns of green resource extraction, and prioritizes inclusive growth (Franchini, 2025). Legal constructs such as benefit-sharing arrangements, free prior and informed consent (FPIC), and social impact assessments are integral to this ethical anchoring.

Ultimately, the role of law and regulation in sustainable finance transcends conventional regulatory paradigms. It is a transformative praxis—an exercise in institutional imagination and normative reconstruction. As climate change, ecological degradation, and social inequities converge into an existential crucible, the legal system stands as both witness and architect of the world to come. By embedding sustainability into the very fabric of financial decision-making, law does not merely respond to crisis; it redefines the ontological premises of finance itself. It constructs a future wherein economic growth is not antithetical to environmental responsibility, but its logical and moral extension.

## LITERATURE REVIEW: THE JURIDICAL-CONCEPTUAL MATRIX OF SUSTAINABLE FINANCE AND INVESTMENT

The corpus of extant scholarship on sustainable finance and investment reveals an intricate, multidimensional evolution of thought that has incrementally displaced the orthodoxy of shareholder primacy with paradigms of stakeholder-centric, ecologically conscious economic praxis. At its conceptual fulcrum lies a profound ontological reorientation—finance, once construed as a neutral, value-agnostic mechanism for capital allocation, is now imbued with normative aspirations toward planetary stewardship, intergenerational justice, and systemic resilience (Guerriero & Tallini, 2025). The literature, in its most sophisticated renderings, interrogates not merely the economic viability of such transitions but the foundational juridical architectures that render them possible, enforceable, and scalable.

An increasing awareness of the interdependence between capital systems and planetary boundaries shapes the intellectual substratum of sustainable finance. This recognition precipitates a radical shift from anthropocentric utilitarianism toward a more integrated, eco-centric rationality. Legal theorists have thus explored the recalibration of fiduciary duties, proposing a reconceptualization of the fiduciary agent not merely as a steward of pecuniary interests but as a custodian of ecological and social continuity (Borowicz, 2025). This entails the juridical institutionalization of long-termism in corporate governance, wherein ESG factors are not discretionary variables but fiduciary imperatives. The emerging literature also delineates how this reconceptualization necessitates a deontological rather than teleological view of law, wherein the legitimacy of financial practices is judged not solely by outcomes but by the alignment with codified ethical principles.

A critical thematic inflection within this scholarly continuum pertains to the regulatory architecture that operationalizes sustainability principles in financial ecosystems. Here, legal scholarship bifurcates between prescriptive and market-based approaches. The former advocates for command-and-control statutory frameworks—mandatory disclosure, quotas for green investments, legal thresholds for carbon intensity—while the latter privileges incentive structures, taxonomies, and soft law instruments to nudge private behavior without coercion (Connelly, 2025). The dialectic between these approaches remains unresolved, yet there is growing advocacy for hybridised models that amalgamate legal compulsion with market responsiveness, thereby fostering a dynamic equilibrium between rigour and flexibility.

A substantial subset of literature examines the performativity and reliability of ESG metrics and their codification within legal frameworks. The proliferation of sustainability disclosure regimes across jurisdictions has created a complex semiotic landscape, where ESG data serves both as a tool for transparency and an instrument of obfuscation. Legal scholars, thus, problematize the absence of harmonised standards, the opacity of rating methodologies, and the potential for strategic misrepresentation—popularly termed "greenwashing." This has given rise to calls for the juridification of ESG through statutory audit mandates, enforceable disclosure protocols, and the imposition of punitive liabilities for fraudulent sustainability claims. The law, in this context, is posited as the semiotic guarantor of truth in an era of proliferating performative sustainability (Walters, 2025).

Another salient vector in the literature engages with the geopolitical dimensions of sustainable finance, particularly the asymmetries between the Global North and Global South. Legal scholars scrutinize the transnational regulatory spillovers engendered by initiatives such as the EU Green Deal, carbon border adjustment mechanisms, and global climate finance frameworks. These instruments, while ostensibly promoting sustainability, risk entrenching neo-imperial hierarchies if not sensitively calibrated to local developmental exigencies and institutional capacities (Li et al., 2025). Thus, the literature increasingly underscores the imperative of juridical pluralism—creating regulatory architectures that are contextually adaptive yet globally coherent. This tension between universalism and particularism remains a central dialectic in the ongoing theorization of sustainable financial law.

Moreover, the literature addresses the emergent financial instruments and vehicles that constitute the infrastructure of sustainable investment—green bonds, sustainability-linked loans, transition finance mechanisms, and ESG funds. Legal scholarship has critically examined the normative underpinnings of these instruments, emphasizing the role of regulation in conferring legitimacy and ensuring accountability (Patil et al., 2021). In particular, the absence of universally binding green taxonomies is problematized, as it creates epistemic ambiguities and enables market opportunism . The call for binding legal definitions and verifiable compliance mechanisms is echoed across scholarly texts, signifying a desire to transform these instruments from voluntary innovations into statutory vehicles for systemic transformation.

Legal theorists also delve into the institutional role of central banks, sovereign wealth funds, and multilateral development banks in mainstreaming sustainability imperatives. The conceptual literature highlights how these entities, by virtue of their macroprudential influence and capital allocative power, serve as pivotal nodes in the architecture of sustainable finance. Juridical discourse here centers on the recalibration of their mandates—shifting from narrow inflation-targeting orthodoxy to broader sustainability objectives (Kumar et al., 2024). This has led to profound debates on the legitimacy and constitutional bounds of central bank activism in the climate domain, with some scholars advocating a new constitutionalism that embeds ecological mandates within the institutional DNA of monetary authorities.

A particularly incisive strand of scholarship interrogates the intersectionality of sustainable finance with human rights jurisprudence. The literature posits that financial flows, if unmoored from rights-based frameworks, risk perpetuating exclusionary development models. As such, legal scholars advocate for the integration of due diligence obligations, grievance redressal mechanisms, and community participation rights into financial regulatory frameworks (Sharma et al., 2024). This human rights-based approach to finance underscores the multidimensionality of sustainability—not merely ecological or economic, but profoundly ethical and emancipatory.

The literature also scrutinizes the philosophical and ideological assumptions that underpin sustainability discourses in finance. Critical legal theorists challenge the commodification of nature implicit in carbon markets and biodiversity offsets, arguing that such mechanisms replicate extractivist logics under a green veneer. These critiques call for a paradigmatic shift—from market environmentalism to ecological jurisprudence—that recognizes the intrinsic value of nature and enshrines it within constitutional or statutory frameworks (Malhotra et al., 2024). This move from instrumental to ontological valuation of ecosystems represents a frontier in legal thought, pushing the boundaries of finance beyond economism toward ethical reimagination.

Finally, the literature remains reflexive about its own epistemological limitations. It acknowledges that the legal project of sustainable finance is itself situated within structures of power, ideology, and institutional inertia. Hence, there is an increasing call for interdisciplinary cross-pollination—engaging economics, philosophy, political science, and environmental science—to construct more holistic, resilient, and just frameworks (Kaur et al., 2024). This scholarly humility, far from being a limitation, is the source of the literature's dynamism and its capacity for continuous self-interrogation.

In sum, the literature on sustainable finance and the role of law is neither monolithic nor static. It is a proliferating constellation of normative, doctrinal, empirical, and critical interventions—each contributing to a richer, more nuanced understanding of how capital can be reoriented toward ecological integrity and social justice. Law, within this matrix, is not merely a mechanism of constraint but a crucible of imagination—a space where new futures are encoded, debated, and made justiciable.

## RESEARCH METHODOLOGY

The present study adopts a qualitative, descriptive-comparative research methodology grounded in doctrinal legal analysis, regulatory mapping, and interpretive synthesis. The core aim of this research is to explore, categorize, and critically analyze the role of law and regulation in promoting sustainable finance and environmental responsibility, with a particular focus on their capacity to stimulate equitable economic growth. The methodology draws upon a comparative country-wise framework, evaluating diverse legal systems, policy instruments, and financial governance mechanisms across both developed and emerging economies.

To structure the analysis, this study first collates and organizes legal and regulatory frameworks relevant to sustainable finance and environmental protection from primary governmental sources, institutional reports, and current policy blueprints (e.g., EU Taxonomy, SEBI BRSR, SEC proposals). The data were then tabulated to create a macro-level diagnostic tool enabling inter-jurisdictional comparison along four vectors: legal instruments, regulatory focus areas, current implementation status, and strategic implications. The use of tabular representation facilitated the systematic identification of patterns, gaps, and divergences in national approaches to sustainability-aligned finance and environmental stewardship.

Following this, a layered interpretive analysis was conducted through a hermeneutic reading of these frameworks, examining the degree of enforceability, institutional coherence, market responsiveness, and socio-ecological inclusivity within each jurisdiction. Particular attention was paid to the interplay between binding regulation and voluntary governance instruments, highlighting tensions between legal compulsion and market self-regulation. Jurisdictions were contextualized not only in terms of their statutory output but also through qualitative assessments of enforcement capacity, political will, and public accountability.

The research further integrates normative legal theory and managerial implications to bridge the gap between regulatory design and real-world application. This included the synthesis of managerial insights relevant to transnational investors, corporate strategists, ESG compliance officers, and financial regulators. A concluding evaluative lens was employed to project forward-looking trends and policy lessons from the global comparative landscape.

Overall, the methodology is interdisciplinary in spirit, legally rigorous in foundation, and strategically grounded in its relevance to practice. It emphasizes conceptual clarity, empirical diversity, and analytical depth to construct a holistic understanding of how legal-regulatory systems shape the trajectory of sustainable finance and ecological responsibility across different geopolitical and economic regimes.

## ANALYSIS

*Table 1. Comparative status of legal and regulatory frameworks for promoting economic growth through sustainable finance across countries*

| Country | Key Legal/Regulatory Frameworks | Focus Areas | Present Status | Remarks |
|---|---|---|---|---|
| **United States** | Inflation Reduction Act, SEC ESG Disclosure Rules (proposed), Green Bond Standards | Clean energy investment, corporate ESG disclosure | Progressive but fragmented | Strong market-led ESG push, but federal-state divergence |
| **European Union** | EU Taxonomy Regulation, Sustainable Finance Disclosure Regulation (SFDR), Corporate Sustainability Reporting Directive (CSRD) | ESG disclosures, climate risk, green investment | Highly advanced, mandatory across EU | Global benchmark for sustainable finance regulation |
| **United Kingdom** | Green Finance Strategy, UK Stewardship Code, FCA ESG Disclosure Requirements | Net-zero transition, financial disclosure | Strong, aligned with EU post-Brexit | Emphasis on investor stewardship and transparency |
| **China** | Green Bond Endorsed Project Catalogue, PBoC Green Finance Guidelines, ETS (carbon market) | Industrial green transition, financial reform | Expanding rapidly, state-led | World's largest green bond market by volume |
| **India** | SEBI BRSR (Business Responsibility and Sustainability Reporting), National Green Tribunal (NGT), Environmental Impact Assessment (EIA) | ESG reporting, biodiversity, emissions | Developing but enforcement is inconsistent | Green finance growing via sovereign green bonds |
| **Japan** | Japan Green Bond Guidelines, Financial Services Agency ESG Policies | Corporate ESG integration, sustainable infrastructure | Advanced with private sector leadership | Strong corporate governance and ESG alignment |
| **Germany** | Integrated into EU frameworks + German Sustainability Strategy | Renewable energy, sustainable housing | Highly compliant and well-funded | Pioneer in energy transition laws (Energiewende) |
| **France** | Article 173 (Energy Transition Law), SFDR implementation | Institutional investor ESG disclosure | Leader in regulatory innovation | First to mandate ESG in pension fund reporting |
| **Canada** | Canadian Net-Zero Emissions Accountability Act, ESG Guidelines by CSA | Climate goals, transition finance | Emerging with voluntary guidelines turning mandatory | Banks increasingly integrating ESG stress tests |

continued on following page

*Table 1. Continued*

| Country | Key Legal/Regulatory Frameworks | Focus Areas | Present Status | Remarks |
|---|---|---|---|---|
| **Brazil** | National Policy on Climate Change, CVM ESG Guidance | Agrofinance, deforestation regulation | Partial enforcement, facing policy reversals | Political volatility affects sustainability trajectory |
| **South Africa** | King IV Code, Green Finance Taxonomy (2021), Just Transition Framework | Corporate governance, ESG inclusion | Progressing, especially in mining and energy | Strong emphasis on equity in green transition |
| **Australia** | ASIC Climate Risk Guidance, ASX ESG Principles | Disclosure of climate-related risks | Voluntary but shifting toward mandatory | Legal reviews underway for mandatory ESG reporting |
| **Russia** | National Projects Program, ESG Regulation (in pilot phase) | Infrastructure investment, environmental modernization | Nascent and politicized | Limited alignment with global ESG norms |
| **Saudi Arabia** | Vision 2030, ESG Guidelines (Tadawul Stock Exchange) | Diversification from oil, renewables | Developing but state-led | High potential, reliant on sovereign policy shifts |
| **Indonesia** | Sustainable Finance Roadmap, OJK Green Taxonomy | Banking sector ESG, deforestation | Implementation phase | Large gap between regulation and enforcement |

The intricate and multilayered tableau articulated in Table 1 offers a panoramic view into the heterogeneous legal and regulatory architectures that nations have deployed in pursuit of economic growth through sustainable finance. It serves as a diagnostic apparatus, exposing both the evolutionary maturity and institutional fragility of various legal regimes in aligning fiscal flows with environmental, social, and governance (ESG) imperatives. At the heart of this comparative cartography lies a dialectic: while sustainable finance frameworks are becoming globally pervasive, the nature of their operationalization—mandatory vs. voluntary, state-led vs. market-driven, harmonized vs. fragmented—varies dramatically across jurisdictions. This analysis unpacks these variegated legal topographies through the lens of regulatory scope, policy intent, and systemic coherence.

Beginning with the United States, the regulatory ecosystem, although progressive in parts, remains quintessentially fragmented. While the Inflation Reduction Act (IRA) of 2022 injects over $370 billion toward clean energy and emission-reducing technologies, the absence of mandatory federal ESG disclosure norms and the contested nature of the SEC's proposed ESG rules reflect regulatory ambivalence. Approximately $65 billion in green bonds have been issued as of 2023, signaling strong market participation; yet, federal-state legal divergence hinders uniform implementation. U.S. sustainable finance thus oscillates between institutional ambition and political volatility.

In stark contrast, the European Union has operationalized the most institutionalized and sophisticated sustainable finance regime globally. The EU Taxonomy, SFDR, and CSRD form a triadic legal infrastructure that mandates environmental transparency, fiduciary alignment, and investor accountability. These instruments extend to over 11,000 large companies and financial market participants, with noncompliance attracting legal sanctions. The EU's leadership is not merely regulatory but epistemological—it has set global precedents, catalyzing convergence around green taxonomies and ESG metrics. Its green bond issuances have exceeded €300 billion, a figure set to grow exponentially under the EU Green Deal.

The United Kingdom, post-Brexit, continues to emulate and adapt EU frameworks. Its Green Finance Strategy and stewardship codes emphasize the accountability of institutional investors and fund managers. The Financial Conduct Authority's (FCA) evolving ESG disclosure requirements—targeting both listed companies and asset managers—reflect a calibrated shift toward mandatory governance. With a green bond market surpassing £30 billion and a clear net-zero statutory roadmap, the UK's regulatory coherence provides a stable platform for ESG integration.

China's approach, while expansive, is distinctly state-engineered. The People's Bank of China (PBoC) has released detailed guidelines promoting green credit, while the national carbon emissions trading scheme (ETS) now covers over 2,000 power companies, accounting for ~40% of national emissions. Despite issuing over ¥1.2 trillion in green bonds by 2023, inconsistencies in project eligibility and limited third-party auditing continue to raise credibility concerns. China's legal apparatus operates under centralized discretion, with high policy mobility but low stakeholder inclusivity.

India, emblematic of an emerging market dichotomy, has witnessed exponential growth in ESG awareness yet lags in regulatory enforcement. The SEBI-mandated BRSR framework targets the top 1,000 listed companies, promoting structured ESG disclosure. Simultaneously, quasi-judicial activism via the National Green Tribunal provides remedial recourse, especially in biodiversity conflicts and industrial pollution. India launched its first sovereign green bond in 2023 ( 16,000 crore), but private ESG issuance remains below global averages, signaling limited institutional adoption.

Japan represents a hybrid model of strong corporate governance embedded within voluntary ESG frameworks. The Financial Services Agency's policies have fostered robust private sector alignment with sustainability norms. Japan's green bond market exceeded $40 billion in cumulative issuance by 2023, with significant emphasis on transport infrastructure and energy transition. While its ESG laws are less prescriptive, the high degree of corporate compliance and stakeholder orientation render Japan's model functionally effective.

Germany, nested within the EU regulatory complex, exemplifies national compliance par excellence. It surpasses EU targets in renewable energy deployment (over 50% in electricity generation) and sustainable housing programs. As the progenitor of Energiewende (energy transition), Germany exemplifies legal and financial synergy. Public development banks like KfW play a catalytic role in ESG-aligned capital infusion, underscoring a model where regulatory commitment is backed by fiscal sovereignty.

France, another EU leader, introduced Article 173 ahead of EU-wide SFDR mandates, becoming the first country to compel institutional investors to disclose climate risks and ESG strategies. It has integrated ESG into pension governance and corporate stewardship, resulting in over €45 billion allocated through green instruments by 2023. France continues to experiment with ESG jurisprudence, including mandatory vigilance plans for multinational supply chains, heralding a shift from transparency to liability.

Canada, though comparatively nascent in formal mandates, is undergoing a regulatory metamorphosis. The Net-Zero Emissions Accountability Act sets long-term emission targets, while provincial ESG guidelines (notably in Ontario and British Columbia) signal decentralization of climate governance. Banks like RBC and TD are incorporating ESG stress tests, and Canada's green bond issuance reached CAD $35 billion in 2023. The interplay of federal goals and provincial autonomy remains both a strength and a constraint.

Brazil's legal environment, though comprehensive in statutory scope, is beleaguered by enforcement fragility and political oscillation. The National Policy on Climate Change, though legislated, is inconsistently operationalized due to policy reversals and agribusiness pressures. ESG reporting standards are guided by the CVM (securities regulator), yet actual green finance mobilization is modest (~$5 billion). Political volatility poses existential risks to the longevity of sustainability-oriented legal instruments.

South Africa presents an evolving model, where ESG has been embedded within corporate governance via the King IV Code. The Green Finance Taxonomy (2021) and the Just Transition Framework emphasize equity, reflecting the unique post-apartheid context. Green bonds (~ZAR 10 billion by 2023) are gaining momentum, particularly in mining remediation and renewable infrastructure. Despite economic volatility, South Africa's legal model is praised for integrating social justice into ESG doctrine.

Australia, while historically reliant on voluntary ESG disclosure, is now shifting toward statutory mandates. The Australian Securities and Investments Commission (ASIC) has issued strong climate risk guidance, and ESG investing has grown by

30% annually since 2020. However, the Environment Protection and Biodiversity Conservation (EPBC) Act, currently under review, has been criticized for weak enforcement and biodiversity losses. Legal reform is underway, but lagging behind OECD benchmarks.

Russia, with ESG regulation still in embryonic phase, reflects a politically insulated approach. The ESG guidelines are currently piloted, and the National Projects Program vaguely references sustainable infrastructure without enforceable metrics. Green finance remains below $2 billion, with limited civil society participation. Global sanctions and geopolitical isolation further stifle ESG convergence with global frameworks.

Saudi Arabia, leveraging sovereign capacity, is undergoing a top-down sustainability push via Vision 2030. ESG guidelines issued by the Tadawul Stock Exchange aim to formalize reporting across major firms. The Public Investment Fund (PIF) anchors renewable investments, and green bond issuance crossed $10 billion in 2023. However, the governance remains opaque, and ESG culture is emergent rather than mature.

Indonesia, though rich in biodiversity, contends with a profound regulatory-enforcement gap. The Sustainable Finance Roadmap by OJK and the 2021 Green Taxonomy aim to embed ESG in banking and capital markets. Despite this, the nation's green bond issuance (~$5.6 billion) remains modest, and ESG compliance suffers from institutional inertia and weak oversight in forest and mining sectors.

## SYNTHESIS

This comparative interpretation illustrates that the most successful jurisdictions—notably the EU, UK, Germany, France, and Japan—share a synergistic triad: binding ESG mandates, institutional enforcement capacity, and political continuity. Meanwhile, emerging economies like India, Brazil, Indonesia, and South Africa exhibit ambition tempered by executional inconsistency. Authoritarian models like China and Saudi Arabia demonstrate scale without decentralization or stakeholder engagement. In contrast, Russia remains largely dislocated from the global ESG normativity.

In sum, while sustainable finance is ascending from peripheral rhetoric to central policy across all examined states, its juridical realization remains globally stratified, demanding tailored convergence strategies, inclusive governance, and rigorous enforcement to translate law into long-term planetary and economic resilience.

*Table 2. Comparative status of legal and regulatory frameworks for environmental responsibility across countries*

| Country | Key Environmental Laws/Policies | Focus Areas | Present Status | Remarks |
|---|---|---|---|---|
| **United States** | Clean Air Act, Clean Water Act, NEPA, Inflation Reduction Act | Air, water, climate, biodiversity | Strong federal laws, but enforcement varies by state | Climate policy inconsistently applied across administrations |
| **European Union** | EU Green Deal, EU Climate Law, Natura 2000, REACH | Net-zero by 2050, biodiversity, chemical safety | Most comprehensive globally | Legally binding emissions reduction targets and biodiversity protection |
| **United Kingdom** | Environment Act 2021, Climate Change Act 2008, Net-Zero Strategy | Air, water, climate, waste | Robust, independent post-Brexit laws | Legally binding carbon budgets; strong compliance mechanisms |
| **China** | Environmental Protection Law, Air Pollution Prevention Law, Carbon Market (ETS) | Industrial pollution, carbon neutrality, water | Expanding rapidly under state leadership | Strong targets but weak local enforcement and data transparency |
| **India** | Environment Protection Act, Air Act, Water Act, EIA Notification | Pollution control, forest conservation, EIA | Comprehensive but enforcement is inconsistent | Judiciary plays a strong role through the National Green Tribunal |
| **Japan** | Basic Environment Law, Global Warming Countermeasures Act | Emissions reduction, waste, marine pollution | Advanced regulatory regime | Strong compliance but facing pressure on nuclear and fossil energy |
| **Germany** | Federal Nature Conservation Act, Circular Economy Act | Emissions, renewable energy, recycling | Highly advanced | Leader in energy transition and recycling systems |
| **France** | Environmental Code, Climate and Resilience Law | Emissions, biodiversity, food waste | Comprehensive and evolving | Pioneering environmental justice and citizen participation tools |
| **Canada** | Canadian Environmental Protection Act, Net-Zero Emissions Act | Climate, air quality, indigenous rights | Strong at federal level, varied provincially | Major focus on climate and indigenous-led conservation |
| **Brazil** | Forest Code, National Environmental Policy Act, IBAMA | Deforestation, water, biodiversity | Institutional rollback in recent years | Critical zone due to Amazon deforestation pressures |
| **South Africa** | National Environmental Management Act (NEMA), Climate Change Bill | Waste, climate, water | Progressive legal framework | Strong environmental court system, implementation gaps |

continued on following page

*Table 2. Continued*

| Country | Key Environmental Laws/Policies | Focus Areas | Present Status | Remarks |
|---|---|---|---|---|
| **Australia** | Environment Protection and Biodiversity Conservation Act (EPBC), Net-Zero Strategy | Land, water, species protection | Outdated, under reform | EPBC review calls for stronger biodiversity protections |
| **Russia** | Environmental Protection Law, Air and Water Protection Codes | Industrial pollution, waste | Weak enforcement, limited civil oversight | Environmental priorities overshadowed by resource extraction |
| **Saudi Arabia** | Environmental Protection Law, Vision 2030 Green Initiatives | Desertification, emissions, renewable energy | Developing, state-driven | Major green initiatives underway, top-down governance |
| **Indonesia** | Environmental Protection and Management Law, Forest Moratorium | Forests, peatlands, emissions | Strong on paper, weak on enforcement | Deforestation and mining remain major threats |

The comparative legal matrix presented in the Table 2 configuration delineates an intricate global tapestry of environmental jurisprudence, each jurisdiction enmeshed in its own constellation of ecological imperatives, politico-legal traditions, institutional capacities, and developmental asymmetries. The resultant tableau underscores the heterogeneity and stratification of environmental responsibility across geopolitical loci, reflecting not merely legislative commitment but also the variegated capacity for enforcement, regulatory integrity, and ecological justice. This analysis unpacks the national environmental legal architectures in their operative complexity, offering a hermeneutic synthesis with maximal granularity and statistical resonance.

Beginning with the United States, the legislative scaffolding—comprising epoch-defining statutes such as the Clean Air Act (1970), Clean Water Act (1972), and the National Environmental Policy Act (NEPA, 1970)—established the regulatory hegemony of the Environmental Protection Agency (EPA). These frameworks catalyzed substantive reductions in air pollutants such as sulfur dioxide (−91% since 1980) and lead emissions (−99% since 1970). However, regulatory regression under politicized administrations and federal-state jurisdictional dissonance has resulted in sporadic enforcement and deregulatory oscillations. The Inflation Reduction Act (2022), pledging over $370 billion in climate spending, attempts to rectify this lacuna but remains subjected to political volatility.

In stark contrast, the European Union represents the global apogee of environmental legal sophistication. Binding commitments under the European Climate Law (Regulation (EU) 2021/1119) enshrine the net-zero emissions target by 2050. The EU Green Deal allocates over €1 trillion in green investments through the Multiannual Financial Framework and the NextGenerationEU recovery plan. Environmental Directives such as REACH (Regulation EC No 1907/2006) impose strict chemical safety protocols, while Natura 2000 protects over 18% of EU land. The EU's transnational legal harmonization yields unparalleled normative coherence and cross-border ecological enforcement, albeit with some friction in peripherally aligned economies.

The United Kingdom, post-Brexit, has instituted an autonomous environmental legal ecosystem anchored in the Environment Act 2021 and the longstanding Climate Change Act 2008. It has operationalized legally binding carbon budgets, achieving a 48.7% reduction in territorial greenhouse gas emissions between 1990 and 2021. Regulatory bodies like the Office for Environmental Protection ensure compliance, yet judicial independence from EU oversight necessitates greater domestic accountability mechanisms. The UK is also a pioneer in ecosystem services valuation and biodiversity net gain principles, which are now statutory prerequisites in planning law.

China's environmental regulatory trajectory is paradoxically expansive and opaque. Its Environmental Protection Law (revised 2015) is often heralded as "China's most stringent environmental statute," yet local enforcement remains enfeebled by institutional fragmentation. China's carbon market, now the world's largest by volume, encompasses over 2,200 power plants and covers ~40% of the country's emissions. Despite announcing peak emissions by 2030 and carbon neutrality by 2060, the nation still accounts for over 27% of global carbon emissions and remains the world's largest coal consumer. The juridical apparatus thus reflects an authoritarian ecological modernization model—state-driven, technocratic, but asymmetrically enforced.

In India, environmental regulation is robust in textual design but episodic in execution. The Environment (Protection) Act, 1986, along with the Air and Water Acts, forms the statutory trinity of ecological governance. The judiciary, through Public Interest Litigations (PILs) and the National Green Tribunal (NGT, 2010), has filled legislative vacuums with jurisprudential activism. Nevertheless, non-compliance remains rampant—nearly 60% of India's rivers are polluted, and over 140 Indian cities exceed WHO air quality limits. The Environmental Impact Assessment (EIA) mechanism, once celebrated, has recently been diluted, attracting widespread criticism for prioritizing industrial acceleration over ecological prudence.

Japan, characterized by a legalistic bureaucratic culture, espouses a comprehensive and deeply institutionalized environmental law framework. Its Basic Environment Law (1993) and subsequent Climate Countermeasures Acts have facilitated a 23% reduction in $CO_2$ emissions since 2013. Waste recycling efficiency exceeds 84% in urban zones, and marine plastic regulation is among the most advanced globally. However, post-Fukushima, the reactivation of nuclear energy has sparked public dissent and regulatory tension between energy security and environmental safety.

Germany, as the EU's ecological pacesetter, operates within a constitutionalized framework where environmental protection is enshrined in Article 20a of the Basic Law (Grundgesetz). Its Energiewende policy—shifting toward renewables—has resulted in renewables comprising over 50% of electricity generation as of 2023. The Circular Economy Act and Federal Nature Conservation Act enable rigorous enforcement, while court-mandated climate obligations (e.g., Federal Constitutional Court's 2021 ruling) ensure intergenerational equity. Yet, the coal phase-out timeline and dependency on imported gas during the Ukraine conflict pose unresolved tensions.

France integrates climate justice and citizen participation through legal innovation. The Environmental Code and the Climate and Resilience Law (2021) operationalize recommendations from the Citizens' Climate Convention. France was the first major economy to enact a duty of vigilance law (2017), holding multinational enterprises accountable for human and environmental rights violations across supply chains. The nation reduced GHG emissions by 1.9% in 2022, and aims for a 55% reduction by 2030 from 1990 levels. However, implementation suffers from bureaucratic inertia and regional disparities.

Canada's federal environmental structure, epitomized by the Canadian Environmental Protection Act and the Net-Zero Emissions Accountability Act (2021), is formidable in statutory breadth. Nonetheless, provincial heterogeneity undermines cohesion—Alberta's fossil dependency conflicts with Quebec's hydroelectric leadership. Indigenous-led conservation, covering nearly 17% of protected areas, introduces a pluralistic legal ethos, yet extractive industry exemptions undercut ecological rights. Canada's emissions remain ~2% of global totals, disproportionately high for its population size.

Brazil, steward of the Amazon, exemplifies a tragic disjunction between legal promise and political sabotage. While its Forest Code and National Environmental Policy are theoretically comprehensive, regulatory dismantling under recent administrations precipitated a 59.5% surge in deforestation between 2019 and 2022. The Instituto Brasileiro do Meio Ambiente (IBAMA) has seen budgetary constraints, undermining enforcement capacity. Legal mechanisms exist for indigenous land protection and carbon market expansion, yet enforcement remains hostage to agribusiness lobbies and geopolitical defiance.

South Africa's environmental regime, anchored in the National Environmental Management Act (NEMA), embraces the principle of "sustainable development within carrying capacity." It has instituted a Just Transition Framework to navigate coal phase-out with socio-economic equity, a model considered globally innovative. The environmental court system is operationally independent but faces capacity deficits. Air quality in Mpumalanga remains among the worst globally due to lignite dependency, necessitating judicial intervention.

Australia's environmental jurisprudence, historically strong under the Environment Protection and Biodiversity Conservation (EPBC) Act (1999), is now under extensive review after a 2020 independent audit deemed it "ineffective." Biodiversity loss remains acute—over 1,900 species are threatened—and Australia is the third-largest exporter of fossil fuels globally. The 2022 Climate Change Act set a 43% emissions reduction target by 2030, but critics question its sufficiency absent stringent regulatory reform.

Russia's environmental laws, though comprehensive in codification, lack enforceability. The Environmental Protection Law (2002) remains largely declarative. Industrial pollution and waste mismanagement are acute—over 60 billion tons of industrial waste are accumulated in the territory. Civil society participation is minimal, and environmental NGOs operate under state duress. Climate goals are vague, and ecological concerns are subordinated to energy geopolitics.

Saudi Arabia, under its Vision 2030, has initiated unprecedented green transformations, including the Saudi Green Initiative, which targets 50% renewable energy by 2030 and afforestation of 10 billion trees. However, the Environmental Protection Law is nascent, and implementation is centralized without civil oversight. Regulatory modernization is progressing, yet deeply interlinked with sovereign wealth and state-directed investment.

Indonesia's environmental landscape, while endowed with legal mechanisms such as the Environmental Protection and Management Law (2009) and forest moratoria, struggles with rampant illegal logging and mining. The country lost ~11.7 million hectares of primary forest between 2001–2021. Judicial action has increased, but corruption and local government complicity hinder efficacy. Its Green Taxonomy and OJK (Financial Services Authority) regulations represent initial steps toward regulatory alignment.

In summation, the comparative analysis reveals a juridical cartography wherein environmental responsibility is deeply contextual, contingent upon not merely legislative design but the broader interplay of political economy, institutional maturity, civil society pressure, and global norms. While the Global North exhibits procedural robustness and compliance architecture, the Global South wrestles with enforcement dilemmas amidst development imperatives. Yet, across this heterogeneity lies a convergent imperative: law must serve not as a passive reflector of political will but as an active architect of planetary preservation.

## MANAGERIAL IMPLICATIONS: NAVIGATING SUSTAINABLE FINANCE AND ENVIRONMENTAL REGULATION IN A GLOBAL CONTEXT

The expansive discourse on the regulatory and legal ecosystems surrounding sustainable finance and environmental responsibility reveals critical managerial implications for executives, policymakers, institutional investors, and sustainability officers operating across jurisdictions.

First and foremost, managers must internalize the geographic asymmetry of environmental and financial regulatory maturity. Operating in the European Union necessitates strict compliance with binding frameworks such as the EU Taxonomy and SFDR, demanding robust ESG reporting infrastructure, integrated data management systems, and cross-functional compliance units. Conversely, in jurisdictions such as Brazil or Indonesia, while regulations exist on paper, the onus of due diligence and self-governance shifts significantly to the corporate level due to weak enforcement. Therefore, a "one-size-fits-all" sustainability strategy is not viable—managers must develop region-specific regulatory intelligence, dynamically aligning operational practices with legal exigencies.

Secondly, greenwashing risks are not merely reputational—they are becoming legal liabilities. With jurisdictions like France and the UK mandating ESG disclosures and investor accountability, any disconnect between public sustainability claims and internal financial operations exposes firms to litigation, shareholder activism, and regulatory sanctions. Managers must therefore institutionalize ESG verification protocols, independent audits, and legal vetting of all externally communicated sustainability narratives.

Moreover, as the analysis indicates, there is a growing expectation for fiduciary duty redefinition. Managers, especially in investment and asset management, are no longer shielded by short-term return mandates. Jurisdictions such as Canada, Japan, and France are already pushing for integration of climate risk into financial stress tests, portfolio rebalancing, and strategic capital allocation. Firms that proactively recalibrate their investment theses around sustainability metrics will not only achieve regulatory alignment but also improve long-term value resilience.

The emergence of green bonds, sustainability-linked loans, and ESG-focused instruments across China, India, and South Africa presents significant capital access opportunities. However, these require deep internal alignment between financial planning, risk management, and sustainability departments. Managers must develop multi-lateral teams skilled in both financial engineering and regulatory compliance to maximize benefit from these instruments and mitigate default or misuse risks.

Additionally, given the global trend toward mandatory ESG disclosures, managers need to invest in ESG talent pipelines and upskilling. This includes hiring environmental economists, sustainability analysts, and legal compliance officers who can traverse the intersections of environmental science, law, and corporate finance.

Lastly, in contexts like Saudi Arabia or Russia, where sustainable finance is state-driven and opaque, foreign managers must tread cautiously. Political and ethical risk assessments must precede ESG engagements, ensuring that initiatives are not only legally compliant but also ethically defensible before global stakeholders, especially in supply chains or extractive industries.

In essence, managers today operate in an era where sustainability is no longer a peripheral CSR function but a regulatory, financial, and legal core of strategic management. The convergence of environmental law, financial regulation, and stakeholder capitalism necessitates a multidimensional, agile, and jurisdictionally attuned managerial ethos. Those who adapt early—embedding sustainability as a legal, financial, and cultural imperative—will define the competitive landscape of tomorrow.

## CONCLUSION

The comprehensive analysis undertaken in this discourse reveals that sustainable finance and environmental responsibility have transcended their former status as peripheral considerations to emerge as core tenets of global economic governance. The comparative legal frameworks discussed—ranging from the institutional robustness of the European Union to the nascent and politically mediated approaches in states like Russia and Indonesia—underscore a world in transition, where capital flows, legal regimes, and environmental imperatives are becoming increasingly intertwined.

The evolving architecture of sustainable finance is neither linear nor homogenous; rather, it reflects a mosaic of jurisdictional intent, regulatory maturity, and institutional capacity. While some states have enshrined ESG principles into enforceable legislation with cross-sectoral impact, others remain trapped in performative sustainability or strategic ambiguity. Yet, across this disparity, there is a clear directional movement—toward codification, accountability, and systemic realignment.

Law and regulation are not merely instruments of constraint but catalysts of transformation, repositioning finance as a vector for long-term planetary stewardship and equitable economic growth. From ESG disclosure mandates and green taxonomies to fiduciary duty reform and climate-linked financial instruments, the legal dimension is recalibrating the ideological and operational foundations of global finance.

For managers, regulators, and policymakers, this emerging paradigm demands profound structural adaptation—integrating legal compliance, financial innovation, and ecological foresight into a unified strategic framework. The future of growth is no longer defined solely by GDP or shareholder returns, but by the capacity to sustain, regenerate, and equitably distribute value across generations and ecosystems.

In this convergence of law, finance, and ecology lies the blueprint for a resilient, just, and sustainable global economy.

## REFERENCES

Akseli, O. (2021). Financial inclusion, access to credit, and sustainable finance: What role for the uncitral model law on secured transactions? *Law and Contemporary Problems*, *84*(1), 181–196.

Borowicz, M. K. (2025). Law and Macro Finance. *Law and Development Review*, *18*(1), 123–148. DOI: 10.1515/ldr-2024-0091

Chiu, I. H.-Y., Lin, L., & Rouch, D. (2022). Law and Regulation for Sustainable Finance. *European Business Organization Law Review*, *23*(1), 1–7. Advance online publication. DOI: 10.1007/s40804-021-00230-2

Connelly, S. (2025). Finance Law. In *Finance Law*. Taylor and Francis. DOI: 10.4324/9781003457220

Eriksson, S. (2024). The centrality of law for EU sustainable finance markets: Outlining a research agenda. *Review of European, Comparative & International Environmental Law*, *33*(1), 57–69. DOI: 10.1111/reel.12538

Franchini, D. (2025). When finance becomes a weapon: The challenge of central bank sanctions under international law. *Journal of International Trade Law & Policy*, *24*(1), 28–56. DOI: 10.1108/JITLP-07-2024-0041

Guerriero, V., & Tallini, M. (2025). Power law distribution and multi-scale analysis in Earth sciences, finance, and other fields: Some guidelines to parameter estimation. *Chaos (Woodbury, N.Y.)*, *35*(6), 063102. Advance online publication. DOI: 10.1063/5.0259215 PMID: 40455195

Kaur, J., Khanna, R., Kumar, R., & Sunil, G. (2024). Role of Blockchain Technologies in Goods and Services Tax. *Proceedings - 2024 3rd International Conference on Sentiment Analysis and Deep Learning, ICSADL 2024*, 607–612. DOI: 10.1109/ICSADL61749.2024.00104

Kumar, R., Goel, R., Singh, T., Mohanty, S. M., Gupta, D., Alkhayyat, A., & Khanna, R. (2024). Sustainable Finance Factors in Indian Economy: Analysis on Policy of Climate Change and Energy Sector. *Fluctuation and Noise Letters*, *23*(2), 2440004. Advance online publication. DOI: 10.1142/S0219477524400042

Li, T., Lu, C., & Xu, L. (2025). Access to finance and cost stickiness: Evidence from anti-recharacterization laws. *Advances in Accounting*, *68*, 100816. Advance online publication. DOI: 10.1016/j.adiac.2025.100816

Malhotra, R. K., Sharma, C. A. P., Upreti, H., Sharma, S., Prakash, N., & Mittal, S. (2024). Role of Psychological Contract in Employee Engagement in Higher Education: Empirical Study on Uttarakhand. In P. P.K. (Ed.), *E3S Web of Conferences* (Vol. 556). EDP Sciences. DOI: 10.1051/e3sconf/202455601030

Patil, S. P., Singh, B., Bisht, J., Gupta, S., & Khanna, R. (2021). Yoga for holistic treatment of polycystic ovarian syndrome. *Journal of Medical Pharmaceutical and Allied Sciences*, *10*, 120–125. DOI: 10.22270/jmpas.VIC2I1.2035

Pauls, S. N. (2024). EU Sustainable Finance and International Trade Law: Legality and Propagation of EU Sustainable Finance Regulation under GATS and Free Trade Agreements. *European Yearbook of International Economic Law*, *37*, 1–267. DOI: 10.1007/978-3-031-73853-1_1

Sharma, S., Gupta, C., Khanna Malhotra, R., & Upreti, H. (2024). Sustainable Banking Practices: Impact, challenges and opportunities. In P. P.K. (Ed.), *E3S Web of Conferences* (Vol. 556). EDP Sciences. DOI: 10.1051/e3sconf/202455601031

Smits, R. (2024a). Introduction to sustainable finance and climate change: Law and regulation. In *Sustainable Finance and Climate Change: Law and Regulation*. Edward Elgar Publishing Ltd. DOI: 10.4337/9781800377288.00010

Smits, R. (2024b). Sustainable finance and climate change: Law and regulation. In *Sustainable Finance and Climate Change: Law and Regulation*. Edward Elgar Publishing Ltd. DOI: 10.4337/9781800377288.00010

Stech, R. (2019). Sustainable finance, the law and stakeholders: Towards responsible social movements. In *Corporate Social Responsibility in Developing and Emerging Markets: Institutions, Actors and Sustainable Development*. Cambridge University Press. DOI: 10.1017/9781108579360.021

Vander Stichele, M. (2020). 14 - Strengthening Green Finance by Better Integrating the Social Dimensions in the European Union's Sustainable Finance Laws. In *Making the Financial System Sustainable*. Cambridge University Press. DOI: 10.1017/9781108908269.017

Walters, R. (2025). Digital Finance Law: Common and Civil Law. In *Digital Finance Law: Common and Civil Law*. Taylor and Francis. DOI: 10.4324/9781003511687

# Chapter 10
# ReCoffee:
## Sustainable Management of Spent Coffee Grounds Using Artificial Intelligence

**Kauser Hameed**
https://orcid.org/0009-0007-7118-8820
*King Faisal University, Saudi Arabia*

**Raazia Saher**
https://orcid.org/0000-0001-7095-5628
*King Faisal University, Saudi Arabia*

**Khutaija Maheen**
https://orcid.org/0009-0009-9741-9724
*Fairleigh Dickinson University, USA*

**Qazi Mudassar Ilyas**
https://orcid.org/0000-0003-4238-8093
*Sultan Sharif Ali Islamic University, Brunei*

## ABSTRACT

*This chapter explores the global issue of food loss and waste, emphasizing its economic and environmental impacts and implications on Sustainable Development Goals, with a specific focus on the coffee industry as a major waste-generating sector. Building on the context, the chapter examines global coffee consumption and production trends, highlighting the substantial volume of spent coffee grounds (SCGs) wasted and their environmental burden. The discussion then introduces Artificial Intelligence (AI) and emerging tools for achieving sustainable waste management in this domain. The chapter investigates AI applications across the coffee value chain, from optimizing*

DOI: 10.4018/979-8-3373-1837-0.ch010

*production and supply to enabling the recycling and valorization of byproducts. It highlights ongoing research and real-world implementations, concluding with a vision for a circular, sustainable future—emphasizing stakeholder collaboration, AI-driven solutions, and actionable policies and industry recommendations.*

## INTRODUCTION

The global crisis of food loss and waste (FLW) pose a significant challenge to the achievement of the United Nations Sustainable Development Goals (SDGs), particularly those related to food security (SDG 2), climate action (SDG 13), responsible consumption and production (SDG 12), and innovation in infrastructure (SDG 9). FLW has garnered widespread attention due to its far-reaching implications for environmental degradation, economic inefficiencies, and social inequalities. Research estimates that by 2030, approximately 2.1 million tonnes of food will be wasted globally, resulting in a financial loss of around $1.5 trillion(Bigdeloo et al., 2021). Currently, about one-third of all food produced for human consumption—approximately 1.3 billion tonnes—is either lost or wasted annually(*More than 1 Billion Tons of Food Lost or Wasted Every Year, UN-Backed Report Finds | UN News*, 2011). Moreover, FLW contributes significantly to environmental deterioration, accounting for 8–10% of global greenhouse gas (GHG) emissions, refer to Table 1. These emissions exacerbate climate-related issues such as extreme weather events, floods, and droughts, ultimately reducing crop yields and disrupting agricultural supply chains.

*Table 1. Food loss and waste statistics*

| Category | Value | Unit |
|---|---|---|
| Annual Food Waste | 1.3 | Billion Tons |
| Economic Loss by 2030 | 1.5 | Trillion Dollars |
| GHG Emissions from FLW | 8–10% | Percentage of Global GHGs |

Given the critical nature of this issue, there is a growing urgency to explore advanced, innovative solutions. Addressing food loss and waste (FLW) represents a triple-win opportunity—mitigating climate change, enhancing food security, and promoting environmental sustainability(*Tackling Food Loss and Waste*, n.d.). Researchers, industry professionals, and policymakers play a pivotal role in implementing sustainable strategies to combat this crisis. In alignment with the 2030 Agenda, the United Nations aims to halve per capita global food waste at the retail and consumer levels and reduce food losses along production and supply chains, (Martin, n.d.).

One of the most pressing areas requiring attention is the coffee industry, which generates a significant amount of global food waste. The sector generates over 40 million tonnes of waste annually, including coffee husks, silverskin, and spent coffee grounds (SCGs)—waste that holds untapped potential for circular economy practices(*2023 U.S. Coffee Impact Report*, n.d.).As the second most widely consumed beverage globally, (Tucker, 2017), coffee production and consumption have increased steadily. Between 2015 and 2017, consumption ranged from 9.1 to 9.4 million tonnes(*2023 U.S. Coffee Impact Report*, n.d.). Global production reached approximately 164.9 million 60-kg bags between 2020 and 2022, (Arya et al., 2022). Figure 1 illustrates these consumption trends. In 2022, the coffee sector contributed $343.2 billion to the U.S. economy, a 52.4% increase since 2015, (Bigdeloo et al., 2021)

*Figure 1. Coffee consumption - worldwide (2015 -2022)*

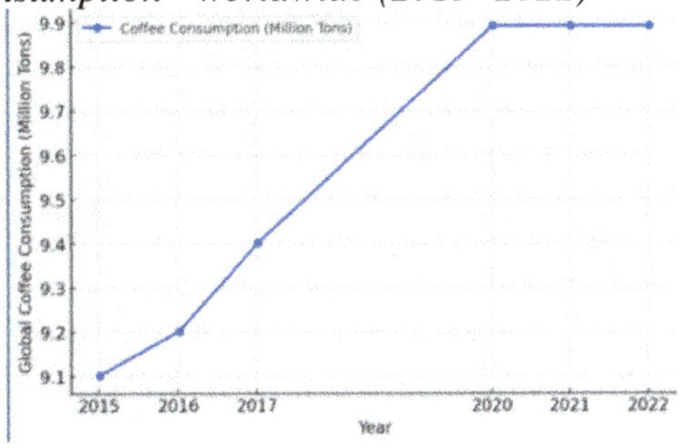


Among the by-products of coffee consumption, SCGs represent a substantial and underutilized waste stream. Approximately 6 million tonnes of SCGs are discarded annually after brewing, (Getachew & Chun, 2017). This waste is commonly disposed of in landfills, leading to methane emissions—a potent GHG—and resulting in significant environmental harm, (Franca & Oliveira, 2019). The failure to valorise SCGs also represents a missed opportunity to extract bioactive compounds and repurpose them for various high-value applications, (Mora-Villalobos et al., 2023). These include the development of bioplastics, biofuels, and compost, among other sustainable products.

As illustrated in Figure 2, the valorisation of coffee by-products, particularly SCGs and coffee silverskin (CS), aligns with the principles of the circular economy. These by-products contain valuable components such as lignin, cellulose, hemicellulose, and various bioactive compounds, including chlorogenic acid and melanoidins, which offer health benefits like cardiovascular protection and anti-inflammatory effect, (Iriondo-DeHond et al., 2020; Paula & Farah, 2022; Gottstein et al., 2021)

*Figure 2. Coffee by-products valorization process*

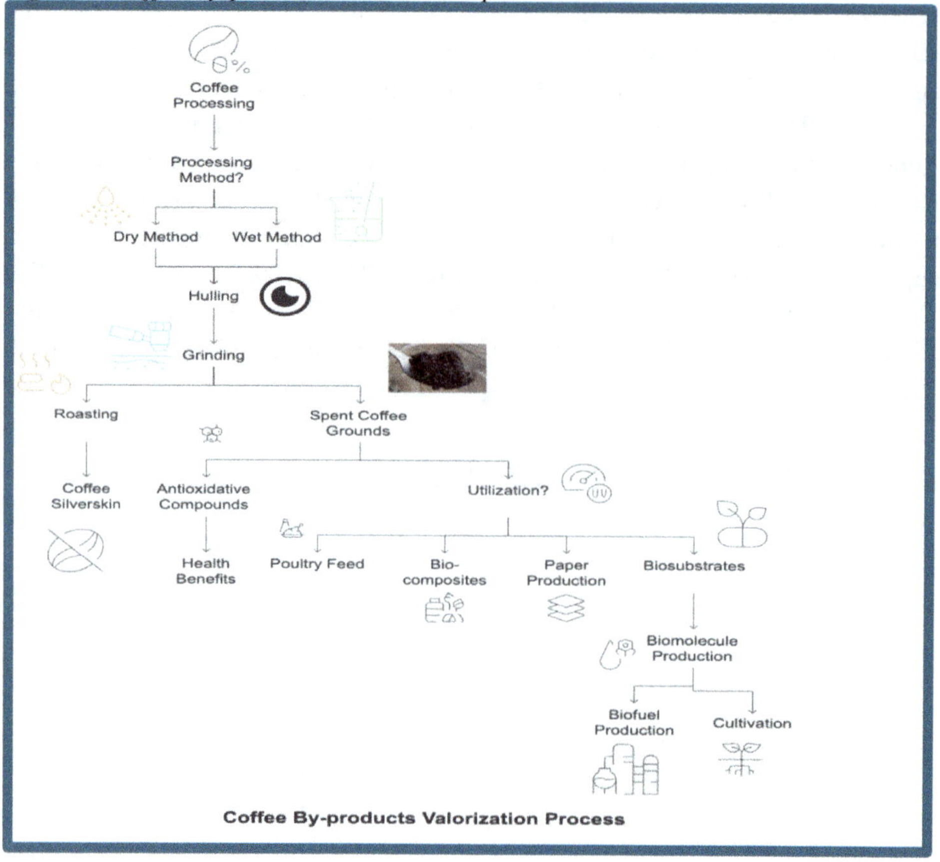


The circular coffee industry framework, depicted in Figure 3, aims to convert these materials into high-value bioproducts, such as food additives, biopolymers, and biofertilizers, thus reducing environmental impact while promoting economic viability, (Kourmentza et al., 2018). Artificial Intelligence (AI) emerges as a transformative tool in this context, offering innovative solutions for the efficient collection, sorting, and transformation of SCGs. AI technologies—such as machine learning, image recognition, predictive analytics, and sensor integration—can optimize waste valorization processes across the coffee supply chain. From automating classification based on bean maturity, roast level, and quality attributes, to predicting optimal processing methods and yield potentials, AI significantly enhances the operational efficiency and sustainability of the industry, (Motta et al., 2024).

*Figure 3. The Circular coffee industry focused on producing valuable bioproducts*

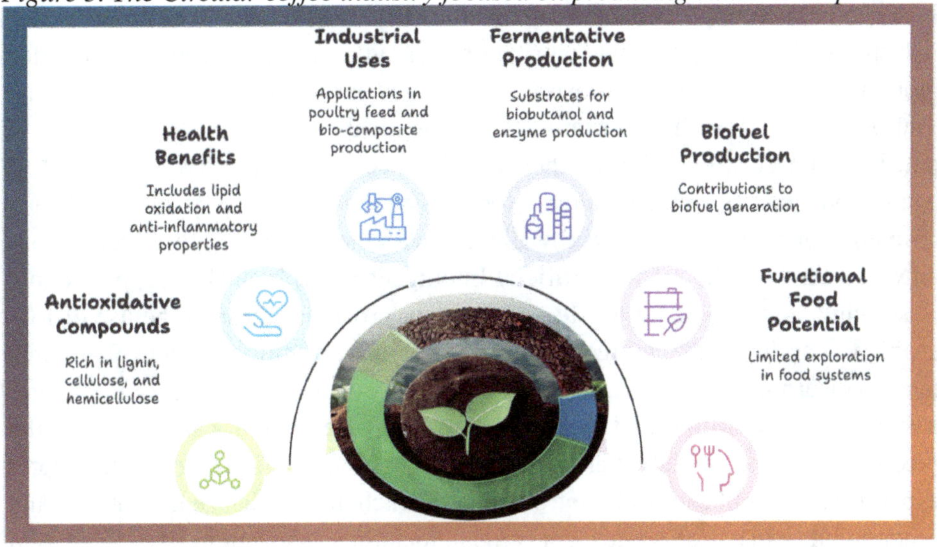


Coffee pulping, drying, roasting, and brewing generate various by-products, including coffee husks, SCGs, and CS, (Mussatto et al., 2011). These by-products, particularly SCGs, are ideal for biorefinery applications due to their dry, powdery nature and robust physicochemical properties. They are increasingly being utilized for producing poultry feed, bio-composites, biofuels, fermentative bio-compounds (such as butanol and isopropanol), and even as substrates for mushroom cultivation and biosorbents for wastewater treatment, (Gouvea et al., 2009; Hijosa-Valsero et al., 2018).

Despite the progress, substantial gaps remain in terms of scalability, consistency, and real-time process optimization. This chapter critically examines how AI can bridge the gaps in the sustainable management of SCGs and other coffee by-products. Emphasizing an integrated approach, the chapter examines how AI-enabled systems can lead to smarter waste segregation, improved quality control, energy-efficient processing, and informed decision-making, thereby advancing the vision of a circular, zero-waste coffee economy. The goals of the chapter are given below:

- To frame the global FLW crisis with a focus on the coffee industry waste.
- To explore the potential of SCG valorisation within a circular economy model.
- To present AI-based strategies for optimizing coffee waste management.
- To recommend governance and policy frameworks enabling sustainable practices.
- To propose integrated innovative technologies for future circular solutions.

The chapter addresses the global food loss and waste (FLW) crisis, highlighting its magnitude and environmental implications with a particular focus on the coffee industry, which is a significant contributor to organic waste, especially spent coffee grounds (SCGs), generated in massive quantities across homes, cafes, and industrial operations. The chapter examines the chemical composition and valorisation potential of SCGs, highlighting their rich lignocellulosic structure and bioactive compounds that make them suitable for applications such as biofuels, fertilizers, cosmetics, and animal feed, thereby aligning with the principles of a circular economy. It highlights the role of Artificial Intelligence (AI) in analyzing, predicting, classifying, and optimizing waste management processes through the use of IoT-enabled smart bins and intelligent collection vehicles. Additionally, it explains how machine learning (ML) techniques—such as regression analysis, time-series forecasting, neural networks, and clustering algorithms—can significantly improve the precision of waste prediction and the efficiency of route optimization. The chapter expands on AI applications by introducing blockchain to enhance traceability and accountability in coffee waste management, including innovations like NFT-based waste trading. It then outlines policy strategies, such as standardized waste classifications, extended producer responsibility, and incentives to support the adoption of AI. Ultimately, it emphasizes the importance of public awareness and cross-sector collaboration, particularly among cafés, households, and institutions, in promoting sustainable practices during high-consumption events. Finally, the chapter concludes with a forward-looking perspective, emphasizing the need to integrate AI, IoT, and blockchain in the development of smart biorefineries, establish inclusive governance systems, and expand interdisciplinary research to make the coffee industry more circular, efficient, and sustainable. The chapter theme is illustrated in Table 2 below:

*Table 2. Thematic structure of the chapter: key areas, subtopics, and technological interventions for sustainable coffee waste management using artificial intelligence*

| Main Theme | Subtopics / Elements |
|---|---|
| 1. Global Context of Food Waste | - Food Loss and Waste (FLW) statistics<br>- SDG challenges (2, 12, 13)<br>- Climate and environmental impacts |
| 2. Coffee Industry and SCG Waste | - Global coffee consumption trends<br>- Waste generation across the coffee chain<br>- Sources of SCG (household, cafes, industrial)<br>- Environmental burden |
| 3. SCG Composition & Valorisation | - Chemical properties (cellulose, lignin, oils, bioactives)<br>- Health and industrial value<br>- Composting, biofuels, cosmetics, fertilizers, bioplastics |

continued on following page

*Table 2. Continued*

| Main Theme | Subtopics / Elements |
|---|---|
| 4. Artificial Intelligence Applications | - AI for SCG analysis & prediction<br>- Waste pattern recognition<br>- Smart bins, IoT, sensors<br>- Smart vehicles & route optimization |
| 5. Machine Learning in Waste Management | - ML models: regression, time series, RNN, SVM, clustering<br>- Sorting, classification, predictive analytics |
| 6. Blockchain and Digital Technologies | - Blockchain for traceability<br>- NFT-based waste trading<br>- Transparent, secure SCG tracking |
| 7. Policy, Governance & Circular Economy | - Sustainable waste classification standards<br>- Producer responsibility schemes<br>- Investment incentives<br>- Circular design thinking |
| 8. Community Engagement & Awareness | - Café and household roles<br>- Public campaigns<br>- Multi-sector collaboration (govt, academia, business)<br>- Event-based waste recovery |
| 9. Conclusion & Recommendations | - Integration of AI, IoT, blockchain<br>- Smart SCG biorefineries<br>- Need for inclusive governance<br>- Research and innovation roadmap |

## BACKGROUND

Coffee is one of the most widely consumed beverages globally and also a significant source of organic waste, particularly in the form of spent coffee grounds (SCGs) generated across households, cafes, and processing units(Motta et al., 2024). Traditionally discarded as waste, SCGs are increasingly recognized for their potential in bioproduct development due to their rich chemical composition and bioactive compounds, (Murthy & Madhava Naidu, 2012). These byproducts, often discarded, possess a rich chemical composition that can be harnessed for various bioproduct applications, (Murthy & Madhava Naidu, 2012).

- Byproducts are secondary products generated during the production of a main product—often from food processing—that can be used to recover chemicals or produce valuable metabolites, (Murthy & Madhava Naidu, 2012).
- Bioproducts, in turn, are derived from biomass or other biological resources, (*Bioproduct Basics*, 2023). They are renewable alternatives to petroleum- or natural gas-based products, including plastics, fertilizers, and industrial

chemicals. The development of bioproducts offers economic, environmental, and health benefits, (*Bioproduct Basics*, 2023).

## Coffee and Its Bioproducts

Spent coffee grounds can be transformed into valuable bioproducts, such as bio-energy, adsorbents, and composite materials. The production of bioproducts often involves breaking down biomass into chemical building blocks and then converting these into marketable products using biological, thermal, and chemical processes, (*Bioproduct Basics*, 2023). The linear consumption model, which results in copious amounts of spent coffee grounds, contrasts with the potential of these wastes as secondary raw materials suitable for circular economy paradigms, (Stufano et al., 2022).

Spent coffee grounds exhibit a complex chemical composition that varies based on the coffee species, roasting conditions, and extraction methods, (Hernández-Varela & Medina, 2023). This complex composition comprises polysaccharides, such as cellulose and hemicellulose, lignin, and soluble sugars, alongside lower quantities of proteins and minerals(Mora-Villalobos et al., 2021). The most prominent components include cellulose, hemicellulose, lignin, and soluble sugars, with minor amounts of proteins and minerals. Lignin, a complex polymer, provides rigidity to plant cell walls but poses challenges in bioprocessing due to its recalcitrant structure. The proportion of oil within spent coffee grounds, which contains triglycerides, free fatty acids, and other lipids, can be converted into biodiesel through transesterification. Moreover, spent coffee grounds contain valuable bioactive compounds, including phenolic acids and melanoidins with antioxidant properties, (Castaldo et al., 2021), Please refer to Figure 4.

*Figure 4. Chemical composition of AI*

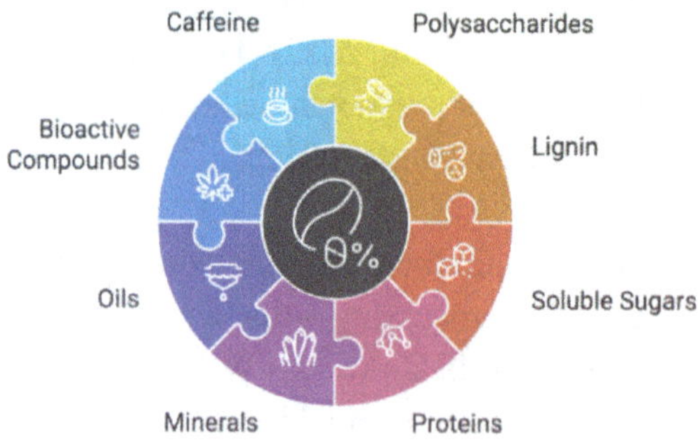

SCGs serve as a versatile feedstock for various sustainable applications, contributing to a circular economy and waste reduction. Biodiesel production from the oil fraction of spent coffee grounds presents a sustainable alternative to fossil fuels, (*Sustainability Issues along the Coffee Chain: From the Field to the Cup - Barreto Peixoto - 2023 - Comprehensive Reviews in Food Science and Food Safety - Wiley Online Library*, n.d.). The oils are extracted using solvents such as n-hexane or petroleum ether(Murthy & Madhava Naidu, 2012). The transesterification reaction, using catalysts, converts triglycerides into fatty acid methyl esters, commonly known as biodiesel. Biogas production through anaerobic digestion of spent coffee grounds provides a renewable energy source while also reducing organic waste. The thermophilic Mycotypha is used to grow coffee husk, an important agro-industrial waste, to promote biomethanation (Murthy & Madhava Naidu, 2012). Activated carbon derived from spent coffee grounds exhibits excellent adsorption properties, making it an ideal material for water treatment and pollutant removal. Using spent coffee grounds as an adsorbent offers a cost-effective and environmentally friendly solution for removing pollutants from wastewater (Murthy & Madhava Naidu, 2012), Please refer to Figure 5.

*Figure 5. Bioproducts from spent coffee grounds*

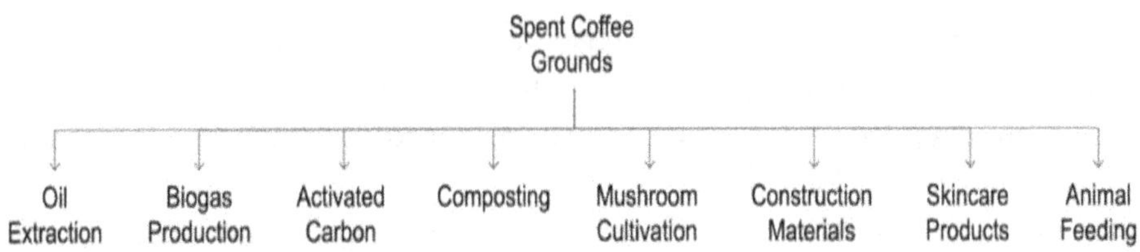


- **Biofuels**: Oils from SCGs are extracted using solvents and converted into biodiesel. Anaerobic digestion of SCGs can also yield biogas(Murthy & Madhava Naidu, 2012; Peixoto et al., 2022)
- **Activated Carbon**: SCG-derived carbon materials offer effective pollutant adsorption for water treatment(Murthy & Madhava Naidu, 2012)
- **Composting and Soil Amendments**: SCGs enrich soil nutrients and structure when composted.
- **Mushroom Cultivation**: Used as a substrate for edible fungi, contributing to food sustainability.

- **Construction Materials**: Added to clay bricks to enhance thermal and mechanical properties(Peixoto et al., 2022)
- **Cosmetics and Skincare**: Rich in antioxidants, SCGs are explored in sunscreen and anti-aging formulations.
- **Animal Feed**: Nutrient-dense residues have shown utility in feed for ruminants, poultry, and rabbits(Murthy & Madhava Naidu, 2012)

These valorisation pathways present a shift from the traditional linear consumption model toward circular strategies that create value while reducing environmental burden, (Stufano et al., 2022)

## Global Trends in AI and Coffee Waste Valorisation

AI algorithms can significantly help sort and segregate coffee grounds from other waste. Machine learning and computer vision aid in waste collection and recycling, enabling the reuse of coffee grounds. AI can predict waste patterns and help cities develop innovative waste collection plans, reduce logistics costs, and reduce environmental impact. Additionally, AI systems can track the decomposition of coffee grounds to optimize methane production for energy and enhance the valorization process of SCGs. AI algorithms can:

- Analyze chemical composition and extraction parameters
- Predict optimal processing conditions for different bioproducts
- Optimize logistics such as waste collection and routing using IoT-enabled smart bins and vehicles
- Improve yield estimation and product quality using machine learning techniques such as regression, time series, neural networks, and clustering(Motta et al., 2024a)

AI adoption for SCG recycling varies globally. For instance, Colombia integrates AI in coffee defect detection and farm management(Largo Avila et al., 2025), while G7 countries and India face implementation gaps despite AI's economic potential (Dave et al., 2025), refer to Table 3.

*Table 3. Country-wise practices*

| Region/ Country | AI Application in Waste Management | Valorisation of Coffee Grounds |
|---|---|---|
| USA | AI optimizes waste collection routes and automates sorting processes (Nwokediegwu et al., 2024) | SCGs used for bioenergy production (de Freitas et al., 2023) |
| Ireland | AI-driven CE initiatives for waste management (Pathan et al., 2023) | N/A |
| Brazil | N/A | SCGs used for bioenergy production(de Freitas et al., 2023) |
| Italy | N/A | CSS used for paper production (Overturf et al., 2021) |
| Africa | AI-powered mobile apps for waste reporting (Nwokediegwu et al., 2024) | N/A |

While countries like the USA and Brazil utilize SCGs for energy, there is a lack of diversity in applications and limited AI integration in many regions. This underlines the need for broader AI adoption and SCG product development.

The USA and Ireland are exploiting AI applications for urban waste management, including optimized collection and automated sorting, as shown in Table 3. In contrast, African nations focus on AI-powered mobile apps for waste reporting. Brazil and Italy show a lack of documented AI applications in waste management. Regarding SCG valorization, the USA and Brazil primarily utilize SCGs for bioenergy, while Italy is exploring alternative uses, such as paper production from coffee silverskin. Ireland and Africa, however, do not report any SCG utilization initiatives. Several research gaps are evident, including the lack of AI-driven waste management in certain regions and the limited diversification of SCG applications beyond bioenergy and paper production. The findings underline the need for further research to explore and expand AI integration in waste management and the sustainable utilization of coffee by-products across diverse geographical contexts, refer to Table 4.

*Table 4. Studies on key applications of spent coffee grounds*

| Product/ Application | Key Findings | Citation |
|---|---|---|
| Biofuel Pellets | High energy content, low ash, suitable for bioenergy production | (Smirnov et al., 2022) |
| Cosmetics | Rich in antioxidants and polyphenols for skincare products | (*Cosmetic Application of Coffee By-Products.*, n.d.) |
| Soil Amendments | Improves soil fertility and plant growth | (*Coffee Waste as an Alternative Fertilizer with Soil Improving Properties for Sandy Soils in Humid Tropical Environments*, n.d.) |
| Fertilizers | Slow-release fertilizers through humification processes | (Zhu et al., 2023) |
| AI-Driven Innovation | AI optimizes IAA production and bioactive compound extraction | (Alloun et al., 2024)(Rajesh Banu et al., 2020) |

Table 4's commentary reveals the numerous applications of repurposed spent coffee grounds (SCG) across various sectors. Studies show that SCG has high energy and low ash content, making it an excellent source for creating biofuel pellets. Antioxidants and polyphenols in SCGs make them a potential systemic substance for skincare formulations. SCG can be used as a soil amendment, promoting plant growth, and can be transformed into slow-release fertilizers through humification. Artificial intelligence is a valuable tool in SCG valorisation, enhancing indole-3-acetic acid (IAA) production and improving the extraction of bioactive compounds. The research findings are inspiring and encouraging. The avenue will further broaden SCG's capabilities as a source of raw materials for renewable energy, agriculture, cosmetics, and many other industries, making the coffee industry circular and sustainable.

## SUSTAINABLE SCG MANAGEMENT

The ubiquitous consumption of coffee, while culturally and economically significant, also raises considerable environmental concerns, including the generation of spent coffee grounds (SCGs). These abundant discarded residues, representing a significant global biomass waste stream, present intricate disposal dilemmas with demonstrable impacts on both public health and ecological integrity. This section initiates a comprehensive inquiry into the genesis and established management methodologies for SCGs, critically evaluating their inherent limitations. Subsequently, it transitions to elucidate the transformative capacity of Artificial Intelligence

(AI) and cognate advanced technologies, including Machine Learning (ML) and Blockchain, in facilitating enhanced SCG management, advancing the principles of a circular economy, and charting a trajectory towards a truly sustainable coffee industry. This exposition is delineated into:

- Current Practices in Coffee Waste Disposal
- Cutting-Edge Practices for Sustainable SCG Management

## Current Practices in Coffee Waste Disposal

The principal sources of Spent Coffee grounds are household, commercial, and industrial. While massive SCG producers are primarily from soluble coffee production, up to 50% of SCGs are produced on a small scale by cafeterias, restaurants, coffee shops, or individuals. (Johnson et al., 2022). Spent coffee grounds from household and commercial users are often either washed down the drain or discarded as general waste, eventually ending up in landfills. However, industrial coffee manufacturers generate large volumes of SCG during production, and their disposal methods vary based on economic feasibility and environmental regulations, as shown in Figure 6.

*Figure 6. Primary sources of spent coffee grounds*

The most widely used methods for the disposal of spent coffee grounds include:

## Landfilling

This involves disposing of spent coffee grounds in designated landfill sites, which are designed to contain waste while minimizing environmental contamination.

## Composting

This aerobic process involves microorganisms breaking down complex, degradable materials and producing organic and inorganic byproducts. In contrast to the landfilling technique of waste disposal, which may pose a threat to underground water, the composting process helps prevent groundwater pollution because fewer microorganisms and chemical contaminants are present during the composting process (Ayilara et al., 2020).

## Incineration

The technique of fully burning waste while maintaining or reducing emission levels below existing emission requirements, and when practical, recovering energy and any byproducts from the combustion process is known as waste incineration. (Buekens, 2013)

## Waterway Disposal

Spent coffee grounds can also be disposed of directly into the waterways by households, coffee shops, and industries. To get rid of the used coffee grounds, many individuals and coffee shops flush them down the sink or into the sewer systems that eventually flow to the lakes, rivers, or the ocean. Additionally, coffee processing facilities generate significant amounts of SCG waste, particularly during the instant coffee preparation process. Fine SCG particles and other liquid debris from coffee processing facilities are occasionally dumped into rivers or municipal water systems. Figure 7, given below, presents the most significant environmental impacts of these SCG disposal methods

*Figure 7. Environmental impacts of the conventional SCG disposal methods*

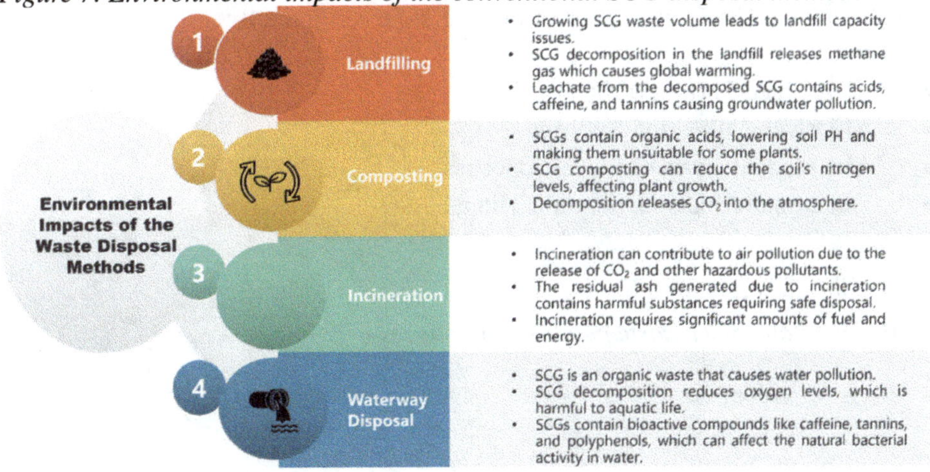


## Cutting-Edge Practices for Sustainable SCG Management

The growing challenge of spent coffee grounds (SCGs), a significant global biomass waste, necessitates a paradigm shift from traditional disposal methods to innovative, sustainable solutions. This section delves into how cutting-edge technologies—Artificial Intelligence (AI), Machine Learning (ML), and Blockchain—are revolutionizing SCG management, promoting a circular economy, and paving the way for a truly sustainable coffee industry. We will explore the direct applications of AI in waste analysis, prediction, and collection; the transformative role of ML in optimizing processes and forecasting trends; and the synergistic integration of AI and Blockchain for enhanced transparency, traceability, and circularity across the coffee supply chain. Innovative solutions for sustainable SCG management are elaborated below:

Artificial Intelligence in SCG Management
Machine Learning in SCG Management
AI and Blockchain Integration for Sustainable Practices

### Artificial Intelligence in SCG Management

AI is revolutionizing the management of spent coffee grounds (SCGs), addressing inefficiencies in conventional methods such as landfilling, incineration, and basic composting. Through the integration of technologies such as IoT, machine learning, and robotics, AI supports a circular economy by enhancing the precision, speed, and quality of waste sorting, collection, analysis, andprediction. Various steps that can facilitate the SCG management include: refer to Figure 8.

- AI-Enabled Sorting of SCGs
- AI-Driven Collection Systems
- AI-Based Analysis of SCG Properties
- Prediction of SCG Generation Trends

*Figure 8. AI and SCG waste management phases*

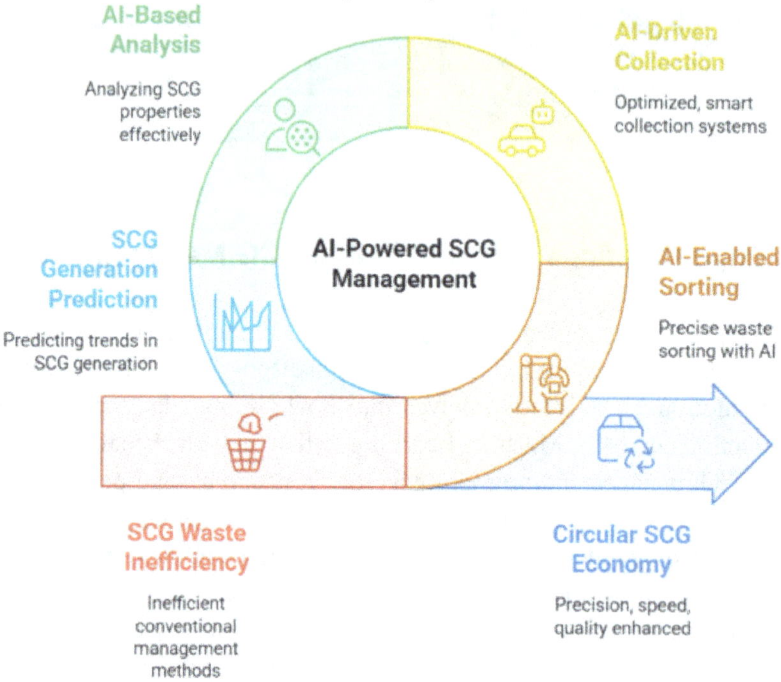


**AI-Enabled Sorting of SCGs.** Efficient SCG management begins with the accurate separation of usable material from contaminants. AI-powered systems integrated with robotics, machine learning, and computer vision enable real-time sorting and quality control:

**Smart Waste Sorting and Robotic Inspection.** Robotic arms equipped with computer vision can identify and remove impurities such as plastics and paper filters from SCGs. These systems ensure cleaner waste streams, improving downstream valorization (Choi et al., 2023; White et al., 2020).

**Integrated Vision and Sensing Systems.** Advanced sensors and imaging technologies evaluate physical attributes such as moisture content and particle size, aiding in the identification of recyclable SCGs and supporting high-quality input for processing (Eron et al., 2024; Motta et al., 2024)

**AI-Driven Collection Systems.** After sorting, efficient collection systems are crucial to

***IoT-Enabled Smart Bins.*** Smart bins use sensors to detect fill levels, temperature, and SCG weight. These devices transmit real-time data to waste collection centers, enabling timely pickups and reducing unnecessary trips.

***Smart Collection Vehicles.*** Collection vehicles equipped with temperature-controlled compartments preserve SCG integrity during transit. Cloud-connected sensors route and guide the vehicle to optimize routes based on bin status and location (GPS integration).

***AI-Driven Route Optimization.*** Machine learning algorithms and cloud-based platforms process data from smart bins to identify the most efficient routes for SCG pickup, factoring in traffic conditions, fill history, and time of day (Saher et al., 2023).

## AI-Based Analysis of SCG Properties

Understanding the composition of SCGs is essential for determining their most suitable reuse path—whether in biofuels, compost, cosmetics, or agriculture.

**Waste Property Characterization.** AI models analyze SCG chemical composition, including moisture levels, oils, lignin, cellulose, and antioxidants, guiding appropriate valorization pathways.

**Application-Based Matching.** AI platforms match SCG chemical profiles with optimal end-use sectors. For example, oil-rich SCGs may be directed toward biodiesel production, while antioxidant-rich material could be used in skincare formulations.

## Prediction of SCG Generation Trends

Proactive waste management requires accurate forecasting of when, where, and how much SCG waste will be generated.

**Predictive Modelling for Waste Volume.** Machine learning algorithms analyze historical data to predict SCG generation patterns based on:

- Coffee consumption rates
- Seasonal variations
- Population density and demographics

**Infrastructure Planning and Resource Allocation.** These predictions support long-term infrastructure development and resource planning for processing facilities, compost sites, and logistics hubs.

## Challenges in AI-Equipped SCG Waste Management

Despite the promise of AI technologies, several real-world barriers affect spent coffee grounds (SCG) management. Urban cafes often lack sufficient space to store wet SCG, leading to rapid decomposition, unpleasant odors, and microbial growth (Rivera & Ortega-Jimenez, 2019). Furthermore, significant infrastructure gaps exist, as traditional waste systems commonly treat SCGs as general waste. Inadequate access to specialized bins, temperature-controlled transport, and appropriate processing units hinders effective SCG reuse (Murthy & Madhava Naidu, 2012) (Campera et al., 2021). Compounding these issues are contamination problems, where improper segregation results in SCGs mixing with non-biodegradable materials, thereby reducing the viability of composting or recycling. Addressing this necessitates solutions such as staff training, improved labeling systems, and the adoption of compostable packaging(Bomfim et al., 2023), *Refer to Figure 9.*

*Figure 9. Challenges in the collection of spent coffee grounds*

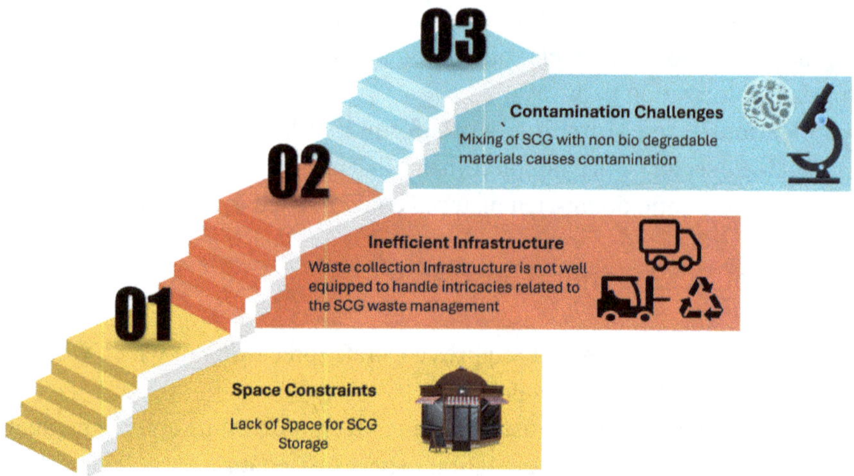

## Machine Learning in SCG Management

The use of machine learning algorithms in waste management represents a paradigm change toward more sustainable and effective approaches(Motta et al., 2024). Traditional waste management systems often face problems such as diverse waste compositions, changing trash generation rates, and logistical difficulties(Sharma et al., 2021). ML provides advanced tools for examining complex patterns in waste data, enabling predictive modelling and optimization techniques(Gunaseelan et al., 2023). Machine learning helps waste management operations move from reactive to proactive techniques, improving resource allocation, reducing environmental impact, and promoting circular economy principles.

**Coffee Waste Prediction Models**. Machine learning algorithms are increasingly important for forecasting garbage generation trends and streamlining collection routes(Xia et al., 2022). As shown in Figure 10, numerous machine learning approaches are available for coffee waste management (Motta et al., 2024)

- **Regression Models.** Linear and polynomial regression models establish relationships between trash generation and determinants such as population density, consumption patterns, and seasonal fluctuations (Pasupuleti et al., 2024).
- **Time Series Analysis.** ARIMA models predict future waste quantities and identify cyclical patterns and trends based on historical data, guiding proactive waste management (Ticona-Salluca et al., 2023)
- **Neural Networks.** Recurrent Neural Networks (RNN) and Long Short-Term Memory (LSTM) networks improve forecast accuracy by managing intricate, non-linear relationships among waste data (Pasupuleti et al., 2024).
- **Support Vector Machines (SVM).** These algorithms handle high-dimensional data, effective for classifying waste materials and optimizing sorting processes (Aghababaei et al., 2025)
- **K-Nearest Neighbors (KNN).** This versatile algorithm is applied in waste classification and regression tasks by grouping data points based on proximity in the feature space(Motta et al., 2024).

*Figure 10. Machine learning in waste management*

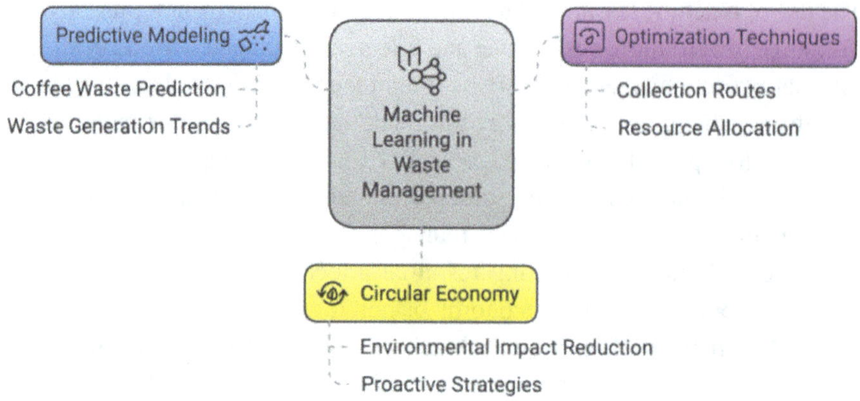


## Optimizing Coffee Waste Collection Routes with Machine Learning

Machine learning algorithms are essential for garbage collection route optimization, resolving shortcomings of conventional techniques. By examining variables such as traffic patterns, waste container fill levels, and vehicle capacity, machine learning (ML) methods provide dynamic routes that save on travel time, fuel consumption, and operating expenses.

- **Clustering Algorithms.** K-means clustering creates effective routes that cut down on redundancy and simplify operations by grouping collection stations according to proximity and waste creation rates.
- **Reinforcement Learning.** These algorithms adapt routes in real time based on changing conditions, such as unexpected traffic congestion or vehicle breakdowns, ensuring continuous optimization and responsiveness.

Integrating machine learning into route optimization enhances waste collection efficiency and contributes to environmental sustainability by reducing greenhouse gas emissions and promoting resource conservation. Although machine learning has the potential to revolutionize coffee waste management, several obstacles and restrictions must be overcome for successful implementation. Key challenges include data quality and availability, as efficient training and validation require large, representative datasets; biased, inconsistent, or lacking data can result in poor decision-making and erroneous forecasts(Motta et al., 2024). Another significant challenge is algorithm interpretability, particularly for deep learning models, where understanding their internal decision-making processes can be difficult due to their inherent complexity. Furthermore, ethical considerations such as data privacy, algorithmic transparency, and fairness must be addressed to maintain public trust and ensure equitable outcomes. Effectively addressing these challenges necessitates investments in robust data collection procedures, stringent quality control measures, and the development of reliable algorithms capable of managing noisy or insufficient data.

## Future Directions for ML in Sustainable Coffee Waste Practices

The integration of machine learning into sustainable coffee waste practices holds immense potential. Future research should focus on:

- **Computer Vision for Automated Sorting.** Automating waste sorting with computer vision and ML increases productivity and lowers contamination (Nwokediegwu et al., 2024). CNNs enable coffee plant image processing, allowing for pre-harvest yield and quality estimation (Eron et al., 2024).
- **IoT Sensors for Real-Time Monitoring.** IoT devices monitor waste levels, temperature, and other parameters, feeding data into machine learning (ML) models for optimized collection schedules and predictive maintenance.
- **AI-Driven Biorefinery Processes.** Machine learning (ML) algorithms analyze biorefinery datasets to optimize SCG conversion into valuable bioproducts and minimize waste. Intelligent classification of recyclable solid waste using machine vision technology is predicted to continue (Chen, 2021). Waste, a mobile application using computer vision and deep learning, shows AI's promise with 92% accuracy in waste material classification (Kunwar, 2023).

## AI and Blockchain in Advancing Sustainable Practices

The integration of Artificial Intelligence (AI) and blockchain technology is transforming numerous industries, with the coffee sector being a key beneficiary. AI plays a critical role in overcoming sustainability issues associated with packaging and the coffee supply chain (Bhagat et al., 2022). The coffee industry faces significant social, economic, and environmental challenges that hinder its sustainability efforts (Peixoto et al., 2022). The complexity of the coffee supply chain and rising demand for sustainable solutions call for innovative approaches to improve efficiency, transparency, and reduce waste (Agnola et al., 2025). AI and blockchain are essential in addressing these challenges and promoting informed decision-making

(Kashem et al., 2023), having already demonstrated their potential in the coffee sector (Kittichotsatsawat et al., 2021).

## Enhancing the Coffee Supply Chain

AI aids in classifying coffee beans based on factors such as ripeness, roasting intensity, disease detection, flavor profiles, and quality (Motta et al., 2024). By applying AI and blockchain, the industry can streamline processes, reduce environmental harm, and ensure ethical practices throughout the supply chain—from cultivation to waste disposal (Motta et al., 2024). AI-driven systems minimize waste by enhancing logistics and optimizing supply chain processes, including route optimization and predictive maintenance (Kittichotsatsawat et al., 2021).

## Sustainable Packaging and Waste Management

## Eco-Friendly Packaging Innovations

AI plays a vital role in developing environmentally friendly packaging solutions. It evaluates material properties like biodegradability, recyclability, and compostability to identify the best options (Hernández-Varela & Medina, 2023). Predictive models assess packaging's environmental impact (carbon emissions, water usage, waste generation) aligned with regulatory standards and consumer expectations (Weber & Wiek, 2021). AI-based simulations optimize packaging designs to minimize material use while maintaining product quality, reducing transportation costs and carbon emissions. Companies like Ansã use AI for roasting consistency, and similar algorithms are applied to food processing and packaging to reduce costs (Motta et al., 2024).

## AI in Logistics and Waste Reduction

AI-based demand forecasting improves supply-demand alignment, helping avoid overproduction and reduce waste. AI-powered logistics optimize routes based on distance, traffic, and capacity, leading to reduced fuel consumption and lower emissions. Predictive maintenance further boosts operational efficiency (Motta et al., 2024)

## Monitoring Waste with AI and Sensors

Sensors throughout the supply chain monitor environmental factors like waste levels and temperature. Data collected is processed by machine learning algorithms to improve waste collection schedules and optimize routes, minimizing spoilage and emissions (Ghahramani et al., 2021). Emerging technologies like AI-driven sorting robots and smart waste containers are also being developed(Pachot & Patissier, 2022).

### Blockchain's Role in Transparency, Traceability, and Accountability

Blockchain technology provides an immutable and transparent record of waste handling, from origin to disposal, ensuring accountability and preventing illegal dumping. Each transaction in the waste management process is secure, verifying proper procedures. Blockchain improves product traceability, especially in regions with less established supply chains, building consumer trust in sustainable sourcing practices (Kshetri, 2021).

### Integrating AI and Blockchain for Circular Waste Management

Combining AI's data analytics with blockchain's transparency creates a comprehensive approach to waste management. AI analyzes data from various sources—such as sensors, waste facilities, and partners—to optimize waste routes and identify recycling opportunities. Pilot projects have shown how this integration can promote a more circular economy, (Bhattacharya, 2021).

### NFT-Based Waste Trading Framework

A blockchain-based framework using Non-Fungible Tokens (NFTs) represents waste units, enabling traceability and dynamic trading. Local governments and recycling centers are adopting this model to improve waste management efficiency. (Kumar et al., 2025). Such frameworks hold promise for expanding to include food donation, animal welfare, and financial transparency in the supply chain (Ellahi et al., 2024).

## Digital Tools Driving the Circular Economy

The circular economy aims to minimize waste generation at the design stage and reduce dependence on raw materials (Bigdeloo et al., 2021; Zanoletti et al., 2021). Digital technologies, including Artificial Intelligence (AI), the Internet of Things (IoT), robotics, cloud computing, and big data analytics, are vital in facilitating this transition (Bhagat et al., 2022). In the context of the coffee industry, integrating physical and digital tools enables the transformation of SCGs into bioproducts such as biofuels, fertilizers, and construction materials. Furthermore, community participation in the bioeconomy is growing, as individuals and businesses increasingly trade their by-products and contribute to local recycling initiatives (Peixoto et al., 2022).

Transparent supply chains supported by blockchain technology promote traceability and trust (Yuzvovich et al., 2024), while sustainability certification schemes align consumer behaviour with ethical production, (Neilson, 2008; Giuliani et al., 2017).

Key enablers for facilitating digital transformation include the following:

- AI for waste prediction and process optimization
- IoT sensors for tracking SCG generation and quality
- Blockchain for supply chain transparency and certification
- Digital platforms for recycling program participation

Sustainability certification schemes have gained prominence in response to consumer demand (Neilson, 2008; Giuliani et al., 2017). Though inconsistencies in certification practices exist, the willingness of consumers to pay more for verified sustainable products has prompted over 93% of major companies to publish sustainability reports(Park & Li, 2021). Nonetheless, the coffee sector continues to face vulnerabilities, including child labor and social inequality (Peixoto et al., 2022), demanding the need for technological and policy interventions. Blockchain can provide decentralized enforcement of sustainability standards, particularly in developing regions(Kshetri, 2021).

## Community Involvement in Sustainable SCG Management

Community engagement is essential for large-scale SCG valorization, particularly during public events where coffee consumption spikes (Chaturvedi et al., 2015). Collaborative networks between cafés, restaurants, households, academic institutions, and government bodies can build infrastructure and create innovation hubs for SCG-based bioproduct development (Campera et al., 2021; Peluso, 2023).

Key actions that can facilitate sustainable SCG management through community involvement include:

Invest in Specialized Collection and Processing Systems

- Including composting and valorization facilities (Murthy & Madhava Naidu, 2012)

Apply the Polluter-Pays Principle

- Incentivize businesses to reduce emissions and manage waste responsibly (Peixoto et al., 2022).

Launch Public Awareness Campaigns

- Promote recycling behavior and environmental responsibility (Tenriawaru et al., 2020).

Integrate SCGs into Circular Models

- Overcome logistical barriers and reduce landfill dependency(Peixoto et al., 2022), refer Figure 11.

*Figure 11. Steps to sustainable coffee waste*

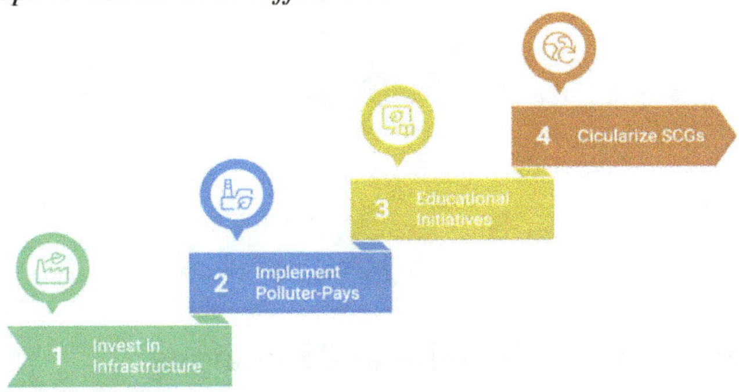


## Policy and Governance for SCG Management

A robust governance framework is essential to mainstream AI-driven solutions and circular practices in SCG management. Policies must support innovation while ensuring accountability and environmental integrity.

Key Governance Measures:

- Standardized waste classification and processing protocols.
- Recognition of SCGs as valuable resources, with defined guidelines for collection and transport.
- Extended Producer Responsibility (EPR) to shift accountability to coffee producers and retailers.
- Incentives for AI and IoT adoption to improve operational efficiency.
- Mandatory source segregation with penalties for non-compliance.
- Smart monitoring infrastructure using IoT to track waste volume, composition, and flow, enabling data-informed decision-making, refer to Figure 12.

*Figure 12. Coffee waste management governance framework*

## SCG Awareness and Educational Campaigns

To build a sustainable coffee ecosystem, education plays a foundational role. Awareness campaigns must be designed to reach multiple audiences, from café owners to individual consumers, emphasizing the benefits of recycling SCGs and transforming them into valuable products, such as biofuels and compost. The following are the educational focus areas:

Train Café Staff and Owners

- On segregation and in-house waste practices.

Guide Households in Proper Disposal and Composting

- Encourage participation in municipal programs (Mora-Villalobos et al., 2021).

Utilize Social Media and Events for Outreach

- Share compelling stories, visuals, and calls-to-action.

Encourage Behavioural Change

- Link recycling practices to environmental impact and policy support (Nepal et al., 2022).

## CONCLUSION AND FUTURE OUTLOOK

The escalating challenge of global food loss and waste, particularly within the coffee industry, poses a significant threat to achieving the United Nations Sustainable Development Goals. As this chapter has comprehensively explored, the extensive consumption and subsequent disposal of spent coffee grounds (SCGs) contribute substantially to environmental degradation and resource inefficiency. Traditional waste management methods, including landfilling and basic composting, prove insufficient to address the sheer volume and unique properties of SCGs, highlighting an urgent need for innovative and sustainable solutions.

This chapter has demonstrated the transformative potential of Artificial Intelligence (AI) and allied technologies in revolutionizing SCG management and fostering a truly circular coffee economy. We have elucidated how AI, through capabilities such as waste analysis, generation pattern prediction, and sophisticated route optimization, can dramatically enhance the efficiency of SCG collection and disposal. Furthermore, the integration of smart sorting systems, robotic arms, and advanced sensing technologies, driven by AI, enables precise contaminant removal and quality control, ensuring that high-quality SCGs are effectively channelled towards valorisation.

Machine Learning (ML) algorithms, as detailed, are pivotal in this paradigm shift. From predicting waste volumes using regression and time series models to optimizing collection routes with clustering and reinforcement learning, ML offers unparalleled tools for proactive waste management. These predictive and adaptive capacities empower stakeholders to make informed decisions, minimize operational costs, and reduce the environmental footprint associated with coffee waste.

Beyond waste management, the strategic convergence of AI and Blockchain technology offers a holistic approach to sustainability across the entire coffee supply chain. AI-driven insights improve coffee bean classification, optimize logistics, enhance sustainable packaging design, and fine-tune demand forecasting. Concurrently, Blockchain ensures unparalleled transparency, traceability, and accountability, from cultivation to waste valorisation, building consumer trust and preventing illicit disposal. The concept of NFT-based waste trading frameworks further exemplifies how digital innovation can create new economic incentives for circular practices.

Despite these promising advancements, the journey toward a fully circular coffee economy presents challenges, including data quality and availability, algorithm interpretability, and ethical considerations. Overcoming these hurdles requires concerted efforts in data standardization, robust algorithm development, and transparent governance frameworks. The future of sustainable coffee management lies in continued interdisciplinary collaboration and technological innovation. Key areas for future research and implementation include:

- Advanced AI-Driven Biorefinery Processes: Leveraging AI and ML to optimize the conversion of SCGs into a wider array of valuable bioproducts (e.g., biofuels, biochemicals, nutraceuticals) with higher efficiency and lower environmental impact. This involves AI-driven process control, yield prediction, and novel compound discovery.

- Integrated Digital Ecosystems: Developing comprehensive platforms that seamlessly combine IoT data from smart bins and collection vehicles with AI analytics and blockchain's immutable ledgers to create a fully traceable and optimized circular waste management system.
- Policy and Economic Incentives: Governments and industry bodies must develop supportive policies, regulatory frameworks, and economic incentives (e.g., subsidies for AI adoption, carbon credits for waste reduction) to accelerate the widespread adoption of these advanced sustainable practices.
- Enhanced Community Engagement: Fostering greater community involvement through educational programs, accessible smart infrastructure, and participatory models that empower citizens and local businesses to actively contribute to SCG collection and valorization.
- Scalability and Replication: Demonstrating successful pilot projects on a larger scale and developing blueprints for replicating these AI and blockchain-driven circular models across diverse geographical regions and agricultural waste streams, establishing the coffee industry as a benchmark for global sustainability.

By embracing these technological advancements and fostering a collaborative ecosystem, the coffee industry can transform its waste problem into a significant opportunity, making substantial contributions to climate action, resource conservation, and a more resilient and circular global economy.

## ACKNOWLEDGMENT

This work was supported by the Deanship of Scientific Research, Vice Presidency for Graduate Studies and Scientific Research, King Faisal University, Saudi Arabia [Grant No. KFU252855].

## REFERENCES

Aghababaei, A., Aghababaei, F., Pignitter, M., & Hadidi, M. (2025). Artificial Intelligence in Agro-Food Systems: From Farm to Fork. *Foods*, *14*(3), 411. DOI: 10.3390/foods14030411 PMID: 39942003

Agnola, T., Ambrosini, L., Beretta, E., & Gremlich, G. (2025). Empowering Global Supply Chains Through Blockchain-Based Platforms: New Evidence from the Coffee Industry. *FinTech*, *4*(1), 3. DOI: 10.3390/fintech4010003

Alloun, W., Berkani, M., Shavandi, A., Beddiar, A., Pellegrini, M., Garzia, M., Lakhdari, D., Ganachari, S. V., Aminabhavi, T. M., Vasseghian, Y., Muddapur, U., & Chaouche, N. K. (2024). Harnessing artificial intelligence-driven approach for enhanced indole-3-acetic acid from the newly isolated *Streptomyces rutgersensis* AW08. *Environmental Research*, *252*, 118933. DOI: 10.1016/j.envres.2024.118933 PMID: 38642645

Arya, S. S., Venkatram, R., More, P. R., & Vijayan, P. (2022). The wastes of coffee bean processing for utilization in food: A review. *Journal of Food Science and Technology*, *59*(2), 429–444. DOI: 10.1007/s13197-021-05032-5 PMID: 35185168

Ayilara, M. S., Olanrewaju, O. S., Babalola, O. O., & Odeyemi, O. (2020). Waste Management through Composting: Challenges and Potentials. *Sustainability (Basel)*, *12*(11), 4456. DOI: 10.3390/su12114456

Bhagat, P. R., Naz, F., & Magda, R. (2022). Artificial intelligence solutions enabling sustainable agriculture: A bibliometric analysis. *PLoS One*, *17*(6), e0268989. Advance online publication. DOI: 10.1371/journal.pone.0268989 PMID: 35679287

Bhattacharya, A. (2021). Blockchain & IoT: A Paradigm Shift for Supply Chain Management. In *Handbook of Blockchain for Sustainable Development* (p. 159). DOI: 10.1002/9781119711063.ch8

Bigdeloo, M., Teymourian, T., Kowsari, E., Ramakrishna, S., & Ehsani, A. (2021). Sustainability and Circular Economy of Food Wastes: Waste Reduction Strategies, Higher Recycling Methods, and Improved Valorization. *Materials Circular Economy*, *3*(1), 3. DOI: 10.1007/s42824-021-00017-3

*Bioproduct Basics*. (2023). https://www.energy.gov/eere/bioenergy/bioproduct-basics

Buekens, A. (2013). *Incineration Technologies*. Springer Science & Business Media. DOI: 10.1007/978-1-4614-5752-7

Campera, M., Budiadi, B., Adinda, E., Ahmad, N., Balestri, M., Hedger, K., Imron, M. A., Manson, S., Nijman, V., & Nekaris, K. A. I. (2021). Fostering a Wildlife-Friendly Program for Sustainable Coffee Farming: The Case of Small-Holder Farmers in Indonesia. *Land (Basel)*, *10*(2), 121. DOI: 10.3390/land10020121

Castaldo, L., Lombardi, S., Gaspari, A., Rubino, M., Izzo, L., Narváez, A., Ritieni, A., & Grosso, M. (2021). In Vitro Bioaccessibility and Antioxidant Activity of Polyphenolic Compounds from Spent Coffee Grounds-Enriched Cookies. *Foods*, *10*(8), 1837. DOI: 10.3390/foods10081837 PMID: 34441614

Chaturvedi, A. K., Arora, R., & Saluja, M. S. (2015). Private Sector and Waste Management in Delhi: A Political Economy Perspective. *IDS Bulletin*, *46*(3), 7–16. DOI: 10.1111/1759-5436.12140

Chen, H. (2021). Optimization of an Intelligent Sorting and Recycling System for Solid Waste Based on Image Recognition Technology. *Advances in Mathematical Physics*, *2021*(1), 4094684. DOI: 10.1155/2021/4094684

Choi, J., Lim, B., & Yoo, Y. (2023). Advancing Plastic Waste Classification and Recycling Efficiency: Integrating Image Sensors and Deep Learning Algorithms. *Applied Sciences (Basel, Switzerland)*, *13*(18), 10224. DOI: 10.3390/app131810224

*Coffee waste as an alternative fertilizer with soil improving properties for sandy soils in humid tropical environments*. (n.d.). ResearchGate. Retrieved October 17, 2025, from https://www.researchgate.net/publication/263375752_Coffee_waste_as_an_alternative_fertilizer_with_soil_improving_properties_for_sandy_soils_in_humid_tropical_environments

*Cosmetic application of coffee by-products*. (n.d.). ResearchGate. Retrieved October 17, 2025, from https://www.researchgate.net/figure/Cosmetic-application-of-coffee-by-products_tbl3_367000924

Dave, G., Patel, T., & Mitra, S. (2025). *Global scenario on renewable energy and net zero goal emphasizing Indian standpoint: A short review*. Energy Systems. DOI: 10.1007/s12667-025-00728-5 de Bomfim, A. S. C., de Oliveira, D. M., Walling, E., Babin, A., Hersant, G., Vaneeckhaute, C., Dumont, M.-J., & Rodrigue, D. (2023). Spent Coffee Grounds Characterization and Reuse in Composting and Soil Amendment. *Waste, 1*(1), 2–20. DOI: 10.3390/waste1010002

de Freitas, C. P. M., Marangon, B. B., Pereira, E. G., & Renato, N. dos S. (2023). Exploring spent coffee grounds energy potential in the Brazilian scenario. *Engenharia Agrícola, 43*(spe), e20220141. DOI: 10.1590/1809-4430-eng.agric.v43nepe20220141/2023

de Paula, J., & Farah, A. (2022). Phenolic compounds in coffee seeds and by-products. In *Coffee Science*. CRC Press. DOI: 10.1201/9781003043133-11

Ellahi, R. M., Wood, L. C., & Bekhit, A. E.-D. A. (2024). Blockchain-Driven Food Supply Chains: A Systematic Review for Unexplored Opportunities. *Applied Sciences (Basel, Switzerland), 14*(19), 8944. DOI: 10.3390/app14198944

Eron, F., Noman, M., de Oliveira, R. R., & Chalfun-Júnior, A. (2024). Computer Vision-Aided Intelligent Monitoring of Coffee: Towards Sustainable Coffee Production. *Scientia Horticulturae, 327*, 112847–112847. DOI: 10.1016/j.scienta.2024.112847

Franca, A. S., & Oliveira, L. S. (2019). Coffee. In Pan, Z., Zhang, R., & Zicari, S. (Eds.), *Integrated Processing Technologies for Food and Agricultural By-Products* (pp. 413–438). Academic Press. DOI: 10.1016/B978-0-12-814138-0.00017-4

Getachew, A. T., & Chun, B. S. (2017). Influence of pretreatment and modifiers on subcritical water liquefaction of spent coffee grounds: A green waste valorization approach. *Journal of Cleaner Production, 142*, 3719–3727. DOI: 10.1016/j.jclepro.2016.10.096

Giuliani, E., Ciravegna, L., Vezzulli, A., & Kilian, B. (2017). Decoupling Standards from Practice: The Impact of In-House Certifications on Coffee Farms' Environmental and Social Conduct. *World Development, 96*, 294–314. DOI: 10.1016/j.worlddev.2017.03.013

Gottstein, V., Bernhardt, M., Dilger, E., Keller, J., Breitling-Utzmann, C. M., Schwarz, S., Kuballa, T., Lachenmeier, D. W., & Bunzel, M. (2021). Coffee Silver Skin: Chemical Characterization with Special Consideration of Dietary Fiber and Heat-Induced Contaminants. *Foods, 10*(8), 1705. DOI: 10.3390/foods10081705 PMID: 34441483

Gouvea, B. M., Torres, C., Franca, A. S., Oliveira, L. S., & Oliveira, E. S. (2009). Feasibility of ethanol production from coffee husks. *Biotechnology Letters*, *31*(9), 1315–1319. DOI: 10.1007/s10529-009-0023-4 PMID: 19466561

Gunaseelan, J., Sundaram, S., & Mariyappan, B. (2023). A Design and Implementation Using an Innovative Deep-Learning Algorithm for Garbage Segregation. *Sensors (Basel)*, *23*(18), 7963–7963. DOI: 10.3390/s23187963 PMID: 37766020

Hernández-Varela, J. D., & Medina, D. I. (2023). Revalorization of Coffee Residues: Advances in the Development of Eco-Friendly Biobased Potential Food Packaging. *Polymers*, *15*(13), 2823. DOI: 10.3390/polym15132823 PMID: 37447469

Hijosa-Valsero, M., Garita-Cambronero, J., Paniagua-García, A. I., & Díez-Antolínez, R. (2018). Biobutanol production from coffee silverskin. *Microbial Cell Factories*, *17*(1), 154. DOI: 10.1186/s12934-018-1002-z PMID: 30261894

Iriondo-DeHond, A., Herrera, T., & Del Castillo, M. D. (2020). Health Benefits of Silverskin. In *Food Wastes and By-products* (pp. 353–371). John Wiley & Sons, Ltd. DOI: 10.1002/9781119534167.ch12

Johnson, K., Liu, Y., & Lu, M. (2022). A Review of Recent Advances in Spent Coffee Grounds Upcycle Technologies and Practices. *Frontiers in Chemical Engineering*, *4*, 838605. Advance online publication. DOI: 10.3389/fceng.2022.838605

Kashem, M. A., Shamsuddoha, M., Nasir, T., & Chowdhury, A. A. (2023). Supply Chain Disruption versus Optimization: A Review on Artificial Intelligence and Blockchain. *Knowledge (Beverly Hills, Calif.)*, *3*(1), 80.

Kittichotsatsawat, Y., Jangkrajarng, V., & Tippayawong, K. Y. (2021). Enhancing Coffee Supply Chain towards Sustainable Growth with Big Data and Modern Agricultural Technologies. *Sustainability (Basel)*, *13*(8), 4593. DOI: 10.3390/su13084593

Kourmentza, C., Economou, Ch. N., Tsafrakidou, P., & Kornaros, M. (2018). Spent coffee grounds make much more than waste: Exploring recent advances and future exploitation strategies for the valorization of an emerging food waste stream. *Journal of Cleaner Production*, *172*, 980–992. DOI: 10.1016/j.jclepro.2017.10.088

Kshetri, N. (2021). Blockchain and sustainable supply chain management in developing countries. *International Journal of Information Management*, *60*, 102376. DOI: 10.1016/j.ijinfomgt.2021.102376

Kumar, C. S., Padhy, A. B., Singh, A. P., & Reddy, K. H. K. (2025). A Dynamic Trading Approach Based on Walrasian Equilibrium in a Blockchain-Based NFT Framework for Sustainable Waste Management. *Mathematics*, *13*(3), 521. DOI: 10.3390/math13030521

Kunwar, S. (2023, April). *MWaste: A Deep Learning Approach to Manage Household Waste*. arXiv. /arXiv.2304.14498DOI: 10.20944/preprints202304.0066.v1

Largo Avila, E., Suárez Rodríguez, C. H., & Arango Espinal, E. (2025). Digital transformation: Evolving applications of artificial intelligence in the coffee industry. *Ingeniería y Desarrollo*, *43*(1), 64–83. DOI: 10.14482/inde.43.01.445.864

Martin. (n.d.). Sustainable consumption and production. *United Nations Sustainable Development*. Retrieved March 6, 2025, from https://www.un.org/sustainabledevelopment/sustainable-consumption-production/

Mora-Villalobos, J.-A., Aguilar, F., Carballo-Arce, A.-F., Vega-Baudrit, J. R., Trimino-Vazquez, H., Villegas-Peñaranda, L. R., Stöbener, A., Eixenberger, D., Bubenheim, P., Sandoval, M., & Liese, A. (2021). Tropical agroindustrial biowaste revalorization through integrative biorefineries—Review part I: Coffee and palm oil by-products. *Biomass Conversion and Biorefinery*, *13*(2), 1469–1487. DOI: 10.1007/s13399-021-01442-9

*More than 1 billion tons of food lost or wasted every year, UN-backed report finds | UN News*. (2011, May 11). https://news.un.org/en/story/2011/05/374722

Motta, I., Vuillerme, N., Pham, H.-H., & de Figueiredo, F. A. P. (2024, November). Machine learning techniques for coffee classification: A comprehensive review of scientific research. In *Artificial Intelligence Review* (Vol. 58, Issue 1). Springer Science+Business Media. DOI: 10.1007/s10462-024-11004-w

Murthy, P. S., & Madhava Naidu, M. (2012). Sustainable management of coffee industry by-products and value addition—A review. *Resources, Conservation and Recycling*, *66*, 45–58. DOI: 10.1016/j.resconrec.2012.06.005

Mussatto, S. I., Machado, E. M. S., Martins, S., & Teixeira, J. A. (2011). Production, Composition, and Application of Coffee and Its Industrial Residues. *Food and Bioprocess Technology*, *4*(5), 661–672. DOI: 10.1007/s11947-011-0565-z

Neilson, J. (2008). Global Private Regulation and Value-Chain Restructuring in Indonesian Smallholder Coffee Systems. *World Development*, *36*(9), 1607–1622. DOI: 10.1016/j.worlddev.2007.09.005

Nepal, M., Nepal, A. K., Khadayat, M. S., Kumar, R., Shyamsundar, P., & Somanathan, E. (2022). Low-Cost Strategies to Improve Municipal Solid Waste Management in Developing Countries: Experimental Evidence from Nepal. *Environmental and Resource Economics*. Advance online publication. DOI: 10.1007/s10640-021-00640-3

Nwokediegwu, Z. Q. S., Ugwuanyi, E. D., Dada, M. A., Majemite, M. T., & Obaigbena, A. (2024). AI-driven waste management systems: A comparative review of innovations in the USA and Africa. *Engineering Science & Technology Journal, 5*(2), 507–516. DOI: 10.51594/estj.v5i2.828

Overturf, E., Pezzutto, S., Boschiero, M., Ravasio, N., & Monegato, A. (2021). The CirCo (Circular Coffee) Project: A Case Study on Valorization of Coffee Silverskin in the Context of Circular Economy in Italy. *Sustainability (Basel), 13*(16), 16. Advance online publication. DOI: 10.3390/su13169069

Pachot, A., & Patissier, C. (2022). Towards Sustainable Artificial Intelligence: An Overview of Environmental Protection Uses and Issues. *arXiv*. /arxiv.2212.11738DOI: 10.48550

Park, A., & Li, H. (2021). The Effect of Blockchain Technology on Supply Chain Sustainability Performances. *Sustainability (Basel), 13*(4), 1726. DOI: 10.3390/su13041726

Pasupuleti, V., Thuraka, B., Kodete, C. S., & Malisetty, S. (2024). Enhancing Supply Chain Agility and Sustainability through Machine Learning: Optimization Techniques for Logistics and Inventory Management. *Logistics (Basel), 8*(3), 73. DOI: 10.3390/logistics8030073

Pathan, M. S., Richardson, E., Galvan, E., & Mooney, P. (2023). The Role of Artificial Intelligence within Circular Economy Activities—A View from Ireland. *Sustainability (Basel), 15*(12), 12. Advance online publication. DOI: 10.3390/su15129451

Peixoto, J. A. B., Silva, J. F., Oliveira, M. B. P. P., & Alves, R. C. (2022, December). Sustainability issues along the coffee chain: From the field to the cup. In *Wiley* (Vol. 22, Issue 1, pp. 287–332). DOI: 10.1111/1541-4337.13069

Peluso, M. (2023). *Coffee By-Products: Economic Opportunities for Sustainability and Innovation in the Coffee Industry*. DOI: 10.3390/ICC2023-14834

Rajesh Banu, J., Kavitha, S., Yukesh Kannah, R., Dinesh Kumar, M., Preethi, , Atabani, A. E., & Kumar, G. (2020). Biorefinery of spent coffee grounds waste: Viable pathway towards circular bioeconomy. *Bioresource Technology, 302*, 122821. DOI: 10.1016/j.biortech.2020.122821 PMID: 32008862

Saher, R., Saleh, M., & Anjum, M. (2023). Holistic Trash Collection System Integrating Human Collaboration with Technology. *Applied Sciences (Basel, Switzerland), 13*(20), 11263. DOI: 10.3390/app132011263

Sharma, P., Gaur, V. K., Sirohi, R., Varjani, S., Kim, S., & Wong, J. W. C. (2021). Sustainable processing of food waste for production of bio-based products for circular bioeconomy. *Bioresource Technology, 325*, 124684. Advance online publication. DOI: 10.1016/j.biortech.2021.124684 PMID: 33493748

Smirnov, Y., Sverchkov, I., & Gabdullina, R. (2022). *Biofuel pellets from spent coffee grounds. Research Square*. DOI: 10.21203/rs.3.rs-1551835/v1

Stufano, P., Perrotta, A., Labarile, R., & Trotta, M. (2022). The second life of coffee can be even more energizing: Circularity of materials for bio-based electrochemical energy storage devices. *MRS Energy & Sustainability : a Review Journal, 9*(2), 443–460. DOI: 10.1557/s43581-022-00036-w

*Sustainability issues along the coffee chain: From the field to the cup—Barreto Peixoto—2023—Comprehensive Reviews in Food Science and Food Safety—Wiley Online Library*. (n.d.). Retrieved October 17, 2025, from https://ift.onlinelibrary.wiley.com/doi/10.1111/1541-4337.13069

*Tackling food loss and waste: A triple win opportunity*. (n.d.). Newsroom. Retrieved March 6, 2025, from https://www.fao.org/newsroom/detail/FAO-UNEP-agriculture-environment-food-loss-waste-day-2022/en

Ticona-Salluca, H., Torres-Cruz, F., & Tumi-Figueroa, E. N. (2023, January). *Machine Learning Applied to Peruvian Vegetables Imports*. arXiv. /arXiv.2301.03587DOI: 10.48550

Tucker, C. M. (2017). *Coffee Culture: Local Experiences, Global Connections* (2nd ed.). Routledge. DOI: 10.4324/9781315678795

2023 . U.S. Coffee Impact Report. (n.d.). Retrieved March 7, 2025, from https://www.ncausa.org/Research-Trends/Economic-Impact

Weber, H., & Wiek, A. (2021). Cooperating With "Open Cards"—The Role of Small Intermediary Businesses in Realizing Sustainable International Coffee Supply. *Frontiers in Sustainable Food Systems, 5*, 663716. Advance online publication. DOI: 10.3389/fsufs.2021.663716

White, G., Cabrera, C., Palade, A., Li, F., & Clarke, S. (2020, June). *WasteNet: Waste Classification at the Edge for Smart Bins*. arXiv. https://doi.org//arXiv.2006.05873DOI: 10.48550

Xia, W., Jiang, Y., Chen, X., & Zhao, R. (2022). Application of machine learning algorithms in municipal solid waste management: A mini review. *Waste Management & Research, 40*(6), 609–624. DOI: 10.1177/0734242X211033716 PMID: 34269157

Yuzvovich, L., Lvova, M. I., & Isakova, N. Y. (2024). Waste management: Environmental strategies and practices. *E3S Web of Conferences, 541*. DOI: 10.1051/e3sconf/202454104004

Zanoletti, A., Cornelio, A., & Bontempi, E. (2021). A post-pandemic sustainable scenario: What actions can be pursued to increase the raw materials availability? *Environmental Research, 202*, 111681. Advance online publication. DOI: 10.1016/j.envres.2021.111681 PMID: 34273363

Zhu, Y., Zhang, K., Hu, Q., Liu, W., Qiao, Y., Cai, D., Zhu, P., Wang, D., Xu, H., Shu, S., & Gao, N. (2023). Accelerated spent coffee grounds humification by heat/base co-activated persulfate and products' fertilization evaluation. *Environmental Technology & Innovation, 32*, 103393. DOI: 10.1016/j.eti.2023.103393

# Chapter 11
# AI-Powered Innovations in Automation for Achieving SDGs:
## Advancing Sustainable Agriculture

**Mrutyunjay Padhiary**
https://orcid.org/0000-0002-2236-568X
*Assam University, Silchar, India*

**Avinash Kumar**
https://orcid.org/0000-0002-0254-3186
*Assam University, Silchar, India*

**Azmirul Hoque**
https://orcid.org/0009-0002-7220-9818
*Assam University, Silchar, India*

**Javed Akhtar Barbhuiya**
https://orcid.org/0000-0002-2235-6695
*Assam University, Silchar, India*

## ABSTRACT

*Agriculture has experienced an important change with the development of artificial intelligence (AI), enabling smarter, more efficient, and sustainable farming operations. This chapter delves into how AI-powered automation could transform agriculture in the context of the Sustainable Development Goals (SDGs). It examines AI applications like precision farming, climate-smart agriculture, and automation technologies, which can improve resource use, increase crop yields, and promote environmental sustainability. These investigations identify cost and lack of access*

DOI: 10.4018/979-8-3373-1837-0.ch011

*as barriers, despite their limitations in reaching a global audience. By focusing on equitable access and inclusive technology, AI can further enhance sustainable practices in several agricultural sectors. These initiatives may contribute to achieving the Sustainable Development Goals (SDGs), such as zero hunger (SDG 2), clean water and sanitation (SDG 6), and climate action (SDG 13). This chapter highlights the potential of AI to change the agricultural sector and assist with sustainability efforts around the world.*

## INTRODUCTION

### Sustainable Agriculture

Sustainable agriculture is essential for ensuring food security, resolving climate change, and enhancing environmental resilience. As the global population is expected to approach 10 billion by 2050, conventional agricultural methods are inadequate to sustainably satisfy this demand (Hemathilake & Gunathilake, 2022). Sustainable agriculture practices attempt to balance productivity with environmental stewardship, resource efficiency, and social equity to face these challenges. Artificial Intelligence (AI) has shifted the agricultural sector, providing innovative solutions for attaining goals associated with sustainability (Padhiary & Kumar, 2024b). AI-driven tools and automation systems offer unique prospects to improve agricultural productivity, optimize resource utilization, and adapt to climate change (Usigbe et al., 2024). These technologies correlate directly with the United Nations sustainable development goals (SDGs), specifically those relevant to zero hunger (SDG 2), clean water and sanitation (SDG 6), and climate action (SDG 13).

Sustainable agriculture is essential for reducing hunger and assuring food security through the efficiency of crop yields, minimization of post-harvest losses, and improvement of food distribution systems. AI-driven technologies, including predictive analytics, yield optimization models, and precision farming techniques, enhance agricultural efficiency and productivity to achieve this goal (Akintuyi, 2024). Sustainable agriculture aids climate action by adopting practices such as agroforestry, organic farming, and minimal tillage. It is linked to other sustainable development goals, including good health and well-being, responsible consumption and production, and life on land. Through the adoption of sustainable practices, agriculture enhances nutrition, minimizes food waste, and preserves biodiversity. The combination of sustainable agricultural methods with AI-driven technologies offers a means to attain the sustainable development goals, benefiting both present and future generations.

## Scope of the Study

Traditional agricultural practices are becoming less sustainable due to modern challenges, such as resource depletion, soil degradation, deforestation, climate change, pest and disease management, shortage of employees, inefficient resource use, lack of technological integration, and economic vulnerabilities (Padhiary & Kumar, 2024a). Inefficient irrigation methods exploit water resources, leading to water shortages in many regions. Deforestation decreases biodiversity and lowers carbon sequestration, while climate change causes more frequent and severe storms and droughts, damaging crops and disrupting planting schedules(Veldkamp et al., 2020). Traditional farming methods contribute to greenhouse gas emissions and worsen climate-related problems for farmers. Conventional methods for managing pests and diseases are often ineffective and can harm the environment, resulting in pesticide resistance and other environmental damage. In developing countries, labor shortages and productivity gaps further restrict productivity and scalability (Gill & Garg, 2014). AI-powered automation is altering agriculture by increasing productivity, maximizing natural resource applications, minimizing environmental impacts, and facilitating the achievement of the United Nations SDGs. It enhances precision agriculture by controlling water, fertilizers, and pesticides using real-time data from sensors, drones, and IoT devices. This reduces resource waste, lowers environmental damage, and ensures optimal crop health and productivity. AI-driven automation improves agriculture's resilience to climate change through predictive analytics and adaptive solutions (Ahamed, 2024). Autonomous agricultural machinery, including self-navigating tractors, harvesters, and robotic weeders, operates with exceptional accuracy and efficiency, reducing reliance on manual labor and expanding productivity (Hoque, Padhiary, et al., 2025). AI-powered automation enables real-time monitoring and decision-making, allowing farmers to make data-driven choices. It goes beyond agricultural production to improve the whole supply chain, using predictive analytics, automated grading and sorting systems, and blockchain-connected AI solutions (Shamshiri et al., 2024). AI-driven automation has also altered livestock management by monitoring animals' health, behavior, and productivity in real time (Spanaki et al., 2022).

Wearable sensors and AI analytics provide early signs of illness to prevent a situation, thus avoiding the use of antibiotics. Automated feeding systems guarantee the appropriate distribution of feed based on the individual animal's needs, thereby promoting sustainability (Lovarelli et al., 2020). The integration of AI-driven automation has connections to many Sustainable development goals, like zero hunger, clean water and sanitation, responsible consumption and production, and climate action. Figure 1 reveals the relationship between various AI applications (e.g., precision farming, smart irrigation, crop monitoring) and the specific SDGs they impact. The visuals emphasize SDG 2 (zero hunger), SDG 6 (clean water and sanitation), and SDG 13 (climate action), showcasing how AI-powered innovations contribute to sustainable agricultural practices

*Figure 1. Infographic on the linkages between AI applications and SDGs in agriculture*

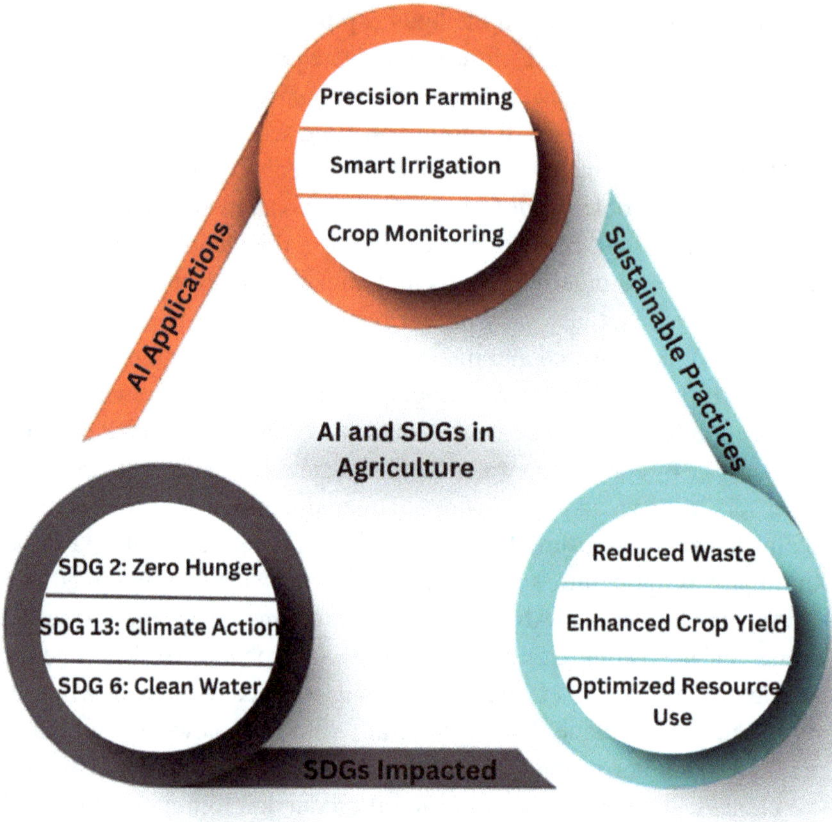


The primary concern of this study is to explore the revolutionary role of AI-driven automation in promoting sustainable agriculture and attaining the United Nations' Sustainable Development Goals (SDGs). The objective is to analyze how AI improves precision agriculture via soil health analysis, crop growth prediction, and yield optimization. The study aims at evaluating the influence of AI-driven technologies, including weather forecasting and crop disease diagnosis, on reducing the effects of climate change and enhancing food safety. The main goal among them is to evaluate the performance of AI-based robots, drones, IoT, and smart sensors in enhancing efficiency in the use of resources and reducing the effects on the environment. The study seeks to identify the barriers to AI adoption in agriculture, including high costs, lack of access in rural regions, and ethical issues. Lastly, it suggests some solutions to these issues in the future, including regulatory incentives, efforts for stakeholders to cooperate, and the creation of open-source AI solutions to allow everyone to benefit from and use AI innovations in sustainable agriculture.

## AI IN SUSTAINABLE AGRICULTURE

AI is a breakthrough technology in agriculture, providing novel solutions for resource improvement, climate adaptability, and sustainable food production. A fundamental function of AI includes data-driven decision-making, precision agriculture, predictive analytics, and automation (Padhiary, 2024). AI technologies are used in diverse agricultural sectors to solve challenges and enhance sustainability, including precision farming, pest and disease control, livestock management, climate adaptation, and supply chain optimization (Javaid et al., 2023). AI-driven solutions offer many benefits that are in line with sustainable farming methods, such as better use of resources, higher output, less damage to the environment, increased toughness, and higher food security (Padhiary, Kumar, et al., 2025). Also, for extensive adoption, we must resolve hurdles such as substantial initial expenses, data accessibility, required technical proficiency, the digital divide, and ethical considerations.

Substantial initial expenses may be expensive for smallholder farmers, yet data accessibility is essential for AI applications. Agriculturalists demand training to use AI tools effectively, which requires capacity-building initiatives (Musungwini et al., 2023). The digital divide makes it harder for developing areas to use AI. This means that data privacy and fairness issues need to be fixed in AI algorithms so that everyone gets the same results. The chances of AI in sustainable agriculture are optimistic, propelled by continuous advancements stimulating innovation. The combination of AI with IoT and robotic systems allows for fully automated, intelligent agricultural systems (Subeesh & Mehta, 2021). AI-driven climate solutions will enhance climate prediction and adaptive strategies, improve resilience, and increase AI uptake among smallholder farmers. Scalable solutions will decrease expenses and enhance accessibility, while connections among governments, academia, and industry will promote innovation and knowledge exchange (Alexander et al., 2020). AI provides significant potential to enhance sustainable agriculture, thereby substantially contributing to global food security and environmental sustainability.

### Precision Agriculture

Precision agriculture (PA), or smart farming, is a modern agricultural technique that applies technology to enhance the efficiency of inputs such as water, fertilizer, and pesticides, thereby improving productivity and reducing negative environmental impacts. The fundamental principles contain site-specific management, resource efficiency, real-time monitoring, and sustainability. Technologies supporting PA encompass the Internet of Things (IoT), AI, Geographic Information Systems (GIS), Remote Sensing Technologies, Variable Rate Technology (VRT), and Robotics and Automation (Padhiary, Saikia, et al., 2025; Sabir et al., 2024). PA has various applications, including soil health management, crop health monitoring, water management, and yield improvement. According to research, AI-powered soil sensors give real-time information about the pH, nutrient levels, and moisture in the soil(Elbasi et al., 2024; Lilhare et al., 2024). This makes it easier to manage nutrients, stop soil erosion and salinity, and keep soil organic matter. Predictive models powered by AI evaluate historical and real-time data to forecast yields and suggest strategies for enhancing productivity. PA provides various advantages that correlate with sustainable farming targets, including resource efficiency, increased productivity, environmental sustainability, climate resilience, and economic benefits. PA is hard to use because it requires a lot of money up front, is hard to integrate data, requires a lot of skills, and is hard for people in rural areas to get to the internet and other technological infrastructure. PA could have a bright future if AI is added, the IoT grows, cost-effective solutions are found, environmentally friendly methods are used, and the government backs the industry with subsidies and training programs (Maraveas, 2022).

AI is advancing agriculture by offering modern techniques for soil health management, crop growth prediction, and yield optimization. AI technologies offer immediate insights into soil conditions, simplifying precision management and improving sustainable agricultural practices. Applications in soil health monitoring include soil quality assessment, soil moisture evaluation, soil erosion estimation, and soil fertility management. AI technologies improve crop growth prediction by delivering precise predictions derived from environmental and physiological data. AI models in crop growth prediction anticipate growth stages, identify diseases and pests, and study weather patterns to evaluate their effects on crop development (Delfani et al., 2024). AI systems recommend optimal planting density, row spacing, and nutrient applications to achieve maximum growth. AI has altered yield planning through the analysis of extensive datasets and the provision of actionable insights to agricultural producers. AI systems use historical and real-time data to calculate crop yields, enhance resource allocations, and deliver instant recommendations based on changing field conditions. AI-powered decision support systems offer timely recommendations based on variable field conditions.

AI-driven irrigation systems have significantly enhanced water-use efficiency and crop productivity in arid regions, solving issues such as water scarcity and resource mismanagement. Case studies indicate that AI-driven smart irrigation systems in Israel, India, and California have decreased water consumption by 30%, enhanced crop yield by 20%, and lowered energy and water pumping expenses by 25% (Nuwarapaksha et al., 2025a). In India, AI-powered drip irrigation systems monitored soil moisture and evaporation rates, achieving a 35% reduction in water usage and a 15% enhancement in sugarcane yield (Vinayaka & Prasad, 2024). California implemented AI-driven precision irrigation systems to conserve water and maintain grape quality. In Australia, AI-powered irrigation systems were implemented to enhance water efficiency for fodder cultivation, resulting in a 25% reduction in water usage and an 18% increase in pasture productivity (Ali & Kaul, 2025). Kenya employed AI-driven rainwater harvesting systems to estimate precipitation patterns and improve the storage and distribution of collected rainwater. These systems provide benefits including water efficiency, cost reduction, climate resilience, and environmental sustainability. AI-driven irrigation systems may considerably enhance water accessibility in resource-limited areas. Table 1 compares the characteristics of traditional farming practices with AI-driven farming methods. Key aspects include water utilization efficiency, yield prediction accuracy, and input optimization. It highlights the advantages of AI in promoting resource efficiency, precision, and sustainability

*Table 1. Comparison of traditional vs. AI-driven farming methods*

| Aspect | Traditional Farming Methods | AI-Driven Farming Methods | Benefits of AI-Driven Methods | References |
|---|---|---|---|---|
| Resource efficiency | High resource wastage | Optimized resource allocation using AI | Reduced water, fertilizer, and pesticide usage | (Adinarayana et al., 2024) |
| Crop monitoring | Manual and time-intensive | Real-time monitoring with sensors and drones | Improved crop health and early issue detection | (Mohyuddin et al., 2024) |
| Irrigation | Fixed schedules, inefficient | AI-based smart irrigation systems | Conserves water and improves irrigation precision | (Nuwarapaksha et al., 2025a) |
| Pest management | Broad-spectrum pesticide application | AI-powered pest prediction and targeted spraying | Reduces pesticide use and environmental harm | (Padhiary, Tikute, et al., 2024; Thangamani et al., 2024) |
| Yield prediction | Based on experience | AI models predicting yields with high accuracy | Better planning and market alignment | (Celis et al., 2024) |
| Climate adaptation | Reactive to weather changes | Predictive models for climate variability | Proactive measures to mitigate risks | (Darjee et al., 2023) |

continued on following page

*Table 1. Continued*

| Aspect | Traditional Farming Methods | AI-Driven Farming Methods | Benefits of AI-Driven Methods | References |
|---|---|---|---|---|
| Labor dependence | High reliance on manual labor | Automated systems for planting and harvesting | Reduced labor costs and time | (Baur & Iles, 2023) |
| Data utilization | Minimal use of data | Big data analytics for decision-making | Informed decisions and precision agriculture | (Farooqui et al., 2024) |
| Sustainability | Limited focus on sustainability | AI-driven focus on sustainable practices | Long-term environmental and economic benefits | (Oladapo et al., 2024) |
| Scalability | Difficult to scale | Easily scalable with AI-driven systems | Expands agricultural potential | (Usigbe et al., 2024) |

## Climate-Smart Agriculture

Climate-smart agriculture (CSA) is a sustainable agricultural technique that promotes the adaptation of farming practices to changing climatic conditions, the reduction of greenhouse gas emissions, and the improvement of agricultural productivity and resilience. It employs AI-driven tools to predict climate risks, optimize resource management, develop resilient crop varieties, evaluate animal health, and monitor soil carbon levels. AI-driven solutions help farmers in making informed decisions about planting schedules, irrigation, and crop selection. In Africa, AI-driven agricultural advisory systems have increased yields by 20% and strengthened resilience to drought conditions (Njuguna et al., 2025). Europe utilizes AI models to evaluate and enhance soil carbon levels through regenerative agricultural practices. In Australia, AI-based livestock monitoring systems have improved animal welfare and reduced methane emissions. The benefits of CSA with AI integration include improved productivity, sustainability, economic viability, and adaptability, allowing farmers to proactively confront climate risks and market demands.

AI changed agriculture by solving issues related to weather prediction and crop disease identification. AI-driven systems combine extensive data and complex modeling methodologies to deliver precise forecasts, targeted predictions, and climate risk evaluations. These tools assist farmers in making data-informed decisions, reducing risks, and enhancing productivity while maintaining sustainability. AI systems in meteorology evaluate extensive datasets from sources such as satellite imagery, terrestrial sensors, historical weather records, and real-time meteorological information (Selvam & Al-Humairi, 2025). Machine learning (ML) models identify patterns and correlations in meteorological phenomena, facilitating highly precise forecasts. AI-driven tools offer hyper localized weather forecasts tailored for individual farms, aiding farmers in planning activities in accordance with favourable weather conditions. In crop disease detection, AI models use image analysis to find early signs of diseases. This makes monitoring more accurate, scalable, and in real time. These models include IoT and remote sensing technologies to estimate potential disease outbreaks and recommend preventive measures. In terms of weather forecasting and disease identification, AI has many benefits, such as higher accuracy, lower costs, higher productivity, better environmental protection, and more power for farmers(Hoque, 2024). Challenges entail data accessibility and quality, scalability, technical proficiency, and integration with conventional practices.

Agriculture significantly contributes to global greenhouse gas emissions through livestock production, fertilizer applications, and land use changes. AI has been used to develop solutions that reduce emissions and enhance the sustainability of agricultural practices. AI-driven systems facilitate better resource utilization, manage agricultural operations, and encourage practices that reduce the environmental impact of farming (Usigbe et al., 2024). Enhanced fertilizer application can lower nitrous oxide emissions by predicting the ideal quantity and timing of fertilizer applications based on soil health, meteorological conditions, and crop needs. Precision livestock management uses AI-driven monitoring systems to improve feeding strategies and lower methane emissions (Hoque & Padhiary, 2024). Creative irrigation systems use real-time meteorological data to improve water efficiency and reduce water waste and energy consumption. AI algorithms aid farmers in applying regenerative agricultural practices, such as cover cropping, reduced tillage, and crop rotation, which increase soil organic carbon and improve carbon sequestration (Hamrani et al., 2020). AI tools facilitate precision planting, increase crop growth under ideal environmental conditions, reduce pesticide and fertilizer use, and reduce emissions from agricultural machinery. Table 2 exhibits the effect of AI technologies on reducing greenhouse gas emissions in agriculture. It focuses applications such as optimized fertilizer application, precision irrigation, lower energy consumption, and enhanced livestock management. The application of AI in promoting climate-smart practices markedly drops the environmental impact of agriculture and contributes to the fulfillment of global climate action targets.

*Table 2. Quantifiable impact of AI on GHG reduction in agriculture*

| AI Application | Reduction in Emissions (%) | GHG Source Addressed | Application | References |
|---|---|---|---|---|
| Precision fertilizer management | 20–30% | Nitrous oxide ($N_2O$) | Variable rate fertilization systems | (Glenn et al., 2021) |
| Livestock methane monitoring | 10–20% | Methane ($CH_4$) | AI-driven Livestock Monitoring | (Neethirajan, 2024) |
| Precision irrigation | 20–25% | Carbon dioxide ($CO_2$) | CropX AI-irrigation system | (Jamal et al., 2024) |
| Carbon sequestration optimization | 30–50% | Carbon dioxide ($CO_2$) | Indigo Ag Carbon monitoring | (Lamb et al., 2018) |
| Methane capture | 50–70% | Methane ($CH_4$) | AI-enabled biogas plants | (Halis et al., 2024) |
| AI for supply chain management | 10–15% | Methane ($CH_4$), $CO_2$ | AgriLedger AI supply chain | (Van Wassenaer et al., 2021) |
| Reduced tillage with AI machines | 15–25% | Carbon dioxide ($CO_2$) | AI-enabled no-till machinery | (Abbasi et al., 2021) |
| AI-based disease detection | 5–10% | Methane ($CH_4$), $CO_2$ | AI for crop disease detection | (Altshuler et al., 2024) |
| AI for water management | 20–30% | Methane ($CH_4$), $CO_2$ | AI for water conservation (e.g., CropX) | (Nie et al., 2023) |
| Precision livestock feeding | 10–20% | Methane ($CH_4$) | AI in livestock feeding optimization | (Kiat et al., 2019) |

## AUTOMATION TECHNOLOGIES FOR SUSTAINABLE AGRICULTURE

Automation technologies are essential to advancing agricultural efficiency, sustainability, and profitability. The technologies include autonomous tractors and machinery merged with GPS and AI systems; drones and aerial imagery; robotic harvesting systems; automated irrigation systems; AI-driven pest and disease detection; automated livestock feeding systems; precision fertilizer application systems; automated weed control systems; and vertical farming automation (Ghobadpour et al., 2022). Autonomous tractors and machinery perform continuously, modifying their operations according to real-time data from sensors and environmental conditions. This results in resource enhancements, improved labor efficiency, reduced soil compaction, and better decision-making. Drones and aerial imaging acquire high-resolution images, measure crop health, and quantify soil moisture, facilitating the precise applications of pesticides, herbicides, and fertilizers.

Robotic harvesters use AI and machine vision to accurately identify and harvest crops, thereby saving labor expenses, decreasing waste, and improving irrigation efficiency. AI-driven pest and disease identification reduces pesticide application, facilitates early intervention, and covers environmental impact. Automated feeding systems enhance feed efficiency, avoid waste, and expand animal productivity. Precision fertilizer application systems evaluate soil health, nutrient concentrations, and crop needs by prescribing exact application rates. These results related to resource efficiency, higher crop yield, and lower greenhouse gas emissions. Automated weed control systems combine cameras and sensors to detect and eliminate weeds, which reduces chemical application and herbicide resistance (Machleb et al., 2020). Vertical farming automation fuses automation with controlled-environment agriculture (CEA) to cultivate crops in complex layers. This strategy improves land application, conserves water resources, and lessens transportation expenses and carbon emissions.

## Robotics and Drones

Robotics and drones are altering the agricultural sector by offering advanced options that improve efficiency, precision, and sustainability. The addition of AI in these technologies allows automation in activities such as planting, harvesting, and weed management, enabling real-time monitoring for crop health and resource efficiency. AI-driven robots for precise crop planting, ensuring optimal seed spacing and minimizing resource consumption. These results in reduced expenses, improved agricultural output, and lowered labour costs. AI-powered harvesting robots, like Octinion'sRubion, collect crops without causing damage, thereby reducing crop loss and keeping uniform harvest quality. AI-powered robotic systems for weed control can precisely find and target weeds, which mean less herbicide use, less damage to the environment, and more crop growth those comprise EcoRobotix and DJI Phantom 4 Multispectral (Dayana et al., 2025).

Farmers use drones for real-time crop monitoring and resource mapping, which provides them with crucial insights into crop health, growth phases, and pest infestations. Figure 2 represents of AI-enabled drones used in agriculture. It includes components such as high-resolution cameras, AI-based analytics for crop health detection, and GPS systems for precise navigation. Itfocuses applications like real-time crop monitoring, pest control, and resource mapping, demonstrating the integration of drone data with automated decision-making systems. These drones facilitate reliable information acquisition, quick issue identification, and enhanced decision-making, resulting in more sustainable agricultural practices. The adoption of drones for AI-driven resource mapping is essential for water conservation, refining fertilizer applications, and determining soil health. Constant drone operations yield ongoing soil health data, enabling farmers to monitor their practices and make necessary adjustments (Guebsi et al., 2024). AI-driven technologies are altering the agricultural sector by improving efficiency, precision, and sustainability.

*Figure 2. AI-powered agricultural drone systems for crop monitoring*

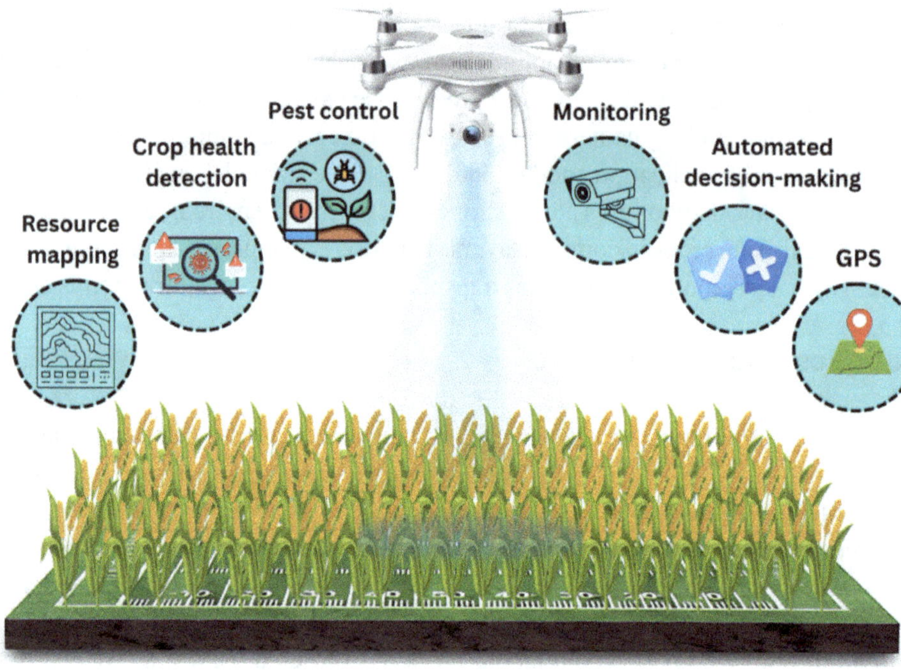


## IoT and Smart Sensors

The combination of IoT devices, smart sensors, and AI is affecting modern agriculture by facilitating real-time data capture from farms. AI analyses this data to facilitate informed decisions that raise resource efficiency, increase crop production, and minimize environmental impacts. Digital sensors integrated into soil, water systems, and crops offer critical insights that empower farmers to improve their resource management efficiently and sustainably (Mgendi, 2024). Real-time inspection of soil, water, and crops is facilitated by IoT sensors that check parameters including moisture levels, temperature, pH, and nutrient composition. AI algorithms evaluate this data and estimate soil response under varying environmental conditions, facilitating accurate soil management. This leads to improved water efficiency, effective fertilizerutilization, soil health maintenance, and prompt actions to sustain soil stability. Table 3 explores various AI-powered tools used in agriculture, such as drones, smart irrigation systems, and autonomous tractors, along with their specific applications and benefits. It provides insights into how these technologies address challenges like resource scarcity, labour shortages, and climate variability.

Innovative water management systems connected with IoT sensors can constantly control water consumption, flow rates, and water quality throughout agricultural fields. This results in water conservation, easing of water stress, enhanced crop health, and lower chemical application. AI-driven, automated feedback systems utilize data from IoT sensors to allocate resources dynamically, facilitating accurate, real-time decision-making that enhances resource efficiency while reducing waste and environmental consequences (Soori et al., 2024). These systems include irrigation feedback systems; fertilizer and nutrient feedback systems; pest and disease control feedback systems; and robotic systems. These systems benefit farmers in resource management, fall fertilizer waste, enhance efficiency, advance sustainable agricultural practices, and limit environmental impact. Integrating IoT sensors and AI enhances agricultural sustainability and helps farmers' overall welfare (Padhiary, Roy, et al., 2024).

*Table 3. AI-powered automation tools and their applications in agriculture*

| AI Tool | Application | Technology Used | Impact on Sustainability | References |
|---|---|---|---|---|
| CropX | Soil moisture monitoring and irrigation control | IoT sensors, AI-driven analytics | Reduces water consumption and optimizes irrigation schedules | (Adinarayana et al., 2024) |
| Ripe robotics | Pest and disease control | AI, Robotics, Image recognition | Minimizes pesticide use and improves crop protection | (Balaska et al., 2023) |
| Arable mark | Real-time crop health monitoring | IoT sensors, AI machine learning | Enhances crop management and early detection of stress | (Ahmad & Nabi, 2021) |
| Teralytic | Soil health and nutrient management | IoT sensors, AI algorithms | Optimizes fertilizer application and prevents overuse | (Choudhary et al., 2024) |
| Netafim | Drip irrigation systems | IoT sensors, AI, automation | Ensures water efficiency and reduces runoff | (Nuwarapaksha et al., 2025b) |
| Yara irix | Fertilizer and nutrient management | IoT sensors, AI analytics | Reduces fertilizer waste and enhances soil health | (Roberts et al., 2023) |
| Fieldin | Farm management and optimization | AI-driven insights, cloud computing | Improves operational efficiency and reduces resource waste | (Elufioye et al., 2024) |

continued on following page

*Table 3. Continued*

| AI Tool | Application | Technology Used | Impact on Sustainability | References |
|---|---|---|---|---|
| John Deere operations center | Precision farming and equipment management | AI, IoT, Machine learning | Enhances farm productivity and equipment utilization | (Polwaththa et al., 2024) |
| Skycision | Aerial monitoring and crop analysis | AI, Drones, Image recognition | Provides early detection of crop issues and optimizes inputs | (Raj et al., 2021) |
| Sensefinity | Environmental monitoring and real-time data collection | IoT sensors, AI machine learning | Promotes sustainability by monitoring environmental factors | (Dominguez-Sanchez et al., 2018) |

## ADVANCING SDGS THROUGH AI INNOVATIONS

The United Nations SDGs aspire to establish a sustainable future for all, with agriculture serving an important function in fulfilling them. AI innovations as useful tools for achieving this goal, as they enhance the sustainability, efficiency, and resilience of agriculture. AI technologies help smallholder farmers obtain resources and information, thereby increasing productivity and income (Javaid et al., 2023). They can predict agricultural yields, assess soil vitality, and identify first signs of pests and diseases, therefore ensuring stable food production and accessibility for those in need. AI-driven systems can also attenuate water consumption in agriculture, aiding in sustainable water resource management. AI can enhance sustainable energy practices in agriculture by exploiting renewable energy sources, including solar and wind. AI can improve resource efficiency and reduce waste in agriculture via precision farming, allowing farmers to utilize the precise quantity of inputs necessary (Getahun et al., 2024). It can help farmers adjust to unpredictable weather patterns and analyze greenhouse gas emissions resulting from agricultural activities. AI technologies enhance the preservation of ecosystems and biodiversity by streamlining land use and reducing deforestation.

### SDG 2: Zero Hunger

AI is significantly contributing to the enhancement of food security by reducing hunger and malnutrition. AI technologies enhance crop yields by improving decision-making regarding resource allocation, pest control, irrigation management, and crop health monitoring (Sharma & Shivandu, 2024). AI systems deliver actionable insights to farmers by integrating data from various sources, including satellite imagery, soil sensors, and weather forecasts, to enhance the use of fertilizer, water, and other resources. These technologies can predict crop performance, detect diseases early, and recommend specific interventions that enhance yields while reducing input costs.

AI increases precision agriculture by allowing farmers to monitor crop conditions in real time, thereby improving their capacity to make timely and informed decisions. This technology helps minimize crop losses caused by pests, diseases, and severe weather events, which can considerably undermine food security. Significant contributions of AI in yield planning cover precision agriculture, crop health testing, climate adaptation, and supply chain enhancement. In Kenya, smallholder farmers use AI-driven platforms, such as Tulezi and iProcure, to enhance crop yields and strengthen food security. These platforms employ AI-driven predictive analytics to supply farmers with insights regarding optimal planting periods, soil health, meteorological forecasts, and pest management. Farmers utilizing Tulezi's AI-driven platform have indicated a crop yield increase of up to 30% (Korir & Kilika, 2023). AI recommendations on irrigation practices have facilitated water conservation while preserving adequate moisture for crops.

## SDG 6: Clean Water and Sanitation

AI-driven irrigation systems represent a viable solution for lowering water wastage in agriculture. These systems use real-time data and predictive analytics to enhance water application, ensuring that crops obtain the appropriate quantity of water at the optimal moment. They are able to predict meteorological patterns, evaluate soil conditions, and quantify evapotranspiration, which aids in determining the exact volume of water required for irrigation. Precision irrigation, weather integration, evaluating soil health, and automated feedback mechanisms are some of the most important features of AI-driven irrigation systems. These systems may decrease water usage, raise agricultural productivity, reduce expenses, and promote environmental sustainability.

In India, CropX created an AI-based Irrigation Management System (IMS) that incorporates soil moisture sensors, regional weather information, and crop-specific water requirements to proactively modify irrigation schedules. The AI algorithms evaluate real-time data to estimate irrigation needs for various crops, considering soil type, climatic conditions, and growth stages of the crops. Findings indicated that farmers using the AI-driven IMS observed a 30–40% decrease in water consumption while sustaining or enhancing crop yields (Ali et al., 2024; Khaleel et al., 2024).

The system assisted farmers in conserving water and energy consumption while reducing dependence on manual labor for irrigation management. The system has enhanced sustainable agricultural practices and conserved water resources in drought-affected areas by avoiding water waste and boosting irrigation efficiency.

These findings show AI's essential function in precision irrigation, enhancing water management, and enabling sustainable agriculture practices.The comparative bar graph data indicates substantial enhancements in water usage efficiency and resource conservation upon the implementation of AI-powered irrigation systems in diverse agricultural practices (Figure 3).

*Figure 3. Water usages before and after AI-powered interventions in agriculture*

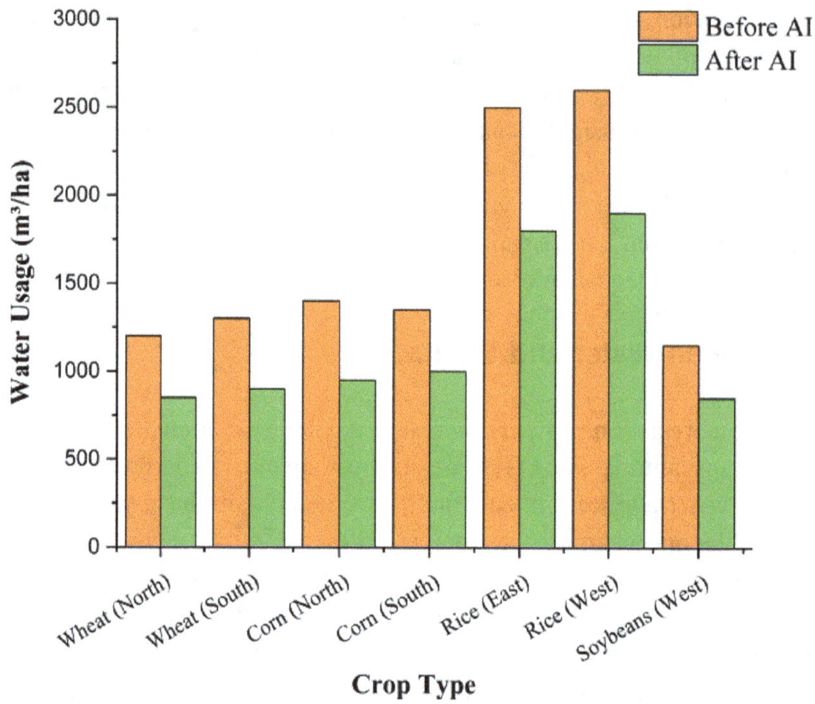


*(Akanbi et al., 2025; Arévalo-Royo et al., 2025; Qamar, 2024)*

## SDG 13: Climate Action

AI is essential in reducing agricultural emissions and enhancing climate resilience. Agriculture is among the most susceptible to climate change, significantly contributing to GHG emissions through practices such as animal husbandry, rice production, and the application of synthetic fertilizers. It can assist in relieving these emissions by enhancing agricultural methods, decreasing greenhouse gases, and improving climate resilience. AI technologies may cut agricultural emissions via precision fertilization, reduction of livestock emissions, efficiency of irrigation, and the use of smart machinery and autonomous vehicles (Padhiary, Kumar, et al., 2024; SaberiKamarposhti et al., 2024). AI systems recommend the ideal type and quantity of nutrients by analyzing soil sensors, weather forecasts, and crop requirements, thereby avoiding emissions. It can monitor the health and behavior of livestock, allowing farmers to optimize animal diets and practices that prevent methane emissions.

AI can make climate resilience better by making agricultural systems more flexible. This can be done by predicting climate change and evaluating risks, choosing and breeding crops that will be resilient to it, using PA to adapt to it, and making the best use of resources to deal with it. The Netherlands is incorporating AI into CSA to reduce emissions and enhance climate change resilience. The AI-driven Greenhouse Climate Control System created by Wageningen University & Research and TNO has decreased greenhouse gas emissions linked to greenhouse agriculture by as much as 25% while enhancing crop yield efficiency (Sarku et al., 2023). By strengthening environmental conditions within the greenhouse, the system ensures that crops experience minimal stress, resulting in improved productivity amid climate change.

## CHALLENGES AND CONSTRAINTS

AI offers the capacity to remake sustainable agriculture, yet it faces numerous challenges and constraints. This covers the substantial expense of AI-driven technologies, limited access to AI resources in rural regions, and ethical issues pertaining to data privacy. The excessive cost of AI-powered tools can render them inaccessible for smallholder farmers, thereby limiting access for numerous individuals in developing nations or small-scale enterprises. Financial assistance denial could impede farmers' ability to implement AI solutions. Poor access to AI tools in remote locations constitutes an additional challenge (Tzachor et al., 2022). Most rural regions are deficient in essential infrastructure and technical proficiency and face obstacles to market access. This situation is compounded by limited access to high-speed internet, unreliable electricity, and often inadequate technical proficiency within rural agricultural communities. Finally, AI-driven agricultural tools frequently lack consideration for rural farmers, hindering their ability to leverage AI innovations.

To solve these challenges, it is essential to improve infrastructure in rural regions and implement training programs to develop local expertise in AI applications. AI developers need to concentrate on creating cost-effective, scalable, and culturally appropriate approaches that address the distinct requirements of rural farmers. Moral issues and data privacy concerns have arisen as significant barriers in the implementation of AI in agriculture. Principal ethical and privacy challenges entail data ownership and access, surveillance and privacy, bias and fairness, transparency and accountability, as well as the necessity for transparent AI systems (Williamson & Prybutok, 2024). To mitigate these issues, effective data privacy regulations and ethical AI frameworks must be instituted to ensure that AI solutions are inclusive, equitable, and uphold farmers' rights and privacy. By handling these challenges, AI developers can formulate strategies that secure the equitable and responsible deployment of AI in agriculture.

The implementation of AI-driven automation in agriculture is essential; still, it requires the resolution of current challenges, including higher expenses, limited accessibility, and knowledge gaps. Governments can facilitate AI adoption via subsidies and grants, tax incentives for innovations, public-private partnerships, regulatory frameworks, and support for market access. Intersectoral collaboration is crucial for solving deficits in research, innovation, and implementation. Governments, industries, and academic institutions need to collaborate to develop innovative AI solutions for agriculture, including joint R&D initiatives focusing on region-specific challenges (Fatemi et al., 2024). Open data platforms enhance the accuracy of AI models, while standard protocols for AI applications in agriculture enable compatibility among tools and systems. International collaborations facilitate funding, learning, expertise sharing, and the transfer of advanced technologies to areas with limited resources.

Capacity-building initiatives for farmers and stakeholders are essential. Workshops for farmer training, digital literacy initiatives, extension services, stakeholder involvement, and online platforms containing multilingual content may provide farmers with the knowledge and skills necessary to use AI tools. Digital literacy projects can improve digital proficiency in rural regions, whereas extension services can incorporate AI-driven decision support systems for immediate assistance in crop management (Naidoo, 2024). Stakeholder engagement could involve all stakeholders in the design and implementation of capacity-building programs.

## APPLICATIONS

AI-driven automation is altering agriculture worldwide, enhancing productivity and sustainability, and achieving the United Nations SDGs. Successful implementations comprise smart irrigation systems in India, AI-enhanced pest management in the United States, AI-based yield prediction in Sub-Saharan Africa, autonomous robotic harvesting in the Netherlands, and AI-integrated livestock monitoring in New Zealand.

AI-driven tools expand productivity through accurate resource allocation and improving the efficiency of crop and livestock management. Yield optimization algorithms and real-time monitoring systems have improved output while reducing input costs (Majumdar et al., 2021). AI technologies reduce the ecological impact of agriculture through decreasing resource depletion and destructive practices. Intelligent irrigation systems lower water consumption by as much as 40%, whereas PA and enhanced fertilizer applications minimize greenhouse gas emissions (Bwambale et al., 2022).

AI-driven predictive analytics support farmers in making informed decisions, thereby avoiding economic risks. The adoption of AI enhances digital literacy and creates employment opportunities in technology-orientated positions, aiding in the achievement of global climate targets(Hoque et al., 2024). The benefits for the economy and society entail income stability, rural empowerment, and access to global markets. Table 4 illustrates the effects of AI-driven automation on essential agricultural metrics, particularly its role in enhancing productivity, sustainability, and conformance with SDG It indicates the quantifiable results of each AI application in practical agricultural environments, highlighting its contribution to improving resource efficiency and sustainability.

AI-driven automation may significantly improve productivity, sustainability, and conformity with SDG goals across diverse agricultural settings. Using AI tools, farmers can attain a 35% decrease in water consumption, a 20% enhancement in crop yields, a 40% reduction in pest damage, a 25% decline in pesticide applications, a 30% boost in productivity, a 50% cut in labor expenses, and a 15% rise in milk output (Ayed & Hanana, 2021; Javaid et al., 2023; Lakhiar et al., 2024).

*Table 4. Impact assessment of AI-powered automation on agricultural outcomes*

| AI Application | Key Metric Improved | Quantitative Impact | Alignment with SDGs | References |
|---|---|---|---|---|
| Smart irrigation systems | Water use efficiency | 35% reduction in water usage | SDG 6: Clean water and sanitation | (Obaideen et al., 2022) |
| AI-driven pest management | Pesticide usage | 25% reduction in pesticide use | SDG 12: Responsible consumption | (Kalirajan et al., 2024) |
| Yield prediction models | Crop productivity | 30% increase in yield | SDG 2: Zero hunger | (Allahyari & Sadeghzadeh, 2020) |
| Robotic harvesting | Labor efficiency | 50% reduction in labor costs | SDG 8: Decent work and economic growth | (Haidegger et al., 2023) |
| Livestock health monitoring | Greenhouse gas emissions | 10% reduction in methane emissions | SDG 13: Climate action | (McGregor et al., 2021) |
| Precision fertilizer application | Soil health | 20% reduction in over-fertilization | SDG 15: Life on land | (Noulas et al., 2023) |

continued on following page

*Table 4. Continued*

| AI Application | Key Metric Improved | Quantitative Impact | Alignment with SDGs | References |
|---|---|---|---|---|
| Drone-based crop surveillance | Crop monitoring accuracy | 40% improvement in pest detection | SDG 9: Industry, innovation, and infrastructure | (Guebsi et al., 2024) |
| Automated greenhouses | Energy use efficiency | 25% reduction in energy consumption | SDG 7: Affordable and clean energy | (Maraveas, 2022) |
| Disease detection algorithms | Early disease identification | 50% improvement in response time | SDG 3: Good health and well-being | (Fernandez, 2020) |
| Market prediction tools | Economic resilience | 15% increase in farmer income | SDG 1: No poverty | (Khanal et al., 2021) |

## PROSPECTIVE DEVELOPMENT

The prospects of AI-driven sustainable agriculture hold significant potential, with continuous advancements capable of solving existing challenges and creating new opportunities for agricultural practices. To fully realize this potential, three critical areas require substantial focus: improving the affordability and accessibility of AI technologies, creating open-source AI tools specifically designed for agriculture, and fostering global collaborations for sustainable agricultural practices. The biggest challenge for the future of AI in agriculture is to enhance the affordability as well as the accessibility of these technologies for farmers across all tiers, especially smallholder and limited-resource farmers.

Researchers and companies can concentrate on creating cheap AI solutions that are less intricate yet still provide valuable insights, including crop disease prediction, irrigation management, and yield management (Redhu et al., 2022; Shaikh et al., 2022). Innovative financing models, including microloans, subsidies, and pay-per-use structures, can facilitate farmers' access to AI technologies without requiring them to spend the entire upfront expense. Governments may provide subsidies or financial incentives to encourage the adoption of AI in agriculture, particularly in rural or developing areas.

Enhanced infrastructure is crucial for allowing access to AI technologies, including high-speed internet, electricity, and digital platforms. Investments in rural regions will empower farmers to use AI tools efficiently, particularly for real-time monitoring, data analysis, and decision-making. Open-source AI tools have the potential to alter the agricultural sector by providing farmers low-cost or free access to advanced technologies that can improve productivity and sustainability (Cob-Parro et al., 2024). To enhance the impact of AI technologies in sustainable agriculture, it is essential to reinforce global collaborations, including partnerships among governments, international organizations, research institutions, private-sector enterprises, and farmers.

Multinational collaboration may successfully address global issues such as food security, climate change, and resource depletion in ways unachievable by individual entities alone. International research partnerships, global standards and guidelines, technology transfer and capacity building, public-private partnerships, and global food security networks can all help make the use of AI technologies in agriculture more responsible and ethical.

## CONCLUSION

AI-driven automation possesses significant potential for improving agriculture, addressing the issues of climate change, resource scarcity, and an expanding global population. AI can significantly contribute to the achievement of the SDGs by optimizing resource utilization, improving crop yields, enhancing sustainability, and promoting climate resilience practices. The addition of AI to agricultural methodologies, such as precision farming, CSA, and automation technologies, offers a chance to improve productivity while reducing environmental impacts.

To realize this innovative potential, it is imperative that we overcome existing challenges. Significant obstacles, including elevated expenses, restricted technological access in rural areas, and moral concerns related to data privacy, must be resolved. It is essential for the widespread adoption of AI tools that they are affordable, accessible, and modified to meet the requirements of smallholder farmers. Also, making open-source solutions, pushing for global partnerships, and encouraging public-private partnerships will help everyone get equal benefits and make sure that AI technologies are used in a way that is fair and includes everyone.

As AI advances, it is crucial to focus on policies, infrastructure, and frameworks that promote collaboration and empower farmers globally. By precisely targeting these challenges, AI possesses the capacity to reinvent agriculture, thereby improving food security, preserving natural resources, and aiding in the attainment of the SDGultimately promoting a more sustainable and prosperous future for all.

## REFERENCES

Abbasi, N. A., Hamrani, A., Madramootoo, C. A., Zhang, T., Tan, C. S., & Goyal, M. K. (2021). Modelling carbon dioxide emissions under a maize-soy rotation using machine learning. *Biosystems Engineering, 212*, 1–18. DOI: 10.1016/j.biosystemseng.2021.09.013

Adinarayana, S., Raju, M. G., Srirangam, D. P., Prasad, D. S., Kumar, M. R., & Veesam, S. B. (2024). Enhancing Resource Management in Precision Farming through AI-Based Irrigation Optimization. In Dey, A., Nayak, S., Kumar, R., & Mohanty, S. N. (Eds.), *How Machine Learning is Innovating Today's World* (1st ed., pp. 221–251). Wiley. DOI: 10.1002/9781394214167.ch15

Ahamed, T. (2024). *IoT and AI in Agriculture: Smart Automation Systems for Increasing Agricultural Productivity to Achieve SDGs and Society 5.0.* Springer Nature. DOI: 10.1007/978-981-97-1263-2

Ahmad, L., & Nabi, F. (2021). *Agriculture 5.0: Artificial intelligence, IoT and machine learning*. CRC Press.

Akanbi, M. B., Adedotun, K. J., Raji, A. K., & Banjoko, I. K. (2025). Optimizing Water Resource Management in Agriculture Using AI-Powered Solar Irrigation Systems. *Journal of Science Innovation and Technology Research.*

Akintuyi, O. B. (2024). AI in agriculture: A comparative review of developments in the USA and Africa. *Research Journal of Science and Engineering, 10*(2), 60–70.

Alexander, A., Martin, D. P., Manolchev, C., & Miller, K. (2020). University–industry collaboration: Using meta-rules to overcome barriers to knowledge transfer. *The Journal of Technology Transfer, 45*(2), 371–392. DOI: 10.1007/s10961-018-9685-1

Ali, A., & Kaul, H.-P. (2025). Monitoring Yield and Quality of Forages and Grassland in the View of Precision Agriculture Applications—A Review. *Remote Sensing (Basel), 17*(2), 279. DOI: 10.3390/rs17020279

Ali, F., Razzaq, A., Tariq, W., Hameed, A., Rehman, A., Razzaq, K., Sarfraz, S., Rajput, N. A., Zaki, H. E., Shahid, M. S., & Ondrasek, G. (2024). Spectral Intelligence: AI-Driven Hyperspectral Imaging for Agricultural and Ecosystem Applications. *Agronomy (Basel), 14*(10), 2260. DOI: 10.3390/agronomy14102260

Allahyari, M. S., & Sadeghzadeh, M. (2020). Agricultural Extension Systems Toward SDGs 2030: Zero Hunger. In Leal Filho, W., Azul, A. M., Brandli, L., Özuyar, P. G., & Wall, T. (Eds.), *Zero Hunger* (pp. 41–52). Springer International Publishing. DOI: 10.1007/978-3-319-95675-6_2

Altshuler, Y., Chebach, T. C., & Cohen, S. (2024). From Microbes to Methane: AI-Based Predictive Modeling of Feed Additive Efficacy in Dairy Cows. In *Applied Swarm Intelligence* (pp. 240–325). CRC Press.

Arévalo-Royo, J., Flor-Montalvo, F.-J., Latorre-Biel, J.-I., Tino-Ramos, R., Martínez-Cámara, E., & Blanco-Fernández, J. (2025). AI Algorithms in the Agrifood Industry: Application Potential in the Spanish Agrifood Context. *Applied Sciences (Basel, Switzerland), 15*(4), 2096. DOI: 10.3390/app15042096

Balaska, V., Adamidou, Z., Vryzas, Z., & Gasteratos, A. (2023). Sustainable crop protection via robotics and artificial intelligence solutions. *Machines (Basel), 11*(8), 774. DOI: 10.3390/machines11080774

Baur, P., & Iles, A. (2023). Inserting machines, displacing people: How automation imaginaries for agriculture promise 'liberation' from the industrialized farm. *Agriculture and Human Values, 40*(3), 815–833. DOI: 10.1007/s10460-023-10435-5

Ben Ayed, R., & Hanana, M. (2021). Artificial Intelligence to Improve the Food and Agriculture Sector. *Journal of Food Quality, 2021*, 1–7. DOI: 10.1155/2021/5584754

Bwambale, E., Abagale, F. K., & Anornu, G. K. (2022). Smart irrigation monitoring and control strategies for improving water use efficiency in precision agriculture: A review. *Agricultural Water Management, 260*, 107324. DOI: 10.1016/j.agwat.2021.107324

Celis, J., Xiao, X., Wagle, P., Adler, P. R., & White, P. (2024). A Review of Yield Forecasting Techniques and Their Impact on Sustainable Agriculture. In Melkonyan-Gottschalk, A., & Daus, D. (Eds.), *Transformation Towards Circular Food Systems* (Vol. 13, pp. 139–168). Springer Nature Switzerland. DOI: 10.1007/978-3-031-63793-3_8

Choudhary, M., Arora, M., & Goyal, N. (2024). Smart agriculture with cloud/fog computing and sensor networks for sustainable development. In *Cloud and Fog Optimization-based Solutions for Sustainable Developments* (pp. 98–117). CRC Press. DOI: 10.1201/9781003494430-5

Cob-Parro, A. C., Lalangui, Y., & Lazcano, R. (2024). Fostering Agricultural Transformation through AI: An Open-Source AI Architecture Exploiting the MLOps Paradigm. *Agronomy (Basel), 14*(2), 259. DOI: 10.3390/agronomy14020259

Darjee, K. B., Neupane, P. R., & Köhl, M. (2023). Proactive Adaptation Responses by Vulnerable Communities to Climate Change Impacts. *Sustainability (Basel), 15*(14), 10952. DOI: 10.3390/su151410952

Dayana, D. S., Venkatamuni, T., Bhagyalakshmi, A., Malleswari, T. N., & Ushasukhanya, S. (2025). AI-Controlled Robotics in Smart Agricultural Systems: Enhancing Precision, Sustainability, and Productivity. In *Edible Electronics for Smart Technology Solutions* (pp. 351–382). IGI Global. https://www.igi-global.com/chapter/ai-controlled-robotics-in-smart-agricultural-systems/360268

Delfani, P., Thuraga, V., Banerjee, B., & Chawade, A. (2024). Integrative approaches in modern agriculture: IoT, ML and AI for disease forecasting amidst climate change. *Precision Agriculture, 25*(5), 2589–2613. DOI: 10.1007/s11119-024-10164-7

Dominguez-Sanchez, A., Cazorla, M., & Orts-Escolano, S. (2018). A new dataset and performance evaluation of a region-based cnn for urban object detection. *Electronics (Basel), 7*(11), 301. DOI: 10.3390/electronics7110301

Elbasi, E., Mostafa, N., Zaki, C., AlArnaout, Z., Topcu, A. E., & Saker, L. (2024). Optimizing agricultural data analysis techniques through ai-powered decision-making processes. *Applied Sciences (Basel, Switzerland), 14*(17), 8018. DOI: 10.3390/app14178018

Elufioye, O. A., Ike, C. U., Odeyemi, O., Usman, F. O., & Mhlongo, N. Z. (2024). Ai-Driven predictive analytics in agricultural supply chains: A review: assessing the benefits and challenges of ai in forecasting demand and optimizing supply in agriculture. *Computer Science & IT Research Journal, 5*(2), 473–497. DOI: 10.51594/csitrj.v5i2.817

Farooqui, N. A., Haleem, M., Khan, W., & Ishrat, M. (2024). Precision Agriculture and Predictive Analytics: Enhancing Agricultural Efficiency and Yield. In N. Singh, S. Birla, M. D. Ansari, & N. K. Shukla (Eds.), *Intelligent Techniques for Predictive Data Analytics* (1st ed., pp. 171–188). Wiley. DOI: 10.1002/9781394227990.ch9

Fatemi, M., Pakzad, M., & Ghazinoory, S. (2024). Implementing RIS3 (Research and Innovation Strategies for Smart Specialization) to unlock Iran's regional potential. *Innovation (Abingdon)*, 1–18. DOI: 10.1080/13511610.2024.2430235

Fernandez, R. M. (2020). SDG3 Good Health and Well-Being: Integration and Connection with Other SDGs. In Leal Filho, W., Wall, T., Azul, A. M., Brandli, L., & Özuyar, P. G. (Eds.), *Good Health and Well-Being* (pp. 629–636). Springer International Publishing. DOI: 10.1007/978-3-319-95681-7_64

Getahun, S., Kefale, H., & Gelaye, Y. (2024). Application of Precision Agriculture Technologies for Sustainable Crop Production and Environmental Sustainability: A Systematic Review. *TheScientificWorldJournal, 2024*(1), 2126734. DOI: 10.1155/2024/2126734 PMID: 39421732

Ghobadpour, A., Monsalve, G., Cardenas, A., & Mousazadeh, H. (2022). Off-road electric vehicles and autonomous robots in agricultural sector: Trends, challenges, and opportunities. *Vehicles (Basel)*, *4*(3), 843–864. DOI: 10.3390/vehicles4030047

Gill, H. K., & Garg, H. (2014). Pesticide: Environmental impacts and management strategies. *Pesticides-Toxic Aspects*, *8*(187), 10–5772.

Glenn, A. J., Moulin, A. P., Roy, A. K., & Wilson, H. F. (2021). Soil nitrous oxide emissions from no-till canola production under variable rate nitrogen fertilizer management. *Geoderma*, *385*, 114857. DOI: 10.1016/j.geoderma.2020.114857

Guebsi, R., Mami, S., & Chokmani, K. (2024). Drones in precision agriculture: A comprehensive review of applications, technologies, and challenges. *Drones (Basel)*, *8*(11), 686. DOI: 10.3390/drones8110686

Haidegger, T., Mai, V., Mörch, C. M., Boesl, D. O., Jacobs, A., Khamis, A., Lach, L., & Vanderborght, B. (2023). Robotics: Enabler and inhibitor of the sustainable development goals. *Sustainable Production and Consumption*, *43*, 422–434. DOI: 10.1016/j.spc.2023.11.011

Halis, R., Ghazali, A., & Zakarya, I. A. (2024). Biofuels from Forest Logging Residues. In Bisaria, V. (Ed.), *Handbook of Biorefinery Research and Technology: Production of Biofuels and Biochemicals* (pp. 593–623). Springer Nature Singapore. DOI: 10.1007/978-94-007-6724-9_41-1

Hamrani, A., Akbarzadeh, A., & Madramootoo, C. A. (2020). Machine learning for predicting greenhouse gas emissions from agricultural soils. *The Science of the Total Environment*, *741*, 140338. DOI: 10.1016/j.scitotenv.2020.140338 PMID: 32610233

Hemathilake, D., & Gunathilake, D. (2022). Agricultural productivity and food supply to meet increased demands. In *Future foods* (pp. 539–553). Elsevier. DOI: 10.1016/B978-0-323-91001-9.00016-5

Hoque, A. (2024). Artificial Intelligence in Post-Harvest Drying Technologies: A Comprehensive Review on Optimization, Quality Enhancement, and Energy Efficiency. *International Journal of Science and Research (Raipur, India)*, *13*(11), 493–502. DOI: 10.21275/SR241107163717

Hoque, A., Mazumder, A. S., Roy, S., Saikia, P., & Kumar, K. (2025). *Transformative Approaches to Agricultural Sustainability: Automation, Smart Greenhouses, and AI*. Academic Press.

Hoque, A., & Padhiary, M. (2024). Automation and AI in Precision Agriculture: Innovations for Enhanced Crop Management and Sustainability. *Asian Journal of Research in Computer Science*, *17*(10), 95–109. DOI: 10.9734/ajrcos/2024/v17i10512

Hoque, A., Padhiary, M., Prasad, G., & Kumar, K. (2025). Real-Time Data Processing in Agricultural Robotics. In Bora, D. J., & Bania, R. K. (Eds.), *Computer Vision Techniques for Agricultural Advancements* (pp. 431–468). IGI Global. DOI: 10.4018/979-8-3693-8019-2.ch014

Jamal, S. M., Yadav, R. K., & Dayal, J. (2024). Innovative Soil Management Technologies for a Changing Climate. In Kanga, S., Singh, S. K., Shevkani, K., Pathak, V., & Sajan, B. (Eds.), *Transforming Agricultural Management for a Sustainable Future* (pp. 203–213). Springer Nature Switzerland. DOI: 10.1007/978-3-031-63430-7_10

Javaid, M., Haleem, A., Khan, I. H., & Suman, R. (2023). Understanding the potential applications of Artificial Intelligence in Agriculture Sector. *Advanced Agrochem*, *2*(1), 15–30. DOI: 10.1016/j.aac.2022.10.001

Kalirajan, M., Mageshen, V. R., Aswitha, K., & Saranya, M. (2024). AI-Based Regulation of Water Supply and Pest Management in Farming. In Chouhan, S. S., Saxena, A., Singh, U. P., & Jain, S. (Eds.), *Artificial Intelligence Techniques in Smart Agriculture* (pp. 195–215). Springer Nature Singapore. DOI: 10.1007/978-981-97-5878-4_12

Khaleel, M., Murtaza, N., Mueen, Q. H., Ahmad, S. A., & Qadri, S. F. (2024). Use of AI in conservation and for understanding climate change. In *A Biologist s Guide to Artificial Intelligence* (pp. 201–240). Elsevier. DOI: 10.1016/B978-0-443-24001-0.00013-0

Khanal, U., Wilson, C., Rahman, S., Lee, B. L., & Hoang, V.-N. (2021). Smallholder farmers' adaptation to climate change and its potential contribution to UN's sustainable development goals of zero hunger and no poverty. *Journal of Cleaner Production*, *281*, 124999. DOI: 10.1016/j.jclepro.2020.124999

Kiat, P. E., Malek, M. A., & Shamsuddin, S. M. (2019). Artificial intelligence projection model for methane emission from livestock in Sarawak. *Sains Malaysiana*, *48*(7), 1325–1332. DOI: 10.17576/jsm-2019-4807-02

Korir, D. J., & Kilika, J. M. (2023). Effect of deployment of strategic leadership in the horticulture industry: A case study of selected flower farms in Kenya. *International Journal of Research in Business and Social Science*, *12*(4), 163–174.

Lakhiar, I. A., Yan, H., Zhang, C., Wang, G., He, B., Hao, B., Han, Y., Wang, B., Bao, R., Syed, T. N., Chauhdary, J. N., & Rakibuzzaman, M. (2024). A Review of Precision Irrigation Water-Saving Technology under Changing Climate for Enhancing Water Use Efficiency, Crop Yield, and Environmental Footprints. *Agriculture*, *14*(7), 1141. DOI: 10.3390/agriculture14071141

Lamb, K. J., Dowsett, M. R., Chatzipanagis, K., Scullion, Z. W., Kröger, R., Lee, J. D., Aguiar, P. M., North, M., & Parkin, A. (2018). Capacitance-Assisted Sustainable Electrochemical Carbon Dioxide Mineralisation. *ChemSusChem*, *11*(1), 137–148. DOI: 10.1002/cssc.201702087 PMID: 29171724

Lilhare, S., Sanodiya, P., Dwivedi, V. K., & Singh, T. (2024). *Leveraging Artificial Intelligence (AI) for Soil Management: A Comprehensive Overview*. Academic Press.

Lovarelli, D., Bacenetti, J., & Guarino, M. (2020). A review on dairy cattle farming: Is precision livestock farming the compromise for an environmental, economic and social sustainable production? *Journal of Cleaner Production*, *262*, 121409. DOI: 10.1016/j.jclepro.2020.121409

Machleb, J., Peteinatos, G. G., Kollenda, B. L., Andújar, D., & Gerhards, R. (2020). Sensor-based mechanical weed control: Present state and prospects. *Computers and Electronics in Agriculture*, *176*, 105638. DOI: 10.1016/j.compag.2020.105638

Majumdar, P., Mitra, S., & Bhattacharya, D. (2021). IoT for Promoting Agriculture 4.0: A Review from the Perspective of Weather Monitoring, Yield Prediction, Security of WSN Protocols, and Hardware Cost Analysis. *Journal of Biosystems Engineering*, *46*(4), 440–461. DOI: 10.1007/s42853-021-00118-6

Maraveas, C. (2022). Incorporating artificial intelligence technology in smart greenhouses: Current State of the Art. *Applied Sciences (Basel, Switzerland)*, *13*(1), 14. DOI: 10.3390/app13010014

McGregor, A., Rickards, L., Houston, D., Goodman, M. K., & Bojovic, M. (2021). The Biopolitics of Cattle Methane Emissions Reduction: Governing Life in a Time of Climate Change. *Antipode*, *53*(4), 1161–1185. DOI: 10.1111/anti.12714

Mgendi, G. (2024). Unlocking the potential of precision agriculture for sustainable farming. *Discover Agriculture*, *2*(1), 87. DOI: 10.1007/s44279-024-00078-3

Mohyuddin, G., Khan, M. A., Haseeb, A., Mahpara, S., Waseem, M., & Saleh, A. M. (2024). Evaluation of Machine Learning approaches for precision Farming in Smart Agriculture System-A comprehensive Review. *IEEE Access : Practical Innovations, Open Solutions*.

Musungwini, S., Gavai, P. V., Munyoro, B., & Chare, A. (2023). Emerging ICT technologies for agriculture, training, and capacity building for farmers in developing countries: A case study in Zimbabwe. In *Applying Drone Technologies and Robotics for Agricultural Sustainability* (pp. 12–30). IGI Global. DOI: 10.4018/978-1-6684-6413-7.ch002

Naidoo, G. M. (2024). The Potential of Artificial Intelligence in South African Rural Development. *OIDA International Journal of Sustainable Development, 17*(11), 207–218.

Neethirajan, S. (2024). Net Zero Dairy Farming—Advancing Climate Goals with Big Data and Artificial Intelligence. *Climate (Basel), 12*(2), 15. DOI: 10.3390/cli12020015

Nie, T., Huang, J., Zhang, Z., Chen, P., Li, T., & Dai, C. (2023). The inhibitory effect of a water-saving irrigation regime on CH4 emission in Mollisols under straw incorporation for 5 consecutive years. *Agricultural Water Management, 278*, 108163. DOI: 10.1016/j.agwat.2023.108163

Njuguna, E., Daum, T., Birner, R., & Mburu, J. (2025). Silicon Savannah and smallholder farming: How can digitalization contribute to sustainable agricultural transformation in Africa? *Agricultural Systems, 222*, 104180. DOI: 10.1016/j.agsy.2024.104180

Noulas, C., Torabian, S., & Qin, R. (2023). Crop Nutrient Requirements and Advanced Fertilizer Management Strategies. In *Agronomy* (Vol. 13, Issue 8, p. 2017). MDPI. https://www.mdpi.com/2073-4395/13/8/2017

Nuwarapaksha, T. D., Udumann, S. S., Dissanayaka, N. S., Dilshan, R. M. N., & Atapattu, A. J. (2025a). AI-Driven Solutions for Sustainable Irrigation: Exploring Smart Technologies to Enhance Conservation and Efficiency. In *Integrating Agriculture, Green Marketing Strategies, and Artificial Intelligence* (pp. 1–32). IGI Global Scientific Publishing.

Nuwarapaksha, T. D., Udumann, S. S., Dissanayaka, N. S., Dilshan, R. M. N., & Atapattu, A. J. (2025b). Revolutionizing Agriculture by Advanced Water and Irrigation Management Technologies. In *Emerging Trends and Technologies in Water Management and Conservation* (pp. 285–318). IGI Global Scientific Publishing.

Obaideen, K., Yousef, B. A., AlMallahi, M. N., Tan, Y. C., Mahmoud, M., Jaber, H., & Ramadan, M. (2022). An overview of smart irrigation systems using IoT. *Energy Nexus, 7*, 100124. DOI: 10.1016/j.nexus.2022.100124

Oladapo, B. I., Olawumi, M. A., & Omigbodun, F. T. (2024). AI-Driven Circular Economy of Enhancing Sustainability and Efficiency in Industrial Operations. *Sustainability (Basel), 16*(23), 10358. DOI: 10.3390/su162310358

Padhiary, M. (2024). The Convergence of Deep Learning, IoT, Sensors, and Farm Machinery in Agriculture. In Thandekkattu, S. G., & Vajjhala, N. R. (Eds.), *Designing Sustainable Internet of Things Solutions for Smart Industries* (pp. 109–142). IGI Global. DOI: 10.4018/979-8-3693-5498-8.ch005

Padhiary, M., Kumar, K., Hussain, N., Roy, D., Barbhuiya, J. A., & Roy, P. (2025). Artificial Intelligence in Farm Management: Integrating Smart Systems for Optimal Agricultural Practices. *International Journal of Smart Agriculture*, *3*(1), 1–11. DOI: 10.54536/ijsa.v3i1.3674

Padhiary, M., & Kumar, R. (2024a). Assessing the Environmental Impacts of Agriculture, Industrial Operations, and Mining on Agro-Ecosystems. In Azrour, M., Mabrouki, J., Alabdulatif, A., Guezzaz, A., & Amounas, F. (Eds.), *Smart Internet of Things for Environment and Healthcare* (pp. 107–126). Springer Nature Switzerland. DOI: 10.1007/978-3-031-70102-3_8

Padhiary, M., & Kumar, R. (2024b). Enhancing Agriculture Through AI Vision and Machine Learning: The Evolution of Smart Farming. In Thangam, D. (Ed.), *Advancements in Intelligent Process Automation* (pp. 295–324). IGI Global. DOI: 10.4018/979-8-3693-5380-6.ch012

Padhiary, M., Kumar, R., & Sethi, L. N. (2024). Navigating the Future of Agriculture: A Comprehensive Review of Automatic All-Terrain Vehicles in Precision Farming. *Journal of The Institution of Engineers (India): Series A, 105*, 767–782. DOI: 10.1007/s40030-024-00816-2

Padhiary, M., Roy, P., Dey, P., & Sahu, B. (2024). Harnessing AI for Automated Decision-Making in Farm Machinery and Operations: Optimizing Agriculture. In Hai-Jew, S. (Ed.), Advances in Computational Intelligence and Robotics. IGI Global. DOI: 10.4018/979-8-3693-6230-3.ch008

Padhiary, M., Saikia, P., Roy, P., Hussain, N., & Kumar, K. (2025). *A Review on Advancing Agricultural Efficiency through Geographic Information Systems, Remote Sensing, and Automated Systems*. Cureus Journal of Engineering. DOI: 10.7759/s44388-024-00559-7

Padhiary, M., Tikute, S. V., Saha, D., Barbhuiya, J. A., & Sethi, L. N. (2024). Development of an IOT-Based Semi-Autonomous Vehicle Sprayer. *Agricultural Research, 13*(3). Advance online publication. DOI: 10.1007/s40003-024-00760-4

Polwaththa, K., Amarasinghe, S. T. C., Amarasinghe, A., & Amarasinghe, A. A. Y. (2024). Exploring Artificial Intelligence and Machine Learning in Precision Agriculture: A Pathway to Improved Efficiency and Economic Outcomes in Crop Production. *American Journal of Agricultural Science, Engineering, and Technology*, *8*(3), 50–59. DOI: 10.54536/ajaset.v8i3.3843

Qamar, A. (2024). AI-Powered Solutions in Climate Change Mitigation and Environmental Sustainability. *Research Corridor Journal of Engineering Science*, *1*(2), 194–209.

Raj, M., Gupta, S., Chamola, V., Elhence, A., Garg, T., Atiquzzaman, M., & Niyato, D. (2021). A survey on the role of Internet of Things for adopting and promoting Agriculture 4.0. *Journal of Network and Computer Applications*, *187*, 103107. DOI: 10.1016/j.jnca.2021.103107

Redhu, N. S., Thakur, Z., Yashveer, S., & Mor, P. (2022). Artificial intelligence: A way forward for agricultural sciences. In *Bioinformatics in Agriculture* (pp. 641–668). Elsevier. DOI: 10.1016/B978-0-323-89778-5.00007-6

Roberts, S., Shedi, O., Tausha, I., Kaonga, K., Nsomba, G., & Tshabalala, N. (2023). *Competition, concentration, and market outcomes in fertiliser markets in East and Southern Africa*. Academic Press.

SaberiKamarposhti, M., Why, N. K., Yadollahi, M., Kamyab, H., Cheng, J., & Khorami, M. (2024). Cultivating a sustainable future in the artificial intelligence era: A comprehensive assessment of greenhouse gas emissions and removals in agriculture. *Environmental Research*, 118528. PMID: 38403150

Sabir, R. M., Mehmood, K., Sarwar, A., Safdar, M., Muhammad, N. E., Gul, N., Athar, F., Majeed, M. D., Sattar, J., Khan, Z., Fatima, M., Hussain, M. A., & Akram, H. M. B. (2024). Remote Sensing and Precision Agriculture: A Sustainable Future. In Kanga, S., Singh, S. K., Shevkani, K., Pathak, V., & Sajan, B. (Eds.), *Transforming Agricultural Management for a Sustainable Future* (pp. 75–103). Springer Nature Switzerland. DOI: 10.1007/978-3-031-63430-7_4

Sarku, R., Clemen, U. A., & Clemen, T. (2023). The application of artificial intelligence models for food security. *Revista de Agricultura (Piracicaba)*, *13*(10), 2037.

Selvam, A. P., & Al-Humairi, S. N. S. (2025). Environmental impact evaluation using smart real-time weather monitoring systems: A systematic review. *Innovative Infrastructure Solutions*, *10*(1), 13. DOI: 10.1007/s41062-024-01817-7

Shaikh, T. A., Rasool, T., & Lone, F. R. (2022). Towards leveraging the role of machine learning and artificial intelligence in precision agriculture and smart farming. *Computers and Electronics in Agriculture, 198*, 107119. DOI: 10.1016/j.compag.2022.107119

Shamshiri, R. R., Rad, A. K., Behjati, M., & Balasundram, S. K. (2024). Sensing and Perception in Robotic Weeding: Innovations and Limitations for Digital Agriculture. *Sensors (Basel), 24*(20), 6743. DOI: 10.3390/s24206743 PMID: 39460222

Sharma, K., & Shivandu, S. K. (2024). Integrating artificial intelligence and internet of things (IoT) for enhanced crop monitoring and management in precision agriculture. *Sensors International, 5*, 100292. DOI: 10.1016/j.sintl.2024.100292

Soori, M., Jough, F. K. G., Dastres, R., & Arezoo, B. (2024). AI-based decision support systems in Industry 4.0, A review. *Journal of Economy and Technology.* https://www.sciencedirect.com/science/article/pii/S2949948824000374

Spanaki, K., Sivarajah, U., Fakhimi, M., Despoudi, S., & Irani, Z. (2022). Disruptive technologies in agricultural operations: A systematic review of AI-driven AgriTech research. *Annals of Operations Research, 308*(1–2), 491–524. DOI: 10.1007/s10479-020-03922-z

Subeesh, A., & Mehta, C. R. (2021). Automation and digitization of agriculture using artificial intelligence and internet of things. *Artificial Intelligence in Agriculture, 5*, 278–291. DOI: 10.1016/j.aiia.2021.11.004

Thangamani, R., Sathya, D., Kamalam, G. K., & Lyer, G. N. (2024). AI Green Revolution: Reshaping Agriculture's Future. In Balasubramanian, S., Natarajan, G., & Chelliah, P. R. (Eds.), *Intelligent Robots and Drones for Precision Agriculture* (pp. 421–461). Springer Nature Switzerland. DOI: 10.1007/978-3-031-51195-0_19

Tzachor, A., Devare, M., King, B., Avin, S., & Ó hÉigeartaigh, S. (2022). Responsible artificial intelligence in agriculture requires systemic understanding of risks and externalities. *Nature Machine Intelligence, 4*(2), 104–109. DOI: 10.1038/s42256-022-00440-4

Usigbe, M. J., Asem-Hiablie, S., Uyeh, D. D., Iyiola, O., Park, T., & Mallipeddi, R. (2024). Enhancing resilience in agricultural production systems with AI-based technologies. *Environment, Development and Sustainability, 26*(9), 21955–21983. DOI: 10.1007/s10668-023-03588-0

Van Wassenaer, L., van Hilten, M., Van Ingen, E., & Van Asseldonk, M. (2021). *Applying blockchain for climate action in agriculture: State of play and outlook.* Food & Agriculture Org.

Veldkamp, E., Schmidt, M., Powers, J. S., & Corre, M. D. (2020). Deforestation and reforestation impacts on soils in the tropics. *Nature Reviews. Earth & Environment*, *1*(11), 590–605. DOI: 10.1038/s43017-020-0091-5

Vinayaka, & Prasad, P. R. C. (2024). AI-Enhanced Remote Sensing Applications in Indian Sugarcane Research: A Comprehensive Review. *Sugar Tech*, 1–20.

Williamson, S. M., & Prybutok, V. (2024). Balancing privacy and progress: A review of privacy challenges, systemic oversight, and patient perceptions in AI-driven healthcare. *Applied Sciences (Basel, Switzerland)*, *14*(2), 675. DOI: 10.3390/app14020675

# Chapter 12
# Skin Cancer Classification Using Hybrid Deep Learning Approaches:
## A Systematic Review

**Zehra Tüfekçi**
https://orcid.org/0000-0002-6410-607X
*Istinye University, Turkey*

**Zeynep Orman**
https://orcid.org/0000-0002-0205-4198
*Istanbul University-Cerrahpasa, Turkey*

**Sibel Senan**
*Istanbul University-Cerrahpasa, Turkey*

## ABSTRACT

*Skin cancer is one of the most common types of cancer worldwide, and early diagnosis is crucial in the fight against the disease. In recent years, deep learning and hybrid approaches have shown significant potential in the diagnosis of skin cancer. This study provides a detailed review of hybrid deep learning methods proposed for skin cancer classification between 2020 and 2024. The methods in the literature are compared in terms of the datasets used, model accuracy rates, and performance-enhancing techniques. The ability of hybrid models to capture time-series dependencies and manage uncertainty makes them an effective tool for skin cancer diagnosis. These findings demonstrate that hybrid approaches provide more comprehensive and reliable results compared to traditional methods in skin*

DOI: 10.4018/979-8-3373-1837-0.ch012

*cancer diagnosis. In the future, the development of larger, more balanced datasets and the integration of explainable artificial intelligence techniques will further support progress in this field.*

## INTRODUCTION

Skin cancer is one of the most common types of cancer, accounting for one in every three diagnosed cancer cases worldwide, according to the World Health Organization (Kousis et al., 2022). Therefore, early detection of skin cancer is of great importance. Skin cancer results from the uncontrolled growth of irregular skin cells, leading to the formation of malignant tumors (Mijwil, 2021). In most cases, it has been observed that the disease develops due to prolonged exposure of unprotected skin to the sun's UV rays. Skin cancers are categorized into two main types: melanoma and non-melanoma. Melanoma is a dangerous, rare, and fatal form of skin cancer. According to the American Cancer Society, melanoma accounts for only 1% of all skin cancer cases but has a significantly higher mortality rate (Dildar et al., 2021). In diagnosing malignant cancers, dermatologists primarily rely on a visual examination of the affected area. However, this method sometimes fails to detect malignant cancers at an early stage. In addition to visual inspection, high-resolution dermoscopic images are also captured. During this process, various filters are applied to control the impact of light on the image and reduce skin reflections, making deeper layers more visible. This technical support has increased detection accuracy by an additional 49% (Kittler et al., 2002).

Computer-Aided Design (CAD) can provide rapid, reliable and consistent diagnosis of a variety of disorders (Gouda et al., 2022). CAD systems enable extraction from lesion images, which is essential for applying machine learning and deep learning techniques. Deep learning can analyze complex structures in images using techniques such as Artificial Neural Networks (ANN) and Convolutional Neural Networks (CNN). Unlike traditional methods, deep learning does not require additional expert intervention for feature extraction; the system can autonomously classify lesions as benign or malignant by analyzing various skin lesion images. This approach significantly enhances the accuracy and speed of early diagnosis, contributing to effective skin cancer treatment. However, challenges such as a lack of sufficient training datasets for high-quality medical imaging and the insufficient labeling of rare cases pose obstacles in this field. Standard CNNs may struggle to perform well on small datasets, making pretraining these models on large datasets (e.g., ImageNet) a common strategy (Bechelli & Delhommelle, 2022).

Traditional image processing and deep learning methods are widely used for skin cancer diagnosis. Reza Ahmadi Mehr and colleagues proposed a deep learning model that assists dermatologists in skin cancer detection by analyzing lesion images along with metadata such as the anatomical location of the lesion, the patient's age, and the gender (Reza Ahmadi Mehr, 2023). The study utilized the ISIC 2019 dataset and applied the Inception-ResNet-v2 CNN model for both binary and multi-class classification. This approach achieved an accuracy rate of 94.5% in distinguishing between benign and malignant lesions. Additionally, it was reported that incorporating metadata into the model improved classification accuracy by at least 5%.

Similarly, in a study conducted by Satin Jain and colleagues, six different transfer learning models were compared for classifying seven types of skin cancer using the HAM10000 dataset (Jain et al., 2021). The study tested models including VGG19, InceptionV3, InceptionResNetV2, ResNet50, Xception, and MobileNet. The highest accuracy, 90.48%, was achieved by the Xception model. These findings highlight that transfer learning-based approaches can yield effective results even when applied to small datasets.

These studies emphasize the significance of integrating deep learning models with traditional image processing techniques for skin cancer diagnosis, as well as their role in improving classification accuracy. Particularly, incorporating patient metadata into models enhances diagnostic processes, making them more comprehensive and reliable. Consequently, hybrid approaches that combine different types of data offer significant advantages in model design.

In recent years, hybrid approaches have emerged as a noteworthy strategy for skin cancer diagnosis. These approaches integrate multiple techniques and algorithms, leveraging the advantages of each method to achieve more effective results. The primary objective of hybrid methods is to enhance classification accuracy by combining different techniques, ultimately enabling early skin cancer detection. By integrating information from various sources and data types, hybrid models improve overall performance. These models are particularly effective in handling small and imbalanced datasets, as they can generate generalized results despite limited data. Furthermore, since hybrid models analyze both pixel-level and high-level (more abstract) features, they offer a broader perspective for diagnosing complex diseases such as skin cancer. The literature suggests that hybrid approaches not only enhance diagnostic accuracy but also provide time- and cost-efficient solutions. As a result, hybrid methods are increasingly preferred in the treatment of critical health conditions such as skin cancer.

This study reviews hybrid methods proposed in the literature for early skin cancer detection between 2020 and 2024. It analyzes the datasets used, applied methodologies, and obtained results. Additionally, the study compares the performance and accuracy rates of various methods. By evaluating the strengths and weaknesses of these studies, recommendations for improving skin cancer diagnostic techniques are provided. The analysis aims to serve as a guide for future research, focusing on enhancing the efficiency of early detection technologies.

The remainder of this study is structured as follows: Section 2 presents a literature review of recent studies. Section 3 outlines the main focus of the chapter, including different types of skin cancer, various datasets, and imaging techniques. Section 4 discusses the results and provides interpretations. Section 5 presents a detailed results analysis. Section 6 highlights the social welfare implications of the work. Section 7 outlines future research directions, and finally, Section 8 concludes the study.

## LITERATURE REVIEW

In the literature, many different studies have been conducted on skin cancer diagnosis using the CNN method.

Shunichi Jinnai and colleagues developed a method using the FRCNN (Faster Region-Based CNN) approach for a six-class classification to determine which class each data belongs to and a binary classification to determine whether the data is benign or malignant (Jinnai et al., 2020). They compared the results obtained with three different groups: dermatologists and assistants. The developed method achieved the highest accuracy for both classifications.

In the study conducted by Syeda Shamaila Zareen and colleagues, 2,239 skin lesions from the ISIC dataset were classified using a hybrid model combining CNN, Recurrent Neural Network (RNN), and Long Short-Term Memory (LSTM) (Zareen et al., 2024). Additionally, this hybrid model was used alongside the ResNet50 architecture. The classification was performed for nine different types of skin cancer: Actinic Keratosis, Basal Cell Carcinoma, Dermatofibroma, Melanoma, Nevus, Pigmented Benign Keratosis, Seborrheic Keratosis, Squamous Cell Carcinoma, and Vascular Lesion. The proposed hybrid model was compared with CNN, ResNet, CRNN, VGGNet, GoogleNet, AlexNet, EfficientNet V2, and MobileNet V2 models and achieved an accuracy of 94.48%, outperforming other models.

According to the study by Priya Kohli, a model combining the strengths of CNN and LSTM networks was developed for the automatic diagnosis of skin lesions (Kohli, 2023). The ISIC 2017 dataset, consisting of 2,000 skin lesions, was used. There are two different classification types: benign and malignant. The proposed model utilized the ResNet50 architecture. The proposed CNN-LSTM hybrid model was compared with the CNN model. While the CNN model achieved an accuracy of 81.08%, the proposed CNN-LSTM model reached an accuracy of 86.75%, demonstrating better results.

In the study conducted by Moloud Abdar and colleagues, the Bayesian Deep Learning (BDL) method was used to measure the uncertainty of traditional deep learning methods (Abdar et al., 2021). Three uncertainty measurement methods were applied during skin cancer image classification: Monte Carlo Dropout (MC Dropout), Ensemble Monte Carlo Dropout (EMC Dropout), and Deep Ensemble (DE). After applying these methods, a new hybrid dynamic BDL model based on the Three-Way Decision (TWD) theory was developed to further reduce uncertainty.

Ebraheem Farea and colleagues proposed a hybrid method using deep learning (Farea et al., 2024). This method involved merging various datasets covering certain disease types and using the Artificial Bee Colony (ABC) algorithm for optimization. The newly created dataset consisted of seven different open datasets, including ISIC-2019, PH2, and MED-NODE, totaling 27,108 images. The classification of nine different types of skin cancer was performed using this dataset. The Xception model, based on transfer learning, was used. In the proposed model, methods such as the Otsu algorithm were used to detect the lesion region in the image, and noise removal techniques were applied to ensure that the model focused only on lesion-related data. The proposed model achieved an accuracy of 93.04%. The study emphasized that combining segmentation and the ABC algorithm significantly improved model performance and that merging images from different data sources positively affected classification accuracy. Additionally, the proposed method was tested on different deep learning models, including DenseNet121, EfficientNetB0, ResNet50, ResNet152V2, MobileNet, VGG16, and InceptionResNetV2. The Xception model combined with the ABC algorithm demonstrated the best performance.

According to the study by Supriya L P and colleagues, a hybrid learning model consisting of two CNNs and one LSTM was proposed using the HAM10000 dataset (Supriya & Khilar, 2024). To address the class imbalance in 1,015 samples, the Target-Specific Augmentation (T-Aug) method was used. The dataset included seven different types of skin cancer: Melanoma, Melanocytic Nevi, Benign Keratosis, Basal Cell Carcinoma, Actinic Keratosis, Vascular Lesion, and Dermatofibroma. CNN and LSTM were used as the primary classifiers, while a Multilayer Perceptron (MLP) was used as the meta-classifier. The proposed model demonstrated significant performance in skin cancer diagnosis, achieving an accuracy of 98.6% through data augmentation and heterogeneous-homogeneous combined learning techniques. It was also compared with other classifiers and achieved higher accuracy.

In their research Arjun K. P. and K. Sampath Kumar proposed a transfer learning approach combining VGG16 and LSTM models was proposed to automatically diagnose skin cancer from dermoscopic images (Arjun & Kumar, 2022). In the developed model, VGG16 was used for deep feature extraction, while LSTM captured long-short-term dependencies, enabling more effective learning of structures. The dataset provided by ISIC contained 30,500 dermoscopic images, including both melanoma and benign lesions. VGG16 consists of 13 convolutional layers, five max-pooling layers, and three fully connected layers. The deep features extracted by VGG16 were transferred to LSTM before classification. LSTM allowed for the classification of more meaningful features by capturing temporal dependencies. The proposed model achieved a test accuracy of 94.39% and a training accuracy of 90.89%. It was compared with other models such as AlexNet, ResNet, DenseNet, and MobileNet and achieved higher accuracy.

In the study conducted by Rabbia Mahum and Suliman Aladhadh, a hybrid approach combining handcrafted and deep learning (DL)-based features was proposed for the early detection and classification of skin lesions (Mahum & Aladhadh, 2022). The DermIS (1,000 images: 500 benign, 500 malignant) and ISIC (1,000 images) datasets were used. Gaussian filtering (GF) was applied to denoise the images. The Local Binary Patterns (LBP) method was used for feature extraction, generating binary patterns based on neighboring pixels to extract texture information. Additionally, the InceptionV3 model was used for automatic feature extraction. The features extracted by LBP and InceptionV3 were combined and transferred to an LSTM network. The proposed method was tested on both datasets, and the results were compared. An accuracy of 99.4% was achieved on the DermIS dataset, while 98.4% accuracy was obtained on the ISIC dataset.

According to the study by Natasha Nigar and colleagues, a deep learning model was developed for skin cancer classification, integrating a LIME-based explainable artificial intelligence (XAI) approach (Nigar et al., 2022). Deep feature extraction was performed using the ResNet-18 transfer learning method. The ISIC 2019 dataset was used, containing 25,331 dermoscopic images classified into eight different lesion categories. The LIME (Local Interpretable Model-Agnostic Explanations) framework was integrated to explain the model's decision-making process. LIME visualized model predictions, making them more interpretable and reliable for dermatologists. The proposed model achieved an accuracy of 94.47%. The ResNet-18 model was compared with the InceptionV3 model and demonstrated superior performance.

Jinen Daghrir and colleagues proposed a hybrid model called Majority Voting, combining CNN with traditional machine learning methods such as K-Nearest Neighbors (KNN) and Support Vector Machines (SVM) to improve skin cancer diagnosis (Daghrir et al., 2020). The ISIC dataset was used, containing a total of 640 images (512 for training and 128 for testing). The classification was binary, distinguishing between malignant and benign lesions. Lesion segmentation was performed using "Morphological Snakes" and thresholding methods. Among the classification methods, KNN achieved 57.3% accuracy, SVM performed better at 71.8% accuracy, and a nine-layer CNN model outperformed both with 85.5% accuracy. By combining the outputs of all methods using Majority Voting, an accuracy of 88.4% was achieved.

In their research Parvathaneni Naga Srinivasu and colleagues, proposed combining MobileNet V2 and Long Short-Term Memory (LSTM) networks to create a lightweight and highly accurate model for skin cancer classification (Srinivasu et al., 2021). The aim of the study is to develop a classifier that achieves high accuracy while being able to operate on devices with low computational power. The HAM10000 dataset, which contains 10,015 dermoscopic images, was used. This dataset includes seven different types of skin cancer. In the proposed method, MobileNet V2 is employed as a lightweight deep learning model capable of delivering high accuracy even with low-resolution images. LSTM helps improve the model's classification performance by learning long-term dependencies. MobileNet V2 is used to extract deep features from the images. The Gray-Level Co-occurrence Matrix (GLCM) is employed to evaluate texture-based features. The proposed method was compared with HARIS, FTNN, CNN, VGG19, MobileNet V1, and MobileNet V2, achieving the highest accuracy of 85.34%.

In the study conducted by Samira Mavaddati, a hybrid classifier called "ResNet50-LSTM" is introduced, which combines the ResNet50 deep model and LSTM networks using transfer learning techniques (Mavaddati, 2025). The objective is to learn both high-level and temporal features of images to classify skin lesions more effectively. The HAM10000 dataset was used to classify seven different types of skin cancer. Three different scenarios were tested in the study: ResNet50 alone, ResNet50 with transfer learning (ResNet50-TL), and the hybrid ResNet50-LSTM method. The ResNet50-LSTM method demonstrated the best performance with an accuracy of 99.09%. When compared with other models such as CNNs, RNNs, and SVMs, the proposed method showed significantly better performance.

According to the study by Puneet Thapar and colleagues, a hybrid deep learning model (CNN + Grasshopper Optimization Algorithm) was tested on dermoscopic images to identify and classify skin cancer (Thapar et al., 2022). The model was developed to automatically distinguish and analyze melanoma and non-melanoma skin lesions. The ISIC 2017, ISIC 2018, and PH-2 datasets were used. Classification was performed between melanoma and non-melanoma (with nevus subcategories). The HR-IQE (Hair Removal - Image Quality Enhancement) algorithm was used to reduce the effects of hair and background in images. The Grasshopper Optimization Algorithm (GOA) was applied for improvement, and segmentation was enhanced using K-means. After segmentation, the Speeded-Up Robust Features (SURF) algorithm was used to extract local features. The model achieved a success rate of 98.42%. When compared with classification and segmentation methods such as K-means, GOA, and CNN, the proposed model provided higher accuracy.

In the study conducted by Dr. Irala Suneetha, a deep learning model that combines the features of VGG16 and InceptionV3 was proposed (Suneetha, 2024). While InceptionV3 can learn details at multiple scales, VGG16 extracts low-level details. A total of 1,253 skin lesion images (benign and malignant) were obtained from Kaggle, with 670 images allocated for training and 583 for testing. In the final layer, the sigmoid activation function was used to perform binary classification (benign or malignant) by combining features obtained from VGG16 and InceptionV3. The Adam optimization algorithm was applied for model optimization. The model was trained for 40 epochs with a batch size of 32. The proposed model achieved an accuracy of 95.71%, significantly outperforming individual models (VGG16: 84.56%, InceptionV3: 89.34%).

According to the study by Maksuda Akter and colleagues, a hybrid deep learning model combining InceptionV3 and DenseNet121 was proposed (Akter et al., 2024). The ISIC dataset, containing 3,297 dermoscopic images, was used. The data was split into 80% for training and 20% for testing. The InceptionV3 model has a comprehensive feature extraction capability with various filter sizes, while DenseNet121 facilitates feature sharing through direct connections between layers, reducing the number of parameters. The outputs of the InceptionV3 and DenseNet121 models were combined using a weighted sum method. Due to its performance, more emphasis was placed on the DenseNet121 model in the proposed hybrid model. The results showed that the hybrid model achieved 92.27% accuracy, outperforming InceptionV3, DenseNet121, EfficientNetB4, the SVM-based method, and the TWDBDL method.

In their research Omneya Attallah proposed an explainable artificial intelligence-based computer-aided diagnosis (CAD) system called Skin-CAD was introduced for skin cancer diagnosis (Attallah, 2024). The HAM10000 dataset, containing 10,015 dermoscopic images with seven different skin cancer types, was used. Four different CNN models—ResNet-50, ResNet-101, Inception, and Xception—were utilized. Features were extracted from the last two layers of CNN models, and the feature dimensions were reduced using Principal Component Analysis (PCA). Additionally, extracted features were processed using feature selection algorithms such as Relief-F and MRMR. Three different SVM models (Linear, Quadratic, Cubic) were used for classification. The obtained results showed that Skin-CAD achieved 97.2% accuracy in binary classification and 96.5% accuracy in multi-class classification.

In the study conducted by Priyanti Paul Tumpa and Md Ahasan Kabir, a computer-aided system was proposed for the accurate classification of skin cancer (Tumpa & Kabir, 2021). The proposed method includes image preprocessing using the Maximum Gradient Intensity (MGI) algorithm, segmentation with Otsu Thresholding, hybrid feature extraction (ABCD, GLCM, LBP), and classification using Artificial Neural Networks (ANN). The ISIC Archive dataset containing 3,600 images and the PH2 dataset containing 200 images were combined. The Otsu Thresholding algorithm was used to isolate skin lesions from images. Feature extraction was performed using ABCD rules (asymmetry, border irregularity, color variation, and diameter), texture-based features (GLCM), and surface texture features with local binary patterning (LBP). ANN was used for classification and was trained using the Levenberg-Marquardt Backpropagation method. The proposed model achieved

97.7% accuracy in binary classification. When compared with methods such as support vector machines, logistic regression, and decision trees, it demonstrated superior performance.

In the study conducted by M. Roshni Thanka and colleagues, a hybrid model combining the VGG16 transfer learning model with XGBoost and LightGBM machine learning algorithms was proposed (Roshni Thanka et al., 2023). The ISIC dataset, consisting of 1,000 benign and 416 malignant melanoma cases, was used. To address data imbalance, Generative Adversarial Networks (GAN) were employed to generate 384 new malignant melanoma images. The VGG16 transfer learning model was used to extract color, border, and texture features of skin lesions. The extracted features from VGG16 were classified using XGBoost and LightGBM models. XGBoost achieved an accuracy of 99.1%, while LightGBM, despite being a faster method, reached an accuracy of 97.2%. XGBoost and LightGBM were compared in terms of precision, specificity, and overall accuracy.

Duggani Keerthana and colleagues developed a hybrid deep learning model by combining features extracted from DenseNet-201 and MobileNet models with a Support Vector Machine (SVM) classifier (Keerthana et al., 2023). The ISBI 2016 dataset was used, divided into 900 training and 379 test samples. The training set included 243 melanoma and 490 benign lesions. The proposed hybrid model achieved 88.02% accuracy in the binary classification task, with an F1 score of 87.43% and a sensitivity of 89.15%. Compared to other CNN-based models like AlexNet and ResNet50, this model produced more accurate results. The study demonstrated that hybrid approaches effectively enhance classification performance and perform well even on small datasets.

Cheng-Hong Yang, Jai-Hong Ren, and colleagues proposed the EfficientUNet++ model which combines the EfficientNet and U-Net++ architectures (Yang et al., 2021). The ISIC and PH2 datasets were used, with ISIC containing 25,331 images, while PH2 was smaller. In image segmentation, EfficientUNet++ achieved 94% Intersection over Union (IoU) and a 93% Dice coefficient. For the PH2 dataset, these values were reported as 96% and 95%, respectively. The proposed model outperformed other segmentation models such as UNet, SegNet, and HRNet. The study emphasized the effectiveness of deep learning-based hybrid models for segmentation tasks; however, the lack of post-segmentation classification was noted as a limitation.

Akhilesh Kumar Sharma and colleagues proposed a classification model that achieves dermatologist-level accuracy in skin cancer diagnosis (Sharma et al., 2022). The proposed model is a Cascaded Ensemble method that combines CNN-based automatic feature extraction with manually extracted color and texture features. The ISIC 2018 and PH2 datasets were used, containing 25,331 and 200 images, respectively. The model integrates features from CNN with color moments and texture-based Gray

Level Co-occurrence Matrix (GLCM). Multi-Layer Perceptron (MLP) was used for final classification. The proposed model achieved 98.3% accuracy, outperforming techniques based on both CNN-derived and manually extracted features.

Mahmoud Ragab and colleagues aimed to enable early diagnosis and accurate classification using a Hybrid Level Set Approach (Ragab et al., 2022). The proposed method successfully segmented lesions in dermoscopic images while reducing the impact of artifacts such as hair, gel, and bubbles. The Melanoma Skin Cancer dataset, containing 10,015 dermoscopic images, was used. The method consists of three stages: artifact removal, image normalization, and segmentation. Before segmentation, artifacts such as hair and blood vessels were removed using oriented wavelet filters and inpainting techniques. A level set function was used to mitigate artifacts and manage uneven contrast. Various CNN models (VGG16, DenseNet121, ResNet50, etc.) were used for classification. Compared to other segmentation methods (Otsu, Geodesic Active Contour, Chan-Vese), the proposed method achieved a higher accuracy of 94.40%.

Azhar Imran, Arslan Nasir, and colleagues proposed a deep learning-based ensemble approach (Imran et al., 2022). In the first stage, malignant and benign images obtained from ISIC skin cancer image repositories were used to train three deep learning models: VGG, CapsNet, and ResNet. In the second stage, the results of these models were combined using majority weighting. The data was split into 80% for training and 20% for testing. Each model was trained separately, and the Majority Voting method was applied. The proposed method achieved 93.5% accuracy, surpassing the performance of individual models.

Md. Kamrul Hasan and colleagues proposed a hybrid Convolutional Neural Network (CNN) model based on a two-stage ensembling method for skin lesion classification (Hasan et al., 2022). The ISIC 2016, ISIC 2017, and ISIC 2018 datasets were used. The proposed model extracted features from pre-trained CNN models via transfer learning, combined channel-based feature maps, and performed ensembling through fully connected layers. The proposed model, named Dermoscopic Expert (DermoExpert), was tested on different datasets and achieved area under the receiver operating characteristic (AUC) values of 96%, 95%, and 97%, respectively. Compared to methods such as Xception, ResNet, and DenseNet, the proposed model provided higher accuracy.

Farhat Afza and colleagues developed a method for multi-class skin lesion classification using hybrid feature selection and an Extreme Learning Machine (ELM) classifier (Afza et al., 2022). The hybrid feature selection approach combined the Whale Optimization Algorithm and mutual information entropy methods. The HAM10000 dataset (10,015 images across 7 classes) and the ISIC 2018 dataset (12,500 images) were used. Features extracted from VGG16 and ResNet50 were refined using the Whale Optimization Algorithm. After optimization, the selected features were processed with the ELM classifier for classification. The proposed method achieved 93.40% accuracy on the HAM10000 dataset and 94.36% accuracy on the ISIC 2018 dataset.

Mohammad Shorfuzzaman proposed an explainable stacking ensemble model for melanoma skin cancer detection (Shorfuzzaman, 2022). Predictions from transfer learning models such as ResNet50, DenseNet121, and EfficientNet were fed into a meta-learner. Classification was performed using an ensemble method. The model was trained on 1,497 malignant and 1,800 benign images from the ISIC Archive (Kaggle) dataset. The decision-making process of the model was made interpretable using SHAP (Shapley Adaptive Explanations). The proposed model achieved an accuracy of 95.76%.

Lisheng Wei and colleagues developed a classification model based on MobileNetV1 and DenseNet-121 for skin cancer detection (Wei et al., 2020). The ISBI 2016 dataset was used, and the U-Net architecture was employed for segmentation. Despite having a low number of parameters, the system designed with MobileNetV1 and DenseNet-121 achieved 97.3% accuracy.

Mohamed A. Elashiri and colleagues developed a hybrid approach for skin cancer classification (Elashiri et al., 2022). The Hybrid Squirrel Butterfly Search (HSBSO) optimization algorithm was used to select the best deep features extracted from ResNet50, VGG16, and DeepLabv3 transfer learning models. The Fuzzy C-means method was employed in the segmentation stage, and the optimized features were transferred to an MLSTM model. The model achieved accuracy rates of 95.8% on the PH2 dataset and 93.2% on the HAM10000 dataset.

Iftiaz A. Alfi and colleagues proposed an ensemble learning-based hybrid model for skin cancer classification (Alfi et al., 2022). The study utilized transfer learning to train deep learning models such as ResNet50V2, DenseNet121, and Xception using the ISIC 2018 dataset. To enhance classification accuracy, the ensemble method combined the outputs of multiple deep learning models. Additionally, SHAP (Shapley Adaptive Explanations) was used to interpret the model's predictions. The proposed method achieved 92% accuracy.

## MAIN FOCUS OF THE CHAPTER

Understanding the modern methods used in the diagnosis of skin cancer is crucial for its early detection and treatment. This chapter addresses the foundational elements necessary for diagnosing skin cancer. It aims to provide readers with comprehensive knowledge of the types of skin cancer, the datasets used for classification, and the image modalities involved in the diagnostic process.

Section 3.1 examines the different types of skin cancer and provides an in-depth explanation of their clinical characteristics, risk factors, and prevalence rates. Both melanoma and non-melanoma skin cancers (such as basal cell carcinoma and squamous cell carcinoma) are explored in detail. The distinctions in their clinical symptoms, visual features, and treatment approaches are highlighted. This information serves as a guide for clinicians and researchers to understand the critical aspects of diagnosing each type of skin cancer.

Section 3.2 focuses on the features of popular datasets used in skin cancer diagnosis. Datasets such as ISIC, HAM10000, PH2, TCGA-SKCM, and PAD-UFES-20 are examined in terms of their size, types of images included (e.g., dermoscopic, clinical, and histopathological images), labeling processes, and diversity. Additionally, the role of these datasets in training, testing, and validating machine learning and deep learning algorithms is emphasized.

Finally, Section 3.3 provides a detailed discussion on the roles and significance of different image types clinical, dermoscopic, and histopathological in skin cancer diagnosis. It explains how each type of image is used to analyze different aspects of the lesion, which features are examined, and how combining these types (multimodal approaches) enhances diagnostic accuracy. The use of artificial intelligence models to process data from these image types and generate more reliable and rapid results is also underscored.

## Skin Cancer Types

Skin cancer lesions can be either benign or malignant, and their accurate diagnosis is crucial for effective treatment and improved survival rates. Early detection plays a vital role in preventing the progression of these lesions into more severe or life-threatening conditions. Below, different types of skin cancer are explained in detail, along with their characteristics, risk factors, and potential treatment options.

### Actinic Keratosis (Solar Keratosis)

This is a precancerous condition caused by prolonged exposure to ultraviolet (UV) radiation from sunlight or artificial sources. It typically appears on areas frequently exposed to the sun, such as hands, face, ears, scalp, and arms. If left untreated, it carries the risk of developing into squamous cell carcinoma, with a conversion rate of approximately 10-15%. Actinic keratosis is more common in fair-skinned individuals, those with a history of excessive sun exposure, and the elderly. Preventive measures, such as consistent use of sunscreen and protective clothing, are crucial for reducing its occurrence. Figure 1 illustrates a representative example of this lesion type.

*Figure 1. Clinical appearance of Actinic Keratosis showing scaly, sun-damaged skin on exposed areas (ISIC Archive)*

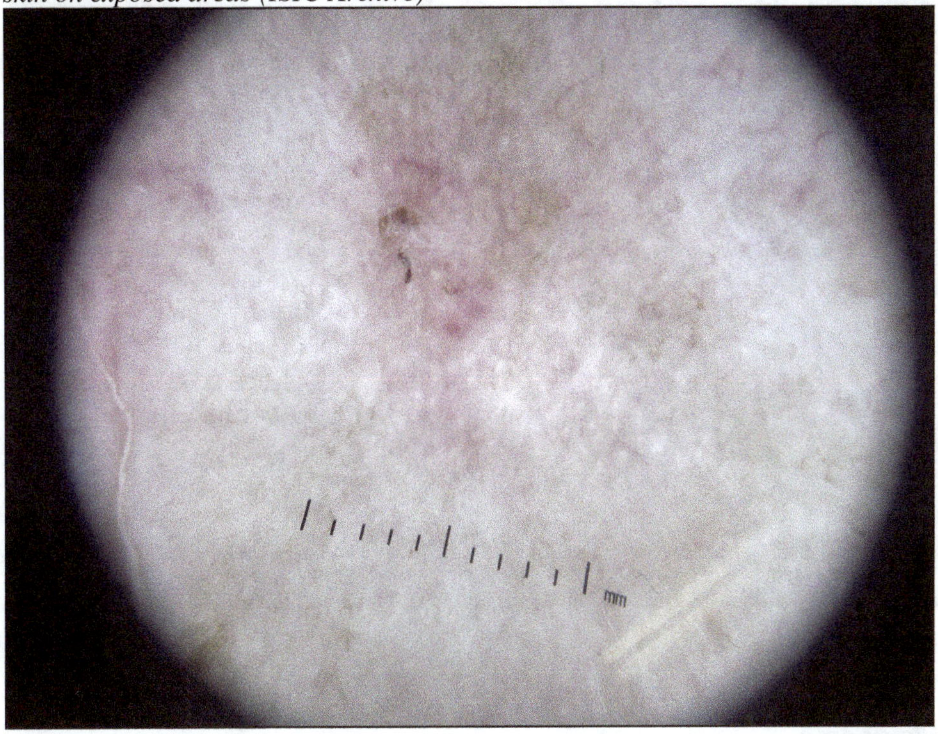


## Basal Cell Carcinoma (BCC)

BCC originates from basal cells located in the deepest layer of the epidermis and is the most common type of skin cancer, accounting for approximately 80% of all cases globally. This slow-growing cancer rarely spreads to other parts of the body but can cause significant tissue damage if untreated. BCC typically appears on sun-exposed areas such as the face, neck, and hands, often presenting as shiny, pearly nodules, or ulcerated lesions. Several subtypes exist, including nodular BCC, superficial BCC, and morpheaform (scar-like) BCC, each with distinct clinical presentations. Treatment options include surgical excision, Mohs micrographic surgery, and topical therapies such as imiquimod. Figure 2 shows a typical appearance associated with this condition.

*Figure 2. Dermoscopic image of Basal Cell Carcinoma illustrating a pearly nodule with visible blood vessels (ISIC Archive)*

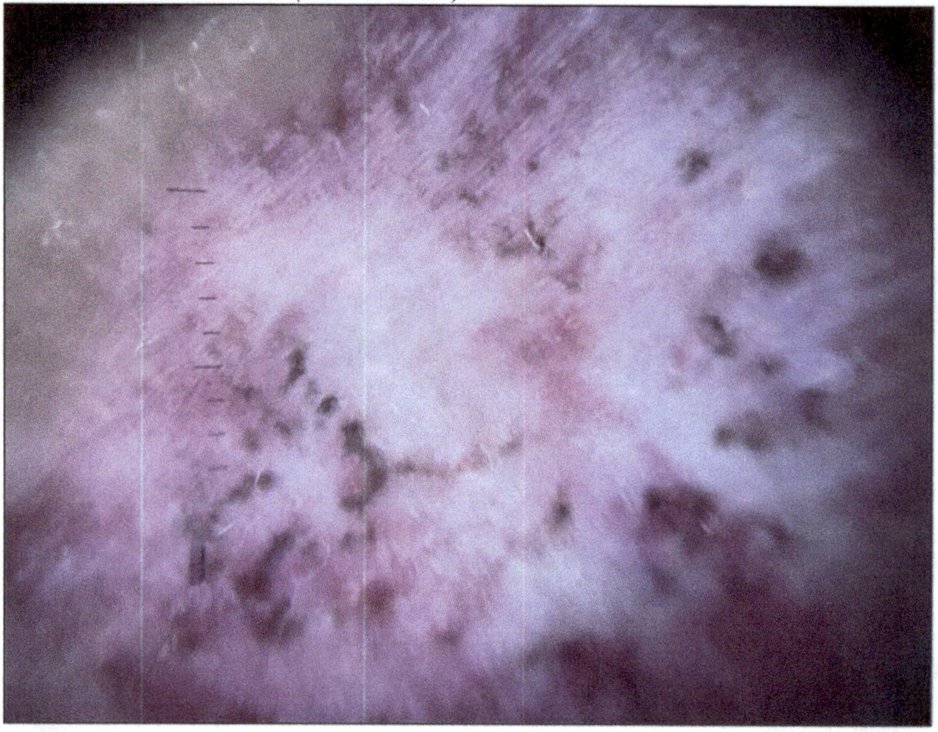

## Melanoma

Melanoma is the deadliest form of skin cancer, arising from the abnormal proliferation of melanocytes, the cells responsible for producing skin pigment. It is identified based on the ABCDEF criteria: Asymmetry, Border irregularity, Color variation, Diameter greater than 6mm, Evolution (changes over time), and changes in the surrounding tissue. Melanoma has two main types: Superficial spreading melanoma, which is the most common, and Acral lentiginous melanoma, which is more prevalent in darker-skinned individuals and appears on palms, soles, or under the nails. Risk factors include a history of sunburns, genetic predisposition, and the presence of atypical moles. Advanced stages of melanoma often require systemic treatments such as immunotherapy or targeted therapy. Figure 3 demonstrates the visual characteristics of this skin abnormality.

*Figure 3. Melanoma exhibiting asymmetry and irregular pigmentation based on the ABCDE criteria (ISIC Archive)*

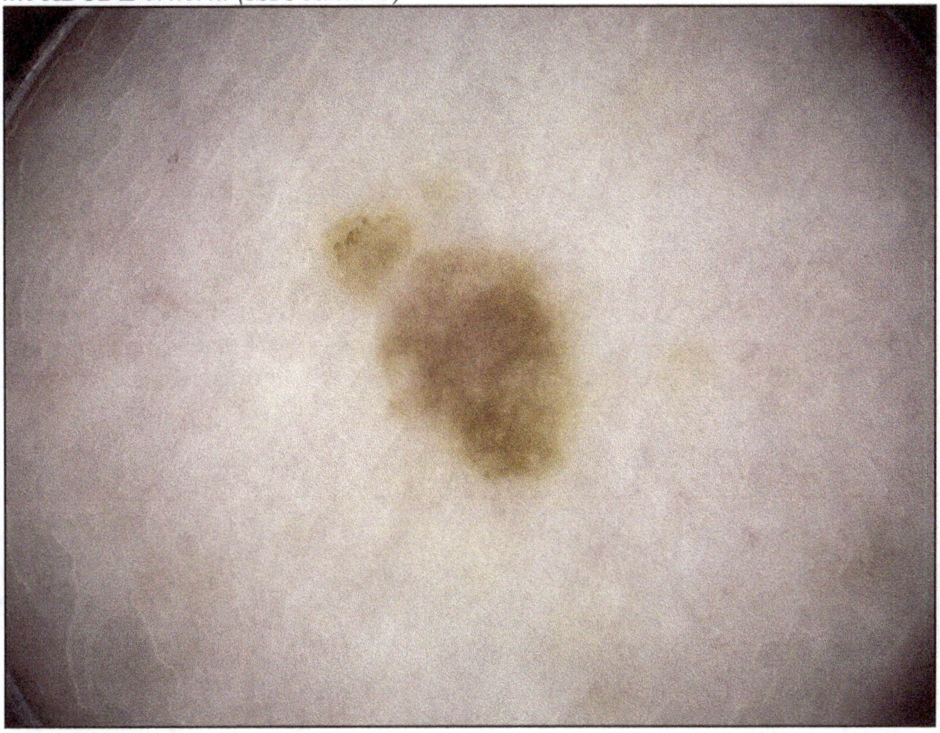

## Nevus

A nevus, commonly known as a mole, is a benign pigmented lesion formed by the clustering of melanocytes. These lesions can appear flat or raised and vary in color from light brown to black. While most nevi are harmless, some may undergo malignant transformation into melanoma, especially if they exhibit rapid growth, irregular borders, or significant color changes. Regular monitoring of atypical nevi is crucial, particularly for individuals with multiple moles or a family history of melanoma. Excisional biopsy is recommended for suspicious lesions to confirm the diagnosis. Figure 4 provides an example of how this lesion presents clinically.

*Figure 4. Visual representation of a benign nevus with regular borders and uniform coloration (ISIC Archive)*

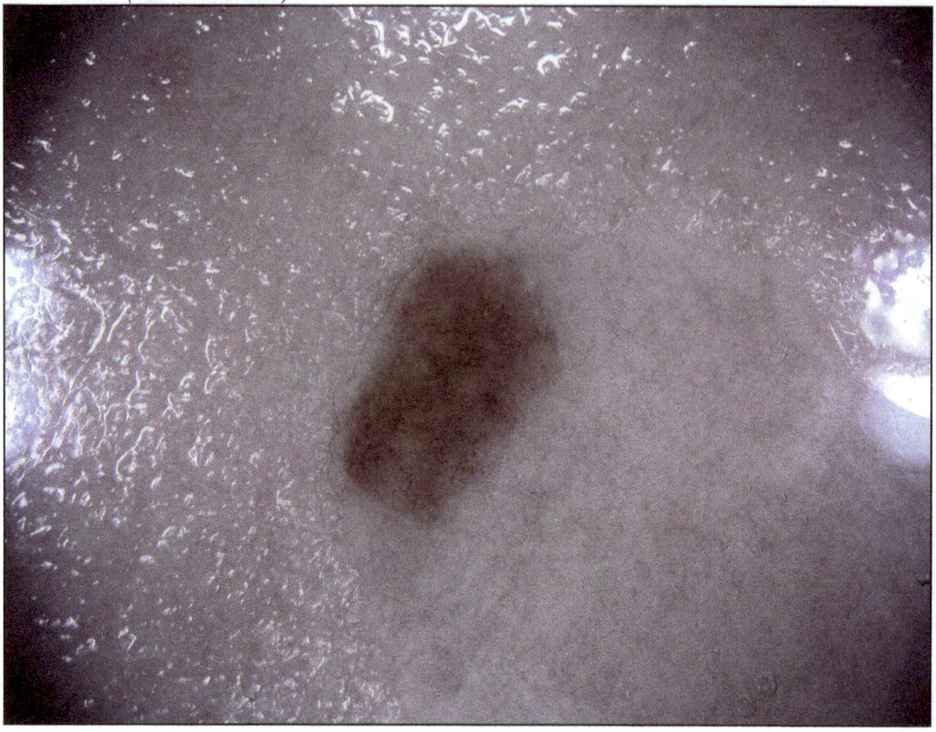

## Pigmented Benign Keratosis (Solar Lentigo)

This is a pigmented, benign lesion caused by cumulative sun damage, often referred to as “age spots” or “liver spots.” It is commonly observed in elderly individuals and appears on sun-exposed areas such as the face, hands, and arms. While these lesions are harmless, they are frequently treated for cosmetic reasons using laser therapy, cryotherapy, or chemical peels. Regular use of sunscreen can prevent the development of new lesions. Figure 5 displays the common dermoscopic features observed in such cases.

*Figure 5. Pigmented Benign Keratosis (Solar Lentigo) appearing as a flat, brown lesion due to sun exposure (ISIC Archive)*

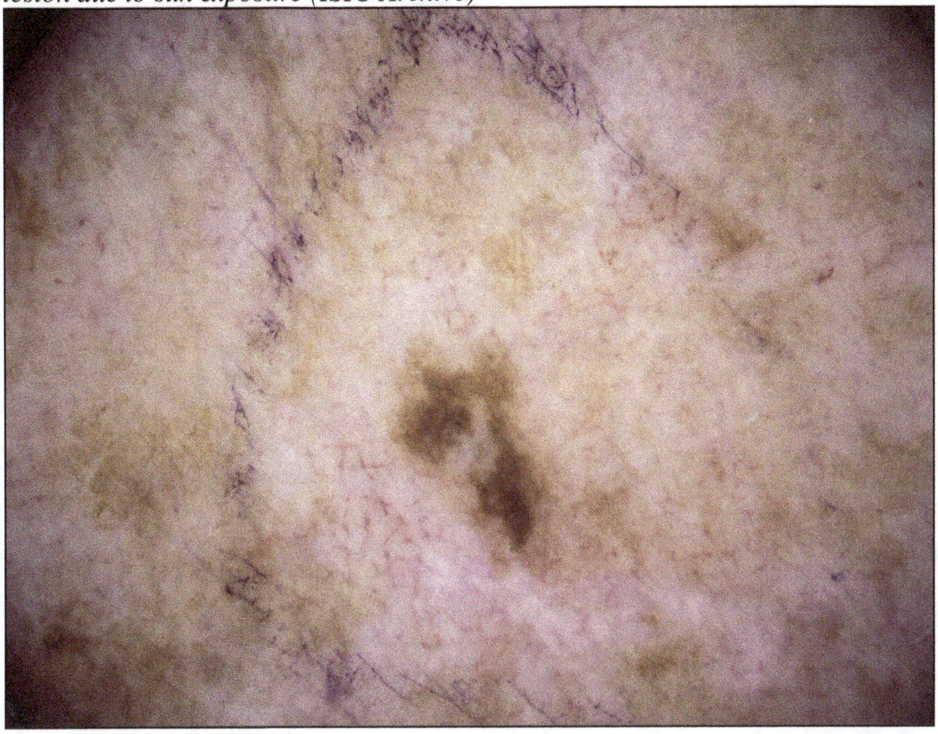

## Seborrheic Keratosis

Seborrheic keratosis is a benign epidermal tumor originating from keratinocytes, most commonly seen in middle-aged and older individuals. These lesions present as greasy, waxy, or wart-like plaques that are brown or black and vary in size. Although seborrheic keratosis is harmless, its appearance can sometimes mimic melanoma, leading to unnecessary concern. Dermoscopic examination is helpful in distinguishing seborrheic keratosis from malignant lesions. Treatments such as cryotherapy, laser ablation, or curettage may be applied for cosmetic purposes. Figure 6 visualizes the lesion morphology associated with this condition.

*Figure 6. Example of Seborrheic Keratosis with waxy surface and typical wart-like morphology (ISIC Archive)*

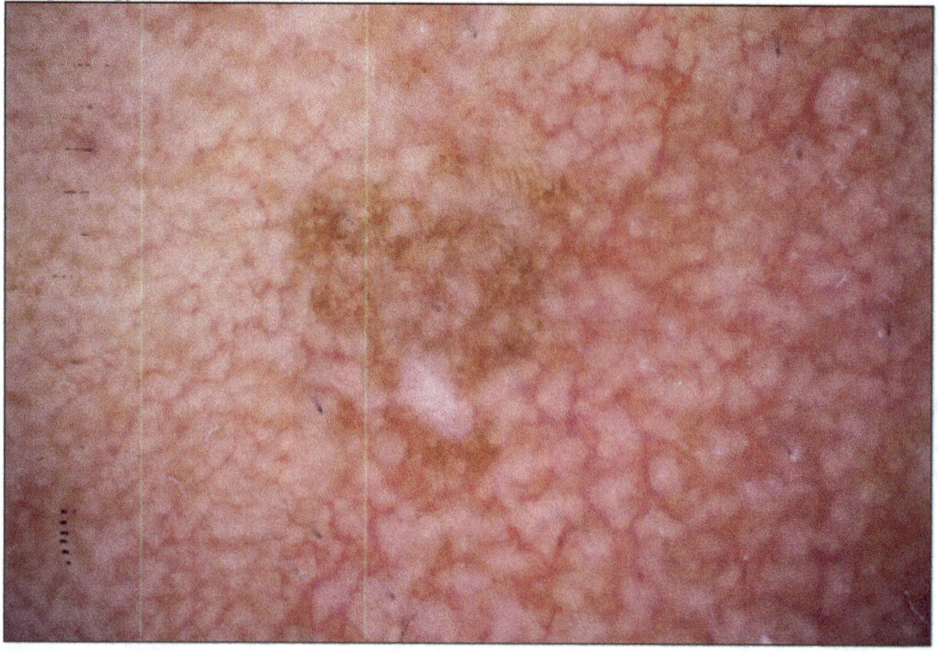

## Squamous Cell Carcinoma (SCC)

Squamous cell carcinoma (SCC) originates from squamous cells in the epidermis and is the second most common type of skin cancer after BCC. Unlike BCC, SCC has a higher risk of metastasis, particularly when left untreated. It commonly appears as red, scaly plaques, firm nodules, or ulcerated lesions on sun-exposed areas. Risk factors include prolonged UV radiation exposure, chronic wounds, immunosuppression, and chemical carcinogen exposure. Treatment typically involves surgical excision, cryotherapy, radiotherapy, or photodynamic therapy, depending on the lesion's size and stage. Early detection and treatment are critical for preventing metastasis. Figure 7 depicts one manifestation of this type of skin cancer.

*Figure 7. Squamous Cell Carcinoma with thickened, crusted surface, commonly seen in sun-exposed regions (ISIC Archive)*

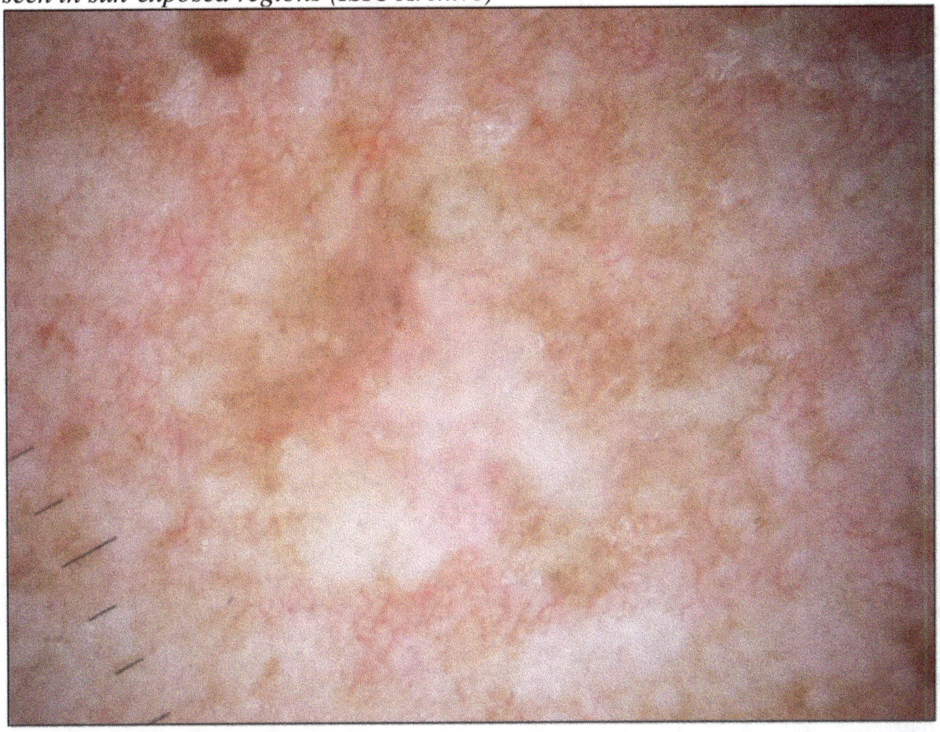

## Vascular Lesions

Vascular lesions result from abnormal growth or malformations of blood vessels and are usually benign. Common types include port-wine stains, hemangiomas, and spider angiomas, which vary in size, shape, and color, typically appearing red, purple, or blue. Although harmless in most cases, vascular lesions may cause discomfort or cosmetic concerns. Treatments such as laser therapy or sclerotherapy can be used to reduce their appearance or alleviate symptoms. Figure 8 highlights the distinguishing features of the lesion.

*Figure 8. Vascular lesion displaying capillary dilation with a reddish-blue hue and irregular pattern (ISIC Archive)*

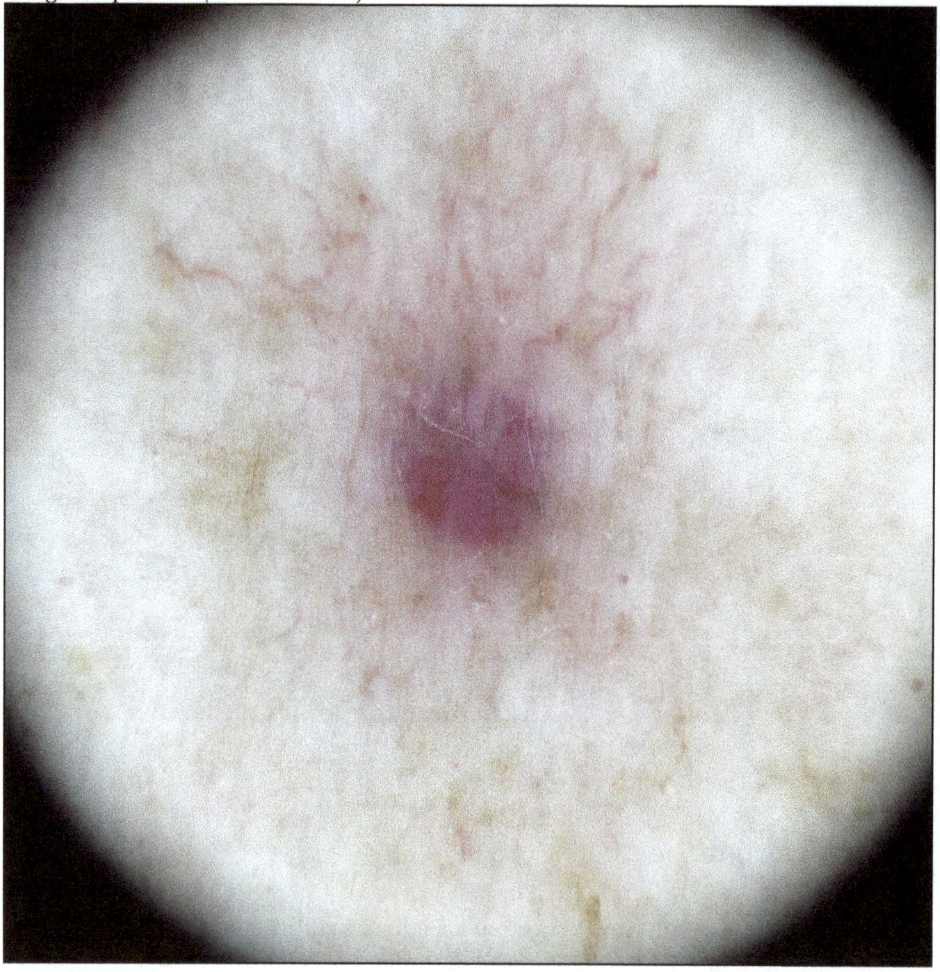

## Datasets

Datasets used for skin cancer classification consist of large and diverse collections designed for recognizing, diagnosing, and categorizing different skin lesions. These datasets typically include clinical photographs, dermoscopic images, histopathological data, and sometimes 3D images. Additionally, the inclusion of demographic diversity, detailed labeling, and metadata (e.g., patient age, gender, lesion location) enhances the utility of these datasets for training and validating machine learning models. Below are some widely used datasets in skin cancer research and their features.

## ISIC (International Skin Imaging Collaboration) Dataset

The ISIC dataset is one of the world's largest and most comprehensive dermoscopic image collections, specifically created for diagnosing and classifying skin lesions. It contains thousands of high-quality dermoscopic images of various malignant and benign skin lesions, including melanoma, basal cell carcinoma, squamous cell carcinoma, actinic keratosis, and benign keratosis. Each image in the dataset is meticulously labeled using standardized protocols, ensuring consistency and reliability in annotations.

The dataset is updated and expanded annually, reflecting advancements in imaging technologies and dermatological expertise. As of 2020, it includes over 70,000 dermoscopic images, along with metadata such as patient demographics, lesion location, and clinical notes. Furthermore, the dataset includes segmentation masks, enabling researchers to perform lesion segmentation tasks. These features make ISIC a valuable resource for training, testing, and benchmarking deep learning models in classification, segmentation, and detection tasks.

The ISIC Archive also organizes annual challenges, such as the ISIC Skin Lesion Classification Challenge, which provides benchmarks for algorithm development and encourages innovation in skin cancer diagnostics.

## HAM10000 (Human Against Machine) Dataset

The HAM10000 dataset is a widely recognized and extensively used dataset in skin cancer classification studies. It contains 10,015 dermoscopic images representing seven distinct skin lesion types: melanoma, basal cell carcinoma, squamous cell carcinoma, actinic keratosis, benign keratosis, dermatofibroma, and nevus.

A unique feature of HAM10000 is its inclusion of both dermoscopic and clinical images, providing a richer and more diverse data source for machine learning applications. This dataset is particularly valuable because it includes individuals from different age groups, skin tones, and ethnic backgrounds, which enhances its generalizability in real-world clinical scenarios.

HAM10000 is designed with a focus on multimodal learning, offering metadata such as patient age, gender, and lesion location alongside the images. These features enable models to utilize additional contextual information for improved classification accuracy. The dataset is widely used in transfer learning applications, where pre-trained models are fine-tuned on smaller, domain-specific datasets for enhanced performance.

## PH2 Dataset

The PH2 dataset is a high-resolution dermoscopic image collection explicitly developed for malignant and pigmented lesion classification. It contains 200 dermoscopic images, all carefully labeled and verified by expert dermatologists. Each image includes detailed annotations for lesion boundaries, texture patterns, and color distribution, making it highly suitable for segmentation tasks.

Although the dataset is relatively small compared to others, its high resolution and precise labeling make it an invaluable resource for training deep learning models that require pixel-level accuracy. Additionally, the dataset categorizes lesions into benign and malignant groups, providing a clear framework for binary classification tasks. The PH2 dataset is often used for validating models trained on larger datasets, as its quality ensures reliable performance evaluation.

## TCGA-SKCM (The Cancer Genome Atlas – Skin Cutaneous Melanoma) Dataset

The TCGA-SKCM dataset is a unique resource providing genetic, molecular, and histopathological data for analyzing malignant melanoma. In addition to over 20,000 histopathological images, the dataset includes genomic sequencing data, mutation profiles, and information on gene expression.

This dataset is particularly valuable for bioinformatics and translational research, as it enables studies on melanoma progression, metastasis mechanisms, and treatment responses. By integrating molecular data with histopathological images, researchers can explore the biological underpinnings of melanoma and develop targeted therapies. The TCGA-SKCM dataset has been instrumental in understanding melanoma heterogeneity and identifying biomarkers for personalized treatment strategies.

## Derm7pt Dataset

The Derm7pt dataset is a specialized dermoscopic dataset designed to mimic the diagnostic criteria used by dermatologists in clinical practice. It classifies skin lesions based on seven criteria: asymmetry, border, color, diameter, dermoscopic structure, pigmentation, and vascular patterns.

With 1,011 labeled dermoscopic images, the dataset provides a structural and descriptive framework for building explainable artificial intelligence models. By using the seven-point checklist, this dataset bridges the gap between machine learning predictions and clinical decision-making processes. Its diverse and detailed annotations make it a valuable educational resource for both researchers and medical professionals.

## Atlas of Dermoscopy Dataset

The Atlas of Dermoscopy dataset is a comprehensive collection of dermoscopic images accompanied by detailed descriptions of dermatological lesions. It includes over 1,500 images, covering a range of benign and malignant conditions such as melanoma, nevus, seborrheic keratosis, and pigmented keratosis.

In addition to the images, the dataset provides essential information for dermoscopic examination, such as lesion morphology, color patterns, and vascular structures. This makes it an excellent resource for training medical students, dermatologists, and machine learning models in dermoscopic interpretation.

## PAD-UFES-20 Dataset

The PAD-UFES-20 dataset is a dermoscopic image collection created in Brazil, focusing on skin lesion types prevalent in tropical regions. It includes 2,298 images representing 20 different skin lesion types, such as actinic keratosis, basal cell carcinoma, and pigmented lesions.

A notable feature of this dataset is its representation of diverse demographic groups, reflecting the population heterogeneity in tropical climates. The dataset also includes metadata such as patient age, gender, and lesion location, making it suitable for multimodal learning approaches. PAD-UFES-20 is particularly valuable for studying the effects of UV radiation in tropical environments and addressing regional healthcare challenges.

# Image Types

The types of images used in the diagnosis and classification of skin cancer vary depending on different analysis methods, datasets, and clinical applications. Each type of image provides unique information that contributes to the accurate detection and classification of skin lesions. This section provides a detailed explanation of the primary image types used in skin cancer diagnosis.

## Dermoscopic Images

Dermoscopic images are obtained using polarized light or liquid surface techniques, enabling detailed visualization of structures beneath the surface of the skin that are invisible to the naked eye. These images are essential for examining pigment networks, vascular patterns, and lesion borders, which are critical features for diagnosing skin cancer.

Dermoscopic imaging is particularly effective for identifying melanomas, pigmented basal cell carcinomas, and other precancerous or cancerous lesions at an early stage. The use of dermoscopic images significantly enhances diagnostic accuracy, as it allows dermatologists and AI algorithms to detect subtle features like asymmetry, irregular borders, and atypical vascular structures.

High-detail dermoscopic images are a cornerstone in datasets such as ISIC, HAM10000, and PH2, where they are used to train machine learning models for tasks like lesion segmentation, feature extraction, and classification. Additionally, these images are increasingly being utilized in telemedicine applications, enabling remote consultations and diagnoses.

Recent advances in AI-based analysis of dermoscopic images have incorporated segmentation algorithms to identify lesion boundaries and hybrid models to improve classification performance. The inclusion of dermoscopic data in AI systems has been shown to increase diagnostic accuracy by up to 49% compared to visual examination alone. Figure 9 displays a dermoscopic image emphasizing pigmentation patterns and structure.

*Figure 9. Dermoscopic image showing pigmentation structures and lesion borders used for diagnosis (ISIC Archive)*

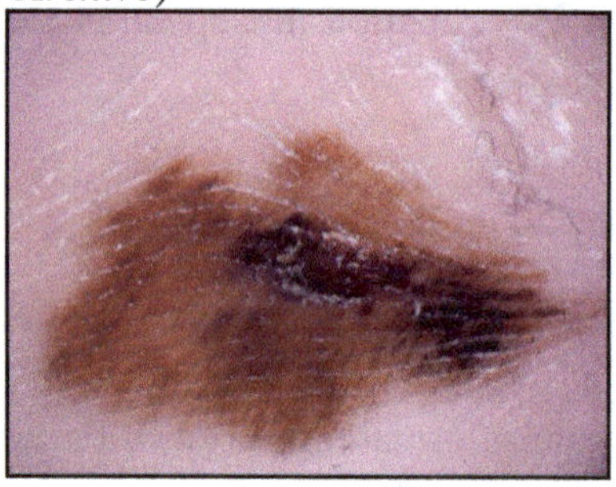

## Clinical Images

Clinical images are macro photographs captured using standard digital cameras, professional equipment, or even mobile phones. These images depict the overall appearance of the skin lesion and the surrounding area, providing valuable context for diagnosis. While clinical images lack the depth of dermoscopic images, they are particularly useful in teledermatology, where patients can send photos to dermatologists for initial evaluations.

These images often complement dermoscopic data by offering a broader perspective of the lesion's location, size, and changes over time. Clinical images can help dermatologists identify skin conditions such as erythema, inflammation, or other surface-level abnormalities that might not be visible in dermoscopic views.

In datasets like HAM10000, clinical images are frequently paired with dermoscopic images to support multimodal diagnostic approaches. AI models that combine clinical and dermoscopic images have demonstrated increased accuracy in distinguishing between benign and malignant lesions, as well as improving the reliability of remote diagnostic systems. Figure 10 shows the clinical presentation of a typical skin lesion.

*Figure 10. Clinical photograph illustrating surface features and color distribution of a skin lesion (ISIC Archive)*

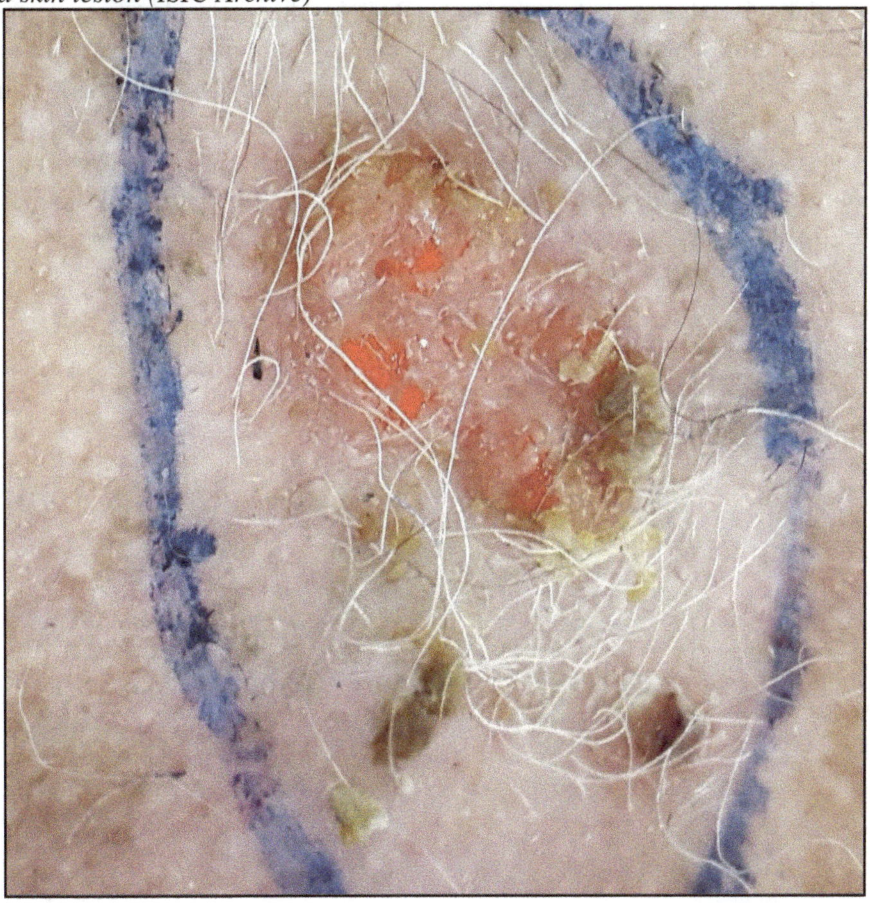

## Histopathological Images

Histopathological images are high-resolution images obtained by examining skin biopsy samples under a microscope. These images are considered the gold standard for confirming cancer diagnoses, as they provide direct insight into the cellular and structural abnormalities associated with malignancies.

Histopathological analysis focuses on identifying key features such as cellular atypia, mitotic activity, growth patterns, and invasion into surrounding tissues. For melanoma and other malignant lesions, histopathological images allow for the evaluation of metastasis potential and treatment planning. These images are also crucial for understanding the biological mechanisms of tumor progression.

The TCGA-SKCM dataset is a prominent source of histopathological images, offering over 20,000 high-resolution images for melanoma research. These images are commonly used in bioinformatics and AI-driven studies to develop models for automated grading, segmentation, and tumor identification. The integration of histopathological data with dermoscopic and clinical images enables a more comprehensive approach to cancer diagnosis.

Recent advancements in AI have led to the development of convolutional neural networks (CNNs) specifically designed for histopathological image analysis. These models are capable of detecting minute details such as nuclear pleomorphism and lymphovascular invasion, which are essential for accurate staging and prognosis. Figure 11 shows histological details obtained through biopsy and sectioning.

*Figure 11. Histopathological image showing abnormal melanocyte proliferation in malignant melanoma (ISIC Archive)*

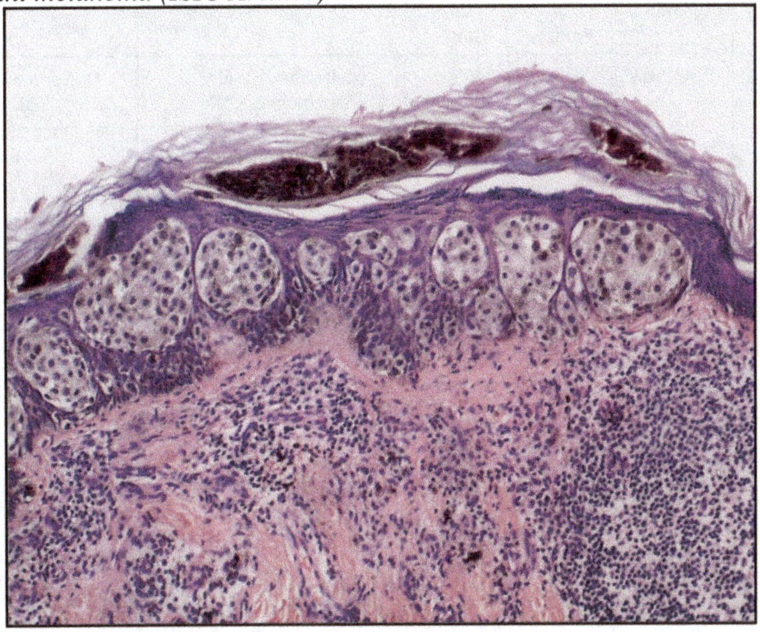

## RESULTS AND DISCUSSION

In this study, the advantages of hybrid deep learning models in skin cancer diagnosis were compared across different datasets and metrics. In Section 4, the accuracy rates of the models, the datasets used, and the strengths and weaknesses of these models are thoroughly examined and discussed. Factors affecting model performance, the optimization techniques used, and the structural characteristics of the datasets were explained. Additionally, comparisons with other studies in the literature were supported by tables to highlight the superior performance of hybrid models. Ultimately, conclusions were drawn regarding the conditions under which models perform better and ways to increase overall accuracy. Table 1 provides a summary of the dataset, Table 2 compares model performance, and Table 3 compares studies found in the literature.

*Table 1. Dataset summary*

| Reference | Dataset Name | Number of Images | Number of Classes | Disease Types | Description |
|---|---|---|---|---|---|
| (Farea et al., 2024) | ISIC 2019 | 27,108 | 9 | Melanoma, Basal Cell Carcinoma, Actinic Keratosis, Nevus, Seborrheic Keratosis, Squamous Cell Carcinoma, Vascular Lesion | One of the largest dermoscopic datasets containing various skin lesions. |
| (Srinivasu et al., 2021) | HAM10000 | 10,015 | 7 | Melanoma, Basal Cell Carcinoma, Nevus, Pigmented Benign Keratosis, Actinic Keratosis, Seborrheic Keratosis, Dermatofibroma | A popular dataset with a balanced distribution of common skin lesions. |
| (Kohli, 2023) | PH2 | 200 | 2 | Melanoma, Benign Nevus | A small dataset containing high-quality images carefully annotated by experts. |
| (Jain et al., 2021) | ISIC 2018 | 11,527 | 7 | Melanoma, Basal Cell Carcinoma, Nevus, Seborrheic Keratosis, Actinic Keratosis, Squamous Cell Carcinoma, Vascular Lesion | A popular dataset frequently used for classification and segmentation. |
| (Farea et al., 2024) | TCGA-SKCM | 20,000+ | 1 | Melanoma | Provides bioinformatics-focused data for genetic and histopathological analyses. |
| (Wei et al., 2020) | ISBI 2016 | 900 | 2 | Melanoma, Benign Lesions | A small dataset that is evenly split for training and testing purposes. |

*Table 2. Model performance comparison*

| Reference | Model Name | Dataset Used | Accuracy (%) | Advantages |
|---|---|---|---|---|
| (Zareen et al., 2024) | ResNet50-LSTM | HAM10000 | 94.48 | Hybrid model; combines the strengths of CNN and LSTM networks. |
| (Jain et al., 2021) | Xception | ISIC 2018 | 90.48 | Transfer learning-based model with the highest accuracy. |
| (Farea et al., 2024) | DenseNet121-ABC | ISIC-2019, PH2, MED-NODE, yedi farklı açık veri seti | 93.04 | Supported by Artificial Bee Colony (ABC) optimization algorithm. |

continued on following page

*Table 2. Continued*

| Reference | Model Name | Dataset Used | Accuracy (%) | Advantages |
|---|---|---|---|---|
| (Yang et al., 2021) | EfficientUNet++ | ISIC + PH2 | 94 | Demonstrated superior performance with a focus on segmentation. |
| (Kohli, 2023) | ResNet50 | ISIC 2017 | 86.75 | Achieved higher accuracy compared to CNN. |
| (Jinnai et al., 2020) | FRCNN | ISIC | 91.5 (Binary), 86.2 (Multi-class) | Better accuracy than dermatologists; high performance for six classes. |
| (Thapar et al., 2022) | CNN-GOA | ISIC 2018 | 98.42 | Developed segmentation and classification using Grasshopper Optimization Algorithm. |
| (Nigar et al., 2022) | ResNet18 + LIME | ISIC 2019 | 94.47 | Model predictions visualized with explainable AI (LIME). |
| (Srinivasu et al., 2021) | MobileNet V2 + LSTM | HAM10000 | 85.34 | Lightweight and fast model; achieved good results even with low-resolution images. |
| (Mavaddati, 2025) | ResNet50-LSTM | HAM10000 | 99.09 | Achieved high accuracy; hybrid model using CNN, RNN, and transfer learning. |
| (Ragab et al., 2022) | Hybrid Level Set | Melanoma Skin Cancer | 94.40 | Integrated with various CNN models after segmentation. |
| (Roshni Thanka et al., 2023) | VGG16 + GAN + XGBoost | ISIC | 99.10 | Used GAN for data augmentation and XGBoost for classification. |
| (Keerthana et al., 2023) | Hybrid SVM + DenseNet121 | ISIC 2016 | 88.02 | Hybrid model; combines features extracted from DenseNet121 with SVM. |
| (Tumpa & Kabir, 2021) | CNN + MGI + ANN | ISIC + PH2 | 97.70 | Hybrid feature extraction (ABCD, GLCM, LBP) with ANN. |
| (Imran et al., 2022) | Ensemble Deep Models | ISIC 2018 | 93.50 | Combined ResNet, CapsNet, and VGG models using majority voting. |
| (Shorfuzzaman, 2022) | Explainable Stacking | ISIC Archive | 95.76 | Used explainable AI (SHAP) with an integrated stacking ensemble method. |

continued on following page

*Table 2. Continued*

| Reference | Model Name | Dataset Used | Accuracy (%) | Advantages |
|---|---|---|---|---|
| (Afza et al., 2022) | Hybrid SVM + Relief-F | HAM10000 | 93.40 | Feature selection and SVM-based classifier used. |
| (Wei et al., 2020) | MobileNetV1-DenseNet121 | ISBI 2016 | 97.30 | Combined low-parameter model with U-Net segmentation. |
| (Daghrir et al., 2020) | CNN-SVM Majority Voting | ISIC | 88.40 | Combined CNN and classical methods using majority voting. |
| (Sharma et al., 2022) | Cascaded Ensemble CNN | ISIC 2018 + PH2 | 98.30 | Combined CNN and hand-extracted features. |

*Table 3. Literature comparison*

| Reference | Year | Model | Dataset | Advantage | Disadvantage |
|---|---|---|---|---|---|
| (Jinnai et al., 2020) | 2020 | FRCNN | ISIC | Performed better than dermatologists; achieved high accuracy for six classes. | Long training time, high computational power. |
| (Kohli, 2023) | 2023 | ResNet50-LSTM | ISIC 2017 | Hybrid model that learns time-series dependencies. | Low performance with small datasets. |
| (Jain et al., 2021) | 2021 | Xception | ISIC 2018 | Lightweight transfer learning-based model used. | Showed low success with more complex lesions. |
| (Mavaddati, 2025) | 2025 | ResNet50-LSTM | HAM10000 | Achieved very high accuracy. | Requires high computational power. |
| (Thapar et al., 2022) | 2022 | CNN-GOA | ISIC 2018 | Improved using Grasshopper Optimization Algorithm. | Lacks classification improvement after segmentation. |
| (Nigar et al., 2022) | 2022 | ResNet18 + LIME | ISIC 2019 | Integrated explainable AI (LIME). | High memory requirements. |
| (Afza et al., 2022) | 2022 | Hybrid SVM + Relief-F | HAM10000 | Model improvement with hybrid feature selection. | Limited performance with small datasets. |
| (Keerthana et al., 2023) | 2023 | Hybrid SVM + DenseNet | ISIC 2016 | Hybrid model combining SVM and CNN. | Not tested on large datasets. |
| (Farea et al., 2024) | 2024 | DenseNet121-ABC | ISIC 2019 + PH2 | Accuracy improvement using optimization algorithms. | Long training time and complex structure. |

continued on following page

*Table 3. Continued*

| Reference | Year | Model | Dataset | Advantage | Disadvantage |
|---|---|---|---|---|---|
| (Wei et al., 2020) | 2020 | MobileNetV1-DenseNet | ISBI 2016 | Low parameter count and integrated segmentation. | Limited data diversity. |
| (Daghrir et al., 2020) | 2020 | CNN-SVM Majority Vote | ISIC | Improved decisions using majority voting. | Provides lower accuracy compared to other methods. |
| (Ragab et al., 2022) | 2022 | Hybrid Level Set | Melanoma Skin | Developed method for managing uncertainty. | Model's generalizability is limited. |

## RESULT ANALYSIS

Hybrid learning techniques present distinct benefits in medical image analysis, particularly in the detection of skin cancer. Unlike approaches that depend solely on deep learning or traditional algorithms, hybrid models integrate various computational methods such as CNNs, RNNs, and conventional machine learning classifiers to build more resilient and adaptive diagnostic systems. This combination allows the extraction of both fine-grained visual cues and abstract, semantic-level information, resulting in more accurate and consistent classification outcomes. Furthermore, hybrid systems are better suited for scenarios with limited or imbalanced data, as they often incorporate ensemble techniques, advanced feature engineering, and data augmentation to enhance model generalization. A significant advantage is their modularity; hybrid approaches can also integrate patient metadata, rule-based logic, or explainability frameworks (e.g., SHAP, LIME), increasing interpretability and clinical trust. Overall, these methods contribute to improved diagnostic precision, reduce algorithmic bias, and offer scalable, flexible solutions for complex healthcare applications.

## SOCIAL WELFARE OF THE PROPOSED WORK

The proposed work has the potential to make a meaningful contribution to public health by enhancing early and accurate detection of skin cancer, which is one of the most common and potentially fatal diseases worldwide. By utilizing advanced hybrid deep learning techniques, this system aims to support dermatologists and healthcare professionals in making faster, more consistent, and more reliable diagnostic decisions. Early diagnosis significantly improves patient outcomes by enabling timely treatment and reducing the likelihood of cancer progression, complications, or mortality. Moreover, the system's ability to operate effectively even with limited data and resources makes it especially beneficial for under-resourced or rural healthcare settings, where access to specialized diagnostic tools and expert consultation may be limited. By improving diagnostic accessibility and efficiency, the proposed work supports the broader goals of preventive medicine and health equity. Additionally, the integration of explainable AI elements contributes to increased transparency and trust in automated decision-making systems, encouraging broader acceptance among clinicians and patients. In this way, the proposed system not only addresses a critical medical challenge but also promotes social welfare by advancing equitable, efficient, and scalable healthcare solutions.

## FUTURE RESEARCH DIRECTIONS

Future research should focus on various areas to make hybrid deep learning models more comprehensive, reliable, and clinically applicable for skin cancer diagnosis. New datasets that are larger, more balanced, and represent diverse ethnic backgrounds should be developed to address class imbalances and increase demographic diversity in existing datasets. Additionally, the use of explainable artificial intelligence (XAI) technologies in clinical applications can help better understand the decision-making processes of the models. Combining patient metadata, such as age, gender, and genetic information, with dermoscopic images more effectively has the potential to enhance diagnostic accuracy. Lightweight model architectures and model compression techniques can be utilized to ensure the computational efficiency required for real-time and cost-effective applications. Lastly, hybrid models should be designed to monitor how lesions evolve over time. These models can be integrated into mobile applications or teledermatology platforms for skin cancer diagnosis.

## CONCLUSION

In this study, hybrid deep learning methods used for skin cancer diagnosis were examined. It has been demonstrated that hybrid deep learning models offer significant advantages over traditional methods in skin cancer diagnosis. Analyses of different datasets and models have shown that hybrid approaches perform particularly well on small and imbalanced datasets. Models such as ResNet50-LSTM demonstrate high accuracy rates, showcasing their success in capturing time-series characteristics. Additionally, transfer learning-based models like Xception and DenseNet121 were found to deliver faster and more consistent results on large datasets. The findings highlight the impact of selecting the right dataset on model performance. For example, when using comprehensive and diverse datasets such as ISIC 2019, it was observed that model accuracy rates improved. Moreover, segmentation-focused approaches (such as EfficientUNet++) were effective in enhancing classification performance by improving the qualitative strength of the datasets. Hybrid models not only increased accuracy rates but also incorporated explainable artificial intelligence (XAI) methods to manage uncertainty and ensure interpretability.

The findings of this study emphasize the potential of hybrid models in skin cancer diagnosis while also pointing to certain limitations and areas for improvement. The size, diversity, and quality of the datasets used significantly affect how well the models perform. In the future, hybrid models, which perform well on small datasets, can be further developed with data augmentation and synthetic data generation techniques. Creating datasets that include different skin types and ethnic groups will improve the generalization capabilities of the models and make them more applicable to a broader user base in clinical settings. The decision-making processes of hybrid models can become more reliable with the inclusion of explainable artificial intelligence (XAI) methods. Explainability techniques like SHAP and LIME can make it easier for dermatologists to understand the models' results and support the diagnostic process. Furthermore, integrating hybrid models with lightweight architectures for use in mobile devices and teledermatology systems can increase the accessibility of diagnostic services.

In conclusion, the findings of this study show that hybrid approaches not only improve accuracy rates but also make skin cancer diagnostic processes more reliable, accessible, and efficient. However, multidisciplinary studies that address ethical, safety, and regulatory considerations are needed for these technologies to reach a wider user base. In the future, more comprehensive datasets, cost-effective applications, and long-term research focused on patient monitoring will support the use of hybrid deep learning models as an indispensable tool in skin cancer diagnosis.

## REFERENCES


Abdar, M., Samami, M., Dehghani Mahmoodabad, S., Doan, T., Mazoure, B., Hashemifesharaki, R., Liu, L., Khosravi, A., Acharya, U. R., Makarenkov, V., & Nahavandi, S. (2021). Uncertainty quantification in skin cancer classification using three-way decision-based Bayesian deep learning. *Computers in Biology and Medicine*, *135*(January), 104418. DOI: 10.1016/j.compbiomed.2021.104418 PMID: 34052016

Afza, F., Sharif, M., Khan, M. A., Tariq, U., Yong, H. S., & Cha, J. (2022). Multiclass Skin Lesion Classification Using Hybrid Deep Features Selection and Extreme Learning Machine. *Sensors (Basel)*, *22*(3), 799. Advance online publication. DOI: 10.3390/s22030799 PMID: 35161553

Akter, M., Khatun, R., Talukder, M. A., Islam, M. M., & Uddin, M. A. (2024). An Integrated Deep Learning Model for Skin Cancer Detection Using Hybrid Feature Fusion Technique. https://arxiv.org/abs/2410.14489

Alfi, I. A., Rahman, M. M., Shorfuzzaman, M., & Nazir, A. (2022). A Non-Invasive Interpretable Diagnosis of Melanoma Skin Cancer Using Deep Learning and Ensemble Stacking of Machine Learning Models. *Diagnostics (Basel)*, *12*(3), 1–18. DOI: 10.3390/diagnostics12030726 PMID: 35328279

Arjun, K. P., & Kumar, K. S. (2022). A combined approach of VGG 16 and LSTM transfer learning technique for skin melanoma classification. *International Journal of Health Sciences*, *6*(May), 13504–13516. DOI: 10.53730/ijhs.v6nS1.8378

Attallah, O. (2024). Skin-CAD: Explainable deep learning classification of skin cancer from dermoscopic images by feature selection of dual high-level CNNs features and transfer learning. *Computers in Biology and Medicine*, *178*(June), 108798. DOI: 10.1016/j.compbiomed.2024.108798 PMID: 38925085

Bechelli, S., & Delhommelle, J. (2022). Machine Learning and Deep Learning Algorithms for Skin Cancer Classification from Dermoscopic Images. *Bioengineering (Basel, Switzerland)*, *9*(3), 1–18. DOI: 10.3390/bioengineering9030097 PMID: 35324786

Daghrir, J., Tlig, L., Bouchouicha, M., & Sayadi, M. (2020). Melanoma skin cancer detection using deep learning and classical machine learning techniques: A hybrid approach. *2020 International Conference on Advanced Technologies for Signal and Image Processing (ATSIP)*. DOI: 10.1109/ATSIP49331.2020.9231544

Dildar, M., Akram, S., Irfan, M., Khan, H. U., Ramzan, M., Mahmood, A. R., Alsaiari, S. A., Saeed, A. H. M., Alraddadi, M. O., & Mahnashi, M. H. (2021). Skin cancer detection: A review using deep learning techniques. *International Journal of Environmental Research and Public Health, 18*(10), 5479. Advance online publication. DOI: 10.3390/ijerph18105479 PMID: 34065430

Elashiri, M. A., Rajesh, A., Nath Pandey, S., Kumar Shukla, S., Urooj, S., & Lay-Ekuakille, A. (2022). Ensemble of weighted deep concatenated features for the skin disease classification model using modified long short term memory. *Biomedical Signal Processing and Control, 76*(April), 103729. DOI: 10.1016/j.bspc.2022.103729

Farea, E., Saleh, R. A. A., AbuAlkebash, H., Farea, A. A. R., & Al-antari, M. A. (2024). A hybrid deep learning skin cancer prediction framework. *Engineering Science and Technology, an International Journal, 57*(August), 101818. DOI: 10.1016/j.jestch.2024.101818

Gouda, W., Sama, N. U., Al-Waakid, G., Humayun, M., & Jhanjhi, N. Z. (2022). Detection of Skin Cancer Based on Skin Lesion Images Using Deep Learning. Healthcare (Basel, Switzerland, 10(7). DOI: 10.3390/healthcare10071183

Hasan, M. K., Elahi, M. T. E., Alam, M. A., Jawad, M. T., & Martí, R. (2022). DermoExpert: Skin lesion classification using a hybrid convolutional neural network through segmentation, transfer learning, and augmentation. *Informatics in Medicine Unlocked, 28*, 100819. DOI: 10.1016/j.imu.2021.100819

Imran, A., Nasir, A., Bilal, M., Sun, G., Alzahrani, A., & Almuhaimeed, A. (2022). Skin Cancer Detection Using Combined Decision of Deep Learners. *IEEE Access : Practical Innovations, Open Solutions, 10*(September), 118198–118212. DOI: 10.1109/ACCESS.2022.3220329

Jain, S., Singhania, U., Tripathy, B., Nasr, E. A., Aboudaif, M. K., & Kamrani, A. K. (2021). Deep Learning-Based Transfer Learning for Classification of Skin Cancer. Sensors (Basel, Switzerland, 21(23). DOI: 10.3390/s21238142

Jinnai, S., Yamazaki, N., Hirano, Y., Sugawara, Y., Ohe, Y., & Hamamoto, R. (2020). The development of a skin cancer classification system for pigmented skin lesions using deep learning. *Biomolecules, 10*(8), 1–13. DOI: 10.3390/biom10081123 PMID: 32751349

Keerthana, D., Venugopal, V., Nath, M. K., & Mishra, M. (2023). Hybrid convolutional neural networks with SVM classifier for classification of skin cancer. Biomedical Engineering Advances, 5(July 2022), 100069. DOI: 10.1016/j.bea.2022.100069

Kittler, H., Pehamberger, H., Wolff, K., & Binder, M. (2002). Diagnostic accuracy of dermoscopy. *The Lancet. Oncology*, *3*(3), 159–165. DOI: 10.1016/S1470-2045(02)00679-4 PMID: 11902502

Kohli, P. (2023). Automated diagnosis of skin lesions using CNN and LSTM. *International Journal of Mechanical Engineering*, *6*(3), 4521–4530. DOI: 10.56452/6-3-667

Kousis, I., Perikos, I., Hatzilygeroudis, I., & Virvou, M. (2022). Deep learning methods for accurate skin cancer recognition and mobile application. *Electronics (Basel)*, *11*(9), 1–19. DOI: 10.3390/electronics11091294

Mahum, R., & Aladhadh, S. (2022). Skin lesion detection using hand-crafted and DL-based features fusion and LSTM. *Diagnostics (Basel)*, *12*(12), 2974. Advance online publication. DOI: 10.3390/diagnostics12122974 PMID: 36552983

Mavaddati, S. (2025). Skin cancer classification based on a hybrid deep model and long short-term memory. Biomedical Signal Processing and Control, 100(PA), 107109. DOI: 10.1016/j.bspc.2024.107109

Mijwil, M. M. (2021). Skin cancer disease images classification using deep learning solutions. *Multimedia Tools and Applications*, *80*(17), 26255–26271. DOI: 10.1007/s11042-021-10952-7

Nigar, N., Umar, M., Shahzad, M. K., Islam, S., & Abalo, D. (2022). A deep learning approach based on explainable artificial intelligence for skin lesion classification. *IEEE Access : Practical Innovations, Open Solutions*, *10*(September), 113715–113725. DOI: 10.1109/ACCESS.2022.3217217

Ragab, M., Choudhry, H., Al-Rabia, M. W., Binyamin, S. S., Aldarmahi, A. A., & Mansour, R. F. (2022). Early and accurate detection of melanoma skin cancer using hybrid level set approach. *Frontiers in Physiology*, *13*(December), 965630. Advance online publication. DOI: 10.3389/fphys.2022.965630 PMID: 36545278

Reza Ahmadi Mehr. (2023). Skin cancer detection based on deep learning methods. In Lecture Notes on Data Engineering and Communications Technologies (Vol. 164, pp. 58–67). DOI: 10.1007/978-3-031-27762-7_6

Roshni Thanka, M., Bijolin Edwin, E., Ebenezer, V., Martin Sagayam, K., Jayakeshav Reddy, B., Günerhan, H., & Emadifar, H. (2023). A hybrid approach for melanoma classification using ensemble machine learning techniques with deep transfer learning. *Computer Methods and Programs in Biomedicine Update*, *3*(April), 100103. DOI: 10.1016/j.cmpbup.2023.100103

Sharma, A. K., Tiwari, S., Aggarwal, G., Goenka, N., Kumar, A., Chakrabarti, P., Chakrabarti, T., Gono, R., Leonowicz, Z., & Jasinski, M. (2022). Dermatologist-level classification of skin cancer using cascaded ensembling of convolutional neural network and handcrafted features based deep neural network. *IEEE Access : Practical Innovations, Open Solutions, 10*, 17920–17932. DOI: 10.1109/ACCESS.2022.3149824

Shorfuzzaman, M. (2022). An explainable stacked ensemble of deep learning models for improved melanoma skin cancer detection. *Multimedia Systems, 28*(4), 1309–1323. DOI: 10.1007/s00530-021-00787-5

Srinivasu, P. N., Sivasai, J. G., Ijaz, M. F., Bhoi, A. K., Kim, W., & Kang, J. J. (2021). Classification of skin disease using deep learning neural networks with MobileNet V2 and LSTM. *Sensors (Basel), 21*(8), 2852. Advance online publication. DOI: 10.3390/s21082852 PMID: 33919583

Suneetha, I. (2024). Hybrid deep learning model for skin cancer classification. *Proceedings of the 2024 International Conference on Artificial Intelligence and Machine Learning* (pp. 90–110). DOI: 10.1051/e3sconf/202459109010

Supriya, L. P., & Khilar, R. (2024). Composite ensemble learning model for skin cancer detection from dermatoscopic images. *Nanotechnology Perceptions, 20*(S9), 111–125. DOI: 10.62441/nano-ntp.v20iS9.9

Thapar, P., Rakhra, M., Cazzato, G., & Hossain, M. S. (2022). A novel hybrid deep learning approach for skin lesion segmentation and classification. *Journal of Healthcare Engineering, 2022*, 1709842. Advance online publication. DOI: 10.1155/2022/1709842 PMID: 35480147

Tumpa, P. P., & Kabir, M. A. (2021). An artificial neural network-based detection and classification of melanoma skin cancer using hybrid texture features. *Sensors International, 2*(August), 100128. DOI: 10.1016/j.sintl.2021.100128

Wei, L., Ding, K., & Hu, H. (2020). Automatic skin cancer detection in dermoscopy images based on ensemble lightweight deep learning network. *IEEE Access : Practical Innovations, Open Solutions, 8*, 99633–99647. DOI: 10.1109/ACCESS.2020.2997710

Yang, C. H., Ren, J. H., Huang, H. C., Chuang, L. Y., & Chang, P. Y. (2021). Deep hybrid convolutional neural network for segmentation of melanoma skin lesion. *Computational Intelligence and Neuroscience, 2021*(1), 9409508. Advance online publication. DOI: 10.1155/2021/9409508 PMID: 34790232

Zareen, S. S., Sun, G., Kundi, M., Qadri, S. F., & Qadri, S. (2024). Enhancing skin cancer diagnosis with deep learning: A hybrid CNN-RNN approach. *Computers, Materials & Continua, 79*(1), 1497–1519. DOI: 10.32604/cmc.2024.047418

## ADDITIONAL READING

Dildar, M., Akram, S., Irfan, M., Khan, H. U., Ramzan, M., Mahmood, A. R., Alsaiari, S. A., Saeed, A. H. M., Alraddadi, M. O., & Mahnashi, M. H. (2021). Skin cancer detection: A review using deep learning techniques. *International Journal of Environmental Research and Public Health, 18*(10), 5479. Advance online publication. DOI: 10.3390/ijerph18105479 PMID: 34065430

Holzinger, A., Goebel, R., & Mengel, M. (2020). *Artificial Intelligence and Machine Learning for Digital Pathology*. Springer. DOI: 10.1007/978-3-030-50402-1

Liopyris, K., Gregoriou, S., Dias, J., & Stratigos, A. J. (2022). Artificial Intelligence in Dermatology: Challenges and Perspectives. *Dermatology and Therapy, 12*(12), 2637–2651. DOI: 10.1007/s13555-022-00833-8 PMID: 36306100

Mazhar, T., Haq, I., Ditta, A., Mohsan, S. A. H., Rehman, F., Zafar, I., & Goh, L. P. W. (2023, February). The role of machine learning and deep learning approaches for the detection of skin cancer. [). MDPI.]. *Health Care, 11*(3), 415. PMID: 36766989

Pacheco, A. G., & Krohling, R. A. (2019). Recent advances in deep learning applied to skin cancer detection. *arXiv preprint arXiv:1912.03280.*

Reza Ahmadi Mehr. (2023). Skin cancer detection based on deep learning methods. In Lecture Notes on Data Engineering and Communications Technologies (Vol. 164, pp. 58–67). DOI: 10.1007/978-3-031-27762-7_6

Wu, Y., Chen, B., Zeng, A., Pan, D., Wang, R., & Zhao, S. (2022). Skin cancer classification with deep learning: A systematic review. *Frontiers in Oncology, 12*, 893972. DOI: 10.3389/fonc.2022.893972 PMID: 35912265

Zhou, S. K., Greenspan, H., & Shen, D. (2020). *Deep Learning for Medical Image Analysis*. Academic Press.

## KEY TERMS AND DEFINITIONS

**Artificial Intelligence (AI):** The simulation of human intelligence by machines to perform tasks such as decision-making, image recognition, and data analysis.

**Computer-Aided Diagnosis (CAD):** A system that assists healthcare professionals in interpreting medical images to improve diagnostic accuracy and efficiency.

**Data Augmentation:** Techniques used to artificially increase the size and diversity of a dataset by applying transformations like rotation, cropping, and scaling to existing images.

**Deep Learning:** A subfield of machine learning that uses artificial neural networks to analyze complex patterns in images, enabling automated diagnosis.

**Dermoscopic Images:** High-resolution images of skin lesions taken using a dermatoscope, which help in distinguishing between lesions.

**Early Detection:** The identification of skin cancer at an initial stage when treatment is most effective, a key goal of AI-driven diagnostic systems.

**Ensemble Learning:** A machine learning technique that combines the predictions of multiple models to improve overall performance and robustness.

**Explainable AI (XAI):** A set of techniques and algorithms designed to make the decision-making processes of AI systems interpretable and transparent.

**Hybrid Models:** Models that combine multiple machine learning or deep learning techniques to leverage the strengths of each method.

**Lesion:** Skin abnormalities, such as moles, spots, or growths, that may be benign or malignant. Lesions are the primary focus of skin cancer diagnosis.

**Melanoma:** The most aggressive form of skin cancer, originating from melanocytes, which produce pigment in the skin.

**Metadata:** Supplementary information about the dataset, such as patient age, gender, or lesion location, which can enhance the model's performance.

**Skin Cancer:** Uncontrolled growth of skin cells leading to malignant tumors. It is classified into melanoma and non-melanoma types.

**Transfer Learning:** A technique in machine learning where a model trained on one task is fine-tuned for a different but related task using a smaller dataset.

# Compilation of References

Abbasi, N. A., Hamrani, A., Madramootoo, C. A., Zhang, T., Tan, C. S., & Goyal, M. K. (2021). Modelling carbon dioxide emissions under a maize-soy rotation using machine learning. *Biosystems Engineering*, *212*, 1–18. DOI: 10.1016/j.biosystemseng.2021.09.013

Abbey, O. (2023). *Artificial intelligence, bias, and sustainable development goals.* University of Virginia. https://example.com/A14-Abbey-Artificial-Intelligence-Bias.pdf

Abdar, M., Samami, M., Dehghani Mahmoodabad, S., Doan, T., Mazoure, B., Hashemifesharaki, R., Liu, L., Khosravi, A., Acharya, U. R., Makarenkov, V., & Nahavandi, S. (2021). Uncertainty quantification in skin cancer classification using three-way decision-based Bayesian deep learning. *Computers in Biology and Medicine*, *135*(January), 104418. DOI: 10.1016/j.compbiomed.2021.104418 PMID: 34052016

Abduh, A., Jayadi, K., Anshari, A., Basri, M., & Arham, M. (2022). Self-efficacy in speaking based activities for art and design students. *International Journal of Language Education*, *6*(1), 91–100. DOI: 10.26858/ijole.v6i1.32384

Abdulmalek, S., Nasir, A., Jabbar, W. A., Almuhaya, M. A., Bairagi, A. K., Khan, M. A. M., & Kee, S. H. (2022). IoT-based healthcare-monitoring system towards improving quality of life: A review. *Health Care*, *10*(10), 1993. DOI: 10.3390/healthcare10101993 PMID: 36292441

Abrardi, L., Cambini, C., & Rondi, L. (2022). Artificial intelligence, firms and consumer behavior: A survey. *Journal of Economic Surveys*, *36*(4), 969–991. DOI: 10.1111/joes.12455

Abulibdeh, A., Zaidan, E., & Abulibdeh, R. (2024). Navigating the confluence of artificial intelligence and education for sustainable development in the era of industry 4.0: Challenges, opportunities, and ethical dimensions. *Journal of Cleaner Production, 437*, 140527. DOI: 10.1016/j.jclepro.2023.140527

Adako, O. P., Adeusi, O. C., & Alaba, P. A. (2024). Revolutionizing Autism Education: Harnessing AI for Tailored Skill Development in Social, Emotional, and Independent Learning Domains. *Journal of Computational and Cognitive Engineering, 3*(4), 348–359. DOI: 10.47852/bonviewJCCE42023414

Adinarayana, S., Raju, M. G., Srirangam, D. P., Prasad, D. S., Kumar, M. R., & Veesam, S. B. (2024). Enhancing Resource Management in Precision Farming through AI-Based Irrigation Optimization. In Dey, A., Nayak, S., Kumar, R., & Mohanty, S. N. (Eds.), *How Machine Learning is Innovating Today's World* (1st ed., pp. 221–251). Wiley. DOI: 10.1002/9781394214167.ch15

Adipat, S., & Chotikapanich, R. (2022). Sustainable Development Goal 4: An education goal to achieve equitable quality education. *Academic Journal of Interdisciplinary Studies, 11*(1), 174. DOI: 10.36941/ajis-2022-0159

Adiyoso, W. (2022). The progress of the SDGs research. *The Journal of Indonesia Sustainable Development Planning, 3*(2), i–iii. DOI: 10.46456/jisdep.v3i2.337

Afza, F., Sharif, M., Khan, M. A., Tariq, U., Yong, H. S., & Cha, J. (2022). Multiclass Skin Lesion Classification Using Hybrid Deep Features Selection and Extreme Learning Machine. *Sensors (Basel), 22*(3), 799. Advance online publication. DOI: 10.3390/s22030799 PMID: 35161553

Aggarwal, D. (2023). Exploring the scope of artificial intelligence (AI) for lifelong education through personalized & adaptive learning. *Journal of Artificial Intelligence, Machine Learning, and Neural Network, 4*(41), 21–26. DOI: 10.55529/jaimlnn.41.21.26

Aghababaei, A., Aghababaei, F., Pignitter, M., & Hadidi, M. (2025). Artificial Intelligence in Agro-Food Systems: From Farm to Fork. *Foods, 14*(3), 411. DOI: 10.3390/foods14030411 PMID: 39942003

Aghdam, Z. N., Rahmani, A. M., & Hosseinzadeh, M. (2021). The role of the Internet of Things in healthcare: Future trends and challenges. *Computer Methods and Programs in Biomedicine, 199*(105903), 1–27. DOI: 10.1016/j.cmpb.2020.105903 PMID: 33348073

Agnola, T., Ambrosini, L., Beretta, E., & Gremlich, G. (2025). Empowering Global Supply Chains Through Blockchain-Based Platforms: New Evidence from the Coffee Industry. *FinTech*, *4*(1), 3. DOI: 10.3390/fintech4010003

Agustiani, R., Zahra, A., Putri, A. D., Hadi, M., Marwan, A., Solehah, A. M., Saputri, A. M., & Sopani, A. (2024). Students' numeracy literacy using artificial intelligence (AI)-based worksheets. *Indiktika: Jurnal Inovasi Pendidikan Matematika*, *7*(1), 173–181. DOI: 10.31851/indiktika.v7i1.17032

Ahamed, T. (2024). *IoT and AI in Agriculture: Smart Automation Systems for Increasing Agricultural Productivity to Achieve SDGs and Society 5.0.* Springer Nature. DOI: 10.1007/978-981-97-1263-2

Ahmad, L., & Nabi, F. (2021). *Agriculture 5.0: Artificial intelligence, IoT and machine learning*. CRC Press.

Ahmad, T., Madonski, R., Zhang, D., Huang, C., & Mujeeb, A. (2022). Data-driven probabilistic machine learning in sustainable smart energy/smart energy systems: Key developments, challenges, and future research opportunities in the context of smart grid paradigm. *Renewable & Sustainable Energy Reviews*, *160*, 112128. DOI: 10.1016/j.rser.2022.112128

Ahmad, T., Zhang, D., Huang, C., Zhang, H., Dai, N., Song, Y., & Chen, H. (2021). Artificial intelligence in sustainable energy industry: Status Quo, challenges and opportunities. *Journal of Cleaner Production*, *289*, 125834. DOI: 10.1016/j.jclepro.2021.125834

Ahmad, T., Zhu, H., Zhang, D., Tariq, R., Bassam, A., Ullah, F., AlGhamdi, A. S., & Alshamrani, S. S. (2022). Energetics Systems and artificial intelligence: Applications of industry 4.0. *Energy Reports*, *8*, 334–361. DOI: 10.1016/j.egyr.2021.11.256

Ahmed, F. (2024). The digital divide and AI in education: Addressing equity and accessibility. *Journal of AI Integration in Education*, *1*(2), 12–23.

Ahn, J., Kim, J., & Sung, Y. (2022). The effect of gender stereotypes on artificial intelligence recommendations. *Journal of Business Research*, *141*, 50–59. DOI: 10.1016/j.jbusres.2021.12.007

Ahrens, A., Zaščerinska, J., Melnikova, J., & Andreeva, N. (2018). An innovative method for data mining in higher education. *Rural Environment. Education. Personality*, *11*, 17–24. DOI: 10.22616/REEP.2018.001

Akanbi, M. B., Adedotun, K. J., Raji, A. K., & Banjoko, I. K. (2025). Optimizing Water Resource Management in Agriculture Using AI-Powered Solar Irrigation Systems. *Journal of Science Innovation and Technology Research.*

Akgun, S., & Greenhow, C. (2022). Artificial intelligence in education: Addressing ethical challenges in K-12 settings. *AI and Ethics*, *2*(3), 431–440. DOI: 10.1007/s43681-021-00096-7

Akindipe, D., & Lalude, O. M. (2025). *Balancing Public Safety and Individual Rights in AI-Driven Public Administration in Nigeria*. DOI: 10.4018/979-8-3693-8372-8.ch003

Akintayo, O. T., Eden, C. A., Ayeni, O. O., & Onyebuchi, N. C. (2024). Integrating AI with emotional and social learning in primary education: Developing a holistic adaptive learning ecosystem. *Computer Science & IT Research Journal*, *5*(5), 1076–1089. DOI: 10.51594/csitrj.v5i5.1116

Akintuyi, O. B. (2024). AI in agriculture: A comparative review of developments in the USA and Africa. *Research Journal of Science and Engineering, 10*(2), 60–70.

Akseli, O. (2021). Financial inclusion, access to credit, and sustainable finance: What role for the uncitral model law on secured transactions? *Law and Contemporary Problems*, *84*(1), 181–196.

Akter, M., Khatun, R., Talukder, M. A., Islam, M. M., & Uddin, M. A. (2024). An Integrated Deep Learning Model for Skin Cancer Detection Using Hybrid Feature Fusion Technique. https://arxiv.org/abs/2410.14489

Alaimo, K., Chilton, M., & Jones, S. J. (2020). Food insecurity, hunger, and malnutrition. In *Present knowledge in nutrition* (pp. 311–326). Academic Press. DOI: 10.1016/B978-0-12-818460-8.00017-4

Alam, A. (2022). *Employing Adaptive Learning and Intelligent Tutoring Robots for Virtual Classrooms and Smart Campuses: Reforming Education in the Age of Artificial Intelligence*. DOI: 10.1007/978-981-19-2980-9_32

Alanazi, A. (2022). Using machine learning for healthcare challenges and opportunities. *Informatics in Medicine Unlocked*, *30*, 100924. DOI: 10.1016/j.imu.2022.100924

Albelda, A. R. (2024). Enhancing sustainability in resource-limited environments: Government, culture, and AI. *IEEE Technology and Society Magazine*, *43*(1), 54–61. DOI: 10.1109/MTS.2024.3365574

Alexander, A., Martin, D. P., Manolchev, C., & Miller, K. (2020). University–industry collaboration: Using meta-rules to overcome barriers to knowledge transfer. *The Journal of Technology Transfer*, *45*(2), 371–392. DOI: 10.1007/s10961-018-9685-1

Alfi, I. A., Rahman, M. M., Shorfuzzaman, M., & Nazir, A. (2022). A Non-Invasive Interpretable Diagnosis of Melanoma Skin Cancer Using Deep Learning and Ensemble Stacking of Machine Learning Models. *Diagnostics (Basel), 12*(3), 1–18. DOI: 10.3390/diagnostics12030726 PMID: 35328279

Alhashmi, S. M. (2024). The evolution and challenges of healthcare policy and research in the Middle East. In *Digital Healthcare in Asia and Gulf Region for Healthy Aging and More Inclusive Societies* (pp. 425–445). Academic Press. DOI: 10.1016/B978-0-443-23637-2.00005-9

Ali, A., & Kaul, H.-P. (2025). Monitoring Yield and Quality of Forages and Grassland in the View of Precision Agriculture Applications—A Review. *Remote Sensing (Basel), 17*(2), 279. DOI: 10.3390/rs17020279

Ali, F., Razzaq, A., Tariq, W., Hameed, A., Rehman, A., Razzaq, K., Sarfraz, S., Rajput, N. A., Zaki, H. E., Shahid, M. S., & Ondrasek, G. (2024). Spectral Intelligence: AI-Driven Hyperspectral Imaging for Agricultural and Ecosystem Applications. *Agronomy (Basel), 14*(10), 2260. DOI: 10.3390/agronomy14102260

Ali, G., Mijwil, M. M., Adamopoulos, I., & Ayad, J. (2025). Leveraging the Internet of Things, Remote Sensing, and Artificial Intelligence for Sustainable Forest Management. *Babylonian Journal of Internet of Things, 2025*, 1–65. DOI: 10.58496/BJIoT/2025/001

Allahyari, M. S., & Sadeghzadeh, M. (2020). Agricultural Extension Systems Toward SDGs 2030: Zero Hunger. In Leal Filho, W., Azul, A. M., Brandli, L., Özuyar, P. G., & Wall, T. (Eds.), *Zero Hunger* (pp. 41–52). Springer International Publishing. DOI: 10.1007/978-3-319-95675-6_2

Allen, C., Metternicht, G., & Wiedmann, T. (2019). Prioritising SDG targets: Assessing baselines, gaps and interlinkages. *Sustainability Science, 14*(2), 421–438. DOI: 10.1007/s11625-018-0596-8

Allgaier, J., Mulansky, L., Draelos, R. L., & Pryss, R. (2023). How does the model make predictions? A systematic literature review on the explainability power of machine learning in healthcare. *Artificial Intelligence in Medicine, 143*, 102616. DOI: 10.1016/j.artmed.2023.102616 PMID: 37673561

Allioui, H., & Mourdi, Y. (2023). Exploring the Full Potentials of IoT for Better Financial Growth and Stability: A Comprehensive Survey. *Sensors (Basel), 23*(19), 8015. DOI: 10.3390/s23198015 PMID: 37836845

Alloun, W., Berkani, M., Shavandi, A., Beddiar, A., Pellegrini, M., Garzia, M., Lakhdari, D., Ganachari, S. V., Aminabhavi, T. M., Vasseghian, Y., Muddapur, U., & Chaouche, N. K. (2024). Harnessing artificial intelligence-driven approach for enhanced indole-3-acetic acid from the newly isolated *Streptomyces rutgersensis* AW08. *Environmental Research*, *252*, 118933. DOI: 10.1016/j.envres.2024.118933 PMID: 38642645

Ally, M., & Perris, K. (2022). Artificial intelligence in the fourth industrial revolution to educate for sustainable development. *Canadian Journal of Learning and Technology*, *48*(4). Advance online publication. DOI: 10.21432/cjlt28287

Almutairi, A. F., Gegov, A., Adda, M., & Arabikhan, F. (2020). Conceptual artificial intelligence framework to improving English as second language. *WSEAS Transactions on Advances in Engineering Education*, *17*, 87–91. DOI: 10.37394/232010.2020.17.11

Alowais, S. A., Alghamdi, S. S., Alsuhebany, N., Alqahtani, T., Alshaya, A. I., Almohareb, S. N., Aldairem, A., Alrashed, M., Bin Saleh, K., Badreldin, H. A., Al Yami, M. S., Al Harbi, S., & Albekairy, A. M. (2023). Revolutionizing healthcare: The role of artificial intelligence in clinical practice. *BMC Medical Education*, *23*(1), 689. DOI: 10.1186/s12909-023-04698-z PMID: 37740191

AlSagri, H. S., & Sohail, S. S. (2024). Evaluating the role of artificial intelligence in sustainable development goals with an emphasis on "quality education." *Discover Sustainability*, *5*(1), 458. DOI: 10.1007/s43621-024-00682-9

Altshuler, Y., Chebach, T. C., & Cohen, S. (2024). From Microbes to Methane: AI-Based Predictive Modeling of Feed Additive Efficacy in Dairy Cows. In *Applied Swarm Intelligence* (pp. 240–325). CRC Press.

Ametepey, S. O., Aigbavboa, C., Thwala, W. D., & Addy, H. (2024). The impact of AI on Sustainable Development Goal implementation: A Delphi study. *Sustainability (Basel)*, *16*(9), 3858. DOI: 10.3390/su16093858

Amiri, Z., Heidari, A., & Navimipour, N. J. (2024). Comprehensive survey of artificial intelligence techniques and strategies for climate change mitigation. *Energy*, *308*, 132827. DOI: 10.1016/j.energy.2024.132827

Anawade, P. A., Sharma, D., & Gahane, S. (2024). A comprehensive review on exploring the impact of telemedicine on healthcare accessibility. *Cureus*, *16*(3), 1–12. DOI: 10.7759/cureus.55996 PMID: 38618307

An, Q., Rahman, S., Zhou, J., & Kang, J. J. (2023). A comprehensive review on machine learning in healthcare industry: Classification, restrictions, opportunities and challenges. *Sensors (Basel)*, *23*(9), 4178. DOI: 10.3390/s23094178 PMID: 37177382

Anshari, M., Hamdan, M., Ahmad, N., & Ali, E. (2025). Public service delivery, artificial intelligence, and the sustainable development goals: Trends, evidence, and complexities. *Journal of Science and Technology Policy Management, 16*(1), 163–181. DOI: 10.1108/JSTPM-07-2023-0123

Arévalo-Royo, J., Flor-Montalvo, F.-J., Latorre-Biel, J.-I., Tino-Ramos, R., Martínez-Cámara, E., & Blanco-Fernández, J. (2025). AI Algorithms in the Agrifood Industry: Application Potential in the Spanish Agrifood Context. *Applied Sciences (Basel, Switzerland), 15*(4), 2096. DOI: 10.3390/app15042096

Arjun, K. P., & Kumar, K. S. (2022). A combined approach of VGG 16 and LSTM transfer learning technique for skin melanoma classification. *International Journal of Health Sciences, 6*(May), 13504–13516. DOI: 10.53730/ijhs.v6nS1.8378

Armutat, S., Wattenberg, M., & Mauritz, N. (2024). Artificial intelligence–gender-specific differences in perception, understanding, and training interest. *International Conference on Gender Research*, 7(1), 36-43. DOI: 10.34190/icgr.7.1.2163

Arslan, M., & Cruz, C. (2024). Business text classification with imbalanced data and moderately large label spaces for digital transformation. *Applied Network Science, 9*(1), 11. Advance online publication. DOI: 10.1007/s41109-024-00623-5

Artyukhov, A., Wołowiec, T., Artyukhova, N., Bogacki, S., & Vasylieva, T. (2024). SDG 4, academic integrity and artificial intelligence: Clash or win-win cooperation? *Sustainability (Basel), 16*(19), 8483. DOI: 10.3390/su16198483

Arya, S. S., Venkatram, R., More, P. R., & Vijayan, P. (2022). The wastes of coffee bean processing for utilization in food: A review. *Journal of Food Science and Technology, 59*(2), 429–444. DOI: 10.1007/s13197-021-05032-5 PMID: 35185168

Attallah, O. (2024). Skin-CAD: Explainable deep learning classification of skin cancer from dermoscopic images by feature selection of dual high-level CNNs features and transfer learning. *Computers in Biology and Medicine, 178*(June), 108798. DOI: 10.1016/j.compbiomed.2024.108798 PMID: 38925085

Ayilara, M. S., Olanrewaju, O. S., Babalola, O. O., & Odeyemi, O. (2020). Waste Management through Composting: Challenges and Potentials. *Sustainability (Basel), 12*(11), 4456. DOI: 10.3390/su12114456

Bachmann, N., Tripathi, S., Brunner, M., & Jodlbauer, H. (2022). The contribution of data driven technologies in achieving sustainable development goals. *Sustainability (Basel), 14*(5), 2497. DOI: 10.3390/su14052497

Bajwa, J., Munir, U., Nori, A., & Williams, B. (2021). Artificial intelligence in healthcare: Transforming the practice of medicine. *Future Healthcare Journal*, *8*(2), 188–194. DOI: 10.7861/fhj.2021-0095 PMID: 34286183

Baker, B., Mills, K. A., McDonald, P., & Wang, L. (2023). AI, Concepts of Intelligence, and Chatbots: The "Figure of Man," the Rise of Emotion, and Future Visions of Education. *Teachers College Record*, *125*(6), 60–84. DOI: 10.1177/01614681231191291

Balaska, V., Adamidou, Z., Vryzas, Z., & Gasteratos, A. (2023). Sustainable crop protection via robotics and artificial intelligence solutions. *Machines (Basel)*, *11*(8), 774. DOI: 10.3390/machines11080774

Baur, P., & Iles, A. (2023). Inserting machines, displacing people: How automation imaginaries for agriculture promise 'liberation'from the industrialized farm. *Agriculture and Human Values*, *40*(3), 815–833. DOI: 10.1007/s10460-023-10435-5

Bayan, F. M. (2024). The Ethics of AI: Navigating the Moral Dilemmas of Artificial Intelligence. *Arab Journal for Scientific Publishing*.

Bayly-Castaneda, K., Ramirez-Montoya, M. S., & Morita-Alexander, A. (2024, August). Crafting personalized learning paths with AI for lifelong learning: A systematic literature review. *Frontiers in Education*, *9*, 1424386. DOI: 10.3389/feduc.2024.1424386

Bechelli, S., & Delhommelle, J. (2022). Machine Learning and Deep Learning Algorithms for Skin Cancer Classification from Dermoscopic Images. *Bioengineering (Basel, Switzerland)*, *9*(3), 1–18. DOI: 10.3390/bioengineering9030097 PMID: 35324786

Bellantuono, L., Monaco, A., Amoroso, N., Aquaro, V., Lombardi, A., Tangaro, S., & Bellotti, R. (2022). Sustainable development goals: Conceptualization, communication and achievement synergies in a complex network framework. *Applied Network Science*, *7*(1), 14. DOI: 10.1007/s41109-022-00455-1

Ben Ayed, R., & Hanana, M. (2021). Artificial Intelligence to Improve the Food and Agriculture Sector. *Journal of Food Quality*, *2021*, 1–7. DOI: 10.1155/2021/5584754

Bennich, T., Persson, Å., Beaussart, R., Allen, C., & Malekpour, S. (2023). Recurring patterns of SDG interlinkages and how they can advance the 2030 Agenda. *One Earth*, *6*(11), 1465–1476. DOI: 10.1016/j.oneear.2023.10.008

Bhagat, P. R., Naz, F., & Magda, R. (2022). Artificial intelligence solutions enabling sustainable agriculture: A bibliometric analysis. *PLoS One*, *17*(6), e0268989. Advance online publication. DOI: 10.1371/journal.pone.0268989 PMID: 35679287

Bhatia, D., & Malik, D. (2021). An Insight into the Potential Role of Artificial Intelligence in Bioinformatics. In Gaur, L., Solanki, A., Wamba, S. F., & Jhanjhi, N. Z. (Eds.), *Advanced AI Techniques and Applications in Bioinformatics* (pp. 17–40). CRC Press. DOI: 10.1201/9781003126164-2

Bhattacharya, A. (2021). Blockchain & IoT: A Paradigm Shift for Supply Chain Management. In *Handbook of Blockchain for Sustainable Development* (p. 159). DOI: 10.1002/9781119711063.ch8

Bibri, S. E., Krogstie, J., Kaboli, A., & Alahi, A. (2024). Smarter eco-cities and their leading-edge artificial intelligence of things solutions for environmental sustainability: A comprehensive systematic review. *Environmental Science and Ecotechnology, 19*, 100330. DOI: 10.1016/j.ese.2023.100330 PMID: 38021367

Biermann, F., Kanie, N., Kim, R. E., Adams, C., Griggs, D., Nilsson, M., & Stafford-Smith, M. (2022). Scientific evidence on the political impact of the Sustainable Development Goals. *Nature Sustainability, 5*(9), 795–800. DOI: 10.1038/s41893-022-00909-5

Bigdeloo, M., Teymourian, T., Kowsari, E., Ramakrishna, S., & Ehsani, A. (2021). Sustainability and Circular Economy of Food Wastes: Waste Reduction Strategies, Higher Recycling Methods, and Improved Valorization. *Materials Circular Economy, 3*(1), 3. DOI: 10.1007/s42824-021-00017-3

Binns, R. (2018). What can political philosophy teach us about algorithmic fairness? *IEEE Security and Privacy, 16*(3), 73–80. DOI: 10.1109/MSP.2018.2701147

*Bioproduct Basics*. (2023). https://www.energy.gov/eere/bioenergy/bioproduct-basics

Blasco, N., Brusca, I., & Barrafón, M. (2020). Drivers for universities' contribution to the sustainable development goals: An analysis of Spanish public universities. *Sustainability (Basel), 13*(1), 89. DOI: 10.3390/su13010089

Blauth, T. F., Gstrein, O. J., & Zwitter, A. (2022). Artificial intelligence crime: An overview of malicious use and abuse of AI. *IEEE Access : Practical Innovations, Open Solutions, 10*, 77110–77122. DOI: 10.1109/ACCESS.2022.3191790

Blicharska, M., Teutschbein, C., & Smithers, R. J. (2021). SDG partnerships may perpetuate the global North–South divide. *Scientific Reports, 11*(1), 22092. DOI: 10.1038/s41598-021-01534-6

Blodgett, S. L., Barocas, S., Daumé, H.III, & Wallach, H. (2020). Language (technology) is power: A critical survey of "bias" in NLP. *Proceedings of the 58th Annual Meeting of the ACL*, 5454-5476. DOI: 10.18653/v1/2020.acl-main.485

Bordalo, P., Coffman, K., Gennaioli, N., & Shleifer, A. (2019). Beliefs about gender. *The American Economic Review*, *109*(3), 739–773. DOI: 10.1257/aer.20170007

Boroujeni, S. P. H., Razi, A., Khoshdel, S., Afghah, F., Coen, J. L., O'Neill, L., Fule, P., Watts, A., Kokolakis, N.-M. T., & Vamvoudakis, K. G. (2024). A comprehensive survey of research towards AI-enabled unmanned aerial systems in pre-, active-, and post-wildfire management. *Information Fusion*, *108*, 102369. DOI: 10.1016/j.inffus.2024.102369

Borowicz, M. K. (2025). Law and Macro Finance. *Law and Development Review*, *18*(1), 123–148. DOI: 10.1515/ldr-2024-0091

Borwein, S., Magistro, B., Loewen, P., Bonikowski, B., & Lee-Whiting, B. (2024). The gender gap in attitudes toward workplace technological change. Socio-. *Economic Review (Kansas City, Mo.)*, *22*, 993–1017.

Buekens, A. (2013). *Incineration Technologies*. Springer Science & Business Media. DOI: 10.1007/978-1-4614-5752-7

Bulathwela, S., Pérez-Ortiz, M., Holloway, C., & Shawe-Taylor, J. (2021). Could AI democratise education? Socio-technical imaginaries of an edtech revolution. *ArXiv Preprint ArXiv:2112.02034*.

Bwambale, E., Abagale, F. K., & Anornu, G. K. (2022). Smart irrigation monitoring and control strategies for improving water use efficiency in precision agriculture: A review. *Agricultural Water Management*, *260*, 107324. DOI: 10.1016/j.agwat.2021.107324

Cai, Z., Fan, X., & Du, J. (2017). Gender and attitudes toward technology use: A meta-analysis. *Computers & Education*, *105*, 1–13. DOI: 10.1016/j.compedu.2016.11.003

Campera, M., Budiadi, B., Adinda, E., Ahmad, N., Balestri, M., Hedger, K., Imron, M. A., Manson, S., Nijman, V., & Nekaris, K. A. I. (2021). Fostering a Wildlife-Friendly Program for Sustainable Coffee Farming: The Case of Small-Holder Farmers in Indonesia. *Land (Basel)*, *10*(2), 121. DOI: 10.3390/land10020121

Carayannis, E. G., & Morawska-Jancelewicz, J. (2022). The futures of Europe: Society 5.0 and Industry 5.0 as driving forces of future universities. *Journal of the Knowledge Economy*, *13*(4), 3445–3471. DOI: 10.1007/s13132-021-00854-2

Castaldo, L., Lombardi, S., Gaspari, A., Rubino, M., Izzo, L., Narváez, A., Ritieni, A., & Grosso, M. (2021). In Vitro Bioaccessibility and Antioxidant Activity of Polyphenolic Compounds from Spent Coffee Grounds-Enriched Cookies. *Foods*, *10*(8), 1837. DOI: 10.3390/foods10081837 PMID: 34441614

Ceia, V., Nothwehr, B., & Wagner, L. (2021). *Gender and Technology: A rights-based and intersectional analysis of key trends*. Academic Press.

Celis, J., Xiao, X., Wagle, P., Adler, P. R., & White, P. (2024). A Review of Yield Forecasting Techniques and Their Impact on Sustainable Agriculture. In Melkonyan-Gottschalk, A., & Daus, D. (Eds.), *Transformation Towards Circular Food Systems* (Vol. 13, pp. 139–168). Springer Nature Switzerland. DOI: 10.1007/978-3-031-63793-3_8

Cembranel, P., Gewehr, L., Dal Moro, L., Fuchs, P. G., Birch, R. S., & Andrade Guerra, J. B. S. O. D. A. (2024). The pivotal role of higher education institutions in cultivating a sustainable development goals-centric culture. *International Journal of Sustainability in Higher Education*, *25*(7), 1385–1411. DOI: 10.1108/IJSHE-01-2024-0057

Ceylan, M., & Mnzile, J. Y. (2025). The integration of artificial intelligence (AI) in educational settings. In *Economic and political consequences of AI: Managing creative destruction* (p. 395). IGI Global Scientific Publishing. DOI: 10.4018/979-8-3693-7036-0.ch017

Chalkidis, I., Fergadiotis, M., Kotitsas, S., Malakasiotis, P., Aletras, N., & Androutsopoulos, I. (2020). An empirical study on large-scale multi-label text classification including few and zero-shot labels. *Proceedings of the 58th Annual Meeting of the Association for Computational Linguistics*, 7503–7515. DOI: 10.18653/v1/2020.emnlp-main.607

Challoumis, C. (2024). AI and economic inequality-addressing the challenges ahead. In *XVIII International Scientific Conference. Dortmund. Germany* (pp. 120-155). Academic Press.

Challoumis, C. (2024, October). Building a sustainable economy-how ai can optimize resource allocation. In *XVI International Scientific Conference* (pp. 190-224).

Chant, S., & Sweetman, C. (2012). Fixing women or fixing the world? 'Smart economics', efficiency approaches, and gender equality in development. *Gender and Development*, *20*(3), 517–529. DOI: 10.1080/13552074.2012.731812

Chaturvedi, A. K., Arora, R., & Saluja, M. S. (2015). Private Sector and Waste Management in Delhi: A Political Economy Perspective. *IDS Bulletin*, *46*(3), 7–16. DOI: 10.1111/1759-5436.12140

Chauhan, P., & Gagandeep, K. (2022). Gender Bias and artificial intelligence: A challenge within the periphery of human rights. *Hasanuddin Law Review*, *8*(1), 46–59. DOI: 10.20956/halrev.v8i1.3569

Che Dalim, C. S., Sunar, M. S., Dey, A., & Billinghurst, M. (2020). Using augmented reality with speech input for non-native children's language learning. *International Journal of Human-Computer Studies, 134*, 44–64. DOI: 10.1016/j.ijhcs.2019.10.002

Chen, H. (2021). Optimization of an Intelligent Sorting and Recycling System for Solid Waste Based on Image Recognition Technology. *Advances in Mathematical Physics, 2021*(1), 4094684. DOI: 10.1155/2021/4094684

Chen, L., Chen, Z., Zhang, Y., Liu, Y., Osman, A. I., Farghali, M., Hua, J., Al-Fatesh, A., Ihara, I., Rooney, D. W., & Yap, P. S. (2023). Artificial intelligence-based solutions for climate change: A review. *Environmental Chemistry Letters, 21*(5), 2525–2557. DOI: 10.1007/s10311-023-01617-y

Chen, S., Huang, J., Xiao, T., Gao, J., Bai, J., Luo, W., & Dong, B. (2020). Carbon emissions under different domestic waste treatment modes induced by garbage classification: Case study in pilot communities in Shanghai, China. *The Science of the Total Environment, 717*, 137193. DOI: 10.1016/j.scitotenv.2020.137193 PMID: 32062281

Chen, Y., Prentice, C., Weaven, S., & Hsiao, A. (2022). A systematic literature review of AI in the sharing economy. *Journal of Global Scholars of Marketing Science, 32*(3), 434–451. DOI: 10.1080/21639159.2020.1808850

Chen, Z., & Liu, B. (2018). *Lifelong machine learning*. Springer International Publishing. DOI: 10.1007/978-3-031-01581-6

Chertow, M., Reck, B. K., Wrzesniewski, A., & Calli, B. (2024). Outlook on the future role of robots and AI in material recovery facilities: Implications for U.S. recycling and the workforce. *Journal of Cleaner Production, 470*, 143234. DOI: 10.1016/j.jclepro.2024.143234

Chiu, I. H.-Y., Lin, L., & Rouch, D. (2022). Law and Regulation for Sustainable Finance. *European Business Organization Law Review, 23*(1), 1–7. Advance online publication. DOI: 10.1007/s40804-021-00230-2

Chohan, S. R., & Hu, G. (2022). Strengthening digital inclusion through e-government: Cohesive ICT training programs to intensify digital competency. *Information Technology for Development, 28*(1), 16–38. DOI: 10.1080/02681102.2020.1841713

Choi, J., Lim, B., & Yoo, Y. (2023). Advancing Plastic Waste Classification and Recycling Efficiency: Integrating Image Sensors and Deep Learning Algorithms. *Applied Sciences (Basel, Switzerland), 13*(18), 10224. DOI: 10.3390/app131810224

Choudhary, M., Arora, M., & Goyal, N. (2024). Smart agriculture with cloud/fog computing and sensor networks for sustainable development. In *Cloud and Fog Optimization-based Solutions for Sustainable Developments* (pp. 98–117). CRC Press. DOI: 10.1201/9781003494430-5

Cingano, F. (2014). Trends in income inequality and its impact on economic growth. *OECD Social, Employment and Migration Working Papers, No. 163*. DOI: 10.1787/5jxrjncwxv6j-en

Cob-Parro, A. C., Lalangui, Y., & Lazcano, R. (2024). Fostering Agricultural Transformation through AI: An Open-Source AI Architecture Exploiting the MLOps Paradigm. *Agronomy (Basel)*, *14*(2), 259. DOI: 10.3390/agronomy14020259

*Coffee waste as an alternative fertilizer with soil improving properties for sandy soils in humid tropical environments.* (n.d.). ResearchGate. Retrieved October 17, 2025, from https://www.researchgate.net/publication/263375752_Coffee_waste_as_an_alternative_fertilizer_with_soil_improving_properties_for_sandy_soils_in_humid_tropical_environments

Community Dataset, O. S. D. G. (2023). *OSDG Community Dataset (OSDG CD)* [Dataset]. Zenodo. https://zenodo.org/records/8397907

Connelly, S. (2025). Finance Law. In *Finance Law*. Taylor and Francis. DOI: 10.4324/9781003457220

Cooke, F. L., Dickmann, M., & Parry, E. (2022). Building sustainable societies through human-centred human resource management: Emerging issues and research opportunities. *International Journal of Human Resource Management*, *33*(1), 1–15. DOI: 10.1080/09585192.2021.2021732

*Cosmetic application of coffee by-products.* (n.d.). ResearchGate. Retrieved October 17, 2025, from https://www.researchgate.net/figure/Cosmetic-application-of-coffee-by-products_tbl3_367000924

Costa, L., Rybski, D., & Kropp, J. P. (2011). A human development framework for $CO_2$ reductions. *PLoS One*, *6*(12), e29262. DOI: 10.1371/journal.pone.0029262

Cowls, J., Tsamados, A., Taddeo, M., & Floridi, L. (2023). The AI gambit: Leveraging artificial intelligence to combat climate change—opportunities, challenges, and recommendations. *AI & Society*, *38*(1), 1–25. DOI: 10.1007/s00146-021-01294-x PMID: 34690449

Craiut, M.-V., & Iancu, I. (2022). Is technology gender neutral? A systematic literature review on gender stereotypes attached to artificial intelligence. *Human Technology*, *18*(3), 297–315. DOI: 10.14254/1795-6889.2022.18-3.6

Curi, Z., Britto, A., & Paraíso, E. (2018). Multi-label classification of user reactions in online news. /arxiv.1809.02811DOI: 10.48550

Da Costa, D., & McMichael, P. (2019). The poverty of the global order. In *Recognition and Redistribution* (pp. 157–171). Routledge. DOI: 10.4324/9781315878263-13

Daghrir, J., Tlig, L., Bouchouicha, M., & Sayadi, M. (2020). Melanoma skin cancer detection using deep learning and classical machine learning techniques: A hybrid approach. *2020 International Conference on Advanced Technologies for Signal and Image Processing (ATSIP)*. DOI: 10.1109/ATSIP49331.2020.9231544

Dang, V. A., Vu Khanh, Q., Nguyen, V. H., Nguyen, T., & Nguyen, D. C. (2023). Intelligent healthcare: Integration of emerging technologies and Internet of Things for humanity. *Sensors*, *23*(9), 4200:1-24. DOI: 10.3390/s23094200

Darjee, K. B., Neupane, P. R., & Köhl, M. (2023). Proactive Adaptation Responses by Vulnerable Communities to Climate Change Impacts. *Sustainability (Basel)*, *15*(14), 10952. DOI: 10.3390/su151410952

Dave, G., Patel, T., & Mitra, S. (2025). *Global scenario on renewable energy and net zero goal emphasizing Indian standpoint: A short review*. Energy Systems. DOI: 10.1007/s12667-025-00728-5

Dayana, D. S., Venkatamuni, T., Bhagyalakshmi, A., Malleswari, T. N., & Ushasukhanya, S. (2025). AI-Controlled Robotics in Smart Agricultural Systems: Enhancing Precision, Sustainability, and Productivity. In *Edible Electronics for Smart Technology Solutions* (pp. 351–382). IGI Global. https://www.igi-global.com/chapter/ai-controlled-robotics-in-smart-agricultural-systems/360268

de Almeida, P. G. R., dos Santos, C. D., & Farias, J. S. (2021). Artificial intelligence regulation: A framework for governance. *Ethics and Information Technology*, *23*(3), 505–525. DOI: 10.1007/s10676-021-09593-z

de Bomfim, A. S. C., de Oliveira, D. M., Walling, E., Babin, A., Hersant, G., Vaneeckhaute, C., Dumont, M.-J., & Rodrigue, D. (2023). Spent Coffee Grounds Characterization and Reuse in Composting and Soil Amendment. *Waste*, *1*(1), 2–20. DOI: 10.3390/waste1010002

de Freitas, C. P. M., Marangon, B. B., Pereira, E. G., & Renato, N. dos S. (2023). Exploring spent coffee grounds energy potential in the Brazilian scenario. *Engenharia Agrícola*, *43*(spe), e20220141. DOI: 10.1590/1809-4430-eng.agric.v43nepe20220141/2023

De Neve, J.-E., & Sachs, J. D. (2020). The SDGs and human well-being: A global analysis of synergies, trade-offs, and regional differences. *Scientific Reports, 10*(1), 15113. DOI: 10.1038/s41598-020-71916-9

de Paula, J., & Farah, A. (2022). Phenolic compounds in coffee seeds and by-products. In *Coffee Science*. CRC Press. DOI: 10.1201/9781003043133-11

Delfani, P., Thuraga, V., Banerjee, B., & Chawade, A. (2024). Integrative approaches in modern agriculture: IoT, ML and AI for disease forecasting amidst climate change. *Precision Agriculture, 25*(5), 2589–2613. DOI: 10.1007/s11119-024-10164-7

Delgado Cadena, M. V. (2020). Gender job gaps and challenges in the digital economy: Findings from global governance entities. *Cuadernos Americanos, 36*(67), 158–171. DOI: 10.25100/cdea.v36i67.8767

Deng, X., & Yu, Z. (2022). A systematic review of machine-translation-assisted language learning for sustainable education. *Sustainability (Basel), 14*(13), 7598. DOI: 10.3390/su14137598

Devlin, J., Chang, M. W., Lee, K., & Toutanova, K. (2019). BERT: Pre-training of deep bidirectional transformers for language understanding. Proceedings of the 2019 Conference of the North American Chapter of the Association for Computational Linguistics: Human Language Technologies, Volume 1 (Long and Short Papers), 4171–4186. DOI: 10.18653/v1/N19-1423

Dhiman, R., Miteff, S., Wang, Y., Ma, S.-C., Amirikas, R., & Fabian, B. (2024). Artificial Intelligence and Sustainability-A Review. *Analytics, 3*(1), 140–164. DOI: 10.3390/analytics3010008

Di Vaio, A., Palladino, R., Hassan, R., & Escobar, O. (2020). Artificial intelligence and business models in the sustainable development goals perspective: A systematic literature review. *Journal of Business Research, 121*, 283–314. DOI: 10.1016/j.jbusres.2020.08.019

Díaz-Rodríguez, N., Del Ser, J., Coeckelbergh, M., de Prado, M. L., Herrera-Viedma, E., & Herrera, F. (2023). Connecting the dots in trustworthy Artificial Intelligence: From AI principles, ethics, and key requirements to responsible AI systems and regulation. *Information Fusion, 99*, 101896. DOI: 10.1016/j.inffus.2023.101896

Dildar, M., Akram, S., Irfan, M., Khan, H. U., Ramzan, M., Mahmood, A. R., Alsaiari, S. A., Saeed, A. H. M., Alraddadi, M. O., & Mahnashi, M. H. (2021). Skin cancer detection: A review using deep learning techniques. *International Journal of Environmental Research and Public Health, 18*(10), 5479. Advance online publication. DOI: 10.3390/ijerph18105479 PMID: 34065430

Dinda, S. (2004). Environmental Kuznets curve hypothesis: A survey. *Ecological Economics, 49*(4), 431–455. DOI: 10.1016/j.ecolecon.2004.02.011

Dobreva, M., Rukavina, T., Stamou, V., Vidaki, A. N., & Zacharopoulou, L. (2023). A Multimodal Installation Exploring Gender Bias in Artificial Intelligence. In Antona, M., & Stephanidis, C., (Eds.), *Proceedings of HCII 2023, Universal access to human-computer interaction* (pp. 27-46). Springer. DOI: 10.1007/978-3-031-35681-0_2

Dodampegama, S., Hou, L., Asadi, E., Zhang, G., & Setunge, S. (2024). Revolutionizing construction and demolition waste sorting: Insights from artificial intelligence and robotic applications. *Resources, Conservation and Recycling, 202*, 107375. DOI: 10.1016/j.resconrec.2023.107375

Dominguez-Sanchez, A., Cazorla, M., & Orts-Escolano, S. (2018). A new dataset and performance evaluation of a region-based cnn for urban object detection. *Electronics (Basel), 7*(11), 301. DOI: 10.3390/electronics7110301

Dwivedi, A., Sahu, S., & Srivastava, A. (2024, December). AI-Powered Real-Time Text Editor with Multilingual Translation and Speech Recognition. In 2024 IEEE 16th International Conference on Computational Intelligence and Communication Networks (CICN) (pp. 1335-1340). IEEE.

Dwivedi, Y. K., Hughes, L., Ismagilova, E., Aarts, G., Coombs, C., Crick, T., Duan, Y., Dwivedi, R., Edwards, J., Eirug, A., Galanos, V., Ilavarasan, P. V., Janssen, M., Jones, P., Kar, A. K., Kizgin, H., Kronemann, B., Lal, B., Lucini, B., & Williams, M. D. (2021). Artificial Intelligence (AI): Multidisciplinary perspectives on emerging challenges, opportunities, and agenda for research, practice and policy. *International Journal of Information Management, 57*, 101994. DOI: 10.1016/j.ijinfomgt.2019.08.002

Ejjami, R. (2024). The future of learning: AI-based curriculum development. International Journal For Multidisciplinary Research, 6(4).

Elashiri, M. A., Rajesh, A., Nath Pandey, S., Kumar Shukla, S., Urooj, S., & Lay-Ekuakille, A. (2022). Ensemble of weighted deep concatenated features for the skin disease classification model using modified long short term memory. *Biomedical Signal Processing and Control, 76*(April), 103729. DOI: 10.1016/j.bspc.2022.103729

Elbasi, E., Mostafa, N., Zaki, C., AlArnaout, Z., Topcu, A. E., & Saker, L. (2024). Optimizing agricultural data analysis techniques through ai-powered decision-making processes. *Applied Sciences (Basel, Switzerland), 14*(17), 8018. DOI: 10.3390/app14178018

Ellahi, R. M., Wood, L. C., & Bekhit, A. E.-D. A. (2024). Blockchain-Driven Food Supply Chains: A Systematic Review for Unexplored Opportunities. *Applied Sciences (Basel, Switzerland)*, *14*(19), 8944. DOI: 10.3390/app14198944

Elson, D. (2017). Recognize, reduce, and redistribute unpaid care work: How to close the gender gap. *New Labor Forum*, *26*(2), 52–61. DOI: 10.1177/1095796017700135

Elufioye, O. A., Ike, C. U., Odeyemi, O., Usman, F. O., & Mhlongo, N. Z. (2024). Ai-Driven predictive analytics in agricultural supply chains: A review: assessing the benefits and challenges of ai in forecasting demand and optimizing supply in agriculture. *Computer Science & IT Research Journal*, *5*(2), 473–497. DOI: 10.51594/csitrj.v5i2.817

Emenike, S. N., & Falcone, G. (2020). A review on energy supply chain resilience through optimization. *Renewable & Sustainable Energy Reviews*, *134*, 110088. DOI: 10.1016/j.rser.2020.110088

Emon, M. M. H. (2025c). Overcoming Hurdles: Navigating Challenges in the Adoption of Smart Logistics. In *Emerging Trends in Smart Logistics Technologies* (pp. 197–228). IGI Global Scientific Publishing. DOI: 10.4018/979-8-3373-2434-0.ch007

Emon, M. M. H., & Chowdhury, M. S. A. (2025). AI and IoT-Powered Smart Logistics: Transforming Supply Chains for Efficiency and Sustainability. In *Emerging Trends in Smart Logistics Technologies* (pp. 45–72). IGI Global Scientific Publishing. DOI: 10.4018/979-8-3373-2434-0.ch002

Emon, M. M. H. (2023). A Systematic Review of the Causes and Consequences of Price Hikes in Bangladesh. *Review of Business and Economics Studies*, *11*(2), 49–58. DOI: 10.26794/2308-944X-2023-11-2-49-58

Emon, M. M. H. (2025a). The Mediating Role of Supply Chain Responsiveness in the Relationship Between Key Supply Chain Drivers and Performance: Evidence from the FMCG Industry. *Brazilian Journal of Operations & Production Management*, *22*(1), 2580. DOI: 10.14488/BJOPM.2580.2025

Emon, M. M. H. (2025b). Leveraging AI on Social Media & Digital Platforms to Enhance English Language Teaching and Learning. In *AI-Powered English Teaching* (pp. 211–238). IGI Global Scientific Publishing., DOI: 10.4018/979-8-3373-1952-0.ch007

Emon, M. M. H., & Khan, T. (2024). A Systematic Literature Review on Sustainability Integration and Marketing Intelligence in the Era of Artificial Intelligence. *Review of Business and Economics Studies*, *12*(4), 6–28. DOI: 10.26794/2308-944X-2024-12-4-6-28

Emon, M. M. H., & Khan, T. (2025a). The mediating role of attitude towards the technology in shaping artificial intelligence usage among professionals. *Telematics and Informatics Reports*, *17*, 100188. DOI: 10.1016/j.teler.2025.100188

Emon, M. M. H., & Khan, T. (2025b). The Rise of Circular Supply Chains: Recycling and Closed-Loop Systems Could Mitigate Inflationary Pressures. In *Supply Chain Disruptions and Impact on Global Inflation* (pp. 195–226). IGI Global. DOI: 10.4018/979-8-3373-1982-7.ch008

Endut, N., Hamzah, W., Ismail, I., Yusof, M., Baker, Y., & Yusoff, H. (2022). A systematic literature review on multi-label classification based on machine learning algorithms. *TEM Journal*, 658–666. https://doi.org/DOI: 10.18421/tem112-20

Eriksson, S. (2024). The centrality of law for EU sustainable finance markets: Outlining a research agenda. *Review of European, Comparative & International Environmental Law*, *33*(1), 57–69. DOI: 10.1111/reel.12538

Erling, E. J., Seargeant, P., & Solly, M. (2014). English in rural Bangladesh: How is language education perceived as a resource for development in rural communities? *English Today*, *30*(4), 15–21. DOI: 10.1017/S0266078414000352

Eron, F., Noman, M., de Oliveira, R. R., & Chalfun-Júnior, A. (2024). Computer Vision-Aided Intelligent Monitoring of Coffee: Towards Sustainable Coffee Production. *Scientia Horticulturae*, *327*, 112847–112847. DOI: 10.1016/j.scienta.2024.112847

Esteva, A., Kuprel, B., Novoa, R. A., Ko, J., Swetter, S. M., Blau, H. M., & Thrun, S. (2017). Dermatologist-level classification of skin cancer with deep neural networks. *Nature*, *542*(7639), 115–118. DOI: 10.1038/nature21056 PMID: 28117445

Facer, K., & Selwyn, N. (2021). *Digital technology and the futures of education: Towards 'Non-Stupid'optimism. Futures of Education initiative*. UNESCO.

Falbo, A., & LaCroix, T. (2021). Est-ce que vous compute? Code-switching, cultural identity, and AI. *ArXiv Preprint ArXiv:2112.08256*.

Faludi, J. (2023). How to create social value through digital social innovation? Unlocking the potential of the social value creation of digital start-ups. *Journal of Social Entrepreneurship*, *14*(1), 73–90. DOI: 10.1080/19420676.2020.1823871

Fan, Z., Yan, Z., & Wen, S. (2023). Deep learning and artificial intelligence in sustainability: A review of SDGs, renewable energy, and environmental health. *Sustainability (Basel)*, *15*(18), 13493. DOI: 10.3390/su151813493

Farahani, M., & Ghasemi, G. (2024). Artificial intelligence and inequality: Challenges and opportunities. *International Journal of Innovation in Education, 9*, 78–99.

Farea, E., Saleh, R. A. A., AbuAlkebash, H., Farea, A. A. R., & Al-antari, M. A. (2024). A hybrid deep learning skin cancer prediction framework. *Engineering Science and Technology, an International Journal, 57*(August), 101818. DOI: 10.1016/j.jestch.2024.101818

Farmanesh, P., Vehbi, A., & Solati Dehkordi, N. (2025). AI literacy in achieving Sustainable Development Goals: The interplay of student engagement and anxiety reduction in Northern Cyprus universities. *Sustainability (Basel), 17*(11), 4763. DOI: 10.3390/su17114763

Farooqui, N. A., Haleem, M., Khan, W., & Ishrat, M. (2024). Precision Agriculture and Predictive Analytics: Enhancing Agricultural Efficiency and Yield. In N. Singh, S. Birla, M. D. Ansari, & N. K. Shukla (Eds.), *Intelligent Techniques for Predictive Data Analytics* (1st ed., pp. 171–188). Wiley. DOI: 10.1002/9781394227990.ch9

Fatemi, M., Pakzad, M., & Ghazinoory, S. (2024). Implementing RIS3 (Research and Innovation Strategies for Smart Specialization) to unlock Iran's regional potential. *Innovation (Abingdon)*, 1–18. DOI: 10.1080/13511610.2024.2430235

Felipe-Lucia, M. R., Soliveres, S., Penone, C., Manning, P., Van der Plas, F., Boch, S., & Fischer, M. (2020). Land-use intensity alters networks between biodiversity, ecosystem functions, and services. *Proceedings of the National Academy of Sciences of the United States of America, 117*(45), 28140–28149. DOI: 10.1073/pnas.2016210117

Feng, S., Shafiei, M. W. M., Ng, T. F., Ren, J., & Jiang, Y. (2024). The intersection of economic growth and environmental sustainability in China: Pathways to achieving SDG. *Energy Strategy Reviews, 55*, 101530. DOI: 10.1016/j.esr.2024.101530

Ferk Savec, V., & Jedrinović, S. (2025). The role of AI implementation in higher education in achieving the Sustainable Development Goals: A case study from Slovenia. *Sustainability (Basel), 17*(1), 183. DOI: 10.3390/su17010183

Fernandez, R. M. (2020). SDG3 good health and well-being: integration and connection with other SDGs. Good Health and Well-Being, 629-636.

Fernandez, R. M. (2020). SDG3 Good Health and Well-Being: Integration and Connection with Other SDGs. In Leal Filho, W., Wall, T., Azul, A. M., Brandli, L., & Özuyar, P. G. (Eds.), *Good Health and Well-Being* (pp. 629–636). Springer International Publishing. DOI: 10.1007/978-3-319-95681-7_64

Filho, W., Salvia, A. L., & Eustachio, J. H. P. P. (2023). An overview of the engagement of higher education institutions in the implementation of the UN Sustainable Development Goals. *Journal of Cleaner Production, 386*, 135694. DOI: 10.1016/j.jclepro.2022.135694

Filho, W., Sálvia, A., Frankenberger, F., Akib, N., Sen, S., Sivapalan, S., & Emblen-Perry, K. (2020). Governance and sustainable development at higher education institutions. *Environment, Development and Sustainability, 23*(4), 6002–6020. DOI: 10.1007/s10668-020-00859-y

Findler, F., Schönherr, N., Lozano, R., Reider, D., & Martinuzzi, A. (2019). The impacts of higher education institutions on sustainable development. *International Journal of Sustainability in Higher Education, 20*(1), 23–38. DOI: 10.1108/IJSHE-07-2017-0114

Franca, A. S., & Oliveira, L. S. (2019). Coffee. In Pan, Z., Zhang, R., & Zicari, S. (Eds.), *Integrated Processing Technologies for Food and Agricultural By-Products* (pp. 413–438). Academic Press. DOI: 10.1016/B978-0-12-814138-0.00017-4

Franchini, D. (2025). When finance becomes a weapon: The challenge of central bank sanctions under international law. *Journal of International Trade Law & Policy, 24*(1), 28–56. DOI: 10.1108/JITLP-07-2024-0041

Fryxell, A. R. (2021). Artificial eye: The modernist origins of AI's gender problem. *Discourse (Berkeley, Calif.), 43*(1), 31–64. DOI: 10.13110/discourse.43.1.0031

Fulton, K., Archibald, A., Hudson, C., Rogers, J., Peecksen, S., & Heap, T. (2023). Cultivating responsible citizenship in a non-traditional degree program through a service-inclusive pedagogy. *Journal of Adult and Continuing Education, 29*(2), 485–504. DOI: 10.1177/14779714231153815

Garcia Ramos, J., & Wilson-Kennedy, Z. (2024). Promoting equity and addressing concerns in teaching and learning with artificial intelligence. *Frontiers in Education, 9*, 1487882. DOI: 10.3389/feduc.2024.1487882

García-Sánchez, I.-M., & García-Sánchez, A. (2020). Corporate Social Responsibility during COVID-19 Pandemic. *Journal of Open Innovation, 6*(4), 126. DOI: 10.3390/joitmc6040126

García-Ull, F. J., & Melero-Lázaro, M. (2023). Gender stereotypes in AI-generated images. *El Profesional de la Información, 32*(5), 1–13.

Geng, Y., & Zhao, N. (2020). Measurement of sustainable higher education development: Evidence from China. *PLoS One, 15*(6), e0233747. DOI: 10.1371/journal.pone.0233747

George, B., & Wooden, O. (2023). Managing the Strategic Transformation of Higher Education through Artificial Intelligence. *Administrative Sciences, 13*(9), 196. DOI: 10.3390/admsci13090196

Getachew, A. T., & Chun, B. S. (2017). Influence of pretreatment and modifiers on subcritical water liquefaction of spent coffee grounds: A green waste valorization approach. *Journal of Cleaner Production, 142*, 3719–3727. DOI: 10.1016/j.jclepro.2016.10.096

Getahun, S., Kefale, H., & Gelaye, Y. (2024). Application of Precision Agriculture Technologies for Sustainable Crop Production and Environmental Sustainability: A Systematic Review. *TheScientificWorldJournal, 2024*(1), 2126734. DOI: 10.1155/2024/2126734 PMID: 39421732

Ghobadpour, A., Monsalve, G., Cardenas, A., & Mousazadeh, H. (2022). Off-road electric vehicles and autonomous robots in agricultural sector: Trends, challenges, and opportunities. *Vehicles (Basel), 4*(3), 843–864. DOI: 10.3390/vehicles4030047

Gikunda, K. (2024). Harnessing Artificial Intelligence for Sustainable Agricultural Development in Africa: Opportunities, Challenges, and Impact. arXiv preprint arXiv:2401.06171.

Gill, S. S., Wu, H., Patros, P., Ottaviani, C., Arora, P., Pujol, V. C., ... Buyya, R. (2024). Modern computing: Vision and challenges. Telematics and Informatics Reports, 100116.

Gill, A. S., & Germann, S. (2022). Conceptual and normative approaches to AI governance for a global digital ecosystem supportive of the UN Sustainable Development Goals (SDGs). *AI and Ethics, 2*(2), 293–301. DOI: 10.1007/s43681-021-00058-z PMID: 34790947

Gill, H. K., & Garg, H. (2014). Pesticide: Environmental impacts and management strategies. *Pesticides-Toxic Aspects, 8*(187), 10–5772.

Giovanola, B., & Tiribelli, S. (2023). Beyond bias and discrimination: Redefining the AI ethics principle of fairness in healthcare machine-learning algorithms. *AI & Society, 38*(2), 549–563. DOI: 10.1007/s00146-022-01455-6 PMID: 35615443

Giuliani, E., Ciravegna, L., Vezzulli, A., & Kilian, B. (2017). Decoupling Standards from Practice: The Impact of In-House Certifications on Coffee Farms' Environmental and Social Conduct. *World Development, 96*, 294–314. DOI: 10.1016/j.worlddev.2017.03.013

Glenn, A. J., Moulin, A. P., Roy, A. K., & Wilson, H. F. (2021). Soil nitrous oxide emissions from no-till canola production under variable rate nitrogen fertilizer management. *Geoderma, 385*, 114857. DOI: 10.1016/j.geoderma.2020.114857

Gligorea, I., Cioca, M., Oancea, R., Gorski, A.-T., Gorski, H., & Tudorache, P. (2023). Adaptive learning using artificial intelligence in e-learning: A literature review. *Education Sciences, 13*(12), 1216. DOI: 10.3390/educsci13121216

Göçoğlu, V., & Göçoğlu, İ. D. (2024). Local potentials for achieving sustainable development goals: Qualitative evidence from local governments in Türkiye. *Local Government Studies*, •••, 1–22.

Golding, N., Burstein, R., Longbottom, J., Browne, A. J., Fullman, N., Sorichetta, A., & Hay, S. I. (2017). Mapping under-5 and neonatal mortality in Africa, 2000–2015: A baseline analysis for the Sustainable Development Goals. *Lancet, 390*(10108), 2171–2182. DOI: 10.1016/S0140-6736(17)31758-0

Gong, J., Ma, H., Teng, Z., Teng, Q., Zhang, H., Du, L., Chen, S., Bhuiyan, M. Z. A., Li, J., & Liu, M. (2020). Hierarchical graph transformer-based deep learning model for large-scale multi-label text classification. *IEEE Access : Practical Innovations, Open Solutions, 8*, 30885–30896. DOI: 10.1109/ACCESS.2020.2972751

Goralski, M. A., & Tan, T. K. (2020). Artificial intelligence and sustainable development. *International Journal of Management Education, 18*(1), 100330. DOI: 10.1016/j.ijme.2019.100330

Gottstein, V., Bernhardt, M., Dilger, E., Keller, J., Breitling-Utzmann, C. M., Schwarz, S., Kuballa, T., Lachenmeier, D. W., & Bunzel, M. (2021). Coffee Silver Skin: Chemical Characterization with Special Consideration of Dietary Fiber and Heat-Induced Contaminants. *Foods, 10*(8), 1705. DOI: 10.3390/foods10081705 PMID: 34441483

Gouda, W., Sama, N. U., Al-Waakid, G., Humayun, M., & Jhanjhi, N. Z. (2022). Detection of Skin Cancer Based on Skin Lesion Images Using Deep Learning. Healthcare (Basel, Switzerland, 10(7). DOI: 10.3390/healthcare10071183

Gouvea, B. M., Torres, C., Franca, A. S., Oliveira, L. S., & Oliveira, E. S. (2009). Feasibility of ethanol production from coffee husks. *Biotechnology Letters, 31*(9), 1315–1319. DOI: 10.1007/s10529-009-0023-4 PMID: 19466561

Griffiths, T. G. (2021). Education to transform the world: Limits and possibilities in and against the SDGs and ESD. *International Studies in Sociology of Education, 30*(1-2), 73–92. Advance online publication. DOI: 10.1080/09620214.2020.1854829

Guebsi, R., Mami, S., & Chokmani, K. (2024). Drones in precision agriculture: A comprehensive review of applications, technologies, and challenges. *Drones (Basel)*, *8*(11), 686. DOI: 10.3390/drones8110686

Guerriero, V., & Tallini, M. (2025). Power law distribution and multi-scale analysis in Earth sciences, finance, and other fields: Some guidelines to parameter estimation. *Chaos (Woodbury, N.Y.)*, *35*(6), 063102. Advance online publication. DOI: 10.1063/5.0259215 PMID: 40455195

Gunaseelan, J., Sundaram, S., & Mariyappan, B. (2023). A Design and Implementation Using an Innovative Deep-Learning Algorithm for Garbage Segregation. *Sensors (Basel)*, *23*(18), 7963–7963. DOI: 10.3390/s23187963 PMID: 37766020

Gunawan, K. D. H., Kaniawati, I., & Setiawan, W. (2021). The responses to artificial intelligence in teacher integrated science learning training program. *Journal of Physics: Conference Series*, *2098*(1), 12034. DOI: 10.1088/1742-6596/2098/1/012034

Gupta, R., Srivastava, D., Sahu, M., Tiwari, S., Ambasta, R. K., & Kumar, P. (2021). Artificial intelligence to deep learning: Machine intelligence approach for drug discovery. *Molecular Diversity*, *25*(3), 1315–1360. DOI: 10.1007/s11030-021-10217-3 PMID: 33844136

Gutierrez-Mijares, M. E., Josa, I., Casanovas-Rubio, M. D. M., & Aguado, A. (2023). Methods for assessing sustainability performance at higher education institutions: A review. *Studies in Higher Education*, *48*(8), 1137–1158. DOI: 10.1080/03075079.2023.2185774

Habehh, H., & Gohel, S. (2021). Machine learning in healthcare. *Current Genomics*, *22*(4), 291–300. DOI: 10.2174/1389202922666210705124359 PMID: 35273459

Haidegger, T., Mai, V., Mörch, C. M., Boesl, D. O., Jacobs, A., Khamis, A., Lach, L., & Vanderborght, B. (2023). Robotics: Enabler and inhibitor of the sustainable development goals. *Sustainable Production and Consumption*, *43*, 422–434. DOI: 10.1016/j.spc.2023.11.011

Haleem, A., Javaid, M., Qadri, M. A., & Suman, R. (2022). Understanding the role of digital technologies in education: A review. *Sustainable Operations and Computers*, *3*, 275–285. DOI: 10.1016/j.susoc.2022.05.004

Haleem, A., Javaid, M., Singh, R. P., & Suman, R. (2021). Telemedicine for healthcare: Capabilities, features, barriers, and applications. *Sensors International*, *2*(100117), 1–12. DOI: 10.1016/j.sintl.2021.100117 PMID: 34806053

Halis, R., Ghazali, A., & Zakarya, I. A. (2024). Biofuels from Forest Logging Residues. In Bisaria, V. (Ed.), *Handbook of Biorefinery Research and Technology: Production of Biofuels and Biochemicals* (pp. 593–623). Springer Nature Singapore. DOI: 10.1007/978-94-007-6724-9_41-1

Halkiopoulos, C., & Gkintoni, E. (2024). Leveraging AI in E-Learning: Personalized Learning and Adaptive Assessment through Cognitive Neuropsychology—A Systematic Analysis. *Electronics (Basel)*, *13*(18), 3762. DOI: 10.3390/electronics13183762

Hall, P., & Ellis, D. (2023). A systematic review of socio-technical gender bias in AI algorithms. *Online Information Review*, *47*(7), 1264–1279. DOI: 10.1108/OIR-08-2021-0452

Hamrani, A., Akbarzadeh, A., & Madramootoo, C. A. (2020). Machine learning for predicting greenhouse gas emissions from agricultural soils. *The Science of the Total Environment*, *741*, 140338. DOI: 10.1016/j.scitotenv.2020.140338 PMID: 32610233

Hasan, M. K., Elahi, M. T. E., Alam, M. A., Jawad, M. T., & Martí, R. (2022). DermoExpert: Skin lesion classification using a hybrid convolutional neural network through segmentation, transfer learning, and augmentation. *Informatics in Medicine Unlocked*, *28*, 100819. DOI: 10.1016/j.imu.2021.100819

Hassani, H., Huang, X., & MacFeely, S. (2022). Impactful digital twin in the healthcare revolution. *Big Data and Cognitive Computing*, *6*(3), 83. DOI: 10.3390/bdcc6030083

Hathaliya, J. J., & Tanwar, S. (2020). An exhaustive survey on security and privacy issues in Healthcare 4.0. *Computer Communications*, *153*, 311–335. DOI: 10.1016/j.comcom.2020.02.018

He, K. Y., Ge, D., & He, M. M. (2017). Big data analytics for genomic medicine. *International Journal of Molecular Sciences*, *18*(2), 412. DOI: 10.3390/ijms18020412 PMID: 28212287

Helm, P., Bella, G., Koch, G., & Giunchiglia, F. (2023). Diversity and language technology: how techno-linguistic bias can cause epistemic injustice. *ArXiv Preprint ArXiv:2307.13714.*

Hemathilake, D., & Gunathilake, D. (2022). Agricultural productivity and food supply to meet increased demands. In *Future foods* (pp. 539–553). Elsevier. DOI: 10.1016/B978-0-323-91001-9.00016-5

Hernández-Varela, J. D., & Medina, D. I. (2023). Revalorization of Coffee Residues: Advances in the Development of Eco-Friendly Biobased Potential Food Packaging. *Polymers*, *15*(13), 2823. DOI: 10.3390/polym15132823 PMID: 37447469

Hickel, J. (2019). The contradiction of the Sustainable Development Goals: Growth versus ecology. *Sustainable Development*, *27*(5), 873–884. DOI: 10.1002/sd.1947

Hijosa-Valsero, M., Garita-Cambronero, J., Paniagua-García, A. I., & Díez-Antolínez, R. (2018). Biobutanol production from coffee silverskin. *Microbial Cell Factories*, *17*(1), 154. DOI: 10.1186/s12934-018-1002-z PMID: 30261894

Hite, K. A., & Seitz, J. L. (2021). *Global issues: an introduction*. John Wiley & Sons.

Hite, R., Childers, G., Jones, G., Corin, E., & Pereyra, M. (2020). Describing the experiences of students with ADHD learning science content with emerging technologies. *Journal of Science Education for Students with Disabilities*, *24*(1), 1–34. DOI: 10.14448/jsesd.13.0012

Holstein, K., & Doroudi, S. (2021). Equity and artificial intelligence in education: will" aied" amplify or alleviate inequities in education? arXiv preprint arXiv:2104.12920.

Hoque, A., Mazumder, A. S., Roy, S., Saikia, P., & Kumar, K. (2025). *Transformative Approaches to Agricultural Sustainability: Automation, Smart Greenhouses, and AI*. Academic Press.

Hoque, A. (2024). Artificial Intelligence in Post-Harvest Drying Technologies: A Comprehensive Review on Optimization, Quality Enhancement, and Energy Efficiency. *International Journal of Science and Research (Raipur, India)*, *13*(11), 493–502. DOI: 10.21275/SR241107163717

Hoque, A., & Padhiary, M. (2024). Automation and AI in Precision Agriculture: Innovations for Enhanced Crop Management and Sustainability. *Asian Journal of Research in Computer Science*, *17*(10), 95–109. DOI: 10.9734/ajrcos/2024/v17i10512

Hoque, A., Padhiary, M., Prasad, G., & Kumar, K. (2025). Real-Time Data Processing in Agricultural Robotics. In Bora, D. J., & Bania, R. K. (Eds.), *Computer Vision Techniques for Agricultural Advancements* (pp. 431–468). IGI Global. DOI: 10.4018/979-8-3693-8019-2.ch014

Horan, D. (2020). Enabling integrated policymaking with the Sustainable Development Goals: An application to Ireland. *Sustainability*, *12*(18), 7800. DOI: 10.3390/su12187800

Hou, Z. (2021). Research on adopting artificial intelligence technology to improve effectiveness of vocational college English learning. *Journal of Physics: Conference Series*, *1744*(4), 42122. DOI: 10.1088/1742-6596/1744/4/042122

How, M. L., Chan, Y. J., & Cheah, S. M. (2020). Predictive insights for improving the resilience of global food security using artificial intelligence. *Sustainability (Basel), 12*(15), 6272. DOI: 10.3390/su12156272

Huadong, G. (2022). *Big Earth data in support of the Sustainable Development Goals*. International Research Center of Big Data for Sustainable Development Goals.

Hussein, A., Sallam, M. E., & Abdalla, M. Y. A. (2023). Exploring New Horizons: Surgical Robots Supported by Artificial Intelligence. *Mesopotamian Journal of Artificial Intelligence in Healthcare, 2022*, 40–44. DOI: 10.58496/MJAIH/2023/008

Hutson, J., & Ceballos, J. (2023). Rethinking Education in the Age of AI: The Importance of Developing Durable Skills in the Industry 4.0. *Journal of Information Economics, 1*, 26-36. .DOI: 10.58567/jie01020002

Imran, A., Nasir, A., Bilal, M., Sun, G., Alzahrani, A., & Almuhaimeed, A. (2022). Skin Cancer Detection Using Combined Decision of Deep Learners. *IEEE Access : Practical Innovations, Open Solutions, 10*(September), 118198–118212. DOI: 10.1109/ACCESS.2022.3220329

International Council for Science. (2017). *A guide to SDG interactions: From science to implementation*. https://council.science/wp-content/uploads/2017/05/SDGs-Guide-to-Interactions.pdf

Ip, K. (2024). The rise of EdTech: Transforming education through entrepreneurial ventures. Advances in Online Education: A Peer-Reviewed Journal, 3(2), 177-193.

Iriondo-DeHond, A., Herrera, T., & Del Castillo, M. D. (2020). Health Benefits of Silverskin. In *Food Wastes and By-products* (pp. 353–371). John Wiley & Sons, Ltd. DOI: 10.1002/9781119534167.ch12

Ismail, I. A., & Aloshi, J. M. (2024). *Data Privacy in AI-Driven Education*. DOI: 10.4018/979-8-3693-5443-8.ch008

Jain, S., Singhania, U., Tripathy, B., Nasr, E. A., Aboudaif, M. K., & Kamrani, A. K. (2021). Deep Learning-Based Transfer Learning for Classification of Skin Cancer. Sensors (Basel, Switzerland, 21(23). DOI: 10.3390/s21238142

Jain, H., Dhupper, R., Shrivastava, A., Kumar, D., & Kumari, M. (2023). AI-enabled strategies for climate change adaptation: Protecting communities, infrastructure, and businesses from the impacts of climate change. *Computational Urban Science, 3*(1), 25. DOI: 10.1007/s43762-023-00100-2

Jamal, S. M., Yadav, R. K., & Dayal, J. (2024). Innovative Soil Management Technologies for a Changing Climate. In Kanga, S., Singh, S. K., Shevkani, K., Pathak, V., & Sajan, B. (Eds.), *Transforming Agricultural Management for a Sustainable Future* (pp. 203–213). Springer Nature Switzerland. DOI: 10.1007/978-3-031-63430-7_10

Javaid, M., Haleem, A., Khan, I. H., & Suman, R. (2023). Understanding the potential applications of Artificial Intelligence in Agriculture Sector. *Advanced Agrochem*, *2*(1), 15–30. DOI: 10.1016/j.aac.2022.10.001

Javaid, M., Haleem, A., Pratap Singh, R., Suman, R., & Rab, S. (2022). Significance of machine learning in healthcare: Features, pillars and applications. *International Journal of Intelligent Networks*, *3*, 58–73. DOI: 10.1016/j.ijin.2022.05.002

Jayachandran, S. (2015). The roots of gender inequality in developing countries. *Annual Review of Economics*, *7*(1), 63–88. DOI: 10.1146/annurev-economics-080614-115404

Jejeniwa, T. O., Mhlongo, N. Z., & Jejeniwa, T. O. (2024). AI solutions for developmental economics: Opportunities and challenges in financial inclusion and poverty alleviation. *International Journal of Advanced Economics*, *6*(4), 108–123. DOI: 10.51594/ijae.v6i4.1073

Jia, F., Sun, D., Ma, Q., & Looi, C.-K. (2022). Developing an AI-based learning system for L2 learners' authentic and ubiquitous learning in English language. *Sustainability (Basel)*, *14*(23), 15527. DOI: 10.3390/su142315527

Jinnai, S., Yamazaki, N., Hirano, Y., Sugawara, Y., Ohe, Y., & Hamamoto, R. (2020). The development of a skin cancer classification system for pigmented skin lesions using deep learning. *Biomolecules*, *10*(8), 1–13. DOI: 10.3390/biom10081123 PMID: 32751349

Johnson, K., Liu, Y., & Lu, M. (2022). A Review of Recent Advances in Spent Coffee Grounds Upcycle Technologies and Practices. *Frontiers in Chemical Engineering*, *4*, 838605. Advance online publication. DOI: 10.3389/fceng.2022.838605

Kaewtubtim, T. (2024). Enhancing AI for gender equality: A multi-stakeholder approach. Feminist AI. https://feministai.pubpub.org/pub/8e8rgs6z

Kalantzis, M., & Cope, B. (2025). Literacy in the Time of Artificial Intelligence. *Reading Research Quarterly*, *60*(1), e591.DOI: 10.1002/rrq.591

Kalirajan, M., Mageshen, V. R., Aswitha, K., & Saranya, M. (2024). AI-Based Regulation of Water Supply and Pest Management in Farming. In Chouhan, S. S., Saxena, A., Singh, U. P., & Jain, S. (Eds.), *Artificial Intelligence Techniques in Smart Agriculture* (pp. 195–215). Springer Nature Singapore. DOI: 10.1007/978-981-97-5878-4_12

Kaplan, A. M., & Haenlein, M. (2019). Siri, Siri, in my hand: Who's the fairest in the land? On the interpretations, illustrations, and implications of artificial intelligence. *Business Horizons, 62*(1), 15–25. DOI: 10.1016/j.bushor.2018.08.004

Karakani, H. M. (2024). Supporting the measurement of the Sustainable Development Goals through the use of geospatial sentiment analysis: A case study of Africa. *IEEE Technology and Society Magazine, 43*(1), 70–85. .DOI: 10.1109/MTS.2024.3377459

Kashem, M. A., Shamsuddoha, M., Nasir, T., & Chowdhury, A. A. (2023). Supply Chain Disruption versus Optimization: A Review on Artificial Intelligence and Blockchain. *Knowledge (Beverly Hills, Calif.), 3*(1), 80.

Kaur, J., Khanna, R., Kumar, R., & Sunil, G. (2024). Role of Blockchain Technologies in Goods and Services Tax. *Proceedings - 2024 3rd International Conference on Sentiment Analysis and Deep Learning, ICSADL 2024*, 607–612. DOI: 10.1109/ICSADL61749.2024.00104

Kaur, R., Gupta, D., Madhukar, M., Singh, A., Abdelhaq, M., Alsaqour, R., Breñosa, J., & Goyal, N. (2022). E-Learning Environment Based Intelligent Profiling System for Enhancing User Adaptation. *Electronics (Basel), 11*(20), 3354. DOI: 10.3390/electronics11203354

Kay, M., Matuszek, C., & Munson, S. A. (2015). Unequal representation by gender in image search results. *CHI, 2015*, 3819–3828.

Kayyali, M. (2025a). AI in Higher Education: Revolutionizing Curriculum and Administration. In AI Adoption and Diffusion in Education (pp. 31-62). IGI Global Scientific Publishing.

Kayyali, M. (2025b). The Future of AI in Education: Predictions and Emerging Trends. Next-Generation AI Methodologies in Education, 367-406.

Kayyali, M. (2026a). AI in Higher Education: The Risk of Excluding Vulnerable Learners. In AI and New Forms of Exclusion (pp. 57-82). IGI Global Scientific Publishing.

Kayyali, M. (2026b). The Impact of AI on Classroom Dynamics in Higher Education: Shifting Roles for Professors and Students. In Responsible AI Integration in Education (pp. 151-180). IGI Global Scientific Publishing.

Kayyali, M. (2026c). Ethical AI and Automation in the Workplace. In Leading Inclusive Workplaces Through Digital Transformation and Organizational Change (pp. 103-138). IGI Global Scientific Publishing.

Kayyali, M. (2026d). Preparing Educators for the Future: Navigating AI Tools in English Language Teaching. In AI-Powered English Teaching (pp. 267-308). IGI Global Scientific Publishing.

Kayyali, M. (2024). Future possibilities and challenges of AI in education. In *Transforming education with generative AI: Prompt engineering and synthetic content creation* (pp. 118–137). IGI Global. DOI: 10.4018/979-8-3693-1351-0.ch006

Kazu, İ. Y., & Kuvvetli, M. (2023). Navigating the challenges of education management: Best practices for improving student outcomes. *European Journal of Science and Technology*, (49), 68–74. DOI: 10.31590/ejosat.1259005

Kebede, A. A., Kalogiannis, T., Van Mierlo, J., & Berecibar, M. (2022). A comprehensive review of stationary energy storage devices for large scale renewable energy sources grid integration. *Renewable & Sustainable Energy Reviews*, *159*, 112213. DOI: 10.1016/j.rser.2022.112213

Keerthana, D., Venugopal, V., Nath, M. K., & Mishra, M. (2023). Hybrid convolutional neural networks with SVM classifier for classification of skin cancer. Biomedical Engineering Advances, 5(July 2022), 100069. DOI: 10.1016/j.bea.2022.100069

Khakurel, J., Penzenstadler, B., Porras, J., Knutas, A., & Zhang, W. (2018). The rise of artificial intelligence under the lens of sustainability. *Technologies*, *6*(4), 1–19. DOI: 10.3390/technologies6040100

Khaleel, M., Murtaza, N., Mueen, Q. H., Ahmad, S. A., & Qadri, S. F. (2024). Use of AI in conservation and for understanding climate change. In *A Biologist s Guide to Artificial Intelligence* (pp. 201–240). Elsevier. DOI: 10.1016/B978-0-443-24001-0.00013-0

Khan, T., & Hasan Emon, M. M. (2024). Determinants of AI Image Generator Adoption Among Marketing Agencies: The Mediating Effects of Perceived Usefulness. *2024 IEEE 3rd International Conference on Robotics, Automation, Artificial-Intelligence and Internet-of-Things (RAAICON)*, 177–182. DOI: 10.1109/RAAICON64172.2024.10928548

Khan, T., Emon, M. M. H., & Nath, A. (2024). Quantifying the Effects of AI-Driven Inventory Management on Operational Efficiency in Online Retail. *2024 27th International Conference on Computer and Information Technology (ICCIT)*, 2092–2097. DOI: 10.1109/ICCIT64611.2024.11021996

Khan, T., Emon, M. M. H., & Rahman, S. (2024). Marketing Strategy Innovation via AI Adoption: A Study on Bangladeshi SMEs in the Context of Industry 5.0. *2024 6th International Conference on Sustainable Technologies for Industry 5.0 (STI)*, 1–6. DOI: 10.1109/STI64222.2024.10951050

Khan, T., Emon, M. M. H., Rahman, M. A., Hamid, A. B. A., & Yaakub, N. I. (2025). Bridging the Gap: Realizing GreenTech Potential. In *AI and Green Technology Applications in Society* (pp. 91–122). IGI Global Scientific Publishing. DOI: 10.4018/979-8-3693-9879-1.ch004

Khanal, U., Wilson, C., Rahman, S., Lee, B. L., & Hoang, V. N. (2021). Smallholder farmers' adaptation to climate change and its potential contribution to UN's sustainable development goals of zero hunger and no poverty. *Journal of Cleaner Production, 281*, 124999. DOI: 10.1016/j.jclepro.2020.124999

Khan, M. A., Saleh, A. M., Waseem, M., & Sajjad, I. A. (2022). Artificial intelligence enabled demand response: Prospects and challenges in smart grid environment. *IEEE Access : Practical Innovations, Open Solutions, 11*, 1477–1505. DOI: 10.1109/ACCESS.2022.3231444

Khan, M. S., Umer, H., & Faruqe, F. (2024). Artificial intelligence for low income countries. *Humanities & Social Sciences Communications, 11*(1), 1–13. DOI: 10.1057/s41599-024-03947-w

Khan, T., & Emon, M. M. H. (2024). Exploring the Potential of the Blue Economy: A Systematic Review of Strategies for Enhancing International Business in Bangladesh in the context of Indo-Pacific Region. *Review of Business and Economics Studies, 12*(2), 55–73. DOI: 10.26794/2308-944X-2024-12-2-55-73

Khan, T., & Emon, M. M. H. (2025). The role of digital supply chain practices in enhancing firm performance: Insights from the manufacturing sector of Bangladesh. *Brazilian Journal of Operations & Production Management, 22*(2), 2493. DOI: 10.14488/BJOPM.2493.2025

Khrais, L. T. (2020). Role of Artificial Intelligence in Shaping Consumer Demand in E-Commerce. *Future Internet, 12*(12), 226. DOI: 10.3390/fi12120226

Khreisat, M. N., Khilani, D., Rusho, M. A., Karkkulainen, E. A., Tabuena, A. C., & Uberas, A. D. (2024). Ethical implications of AI integration in educational decision-making: A systematic review. *Educational Administration: Theory and Practice, 30*(5), 8521–8527.

Kiat, P. E., Malek, M. A., & Shamsuddin, S. M. (2019). Artificial intelligence projection model for methane emission from livestock in Sarawak. *Sains Malaysiana, 48*(7), 1325–1332. DOI: 10.17576/jsm-2019-4807-02

Kibar, A. H., Ampa, A. T., & Nappu, S. (2023). A Study on EFL Teacher Strategies in Utilizing ICT for Regional Public Highschool of Indonesia. *Tamaddun, 22*(1), 1–10. DOI: 10.33096/tamaddun.v22i1.205

Kickbusch, I., & Alakija, A. (2023). The Sustainable Development Goals should be reset to prioritize poverty, health and climate. *Nature Medicine, 29*(10), 2399–2401. DOI: 10.1038/s41591-023-02546-7

Kim, J. (2025). Artificial intelligence in achieving sustainable development: Expectations of undergraduate students. *TechTrends, 69*(1), 138–148. DOI: 10.1007/s11528-024-01025-1

Kim, J., Lee, H., & Cho, Y. H. (2022). Learning design to support student-AI collaboration: Perspectives of leading teachers for AI in education. *Education and Information Technologies, 27*(5), 6069–6104. DOI: 10.1007/s10639-021-10831-6

Kiritchenko, S., & Mohammad, S. M. (2018). Examining gender and race bias in two hundred sentiment analysis systems. *Proceedings of NAACL-HLT,* 43-53. DOI: 10.18653/v1/S18-2005

Kirubakaran, S. J., Gunasekaran, A., Dolly, D. R. J., Jagannath, D. J., & Peter, J. D. (2023). A feasible approach to smart remote health monitoring: Subscription-based model. *Frontiers in Public Health, 11,* 1150455. DOI: 10.3389/fpubh.2023.1150455 PMID: 37113166

Kittichotsatsawat, Y., Jangkrajarng, V., & Tippayawong, K. Y. (2021). Enhancing Coffee Supply Chain towards Sustainable Growth with Big Data and Modern Agricultural Technologies. *Sustainability (Basel), 13*(8), 4593. DOI: 10.3390/su13084593

Kittler, H., Pehamberger, H., Wolff, K., & Binder, M. (2002). Diagnostic accuracy of dermoscopy. *The Lancet. Oncology, 3*(3), 159–165. DOI: 10.1016/S1470-2045(02)00679-4 PMID: 11902502

Kizilcec, R. F. (2024). To advance AI use in education, focus on understanding educators. *International Journal of Artificial Intelligence in Education, 34*(1), 12–19. DOI: 10.1007/s40593-023-00351-4

Kleespies, M. W., & Dierkes, P. W. (2022). The importance of the Sustainable Development Goals to students of environmental and sustainability studies—A global survey in 41 countries. *Humanities & Social Sciences Communications, 9*(1), 218. Advance online publication. DOI: 10.1057/s41599-022-01242-0

Knox, J., Wang, Y., & Gallagher, M. (2019). *Artificial intelligence and inclusive education*. Springer. DOI: 10.1007/978-981-13-8161-4

Koene, A. (2017). Algorithmic bias: Addressing growing concerns. *IEEE Technology and Society Magazine*, *36*(2), 31–32. DOI: 10.1109/MTS.2017.2697080

Kohli, P. (2023). Automated diagnosis of skin lesions using CNN and LSTM. *International Journal of Mechanical Engineering*, *6*(3), 4521–4530. DOI: 10.56452/6-3-667

Kollewe, J. (2018, July 9). Artificial intelligence will be a net UK jobs creator, finds report. *The Guardian*. https://www.theguardian.com/technology/2018/jul/09/artificial-intelligenceuk-jobs-report

Kordzadeh, N., & Ghasemaghaei, M. (2021). Algorithmic bias: Review, synthesis, and future research directions. *European Journal of Information Systems*, *1*, 1–23.

Korir, D. J., & Kilika, J. M. (2023). Effect of deployment of strategic leadership in the horticulture industry: A case study of selected flower farms in Kenya. *International Journal of Research in Business and Social Science, 12*(4), 163–174.

Kourmentza, C., Economou, Ch. N., Tsafrakidou, P., & Kornaros, M. (2018). Spent coffee grounds make much more than waste: Exploring recent advances and future exploitation strategies for the valorization of an emerging food waste stream. *Journal of Cleaner Production*, *172*, 980–992. DOI: 10.1016/j.jclepro.2017.10.088

Kousis, I., Perikos, I., Hatzilygeroudis, I., & Virvou, M. (2022). Deep learning methods for accurate skin cancer recognition and mobile application. *Electronics (Basel)*, *11*(9), 1–19. DOI: 10.3390/electronics11091294

Kroll, C., Warchold, A., & Pradhan, P. (2019). Sustainable Development Goals (SDGs): Are we successful in turning trade-offs into synergies? *Palgrave Communications*, *5*(1), 140. DOI: 10.1057/s41599-019-0335-5

Kshetri, N. (2021). Blockchain and sustainable supply chain management in developing countries. *International Journal of Information Management*, *60*, 102376. DOI: 10.1016/j.ijinfomgt.2021.102376

Kuleto, V., Ilić, M., Dumangiu, M., Ranković, M., Martins, O. M. D., Păun, D., & Mihoreanu, L. (2021). Exploring Opportunities and Challenges of Artificial Intelligence and Machine Learning in Higher Education Institutions. *Sustainability (Basel)*, *13*(18), 10424. DOI: 10.3390/su131810424

Kulkarni, A., Ramanathan, C., & Venugopal, V. (2024). Toward sustainable data practices: Integrating open data with SDG-based data lake frameworks. *IEEE Technology and Society Magazine*, *43*(1), 62–69. DOI: 10.1109/MTS.2024.3365591

Kumar, C. S., Padhy, A. B., Singh, A. P., & Reddy, K. H. K. (2025). A Dynamic Trading Approach Based on Walrasian Equilibrium in a Blockchain-Based NFT Framework for Sustainable Waste Management. *Mathematics, 13*(3), 521. DOI: 10.3390/math13030521

Kumar, R., Goel, R., Singh, T., Mohanty, S. M., Gupta, D., Alkhayyat, A., & Khanna, R. (2024). Sustainable Finance Factors in Indian Economy: Analysis on Policy of Climate Change and Energy Sector. *Fluctuation and Noise Letters, 23*(2), 2440004. Advance online publication. DOI: 10.1142/S0219477524400042

Kumar, V., Ashraf, A. R., & Nadeem, W. (2024). AI-powered marketing: What, where, and how? *International Journal of Information Management, 77*, 102783. DOI: 10.1016/j.ijinfomgt.2024.102783

Kunjumuhammed, S. K. (2024). Artificial Intelligence in Addressing Educational Inequality Dimensions in Higher Education Institutions (HEIs): A Critical Review. Risks and Challenges of AI-Driven Finance: Bias, Ethics, and Security, 146-164.

Kunwar, S. (2023, April). *MWaste: A Deep Learning Approach to Manage Household Waste*. arXiv. /arXiv.2304.14498DOI: 10.20944/preprints202304.0066.v1

Kuteesa, K. N., Akpuokwe, C. U., & Udeh, C. A. (2024). Gender equity in education: Addressing challenges and promoting opportunities for social empowerment. *International Journal of Applied Research in Social Sciences, 6*(4), 631–641. DOI: 10.51594/ijarss.v6i4.1034

Labadze, L., Grigolia, M., & Machaidze, L. (2023). Role of AI chatbots in education: Systematic literature review. *International Journal of Educational Technology in Higher Education, 20*(1), 56. DOI: 10.1186/s41239-023-00426-1

Lakhiar, I. A., Yan, H., Zhang, C., Wang, G., He, B., Hao, B., Han, Y., Wang, B., Bao, R., Syed, T. N., Chauhdary, J. N., & Rakibuzzaman, M. (2024). A Review of Precision Irrigation Water-Saving Technology under Changing Climate for Enhancing Water Use Efficiency, Crop Yield, and Environmental Footprints. *Agriculture, 14*(7), 1141. DOI: 10.3390/agriculture14071141

Lamb, K. J., Dowsett, M. R., Chatzipanagis, K., Scullion, Z. W., Kröger, R., Lee, J. D., Aguiar, P. M., North, M., & Parkin, A. (2018). Capacitance-Assisted Sustainable Electrochemical Carbon Dioxide Mineralisation. *ChemSusChem, 11*(1), 137–148. DOI: 10.1002/cssc.201702087 PMID: 29171724

Lambrecht, A., & Tucker, C. (2019). Algorithmic bias? An empirical study of apparent gender-based discrimination in the display of STEM career ads. *Management Science, 65*(7), 2966–2981. DOI: 10.1287/mnsc.2018.3093

Langeveldt, D. C. (2021). AI-driven leadership: A conceptual framework for educational decision making in the AI era. *Journal of Educational Administration, 59*(3), 256–270.

Largo Avila, E., Suárez Rodríguez, C. H., & Arango Espinal, E. (2025). Digital transformation: Evolving applications of artificial intelligence in the coffee industry. *Ingeniería y Desarrollo, 43*(1), 64–83. DOI: 10.14482/inde.43.01.445.864

Larson, P. D. (2020). Corruption, gender inequality and logistics performance. *International Journal of Logistics Management, 31*(2), 381–397. DOI: 10.1108/IJLM-02-2019-0062

Laudisa, F. (2024). The Epistemology of Models in the Era of Pandemic. In Nicoletti, M., & Palazzo, A. (Eds.), *Epidemics and Pandemics: Philosophical Perspectives* (pp. 297–308). Brepols Publishers., DOI: 10.1484/M.STPH-EB.5.136416

Leach, M., & Green, C. (2021). Gender and the SDGs: Mainstreaming, intersectionality and the transformative potential of the 2030 Agenda. *Sustainable Development, 29*(4), 617–630.

Leal Filho, W., Tripathi, S. K., Andrade Guerra, J. B. S. O. D., Giné-Garriga, R., Orlovic Lovren, V., & Willats, J. (2019). Using the sustainable development goals towards a better understanding of sustainability challenges. *International Journal of Sustainable Development and World Ecology, 26*(2), 179–190. DOI: 10.1080/13504509.2018.1505674

Leal Filho, W., Wall, T., Mucova, S. A. R., Nagy, G. J., Balogun, A. L., Luetz, J. M., & Gandhi, O. (2022). Deploying artificial intelligence for climate change adaptation. *Technological Forecasting and Social Change, 180*, 121662. DOI: 10.1016/j.techfore.2022.121662

Leavy, S. (2018). Gender Bias in Artificial Intelligence: The Need for Diversity and Gender Theory in Machine Learning. In *Proceedings of the 1st International Workshop on Gender Equality in Software Engineering* (pp. 14-16). ACM/IEEE. DOI: 10.1145/3195570.3195580

Lee, C.-C., Chiu, Y.-B., & Sun, C.-H. (2010). The environmental Kuznets curve hypothesis for water pollution: Do regions matter? *Energy Policy, 38*(1), 12–23. DOI: 10.1016/j.enpol.2009.05.004

Lee, N. (2018). Detecting racial bias in algorithms and machine learning. Journal of Information. *Communication and Ethics in Society, 16*(3), 252–260. DOI: 10.1108/JICES-06-2018-0056

Lilhare, S., Sanodiya, P., Dwivedi, V. K., & Singh, T. (2024). *Leveraging Artificial Intelligence (AI) for Soil Management: A Comprehensive Overview*. Academic Press.

Li, M. (2024). Exploring the digital divide in primary education: A comparative study of urban and rural mathematics teachers' TPACK and attitudes towards technology integration in post-pandemic China. *Education and Information Technologies*, 1–33.

Lim, C. P., Ra, S., Chin, B., & Wang, T. (2020). Information and communication technologies (ICT) for access to quality education in the global south: A case study of Sri Lanka. *Education and Information Technologies, 25*(4), 2447–2462. DOI: 10.1007/s10639-019-10069-3

Li, T., Lu, C., & Xu, L. (2025). Access to finance and cost stickiness: Evidence from anti-recharacterization laws. *Advances in Accounting, 68*, 100816. Advance online publication. DOI: 10.1016/j.adiac.2025.100816

Liu, M. (2023). Exploring the application of artificial intelligence in foreign language teaching: Challenges and future development. *SHS Web of Conferences, 168*, 3025.

Liu, J. (2018). An integrated framework for achieving sustainable development goals around the world. *Ecology Economy and Society–The INSEE Journal, 1*(2), 11–17.

Liu, X., & Huang, X. (2022). [Retracted] Design of Artificial Intelligence-Based English Network Teaching (AI-ENT) System. *Mathematical Problems in Engineering, 2022*(1), 1849430.

Liu, Y. (2024). Research on Algorithmic Gender Bias under the Paradigm of Machine Behavior Studies. *Lecture Notes in Education Psychology and Public Media, 50*(1), 13–22. DOI: 10.54254/2753-7048/50/20240802

Liu, Y., Huang, B., Guo, H., & Liu, J. (2023). A big data approach to assess progress towards Sustainable Development Goals for cities of varying sizes. *Communications Earth & Environment, 4*(1), 66. DOI: 10.1038/s43247-023-00730-8

Liu, Y., & Ren, L. (2022). The influence of artificial intelligence technology on teaching under the threshold of "Internet+": Based on the application example of an English education platform. *Wireless Communications and Mobile Computing, 2022*(1), 5728569. DOI: 10.1155/2022/5728569

Lomborg, B. (2020). Welfare in the 21st century: Increasing development, reducing inequality, the impact of climate change, and the cost of climate policies. *Technological Forecasting and Social Change, 156*, 119981. DOI: 10.1016/j.techfore.2020.119981

Lovarelli, D., Bacenetti, J., & Guarino, M. (2020). A review on dairy cattle farming: Is precision livestock farming the compromise for an environmental, economic and social sustainable production? *Journal of Cleaner Production, 262*, 121409. DOI: 10.1016/j.jclepro.2020.121409

Lütz, F. (2022). Gender equality and artificial intelligence in Europe. Addressing direct and indirect impacts of algorithms on gender-based discrimination. *ERA Forum, 23*, 33-52.

Lütz, F. (2024). The AI act, gender equality and non-discrimination: What role for the AI office? *ERA Forum, 25*, 79-95.

Lutz, C. (2019). Digital inequalities in the age of artificial intelligence and big data. *Human Behavior and Emerging Technologies, 1*(2), 141–148. DOI: 10.1002/hbe2.140

Lysaght, T., Lim, H. Y., Xafis, V., & Ngiam, K. Y. (2019). AIassisted decision-making in healthcare. *Asian Bioethics Review, 11*(3), 299–314. DOI: 10.1007/s41649-019-00096-0

Machado, T. M., & Berssaneti, F. T. (2023). Literature review of digital twin in health-care. *Heliyon, 9*(9), 1–12. DOI: 10.1016/j.heliyon.2023.e19390 PMID: 37809792

Machleb, J., Peteinatos, G. G., Kollenda, B. L., Andújar, D., & Gerhards, R. (2020). Sensor-based mechanical weed control: Present state and prospects. *Computers and Electronics in Agriculture, 176*, 105638. DOI: 10.1016/j.compag.2020.105638

Maghsudi, S., Lan, A., Xu, J., & van Der Schaar, M. (2021). Personalized education in the artificial intelligence era: What to expect next. *IEEE Signal Processing Magazine, 38*(3), 37–50. DOI: 10.1109/MSP.2021.3055032

Mahani, A. (2023). Classification in multi-label datasets. DOI: 10.5772/intechopen.109352

Mahum, R., & Aladhadh, S. (2022). Skin lesion detection using hand-crafted and DL-based features fusion and LSTM. *Diagnostics (Basel), 12*(12), 2974. Advance online publication. DOI: 10.3390/diagnostics12122974 PMID: 36552983

Majumdar, P., Mitra, S., & Bhattacharya, D. (2021). IoT for Promoting Agriculture 4.0: A Review from the Perspective of Weather Monitoring, Yield Prediction, Security of WSN Protocols, and Hardware Cost Analysis. *Journal of Biosystems Engineering, 46*(4), 440–461. DOI: 10.1007/s42853-021-00118-6

Makridakis, S. (2017). The forthcoming artificial intelligence (AI) revolution: Its impact on society and firms. *Futures, 90*, 46–60. DOI: 10.1016/j.futures.2017.03.006

Malarvizhi, D. K., Priyadharshini, K., & Manasa, B. (2024). Uncovering biases, unlocking the potential of AI education, and digital inclusion for marginalized communities. *Cuestiones de Fisioterapia*, *53*(3), 1928–1937.

Malekpour, S., Allen, C., Sagar, A., Scholz, I., Persson, Å., Miranda, J. J., & Al-Ghanim, K. (2023). What scientists need to do to accelerate progress on the SDGs. *Nature*, *621*, 250.

Malhi, Y., Franklin, J., Seddon, N., Solan, M., Turner, M. G., Field, C. B., & Knowlton, N. (2020). Climate change and ecosystems: threats, opportunities and solutions. Philosophical Transactions of the Royal Society B, 375(1794), 20190104.

Malhotra, R. K., Sharma, C. A. P., Upreti, H., Sharma, S., Prakash, N., & Mittal, S. (2024). Role of Psychological Contract in Employee Engagement in Higher Education: Empirical Study on Uttarakhand. In P. P.K. (Ed.), *E3S Web of Conferences* (Vol. 556). EDP Sciences. DOI: 10.1051/e3sconf/202455601030

Maliki, K., & Naji, F. (2024). Gender inequality in the sphere of artificial intelligence: Theoretical approach. *Journal of Autonomous Intelligence*, *7*(3), 1–12. DOI: 10.32629/jai.v7i3.1394

Manasi, A., Panchanadeswaran, S., Sours, E., & Lee, S. J. (2022). Mirroring the bias: Gender and artificial intelligence. *Gender, Technology and Development*, *26*(3), 295–305. DOI: 10.1080/09718524.2022.2128254

Maphosa, V. (2024). The rise of artificial intelligence and emerging ethical and social concerns. *AI, Computer Science, and Robotics Technology*, *3*, 1–20. DOI: 10.5772/acrt.20240020

Maraveas, C. (2022). Incorporating artificial intelligence technology in smart greenhouses: Current State of the Art. *Applied Sciences (Basel, Switzerland)*, *13*(1), 14. DOI: 10.3390/app13010014

Martin. (n.d.). Sustainable consumption and production. *United Nations Sustainable Development*. Retrieved March 6, 2025, from https://www.un.org/sustainabledevelopment/sustainable-consumption-production/

Marwan, A. (2020). *Impact of artificial intelligence on education for employment: Learning and employability framework*. Academic Press.

Matsui, T., Suzuki, K., Ando, K., Kitai, Y., Haga, C., Masuhara, N., & Kawakubo, S. (2022). A natural language processing model for supporting sustainable development goals: Translating semantics, visualizing nexus, and connecting stakeholders. *Sustainability Science*, *17*(3), 969–985. DOI: 10.1007/s11625-022-01093-3

Mavaddati, S. (2025). Skin cancer classification based on a hybrid deep model and long short-term memory. Biomedical Signal Processing and Control, 100(PA), 107109. DOI: 10.1016/j.bspc.2024.107109

Mazzi, F. (2024). Artificial Intelligence and Sustainability Considerations: National, Regional and Supra National Perspective. Regional and Supra National Perspective.

McGregor, A., Rickards, L., Houston, D., Goodman, M. K., & Bojovic, M. (2021). The Biopolitics of Cattle Methane Emissions Reduction: Governing Life in a Time of Climate Change. *Antipode*, *53*(4), 1161–1185. DOI: 10.1111/anti.12714

McMahon, D. D., Barrio, B., McMahon, A. K., Tutt, K., & Firestone, J. (2020). Virtual reality exercise games for high school students with intellectual and developmental disabilities. *Journal of Special Education Technology*, *35*(2), 87–96. DOI: 10.1177/0162643419836416

Mehrabi, N., Morstatter, F., Saxena, N., Lerman, K., & Galstyan, A. (2021). A survey on bias and fairness in machine learning. *ACM Computing Surveys*, *54*(6), 1–35. DOI: 10.1145/3457607

Mello, R. F., Freitas, E., Pereira, F. D., Cabral, L., Tedesco, P., & Ramalho, G. (2023). Education in the age of Generative AI: Context and Recent Developments. *ArXiv Preprint ArXiv:2309.12332*.

Mgendi, G. (2024). Unlocking the potential of precision agriculture for sustainable farming. *Discover Agriculture*, *2*(1), 87. DOI: 10.1007/s44279-024-00078-3

Mhlanga, D. (2021). Artificial intelligence in the industry 4.0, and its impact on poverty, innovation, infrastructure development, and the sustainable development goals: Lessons from emerging economies? *Sustainability (Basel)*, *13*(11), 5788. DOI: 10.3390/su13115788

Mhlanga, D. (2022). Human-centered artificial intelligence: The superlative approach to achieve sustainable development goals in the fourth industrial revolution. *Sustainability (Basel)*, *14*(13), 7804. DOI: 10.3390/su14137804

Mijwil, M. M. (2021). Skin cancer disease images classification using deep learning solutions. *Multimedia Tools and Applications*, *80*(17), 26255–26271. DOI: 10.1007/s11042-021-10952-7

Miller, K., Cunningham, J., & Lehmann, E. (2021). Extending the university mission and business model: Influences and implications. *Studies in Higher Education*, *46*(5), 915–925. DOI: 10.1080/03075079.2021.1896799

Minghai, Y., Saliu, F., & Khan, W. A. (2025). AI-powered decision-making applications for sustainable development. In *Multi-criteria decision-making and optimum design with machine learning* (pp. 233–251). CRC Press.

Miola, A., Borchardt, S., Neher, F., & Buscaglia, D. (2019). *Interlinkages and policy coherence for the Sustainable Development Goals implementation: An operational method to identify trade-offs and co-benefits in a systemic way*. Publications Office of the European Union. DOI: 10.2760/472928

Mishra, D. (2024). Strategic Communication for AI-Driven Sustainability Initiatives: Bridging Technology, Policy, and Public Engagement in Achieving SDGs. In AI Applications for Clean Energy and Sustainability (pp. 187-211). IGI Global.

Mishra, S. K., Jeba Praba, J., & Georrge, J. J. (2024). An emerging trends of bioinformatics and big data analytics in healthcare. In *Digital Transformation in Healthcare* e 5.0: Volume 2: Metaverse, Nanorobots and Machine Learning (p. 159-188). Walter de Gruyter GmbH & Co KG.

Mitchell, S. A., & Sok, D. K. (2023). Precision Livestock Farming in the Digital Age: Sensors and Microfluidics Paving the Way for Sustainable Agriculture. *Sage Science Review of Educational Technology*, *6*(1), 71–87.

Mogaji, E., Soetan, T. O., & Kieu, T. A. (2020). The implications of artificial intelligence on the digital marketing of financial services to vulnerable customers. Australasian Marketing Journal.

Mohammadi Lanbaran, N., Naujokaitis, D., Kairaitis, G., Jenciūtė, G., & Radziukynienė, N. (2024). Overview of Startups Developing Artificial Intelligence for the Energy Sector. *Applied Sciences (Basel, Switzerland)*, *14*(18), 8294. DOI: 10.3390/app14188294

Mohyuddin, G., Khan, M. A., Haseeb, A., Mahpara, S., Waseem, M., & Saleh, A. M. (2024). Evaluation of Machine Learning approaches for precision Farming in Smart Agriculture System-A comprehensive Review. *IEEE Access : Practical Innovations, Open Solutions*.

Mok, K. H., & Wu, A. M. (2016). Higher education, changing labour market and social mobility in the era of massification in China. *Journal of Education and Work*, *29*(1), 77–97. DOI: 10.1080/13639080.2015.1049028

Mondejar, M. E., Avtar, R., Diaz, H. L. B., Dubey, R. K., Esteban, J., Gómez-Morales, A., Hallam, B., Mbungu, N. T., Okolo, C. C., Prasad, K. A., She, Q., & Garcia-Segura, S. (2021). Digitalization to achieve sustainable development goals: Steps towards a Smart Green Planet. *The Science of the Total Environment, 794*, 148539. DOI: 10.1016/j.scitotenv.2021.148539 PMID: 34323742

Mora-Villalobos, J.-A., Aguilar, F., Carballo-Arce, A.-F., Vega-Baudrit, J. R., Trimino-Vazquez, H., Villegas-Peñaranda, L. R., Stöbener, A., Eixenberger, D., Bubenheim, P., Sandoval, M., & Liese, A. (2021). Tropical agroindustrial biowaste revalorization through integrative biorefineries—Review part I: Coffee and palm oil by-products. *Biomass Conversion and Biorefinery, 13*(2), 1469–1487. DOI: 10.1007/s13399-021-01442-9

*More than 1 billion tons of food lost or wasted every year, UN-backed report finds | UN News*. (2011, May 11). https://news.un.org/en/story/2011/05/374722

Mor, S., & Ravindra, K. (2023). Municipal solid waste landfills in lower-and middle-income countries: Environmental impacts, challenges and sustainable management practices. *Process Safety and Environmental Protection, 174*, 510–530. DOI: 10.1016/j.psep.2023.04.014

Morze, N., Varchenko-Trotsenko, L., Terletska, T., & Smyrnova-Trybulska, E. (2021). Implementation of adaptive learning at higher education institutions by means of Moodle LMS. *Journal of Physics: Conference Series, 1840*(1), 12062. DOI: 10.1088/1742-6596/1840/1/012062

Motta, I., Vuillerme, N., Pham, H.-H., & de Figueiredo, F. A. P. (2024, November). Machine learning techniques for coffee classification: A comprehensive review of scientific research. In *Artificial Intelligence Review* (Vol. 58, Issue 1). Springer Science+Business Media. DOI: 10.1007/s10462-024-11004-w

Mousaei, A., Naderi, Y., & Bayram, I. S. (2024). Advancing state of charge management in electric vehicles with machine learning: A technological review. *IEEE Access : Practical Innovations, Open Solutions, 12*, 43255–43283. DOI: 10.1109/ACCESS.2024.3378527

Muhammad, F., & Orji, C. M. (2024). Revolutionizing education in the digital era: The role of AI in promoting inclusivity, equality, and ethical innovation. *The American Journal of Social Science and Education Innovations, 6*(9), 151–157. DOI: 10.37547/tajssei/Volume06Issue09-16

Mukhallafi, T. R. A. (2020). Using artificial intelligence for developing English language teaching/learning: An analytical study from university students' perspective. *International Journal of English Linguistics, 10*(6), 40. DOI: 10.5539/ijel.v10n6p40

Murthy, P. S., & Madhava Naidu, M. (2012). Sustainable management of coffee industry by-products and value addition—A review. *Resources, Conservation and Recycling*, *66*, 45–58. DOI: 10.1016/j.resconrec.2012.06.005

Mussatto, S. I., Machado, E. M. S., Martins, S., & Teixeira, J. A. (2011). Production, Composition, and Application of Coffee and Its Industrial Residues. *Food and Bioprocess Technology*, *4*(5), 661–672. DOI: 10.1007/s11947-011-0565-z

Mustafawi, E., Shaaban, K., Khwaileh, T., & Ata, K. (2022). Perceptions and attitudes of Qatar University students regarding the utility of arabic and english in communication and education in Qatar. *Language Policy*, *21*(1), 75–119. DOI: 10.1007/s10993-021-09590-4

Musungwini, S., Gavai, P. V., Munyoro, B., & Chare, A. (2023). Emerging ICT technologies for agriculture, training, and capacity building for farmers in developing countries: A case study in Zimbabwe. In *Applying Drone Technologies and Robotics for Agricultural Sustainability* (pp. 12–30). IGI Global. DOI: 10.4018/978-1-6684-6413-7.ch002

Mwitondi, K. S., Munyakazi, I., & Gatsheni, B. N. (2020). A robust machine learning approach to SDG data segmentation. *Journal of Big Data*, *7*(1), 97. DOI: 10.1186/s40537-020-00373-y

Nagaraj, K., Sharvani, G. S., & Sridhar, A. (2018). Emerging trend of big data analytics in bioinformatics: A literature review. *International Journal of Bioinformatics Research and Applications*, *14*(1-2), 144–205. DOI: 10.1504/IJBRA.2018.089175

Nahar, S. (2024). Modeling the effects of artificial intelligence (AI)-based innovation on sustainable development goals (SDGs): Applying a system dynamics perspective in a cross-country setting. *Technological Forecasting and Social Change*, *201*, 123203. DOI: 10.1016/j.techfore.2023.123203

Naidoo, G. M. (2024). The Potential of Artificial Intelligence in South African Rural Development. *OIDA International Journal of Sustainable Development*, *17*(11), 207–218.

Nayyar, A., Gadhavi, L., & Zaman, N. (2021). Machine learning in healthcare: review, opportunities and challenges. In Singh, K. K., Elhoseny, M., Singh, A., & Elngar, A. A. (Eds.), *Machine learning and the internet of medical things in healthcare* (pp. 23–45). Academic Press. DOI: 10.1016/B978-0-12-821229-5.00011-2

Nedungadi, P., Tang, K.-Y., & Raman, R. (2024). The transformative power of generative artificial intelligence for achieving the Sustainable Development Goal of quality education. *Sustainability (Basel)*, *16*(22), 9779. DOI: 10.3390/su16229779

Neethirajan, S. (2024). Net Zero Dairy Farming—Advancing Climate Goals with Big Data and Artificial Intelligence. *Climate (Basel), 12*(2), 15. DOI: 10.3390/cli12020015

Neilson, J. (2008). Global Private Regulation and Value-Chain Restructuring in Indonesian Smallholder Coffee Systems. *World Development, 36*(9), 1607–1622. DOI: 10.1016/j.worlddev.2007.09.005

Nepal, M., Nepal, A. K., Khadayat, M. S., Kumar, R., Shyamsundar, P., & Somanathan, E. (2022). Low-Cost Strategies to Improve Municipal Solid Waste Management in Developing Countries: Experimental Evidence from Nepal. *Environmental and Resource Economics*. Advance online publication. DOI: 10.1007/s10640-021-00640-3

Ng, D. T. K., Leung, J. K. L., Su, J., Ng, R. C. W., & Chu, S. K. W. (2023). Teachers' AI digital competencies and twenty-first century skills in the post-pandemic world. *Educational Technology Research and Development, 71*(1), 137–161. DOI: 10.1007/s11423-023-10203-6

Nie, T., Huang, J., Zhang, Z., Chen, P., Li, T., & Dai, C. (2023). The inhibitory effect of a water-saving irrigation regime on CH4 emission in Mollisols under straw incorporation for 5 consecutive years. *Agricultural Water Management, 278*, 108163. DOI: 10.1016/j.agwat.2023.108163

Nigar, N., Umar, M., Shahzad, M. K., Islam, S., & Abalo, D. (2022). A deep learning approach based on explainable artificial intelligence for skin lesion classification. *IEEE Access : Practical Innovations, Open Solutions, 10*(September), 113715–113725. DOI: 10.1109/ACCESS.2022.3217217

Nishant, R., Kennedy, M., & Corbett, J. (2020). Artificial intelligence for sustainability: Challenges, opportunities, and a research agenda. *International Journal of Information Management, 53*, 102104. DOI: 10.1016/j.ijinfomgt.2020.102104

Nižetić, S., Šolić, P., López-de-Ipiña González-de-Artaza, D., & Patrono, L. (2020). Internet of Things (IoT): Opportunities, issues and challenges towards a smart and sustainable future. *Journal of Cleaner Production, 274*, 122877. DOI: 10.1016/j.jclepro.2020.122877 PMID: 32834567

Njuguna, E., Daum, T., Birner, R., & Mburu, J. (2025). Silicon Savannah and smallholder farming: How can digitalization contribute to sustainable agricultural transformation in Africa? *Agricultural Systems, 222*, 104180. DOI: 10.1016/j.agsy.2024.104180

Nkechi, A. A., Ojo, A. O., & Eneh, O. A. (2024). Impact of artificial intelligence in achieving quality education. *Artificial Intelligence and Education-Shaping the Future of Learning: Shaping the Future of Learning*, 73.

Noulas, C., Torabian, S., & Qin, R. (2023). Crop Nutrient Requirements and Advanced Fertilizer Management Strategies. In *Agronomy* (Vol. 13, Issue 8, p. 2017). MDPI. https://www.mdpi.com/2073-4395/13/8/2017

Nuwarapaksha, T. D., Udumann, S. S., Dissanayaka, N. S., Dilshan, R. M. N., & Atapattu, A. J. (2025a). AI-Driven Solutions for Sustainable Irrigation: Exploring Smart Technologies to Enhance Conservation and Efficiency. In *Integrating Agriculture, Green Marketing Strategies, and Artificial Intelligence* (pp. 1–32). IGI Global Scientific Publishing.

Nuwarapaksha, T. D., Udumann, S. S., Dissanayaka, N. S., Dilshan, R. M. N., & Atapattu, A. J. (2025b). Revolutionizing Agriculture by Advanced Water and Irrigation Management Technologies. In *Emerging Trends and Technologies in Water Management and Conservation* (pp. 285–318). IGI Global Scientific Publishing.

Nwokediegwu, Z. Q. S., Ugwuanyi, E. D., Dada, M. A., Majemite, M. T., & Obaigbena, A. (2024). AI-driven waste management systems: A comparative review of innovations in the USA and Africa. *Engineering Science & Technology Journal*, *5*(2), 507–516. DOI: 10.51594/estj.v5i2.828

O'Connor, S., & Liu, H. (2023). Gender bias perpetuation and mitigation in AI technologies: Challenges and opportunities. *AI & Society*, *39*(4), 2045–2057. DOI: 10.1007/s00146-023-01675-4

Obaideen, K., Albasha, L., Iqbal, U., & Mir, H. (2024). Wireless power transfer: Applications, challenges, barriers, and the role of AI in achieving sustainable development goals-A bibliometric analysis. *Energy Strategy Reviews*, *53*, 101376. DOI: 10.1016/j.esr.2024.101376

Obaideen, K., Yousef, B. A., AlMallahi, M. N., Tan, Y. C., Mahmoud, M., Jaber, H., & Ramadan, M. (2022). An overview of smart irrigation systems using IoT. *Energy Nexus*, *7*, 100124. DOI: 10.1016/j.nexus.2022.100124

Ofosu-Ampong, K. (2023). Gender differences in perception of artificial intelligence-based tools. *Journal of Digital Art & Humanities*, *4*(2), 52–56. DOI: 10.33847/2712-8149.4.2_6

Oladapo, B. I., Olawumi, M. A., & Omigbodun, F. T. (2024). AI-Driven Circular Economy of Enhancing Sustainability and Efficiency in Industrial Operations. *Sustainability (Basel)*, *16*(23), 10358. DOI: 10.3390/su162310358

Oleksy, W., Just, E., & Zapedowska-Kling, K. (2012). Gender issues in information and communication technologies (ICTs). *Journal of Information Communication and Ethics in Society*, *10*(2), 107–120. DOI: 10.1108/14779961211227010

Onyezere, C. V., Oforleta, C. M., & Onyezere, C. E. (2024). Artificial intelligence and sustainable development in Nigeria, West Africa (2015-2024). *International Journal of Public Administration and Development Studies*, *1*(1), 1–16.

Opesemowo, O. A. G., & Adekomaya, V. (2024). Harnessing Artificial Intelligence for Advancing Sustainable Development Goals in South Africa's Higher Education System: A Qualitative Study. *International Journal of Learning. Teaching and Educational Research*, *23*(3), 67–86. DOI: 10.26803/ijlter.23.3.4

Ospina-Forero, L., Castañeda, G., & Guerrero, O. A. (2022). Estimating networks of sustainable development goals. *Information & Management*, *59*(5), 103342. DOI: 10.1016/j.im.2020.103342

Otis, N. G., Delecourt, S., Cranney, K., & Koning, R. (2024). Global evidence on gender gaps and generative AI. *Harvard Business School*. https://www.hbs.edu/

Otterbacher, J., Bates, J., & Clough, P. (2017). Competent men and warm women: Gender stereotypes in image search. *Information Processing & Management*, *53*(6), 1182–1195.

Overturf, E., Pezzutto, S., Boschiero, M., Ravasio, N., & Monegato, A. (2021). The CirCo (Circular Coffee) Project: A Case Study on Valorization of Coffee Silverskin in the Context of Circular Economy in Italy. *Sustainability (Basel)*, *13*(16), 16. Advance online publication. DOI: 10.3390/su13169069

Ozkan, M. A. (2025). Telemedicine and the Future of Healthcare: Challenges and Opportunities in Remote Patient Management. *The Open European Journal for Research in Medical and Basic Sciences (OEJRMBS)*, 1(1), 55-65. https://easdjournals.com/index.php/oejrmbs/index

Pachava, V., Lasekan, O. A., Méndez-Alarcón, C. M., Pena, M. T. G., & Golla, S. K. (2025). Advancing SDG 4: Harnessing generative AI to transform learning, teaching, and educational equity in higher education. *Journal of Lifestyle and SDGs Review*, *5*(2), e03774. DOI: 10.47172/2965-730X.SDGsReview.v5.n02.pe03774

Pactwa, K., Woźniak, J., Jach, K., & Brdulak, A. (2024). Including the social responsibility of universities and sustainable development goals in the strategic plans of universities in europe. *Sustainable Development (Bradford)*, *32*(5), 4593–4605. DOI: 10.1002/sd.2924

Padhiary, M., Kumar, R., & Sethi, L. N. (2024). Navigating the Future of Agriculture: A Comprehensive Review of Automatic All-Terrain Vehicles in Precision Farming. *Journal of The Institution of Engineers (India): Series A, 105*, 767–782. DOI: 10.1007/s40030-024-00816-2

Padhiary, M. (2024). The Convergence of Deep Learning, IoT, Sensors, and Farm Machinery in Agriculture. In Thandekkattu, S. G., & Vajjhala, N. R. (Eds.), *Designing Sustainable Internet of Things Solutions for Smart Industries* (pp. 109–142). IGI Global. DOI: 10.4018/979-8-3693-5498-8.ch005

Padhiary, M., Kumar, K., Hussain, N., Roy, D., Barbhuiya, J. A., & Roy, P. (2025). Artificial Intelligence in Farm Management: Integrating Smart Systems for Optimal Agricultural Practices. *International Journal of Smart Agriculture, 3*(1), 1–11. DOI: 10.54536/ijsa.v3i1.3674

Padhiary, M., & Kumar, R. (2024a). Assessing the Environmental Impacts of Agriculture, Industrial Operations, and Mining on Agro-Ecosystems. In Azrour, M., Mabrouki, J., Alabdulatif, A., Guezzaz, A., & Amounas, F. (Eds.), *Smart Internet of Things for Environment and Healthcare* (pp. 107–126). Springer Nature Switzerland. DOI: 10.1007/978-3-031-70102-3_8

Padhiary, M., & Kumar, R. (2024b). Enhancing Agriculture Through AI Vision and Machine Learning: The Evolution of Smart Farming. In Thangam, D. (Ed.), *Advancements in Intelligent Process Automation* (pp. 295–324). IGI Global. DOI: 10.4018/979-8-3693-5380-6.ch012

Padhiary, M., Roy, P., Dey, P., & Sahu, B. (2024). Harnessing AI for Automated Decision-Making in Farm Machinery and Operations: Optimizing Agriculture. In Hai-Jew, S. (Ed.), Advances in Computational Intelligence and Robotics. IGI Global. DOI: 10.4018/979-8-3693-6230-3.ch008

Padhiary, M., Saikia, P., Roy, P., Hussain, N., & Kumar, K. (2025). *A Review on Advancing Agricultural Efficiency through Geographic Information Systems, Remote Sensing, and Automated Systems*. Cureus Journal of Engineering. DOI: 10.7759/s44388-024-00559-7

Padhiary, M., Tikute, S. V., Saha, D., Barbhuiya, J. A., & Sethi, L. N. (2024). Development of an IOT-Based Semi-Autonomous Vehicle Sprayer. *Agricultural Research, 13*(3). Advance online publication. DOI: 10.1007/s40003-024-00760-4

Paknejad Rizi, S. M., Torabi, F., & Jafari Pavarsi, H. (2022). Challenges of Performance-Based Payment Methods in Health Care System: A Systematic Review. *Evidence Based Health Policy. Management and Economics*, *6*(4), 285–297. DOI: 10.18502/jebhpme.v6i4.11541

Pandey, D. K., & Mishra, R. (2024). Towards sustainable agriculture: Harnessing AI for global food security. *Artificial Intelligence in Agriculture*, *12*, 72–84. DOI: 10.1016/j.aiia.2024.04.003

Panesar, A. (2019). Ethics of intelligence. In *Machine learning and AI for healthcare: big data for improved health outcomes* (pp. 207–254). Apress. DOI: 10.1007/978-1-4842-3799-1_6

Park, A., & Li, H. (2021). The Effect of Blockchain Technology on Supply Chain Sustainability Performances. *Sustainability (Basel)*, *13*(4), 1726. DOI: 10.3390/su13041726

Park, K., Mott, B., Lee, S., Gupta, A., Jantaraweragul, K., Glazewski, K., Scribner, A. J., Ottenbreit-Leftwich, A., Hmelo-Silver, C., & Lester, J. (2022). Investigating a visual interface for elementary students to formulate AI planning tasks. *Journal of Computer Languages*, *73*, 101157. DOI: 10.1016/j.cola.2022.101157

Pasupuleti, V., Thuraka, B., Kodete, C. S., & Malisetty, S. (2024). Enhancing Supply Chain Agility and Sustainability through Machine Learning: Optimization Techniques for Logistics and Inventory Management. *Logistics (Basel)*, *8*(3), 73. DOI: 10.3390/logistics8030073

Pathan, M. S., Richardson, E., Galvan, E., & Mooney, P. (2023). The Role of Artificial Intelligence within Circular Economy Activities—A View from Ireland. *Sustainability (Basel)*, *15*(12), 12. Advance online publication. DOI: 10.3390/su15129451

Patil, S. P., Singh, B., Bisht, J., Gupta, S., & Khanna, R. (2021). Yoga for holistic treatment of polycystic ovarian syndrome. *Journal of Medical Pharmaceutical and Allied Sciences*, *10*, 120–125. DOI: 10.22270/jmpas.VIC2I1.2035

Pauls, S. N. (2024). EU Sustainable Finance and International Trade Law: Legality and Propagation of EU Sustainable Finance Regulation under GATS and Free Trade Agreements. *European Yearbook of International Economic Law*, *37*, 1–267. DOI: 10.1007/978-3-031-73853-1_1

Pedro, F., Subosa, M., Rivas, A., & Valverde, P. (2019). Artificial intelligence in education: Challenges and opportunities for sustainable development. Academic Press.

Peixoto, J. A. B., Silva, J. F., Oliveira, M. B. P. P., & Alves, R. C. (2022, December). Sustainability issues along the coffee chain: From the field to the cup. In *Wiley* (Vol. 22, Issue 1, pp. 287–332). DOI: 10.1111/1541-4337.13069

Pelton, J. N. (2020). UN Sustainable Development Goals for 2030. In *Handbook of Small Satellites: Technology, Design, Manufacture, Applications, Economics, and Regulation* (pp. 1537–1566). Springer International Publishing.

Peluso, M. (2023). *Coffee By-Products: Economic Opportunities for Sustainability and Innovation in the Coffee Industry*. DOI: 10.3390/ICC2023-14834

Piñeros, V. J., Reveles-Espinoza, A. M., & Monroy, J. A. (2024). From Remote Sensing to Artificial Intelligence in Coral Reef Monitoring. *Machines (Basel)*, *12*(10), 693. DOI: 10.3390/machines12100693

Pinski, M., & Benlian, A. (2024). AI literacy for users: A comprehensive review and future research directions of learning methods, components, and effects. *Computers in Human Behavior: Artificial Humans*, 100062.

Polwaththa, K., Amarasinghe, S. T. C., Amarasinghe, A., & Amarasinghe, A. A. Y. (2024). Exploring Artificial Intelligence and Machine Learning in Precision Agriculture: A Pathway to Improved Efficiency and Economic Outcomes in Crop Production. *American Journal of Agricultural Science, Engineering, and Technology*, *8*(3), 50–59. DOI: 10.54536/ajaset.v8i3.3843

Prabhakar, A. C. (2025). AI Strategies for Sustainable Development Goals: Collective Action for Poverty Alleviation. In AI Strategies for Social Entrepreneurship and Sustainable Economic Development (pp. 393-442). IGI Global Scientific Publishing.

Prior, D. D., Mysore Seshadrinath, S., Zhang, M., & McCormack, M. (2024). Measuring sustainable development goals (SDGs) in higher education through semantic matching. *Studies in Higher Education*, 1–14. DOI: 10.1080/03075079.2024.2386625

Qamar, A. (2024). AI-Powered Solutions in Climate Change Mitigation and Environmental Sustainability. *Research Corridor Journal of Engineering Science*, *1*(2), 194–209.

Qasim, S. H. (2024). Beyond the Classroom: Emerging Technologies to Enhance Learning. Academic Press.

Radwan, N., & Farouk, M. (2021). The growth of internet of things (IoT) in the management of healthcare issues and healthcare policy development. *International Journal of Technology Innovation and Management*, *1*(1), 69–84. DOI: 10.54489/ijtim.v1i1.8

Ragab, M., Choudhry, H., Al-Rabia, M. W., Binyamin, S. S., Aldarmahi, A. A., & Mansour, R. F. (2022). Early and accurate detection of melanoma skin cancer using hybrid level set approach. *Frontiers in Physiology*, *13*(December), 965630. Advance online publication. DOI: 10.3389/fphys.2022.965630 PMID: 36545278

Rahman, A., Debnath, T., Kundu, D., Khan, M. S. I., Aishi, A. A., Sazzad, S., Sayduzzaman, M., & Band, S. S. (2024). Machine learning and deep learning-based approach in smart healthcare: Recent advances, applications, challenges and opportunities. *AIMS Public Health, 11*(1), 58–109. DOI: 10.3934/publichealth.2024004 PMID: 38617415

Rajesh Banu, J., Kavitha, S., Yukesh Kannah, R., Dinesh Kumar, M., Preethi, , Atabani, A. E., & Kumar, G. (2020). Biorefinery of spent coffee grounds waste: Viable pathway towards circular bioeconomy. *Bioresource Technology, 302*, 122821. DOI: 10.1016/j.biortech.2020.122821 PMID: 32008862

Raji, I. D., Yang, J., Bornstein, S., & Marcus, J. (2022). The AI auditing ecosystem. *Proceedings of the 2022 ACM FAccT Conference*, 923-936.

Raj, M., Gupta, S., Chamola, V., Elhence, A., Garg, T., Atiquzzaman, M., & Niyato, D. (2021). A survey on the role of Internet of Things for adopting and promoting Agriculture 4.0. *Journal of Network and Computer Applications, 187*, 103107. DOI: 10.1016/j.jnca.2021.103107

Ramadan, M. N., Ali, M. A., Khoo, S. Y., Alkhedher, M., & Alherbawi, M. (2024). Real-time IoT-powered AI system for monitoring and forecasting of air pollution in industrial environment. *Ecotoxicology and Environmental Safety, 283*, 116856. DOI: 10.1016/j.ecoenv.2024.116856 PMID: 39151373

Raman, R., Pattnaik, D., Kumar, C., & Nedungadi, P. (2024). Advancing sustainable energy systems: A decade of SETA research contribution to sustainable development goals. *Sustainable Energy Technologies and Assessments, 71*, 103978. DOI: 10.1016/j.seta.2024.103978

Rane, N., Choudhary, S., & Rane, J. (2023b). Hyper-personalization for enhancing customer loyalty and satisfaction in Customer Relationship Management (CRM) systems. SSRN *Electronic Journal*. DOI: 10.2139/ssrn.4641044

Rane, N., Choudhary, S., & Rane, J. (2023a). Education 4.0 and 5.0: Integrating Artificial Intelligence (AI) for personalized and adaptive learning. *Available at SSRN* 4638365. DOI: 10.2139/ssrn.4638365

Rashmi, D. (2023). Unlocking the Potential of AI in Education: Challenges and Opportunities. *International Journal for Multidisciplinary Research, 5*(4), 1–11.

Razavi, S. (2016). The 2030 Agenda: Challenges of implementation to attain gender equality and women's rights. *Gender and Development, 24*(1), 25–41. https://doi .org/. DOI: 10.1080/13552074.2016.1142229

Redhu, N. S., Thakur, Z., Yashveer, S., & Mor, P. (2022). Artificial intelligence: A way forward for agricultural sciences. In *Bioinformatics in Agriculture* (pp. 641–668). Elsevier. DOI: 10.1016/B978-0-323-89778-5.00007-6

Rehman, A., Naz, S., & Razzak, I. (2022). Leveraging big data analytics in healthcare enhancement: Trends, challenges and opportunities. *Multimedia Systems, 28*(4), 1339–1371. DOI: 10.1007/s00530-020-00736-8

Report, W. H. (2023). *World Happiness Index 2023* [Dataset]. https://worldhappiness.report/data

Reza Ahmadi Mehr. (2023). Skin cancer detection based on deep learning methods. In Lecture Notes on Data Engineering and Communications Technologies (Vol. 164, pp. 58–67). DOI: 10.1007/978-3-031-27762-7_6

Robert, L., Pierce, C., Morris, L., Kim, S., & Alahmad, R. (2020). Designing Fair AI for Managing Employees in Organizations: A Review. *Human-Computer Interaction, 35*(5-6), 545–575. DOI: 10.1080/07370024.2020.1735391

Roberts, S., Shedi, O., Tausha, I., Kaonga, K., Nsomba, G., & Tshabalala, N. (2023). *Competition, concentration, and market outcomes in fertiliser markets in East and Southern Africa.* Academic Press.

Rodríguez-Zurita, D., Jaya-Montalvo, M., Moreira-Arboleda, J., Raya-Diez, E., & Carrión-Mero, P. (2024). Sustainable development through service learning and community engagement in higher education: A systematic literature review. *International Journal of Sustainability in Higher Education, 26*(1), 158–201. DOI: 10.1108/IJSHE-10-2023-0461

Rose Taylor, S. (2020). UN Women's feminist engagement with governance by indicators in the Millennium and Sustainable Development Goals. *Global Social Policy, 20*(3), 352–366. DOI: 10.1177/1468018120931696

Roshanaei, M., Olivares, H., & Lopez, R. R. (2023). Harnessing AI to foster equity in education: Opportunities, challenges, and emerging strategies. *Journal of Intelligent Learning Systems and Applications, 15*(04), 123–143. DOI: 10.4236/jilsa.2023.154009

Roshni Thanka, M., Bijolin Edwin, E., Ebenezer, V., Martin Sagayam, K., Jayakeshav Reddy, B., Günerhan, H., & Emadifar, H. (2023). A hybrid approach for melanoma classification using ensemble machine learning techniques with deep transfer learning. *Computer Methods and Programs in Biomedicine Update, 3*(April), 100103. DOI: 10.1016/j.cmpbup.2023.100103

Rosmayanti, V., Noni, N., & Patak, A. A. (2022). Students' acceptance of technology use in learning English pharmacy. *International Journal of Language Education, 6*(3), 314–331. DOI: 10.26858/ijole.v6i3.24144

Rosmayanti, V., Patak, A. A., & Noni, N. (2023). Integrating technology into ESP instruction: Teaching English for pharmacy students. *The Journal of AsiaTEFL, 20*(2), 475–484. DOI: 10.18823/asiatefl.2023.20.2.18.475

Rossi, F. (2019). Building trust in artificial intelligence. *Journal of International Affairs, 72*(1), 127–134.

Russell, S., & Norvig, P. (2021). *Artificial Intelligence: A Modern Approach* (4th ed.). Pearson Education Limited.

Ryan, M., Antoniou, J., Brooks, L., Jiya, T., Macnish, K., & Stahl, B. (2020). The ethical balance of using smart information systems for promoting the United Nations' Sustainable Development Goals. *Sustainability (Basel), 12*(12), 4826. DOI: 10.3390/su12124826

SaberiKamarposhti, M., Why, N. K., Yadollahi, M., Kamyab, H., Cheng, J., & Khorami, M. (2024). Cultivating a sustainable future in the artificial intelligence era: A comprehensive assessment of greenhouse gas emissions and removals in agriculture. *Environmental Research*, 118528. PMID: 38403150

Sachs, J., Lafortune, G., Kroll, C., Fuller, G., & Woelm, F. (2016–2023). *Sustainable Development Reports (SDG Index and Dashboards).* Cambridge University Press. https://dashboards.sdgindex.org/

Sachs, J., Kroll, C., Lafortune, G., Fuller, G., & Woelm, F. (2022). *Sustainable Development Report 2022: From crises to sustainable development: The SDGs as roadmap to 2030 and beyond.* Cambridge University Press., DOI: 10.1017/9781009210058

Sadick, A.-M. (n.d.). *sdgBERT* [Pre-trained model]. Hugging Face. https://huggingface.co/sadickam/sdgBERT

Sætra, H. S. (2021). AI in Context and the Sustainable Development Goals: Factoring in the Unsustainability of the Sociotechnical System. *Sustainability (Basel), 13*(4), 1–18. DOI: 10.3390/su13041738

Saher, R., Saleh, M., & Anjum, M. (2023). Holistic Trash Collection System Integrating Human Collaboration with Technology. *Applied Sciences (Basel, Switzerland), 13*(20), 11263. DOI: 10.3390/app132011263

Saini, M., Sengupta, E., Singh, M., Singh, H., & Singh, J. (2023). Sustainable Development Goal for quality education (SDG 4): A study on SDG 4 to extract the pattern of association among the indicators of SDG 4 employing a genetic algorithm. *Education and Information Technologies*, *28*(2), 2031–2069. DOI: 10.1007/s10639-022-11265-4

Sakkir, G., Al Amir, F., Atmowardoyo, H., Weda, S., & Rosmayanti, V. (2024). An analysis of translanguaging practices in an Indonesian EFL classroom : Teacher perception Geminastiti. *Xlinguae*, *17*(2), 3–15. DOI: 10.18355/XL.2024.17.02.01

Saleh, S. A., & Adly, H. M. (2024). Measuring the impact of higher education in promoting sustainable development goals: Analysis of the Arab universities' performance. *Problemy Ekorozwoju*, *19*(1), 261–274. DOI: 10.35784/preko.5384

Samad, A., Kim, S. H., Kim, C. J., Lee, E. Y., Kumari, S., Hossain, M. J., Alam, A. M. M. N., Muazzam, A., Hwang, Y.-H., & Joo, S. T. (2025). From Farms to Labs: The New Trend of Sustainable Meat Alternatives. *Food Science of Animal Resources*, *45*(1), 13–30. DOI: 10.5851/kosfa.2024.e105 PMID: 39840251

Sanabria, Z. J., Alfaro Ponce, B., Argüelles Cruz, A., & Ramírez Montoya, M. S. (2023). AI-based platform design for complex thinking assessment: A case study of an ideation using the transition design approach. https://repositorio.tec.mx/handle/11285/651579

Sarku, R., Clemen, U. A., & Clemen, T. (2023). The application of artificial intelligence models for food security. *Revista de Agricultura (Piracicaba)*, *13*(10), 2037.

Saxena, R. R. (2024). Artificial Intelligence in Traffic Systems. arXiv preprint arXiv:2412.12046.

Selvam, A. P., & Al-Humairi, S. N. S. (2025). Environmental impact evaluation using smart real-time weather monitoring systems: A systematic review. *Innovative Infrastructure Solutions*, *10*(1), 13. DOI: 10.1007/s41062-024-01817-7

Seo, K., Tang, J., Roll, I., Fels, S., & Yoon, D. (2021). The impact of artificial intelligence on learner–instructor interaction in online learning. *International Journal of Educational Technology in Higher Education*, *18*(1), 54. DOI: 10.1186/s41239-021-00292-9 PMID: 34778540

Serafini, P. G., de Moura, J. M., de Almeida, M. R., & de Rezende, J. F. D. (2022). Sustainable development goals in higher education institutions: A systematic literature review. *Journal of Cleaner Production*, *370*, 133473. DOI: 10.1016/j.jclepro.2022.133473

Şerban, A. C., & Lytras, M. D. (2020). Artificial intelligence for smart renewable energy sector in europe—Smart energy infrastructures for next generation smart cities. *IEEE Access : Practical Innovations, Open Solutions*, *8*, 77364–77377. DOI: 10.1109/ACCESS.2020.2990123

Shaikh, T. A., Rasool, T., & Lone, F. R. (2022). Towards leveraging the role of machine learning and artificial intelligence in precision agriculture and smart farming. *Computers and Electronics in Agriculture*, *198*, 107119. DOI: 10.1016/j.compag.2022.107119

Shamshiri, R. R., Rad, A. K., Behjati, M., & Balasundram, S. K. (2024). Sensing and Perception in Robotic Weeding: Innovations and Limitations for Digital Agriculture. *Sensors (Basel)*, *24*(20), 6743. DOI: 10.3390/s24206743 PMID: 39460222

Sharma, S., Gupta, C., Khanna Malhotra, R., & Upreti, H. (2024). Sustainable Banking Practices: Impact, challenges and opportunities. In P. P.K. (Ed.), *E3S Web of Conferences* (Vol. 556). EDP Sciences. DOI: 10.1051/e3sconf/202455601031

Sharma, A. K., Tiwari, S., Aggarwal, G., Goenka, N., Kumar, A., Chakrabarti, P., Chakrabarti, T., Gono, R., Leonowicz, Z., & Jasinski, M. (2022). Dermatologist-level classification of skin cancer using cascaded ensembling of convolutional neural network and handcrafted features based deep neural network. *IEEE Access : Practical Innovations, Open Solutions*, *10*, 17920–17932. DOI: 10.1109/ACCESS.2022.3149824

Sharma, K., & Shivandu, S. K. (2024). Integrating artificial intelligence and internet of things (IoT) for enhanced crop monitoring and management in precision agriculture. *Sensors International*, *5*, 100292. DOI: 10.1016/j.sintl.2024.100292

Sharma, P., Gaur, V. K., Sirohi, R., Varjani, S., Kim, S., & Wong, J. W. C. (2021). Sustainable processing of food waste for production of bio-based products for circular bioeconomy. *Bioresource Technology*, *325*, 124684. Advance online publication. DOI: 10.1016/j.biortech.2021.124684 PMID: 33493748

Sharma, S., Rawal, R., & Shah, D. (2023). Addressing the challenges of AI-based telemedicine: Best practices and lessons learned. *Journal of Education and Health Promotion*, *12*(1), 338. DOI: 10.4103/jehp.jehp_402_23 PMID: 38023098

Shetty, S., Gali, S., Augustine, D., & Sv, S. (2024). Artificial intelligence systems in dental shade-matching: A systematic review. *Journal of Prosthodontics*, *33*(6), 519–532. DOI: 10.1111/jopr.13805

Shivaprakash, K. N., Swami, N., Mysorekar, S., Arora, R., Gangadharan, A., Vohra, K., Jadeyegowda, M., & Kiesecker, J. M. (2022). Potential for artificial intelligence (AI) and machine learning (ML) applications in biodiversity conservation, managing forests, and related services in India. *Sustainability (Basel), 14*(12), 7154. DOI: 10.3390/su14127154

Shorfuzzaman, M. (2022). An explainable stacked ensemble of deep learning models for improved melanoma skin cancer detection. *Multimedia Systems, 28*(4), 1309–1323. DOI: 10.1007/s00530-021-00787-5

Sishodia, R. P., Ray, R. L., & Singh, S. K. (2020). Applications of remote sensing in precision agriculture: A review. *Remote Sensing (Basel), 12*(19), 3136. DOI: 10.3390/rs12193136

Smirnov, Y., Sverchkov, I., & Gabdullina, R. (2022). *Biofuel pellets from spent coffee grounds. Research Square*. DOI: 10.21203/rs.3.rs-1551835/v1

Smits, R. (2024a). Introduction to sustainable finance and climate change: Law and regulation. In *Sustainable Finance and Climate Change: Law and Regulation*. Edward Elgar Publishing Ltd. DOI: 10.4337/9781800377288.00010

Snezhana, D. (2023). Applying artificial intelligence (AI) for mitigation climate change consequences of the natural disasters. *Research Journal of Ecology and Environmental Sciences, 3*(1), 1–8.

Solaja, O. M. (2024). Unleashing the Power of AI: Revolutionizing Plastic Waste Management for Sustainable Development in Developing Nations. *Water Technology, 12*(1), 28–38.

Someh, I., Davern, M., Breidbach, C. F., & Shanks, G. (2019). Ethical issues in big data analytics: A stakeholder perspective. *Communications of the Association for Information Systems, 44*(1), 1–20. DOI: 10.17705/1CAIS.04434

Soori, M., Jough, F. K. G., Dastres, R., & Arezoo, B. (2024). AI-based decision support systems in Industry 4.0, A review. *Journal of Economy and Technology*. https://www.sciencedirect.com/science/article/pii/S2949948824000374

Sovrano, F., Palmirani, M., & Vitali, F. (2020). Deep learning based multi-label text classification of unga resolutions. *Proceedings of the 13th International Conference on Theory and Practice of Electronic Governance*, 686-695. DOI: 10.1145/3428502.3428604

Spanaki, K., Sivarajah, U., Fakhimi, M., Despoudi, S., & Irani, Z. (2022). Disruptive technologies in agricultural operations: A systematic review of AI-driven Agri-Tech research. *Annals of Operations Research, 308*(1–2), 491–524. DOI: 10.1007/s10479-020-03922-z

Srinivasu, P. N., Sivasai, J. G., Ijaz, M. F., Bhoi, A. K., Kim, W., & Kang, J. J. (2021). Classification of skin disease using deep learning neural networks with MobileNet V2 and LSTM. *Sensors (Basel), 21*(8), 2852. Advance online publication. DOI: 10.3390/s21082852 PMID: 33919583

Stahl, B. C. (2021). *Artificial intelligence for a better future: an ecosystem perspective on the ethics of AI and emerging digital technologies.* Springer Nature. DOI: 10.1007/978-3-030-69978-9

Stahl, B. C., & Leach, T. (2023). Assessing the ethical and social concerns of artificial intelligence in neuroinformatics research: An empirical test of the European Union Assessment List for Trustworthy AI (ALTAI). *AI and Ethics, 3*(3), 745–767. DOI: 10.1007/s43681-022-00201-4

Stech, R. (2019). Sustainable finance, the law and stakeholders: Towards responsible social movements. In *Corporate Social Responsibility in Developing and Emerging Markets: Institutions, Actors and Sustainable Development.* Cambridge University Press. DOI: 10.1017/9781108579360.021

Stecuła, K., Wolniak, R., & Grebski, W. W. (2023). AI-Driven Urban Energy Solutions—From Individuals to Society: A Review. *Energies, 16*(24), 7988. DOI: 10.3390/en16247988

St-Hilaire, F., Do Vu, D., Frau, A., Burns, N., Faraji, F., Potochny, J., Robert, S., Roussel, A., Zheng, S., & Glazier, T. (2022). A new era: Intelligent tutoring systems will transform online learning for millions. *ArXiv Preprint ArXiv:2203.03724.*

Stoltzfus, M., Kaur, A., Chawla, A., Gupta, V., Anamika, F. N. U., & Jain, R. (2023). The role of telemedicine in healthcare: An overview and update. *The Egyptian Journal of Internal Medicine, 35*(1), 1–5. DOI: 10.1186/s43162-023-00234-z

Stufano, P., Perrotta, A., Labarile, R., & Trotta, M. (2022). The second life of coffee can be even more energizing: Circularity of materials for bio-based electrochemical energy storage devices. *MRS Energy & Sustainability : a Review Journal, 9*(2), 443–460. DOI: 10.1557/s43581-022-00036-w

Subeesh, A., & Mehta, C. R. (2021). Automation and digitization of agriculture using artificial intelligence and internet of things. *Artificial Intelligence in Agriculture, 5,* 278–291. DOI: 10.1016/j.aiia.2021.11.004

Suneetha, I. (2024). Hybrid deep learning model for skin cancer classification. *Proceedings of the 2024 International Conference on Artificial Intelligence and Machine Learning* (pp. 90–110). DOI: 10.1051/e3sconf/202459109010

Sun, T., He, X., & Li, Z. (2023a). Digital twin in healthcare: Recent updates and challenges. *Digital Health, 9*, 1–13. DOI: 10.1177/20552076221149651 PMID: 36636729

Sun, T., Wang, J., Suo, M., Liu, X., Huang, H., Zhang, J., Zhang, W., & Li, Z. (2023b). The digital twin: A potential solution for the personalized diagnosis and treatment of musculoskeletal system diseases. *Bioengineering (Basel, Switzerland), 10*(6), 627. DOI: 10.3390/bioengineering10060627 PMID: 37370558

Supriya, L. P., & Khilar, R. (2024). Composite ensemble learning model for skin cancer detection from dermatoscopic images. *Nanotechnology Perceptions, 20*(S9), 111–125. DOI: 10.62441/nano-ntp.v20iS9.9

*Sustainability issues along the coffee chain: From the field to the cup—Barreto Peixoto—2023—Comprehensive Reviews in Food Science and Food Safety—Wiley Online Library*. (n.d.). Retrieved October 17, 2025, from https://ift.onlinelibrary.wiley.com/doi/10.1111/1541-4337.13069

Sutko, D. M. (2020). Theorizing femininity in artificial intelligence: A framework for undoing technology's gender troubles. *Cultural Studies, 34*(4), 567–592. DOI: 10.1080/09502386.2019.1671469

*Tackling food loss and waste: A triple win opportunity*. (n.d.). Newsroom. Retrieved March 6, 2025, from https://www.fao.org/newsroom/detail/FAO-UNEP-agriculture-environment-food-loss-waste-day-2022/en

Tang, J., & Deng, Y. (2022). The design model of the English-graded teaching assistant expert system is based on an improved B/S three-tier structure system. *Mobile Information Systems, 2022*, Article e4167760, 1–9. DOI: 10.1155/2022/4167760

Tan, M., & Subramonyam, H. (2024). More than model documentation: uncovering teachers' bespoke information needs for informed classroom integration of ChatGPT. *Proceedings of the CHI Conference on Human Factors in Computing Systems*, 1–19. DOI: 10.1145/3613904.3642592

Tanveer, M., Hassan, S., & Bhaumik, A. (2020). Academic policy regarding sustainability and artificial intelligence (AI). *Sustainability (Basel), 12*(22), 9435. DOI: 10.3390/su12229435

Thangamani, R., Sathya, D., Kamalam, G. K., & Lyer, G. N. (2024). AI Green Revolution: Reshaping Agriculture's Future. In Balasubramanian, S., Natarajan, G., & Chelliah, P. R. (Eds.), *Intelligent Robots and Drones for Precision Agriculture* (pp. 421–461). Springer Nature Switzerland. DOI: 10.1007/978-3-031-51195-0_19

Thapar, P., Rakhra, M., Cazzato, G., & Hossain, M. S. (2022). A novel hybrid deep learning approach for skin lesion segmentation and classification. *Journal of Healthcare Engineering*, *2022*, 1709842. Advance online publication. DOI: 10.1155/2022/1709842 PMID: 35480147

Thuy, H. N., Ngoc, Q. N., & Ngoc, H. L. (2022). A case study of integrating SDG indicators into GIS for planning and developing urban. In *International Conference: Sustainable University Development: Opportunity and Challenge (SUDOC 2022)*, University of Economics Ho Chi Minh City (UEH), Ho Chi Minh City, Vietnam.

Toniolo, K., Masiero, E., Massaro, M., & Bagnoli, C. (2020). Sustainable business models and artificial intelligence: Opportunities and challenges. In *Knowledge, People, and Digital Transformation* (pp. 103–117). Springer. DOI: 10.1007/978-3-030-40390-4_8

Topol, E. (2019). *Deep Medicine: How Artificial Intelligence Can Make Healthcare Human Again*. Basic Book.

Truby, J. (2020). Governing artificial intelligence to benefit the UN sustainable development goals. *Sustainable Development (Bradford)*, *28*(4), 946–959. DOI: 10.1002/sd.2048

Trung, N. D., Huy, D. T. N., Le, T. H., Huong, D. T., & Hoa, N. T. (2021). ICT, AI, IOTs and technology applications in education- A case with accelerometer and internet learner gender prediction. *Advances in Mechanics*, *9*(3), 1288–1296.

Truong, Y., & Papagiannidis, S. (2022). Artificial intelligence as an enabler for innovation: A review and future research agenda. *Technological Forecasting and Social Change*, *183*, 121852. DOI: 10.1016/j.techfore.2022.121852

Tucker, C. M. (2017). *Coffee Culture: Local Experiences, Global Connections* (2nd ed.). Routledge. DOI: 10.4324/9781315678795

Tumpa, P. P., & Kabir, M. A. (2021). An artificial neural network-based detection and classification of melanoma skin cancer using hybrid texture features. *Sensors International*, *2*(August), 100128. DOI: 10.1016/j.sintl.2021.100128

Turienzo, J., Cabanelas, P., & Lampón, J. F. (2023). Business models in times of disruption: The connected and autonomous vehicles (uncertain) domino effect. *Journal of Business Research*, *156*, 113481. DOI: 10.1016/j.jbusres.2022.113481

Tzachor, A., Devare, M., King, B., Avin, S., & Ó hÉigeartaigh, S. (2022). Responsible artificial intelligence in agriculture requires systemic understanding of risks and externalities. *Nature Machine Intelligence*, *4*(2), 104–109. DOI: 10.1038/s42256-022-00440-4

United Nations (UN). (2015). *Transforming our world: The 2030 Agenda for Sustainable Development.* Available from: https://sdgs.un.org/goals

United Nations. (2017). *Resolution adopted by the General Assembly on 6 July 2017: Work of the Statistical Commission pertaining to the 2030 Agenda for Sustainable Development (A/RES/71/313).* https://unstats.un.org/sdgs/indicators/indicators-list/

United Nations. (2020). *The Sustainable Development Goals Report 2020: The 2030 Agenda for Sustainable Development.*

United Nations. (2020a). *The Sustainable Development Goals report 2020.* https://unstats.un.org/sdgs/report/2020/The-Sustainable-Development-Goals-Report 2020.pdf

United Nations. (2023). *The Sustainable Development Goals Report 2023: Special Edition.*

Usigbe, M. J., Asem-Hiablie, S., Uyeh, D. D., Iyiola, O., Park, T., & Mallipeddi, R. (2024). Enhancing resilience in agricultural production systems with AI-based technologies. *Environment, Development and Sustainability*, *26*(9), 21955–21983. DOI: 10.1007/s10668-023-03588-0

Vallée, A. (2023). Digital twin for healthcare systems. *Frontiers in Digital Health*, *5*, 1253050. DOI: 10.3389/fdgth.2023.1253050 PMID: 37744683

van Niekerk, A. J. (2020). Inclusive economic sustainability: SDGs and global inequality. *Sustainability (Basel)*, *12*(13), 5427. DOI: 10.3390/su12135427

Van Wassenaer, L., van Hilten, M., Van Ingen, E., & Van Asseldonk, M. (2021). *Applying blockchain for climate action in agriculture: State of play and outlook.* Food & Agriculture Org.

van Zanten, J. A., & Putintseva, M. (2025). Evaluating governmental policies for the sustainable development goals using hierarchical clustering. *International Journal of Sustainable Development and World Ecology*, *32*(3), 322–340. DOI: 10.1080/13504509.2024.2448669

Vander Stichele, M. (2020). 14 - Strengthening Green Finance by Better Integrating the Social Dimensions in the European Union's Sustainable Finance Laws. In *Making the Financial System Sustainable*. Cambridge University Press. DOI: 10.1017/9781108908269.017

Veale, M., Van Kleek, M., & Binns, R. (2018). Fairness and accountability design needs for algorithmic support in high-stakes public sector decision-making. *Proceedings of the 2018 CHI conference on human factors in computing systems*. DOI: 10.1145/3173574.3174014

Vecchio, G., Tiznado-Aitken, I., & Hurtubia, R. (2020). Transport and equity in Latin America: A critical review of socially oriented accessibility assessments. *Transport Reviews*, *40*(3), 354–381. DOI: 10.1080/01441647.2020.1711828

Veldkamp, E., Schmidt, M., Powers, J. S., & Corre, M. D. (2020). Deforestation and reforestation impacts on soils in the tropics. *Nature Reviews. Earth & Environment*, *1*(11), 590–605. DOI: 10.1038/s43017-020-0091-5

Venturelli, A., & Pizzi, S. (2023). United Nations Agenda 2030 on Sustainable Development Goals, The. In *Encyclopedia of Sustainable Management* (pp. 3830–3832). Springer International Publishing. DOI: 10.1007/978-3-031-25984-5_990

Verma, R. K., Kishor, K., & Jha, S. K. (2024). Big Data Analytics in Bioinformatics and Healthcare. In *Applications of Parallel Data Processing for Biomedical Imaging* (pp. 25–43). DOI: 10.4018/979-8-3693-2426-4.ch002

Villafuerte, N., Manzano, S., Ayala, P., & García, M. V. (2023). Artificial Intelligence in Virtual Telemedicine Triage: A Respiratory Infection Diagnosis Tool with Electronic Measuring Device. *Future Internet*, *15*(7), 227. DOI: 10.3390/fi15070227

Vinayaka, & Prasad, P. R. C. (2024). AI-Enhanced Remote Sensing Applications in Indian Sugarcane Research: A Comprehensive Review. *Sugar Tech*, 1–20.

Vincent, G., Narashimman, G., Suresh, M., Kingsly, P. J., Rajendhiran, M., & Rajalakshmi, M. (2024). Examine Ai Models For Credit Scoring And Risk Assessment, Integrating Nontraditional Data Sources Such As Social Media And Transaction Histories To Enhance Accuracy And Inclusivity. *Educational Administration: Theory and Practice*, *30*(5), 13931–13940.

Vinuesa, R., Azizpour, H., Leite, I., Balaam, M., Dignum, V., Domisch, S., Felländer, A., Langhans, S. D., Tegmark, M., & Fuso Nerini, F. (2020). The role of artificial intelligence in achieving the Sustainable Development Goals. *Nature Communications*, *11*(1), 1–10. DOI: 10.1038/s41467-019-14108-y PMID: 31932590

Walker, J., Pearce, C., Boe, K., & Lawson, M. (2019). *The power of education to fight inequality: How increasing educational equality and quality is crucial to fighting economic and gender inequality*. Oxfam. https://policy-practice.oxfam.org/resources/the-power-of education-to-fight-inequality-620867/

Walters, R. (2025). Digital Finance Law: Common and Civil Law. In *Digital Finance Law: Common and Civil Law*. Taylor and Francis. DOI: 10.4324/9781003511687

Walter, Y. (2024). Embracing the future of artificial intelligence in the classroom: The relevance of AI literacy, prompt engineering, and critical thinking in modern education. *International Journal of Educational Technology in Higher Education*, *21*(1), 15. DOI: 10.1186/s41239-024-00448-3

Wamba-Taguimdje, S. L., Wamba, S. F., Kamdjoug, J. R. K., & Wanko, C. E. T. (2020). Influence of artificial intelligence (AI) on firm performance: The business value of AI-based transformation projects. *Business Process Management Journal*, *26*(7), 1893–1924. DOI: 10.1108/BPMJ-10-2019-0411

Wang, Y. (2020). When artificial intelligence meets educational leaders' data-informed decision making: A cautionary tale. *Educational Policy Studies Faculty Publications*, 40. https://scholarworks.gsu.edu/eps_facpub/40

Wang, J., Cao, Y., & Shu, X. (2023). Decision models for sustainable development goals based on a relational network approach. Highlights in Science. *Engineering and Technology*, *60*, 167–175. DOI: 10.54097/hset.v60i.10353

Wang, T., Lund, B. D., Marengo, A., Pagano, A., Mannuru, N. R., Teel, Z. A., & Pange, J. (2023). Exploring the potential impact of artificial intelligence (AI) on international students in higher education: Generative AI, chatbots, analytics, and international student success. *Applied Sciences (Basel, Switzerland)*, *13*(11), 6716. DOI: 10.3390/app13116716

Wan, X., Zhou, X., Ye, Z., Mortensen, C. K., & Bai, Z. (2020, June). Smiley-Cluster: Supporting accessible machine learning in K-12 scientific discovery. In *Proceedings of the Interaction Design and Children Conference* (pp. 23–35). DOI: 10.1145/3392063.3394440

Wanyama, J., Bwambale, E., Kiraga, S., Katimbo, A., Nakawuka, P., Kabenge, I., & Oluk, I. (2024). A systematic review of fourth industrial revolution technologies in smart irrigation: Constraints, opportunities, and future prospects for sub-Saharan Africa. *Smart Agricultural Technology*, *7*, 100412. DOI: 10.1016/j.atech.2024.100412

Weber, H., & Wiek, A. (2021). Cooperating With "Open Cards"—The Role of Small Intermediary Businesses in Realizing Sustainable International Coffee Supply. *Frontiers in Sustainable Food Systems*, *5*, 663716. Advance online publication. DOI: 10.3389/fsufs.2021.663716

Wei, L., Ding, K., & Hu, H. (2020). Automatic skin cancer detection in dermoscopy images based on ensemble lightweight deep learning network. *IEEE Access : Practical Innovations, Open Solutions*, *8*, 99633–99647. DOI: 10.1109/ACCESS.2020.2997710

Weiskopf, S. R., Rubenstein, M. A., Crozier, L. G., Gaichas, S., Griffis, R., Halofsky, J. E., Hyde, K. J. W., Morelli, T. L., Morisette, J. T., Muñoz, R. C., Pershing, A. J., Peterson, D. L., Poudel, R., Staudinger, M. D., Sutton-Grier, A. E., Thompson, L., Vose, J., Weltzin, J. F., & Whyte, K. P. (2020). Climate change effects on biodiversity, ecosystems, ecosystem services, and natural resource management in the United States. *The Science of the Total Environment*, *733*, 137782. DOI: 10.1016/j.scitotenv.2020.137782 PMID: 32209235

West, S. M., Whittaker, M., & Crawford, K. (2019). Discriminating systems: Gender, race, and power in AI. *AI Now Institute Report*, 1-33.

Willcocks, L. (2020). Robo-Apocalypse cancelled? Reframing the automation and future of work debate. *Journal of Information Technology*, *35*(4), 286–302. DOI: 10.1177/0268396220925830

Williams, R. (2024). Impact. AI: Democratizing AI through K-12 Artificial Intelligence Education (Doctoral dissertation, Massachusetts Institute of Technology).

Williamson, S. M., & Prybutok, V. (2024). Balancing privacy and progress: A review of privacy challenges, systemic oversight, and patient perceptions in AI-driven healthcare. *Applied Sciences (Basel, Switzerland)*, *14*(2), 675. DOI: 10.3390/app14020675

Wong, P.-H. (2019). Democratizing Algorithmic Fairness. *Philosophy & Technology*, *33*(2), 225–244. DOI: 10.1007/s13347-019-00355-w

Woo, J. H., & Choi, H. (2021). Systematic review for AI-based language learning tools. *ArXiv Preprint ArXiv:2111.04455*.

World Bank. (2021). *Social dimensions of climate change*. https://www.worldbank.org/en/topic/social-dimensions-of-climate-change

World Bank. (2022). *GDP per capita (current US$)* [Dataset]. https://data.worldbank.org/indicator/NY.GDP.PCAP.CD

World Bank. (2023). *Providing sustainable development solutions.*https://www.worldbank.org/en/about/annual-report/supporting-clients

Wulf, C., Werker, J., Zapp, P., Schreiber, A., Schlör, H., & Kuckshinrichs, W. (2018). Sustainable development goals as a guideline for indicator selection in life cycle sustainability assessment. In *Proceedings of the 25th CIRP Life Cycle Engineering (LCE) Conference* (pp. 59-65). DOI: 10.1016/j.procir.2017.11.144

Xianhua, L. (2019). Research on the effect of artificial intelligence technology on English learning efficiency. *2019 12th International Conference on Intelligent Computation Technology and Automation (ICICTA)*, 548–551.

Xia, W., Jiang, Y., Chen, X., & Zhao, R. (2022). Application of machine learning algorithms in municipal solid waste management: A mini review. *Waste Management & Research, 40*(6), 609–624. DOI: 10.1177/0734242X211033716 PMID: 34269157

Xia, Y., Zhang, M., Tsang, D. C. W., Geng, N., Lu, D., Zhu, L., Igalavithana, A. D., Dissanayake, P. D., Rinklebe, J., Yang, X., & Ok, Y. S. (2020). Recent advances in control technologies for non-point source pollution with nitrogen and phosphorous from agricultural runoff: Current practices and future prospects. *Applied Biological Chemistry, 63*(1), 8. DOI: 10.1186/s13765-020-0493-6

Xu, L. D., He, W., & Li, S. (2014). Internet of things in industries: A survey. *IEEE Transactions on Industrial Informatics, 10*(4), 2233–2243. DOI: 10.1109/TII.2014.2300753

Xu, X., Wang, X., Zhang, Y., & Zheng, R. (2024). Applying ChatGPT to tackle the side effects of personal learning environments from learner and learning perspective: An interview of experts in higher education. *PLoS One, 19*(1), e0295646. DOI: 10.1371/journal.pone.0295646

Yadav, P., Tudela, L., & Marco-Lajara, B. (2024). The role of AI in assessing and achieving the Sustainable Development Goals (SDGs). IGI Global. DOI: 10.4018/979-8-3693-3282-5.ch001

Yale Center for Environmental Law & Policy, & Center for International Earth Science Information Network (CIESIN) – Columbia University. (2022). *Environmental Performance Index 2022* [Dataset]. https://sedac.ciesin.columbia.edu/data/set/epi-environmental-performance-index-2022/data-download

Yang, C. H., Ren, J. H., Huang, H. C., Chuang, L. Y., & Chang, P. Y. (2021). Deep hybrid convolutional neural network for segmentation of melanoma skin lesion. *Computational Intelligence and Neuroscience, 2021*(1), 9409508. Advance online publication. DOI: 10.1155/2021/9409508 PMID: 34790232

Yekollu, R. K., Bhimraj Ghuge, T., Sunil Biradar, S., Haldikar, S. V., & Farook Mohideen Abdul Kader, O. (2024). *AI-Driven Personalized Learning Paths: Enhancing Education Through Adaptive Systems*. DOI: 10.1007/978-981-97-3191-6_38

Yigitcanlar, T., & Cugurullo, F. (2020). The sustainability of artificial intelligence: An urbanistic viewpoint from the lens of smart and sustainable cities. *Sustainability (Basel)*, *12*(20), 8548. DOI: 10.3390/su12208548

Yu, C. (2024). Gender inequality in the age of AI: Predictions, perspectives, and policy recommendations (No. 5zrh9_v1). *Center for Open Science*.

Yumnam, G., Gyanendra, Y., & Singh, C. I. (2024). A systematic bibliometric review of the global research dynamics of United Nations Sustainable Development Goals 2030. *Sustainable Futures : An Applied Journal of Technology, Environment and Society*, *7*, 100192. DOI: 10.1016/j.sftr.2024.100192

Yuzvovich, L., Lvova, M. I., & Isakova, N. Y. (2024). Waste management: Environmental strategies and practices. *E3S Web of Conferences, 541*. DOI: 10.1051/e3sconf/202454104004

Zaman, Q. (2024). The Role of Artificial Intelligence in Early Disease Detection: Transforming Diagnostics and Treatment. *Multidisciplinary Journal of Healthcare*, *1*(2), 43–54.

Zanoletti, A., Cornelio, A., & Bontempi, E. (2021). A post-pandemic sustainable scenario: What actions can be pursued to increase the raw materials availability? *Environmental Research*, *202*, 111681. Advance online publication. DOI: 10.1016/j.envres.2021.111681 PMID: 34273363

Zareen, S. S., Sun, G., Kundi, M., Qadri, S. F., & Qadri, S. (2024). Enhancing skin cancer diagnosis with deep learning: A hybrid CNN-RNN approach. *Computers, Materials & Continua*, *79*(1), 1497–1519. DOI: 10.32604/cmc.2024.047418

Zastudil, C., Rogalska, M., Kapp, C., Vaughn, J., & MacNeil, S. (2023). Generative ai in computing education: Perspectives of students and instructors. *2023 IEEE Frontiers in Education Conference (FIE)*, 1–9.

Zhang, H., Meng, Y., Zeng, Z., & Zhao, L. (2025). The white-hot international standards competition (the Fourth Industrial Revolution). In *Brief History of Standards* (pp. 187 249). Singapore: Springer Nature Singapore.

Zhang, K., & Aslan, A. B. (2021). AI technologies for education: Recent research & future directions. *Computers and Education: Artificial Intelligence*, *2*, 100025. DOI: 10.1016/j.caeai.2021.100025

Zhang, W., Zhu, X., Fu, Y., Tsuji, J., & Weng, Z. (2017). Predicting human splicing branchpoints by combining sequence-derived features and multi-label learning methods. *BMC Bioinformatics, 18*(S13), 464. Advance online publication. DOI: 10.1186/s12859-017-1875-6

Zhang, Y., Zhang, M., Wu, L., & Li, J. (2024). Digital Transition Framework for Higher Education in AI-Assisted Engineering Teaching. *Science & Education*, 1–22.

Zhou, W. (2020). Sociocultural theory and its implications in college English teaching and learning in the age of artificial intelligence. *Journal of Physics: Conference Series, 1646*(1), 12142. DOI: 10.1088/1742-6596/1646/1/012142

Zhu, Y. (2021). Research on English teaching of professional skilled talents training based on artificial intelligence. *Journal of Intelligent & Fuzzy Systems, Preprint*, 1–12.

Zhu, Y., Zhang, K., Hu, Q., Liu, W., Qiao, Y., Cai, D., Zhu, P., Wang, D., Xu, H., Shu, S., & Gao, N. (2023). Accelerated spent coffee grounds humification by heat/base co-activated persulfate and products' fertilization evaluation. *Environmental Technology & Innovation, 32*, 103393. DOI: 10.1016/j.eti.2023.103393

Ziolo, M., Filipiak, B. Z., Bąk, I., & Cheba, K. (2019). How to design more sustainable financial systems: The roles of environmental, social, and governance factors in the decision-making process. *Sustainability (Basel), 11*(20), 5604. DOI: 10.3390/su11205604

Zohuri, B., Behgounia, F., & Nezam, Z. Z. (2020). Artificial Intelligence Integration with Energy Sources (Renewable and Non-renewable). *Journal of Energy and Power Engineering, 14*, 193–210.

# About the Contributors

**Gamze Sart** was awarded the PhD degree in the field of Educational Sciences in Bogazici University in 2013. She worked as an Assistant Professor in the Faculty of Education, Yeditepe University in 2013 and Hasan Ali Yucel Faculty of Education, Istanbul University during the period 2014-2018, as an Associate Professor in the Hasan Ali Yucel Faculty of Education, Istanbul University-Cerrahpaşa between 2018 and 2024 and as a Professor in the Hasan Ali Yucel Faculty of Education since 2024. Her main research areas: Educational Studies, Higher Education Policies, Higher Education Management, Lifelong Learning, Sustainable Development.

**Yilmaz Bayar** awarded the PhD degree in the field of Economics in Istanbul University Institute of Social Sciences in 2012. He worked as an Assistant Professor in the Faculty of Business Administration, Karabuk University during the period September 2012-March 2015 and as an Associate Professor in the Faculty of Economics and Administrative Sciences, Usak University, during the period March 2015-October 2020 and now working as a Professor in the Faculty of Economics and Administrative Sciences, Bandirma Onyedi Eylul University, since October 2020.

**Funda Hatice Sezgin** completed her undergraduate education in Faculty of economics in University of Istanbul. She did master of business administration degree (MBA) in Econometrics of University of Istanbul, and doctor of econometrics in Marmara University. Her research interests are time series analysis, panel data analysis and statistical methods. She works in the department of industrial engineering at Istanbul University-Cerrahpasa.

* * *

**Canan Hazal Akarsu** graduated from the Ph.D. program in Industrial Engineering at Istanbul University-Cerrahpaşa in 2024. She is currently a data scientist in the Corporate Data Management Office at Istanbul University-

Cerrahpaşa. Her research interests include machine learning, heuristic methods, production planning, scheduling, multi-criteria decision making, supply chain, and logistics management.

**Ibtisamatul Aminah** was born in Ujung Pandang on November 19, 1992. She earned her Bachelor's degree in Chemistry from the Faculty of Mathematics and Natural Sciences (FMIPA), Hasanuddin University, in 2015 through the Bidikmisi scholarship program. She obtained her Doctorate in Biomedical Sciences in 2021 from the Faculty of Medicine, Andalas University, supported by the Superior Undergraduate to Doctoral Scholarship Program (PMDSU). Her research focuses on integrating marine natural product chemistry, biochemistry, biotechnology, and bioinformatics. The author has experience as a volunteer laboratory analyst for COVID-19 testing at the Central Laboratory and Research Center for Infectious Diseases (PDRPI), Faculty of Medicine, Andalas University (March 2020–June 2022). Additionally, she served as a PCR Laboratory Supervisor at Budi Mulia Mother and Child Hospital, Makassar (September 2021–August 2022).

**Sinem Buyuksaatci Kiris** obtained her Ph.D. in Industrial Engineering from Istanbul University. Her research focuses on areas including Supply Chain Management, Sustainability, Circular Economy, Simulation and Multi-Criteria Decision Making. Her scholarly works have been published in reputable journals such as Annals of Operations Research, IMA Journal of Management Mathematics, and the International Journal of Information Technology & Decision Making. She currently serves as an Assistant Professor in the Department of Industrial Engineering at Istanbul University-Cerrahpasa and, since 2023, as Vice Chair, where she supports program oversight, accreditation efforts, and research–teaching coordination.

**Susanta Das** is a seasoned educator with a proven record of teaching and mentoring diverse students, working at multiple institutions, and providing service to the various initiatives of organizations. He received his Ph.D. and M.A. degrees from Western Michigan University (WMU), USA, and M.Sc. degree from Banaras Hindu University (BHU), India all in Physics. He continued his research as a Marie-Curie post-doctoral fellow at Stockholm University, Stockholm, Sweden on beam diagnostics for the DESIREE (Double ElectroStatic Ion Ring ExpEriment) in the project DITANET (Diagnostic Techniques for particle Accelerators – a Marie-Curie initial training NETwork), at the Indian Institute of Science Education and Research-Kolkata, India on high-pressure physics as a Project Scientist-B, and at the University of Electro-Communications, Tokyo, Japan on ion-surface interactions as a Post-doctoral fellow. Throughout his career, Dr. Das worked and collaborated with many researchers, Ph.D., master, and visiting students from different countries. He further visited many countries to discuss research and an international conference participant (UK, Italy, Germany, Greece, Belgium, Bulgaria, Romania, Brazil etc.). He worked at several institutions before assuming his current role at Ajeenkya D Y Patil University. He received the Marie-Curie post-doctoral fellowship in Sweden, Science Academies' Summer Research Fellowship in India, Gowen Frostic Doctoral Fellowship, Department Graduate Research and Creative Scholar Award by WMU, and Leo R. Parpart Doctoral Fellowship by Dept. of Physics, WMU, among many others, throughout his academic journey. He co-authored several research articles in WoS/Scopus indexed international journals, conference proceedings, and scholarly book chapters and co-edited several books published by renowned international publishing houses (IGI-Global, Springer Nature, Nova Science Publishers, Wiley, Scrivener-Wiley, Notion Press). At present, Dr. Das continues to delve into cutting-edge fields, with a keen interest in nanotechnology, UN SDGs, and data science. His multifaceted contributions, spanning teaching, research, and administrative leadership, showcase a dedicated professional who is instrumental in advancing the vision and mission of the institutions he serves.

**Aditya Deshpande** is presently enrolled at Ajeenkya D. Y. Patil University to pursue a B.Tech in Computer Science and Engineering. They have developed a solid foundation in programming languages like C, C++, Java, and Python during their academic career. Their main areas of interest are cybersecurity, software development, agentic systems, and artificial intelligence. They have created a number of projects that demonstrate their technical proficiency and problem-solving skills. Notably, they oversaw the creation of the "Mental Health Tester" project, which combined Android-based tools and AI-driven evaluation to support mental health. This sponsored project was a key component of their investigation into applied AI in practical settings and was published as a technical paper and survey. Additionally, they have worked on multiple micro-projects across various domains, including banking systems, aircraft management, and interactive games like Tic-Tac-Toe. Furthermore, they have contributed to numerous micro-projects throughout In addition to project work, they have written and conducted research on agentic AI, neural architectures, and autonomous intelligent systems, which have helped the academic community. They recently explored the future potential of multimodal and service-oriented intelligent frameworks in a technical paper and research proposal on Technological Advancements in Agentic AI. Their experiences have improved their teamwork, algorithmic thinking, and innovation-driven development abilities. They are excited about using AI and technology to develop scalable, human-centered solutions, and they want to keep advancing computer science through both practical applications and research.

**Md Mehedi Hasan Emon** is a research practitioner in Business and Management, with specialized in Supply Chain Management, Digital Transformation, Marketing, Information Systems, and Educational Technology (Edutech). His work bridges a diverse range of domains including Artificial Intelligence in Business, Human-Computer Interaction, Cognitive Behaviour, E-commerce, and Smart Logistics. His research extensively explores the integration of emerging technologies in business ecosystems focusing on AI-driven innovation, behavioral responses to technology adoption, and digital marketing strategies. He has also contributed significantly to sustainability-focused fields such as GreenTech, Green Finance, Renewable Energy, and Blockchain-enabled financial innovation. Additionally, his work in Smart Cities and IoT adoption emphasizes the importance of user trust, security, and operational efficiency. Emon has authored numerous peer-reviewed publications on topics including AI adoption intention, supply chain visibility, digital learning acceptance, and crisis-resilient supply chains. Many of his studies adopt behavioral and cognitive perspectives to understand how professionals and consumers interact with technology highlighting the psychological and user-centric aspects of digital transformation. He has participated in several research initiatives funded by the University Grants Commission of Bangladesh and the European Union. His work aligns closely with the United Nations Sustainable Development Goals (SDGs), particularly in areas such as poverty reduction, access to quality education, clean and affordable energy, inclusive economic growth, sustainable industrialization, responsible consumption, climate resilience, and ocean sustainability. His work also reflects a commitment to reducing inequalities and fostering international partnerships for sustainable development. In addition to his research contributions, he serves as a peer reviewer for several high-impact academic journals and is widely recognized for promoting academic rigor and ethical scholarship. As a prolific author, he continues to shape the discourse on sustainability, innovation, and digital advancement through his research, writing, and knowledge dissemination.

**Guntur Roryngosan Fara** is a dedicated medical professional and academician committed to the fields of healthcare and education. He earned his Bachelor's degree in Medicine and obtained his medical doctor (dr.) qualification from Universitas Muslim Indonesia. His passion for healthcare led him to pursue further studies, completing a Master's degree in Health Sciences (M.Kes) at Universitas Hasanuddin. Beyond his role as a physician, Dr. Guntur is also actively involved in academia. Since 2020, he has been serving as a lecturer at Universitas Megarezky, sharing his knowledge and expertise with aspiring medical students. With his combined clinical experience and educational contributions, he continues to inspire future healthcare professionals.

**Binnur Akıf Gurul** completed her undergraduate education at Istanbul Technical University in the Department of Management Engineering. She received her master's degree in the Institute of Social Sciences, Department of Business Administration in Istanbul Aydin University. She completed her first doctoral degree in the Institute of Social Sciences, Department of Business Administration in Istanbul Gelisim University. She completed her second doctoral degree in the Postgraduate Education Institute, Department of Industrial Engineering in Istanbul University – Cerrahpasa. Her research interests are manufacturing and service systems, multi-criteria decision making, quality management systems, supply chain management, sustainability, management organization, and organizational behavior. Currently, she is Assistant Prof. Dr. in Istanbul Gelisim University, Faculty of Engineering and Architecture, Department of Industrial Engineering.

**Kauser Hameed**, with a master's in computer applications, is a dedicated researcher and active IT professional bridging theoretical and practical aspects in both academic and industry settings. Her career includes roles as an IT Business Analyst at General Electrical Internation and a Technical Trainer at SumTotal-Multinational. Currently, working as a senior lecturer in the College of Computer Sciences and Information Systems at King Faisal University, KSA, she has supervised diverse projects and contributed to number of grant-winning researches. She has also co-edited book, co-authored chapters and made scientific contributions, and has won hackathon and competitions. While remaining open to exploring emerging technologies, her research interests include artificial intelligence, machine learning, knowledge management, and information retrieval. Furthermore, she has actively contributed to academic leadership, curriculum development, and quality assurance initiatives at her workplaces.

**Qazi Mudassar Ilyas** received his Ph.D. in Information and Communication Engineering from Huazhong University of Science and Technology, China, in 2005. Over the years, he has held academic positions at several leading institutions in Pakistan, including Ghulam Ishaq Khan Institute (GIKI), Topi; the University of the Punjab, Lahore; and COMSATS Institute of Information Technology, Abbottabad. He is currently serving as an Associate Professor at Sultan Sharif Ali Islamic University, Brunei Darussalam. His research spans artificial intelligence, machine learning, knowledge management, and information retrieval. He has also contributed to academic leadership, curriculum development, and quality assurance initiatives across multiple institutions.

**Kian Jazayeri** holds a PhD in Electrical and Electronic Engineering from Eastern Mediterranean University, where he also completed his undergraduate and master's studies. His research focuses on data analysis, machine learning, natural language processing, and solar energy systems, with publications in international journals and conferences. He currently serves as the Head of the Management Information Systems Department at Cyprus International University and has coordinated undergraduate and graduate programs in Data Science. Dr. Jazayeri is also involved in supervising graduate theses and advising the university's Digital Technologies Club.

**Moein Jazayeri** holds a PhD in Electrical and Electronic Engineering from Eastern Mediterranean University, with a master's and undergraduate degree in Electrical Engineering from Istanbul Technical University and Yıldız Technical University. His research focuses on solar energy systems, power system optimization, and renewable energy integration, with publications in international journals and conferences. He currently serves as the Vice Dean of the Faculty of Engineering and Program Director for Mechatronics Engineering, while also coordinating multiple associate programs in engineering and renewable energy. Dr. Jazayeri has supervised several graduate theses and received awards for research excellence, including the IEEE PES T&D Best Paper Award.

**Mustafa Kayyali** is an ardent advocate for excellence in higher education, driven by a relentless pursuit of quality, recognition, and innovation. Their journey in academia started with a Master's in Quality Management and Evaluation in Higher Education from Universitat Oberta de Catalunya, followed by a Ph.D. in Quality Management from Azteca University. These academic pursuits have laid a strong foundation for their expertise in Accreditation, Quality Assurance, and Higher Education Rankings. As an entrepreneur, researcher, translator, and publisher, they are deeply involved in various facets of the academic world. Their diverse interests encompass Management, Translation, Interpretation, and Academic consulting, contributing to a well-rounded understanding of the industry. Throughout their career, they have made significant contributions to academic literature, with more than 40 published papers and 30 book chapters to my name. Additionally, they take pride in having translated 6 books, bridging language gaps, and promoting knowledge exchange on a global scale. They are committed to fostering positive change in higher education and contributing to its continuous improvement.

**Tahsina Khan** is serving as Deputy Director (Research) at the Centre for Higher Studies and Research in Bangladesh University of Professionals (BUP). In addition, she is also serving as the Assistant Editor of the BUP Journal. She is an Academician in Business Studies with more than 14 years of teaching, research & consulting experience in Higher Education Institutions. Over the years, she has successfully supervised multilateral academic programs in collaboration with the Government, NGOs, and Corporations from the Business sector. As a Visiting Lecturer, she has taught in the MBA program of the University of Gavle, Sweden. She has worked as Director of the research projects funded by the University Grants Commission (UGC) under the Ministry of Education. Her research papers were presented in National and International Conferences in Canada, France, Malaysia and Indonesia. As Session Chair, she presided over the conference organized by Higher Education and Innovation Group (HEAIG). She has also been invited as a resource speaker at the United Nations affiliated conference at the Yonsei University in Wonju, South Korea. She has published a number of peer-reviewed articles in reputed international journals and her policy brief paper on Rural Development has been included in the knowledge hub of the UN Task Force on SDG implementation. She is a member of International Sociological Association (ISA) which is associated with UNESCO, Economic & Social Council of the United Nations.

**Tarık Küçükdeniz** completed his Ph.D. in Industrial Engineering at Istanbul University in 2009. He currently works as a Professor at Istanbul University-Cerrahpaşa. His research interests include production management, computer science, algorithms, industrial engineering, stochastic modeling, queueing theory and applications, optimization theory and methods, multi-objective optimization, simulation optimization, system dynamics, production planning and control, inventory systems.

**Khutaija Maheen** is a Canadian technology professional who holds a Master's degree in Computer Science from the United States and brings over a decade of international experience in the IT industry, including roles in the United States and Canada. She started her career as a software developer and transitioned into Project Management, earning both PMP and PMI-ACP certifications. Over the years, she has led diverse client-focused software initiatives and driven Agile transformations across enterprise environments. Her recent focus lies in leveraging Artificial Intelligence for sustainable innovation, particularly in the domains of speech recognition and bioproduct development. She is also actively involved in academic research, with publications exploring the intersection of AI, natural language processing, and environmental technology. Currently, she is exploring doctoral opportunities with a focus on AI-driven solutions for global impact.

**Zeynep Orman** received her BSc in Computer Science Engineering in 2001 and her MSc and Ph.D. degrees in Computer Engineering in 2003 and 2007, respectively from Istanbul University, Istanbul, Turkey. She has studied as a postdoctoral research fellow in the Department of Information Systems and Computing, Brunel University,

London, UK in 2009. She is currently working as a Professor in the Department of Computer Engineering, Istanbul University-Cerrahpasa. She is also the head of the Computer Science branch. Her research interests include artificial intelligence, neural networks, nonlinear systems, machine learning, optimization, and data science.

**Mrutyunjay Padhiary** is an Assistant Professor in the Department of Agricultural Engineering at Assam University, Silchar, India, with a deep academic background. His previous positions included significant teaching and research duties at the Faculty of Technology, UBKV in West Bengal, and Tribhuvan University in Nepal, as well as research experience at IIT Kharagpur. He has been awarded multiple awards, including an International NUS Research Fellowship and an excellent score on the 2001 GATE Exam, demonstrating his proficiency in precision agriculture. He has made substantial contributions to biofuel production, artificial intelligence vision, aquaculture, precision agriculture, agricultural automation, and artificial intelligence. He is currently working on several research projects, which range from autonomous surface vessels to precision agriculture all-terrain vehicles.

**Vivit Rosmayanti**, S.Pd.I., M.Pd, was born in Botta on June 26, 1987. She has over 10 years of experience teaching at the University. She obtained a bachelor's degree in English Education from Alauddin State Islamic University. She completed her master's and doctoral degrees in English Education from Makassar State University. She is currently a lecturer in the Post Graduate Program, Department of English Education at Makassar State University, South Sulawesi, Indonesia. She is also actively writing research articles to be published in nationally and internationally accredited journals. She has written in some chapter books, monographs, and reference books. She is interested in teaching methods for teaching English. Her research interests include language teaching methodology, ICT instruction, and ESP teaching.

**Safaruddin** is a dedicated senior lecturer at the Faculty of Pharmacy, Universitas Megarezky, South Sulawesi, Indonesia, with over 12 years of experience shaping the future of pharmacy professionals. A certified pharmacist, he began his academic journey with a Bachelor's degree from the Islamic University of Makassar. He later advanced his expertise by earning a Master's degree and completing his Pharmacist Profession Program at Universitas Hasanuddin. Passionate about contributing to the field, Safaruddin actively engages in community service, teaching, and publishing research articles and books in accredited journals. As an active member of several professional pharmacist organizations, he stays committed to continuous professional development by participating in conferences, workshops, and seminars/webinars. His dedication to education, research, and professional growth makes him a respected figure in the pharmacy community.

**Raazia Saher** is a lecturer in the Department of Computer Science and Information Technology at King Faisal University, Saudi Arabia, where she has been actively engaged in teaching and academic service for over 13 years. In addition to her teaching responsibilities, she has contributed to institutional development through her involvement in quality assurance, student advising, and extracurricular activities. She holds an M.Sc. in Electrical Engineering from the University of Engineering and Technology, Taxila, Pakistan, awarded in 2009, and is a registered professional engineer with the Pakistan Engineering Council. Prior to her academic career, she gained hands-on technical experience as an operational engineer at Pakistan Telecommunications Company Limited, where she developed expertise in Next Generation Networks and Soft Switches. Her research interests include artificial intelligence, machine learning, the Internet of Things (IoT), and cybersecurity. She has numerous notable publications in these areas and also holds an accepted patent related to her research work.

**Atharva Saraf** is currently pursuing a B. Tech degree in Computer Science Engineering at Ajeenkya D Y Patil University. Throughout his academic journey, he has developed a strong foundation in various programming languages, including C, C++, and Python. His interests and focus areas lie in algorithm-based programs, artificial intelligence (with a special emphasis on neural networks), and cybersecurity. His has successfully undertaken several projects that reflect my proficiency and passion in these domains. For instance, he developed a PC-Tuner application aimed at optimizing system performance by employing various methods such as defragmentation. Additionally, he created an automated backup utility capable of securely backing up selected files, folders, and stores them in compressed backup folder in system itself it can also store backups on external hard disk and cloud storages. Beyond project work, he has contributed to the academic community through research articles and book chapters. Notable among these is my co-authored chapter on federated learning techniques, exploring their applications and advancements in the field of machine learning. Moreover, he is currently working on writing a book chapter focusing on federated learning, delving deeper into its methodologies and practical implementations. His academic experiences have honed his skills in problem-solving, critical thinking, and collaborative teamwork. He is eager to further expand His knowledge and expertise in computer science, particularly in areas that intersect with his interests in algorithms, artificial intelligence, and their practical applications.

**Sabina Sehajpal** is working as an Associate Professor at Chandigarh University.

**Sibel Senan** is currently an Associate Professor at the Dept. Of Computer Engineering in Istanbul University-Cerrahpasa. She received her M.Sc. and Ph.D. degrees at the same department in 2005 and in 2010, respectively. Her main interests are Artificial Intelligence, Machine Learning, Neural Networks, Nonlinear Systems, Computational Intelligence.

**Melike Solak** is a Ph.D. student in the Mathematics Department at Istanbul University. Since 2024, she has been a data scientist in the Corporate Data Management Office at Istanbul University-Cerrahpaşa. Her research interests include machine learning, stability analysis, nonlinear systems, and artificial neural networks.

**Besse Yuliana** is a senior lecturer at the Faculty of Pharmacy, Universitas Megarezky, South Sulawesi, Indonesia, with over a decade of experience in teaching and mentoring future pharmacists. A certified professional pharmacist, she holds a doctorate in Pharmaceutical Science and Technology from the Faculty of Pharmacy, Hasanuddin University. Committed to lifelong learning and professional growth, Besse actively engages in community service, academic teaching, and publishing research articles and books in accredited journals. She is an active member of several professional pharmacist organizations and regularly participates in conferences, workshops, and seminars/webinars to stay at the forefront of developments in the pharmaceutical field. Her dedication to education and research continues to make a significant impact on her students and the broader pharmacy community.

# Index


## A

AI-Driven Innovation 17, 122, 266
AI-Powered Automation 291, 293, 303, 309
AI-Powered Tools 121, 144, 183, 192, 194, 303, 307
AI Technologies 3, 6, 13, 14, 16, 18, 21, 23, 24, 25, 49, 54, 102, 103, 104, 105, 109, 115, 119, 123, 134, 135, 139, 140, 141, 143, 144, 146, 183, 184, 194, 196, 197, 198, 200, 201, 205, 258, 272, 295, 296, 299, 304, 306, 309, 310, 311
Assistive Technologies 182

## B

Bioinformatics 180, 207, 209, 210, 218, 219, 226, 227, 229, 320, 344, 348, 350

## C

Circular economy 14, 40, 244, 247, 257, 259, 260, 261, 262, 263, 267, 269, 273, 277, 284, 288, 318
Climate Action 1, 5, 6, 12, 13, 14, 17, 19, 24, 58, 59, 63, 76, 83, 108, 114, 115, 134, 136, 168, 171, 174, 225, 256, 282, 292, 293, 294, 299, 306, 309, 321
Climate-Smart Agriculture 291, 298
Clustering Analysis 72
Coffee Industry 255, 257, 258, 259, 260, 266, 267, 269, 275, 277, 280, 282, 283, 287, 288

## D

Decision-Support Systems 49, 94
Deep Learning 25, 29, 56, 93, 127, 178, 179, 186, 210, 220, 228, 252, 275, 284, 287, 319, 323, 324, 325, 326, 327, 328, 329, 330, 331, 332, 333, 334, 343, 344, 349, 353, 354, 355, 356, 357, 358, 359, 360, 361
Digital Engagement 231
Digital Twins 207, 209, 210, 215, 216, 222

## E

Economic Empowerment 40
Educational Inequalities 103, 116
ELT 181, 184
Equal Access to Education 37
Ethical AI 17, 30, 122, 308

## F

Femtech 231

## G

Gender 16, 27, 31, 37, 38, 39, 40, 41, 42, 43, 44, 45, 46, 47, 48, 49, 50, 51, 52, 53, 54, 55, 56, 58, 60, 63, 97, 101, 111, 134, 136, 138, 142, 143, 144, 145, 150, 152, 153, 154, 158, 171, 174, 231, 232, 325, 342, 343, 345, 354, 361
Global Sustainability 2, 3, 4, 21, 22, 23, 24, 25, 26, 78, 83, 93, 95, 135, 139, 159, 176, 282

## H

Higher Education Sustainability 161
Hybrid Models 219, 323, 325, 331, 346, 349, 353, 354, 355, 361

## I

Inclusivity 35, 40, 42, 43, 44, 46, 47, 49, 133, 136, 138, 142, 143, 145, 152, 181, 190, 192, 193, 196, 200, 238, 241

## L

Language Learning Technologies 181
Lifelong Learning Opportunities 140, 142, 146

## M

Machine Learning 1, 4, 5, 7, 12, 13, 14, 18, 20, 32, 34, 36, 37, 38, 40, 43, 53, 54, 56, 57, 58, 59, 60, 61, 67, 92, 94, 98, 99, 103, 104, 105, 107, 108, 109, 110, 111, 115, 120, 124, 127, 129, 134, 139, 140, 142, 144, 148, 149, 151, 154, 168, 177, 196, 207, 209, 210, 216, 217, 219, 220, 221, 226, 227, 228, 258, 260, 261, 264, 267, 269, 270, 271, 273, 274, 275, 276, 281, 287, 288, 289, 298, 303, 304, 312, 315, 317, 319, 320, 321, 324, 328, 331, 334, 342, 343, 344, 345, 346, 353, 356, 358, 359, 360, 361

Metadata 325, 342, 343, 345, 353, 354, 361

## P

Poverty Alleviation 6, 7, 24, 30, 33, 91

Precision Farming 291, 292, 293, 295, 304, 311, 312, 317, 319

## R

Recycling 14, 22, 109, 125, 127, 131, 244, 246, 256, 264, 272, 277, 278, 280, 284, 287

Reduced Inequalities 9, 15, 76, 122, 136, 162, 171, 173, 174, 182

## S

Skin Cancer 226, 323, 324, 325, 326, 327, 328, 329, 330, 331, 332, 333, 334, 335, 336, 340, 342, 343, 345, 346, 349, 350, 351, 353, 354, 355, 356, 357, 358, 359, 360, 361

Smart Health Technologies 209

Social Development 111, 113, 131

Strategic Planning 59, 90, 94, 163, 174

Supply Chain Optimization 295

Sustainability 2, 3, 4, 12, 13, 14, 15, 17, 18, 21, 22, 23, 24, 25, 26, 27, 29, 31, 32, 33, 34, 35, 40, 41, 52, 54, 55, 58, 59, 60, 67, 74, 78, 83, 88, 93, 94, 95, 96, 97, 99, 101, 106, 107, 108, 109, 126, 129, 131, 134, 135, 136, 137, 139, 148, 149, 150, 151, 152, 157, 158, 159, 160, 161, 162, 163, 164, 165, 166, 167, 168, 169, 170, 171, 172, 173, 174, 175, 176, 177, 178, 179, 198, 199, 200, 202, 203, 204, 208, 210, 224, 229, 232, 233, 234, 235, 236, 237, 238, 239, 240, 241, 242, 243, 249, 250, 256, 258, 263, 274, 275, 278, 281, 282, 283, 284, 286, 288, 289, 291, 292, 293, 295, 296, 297, 298, 299, 300, 301, 302, 303, 304, 305, 308, 309, 310, 311, 313, 314, 315, 317, 318, 320, 321

Sustainable Cities and Communities 20, 76, 114, 136, 171, 174

Sustainable Development 1, 2, 3, 4, 5, 6, 8, 9, 15, 18, 21, 24, 25, 26, 28, 29, 30, 31, 32, 33, 34, 35, 36, 37, 38, 39, 40, 41, 42, 45, 49, 50, 52, 53, 54, 55, 56, 57, 58, 59, 61, 62, 70, 71, 72, 73, 76, 78, 83, 88, 89, 90, 93, 94, 96, 97, 98, 99, 101, 108, 114, 115, 123, 124, 129, 133, 134, 135, 136, 137, 138, 139, 140, 142, 146, 148, 149, 150, 151, 152, 153, 154, 157, 158, 160, 161, 162, 163, 166, 169, 175, 176, 177, 178, 179, 180, 181, 182, 190, 199, 201, 207, 208, 209, 210, 224, 228, 229, 231, 247, 253, 255, 256, 280, 283, 287, 291, 292, 293, 294, 313, 315, 316, 318

Sustainable Development Goals (SDGs) 18

## T

Telemedicine 3, 5, 19, 34, 46, 207, 209, 210, 211, 212, 213, 224, 226, 227, 228, 229, 346

Time Series Forecasting 59, 61, 69, 99

Transfer Learning 325, 327, 328, 329, 331, 332, 333, 343, 350, 351, 352, 354, 356, 357, 358, 361

## V

Valorization 256, 258, 264, 265, 270, 271, 278, 282, 284, 285, 286, 288

## W

Women's Health 39, 48, 231

## Z

Zero Hunger 7, 8, 18, 30, 76, 134, 136, 171, 173, 292, 293, 294, 304, 309, 312, 316

www.ingramcontent.com/pod-product-compliance
Lightning Source LLC
LaVergne TN
LVHW062327300926
849161LV00007B/1609
* 9 7 9 8 3 3 7 3 1 8 3 7 0 *